CIMA

STUDY TEXT

Final Paper 12

Business Strategy

IN THIS JULY 2002 EDITION

- Targeted to the **syllabus** and **learning outcomes**

- **Quizzes** and **questions** to check your understanding

- **Clear layout** and **style** designed to save you time

- Plenty of **exam-style questions**

- **Chapter Roundups** and summaries to help revision

- **Mind Maps** to integrate the key points

NEW IN THIS JULY 2002 EDITION

- Thoroughly reviewed and updated in light of the May 2002 exam

- Links to help you with the Final Level Case Study

BPP Publishing
July 2002

First edition July 2000
Third edition July 2002

ISBN 0 7517 3766 6 (*Previous edition 0 7517 3168 4*)

British Library Cataloguing-in-Publication Data
A catalogue record for this book
is available from the British Library

Published by

BPP Publishing Ltd
Aldine House, Aldine Place
London W12 8AW

www.bpp.com

Printed in Great Britain by Ashford Colour Press Ltd

We are grateful to the Chartered Institute of Management Accountants for permission to reproduce past examination questions and questions from the pilot paper. The suggested solutions to the illustrative questions have been prepared by BPP Publishing Limited.

Contents

Page

PAGES   VIDEO

BPP
PUBLISHING

LEARNING TO LEARN ACCOUNTANCY

BPP's ground-breaking **Learning to learn accountancy** book is designed to be used both at the outset of your CIMA studies and throughout the process of learning accountancy. It challenges you to consider how you study and gives you helpful hints about how to approach the various types of paper which you will encounter. It can help you **get your studies both subject and exam focused**, enabling you to **acquire knowledge**, **practice and revise efficiently and effectively**.

THE BPP STUDY TEXT

Aims of this Study Text

To provide you with the knowledge and understanding, skills and application techniques that you need if you are to be successful in your exams

This Study Text has been written around the **Business Strategy** syllabus.

- It is **comprehensive**. It covers the syllabus content. No more, no less.

- It is written at the **right level**. Each chapter is written with CIMA's precise learning outcomes in mind.

- It is targeted to the **exam**. We have taken account of the pilot paper and the papers set to date, questions put to the examiner and the assessment methodology.

To allow you to study in the way that best suits your learning style and the time you have available, by following your personal Study Plan (see page (ix))

You may be studying at home on your own until the date of the exam, or you may be attending a full-time course. You may like to (and have time to) read every word, or you may prefer to (or only have time to) skim-read and devote the remainder of your time to question practice. Wherever you fall in the spectrum, you will find the BPP Study Text meets your needs in designing and following your personal Study Plan.

To tie in with the other components of the BPP Effective Study Package to ensure you have the best possible chance of passing the exam (see page (vi))

BPP PUBLISHING

Recommended period of use	Elements of the BPP Effective Study Package
From the outset and throughout	**Learning to learn accountancy** Read this invaluable book as you begin your studies and refer to it as you work through the various elements of the BPP Effective Study Package. It will help you to acquire knowledge, practice and revise, both efficiently and effectively.
Three to twelve months before the exam	**Study Text** Use the Study Text to acquire knowledge, understanding, skills and the ability to use application techniques.
Throughout	**Virtual Campus** Study, practice, revise and take advantage of other useful resources with BPP's fully interactive e-learning site with comprehensive tutor support.
One to six months before the exam	**Practice & Revision Kit** Try the numerous examination-format questions, for which there are realistic suggested solutions prepared by BPP's own authors. Then attempt the two mock exams.
From three months before the exam until the last minute	**Passcards** Work through these short, memorable notes which are focused on what is most likely to come up in the exam you will be sitting.
One to six months before the exam	**Success Tapes** These audio tapes cover the vital elements of your syllabus in less than 90 minutes per subject. Each tape also contains exam hints to help you fine tune your strategy.
Three to twelve months before the exam	**Breakthrough Videos** Use a Breakthrough Video to supplement your Study Text. They give you clear tuition on key exam subjects and allow you the luxury of being able to pause or repeat sections until you have fully grasped the topic.

HELP YOURSELF STUDY FOR YOUR CIMA EXAMS

Exams for professional bodies such as CIMA are very different from those you have taken at college or university. You will be under **greater time pressure before** the exam - as you may be combining your study with work. There are many different ways of learning and so the BPP Study Text offers you a number of different tools to help you through. Here are some hints and tips: they are not plucked out of the air, but **based on research and experience**. (You don't need to know that long-term memory is in the same part of the brain as emotions and feelings - but it's a fact anyway.)

The right approach

1   The right attitude

Believe in yourself	Yes, there is a lot to learn. Yes, it is a challenge. But thousands have succeeded before and you can too.
Remember why you're doing it	Studying might seem a grind at times, but you are doing it for a reason: to advance your career.

2   The right focus

Read through the Syllabus and learning outcomes	These tell you what you are expected to know and are supplemented by Exam Focus Points in the text.
Study the Exam Paper section	Past papers are a reasonable guide of what you should expect in the exam.

3   The right method

The big picture	You need to grasp the detail - but keeping in mind how everything fits into the big picture will help you understand better. • The **Introduction** of each chapter puts the material in context. • The **Syllabus content, learning outcomes** and **Exam focus points** show you what you need to **grasp**. • **Mind Maps** show the links and key issues in key topics.
In your own words	To absorb the information (and to practise your written communication skills), it helps to **put it into your own words.** • **Take notes.** • Answer the **questions** in each chapter. As well as helping you absorb the information, you will practise the assessment formats used in the exam and your written communication skills, which become increasingly important as you progress through your CIMA exams. • Draw **mind maps**. We have some examples. • Try 'teaching' a subject to a colleague or friend.

Give yourself cues to jog your memory	The BPP Study Text uses **bold** to **highlight key points** and **icons** to identify key features, such as **Exam focus points** and **Key terms.** • Try **colour coding** with a highlighter pen. • Write **key points** on cards.

4   **The right review**

Review, review, review	It is a **fact** that regularly reviewing a topic in summary form can **fix it in your memory**. Because **review** is so important, the BPP Study Text helps you to do so in many ways. • **Chapter roundups** summarise the key points in each chapter. Use them to recap each study session. • The **Quick quiz** is another review technique to ensure that you have grasped the essentials. • Go through the **Examples** in each chapter a second or third time.

Developing your personal Study Plan

One thing that the BPP Learning to learn accountancy book emphasises (see page (iv)) is the need to prepare (and use) a study plan. Planning and sticking to the plan are key elements of learning success.

There are four steps you should work through.

Step 1. **How do you learn?**

First you need to be aware of your style of learning. The BPP Learning to learn accountancy book commits a chapter to this **self-discovery**. What types of intelligence do you display when learning? You might be advised to brush up on certain study skills before launching into this Study Text.

> BPP's **Learning to learn accountancy** book helps you to identify what intelligences you show more strongly and then details how you can tailor your study process through your preferences. It also includes handy hints on how to develop intelligences you exhibit less strongly, but which might be needed as you study accountancy.

Are you a **theorist** or are you more **practical**? If you would rather get to grips with a theory before trying to apply it in practice, you should follow the study sequence on page X. If the reverse is true (you like to know why you are learning theory before you do so), you might be advised to flick through Study Text chapters and look at questions, case studies and examples (Steps 7, 8 and 9 in the **suggested study sequence**) before reading through the detailed theory.

Step 2. **How much time do you have?**

Work out the time you have available per week, given the following.

• The standard you have set yourself
• The time you need to set aside later for work on the Practice & Revision Kit and Passcards
• The other exam(s) you are sitting

- Very importantly, practical matters such as work, travel, exercise, sleep and social life

Note your time available in box A.

Hours

A [   ]

Step 3. Allocate your time

- Take the time you have available per week for this Study Text
  shown in box A, multiply it by the number of weeks available and
  insert the result in box B.

B [   ]

- Divide the figure in Box B by the number of chapters in this text
  and insert the result in box C.

C [   ]

Remember that this is only a rough guide. Some of the chapters in this book are longer and more complicated than others, and you will find some subjects easier to understand than others.

Step 4. Implement

Set about studying each chapter in the time shown in box C, following the key study steps in the order suggested by your particular learning style.

This is your personal **Study Plan**. You should try and combine it with the study sequence outlined below. You may want to modify the sequence a little (as has been suggested above) to adapt it to your **personal style**.

Suggested study sequence

It is likely that the best way to approach this Study Text is to tackle the chapters in the order in which you find them. Taking into account your individual learning style, you could follow this sequence.

Key study steps	Activity
Step 1 **Topic list**	Each numbered topic is a numbered section in the chapter.
Step 2 **Introduction**	This gives you the **big picture** in terms of the **context** of the chapter, the **content** you will cover, and the **learning outcomes** the chapter assesses - in other words, it sets your **objectives for study.**
Step 3 **Explanations**	Proceed methodically through the chapter, reading each section thoroughly and making sure you understand.
Step 4 **Key terms and Exam focus points**	• **Key terms** can often earn you *easy marks* if you state them clearly and correctly in an appropriate exam answer (and they are highlighted in the index at the back of the text). • **Exam focus points** give you a good idea of how we think the examiner intends to examine certain topics.
Step 5 **Note taking**	Take brief notes, if you wish. Avoid the temptation to copy out too much. Remember that being able to put something into your own words is a sign of being able to understand it. If you find you cannot explain something you have read, read it again before you make the notes.

BPP
PUBLISHING

Key study steps	Activity
Step 6 **Examples**	Follow each through to its solution very carefully.
Step 7 **Case examples**	Study each one, and try to add flesh to them from your own experience – they are designed to show how the topics you are studying come alive (and often come unstuck) in the real world.
Step 8 **Questions**	Make a very good attempt at each one.
Step 9 **Answers**	Check yours against ours, and make sure you understand any discrepancies.
Step 10 **Chapter roundup**	Work through it very carefully, to make sure you have grasped the major points it is highlighting.
Step 11 **Quick quiz**	When you are happy that you have covered the chapter, use the **Quick quiz** to check how much you have remembered of the topics covered and to practise questions in a variety of formats.
Step 12 **Question(s) in the Exam Question bank**	Either at this point, or later when you are thinking about revising, make a full attempt at the **Question(s)** suggested at the very end of the chapter. You can find these at the end of the Study Text, along with the **Answers** so you can see how you did. We highlight those that are introductory, and those which are of the standard you would expect to find in an exam.

Short of time: Skim study technique?

You may find you simply do not have the time available to follow all the key study steps for each chapter, however you adapt them for your particular learning style. If this is the case, follow the **skim study** technique below (the icons in the Study Text will help you to do this).

- Study the chapters in the order you find them in the Study Text.

- For each chapter, follow the key study steps 1/2, and then skim-read through step 3. Jump to step 10, and then go back to step 4. Follow through steps 6 and 7, and prepare outline answers to questions (steps 8/9). Try the Quick quiz (step 11), following up any items you can't answer, then do a plan for the Question (step 12), comparing it against our answers. You should probably still follow step 5 (note-taking), although you may decide simply to rely on the BPP Passcards for this.

Moving on...

However you study, when you are ready to embark on the practice and revision phase of the BPP Effective Study Package, you should still refer back to this Study Text, both as a source of **reference** (you should find the index particularly helpful for this) and as a way to **review** (the Chapter roundups and Quick quizzes help you here).

And remember to keep careful hold of this Study Text – you will find it invaluable in your work.

SYLLABUS AND LEARNING OUTCOMES

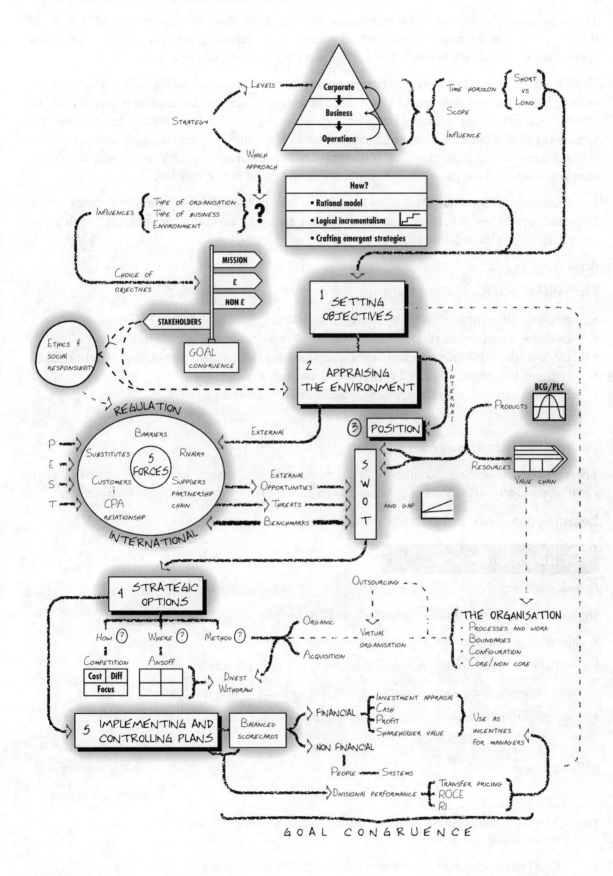

BPP PUBLISHING

Syllabus overview

The syllabus emphasises both the importance of the organisation's environment and the role of the Chartered Management Accountant in setting and evaluating strategic options. Differing approaches to strategy are presented as a response to the need to fulfil objectives.

The Chartered Management Accountant can play a major role in enhancing understanding of the relative importance of competitive forces and influences. Once this framework is established the relative position of the organisation within this setting can be attempted. Then follows the assessment of possible actions to enhance performance within this context, some steps having an external focus, for example branding and supply chain partnerships, others an internal focus. The question of where the organisation's boundaries should be set is also considered.

The Chartered Management Accountant is a key player in the implementation of strategic plans. Different approaches to performance measurement are considered and the inherent problems in measuring a complex organisation are raised.

Aims

This syllabus tests the student's ability to:

- Evaluate different approaches to strategy formulation
- Evaluate the environmental influences on the organisation and evaluate its position
- Evaluate the role of management accounting techniques in a changing business environment
- Evaluate strategic options and make appropriate recommendations
- Evaluate performance measurement systems for an organisation

Assessment

There will be a written paper of 3 hours.

There will be two sections. Section A will have a compulsory question based upon a scenario up to a maximum of 50 marks. Section B will contain a choice of questions, normally two from four.

Learning outcomes and syllabus content

(i) Setting objectives- 10%

Learning outcomes

On completion of their studies students should be able to:

- Identify the importance of objectives and objective setting

- Evaluate and contrast differing corporate frameworks and objectives

- Evaluate an organisation's mission, goals and aims and recommend appropriate changes

- Evaluate different approaches to strategy formulation and recommend the most appropriate

Syllabus content

	Covered in chapter
• The importance of developing achievable objectives for the organisation	2
• Competing objectives for the organisation: profit motive, short term and long term, sustainable growth, stakeholders and social responsibility. The objectives of not for profit organisations are also considered	3

	Covered in chapter
• Formulating the organisation's mission, goals, aims and critical success factors	3
• The rational model of strategy formulation	2
• Other less formal approaches to strategy formulation, including incrementalism and emergent approaches	2

Learning outcomes

On completion of their studies students should be able to:

• Evaluate the competitive forces in the market place

• Evaluate the importance of international issues including competition, management and regulation

• Explain the role and activities of pressure groups

• Evaluate the availability and quality of data for environmental analysis

• Analyse and evaluate the organisation's customer portfolio

• Prepare and evaluate competitor analysis

• Evaluate relationships with customers and suppliers and recommend appropriate changes or improvements

Syllabus content

	Covered in chapter
• The importance of relating the organisation to its environment when assessing its competitive position and consideration of the level of uncertainty and risks that the organisation faces	4
• Classifying and assessing the changing national and international influences on the organisation carefully using appropriate models and techniques (eg PEST). This would include such issues as EU regulation, GATT agreements and trade cycles	4,5
• The influence of industry forces in the market place (eg Porter's 5 forces model)	5
• International factors affecting the market place: country advantages and global factors	5
• The role and activities of interest groups and pressure groups (eg self-interest groups, such as industry associations, as well as environmental and ethical pressure groups). This topic is concerned with the recognition of additional stakeholders	4
• The availability and quality of data and information for environmental analysis. This includes the need for Internet and database interrogation	4
• The customer portfolio: customer analysis and behaviour, including the marketing audit and customer profitability analysis as well as customer retention and loyalty. The concept of relationship marketing	6

BPP PUBLISHING

Covered in chapter

- The importance of relationships with customers and suppliers, adversarial relationships or partnerships in the supply chain   6

- The implications of the above for the Chartered Management Accountant and the management accounting information system   4, 5, 6

Learning outcomes

On completion of their studies students should be able to:

- Evaluate the strengths, weaknesses, opportunities and threats of an organisation
- Evaluate and produce a comprehensive review of performance, resources and capabilities
- Evaluate the product portfolio of the organisation and advise on appropriate action
- Produce a benchmarking exercise and evaluate the outcomes
- Identify and evaluate an organisation's value chain and the accounting implications thereof
- Evaluate the impact of the external environment and the strategic objectives of an organisation
- Identify the position of organisational boundaries

Syllabus content

- The current state of the organisation and its advantages and disadvantages (eg SWOT analysis)   8

- Auditing an organisation's resources; considering intangible resources, products, services, people, structure, finance, stakeholder relations and systems   7

- The product portfolio, product life cycle and BCG analysis   7

- Benchmarking performance with best practice organisations   7

- Value chain analysis and the implications for the organisation and the accounting system   7

Learning outcomes

On completion of their studies students should be able to:

- Identify and evaluate an organisation's planning gap
- Evaluate and recommend growth and divestment strategies
- Evaluate and recommend response strategies to competitors' actions
- Prepare and evaluate strategic scenario plans
- Evaluate and recommend appropriate changes in organisational structure
- Identify and evaluate approaches to the design and operation of the management accounting systems
- Apply investment techniques to marketing and strategy decisions

Syllabus content

	Covered in chapter
• The importance of the planning gap and the use of scenario planning	8
• Competitor analysis including generic competitive strategies, product-market strategies (Ansoff) and competitor response profiles	9
• Branding and brand switching strategies	9
• Advantages and disadvantages of different methods of growth, including international acquisitions. The evaluation of growth strategies	10
• Divestment strategies and demergers and the evaluation of such actions	10
• The development and evaluation of response strategies to the actions of competitive forces (eg competitor price changes)	9
• The implications for the internal organisation of the entity of the environment and corporate objectives	12
• Alternative forms of organisation (core and non-core activities) and the effects of changes in technology (eg home working) and the labour market (flexible employment relationships)	12
• The application of business process re-engineering and the need for customer responsiveness	12
• The role of the management accounting and information systems in supporting management and the appropriateness of management accounting techniques for alternative organisational structures and philosophies	1, 12
• The concept and design of a strategic management accounting information system to assist strategy formulation, implementation and control	1
• The use of investment appraisal techniques in marketing and strategy selection, eg. volume enhancing marketing spends and decay reducing marketing spends	11
• The basics of transaction cost analysis and the implications for the location of assets, knowledge, people and activities inside or outside the organisation	12
• Contracting and outsourcing decisions and their financial effects	12
• The potential problems and advantages in contracting out the finance function as a whole or of some elements of the function	12
• The implications of the above for the Chartered Management Accountant and the management accounting information system	12

BPP PUBLISHING

On completion of their studies students should be able to:

- Evaluate and recommend appropriate control measures
- Evaluate and produce multidimensional models of performance measurement
- Discuss the effect of regulation on performance
- Evaluate the use of shareholder value analysis
- Identify problems in performance measurement and recommend solutions
- Evaluate performance from different time and stakeholder perspectives

Syllabus content

	Covered in chapter
• The problem of assessing strategic performance; the use of profit and cash measures and the concept of appropriate measures for an industry and contingent on environmental factors	13, 14
• Non-financial measures and their interaction with financial measures. Consider the need for ethical and environmental measures	13
• Multidimensional models of performance: including the balanced scorecard, the results and determinants framework (six dimensional performance matrix) and the performance pyramid	13
• The effect of regulation, both voluntary and legal, on corporate performance	4, 13
• The achieving of success for the shareholder; shareholder value analysis and value drivers. The strategic use of shareholder value analysis in resource allocation and re-balancing the portfolio	15
• Strategic business unit performance: transfer pricing, reward systems and agency theory	15
• The appraisal and comparison of international subsidiaries	15
• Short versus long term achievement: research and development, changing technology, outsourcing and capital investment	15

THE EXAM PAPER

Format of the paper

		Number of marks
Section A:	Compulsory case study scenario	50
Section B:	Two questions from four	50
		100

Time allowed: 3 hours

Analysis of papers

May 2002

Section A

1   Computer software and data retrieval company looking to develop its services, but hampered by inadequate management information systems.
   (a)   Corporate objectives and shareholders
   (b)   Relevance of management information in a dynamic environment
   (c)   Turnover and cost analysis
   (d)   Recommendation on contract bid

Section B

2   Evaluation of SWOT analysis
3   Application of the Ms model (position audit)
4   Competitive forces and performance indicators
5   Transaction cost analysis and networks

November 2001

Section A

1   Family entertainment company, already operating two theme parks in the USA and Europe, wants to open one in the Far East.
   (a)   Application of Porter's diamond
   (b)   (i)   DCF calculation; return on investment
       (ii)   Appraise DCF calculation and make recommendations
   (c)   Use of shareholder value analysis

Section B

2   Overseas expansion strategy – rationale, strategic and operational issues
3   Formal and informal strategy approaches
4   Usefulness of the balanced scorecard
5   Value chain analysis for a university

May 2001

Section A

1   Merger deal between music company and large entertainments group
   (a)   Nature of the business environment, and rationale for the merger
   (b)   (i)   Analysis of performance by business area
       (ii)   Calculation of contribution volume variance
       (iii)   Recommendations for strategic development
   (c)   Shareholder value: theory and application

Section B

2   Factors to consider in an international product launch; Porter's diamond
3   Strategic information required when planning service provision; role of the management accountant in providing reports
4   Stakeholder relationships; benchmarking
5   Public v private sector: objective setting and performance measurement

Pilot paper

Section A

1   Highly profitable and diverse international conglomerate company, whose main objective is to increase shareholder value, conducts careful divisional performance measurement using ROCE. Transfer prices are set centrally. One division in particular appears to be deteriorating, although its manager has submitted proposals for a strategic acquisition.

    (a)   Sources, uses and quality of environmental information
    (b)   Critical appraisal of performance assessment methods
    (c)   Factors in assessing the proposed acquisition
    (d)   Improved performance measurement for the new division

Section B

2   Industry life cycle and the Ansoff matrix
3   Organisational objectives at different stages of company growth
4   Management accounting: traditional criticisms and information collection
5   Financial and non-financial factors for investment appraisal

WHAT THE EXAMINER MEANS

The table below has been prepared by CIMA to help you interpret exam questions.

Learning objective	Verbs used	Definition
1 Knowledge What you are expected to know	• List • State • Define	• Make a list of • Express, fully or clearly, the details of/facts of • Give the exact meaning of
2 Comprehension What you are expected to understand	• Describe • Distinguish • Explain • Identify • Illustrate	• Communicate the key features of • Highlight the differences between • Make clear or intelligible/state the meaning of • Recognise, establish or select after consideration • Use an example to describe or explain something
3 Application Can you apply your knowledge?	• Apply • Calculate/compute • Demonstrate • Prepare • Reconcile • Solve • Tabulate	• To put to practical use • To ascertain or reckon mathematically • To prove with certainty or to exhibit by practical means • To make or get ready for use • To make or prove consistent/compatible • Find an answer to • Arrange in a table
4 Analysis Can you analyse the detail of what you have learned?	• Analyse • Categorise • Compare and contrast • Construct • Discuss • Interpret • Produce	• Examine in detail the structure of • Place into a defined class or division • Show the similarities and/or differences between • To build up or compile • To examine in detail by argument • To translate into intelligible or familiar terms • To create or bring into existence
5 Evaluation Can you use your learning to evaluate, make decisions or recommendations?	• Advise • Evaluate • Recommend	• To counsel, inform or notify • To appraise or assess the value of • To advise on a course of action

CASE STUDY: UNITY BICYCLES PLC

Why have a case study?

Fifty per cent of the marks in the Business Strategy paper are earned by a compulsory case study. The two other questions you have to do may also have a scenario element to them. The examiner can choose companies from many industries with many different problems. Your job is to make sense of them.

Students have difficulties with scenario-based questions for a variety of reasons.

- Students have problems applying their technical knowledge to the circumstances of the case study.

- Students are uncomfortable with the uncertainties, guesswork and judgement involved in the case study.

- Many accountancy papers involve the application of rules to data to achieve a defined result which is either right or wrong. In the Business Strategy paper you use models to interpret the data in order to understand it better and to develop your answers.

- More often than not in case studies, there is no right answer and no wrong answer. But some answers are much more relevant than others.

- As a management accountant, you will be applying some of the techniques you have learned at earlier stages to the scenario described. For the purposes of strategic decision-making, you may have to treat numerical data in a more flexible way.

- The case study might cover a number of areas of the syllabus in an integrated way. The issues are not easily put into compartments.

- Finally, there is a fair amount of new technical material to be covered in Business Strategy.

Unity Bicycles plc is our attempt to help you deal with these problems as you study, and before you sit down to do exam-style questions.

Using the case study

Unity Bicycles plc is a fictitious company facing a number of issues relating to strategic choices and strategic management in approaching its products and markets. The market and environmental data has been developed for the case study.

- At the end of each chapter, you will find a number of questions relating to Unity Bicycles plc which are relevant to the content of that chapter.

- The Unity Bicycles Review contains a few pointers to how the chapter content relates to the questions raised. These are not full answers to the questions, but are supposed to kick-start your own thought processes.

Unity Bicycles plc is a learning aid to help you develop some of the mental disciplines necessary to succeed in case study questions. It is integrative and does not fall into simple compartments.

For lecturers

- Unity Bicycles plc might be useful in stimulating classroom discussion, either before or after you cover a topic. You might wish to pose additional questions on it, or develop your own material to explore some topic areas in more detail.

For students, without classroom tuition

You can use Unity Bicycles plc in a number of ways.

- Before you cover a topic, to get you thinking
- After you have covered a topic, to apply your learning
- After you have completed the whole Study Text
- During your revision, once you have mastered the technical material
- In discussions with your fellow students

A good way of getting to grips with case study material is to skim read it twice, and perhaps highlight key issues as you go along.

Unity Bicycles plc

History

Unity Bicycles plc (UB) is the only firm that still makes pedal bicycles in the UK. Founded in 1902, it was once the world's biggest bicycle maker. After World War II, overseas governments, especially in developing countries, preferred to make bicycles themselves rather than import them.

The firm still prospered in the UK and Europe. In the early 1970s, when the price of oil quadrupled overnight, the company ran into financial difficulties. UB could not make enough bicycles to cope with the temporary surge in demand, ran into working capital problems and went into receivership.

In 1975, the firm was taken over by a former supplier, the metal and materials processing company Metal Technologies plc (MT), which provided specialist materials and metals to the car, aerospace, energy and construction industries. MT's bosses felt that bicycle-making was just another type of metal processing, which tied in neatly with MT's metallurgical skills. UB sourced all its components from MT. It retained a separate sales department, and had its own budgets for advertising and product development. MT saw UB's stable business as a useful source of cash, to compensate for the more volatile demand for specialist metals.

For several years UB did fairly well in the UK, as there was little competition. In the early 1980s, however, a number of developments put the firm's future survival in doubt.

The overvalued sterling exchange rate of the early 1980s drove many of MT's British customers to the wall. MT was affected, and had to raise cash.

UB began to face competition in the UK from manufacturers in Taiwan, and MT underestimated the demand for new kinds of bicycle. UB fell into loss. Overseas competition remains a problem. In 1991, over 2.5m cheap Chinese-made bikes flooded the European market. The European Bicycle Manufacturers Association, of which Unity is a member, persuaded the EU to impose anti-dumping duties of 34%. With GATT, import duties will have to come down anyway, and it will be much harder to launch legal actions in future. Chinese bikes are still imported in kit form.

In 1990 MT decided to focus on its core business of metallurgy and producing specialist materials and to divest itself of UB. MT sold UB for £50m to a management buyout team led by Walter Drake: the management team provided 10% of the capital. A venture capitalist from Hong Kong, Mr Wang Wei, provided a further 30%, and the final £30m was raised by bonds and long-term bank loans, to be repaid in full at the end of 2002.

Walter Drake persuaded the EU to give some grant money and, with tax incentives, UB moved all its equipment to an enterprise zone in Wales early in 1992. Walter Drake used the move to slash costs and reduce the size of the UK workforce by 75%. UB also started a global sourcing policy (see below), which again enabled UB to cut costs, and reduce supplies from MT. Two years after the buyout the company was making profits again and was generating cash.

Some of the cash was spent acquiring a plant in Tijuana, Mexico (see below), near the US border, which Walter had seen on holiday. UB has acquired a bicycle making plant in Romania, formerly a state-run concern, and still managed by the people who ran it in communist times.

In 1998, UB was refloated on the Stock Market. The venture capitalist sold all his shares. 60% of the shares are now owned by outside investors: Walter believes very strongly that managers and directors should own shares. In July 2001, the market value of the shares in issue suggested that the company had a value of £200m. Walter and the management team are very reluctant to dilute their shareholdings further. They enjoy the control that comes of being owner directors and they think this enables them to take a longer-term view.

The firm's price/earnings ratio is high for the sector, at 6.6. Investors look forward to increased dividends.

Profits come from sales of bikes UB makes itself and from licenses and royalties paid by overseas producers. (More about this later.)

World bike production

World production of bikes is about 120m each year, of which about 40m are made in China. Of this, China exports 10m. UB itself makes 3m bikes per annum (of which 2m are made in the UK, the remainder in Mexico and Romania), although licensing agreements (see below) account for 3m more. UB makes a wider product range than most other manufacturers.

Workforce

Worldwide, UB employs 4,000 staff of whom 1,000 work on a number of temporary and part-time arrangements to cope with seasonal peaks and troughs in demand.

UB is considering changing these arrangements. A small New Zealand firm [cited by B R Lord in *Management Accounting Research*] has the following arrangement:

> 'To stabilise labour cost and provide employees with a steady income, management offer employees a contract whereupon they work only a 5 hour day in low season, but are paid for an 8 hour day. The difference in pay between a 5 hour and an 8 hour day is recorded as a debt to the company. In the busy season they work more than an 8 hour day, but only receive cash wages for 8 hours. The overtime, at overtime rates, is applied to reducing their debt. Any debt not repaid by Christmas is forgiven. The scheme benefits the employees, as they have a steady income all year round. The scheme also benefits the company, as it has a stable work-force, and the smoothed pay rate simplifies the estimation of direct labour costs.'

Supplies and suppliers: sourcing

'Nobody wants to compete on price. But I have to. I take the view that I cannot ignore low cost competition: I don't want to give them a foothold': says Walter Drake.

'About 70% of components are bought in. At the moment, the cheapest supplies come from Asia. I've got a team in Hong Kong dealing with component manufacturers, and we deal with 150 or so different firms. I'm not entirely happy about this, because we do spend a lot of money on inspection and it costs time and money to ship the components over, but the economics of it are overwhelming. If that changed, I might change my mind. I'm interested in suppliers in Eastern Europe, but they're too slow, bureaucratic and the quality isn't good enough.'

In the past UB purchased gears from Bowman Storm, but it now designs its own. Some gears it makes in-house. Standard gears it subcontracts to its Asian suppliers, who make the product to strict specifications. Walter Drake regards gears as a key part of the product technology.

UB also benefits from its past history with MT. Having suffered as a result of UB's global sourcing policy, MT wants to win back some of the business, by applying its knowledge of materials and metals. It has developed some new lightweight but extremely strong alloys, which might be useful in some bike models. Although kilogram per kilogram they are more expensive than the materials currently used, less of each material is needed to give bicycles the required strength, provided the right equipment is used in manufacture.

Costs and prices

The bikes from UB's Welsh factory sell at between £100 for the cheapest model to £1,800 for the most expensive, but on average they sell for £120. The more expensive bikes are designed for special conditions, and are made out of special alloys. On average, variable production costs account for 40%-50% of the selling price. At current production volumes, fixed production costs amount to a further 30% of sales, leaving a profit of 20%. In Mexico (and Romania), the firm in the short term intends to benefit from cheap labour. Variable production costs here are 60% of the selling price as the factories are less automated.

After marketing and distribution costs, in 2002 UB expects to make a profit of £30m.

New investment and improvements

UB is planning a £30m investment in new machinery of which £20m will be spent in Wales, £7m in Tijuana and £3m in Romania. This will double capacity, enable a 20% cut in the UK labour force, and introduce flexibility. It will enable Mexico and Romania to produce better quality bikes as well. 'Mexico is a bit more stable and the government is more pro-business than Romania in my view. And it's next to the USA. Romania is more risky altogether,' Walter feels.

In particular, the Romanian plant requires a complete change in the way it is run.

'At the moment, the Romanian managers don't seem to understand the concept of profit, or the fact that they are accountable to Unity Bicycles and shareholders far away in England. They still defer to local party functionaries or even the town council. I've sacked a few of the managers. The workforce are just used to obeying orders to fulfil the plan. The new lot are keen, but completely inexperienced in modern market and production disciplines. They want to learn but they just don't know how to take commercial decisions. You ask them for profits, and they cut down on machine maintenance. You ask them for quality, and they spend huge amounts polishing each bike by hand. I've introduced a bonus scheme based on Return on Investment.'

The Tijuana plant is a problem and an opportunity. Mexican workers are cheaper than their American counterparts, but the productivity gap is huge. Walter Drake realises that the Mexican managers are committed, but he needs to motivate them better.

All UB's state of the art production expertise is concentrated in Wales, and the managers of the UK plant are reluctant for an overseas posting.

£10m of the investment will be funded from retained profits, and the remaining £20m borrowed from the bank, at a variable interest rate of 1% over base rate, to be repaid in 2008.

Physical distribution

The factory in Wales is near the M4 motorway, within easy reach of sea ports, and Wales and west England are shortly to have a freight link directly through the Channel Tunnel. In the UK, UB still uses MT's warehouses for delivery to the Midlands and the North. For the rest of the UK it has a dedicated distribution network, direct from the factory.

For European deliveries it employs a logistics firm. Elsewhere in the world, it has joint ventures with local distributors and a variety of warehousing arrangements. Small warehouses with reserve stock are necessary in markets where infrastructure is poor.

Expansion in Asia

Walter has further ambitions. 'I really want to get back to speed in Asia. After all, that's where the biggest markets are, but it's a bit like selling coals to Newcastle. They've been making bikes for ages. In India, they're making the same models that we used to produce 30 years ago, on the same equipment. China, too. Consumers want something a bit more - and affordable cars for all are a long way off.'

UB has arrangements with many manufacturers in China. As well as sourcing supplies from Asia, the company has licensing arrangements with two firms, Li Po Bicycles and Tu Fu Cycle Co. UB collects royalties on sales of about 1.5 million bikes produced by them, amounting to £1 per bicycle. These arrangements enable UB to maintain a presence in this market, with the minimum of technology transfer for the time being, and they are a useful source of cash.

In the long-term UB is worried about overcapacity. In March 1997, The *Financial Times* carried the following report.

> The Shanghai Forever Bicycle Company, which has built 100m bicycles since 1949, is making low profits as China's bicycle market is oversupplied. To use the capacity, the firm is investing in new types of bike and, as importantly, has been exporting heavily to Africa and South America. Excess domestic capacity makes establishing overseas plants a waste of money.

In China, Walter hopes to set up a joint venture with the Bao Yu Bike Company, based in the Shenzhen special economic zone near Hong Kong. The joint venture will not make bikes but instead will provide consultancy, technology and design ideas to the many Chinese bike manufacturers, in return for more royalties, depending on the technology sold. The joint venture will eventually result in cheaper versions of mountain bikes common in the West.

In India, Walter hopes to rebuild the relationship with Unity (India) Pty, a former subsidiary nationalised in 1948. Unity (India) Pty has been making the same model of bike since that date, on UB's old equipment. UB intends to transfer to India the old equipment to be replaced in Wales, which will enable a broader product range to be sold in the Indian market.

Product range

UB and its licensees produce a huge variety of bikes. These fall into the following basic categories.

(a) High performance bicycles. UB has produced bikes for the British Olympic team, and it employs three designers who are experts in materials technology. These involve novel designs, aerodynamics and very lightweight metals. Drake regards them as a source of publicity and also a test bed for innovations that can be adopted elsewhere on the range. Walter Drake is pleased that UB bikes were ridden by the victors of the Tour de France in two successive years.

(b) Sports bikes. These are sold to cycling enthusiasts, are tough and lightweight. Product innovations are expected. UB provides sponsorship to the Bicyclists Travel Club in the UK, which promotes cycling as a recreational activity.

(c) UB is heavily promoting its mountain bikes at the moment. They partly function as a fashion statement, and are suitable for rougher roads and tracks. They are popular with hikers and ramblers, and with young people. However, fashion being what it is, demand is beginning to tail off, as the market is maturing.

(d) Commuter bikes. These are standard bicycles for general use, with an option for baskets etc. People use them to go to work, and do short trips. They are popular in the Netherlands and Germany, and countries whose governments actively promote cycling as an alternative to the car.

(e) In the UK, the company has recently introduced a collapsible bike. This folds up easily, and can be carried on the bus, train or in the back of the car. This has been successfully introduced in the Netherlands, and the firm has begun to sell these in London, on a test basis, by mail order, after a heavy advertising campaign in the Evening Standard (London's evening paper) and public relations (on Tvnews).

All UB's bikes come in a range of features and colours.

UB also provides other accessories such as reflector belts, water bottles etc. These Walter subcontracts to manufacturers in Asia. 'They are easy to make, and I can't be bothered to do them in-house'.

New products: battery powered bikes?

Recently, R&D have shown Walter Drake a new product idea. This is a battery and motor which can be fitted on the back of the bike for the rider to use when he or she needs more power, going up hill. UB has estimated these would cost £200 to make, but with experience curve effects and economies of scale, could be produced for £100 if 2 million were made each year. R&D believe these motors would encourage people to cycle who lived in hilly areas, or who were worried about getting tired. The batteries would require new chemicals and miniature components, and could be easily recharged from the mains electricity supply. Walter Drake dreams of a whole new market opening before him...

The R&D director says: 'I've lined up a possible battery manufacturer for the electric bike. Technically speaking I think this project is do-able. It would create a splash. Again, we could test it in the Netherlands, or perhaps smaller towns in the UK. Cambridge has introduced a road pricing scheme, charging car users for access to the city centre. This might be the environment for us.'

Competitors

Apart from 20 or so Chinese bike companies, UB has four competitors in Europe competing over the same product range, and three specialising in the sports bike market. UB is not too concerned with the European competitors. None of them have copied UB's licensing agreements in China. The four mainstream producers are subsidiaries of much larger firms, either in engineering or in the motor industries, much in the same way as UB was, when owned by MT. The specialist sports bike firms produce in small volumes.

EU countries

Demand is fairly stable at 15m units a year, and is expected to remain so, especially as the population 'ages'. UB has a market share of 10%. Walter believes that European customers are the most demanding in the world. Bikes are leisure products, are used for commuting, and are well within people's price range. Walter sees the following opportunities.

(a) More highly specified bikes, at premium prices, will become popular.

(b)   A possible increase in usage in some countries, as governments control the use of cars. Although in the UK commuting to work by bike is in decline, this is not necessarily the case elsewhere.

(c)   Some people are worried that their bikes will be stolen.

The EU market takes about 75% of the production of the Welsh factory. Distribution channels in the UK and France have undergone some changes. The growth of out-of-town shopping centres and other retail developments has meant that sales of bicycles, as with other leisure goods, have become concentrated amongst a number of larger firms, of which a good example is Barfields, which has large number of Bike Centres over the UK. However, 75% of bikes sold in Europe are through specialist dealers, as before: there are fewer large retail complexes in Germany. In a way this suits UB.

The firm keeps a database of dealers and retailers and monitors demand and sales. It ensures retailers have stocks of standard ranges. For high performance and some sports bikes, UB supplies a catalogue, from which customers can choose. The order is delivered as soon as possible.

Walter gets a lot of his market information from dealers, and the firm's market research staff regularly talk to them. He is aware that IT systems could be used to develop a database of individual customers, especially those who buy premium bikes.

Competition from European producers is hardly cut-throat. They are all worried about cheap imports. Some temporary protection has been offered by the EU.

Eastern Europe, Russia and the Middle East

Demand is an unknown quantity. Walter believes that there is a demand for goods of a high quality, which the UK factory will supply. In fact, at present there is a flourishing import trade for Russia's 'new rich' (the richest 10%), but at present they buy bikes made by UB's French and German competitors. Cheaper basic bikes will eventually be sourced from Romania. Walter knows that distribution is poor, especially for finished goods. He is trying to consider ways of making it easier for customers to get hold of UB's bikes.

There is one manufacturer in Russia, but there have been quality problems, particularly in relation to bike design. Walter has heard that a Russian tank factory has decided to make money by building bikes instead.

Each country in Russia and Eastern Europe will be treated as a separate market with its own sales office.

The Americas

In North America (countries covered by the NAFTA agreement, ie USA, Canada and Mexico) sales amount to about 15m bikes per year. There is less demand for bikes as commuting necessities and more as leisure vehicles. Mountain bikes are particularly popular here. The Welsh plant exports 300,000 bikes a year to North America. The entire production of the Tijuana plant goes to NAFTA countries. The US and Canada have well developed retail chains. Most of the car companies have bike subsidiaries, and there are specialist bike firms too. Unity's branded bikes have a quality image as the 'Rolls Royce' of cycling.

Walter regards America as an important growth market, and great things are expected of the Tijuana factory. Currently, bikes made at Tijuana do not use the UB brand.

India

Annual sales are about 20m. Until recently, import controls meant that bicycles were impossible to import, and all bikes were made at home. In rural India, bicycles are necessary commuting vehicles, not leisure goods. However, there is a 70 million strong middle class, who might be receptive to Western fashions. Owing to the difficulties and expense of travelling, bikes are sold through a very large number of small shops, each with a small number of models. In many villages and small towns, bikes will be sold by local garages or other tradesmen dealing with metal goods. However, in the large towns, distribution is carried out more often by specialist bike shops.

Four firms are licensed to manufacture bikes in India. One is Unity's former subsidiary, Unity (India) Pty, mentioned above.

China

Annual sales are about 30m units. (China produces 40m bikes a year, but exports 10m of these.) Again, in rural areas, bikes are a basic means of transport, and people are well served by local manufacturers. Walter hopes that the Bao Yu joint venture will account for 10% of the market. There are twenty companies making basic bikes.

Other

Annual sales elsewhere amount to about 40m bicycles although, as in Russia, Eastern Europe and the Middle East, no-one knows for sure. However, 10% of the production of the Welsh factory is exported, as premium products, to Australia, Japan, New Zealand and South Africa.

Marketing and advertising

UB has a sales department, and employs a single advertising agency in Europe. In the past, all bikes were sold under the Unity name. Some marketing consultants suggested that UB develop a number of brands for the different types of bikes and in the different markets.

Customers know that UB is an established British firm, but otherwise, they seem confused as to what UB stand for, in particular, the variety of UB's products. The marketing director wants to streamline UB's brand management.

The Mexican and Romanian plants 'still have a mountain to climb on quality management,' says Walter, 'so they're low range. Of course, once they start getting any good, it'll cost us more to make them there. I've developed a couple of low-end brand names so that people don't get the wrong idea about the Unity brand. Of course, I'll introduce Unity branding once they get any good. It means I won't be out-marketed by cheap imports, which I can make myself'.

Walter Drake takes pricing issues very seriously, hence his concern for low-cost components. He sees pricing policy as a means to ensure economies of scale in output, and in some markets it is the most important factor in a purchase decision. In competitive terms, he does not want to be driven out of the market by low cost competition. However: 'I invoice in sterling. I can't be bothered fiddling around with 20 or 30 currencies.'

Management organisation and processes

When UB was sold by MT it had an old fashioned and top heavy management structure. Sales managers were paid largely by commission on sales, but all other managers received a fixed salary. UB was regarded as a profit centre by MT, with no account taken of its on-going investment and capital needs. MT had no global ambitions for UB, seeing it, as mentioned earlier, as a steady source of cash. UB was regarded as, and was expected to be, a low risk business. Investment projects were judged on a conservative pay-back period.

As part of MT, UB hid behind the systems of a much larger business. Its revenues were supposed to cover its costs, and the firm was expected to make a profit, but there was no effort to relate this to the investment made in the company.

As far as the current organisation is concerned, each factory operates as a separate division, broadly in line with where the goods are distributed. There is some confusion in North America, where marketing is directed from Tijuana, for the cheaper bikes, and from Wales for the more expensive bikes. There is a purchasing office in Hong Kong, which sources components for the Welsh and Mexican operations. The purchasing office earns its profits by adding a 10% mark-up on cost to the components it supplies.

Walter Drake is suspicious of people he regards as 'unproductive bean counters' and likes to keep administration and accounting systems simple and streamlined. Broadly speaking, he wants to know:

On a weekly basis

- Volume sales for each country
- Sterling value of sales

Monthly and annually

- Total revenue per country
- Total production costs
- Gross profit
- Market share

UB's accountants prepare budgets on a rolling twelve month basis. These budgets can be flexed for different levels of demand. Every year there is a thorough budget review, normally in February.

Overheads are absorbed over the volume of bikes produced on the basis of direct labour hours. Walter Drake takes great care to monitor costs, especially at the Hong Kong buying centre. 'I know what the competition are paying as I pay the same price myself.'

A standard costing system is used to keep track of costs. Standards are set annually, at the same time as the annual budget review. Actual results are always meticulously reconciled to standard.

Walter Drake reviews marketing expenses, in particular the costs of distribution, with a view to driving them down further. At the moment, many of the retailers hold the bikes on a consignment basis until they are sold. This means that UB is financing their stock. Walter feels that this is the best way of ensuring that retailers carry the stock and display it to customers, even though this is expensive, but he would much rather the shopkeepers paid up front. He regards advertising as an expense, and does a rough and ready calculation, apportioning advertising expenditure by the size of the market, and generally uses print media. Walter Drake has no time for TV advertisements or other communications innovations: 'They cost too much'.

Strategic anxieties

The management buyout team are pleased with the direction the company is taking. It has a toehold in most of the major growth markets, and it is addressing seriously the problem of low cost competition. At a board meeting in June 2000, the following points were made.

By the production director of the Wales plant: 'We need some idea as to where the company is going. I know you're investing all this money over here, but are you going to invest even more in

China? What am I going to do with all the capacity? The new machines will enable us to develop different types of bike more quickly.'

By the finance director: 'I know we would all like to hold on to our shares, but I feel that borrowing as a means of expansion is a risky option. I don't see why we can't put a further 20% of the shares into the market. We'd still retain control on crucial decisions. It also concerns me that we have not discussed what we will achieve from the factory investment. We're doubling capacity in the UK and Europe; that's fine, but can we make it pay? Not even the Chancellor of the Exchequer can predict interest rates 8 years from now. What return do we expect on this investment?'

By Walter Drake: 'Now we're a bigger company, we need to give our new plants a sense of direction, to motivate the managers if nothing else, especially in North America. I feel we need to look at some of our operations, in particular quality and how we build our brands. Also the current divisional structure has got to change into something more in line with how the business actually works'.

BPP PUBLISHING

Part A
Setting objectives

Chapter 1

BUSINESS STRATEGY AND THE MANAGEMENT ACCOUNTANT

Topic list	Syllabus reference	Ability required
1 Management accounting and business strategy - an introductory note	(iv)	Comprehension/evaluation
2 The design of management accounting systems	(iv)	Comprehension/evaluation
3 System design: contingency theory	(iv)	Comprehension/evaluation
4 Strategy and management control	(iv)	Comprehension/evaluation

Introduction

This chapter introduces the **role** of the management accountant in **strategic planning**. Even though the design and operation of the **management accounting system** appears in part (iv) of the syllabus, it is important to realise that many management accounting issues underpin the strategic planning process and their relationship must be clear from the outset, when **objectives** are being set.

In section 1 we discuss the role of the management accountant in strategy formulation. The role of the management accountant in preparing and presenting information for decision making, laying particular emphasis on **external factors**, is central to this study text.

In sections 2 and 3 we look at the **design** of management accounting systems, including **contingency theory**.

Section 4 considers the importance of **management control systems** in the strategy process.

Learning outcomes covered in this chapter

- **Identify** and **evaluate** approaches to the design and operation of the management accounting systems

Syllabus content covered in this chapter

- The role of the management accounting and information systems in supporting management and the appropriateness of management accounting techniques for alternative organisational structures and philosophies

- The concept and design of a strategic management accounting information system to assist strategy formulation, implementation and control

1 MANAGEMENT ACCOUNTING AND BUSINESS STRATEGY: AN INTRODUCTORY NOTE

Management accounting and planned strategies

1.1 The role of the **management accountant in strategic planning** is to provide management information in order that strategic planning and control decisions can be made. Particular examples of the role of the management accountant are found throughout this text.

KEY TERM

Management accounting. 'The application of the principles of accounting and financial management to create, protect, preserve and increase value so as to deliver that value to the stakeholders of profit and not-for-profit enterprises, both public and private. Management accounting is an integral part of management, requiring the identification, generation, presentation, interpretation and use of information relevant to:

- formulating business strategy
- planning and controlling activities
- decision making
- efficient resource usage
- performance improvement and value enhancement
- Safeguarding tangible and intangible assets
- corporate governance and internal control'

(CIMA *Official Terminology*)

Future uncertainty

1.2 It is worth emphasising the **uncertainty** in much strategic planning.

   (a) Strategic plans may cover a **long period** into the future.

   (b) Many strategic plans involve big changes and **new ventures,** such as capacity expansion decisions or decisions to develop into new product areas and new markets.

1.3 Inevitably, management accounting information for strategic planning will be based on incomplete data and will use **forecasts** and **estimates.**

   (a) It follows that strategic management accounting information is unlikely to give clear guidelines for management decisions and should incorporate some **risk and uncertainty analysis** (eg sensitivity analysis).

   (b) For longer term plans, DCF techniques ought to be used in financial evaluation.

   (c) The management accountant will be involved in the following.

   - Project evaluation
   - Managing cash and operational matters
   - Reviewing the outcome of the project (post implementation review)

External and competitor orientation

1.4 Much management accounting information has been devised for internal consumption.

   - Strategic management involves **environmental considerations**
   - A strategy is pursued in relation to **competitors**

Case example

A survey by the University of Manchester discovered that the following factors are seen as important in defining the role of the management accountant.

	% of respondents
Information technology	73
Organisational restructuring	53
New accounting software	41
Customer orientated initiatives	39
New management styles	36
E-commerce/electronic business	32
External reporting requirements	24
Core competency aims	23
Globalisation	23
Takeover/merger	20
Quality-orientated initiatives	18
New accounting techniques	16
External consultants advice	12
Production technologies	8

The challenge for management accountants

1.5   The challenge lies in providing more relevant information for decision making. Traditional management accounting systems may not always provide this.

(a)   **Historical costs** are not necessarily the best guide to decision-making. One of the criticisms of management accounting outlined by Kaplan, Bromwich and Bhimani, and so on is that management accounting information is biased towards the **past rather than the future.**

(b)   **Strategic issues** are not easily detected by management accounting systems.

(c)   **Financial models** of some sophistication are needed to enable management accountants to provide useful information.

The characteristics of a strategic management accounting system are discussed in some detail later in this chapter.

What is strategy?

1.6   Strategy is a concept that has many shades of meaning.

KEY TERM

A **strategy** is 'a course of action, including the specification of resources required, to achieve a specific objective'. (CIMA *Official Terminology*)

1.7   A basic premise is that strategy is concerned with **long-term direction**. Johnson and Scholes (1999) develop this idea.

'Strategy is the **direction and scope** of an organisation over the **long term** which **achieves advantage** for the organisation through its **configuration of resources** within a **changing environment,** to meet the **needs of markets** and to fulfil **stakeholder expectations**.'

BPP PUBLISHING

1.8 We can take the highlighted phrases out of this definition, and expand them to indicate that there is general agreement on what constitutes the key elements of strategy.

Phrase	Comment
Direction and scope	Strategy gives at least an **initial deliberate direction**, range of **activities** and **future** for the company to aim at, even if environmental circumstances conspire to send it off course and demand management action.
Long term	Most organisations are 'in it' for the **achievement of objectives** that will go beyond short-term profit targets. What constitutes 'long term' in business strategy is open to debate; Stacey (2000) claims that the average lifespan of commercial organisations in Western countries is about 40 years. Bear in mind that: • Time horizons are culturally determined; the 'long-term' means different things in different cultures. • The 'long-term' varies from industry to industry: compare fashion retailing with mining. A turnround strategy for a fashion retailer depends on success in one or two seasons.
Achieves advantage	Strategy affects the overall **welfare** of the organisation and its **position against competitors**.
Configuration of resources	Strategies require **processes** to guide the **effective utilisation** of resources and competences.
Changing environment	It is a tenet of business strategy that an organisation is inextricably linked with its environment, and strategy can help the organisation to cope with **changes** and **complexity**.
Needs of markets	The satisfaction of market demands is a key factor in any business strategy. '**What business are we in?**' is an important starting point.
Stakeholder expectations	As well as **customers**, other stakeholders (in particular **shareholders**) have their own interests in the organisation. Should the pursuit of shareholder wealth be the main concern of management?

1.9 Mintzberg (1998) argues that five definitions of strategy are needed. These are represented on the diagram which we have developed below.

POINT TO NOTE

The diagram goes beyond giving a definition of strategy; it indicates some of the issues in the development of strategic thinking that we will be examining in the next chapter. The basic distinction is between planning a strategy (being 'rational'), and allowing it to emerge ('crafting' and learning).

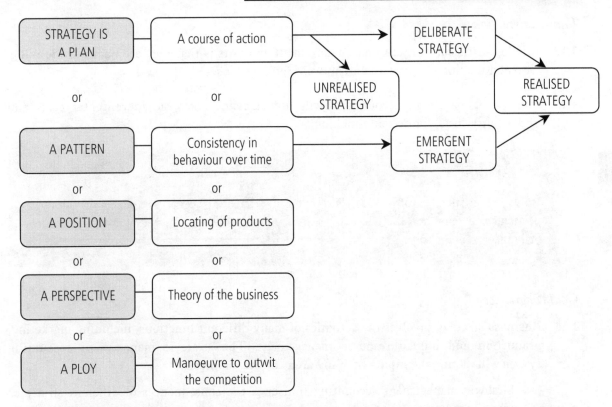

What is strategic management accounting?

> **KEY TERM**
>
> CIMA has defined **strategic management accounting** as follows: 'A form of management accounting in which emphasis is placed on information which relates to factors external to the firm, as well as non-financial information and internally-generated information'.

1.10   Ward suggests that the role of the strategic management accountant can be analysed as follows.

    (a)   **Financial analysis** indicates the **current position** of a business and its financial performance in comparison with competitors, as well as breaking it down into product and customer profitability analyses. (These are discussed in later chapters.)

    (b)   **Financial planning** quantifies the goals and objectives of the business, normally in a budget.

    (c)   **Financial control**. Financial information is an essential part of the **feedback** mechanism comparing planned with actual performance.

External orientation

1.11   The important fact which distinguishes strategic management accounting from other management accounting activities is its **external orientation**, towards customers and competitors, suppliers and perhaps other stakeholders.

    (a)   **Competitive advantage is relative**. Understanding competitors is therefore of prime importance.

    (b)   **Customers** determine if a firm has competitive advantage.

Future orientation

1.12 Another criticism of traditional management accounts is that they are **backward-looking**. Decision-making is a forward and outward looking process.

1.13 Strategic management accountants will use **relevant costs** (ie **incremental** costs and **opportunity** costs) for decision-making.

> ### KEY TERM
>
> **Relevant costs** are future cash flows arising as a direct consequence of taking a particular decision and include extra cash payments, savings in cash payments and extra or reduced revenues.

Goal congruence

1.14 **Business strategy** involves the activities of many different functions, including marketing, production and human resource management. The strategic management accounting system will require the **inputs of many areas of the business**.

(a) Strategic management accounting translates the consequences of different strategies into a **common accounting language for comparison**.

(b) It **relates business operations to financial performance**, and therefore helps ensure that business activities are focused on shareholders' needs for profit.

(c) It **helps to ensure goal congruence**, again by translating business activities into the common language of finance.

> ### KEY TERM
>
> **Goal congruence.** 'In a control system, the state which leads individuals or groups to take actions which are in their self-interest and also in the best interest of the entity. Goal incongruence exists when the interests of individuals or of groups associated with an entity are not in harmony.'
>
> (CIMA *Official Terminology*)

What information could strategic management accounting provide?

1.15 Bearing in mind the need for **goal congruence**, **external orientation** and **future orientation**, some **examples** of strategic management accounting are provided below.

(a) **Competitors' costs**. What are they? How do they compare with ours? Can we beat them? Are competitors vulnerable because of their cost structure?

(b) **Financial effect of competitor response**.

(c) **Product profitability**. A firm should want to know what profits or losses are being made by each of its products, and why.

(d) **Customer profitability**. Some customers or groups of customers are worth more than others.

(e) **Pricing decisions**. Accounting information can help to analyse how profits and cash flows will vary according to price and prospective demand.

(f) The **value of market share**. A firm ought to be aware of what it is worth to increase the market share of one of its products.

(g) **Capacity expansion**. Should the firm expand its capacity, and if so by how much?

(h) **Brand values**. How much is it worth investing in a 'brand' which customers will choose over competitors' brands?

(i) **Shareholder wealth**. Future profitability determines the value of a business.

(j) **Cash-flow**. A loss-making company can survive if it has adequate cash resources, but a profitable company cannot survive unless it has sufficient liquidity.

(k) Effect of **acquisitions** and **mergers**.

(l) Decisions to **enter or leave a business area**.

(m) Introduction of **new technology**.

POINT TO NOTE

Most strategic decisions are unique, so the information needed to support them is likely to be ad hoc and specially tailored.

Useful cost categories for strategic management accounting

1.16 Some cost classifications are particularly relevant.

KEY TERMS

Incremental/differential costs. These are the differences in total cost between alternatives. For strategic decision-making they can be considered as the extra cost that would be incurred by a decision.

Avoidable/unavoidable costs. These are the specific costs of an activity or sector of a business which would be avoided if that activity or sector did not exist.

Committed costs. For strategic decision-making purposes, a committed cost is 'any cost which cannot be changed at the behest of the business during the time-scale of the decision'.

Controllable/uncontrollable costs. Some costs are susceptible to control by managers and some are not.

Opportunity cost is the value of a benefit sacrificed in favour of an alternative course of action. For example, a firm might save £100,000 by cutting its advertising expenditure, but there might be an opportunity cost in that sales revenue (and profits) might be lost.

Success factors for a strategic management accounting system (SMAS)

1.17 Strategic management accounting has to bridge a gap between financial reporting on the one hand and the uncertainties of the future on the other. We can now go on to identify the success factors of a strategic management accounting system (as outlined by Ward). It should:

- Aid strategic decisions
- Close the communication gap between accountants and managers

- Identify the type of decision
- Offer appropriate financial performance indicators
- Distinguish between economic and managerial performance
- Provide relevant information
- Separate committed from discretionary costs
- Distinguish discretionary from engineered costs
- Use standard costs strategically
- Allow for changes over time

These are now discussed in more detail.

Aid strategic decisions

1.18 As part of a strategic management system, the SMAS will provide one-off information to support and evaluate particular strategic decisions and information for strategic management, in order to monitor strategies and the firm's overall competitive position. Changes in the external environment and competitor responses should be easily incorporated into the system.

Question 1

Gamma Ltd produces seven products A, B, C, D, E, F, G. Of this product range G is heavily loss-making, but it shares a distribution channel with E and F, both of which make reasonable profits. If necessary, product E can be distributed, at some extra costs, in the distribution channel currently serving A, B, C and D. What are the relevant issues behind any production decision?

Answer

(a) If G is not sold, the distribution channel would still be used by E and F, therefore most of the costs of *distributing* G are unavoidable.

(b) It might be cheaper, then, to stop selling F and G entirely and incur the extra costs of delivering E. This is because G's losses would be avoided, as would all the costs of the distribution channel for E, F and G; and the only sacrifice would be F's small profit.

(c) On the other hand, sales of G, whilst loss-making, might make it harder for a competitor to 'invade' the distribution channel, firstly with a replacement for G and then with more serious competition for profitable E and F.

Close the communication gap

1.19 The SMAS converts financial data into information for strategic decision-making. Financial data is off-putting to many people. Consequently, the preparer of such information should make sure that it is tailored.

- Ask the recipient how he or she would like the **format** of the report
- Provide only the **relevant** supporting financial data
- Identify the **key assumptions** on which the information is prepared

Identify the types of the decision

1.20 Ward states that, despite the one-off nature of many strategic decisions, it is possible to identify the following types of financial decision.

(a) **Changing the balance of resource allocation** between different business areas, for example by increasing spending in one area.

(b) **Entering a new business area** (eg new product development, new markets). Some account will have to be taken of the timescale in which the strategy is expected to consume resources, as benefits may be some time in coming.

(c) **Exit decisions** which come in two forms.

- **Closing down** part of the business and selling off the assets
- Selling the business as a **going concern**

1.21 To support such decisions, the SMAS should:

- Incorporate **future cash flows** rather than historic costs
- Include only those items which will be **changed** by the particular decision

Suitable financial performance measures

1.22 Two general points can be made.

(a) **Financial data is not enough**. Customers drive a business, and competitors can ruin it, so performance measures which ignore key variables of customer satisfaction or competitor activity ignore critical strategic issues.

(b) **The financial information must suit the competitive strategies**. A report complaining about the expense of an advertising campaign ignores the fact that failing to advertise could lead to loss of market share.

Economic versus managerial performance

1.23 A business's **overall economic performance** results from both controllable factors and uncontrollable factors.

(a) **Risk**. Shareholders may be happy with the risk, if it is balanced by suitable return, but a manager may be unhappy if his or her career is at risk from pursuing a strategy whose success is outside his or her control.

(b) **Performance**. Judging a manager's contribution on the basis of the overall economic performance of the business may not reflect his or her contribution at all. Managers should therefore be judged on their contribution over areas over which they have control.

Provide relevant information

1.24 **Relevant financial information** should be provided, which presents strategic decisions from the organisation's viewpoint. Specific, tailored reports should support individual decisions and activities, perhaps with **profitability analyses** for each market segment.

Separate committed from discretionary costs

1.25 **Ignore sunk costs**. This has a number of ramifications for the making of business strategies.

- A cost may be **committed** even though it has not actually been incurred.
- **Discretionary costs** are those over which the decision-maker still has choice.

Distinguish between discretionary and engineered costs

1.26 **Engineered costs** are those which derive from a relatively predictable relationship between input materials and output units of production.

11

Use standard costs strategically

1.27 **Standard costs** consist of a physical usage element (eg volume of materials) and a price element. The split between the **price** and **usage** elements is indicative.

- The extent to which the firm is **vulnerable** to suppliers raising prices
- The possible impact of **trade-offs** between, say, labour and materials

1.28 **Trade-offs.** If the relationships between the input material and output quantities are known, or variable, then standard costing can show the financial effects of different mixes.

(a) For example, if there is a trade off between labour and raw materials, changes in the relative costs of these factors can indicate a suitable mix: more expensive labour would result in less of a valued raw material being used.

(b) If the price of a raw material escalates suddenly, the standard costing system can be amended with the new price, and a new mix analysis calculated which takes it into account.

1.29 **Absorbing indirect/fixed overheads** into products can lead to poor pricing decisions, in the short term. If a factory is working at 60% capacity utilisation, this could lead to higher indirect costs being absorbed per unit. This information, if wrongly interpreted, could be used to suggest a price rise, rather than a reduction to encourage more sales and hence an increased utilisation of capacity.

2 THE DESIGN OF MANAGEMENT ACCOUNTING SYSTEMS   Pilot paper

What is a management accounting system (MAS)?

Exam focus point

Textbooks at this level generally do not ask such basic questions as this, but if you are asked in the exam (and you will be!) to select an appropriate management accounting system for a specific purpose it is helpful to have some concrete ideas.

2.1 Let us define a MAS by means of its more tangible components.

(a) Some **people** with accounting knowledge

(b) The **equipment** they use

(c) Paper or computer **records of financial transactions**

(d) **Codes** or **titles** describing the purpose of the financial transaction ('Rent') and who it was incurred on behalf of ('Factory A')

(e) **Records of the usage of resources** other than money, such as time, physical materials, energy and so forth

(f) A large variety of simple and complex **mathematical techniques** for arranging and analysing information.

- Double-entry analysis
- Percentages and ratios
- Tabulation of figures
- Budgets
- DCF calculations
- Adding up and subtracting
- Linear programming
- Methods of allocating costs
- Risk analysis (probabilities etc)
- Relevant costing

(g) **Reports** that are produced by the staff in (a), using (b) to (f).

(h) **People** to whom the reports are given

This is a **system because it has inputs** (items (a) to (e)), **processes** (item (f)) and **outputs** (item (g)).

Designing a management accounting system

2.2 The following factors should be considered when designing a management accounting system.

Factor	Detail
Output required	The management accountant must identify the information needs of managers. If a particular manager finds pie-charts most useful the system should be able to produce them.
Response required	A further, vitally important issue is how managers are likely to behave, depending on what factors or figures are stressed in the information they are given.
When the output is required	If information is needed within the hour the system should be capable of producing it at this speed.
Sources of input information	The production manager may require a report detailing the precise operations of his machines. The management accounting system could only acquire this information if suitable production technology had been installed.
Processing involved	This is generally a cost/benefit calculation: some of the information that could be provided would cost more to produce than the benefit obtained from having it.

2.3 **Designing a management accounting system effectively means devising ways to provide accounting information for managers to use.** Remember however that managers need information that financial accounting systems and cost accounting systems on their own do not provide.

- They need **detailed** information, to help them to run the business.
- They also need **forward-looking** information, for planning.
- They will want data to be **analysed differently**, to suit their specific requirements.

Question 2

What are the features of good (management accounting) information?

Answer

All good information should have the following features.

- It should be **relevant** to the user's needs
- It should be **accurate** within the user's needs
- It should inspire the user's **confidence**
- It should be **timely**
- It should be **appropriately communicated**
- It should be **cost-effective**

We may further identify features that pertain particularly to management accounting information.

- It is generally **forward-looking**
- It can be **financial or non-financial, quantitative or qualitative**
- It should be **free from bias**
- It is often **comparative**

2.4 Management accounting information is used by managers for a variety of purposes.

  (a) To **make decisions**. Managers are faced with several types of decision.

    (i) **Strategic decisions** (which relate to the longer term objectives of a business) require information which tends to relate to the organisation as a whole, is in summary form and is derived from both internal and external sources.

    (ii) **Tactical and operational decisions** (which relate to the short or medium term and to a department, product or division rather than the organisation as a whole) require information which is more detailed and more restricted in its sources.

  (b) To **plan** for the future. Managers have to plan and they need information to do this, much of it management accounting information.

  (c) To **monitor the performance** of the business. Managers need to know what they want the business to achieve (targets or standards) and what the business is actually achieving. By comparing the actual achievements with targeted performance, management can decide whether control action is needed.

  (d) To **measure profits** and put a **value to stocks**. Management accounting systems can be used to analyse the profitability of the business as a whole, and of the individual divisions, departments or products within the business. Putting a value to closing stocks is an element in the measurement of profits in a period (as well as for balance sheet valuation purposes) and costing systems are used to derive stock values.

Strategic planning, management control and operational control 5/01

2.5 Another way of looking at the information that a MAS may be required to produce is to consider the question under three headings put forward by Anthony: strategic planning, management control and operational control.

Question 3

Explain how information needs may differ at these three levels. If you can't you need to do some revision!

Exam focus point

The May 2001 paper contained a question on how the management accountant of a passenger ferry service company should provide reports for operational and strategic planning purposes.

Strategic planning information

KEY TERM

Strategic plan. 'A statement of long term goals, along with a definition of the strategies and policies which will ensure achievement of these goals.'

(CIMA *Official Terminology*)

2.6 **Strategic plans** include such matters as the selection of products and markets, the required levels of company profitability and the purchase and disposal of subsidiary companies or major fixed assets.

2.7 **Strategic planning information** is generally **external data** about competitors, customers, suppliers, new technology, the state of markets and the economy, government legislation, political unrest and so on.

2.8 Such information includes overall profitability, the profitability of different segments of the business, future market prospects, the availability and cost of raising new funds, total manning levels and capital equipment needs. Much of this information must come from **environmental sources,** although internally generated information will always be used.

POINT TO NOTE

Strategic information is prepared on an **ad hoc basis**. It also tends to be more **approximate** and **imprecise** than management control information.

Management control information

KEY TERM

Management control. 'All of the processes used by managers to ensure that organisational goals are achieved and procedures adhered to, and that the organisation responds appropriately to changes in the environment.

Closed loop system
A control system which includes a provision for corrective action, taken on either a feedforward or a feedback basis

Feedback control
The measurement of differences between planned outputs and actual outputs achieved, and the modification of subsequent action and/or plans to achieve future required results

Feedforward control
The forecasting of differences between actual and planned outcomes, and the implementation of action, before the event, to avoid such differences

Open loop system
A control system which includes no provision for corrective action to be applied to the sequence of activities.'

(CIMA *Official Terminology*)

2.9 The information required for management control **embraces the entire organisation** and **provides a comparison between actual results and the plan.** The information is often **quantitative** (labour hours, quantities of materials consumed, volumes of sales and production) and is commonly **expressed in money terms**.

2.10 Such information includes productivity measurements, budgetary control or variance analysis reports, cash flow forecasts, profit results within a particular department of the organisation, labour turnover statistics within a department and so on. A large proportion of this information will be **generated from within the organisation** and it will often have an **accounting emphasis**.

PUBLISHING

Operational control information

2.11 Operational information is information which is **needed for the conduct of day-to-day implementation of plans**. It will include much 'transaction data' such as data about customer orders, purchase orders, cash receipts and payments.

2.12 The amount of **detail** provided in information is likely to vary with the purpose for which it is needed, and operational information is likely to go into much more detail than management control information. Operational information is often **expressed in terms of units, hours, quantities of material and so on.**

3 SYSTEM DESIGN: CONTINGENCY THEORY   5/02

KEY TERM

Contingency theory is the 'Hypothesis that there can be no universally applicable best practice in the design of organisational units or of control systems such as management accounting systems. The efficient design and functioning of such systems is dependent on an awareness by the system designer of the specific environmental factors which influence their operation, such as organisational structure, technology base and market situation'.

(CIMA *Official Terminology*)

3.1 As Emmanuel et al say, 'what contingency theorists have done is to try to identify the specific features of an organisation's context that impact on particular features of accounting system design'.

Exam focus point

This is directly relevant to the exam, when you will be asked about accounting system design in very specific contexts. The May 2002 exam scenario question asked candidates to identify useful pieces of further management accounting information after undertaking preliminary analysis of turnover and costs.

3.2 The major factors that have been identified are classified by Emmanuel et al as follows.

(a) **The environment**

- Its degree of predictability
- The degree of competition faced
- The number of different product markets faced
- The degree of hostility exhibited by competing organisations

(b) **Organisational structure**

- Size
- Interdependence of parts
- Degree of decentralisation
- Availability of resources

(c) **Technology**

- The nature of the production process
- The routineness/complexity of the production process

- How well the relationship between ends and means is understood
- The amount of variety in each task that has to be performed

3.3 The following example is a highly simplistic application of the theory but it may help you to grasp ideas that are generally presented in a highly abstract way by accounting academics.

3.4 EXAMPLE: CONTINGENCY THEORY AND MANAGEMENT ACCOUNTING SYSTEMS

Stable Ltd makes three different products, X, Y and Z. It has never had any competitors. Every month the managing director receives a report from the management accountant in the following form (the numbers are for illustration only).

	£
Sales	10,000
Production costs	5,000
Gross profit	5,000
Administrative costs	1,000
Net profit	4,000

A few months ago **another company**, Turbulence & Co, **entered the market** for products X and Y, **undercutting the prices** charged by Stable Ltd. Turbulence has now started to **win some of Stable's customers**.

The managing director asks the management accountant for **information about the profitability of its own versions of products X and Y**. Sales information is easy to reanalyse, but to analyse production information in this way requires a **new system of coding** to be introduced. Eventually the management accountant comes up with the following report.

	X	Y	Z	Total
	£	£	£	£
Sales	3,000	3,000	4,000	10,000
Production costs	500	500	4,000	5,000
Gross profit	2,500	2,500	-	5,000
Administrative costs				1,000
Net profit				4,000

As a result of receiving this information the MD **drops the price** of Stable's products X and Y. He **divides the production function into two divisions**, one of which will concentrate exclusively upon reducing the costs of product Z while maintaining quality.

The **management accountant** is asked to **work closely** with the division Z **production manager** in designing a system that will help to monitor and control costs. He is also to work closely with the **marketing managers** of products X and Y so that the organisation can respond rapidly to any further competitive pressures. **Reports** are to be made **weekly** and are to include as **much information** as can be determined about Turbulence's financial performance, pricing, marketing penetration and so on.

This example may be **explained in terms of contingency theory** as follows.

(a) **Originally the design of the accounting system** is determined by the facts that Stable Ltd faces a **highly predictable environment**, and that it is a **highly centralised organisation**.

(b) The **design of the new system** is the **result of a new set of contingent variables:** the entry of Turbulence into two of Stable's markets requires the system to adopt a product-based reporting structure with more externally-derived information in the case of products X and Y and more detailed analysis of internal information in the case of product Z. This is matched by a change in the structure of the organisation as a whole.

> **REMEMBER**
>
> Contingency theorists' aim is to identify specific features of an organisation's context that affect the design of particular features of that organisation's accounting system

Contingent variables

3.5 In the 1990 edition of Emmanuel et al's book there is a review of the major studies in the contingency theory tradition up until that time. These are classified under the headings 'environment' and technology' (as before), with 'organisation' being sub-divided into 'size', 'strategy' and 'culture'. In the remainder of this section we give a summary of the main points made in this discussion.

> **Exam focus point**
>
> It is certainly worth spending some time reading through these lists of points. Once you have glanced through a few examination questions asking you to suggest an appropriate control system for a particular scenario you will be very glad to have a head full of ideas such as the following.

Environment

3.6 Emmanuel et al identify **uncertainty as the major factor in the environment affecting the design of accounting control systems.**

(a) The **sophistication** of an accounting system is influenced by the intensity of **competition** faced.

(b) Organisations use accounting information in different ways depending upon the **type of competition faced** (for example competition on price as opposed to product rivalry).

(c) **Budget information is evaluated** by senior managers **rigidly in 'tough' environments,** but more flexibly in 'liberal' environments.

(d) The **more dynamic** the environment (that is the more rapidly it changes), the **more frequently accounting control reports** will be required.

(e) The **larger the number of product markets** an organisation is in, the **more decentralised its control system** will be, with quasi-independent responsibility centres.

(f) The more **severe** the **competition,** the **more sophisticated the accounting information system** will be, for example incorporating non-financial information.

(g) The design of an organisation's accounting system will be affected by its environment. An organisation's **environment** will be somewhere **between** the **two extremes simple/complex** and somewhere between the **two extremes static/dynamic.**

(h) The **more complex the structure** of an organisation the **more accounting control 'tools'** it will have.

(i) **'Turbulence'** or discontinuity in an organisation's environment often requires the **replacement of control tools** which have been rendered obsolete by new ones.

(j) Control systems are not determined by organisation structure: **both structure and control systems are dependent on the environment.** In an **uncertain environment** more use will be made of **external, non-financial and projected information.**

(k) In conditions of **uncertainty, subjective methods of performance evaluation** are more effective.

(l) Accounting systems are **affected by** the extent to which the organisation is **manipulated by other organisations** such as competitors, suppliers, customers or government bodies.

Exam focus point

A question on the May 2002 paper approached the uncertainty of the environment from another angle, by asking how management information can ever hope to be relevant in a rapidly changing environment such as that experienced by 21st century computer companies.

Technology

3.7 (a) The nature of the **production process** (for example jobbing on the one hand or mass production on the other) determines the **amount of cost allocation** rather than **cost apportionment** that can be done.

(b) The **complexity of the 'task'** that an organisation performs **affects the financial control structure**.

(c) The **amount of data** produced, **what** that data is **about** and **how it is used** closely **correlates** with the **number of things that go wrong in a production process and the procedures used to investigate the problems**.

(d) The **more automated** a production process is, the **more 'formality'** there will be in the use of budget systems.

(e) The structure and processes of (and so, presumably, the method of accounting for) **operational units** tend to be related to **technological variables** while the structure and processes of **managerial/planning units** tend to be related to **environmental variables**.

Size

3.8 (a) As an organisation grows it will initially organise on a **functional basis** (see Chapter 12 for more on organisational structure). If it diversifies into different products or markets it will re-organise into **semi-autonomous divisions**. The **same accounting system** that is used to measure overall performance can then be **applied en bloc to each individual division**.

(b) In larger organisations the greater degree of **decentralisation** seems to lead to greater **participation** in budgeting.

Culture

3.9 (a) Control systems which are inconsistent with an organisation's value system or with the language or symbols that help to make up its culture are likely to create **resistance**: typically people would develop informal ways to get round controls that were regarded as intrusive.

(b) New control systems that **threaten to alter existing power relationships** may be **thwarted** by those affected.

(c) Control processes will be most **effective** if they operate by generating a corporate culture that is **supportive** of organisational aims, objectives and methods of working, and which is **consistent** with the demands of the environment in which the organisation operates.

4   STRATEGY AND MANAGEMENT CONTROL

Strategy

4.1   We offered some definitions of strategy earlier in this chapter.

Management control systems and competitive advantage

4.2   Robert Simons conducted a study that examined the **effects of strategy on management control systems and vice versa**. He looked at two companies competing in the same industry. One followed a '**cost leadership**' strategy, the other a '**differentiation**' strategy (see Chapter 9). He found that there were significant differences in the way that the two companies used basically similar control systems.

Top management control systems	Cost leadership strategy	Differentiation strategy
Strategic planning review	Sporadic. Last update 2 years ago. Does not motivate a lot of discussion in the company.	Intensive annual process. Business managers prepare strategic plans for debate by top management committee.
Financial goals	Set by top management and communicated down through organisation.	Established by each business unit and rolled up after a series of review and challenge meetings.
Budget preparation and review	Budgets prepared to meet financial goals. Budgets coordinated by Finance Dept and presented to top management when assured that goals will be met.	Market segment prepares budgets with focus on strategy and tactics. Intensive debate at presentations to top management committee.
Budget revisions and updates	Not revised during budget year	Business units rebudget from lowest expense three times during year with action plans to deal with changes.
Program reviews	Intensive monitoring of product and process-related programs. Programs cut across organisational boundaries and affect all layers of company.	Programs limited to R&D which is delegated to local operating companies.
Evaluation and reward	Percentage of bonus based on contribution to generating profit in excess of plan based on personal goals (usually quantified).	Bonus based on subjective evaluation of effort, MBO system used throughout organisation.

Source: R Simons, 'The role of management control systems in creating competitive advantage: new perspectives,' *Accounting, Organisations and Society*, (1990)

Types of control system

4.3   Simons went on in 1995 (*Levels of Control: How Management use Innovative Control Systems to Drive Strategic Renewal*) to identify **four types of control system** used by top managers.

Type of control system	Detail
Beliefs systems	Determine purpose from such [documents] as mission statements or statements of purpose, and guide or limit the search for opportunities.
Boundary systems	Define limits. These vary from codes of conduct to operational guidelines, but include strategic planning systems and capital expenditure authorisation systems which define the limits of areas in which the search for opportunities can be conducted.
Diagnostic control systems	Monitor operations against preset standards of performance - typically budgeting systems and operating statements.
Interactive control systems	Typically profit-planning systems, project and brand management systems, budget formulation and planning - focusing on forecast information and possible opportunities.

Simons also distinguishes **internal control systems** as essential to **ensure the integrity and reliability of all other systems**.

Strategies and styles

4.4   Goold and Campbell conducted a study of a large number of high profile diversified companies to examine **how different companies cope with the problem of managing diversity** (*Strategies and Styles*: *The Role of the Centre in Managing Diversified Corporations*, 1987).

4.5   They discovered three main philosophies and three corresponding styles of strategic management.

Philosophy	Example	Style of management
Core businesses	Cadbury's. 'The company commits itself to a few industries and sets out to win big in those industries.'	Strategic planning style
Manageable businesses	Hanson Trust. 'The emphasis is on selecting businesses for the portfolio which can be effectively managed using short-term financial controls...' The businesses have few linkages with each other, should be in relatively stable competitive environments and should not involve large or long-term investment decisions.	Financial control style
Diverse businesses	ICI before demerger. 'The centre seeks to build a portfolio that spreads risk across industries and geographic areas as well as ensuring that the portfolio is balanced in terms of growth, profitability and cash flow.'	Strategic control style

4.6 Goold and Campbell describe the features of the different styles of central management as follows.

Style of central management	Features
Strategic planning	Entails the centre participating in and influencing the strategies of the core businesses. The centre establishes a planning process and contributes to strategic thinking. Rather less emphasis is placed on financial controls and performance targets are set flexibly and reviewed within the context of long-term progress.
Financial control	As the name suggests, focuses on annual profit targets. There are no long-term planning documents and no strategy documents. The role of the centre is limited to approving budgets and monitoring performance.
Strategic control	Concerned with the plans of its business units but believes in autonomy for business unit managers. Plans are therefore made locally but reviewed in a formal planning process to upgrade the quality of the thinking. The centre does not advocate strategies or interfere with major decisions but maintains control through financial targets and strategic objectives.

4.7 Since they conducted their original work Goold and Campbell have periodically reviewed the companies they visited. Several found it necessary to **change their style in response to factors** such as the **recession** in the late 80s and early 90s. Some had changed style in association with a **new chief executive** and **top management team**.

The limitations of contingency theory

4.8 Logically, one would expect those researching into the field of contingency theory and management accounting to have put forward suggestions as to how accounting systems could be improved by demonstrating what systems work well in what circumstances. So far, however, **contingency theory** seems to have **provided no more than a framework for describing existing accounting systems.**

4.9 There has been no better summary of the pros and cons of contingency theory than the conclusion to Otley's 1980 article 'The contingency theory of management accounting: achievement and prognosis' (*Accounting, Organisations and Society*) on which much of the relevant chapter in the later book by Emmanuel, Otley and Merchant is based. Otley's conclusion is quoted below, with emphasis added by BPP for clarity.

> 'A contingency theory of management accounting has a **great deal of appeal**. It is in **accord with practical wisdom** and appears to afford a **potential explanation for the bewildering variety of management accounting systems actually observed in practice**. In addition, the **relevance of organisation theory to management accounting is being increasingly recognised.**'

4.10 Some objections may be added.

(a) It is by **no means clear how the various contingent variables** proposed **affect the management accounting system**. It often seems that it is the organisation structure that adapts to its environment and the management accounting system simply reflects the organisation structure.

(b) For **financial accounting** purposes accountants are expected to follow the rules and regulations of accounting standards and company law. Although financial accounting does not insist upon one best way, it does not allow many alternatives for external reporting purposes. This is quite at **odds with the contingency approach**.

(c) The theory tends to **ignore the influence of aspects of an organisation's context which are more difficult to quantify**. It fails to recognise the impact of the people within an organisation, of management structure, managerial style and, particularly, organisational culture - those factors that make an organisation unique.

POINT TO NOTE

It is evidently true that there is not 'one best way' of designing an organisation or its accounting system: otherwise all successful organisations (and their accounting systems) would be identical. Following Chapter 12 (Organisational Structure and Strategy), you will find a mind map summarising the many influences on the design of management accounting systems.

Unity Bicycles plc

(1) Briefly give examples of how, as a management accountant, you could usefully provide information to UB.

(2) What do you consider to be the key risks of UB's plans?

(3) How would you appraise strategically the proposed new 'electric battery' for push bikes, on the assumption the firm has yet to make up its mind?

Chapter roundup

- Strategic management accounting information should have an **external and future orientation** and should provide **decision-relevant** information on issues such as product profitability, competition costs, the value of market share etc.

- Management accounting information can be used to support **strategic decision making**. A strategic management accounting system should provide relevant information in a useful way, identifying the *real* costs and revenues in a decision.

- **Contingency theorists** try to identify the specific features of an organisation's context that impact on particular features of accounting system design – notably the environment, organisation structure and technology.

- **Simons** has shown how **strategy impinges on management control systems and vice versa. Goold and Campbell** describe **three strategies and styles: strategic planning, financial control and strategic control.**

- **Management accounting system design** needs to consider **inputs, processes and outputs.** The required outputs are the starting point. Information requirements differ depending upon the decision-making level that is being supplied.

Quick quiz

1 What is strategic management accounting?

2 How does Ward analyse the role of the strategic management accountant?

3 Decision making is a

   A forward and inward looking process
   B backward and outward looking process
   C forward and outward looking process
   D backward and inward looking process

BPP
PUBLISHING

4 Define relevant costs.

5 Standard costs consist of a (1) ………….. element and a (2) …………… element.

6 MAS information, including to Anthony's three headings, can assist with

(1) ….

(2) ….

(3) ….

7 According to Emmanuel et al, what (1) ………….. have done is to try and identify the specific features of an organisation's (2) ………….. that impact on particular features of (3) ………….. design. The major factors are:

(4) ….

(5) ….

(6) ….

8 Define strategy.

9 Give four success factors of a strategic management accounting system.

10 What are the four types of control system used by top managers, identified by Simons?

Answers to quick quiz

1 CIMA has defined strategic management accounting as follows: 'A form of management accounting in which emphasis is placed on information which relates to factors external to the firm as well as non-financial information and internally-generated information'.

2 Financial analysis, financial planning and financial control.

3 C

4 Relevant costs are future cash flows arising as a direct consequence of taking a particular decision and include extra cash payments, savings in cash payments and extra or reduced revenues.

5 (1) physical usage (2) price

6 (1) Strategic planning
(2) Management control
(3) Operational control

7 (1) contingency theorists (2) context (3) accounting system (4) environment (5) organisational structure (6) technology

8 A strategy is a plan for interacting with the competitive environment, using available resources, to achieve organisation objectives.

9 Any four from the following

- Aid strategic decisions
- Close the communication gap between accountants and managers
- Identify the type of decision
- Offer appropriate financial performance indicators
- Distinguish between economic and managerial performance
- Provide relevant information
- Separate committed from discretionary costs
- Distinguish discretionary from engineered costs
- Use standard costs strategically
- Allow for changes over time

10 Beliefs systems
Boundary systems
Diagnostic control
Interactive control systems

Unity Bicycles plc review

Question 1. The firm *already* has some of the makings of an informal SMAS even though it is not embedded in accounting data. Here are some examples.

(a) **Competitors**. Walter Drake is focused on competitors, and already has a good idea already what *their* component costs are. UB is sensitive to component costs, so the standard costing system reflects this.

(b) **Committed costs**? We do not know the nature of the supply agreements. Perhaps they commit the firm to future expenditure.

(c) The **standard costing system** is not being used flexibly. After all, the new materials offered by MT may be less expensive than they appear if less of them are used, or if there is less waste. The standard costing system could be used to model the effect of using the new materials suggested by MT.

Question 2. UB faces every sort of risk under the sun.

(a) **Financial**. UB depends on borrowing.

(b) **Political**. Relations between mainland China and Taiwan could become a problem.

(c) **Exchange risk**. UB invoices in sterling, and no mention is made of hedging instruments.

(d) **Business**. UB is investing in new capacity. Unless it is going to expand the market, what will it do? Its markets in Europe seen stable. It might be trying to drive out a competitor.

Question 3. The new electric battery needs strategic appraisal.

(a) How popular is it? Will there be a demand?

(b) UB knows nothing about batteries - it would have to buy them in.

(c) Has any analysis been done of demand?

(d) Is it easy to copy?

Now try the question below from the Exam Question Bank

Question to try	Level	Marks	Time
1	Introductory	n/a	30 mins

Chapter 2

DEVELOPING OBJECTIVES

Topic list		Syllabus reference	Ability required
1	Strategic planning	(i)	Comprehension
2	Strategic planning: the rational model	(i)	Comprehension/evaluation
3	Less formal strategic planning	(i)	Comprehension/evaluation
4	Flexibility in strategic planning	(i)	Comprehension/evaluation
5	Evaluating strategic choices	(i)	Comprehension/evaluation
6	Budgets and financial resources	(i)	Comprehension/evaluation
7	Contingency plans	(i)	Comprehension/evaluation

Introduction

This chapter proposes a **model of the strategic planning process** to which you should refer as you proceed through this Study Text. It also deals with a number of **approaches** to and **definitions of strategy**.

The **rational model** is introduced in this chapter, and the key importance of **objectives** in the development of a business strategy. The rational model has its critics, so we examine some **alternatives** to it (section 3), and the need for **flexibility** (section 4).

The chapter continues in section 5 with a consideration of the issues involved in **evaluating** strategic choices. Sections 6 and 7 discuss **budgeting** and its relevance to the strategic planning exercise, and the need for **contingency planning**.

Learning outcomes covered in this chapter

- **Identify** the importance of objectives and objective setting

- **Evaluate** different approaches to strategy formulation and **recommend** the most appropriate

Syllabus content covered in this chapter

- The importance of developing achievable objectives for the organisation

- The rational model of strategy formulation

- Other less formal approaches to strategy formulation, including incrementalism and emergent approaches

1 STRATEGIC PLANNING

1.1 Managing business strategy involves the entire cycle of **planning and control**, at a **strategic** level.

- Strategic analysis
- Strategic choice
- Implementation of chosen strategies
- Review and control

KEY TERM

The CIMA Management Accounting Official Terminology defines **planning** as 'the establishment of objectives and the formulation, evaluation and selection of the policies, strategies, tactics and action required to achieve these objectives. **Planning comprises long-term/strategic planning, and short-term operation planning**.

1.2 How does this relate to the management of business strategy?

KEY TERMS

A **strategy** is defined by the CIMA as 'a course of action including the specification of resources required, to achieve a specific objective'.

A **strategic plan** is 'a statement of **long term** goals along with a definition of the strategies and policies which will achieve these goals'. It has an **external** rather than an internal focus.

Strategic management is the implementation and control of an agreed strategy.

Tactics are defined by the CIMA as the 'short term plan for achieving an entity's objectives'.

1.3 Keep in mind that there are a **number of approaches** to strategic decision-making: you do not need to have a formal planning process to have a strategy.

1.4 A strategic thinker should have a **vision** of:

- What the business is now
- What it could be in an ideal world
- What the ideal world would be like

2 STRATEGIC PLANNING: THE RATIONAL MODEL   11/01

2.1 To develop a business strategy, an organisation has to decide the following.

- What it is **good at**
- How the market might **change**
- How **customer satisfaction** can be delivered
- What might **constrain** realisation of the plan
- What should be done to **minimise risk**
- What **actions** should be put in place

Characteristics of strategic decisions

2.2 Johnson and Scholes (*Exploring Corporate Strategy*) have summarised the characteristics of strategic decisions for an organisation as follows.

- The **scope** of the organisation's activities

- Matching of an organisation's activities to its **capabilities** and the **environment** in which it operates

- Major decisions about the allocation of **resources**

- **Operational** decisions, because they will set off a chain of 'lesser' decisions

- The **values** and expectations of senior management

- The long-term **direction** that the organisation takes

- **Change** in the organisation

A strategic planning model

2.3 Strategic planning divides into a number of different stages: strategic **analysis**, strategic **choice** and **implementation**. This is represented on the diagram on page 30.

(a) **Strategic analysis**

	Stage	Comment	Key tools, models, techniques
Step 1.	Mission and/or vision	Mission denotes values, the business's rationale for existing; vision refers to where the organisation intends to be in a few years time	• Mission statement
Step 2.	Goals	Interpret the mission to different stakeholders	• Stakeholder analysis
Step 3.	Objectives	Quantified embodiments of mission	• Measures such as profitability, time scale, deadlines
Step 4.	Environmental analysis	Identify opportunities and threats	• PEST analysis • Porter's 5 force analysis; 'diamond' (competitive advantage of nations) • Scenario building

	Stage	Comment	Key tools, models, techniques
Step 5.	Position audit or situation analysis	Identify strengths and weaknesses Firm's **current** resources, products, customers, systems, structure, results, efficiency, effectiveness	• Resource audit • Distinctive competence • Value chain • Product life cycle • BCG matrix • Marketing audit
Step 6.	Corporate appraisal	Combines Steps 4 and 5	• SWOT analysis charts
Step 7.	Gap analysis	Compares outcomes of Step 6 with Step 3	• Gap analysis

(b) Strategic choice

Stage	Comment	Key tools, models, techniques
Strategic options generation	Come up with new ideas: • How to compete (competitive advantage) • Where to compete • Method of growth	• Value chain analysis • Scenario building • Porter's generic strategic choices • Ansoff's growth vector matrix • Acquisition vs organic growth
Strategic options evaluation	Normally, each strategy has to be evaluated on the basis of • Acceptability • Suitability • Feasibility • Environmental fit	• Stakeholder analysis • Risk analysis • Decision-making tools such as decision trees, matrices, ranking and scoring methods • Financial measures (eg ROCE, DCF)

(c) **Strategy selection** involves choosing between the alternative strategies.

    (i)   The **competitive strategies** are the generic strategies for competitive advantage an organisation will pursue. They determine **how you compete**.

    (ii)   **Product-market strategies** (which markets you should enter or leave) determine **where you compete** and the direction of growth.

    (iii)   **Institutional strategies** (ie relationships with other organisations) determine the **method of growth**.

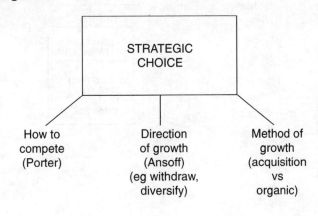

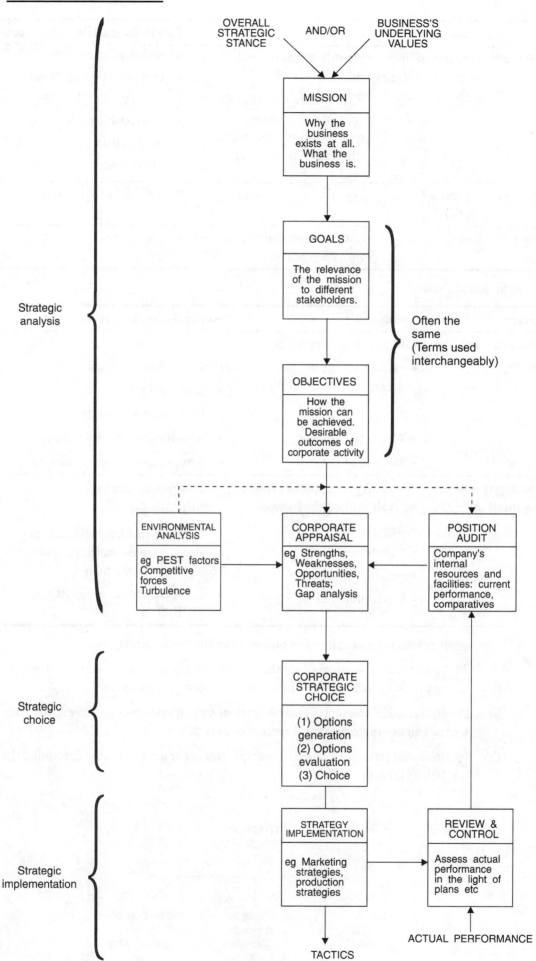

Strategy implementation

2.4 Strategy implementation is the **conversion** of the strategy into detailed plans or objectives for operating units.

2.5 The planning of implementation has several aspects.

- **Resource** planning
- **Operations** planning
- **Organisation** structure and control systems

Types of strategy

2.6 **Corporate strategy** is the most general level of strategy in an organisation, identifying the strategy for the business as a whole.

2.7 **Business strategy**. This relates to how an organisation approaches a particular market, or the activity of a particular business unit.

2.8 **Operational and functional strategies** involve decisions which are made at operational level. These decisions include product pricing, investment in plant, personnel policy and so forth. The contributions of these different functions determine the success of the strategy.

Question 1

Ganymede Ltd is a company selling widgets. The finance director says: 'We plan to issue more shares to raise money for new plant capacity - we don't want loan finance - which will enable us to compete better in the vital and growing widget markets of Latin America. After all, we've promised the shareholders 5% profit growth this year, and trading is tough'.

Identify the corporate, business and functional strategies in the above quotation.

Answer

The corporate objective is profit growth. The corporate strategy is the decision that this will be achieved by entering new markets, rather than producing new products. The business strategy suggests that those markets include Latin America. The operational or functional strategy involves the decision to invest in new plant (the production function) which is to be financed by shares rather than loans (the finance function).

Exam focus point

Do not be too sequential and inflexible in your approach to answering a question on evaluating strategy. You may want to establish objectives and analyse the environment before you make choices, but allow yourself some flexibility in your thinking in case circumstances change beyond all recognition!

BPP
PUBLISHING

3   LESS FORMAL STRATEGIC PLANNING   11/01

3.1   These are the advantages of a formal system of strategic planning.

Advantages	Comment
Identifies risks	Strategic planning helps in managing these risks.
Forces managers to think	Strategic planning can encourage creativity and initiative by tapping the ideas of the management team.
Forces decision-making	Companies cannot remain static - they have to cope with changes in the environment. A strategic plan draws attention to the need to change and adapt, not just to 'stand still' and survive.
Better control	Management control can be better exercised if targets are explicit.
Enforces consistency at all levels	Long-term, medium-term and short-term objectives, plans and controls can be made consistent with one another. Otherwise, strategies can be rendered ineffective by budgeting systems and performance measures which have no strategic content.
Public knowledge	Drucker has argued that an entrepreneur who builds a long-lasting business has 'a theory of the business' which informs his or her business decisions. In large organisations, that theory of the business has to become public knowledge, as decisions cannot be taken only by one person.
Time horizon	Some plans are needed for the long term.
Co-ordinates	Activities of different business functions need to be directed towards a common goal.
Clarifies objectives	Managers are forced to define what they want to achieve.
Allocates responsibility	A plan shows people where they fit in.

Case example

UK defence firms

The UK *defence industry* faces lower government spending and greater competition as contracts are put out to open tender. There is greater competition in export markets. Having failed to diversify into civil areas, companies are changing the way they work.

Planning

A number of assumptions can be made about the environment and customer demands.

(a)   Military needs are for mobile and flexible forces.

(b)   For economic reasons, reliability and maintainability are desired.

(c)   There should be military applications of civilian technology.

(d)   The Ministry of Defence has also tightened up on procurement, replacing cost-plus contracts with competitive tenders.

European defence is likely to consolidate, and defence firms are undertaking strategic management, perhaps for the first time. All firms are concerned with cash flow and productivity. Strategic planning departments have been set up to provide necessary inputs and analyses. The planners emphasise the threat from arms manufacturers in Russia, Germany and Japan. Analysts have identified that improvements in productivity and quality, to ensure the systems work, is of key importance.

3.2 Recently, the very notion that strategy-making can be reduced to planning processes has come under attack from Henry Mintzberg, in his book *The Rise and Fall of Strategic Planning.*

Criticisms of strategic planning in practice (Mintzberg)

Problem	Comments
Practical failure	Empirical studies have not proved that **formal planning** processes contribute to success
Routine and regular	Strategic planning occurs often in an **annual cycle**. But a firm 'cannot allow itself to wait every year for the month of February to address its problems.'
Reduces initiative	Formal planning discourages **strategic thinking**. Once a plan is locked in place, people are unwilling to question it.
Internal politics	The assumption of 'objectivity' in evaluation ignores political battles between different managers and departments.
Exaggerates power	Managers are not all-knowing, and there are limits to the extent to which they can control the behaviour of the organisation.

No strategic planning: 'freewheeling opportunism'

3.3 The **freewheeling opportunism approach** suggests firms should not bother with strategic plans and should exploit opportunities as they arise.

(a) **Advantages**

   (i) Good opportunities are not lost.

   (ii) A freewheeling opportunistic approach would **adapt to change** (eg a very steep rise in the price of a key commodity) more quickly.

   (iii) It might encourage a more **flexible, creative attitude**.

(b) **Disadvantages**

   (i) **No co-ordinating framework** for the organisation, so that some opportunities get missed anyway.

   (ii) It emphasises the **profit motive** to the exclusion of all other considerations.

   (iii) The firm ends up **reacting** all the time rather than acting purposively.

Management accounting and freewheeling opportunism

3.4 **A freewheeling opportunism** approach eschews the careful routine of planning, and instead seizes such opportunities that arise. Not all 'opportunities' will work out, and there may be problems sustaining this policy.

3.5 The management accountant's role will be **investigative**.

(a) What are the financial characteristics of the proposed strategy? For example, in an acquisition, what is the effect on **cash flow**?

(b) How does the proposed strategy affect the firm's **risk profile**?

(c) What **new markets** will the firm be entering by pursuing this strategy? If so, what is the likely response of competitors?

No strategic planning: incrementalism

3.6   Herbert Simon suggested that managers muddle through with a solution which is reasonable, if not ideal. Managers are limited by **time**, by the **information** they have and by their own skills, habits and reflexes.

3.7   This has the following implications.

(a) Strategic managers do not evaluate all the possible options but choose between relatively few alternatives.

(b) Strategy making tends to involve small scale extensions of past policy - **incrementalism** - rather than radical shifts.

> ### KEY TERM
>
> **Incrementalism** is an approach to strategy and decision making highlighting small and slow changes rather than one-off changes in direction. The danger is that such small scale adjustments may not be enough to move with customers and their needs.

3.8   Quinn coined the term **logical incrementalism** to mean that strategies might not be formulated by planning, but using an incremental process with an underlying logic. Top managers guide internal activities (as with the rational approach) while at the same time responding to external events, and develop their conscious strategies this way.

No strategic planning: crafting emergent strategies

3.9   Some strategies emerge 'from below'. They can result from a number of **ad hoc choices**, perhaps made lower down the hierarchy.

> ### KEY TERM
>
> An **emergent strategy** is one developed out of a pattern of behaviour not consciously imposed by senior management.

3.10 The diagram below should help to explain the point.

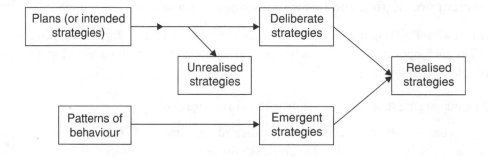

Question 2

Aldebaran Ltd is a public relations agency founded by an entrepreneur, Estella Grande, who has employed various talented individuals from other agencies to set up in business. Estella Grande wants Aldebaran Ltd to become the largest public relations agency in North London. Management consultants, in a planning document, have suggested 'growth by acquisition'. In other words, Aldebaran should buy up the other public relations agencies in the area. These would be retained as semi-independent business units, as the Aldebaran Ltd group could benefit from the goodwill of the newly acquired agencies. When Estella presents these ideas to the Board there is general consensus with one significant exception. Livia Strange, the marketing director, is horrified. 'How am I going to sell this to my staff? Ever since we've been in business, we've won business by undercutting and slagging off the competition. My team have a whole culture based on it. I give them champagne if they pinch a high value client. Why acquire these new businesses - why not stick to pinching their clients instead?'

What is the source of the conflict?

Answer

Livia Strange's department has generated its own pattern of competitive behaviour. It is an emergent strategy. It conflicts directly with the planned strategy proposed by the consultants. This little case history also makes the additional point that strategies are not only about numbers, targets and grand plans, but about the organisational cultures influencing a people's behaviour.

3.11 There are dangers in following an emergent strategy. It may involve **risks,** or it may **interfere** with other strategies. It will need to be **managed** if it commits the organisation to using resources.

Crafting strategy

3.12 Mintzberg uses the metaphor of **crafting strategy** to help understand the idea.

Case example

Honda

Honda is now one of the leading manufacturers of motorbikes. The company is credited with identifying and targeting an untapped market for small 50cc bikes in the US, which enabled it to expand, trounce European competition and severely damage indigenous US bike manufacturers. By 1965, Honda had 63% of the US market. But this occurred by accident.

On entering the US market, Honda had wanted to compete with the larger European and US bikes of 250ccs and over. These bikes had a defined market, and were sold through dedicated motorbike dealerships. Disaster struck when Honda's larger machines developed faults - they had not been designed for the hard wear and tear imposed by US motorcyclists. Honda had to recall the larger machines.

Honda had made little effort to sell its small 50 cc motorbikes - its staff rode them on errands around Los Angeles. Sports goods shops, ordinary bicycle and department stores had expressed an interest, but Honda did not want to confuse its image in its 'target' market of men who bought the larger bikes.

The faults in Honda's larger machines meant that *reluctantly*, Honda *had* to sell the small 50cc bikes just to raise money. They proved very popular with people who would never have bought motorbikes before. *Eventually* the company adopted this new market with enthusiasm with the slogan: 'You meet the nicest people on a Honda'. The strategy had emerged, *against* managers' conscious intentions, but they eventually responded to the new situation.

How to craft strategy

3.13 Mintzberg mentions the following essential activities in strategic management.

BPP
PUBLISHING

(a) **Manage stability.**

(b) **Detect discontinuity.** Environments do not change regularly, nor are they always turbulent. Some changes are more important than others.

(c) **Know the business.** This has to include an awareness and understanding of operations.

3.14 Following these, **crafting strategy** might involve the following roles for management accounting.

(a) **Managing stability.** Standard management accounting information in stable environments enables the business to **control its activities** and use its resources effectively.

(b) **Detecting discontinuity.** Management accountants are probably not the best source of information for detecting **environmental change.** Concerns such as the failure of a major customer may be picked up through debtors' age analysis.

(c) **Know the business**

(i) Management accounting information can model the operations of the business in financial terms.

(ii) Many of a business's **critical success factors,** such as customer confidence, are not easily susceptible to management accounting analysis.

(d) **Managing patterns.** The management accounting system must enable 'patterns' to be detected. All this would suggest an aggregation of financial and non-financial information in a **relational database,** with a variety of tools and techniques (eg graphical systems).

(e) **Reconciling change and continuity.** The inflexibility of management accounting information makes it inappropriate for this purpose.

Question 3

How do you think strategy is made in your organisation? Do you think that, in practice, strategy is a deliberate process, determined by senior management in a full scale planning exercise, or does it 'emerge' from the decisions made by more junior staff, which senior managers simply endorse?

POINT TO NOTE

While the rational approach may mean that there is no room for **learning** in the strategy formulation process, the emergent approach could mean that there is no overall **control** over the strategy. Perhaps the best strategy is one that combines elements of both.

Chaos theory, strategy and organisations

3.15 Organisations can be seen as structures to be made as **automatic and machine-like** as possible, but alternative (and more recent) views recognise the challenge presented by a **dynamic and complex environment.** Stacey (2000) discerns a further layer of complication in the way that organisations work, which he explores in terms of **chaos theory.** He proposes a radical theory of how strategy emerges, based on a view of the organisation as a

self-organising complex process, formed by human relationships. This view contrasts sharply with what Stacey sees as orthodox theory built around **cybernetic** systems.

Case example

In organisational terms we can see a simple example of a **cybernetic system** in monthly comparison between budget and actual figures. If there is a shortfall in retail turnover, for example, control action in the form of a sales promotion campaign might be undertaken. The rational model of strategy, with which you are familiar, can also be seen as a feedback system, in which the corporate mission is the desired end state, which is compared with actual strategic performance through the process of corporate appraisal.

This view of strategy postulates that organisations are driven by two main forces.

- The need to satisfy a **specific goal**
- The goal itself must lead to **stable adaptation** to the environment

---

3.16 Stacey suggests that modern thinking about complexity can offer us a useful insight into the way organisations actually work, and how they move towards learning, innovation and adaptation to a complex and unstable global environment. Very complex systems, such as organisations, can (and do) undergo **unpredictable changes in their behaviour**, such as the adoption of a radical new strategy. **Organisations are chaotic systems**. Chaos theory holds that, although it is true that the environment is vast and is hard to model, behaviour is not random, nor is it totally unpredictable.

Case example

Consumer credit and banking strategies in China

The weather system is enormously complex and so, indeed, are human societies. A possible example of a small scale event or innovation, causing significant change and shifts in cultural preference, is perhaps the market for credit. According to The Economist (April 20th 2002), the market for consumer credit in East Asia is growing, and is evidenced in demand for credit cards, mortgages and so forth.

'It adds up to a seismic shift in the region's economies, banks and consumer patterns. For decades, the 'Asian' model of export-led development was based on high rates of saving and investment, with consumption suppressed. China's saving rate, at about 40 percent, is one of the highest in the world, and other East and South-east Asian countries are not far behind.'

Banks used to lend money to business conglomerates, but many loans are bad, hence the banks' wish to shift attention **from** firms **to** consumers (who are more profitable and less risky). Cultural barriers to borrowing have fallen. The main obstacles are poor payment infrastructures and limited information available to banks to assess consumers' credit risks. So, having changed strategy from lending to firms to targeting consumers – facilitated by changes in the law – the banks may still suffer from making imprudent lending decisions.

This example of self-organising change is a **collective response** of the whole system. Environmental change on the part of Asia's banks seems to have led to strategic change in their lending policies.

3.17 Below the level of the collective response, it should be remembered that organisations rely heavily on the individual **people** they contain. Those people interact according to common rules that are laid down in various ways.

- The formal organisation structure
- The organisation's culture
- The informal organisation
- Legal presumptions
- Cultural norms of the industry/national origin

The organisation is thus a **complex adaptive system**.

3.18 Stacey sees the behaviour of the organisation as taking place both at the level of its people, and the collective level, simultaneously. He suggests that organisations that are capable of learning and adapting do so because, as systems, they are operating in the **chaotic region between stability and instability**. They will be poised in a state of 'bounded instability', or chaos, and as a result, a new preferred state will be spontaneously created within it, allowing it to adapt and evolve through a process of self-organisation.

3.19 Stacey pays considerable attention to the **position of the manager** in all this, and particularly the manager or managers at the strategic apex. Management has a very important role to play. They are in a position to see how things are going and to interact with many more other agents than most members of the organisation.

4 FLEXIBILITY IN STRATEGIC PLANNING

4.1 All companies must make allowances for the possible need to make changes. Planning must therefore have the following characteristics.

- It must be **flexible**.
- It must establish **controls** for measuring performance.

4.2 Thus, an objective of increasing turnover from £5 million in the past year to £10 million in five years' time, and raising profits from £1 million to £1.5 million, contains sufficient flexibility to permit growth by various options.

Example of flexibility in planning

4.3 Suppose that XYZ plc has been asked to tender for a contract. The estimated cost of the contract is £2,000,000 although there is a 10% probability that costs will exceed this amount by up to £200,000. The average amount of capital tied up in the project would be one half of the total cost - ie £1,000,000. The company's directors have set a minimum target return of 30% on capital for all contracts of this type. In this case, however, the directors are aware that a competitor is keen to win the contract, and could put in a tender price as low as £2,100,000. What should XYZ plc's tender price be?

4.4 If the company's price objective of a 30% return on capital is regarded as rigid, the tender price should be as follows.

	£
Cost - most likely estimate	2,000,000
Minimum return (30% of £1,000,000)	300,000
Price	2,300,000

4.5 At this price, however, XYZ plc might fail to win the contract since the rival bidder might put in a tender of £2,100,000.

4.6 XYZ plc should therefore consider the following options.

(a) Put in a tender of £2,300,000 and try to justify the higher price with the promise of a better quality product or service to the customer.

(b) Depending on how important the contract is to XYZ plc, the directors may agree to compromise on the target return of 30% and put in a tender below £2,300,000.

    (i) A tender of £2,200,000 should be sufficient to provide a return of 20%, and if costs do overrun, the contract would still just break even.

(ii) A tender in the region of £2,100,000, the expected rival bid, would provide a return of only 10% and the possibility of making a loss if costs overrun.

5 EVALUATING STRATEGIC CHOICES

5.1 According to the rational model, individual strategies have to be **evaluated**, according to a number of criteria, before a strategy or a mixture of strategies is chosen. Johnson and Scholes narrow these down to **suitability, feasibility** and **acceptability**.

Suitability

5.2 **Suitability** relates to the **strategic logic** of the strategy. The strategy should fit the situation of the firm. Does it:

- **Exploit** company strengths and distinctive **competences**?
- Rectify company **weaknesses**?
- **Neutralise** or deflect environmental **threats**?
- Help the firm to seize **opportunities**?
- **Satisfy the goals** of the organisation?
- **Fill the gap** identified by gap analysis?
- Generate/maintain **competitive advantage**?
- Involve an acceptable level of **risk**?
- Suit the **politics** and corporate **culture**?

Feasibility

5.3 **Feasibility** asks whether the strategy can in fact be implemented.

- Is there enough **money**?
- Is there the **ability** to deliver the goods/services specified in the strategy?
- Can we deal with the likely **responses that competitors** will make?
- Do we have access to **technology, materials and resources**?
- Do we have enough **time** to implement the strategy?

5.4 Strategies which do not make use of the existing competences, and which therefore call for new competences to be acquired, might not be feasible.

- Gaining competences via organic growth takes time
- Acquiring new competences can be costly

5.5 We look at budgets and financial resources in the next section.

Acceptability (to stakeholders)

5.6 **The acceptability** of a strategy relates to people's expectations of it. It is here that stakeholder analysis can be brought in.

(a) **Financial considerations**. Strategies will be evaluated by considering how far they contribute to meeting the dominant objective of increasing shareholder wealth.

- Return on investment
- Profits
- Growth
- EPS

- Cash flow
- Price/Earnings
- Market capitalisation

(b) **Customers** may object to a strategy if it means reducing service, but on the other hand they may have no choice.

(c) **Banks** are interested in the implications for cash resources, debt levels etc.

(d) **Government**. A strategy involving a takeover may be prohibited under monopolies and mergers legislation. Similarly, the environmental impact may cause key stakeholders to withhold consent.

Case example

The Irish government in 1998 imposed a temporary ban on superstores in excess of 32,000 square feet. Such constraints have led to interest in overseas development. Tesco has expanded into Thailand and South Korea in addition to its stores in Eastern Europe, in pursuit of an avowedly 'global' strategy.

(e) **The public**. The environmental impact may cause key stakeholders to protest.

(f) **Risk**. Different shareholders have different attitudes to risk. A strategy which changed the risk/return profile, for whatever reason, may not be acceptable.

6 BUDGETS AND FINANCIAL RESOURCES

Budgets

> **KEY TERM**
>
> The CIMA definition of a **budget** is 'a quantitative statement, for a defined period of time, which may include planned revenues, expenses, assets, liabilities and cash flows. A budget provides a focus for the organisation, aids the co-ordination of activities, and facilitates control. Planning is achieved by means of a fixed master budget, whereas control is generally exercised through the comparison of actual costs with a flexible budget'.
>
> (CIMA *Official Terminology*)

6.1 Johnson and Scholes see four aspects of the budgeting process which are relevant to the strategic planning exercise.

(a) **Capital budgeting**, to determine:

- The outflow and inflow of funds associated with capital projects

- The implications of different funding methods for a project

- The method of assessing how worthwhile a project might be in terms of return on funds invested

(b) **Working capital budgets** to express outcomes of decisions in terms of inventory levels, cash, debtors and creditors, and the implications for future working capital policy.

(c) **Departmental budgets** may be important if strategic changes are likely to affect parts of a business in different ways.

(d) **Consolidated budgets** are useful to project the implications of the corporate decision process.

Budgets, objectives and organisation

6.2 However, the relationship between **budgeting** and **planning** is problematic. According to Bunce and Fraser (*Management Accounting*, February 1997):

> 'Budgeting was designed by accountants principally as a mechanism for financial forecasting, managing cashflow and capital expenditure and controlling costs. It is not the ideal vehicle for the management functions which have been piled onto it, such as communicating corporate goals, setting objectives, continuous improvement, resource allocation and as a basis for performance appraisal. Times have changed.'

6.3 According to Hope and Fraser (*Management Accounting*, December 1997), firms are trying to focus more on the customer, and the new climate where innovation, intellectual capital and knowledge sharing are key factors is not easily planned for using traditional accounting systems. This shift in emphasis requires new ways of managing performance, but most companies in Europe still operate with formal budgeting systems.

Case example

Budgeting is coming to be regarded by some as 'an unnecessary evil'. Svenska Handelsbanken abandoned traditional budgeting as long ago as 1979 with dramatic success.

It is now the largest bank in Scandinavia and the most efficient of the big banks in Europe. Each bank is operated like an independent business. There is a profit-sharing scheme based on performance relative to competitors and each branch can easily compare its performance to another. Its cost/income ratio has been reduced to 45%, compared to 70% for many of its rivals.

The budget period and strategic plans

6.4 If the budget is to be properly related to the strategic plan the factors which should influence the budget period are as follows.

(a) A plan decided upon now might need a considerable time to be put into operation.

(b) A distinction can be made between long-term planning and short-term budgeting according to the 'fixed' or 'variable' nature of the resources of the business.

(c) All budgets involve some element of forecasting and guesswork.

(d) Unforeseen events might occur which transform the commercial situation.

Strategic cash flow planning

6.5 It is essential for the survival of any business to have an adequate inflow of cash, but there are different planning issues involved.

(a) The **planning horizon** is longer.

(b) The **uncertainties** about future cash inflows and cash outflows are much greater.

(c) The business should be able to respond, if necessary, to an **unexpected need** for cash. Where could extra cash be raised, and in what amounts?

(d) A company should have planned cash flows which are consistent with its:

- Dividend payment policy
- Policy for financial structuring, debt and gearing

7 CONTINGENCY PLANS

> **KEY TERMS**
>
> A **contingency** is a possible future event which, if it were to happen, would be beyond management's control. It is uncontrollable, and not provided for in the main corporate plan.
>
> A **contingency plan** is defined by CIMA as 'action to be implemented only upon the occurrence of future events other than those in the accepted plan'.

7.1 Where contingencies are known about, contingency plans should be prepared in advance.

7.2 As an example, a company heavily involved in exporting or importing goods in a competitive market will be susceptible to fluctuations in **foreign exchange rates**. Although the **risks** of foreign exchange exposure can be reduced, with various financial instruments, the company will almost certainly be unable to eliminate foreign exchange risks over its longer-term corporate planning period. Contingency plans can be prepared to deal with adverse exchange rate movements, by speculating how far rates might alter and calculating the implications of various degrees of change.

7.3 Contingency plans might also be needed for the following reasons.

(a) **Crisis management.** A contingency might be something like product contamination, and the need for a product recall. Plans can enable 'crises' of this nature to be dealt with effectively.

(b) **Uncertain outcomes of legal action.** Supermarket chains have been taken to court over alleged breaches of brand owner's trade marks.

(c) **Breakdowns.** Many firms have contingency plans in the event of disasters such as fires or major IT breakdowns.

Unity Bicycles plc

(1) What do you consider to be the most important strategic decisions taken by MT?

(2) What do you think of the way in which strategic decisions appear to be taken at UB? Can you suggest a better way?

Chapter roundup

- Strategic decisions relate to the scope of a firm's activities, the long-term direction of the organisation, and allocation of resources.

- The rational model of strategy formation suggest a logical sequence which involves analysing the current situation, generating choices (relating to competitors, products and markets) strategies and implementing the chosen strategies.

- Alternative models include incrementalism, freewheeling opportunism and crafting emergent strategies. The management accountant's role differs in each case.

- Chaos theory is a radical theory of how strategy emerges, based on the idea of the organisation as a complex self-organising system, formed by human relationships.

- Strategic choices are evaluated according to their suitability (to the organisation and its current situation), their feasibility (eg in terms of usefulness or competences) and their acceptability (eg to relevant stakeholder groups).

- The budgeting process is relevant to the strategic planning exercise as it can project the resource implications of strategic decisions.

- When contingencies are known about, plans should be made in advance. Outstanding legal action or systems failures provide examples of when contingency plans may be required.

Quick quiz

1   Fill in the gaps in the statements below, using the words in the box.

- Managing business strategy involves the entire cycle of (1) .... , at a (2) .... level. This cycle involves:

  ° strategic (3) ....

  ° strategic (4) ....

  ° (5) .... of chosen strategies

  ° (6) .... and (7) ....

- Planning comprises (8) .... planning and (9) .... planning.

⊙ choice	⊙ analysis	⊙ planning and control
⊙ long term/strategic	⊙ strategic	⊙ short term/operation
⊙ review	⊙ control	⊙ implementation

2   What are the seven steps in strategic analysis?

3   What is strategy implementation?

4   Operational and functional strategies identify the strategy for the business as a whole.

☐ True

☐ False

5   One approach to strategy formulation suggests that firms should not bother with strategic plans and should exploit opportunities as they arise. This approach is known as

incrementalism	freewheeling opportunism
rational model	strategic choice

6   What are the Johnson and Scholes criteria for evaluating individual strategies?

7   Why is a capital budget relevant to a strategic planning exercise?

8 Product-market strategies determine where you compete and the direction of growth

 ☐ True

 ☐ False

9 Give five advantages of a formal system of strategic planning.

10 Who has attacked the idea that strategy making can be reduced to planning processes?

Answers to quick quiz

1 (1) planning and control (2) strategic (3) analysis (4) choice (5) implementation (6) review (7) control (8) long term/strategic (9) short term/operation

2 Mission/vision

 Goals

 Objectives

 Environmental analysis

 Position audit

 Corporate appraisal

 Gap analysis

3 Strategy implementation is the conversion of the strategy into detailed plans or objectives for operating units.

4 False

5 Freewheeling opportunism

6 Suitability, feasibility and acceptability

7 Because it determines:

- The outflow and inflow of funds associated with capital projects
- The implications of different funding methods for a project
- The method of assessing how worthwhile a project might be in terms of return on funds invested

8 True

9 Five from the following

- Identifies risks
- Forces managers to think
- Forces decision-making
- Better control
- Enforces consistency at all levels
- Public knowledge
- Time horizon
- Co-ordinates
- Clarifies objectives
- Allocates responsibility

10 Henry Mintzberg

Unity Bicycles plc review

Question 1. MT's strategic decisions were related to acquiring and disposing of UB.

Question 2. Strategic decision-making at UB.

(a) Walter Drake appears to have a theory of the business. UB does seem to have an external focus, in that management review environmental trends and, in the case of world trade, try to anticipate them. UB has also made strategic choices, in factory location, the decision to license firms in China, as well as to become, effectively, a global firm.

(b) However, too much of the strategy-making process seems to occur in Walter Drakes' brain. Some formality is needed, simply to communicate strategic decisions and to lessen dependence on Walter.

Now try the question below from the Exam Question Bank

Question to try	Level	Marks	Time
2	Introductory	n/a	30 mins

BPP PUBLISHING

Chapter 3

DIFFERING OBJECTIVES

Topic list	Syllabus reference	Ability required
1 Mission, goals and strategy	(i)	Evaluation
2 Resources and CSFs	(i)	Evaluation
3 Business goals and objectives	(i)	Evaluation
4 Stakeholder goals and objectives	(i)	Evaluation
5 The short and long term	(i)	Evaluation
6 Social responsibility and sustainability	(i)	Evaluation
7 Not for profit organisations	(i)	Evaluation
8 The public sector	(i)	Evaluation

Introduction

In this chapter we consider the **objectives and goals** of an organisation. A **mission** (section 1) describes what the organisation is for and how it relates to the wider society. Many organisations, especially public sector ones, have to juggle a number of conflicting objectives, and so developing a mission may be difficult. Businesses (section 3) generally pursue some kind of **financial return**, although a number of measures can be used. **Secondary objectives** support this return. Trade-offs have to be made between goals.

Various groups of **stakeholders** (section 4) have their own expectations of the organisation. Managers' and employees goals are not the same as the shareholder goals. Different stakeholder groups exercise different degrees of power.

Allied to a consideration of stakeholders is the question of **short versus long term perspectives** on business performance (section 5). Many writers believe this is a particular problem for the UK and that one of its causes is how performance is rewarded.

The theme of **social responsibility and sustainability** (section 6) is the question of how far a business is accountable to the wider community for the effects of its operations, and the fact that resources are finite and need to be replaced. Every action represents a use of resources and the organisation needs to develop strategies to take account of this.

The chapter closes with a look at the specific issues relating to the **not-for-profit** and **public sector** objectives.

Learning outcomes covered in this chapter

- **Evaluate** and **contrast** differing corporate frameworks and objectives
- **Evaluate** an organisation's mission, goals and aims and **recommend** appropriate changes

Syllabus content covered in this chapter

- Formulating the organisation's mission, goals, aims and critical success factors
- Competing objectives for the organisation: profit motive, short term and long term, sustainable growth, stakeholders and social responsibility. The objectives of not for profit organisations are also considered

1   MISSION, GOALS AND STRATEGY

1.1   In the previous chapter, we identified the concept of **mission** as the logical starting point of the process of strategy.

KEY TERM

An expanded definition of **mission** includes four elements.

(a)   **Purpose.** Why does the company exist? Who does it exist for?

- To create wealth for shareholders, who take priority over all other stakeholders?

- To satisfy the needs of all stakeholders (including employees, society at large, for example)?

- To reach some higher goal and objective ('the advancement of society')?

(b)   **Strategy.** This provides the commercial logic for the company, and so addresses the following question: 'What is our business? What should it be?'

(c)   **Policies and standards of behaviour.** For example, a service industry that wishes to be the best in its market must aim for standards of service, in all its operations, which are at least as good as those found in its competitors.

(d)   **Values.** Values relate to the organisation's culture, and are the basic beliefs of the people who work in the organisation.

Case study link

It could be argued in the May 2002 case study scenario that Global Inc. lacks a mission, or indeed any clear strategy driven by the top. The CEO knows who his competitors are, but lacks ideas.

The importance of mission for corporate strategy

1.2   Mission and values are taken seriously by many businesses.

(a)   Values are integral elements of consumers' buying decisions, as evidenced by advertising, branding and market research. Customers ask not only 'What do you sell?' but 'What do you stand for?'

(b)   Studies into organisational behaviour show that people are motivated by more than money.

(c)   Some writers believe there is an empirical relationship between strong corporate values and profitability.

Case example

The *Financial Times* reported the result of research by the Digital Equipment Corporation into a sample of 429 company executives.

- 80% of the sample have a formal mission statement
- 80% believed mission contributes to profitability
- 75% believe they have a responsibility to implement the mission statement

---

BPP PUBLISHING

Mission statements

1.3 **Mission statements** are formal documents which state the organisation's mission. There is no standard format, but they should be easy to remember, flexible and distinctive.

Case examples

Evaluate the following mission statements against the three criteria above.

(a) *Glaxo* 'is an integrated research-based group of companies whose corporate purpose is to create, discover, develop, manufacture and market throughout the world, safe, effective medicines of the highest quality which will bring benefit to patients through improved longevity and quality of life, and to society through economic value.'

(b) *IBM (UK):* 'We shall increase the pace of change. Market-driven quality is our aim. It means listening and responding more sensitively to our customers. It means eliminating defects and errors, speeding up all our processes, measuring everything we do against a common standard, and it means involving employees totally in our aims'.

(c) *Matsushita:* 'the duty of the manufacturer is to serve the foundation of man's happiness by making man's life affluent with an inexpensive and inexhaustible supply of life's necessities.'

1.4 Some are suspicious of mission statements.

(a) They are often **public relations** exercises rather than an accurate portrayal of the firm's actual values.

(b) They can often be full of **generalisations** which are impossible to tie down to specific strategic implications.

(c) They may be ignored by the people responsible for formulating or implementing strategy.

Mission and planning

1.5 The mission statement can play an important role in the strategic planning process.

(a) **Inspires planning.** Plans should develop activities and programmes consistent with the organisation's mission.

(b) **Screening.** Mission also acts as a yardstick by which plans are judged.

(c) Mission also affects the **implementation** of a planned strategy in terms of the ways in which the firm carries out its business and the culture of the organisation.

Case example

The Co-op has explicit social objectives. In some cases it will retain stores which, although too small to be as profitable as a large supermarket, fulfil an important social role in the communities which host them.

---

2 RESOURCES AND CSFs

Resource planning at corporate level

2.1 The strategic plan, overall, might require a total change in the organisation's resources.

- The degree of change
- The extent of central direction

2.2 Clearly, in times of scarce resources the degree of central control might be increased. Powerful interest groups might support the current state of affairs. Different divisions can compete for resources and powerful political forces can come into play.

Resource planning at operational level

2.3 At operational level the stages in **resource planning** are as follows.

(a) Establishing currently obtainable resources - making a **resource audit**.

(b) **Estimating the resources needed** to pursue a particular strategy.

(c) Assigning **responsibilities** to managers for the acquisition, use and control of resources.

(d) Identifying all **factors** influencing the availability of resources.

2.4 Johnson and Scholes suggest that there are three central questions in operational resource planning that must be resolved.

(a) **Resource identification**. What resources will be needed to implement the strategy?

(b) **Fit with existing resources**.

(c) **Fit between required resources**. For example, increasing output might require more people and more machines, and extra resources might be needed for training.

Preparing resource plans

Planning issues: critical success factors

2.5 Resource plans can be prepared in detail, providing organisations know what they need to achieve.

> ### KEY TERMS
>
> A **critical success factor** (CSF) is defined by the CIMA as 'an element of organisational activity which is central to its future success. Critical success factors may change over time, and may include items such as product quality, employee attitudes, manufacturing flexibility and brand awareness'.
>
> **Key tasks** are what must be done to ensure each critical success factor is achieved.
>
> **Priorities** indicate the order in which tasks are performed.

2.6 For example, the critical success factor to run a successful mail order business is speedy delivery. A CSF of a parcel delivery service is that it must be quicker than the normal post. Underpinning critical success factors are key tasks. If customer care is a CSF, then a key task, and hence a measure of performance, would include responding to enquiries within a given time period.

Question 1

Draw up a list of four critical success factors for the strategy of the organisation for which you work.

2.7 CSFs can be used to translate strategic objectives into performance targets and tactical plans.

Example

(a) Dogger Bank plc has defined increased profit as a **business objective**.

(b) The **strategy** for increased profits is to increase revenue per customer.

(c) Increasing revenue per customer might not be possible unless customers buy other services from the bank.

    (i) The **critical success factor** will be the number of extra services sold to each customer.

    (ii) A **key task** might involve developing a customer database.

Components of the resource plan

2.8 The resource plan might use the following tools.

- Budgets
- Plans for human resources, such as recruitment, selection and training
- Network analysis, indicating how resources will be deployed in a particular sequence

Management accountant's role

2.9 The management accountant has an obvious role in resource planning.

(a) **Resources in any organisation are scarce**, and there will be a whole host of ideas or projects competing for resources.

(b) The accountant will be involved in selecting those which make the **most efficient use of resources available**. Measures such as contribution per unit of limiting factor might be useful.

Financial resources

2.10 Finance is virtually always in short supply.

- The main source of funds for most companies is **retained profits** where these are sufficient for needs.
- New issues of **share capital** to raise funds will only be feasible if investors are willing.
- Acquisitions might be financed by issuing **new shares**.
- Firms can **borrow**, but their ability to borrow will be limited.

2.11 **Leasing** is a method of acquiring fixed assets without having to incur capital expenditure. Leases do in some cases give the lessee a **cashflow advantage**, although the lease has to be accounted for in accordance with SSAP 21 in the annual published financial statements.

(a) With operating leases, capital equipment is hired for a lease period, and the lessee pays lease charges (rental) to the lessor. The legal owner of the equipment is the lessor, and at the end of the lease period, the equipment is surrendered to the lessor by the lessee.

(b) With finance leases, the lease period is most or all of the expected operating life of the asset. The lessee treats the asset as his in the accounts, and it does not revert to the lessor at the end of the lease period.

Working capital strategy

2.12 In general terms, working capital strategy should be directed towards avoiding the **cash flow** difficulties that might beset a firm with too many **current liabilities** and not enough **current assets**.

2.13 At a strategic level, **debtors control** is more concerned with the following.

- How much credit should be allowed?
- What **customer-vetting procedures** ought to be established?

2.14 Credit should be taken where it is reasonable to do so. **Trade creditors** are a cheap source of finance (unless they offer attractive discounts for early payment).

3 BUSINESS GOALS AND OBJECTIVES   Pilot paper, 5/01

General characteristics of objectives and goals

> **KEY TERMS**
>
> Mintzberg defines **goals** as 'the intentions behind decisions or actions, the states of mind that drive individuals or collectives of individuals called organisations to do what they do.'
>
> (a) **Operational goals** can be expressed as objectives. Here is an example.
>
>   (i) An operational goal: 'Cut costs'
>   (ii) The objective: 'Reduce budget by 5%'
>
> (b) **Non-operational goals** A university's goal might be to 'seek truth'.
>
> Not all goals can be measured.

3.1 In practice most organisations set themselves **quantified objectives** in order to enact the corporate mission. Many objectives are:

- **S**pecific
- **M**easurable
- **A**ttainable
- **R**esults-orientated
- **T**ime-bounded

3.2 There should be **goal congruence,** which we defined in Chapter 1. The goals set for different parts of the organisation should be consistent with each other.

Primary and secondary objectives

3.3 Some objectives are more important than others. In the hierarchy of objectives, there is a **primary corporate objective** and other **secondary objectives** which should combine to ensure the achievement of the overall corporate objective.

3.4 For example, if a company sets itself an objective of growth in profits, as its primary aim, it will then have to develop strategies by which this primary objective can be achieved. An objective must then be set for each individual strategy. Secondary objectives might then be concerned with sales growth, continual technological innovation, customer service, product quality, efficient resource management or reducing the company's reliance on debt capital.

Case example

British Airways publicity once indicated the following corporate goals. What do you think of them? Which is most important? Will they have changed since the events of September 11 2001 and the subsequent turmoil in the airline industry?

- Safety and security
- Strong and consistent financial performance
- Global reach
- Superior services
- Good value for money
- Healthy working environment
- Good neighbourliness

'Overall, our aim is to be the best and most successful company in the airline industry.'

Long-term objectives and short-term objectives

3.5 Objectives may be long-term and short-term. A company that is suffering from a recession in its core industries and making losses in the short term might continue to have a long term primary objective of achieving a growth in profits, but in the short term its primary objective might be survival.

Financial objectives

3.6 For business in the UK, the primary objective is concerned with the return to shareholders.

(a) A satisfactory return for a company must be sufficient to **reward shareholders adequately** in the long run for the risks they take. The reward will take the form of **profits,** which can lead to **dividends** or to **increases in the market value** of the shares.

(b) The size of return which is adequate for ordinary shareholders will vary according to the risk involved.

3.7 There are different ways of expressing a financial objective in quantitative terms. Financial objectives would include the following.

- Profitability
- Return on investment (ROI) or return on capital employed (ROCE)
- Share price, earnings per share, dividends
- Growth

Profitability

3.8 Profitability on its own is not satisfactory as an overall long-term corporate objective.

(a) It fails to allow for the size of the capital investment required to make the profit.

(b) Shareholders should be interested in maximising profits over time. In order to maximise profits over time, costs will have to be incurred today in order to generate returns in the future.

Return on investment (ROI) or return on capital employed (ROCE)

3.9 Many companies use an **accounting ROI** (profits as a percentage of capital invested) as a primary objective. Although it relates the return to the capital, it has these drawbacks.

(a) **Unreliable data.** Capital employed is notoriously suspect as a financial measure, since a book value in the balance sheet will probably bear little or no comparison with the 'true' value - net replacement cost, gross replacement cost, net realisable value or economic value of the asset.

(b) **Short vs long term.** There will be difficulty in balancing short-term results against long-term requirements.

(c) **Risk.** High risk projects might promise a high return but it may be safer to opt for a project with a lower return but a greater guarantee of success.

Share price, earnings, dividends and market value

3.10 **Earnings per share** or **dividend payments** are measures which recognise that a company is owned by its shareholder-investors. Failure to provide a satisfactory EPS or dividend could lead the shareholders to sell their shares.

3.11 **Market capitalisation** is the total value of the businesses shares on the stock market. When earnings and dividends are low, the **market value** of shares will also be depressed unless there is a strong prospect of dividend growth.

3.12 Shareholders are concerned with the size of the return they get, but also with the size of the investment they must make to achieve the return. To overcome this problem, earnings and dividend growth could be expressed as **dividends received plus the capital growth** in market value.

3.13 The **price/earnings ratio** measures the relationship between earnings per share and the price at which shares are traded. It is the market value divided by earnings per share.

Growth

3.14 There are some difficulties in accepting growth as an overall objective.

(a) **Growth of what?** In the long run, some elements must be expected to grow faster than others because of the dynamics of the business environment.

(b) In the long run, growth might lead to **diseconomies of scale** so that inefficiencies will occur.

3.15 **Smaller companies** will usually have a greater potential for significant rates of growth, especially in new industries, and growth will be a prime objective. Larger companies grow to achieve a size which will enable them to compete with other multinationals in world markets.

Multiple objectives

3.16 A firm might identify several objectives.

- Scope for growth and enhanced **corporate wealth**
- Maintaining a policy of paying attractive but not over-generous **dividends**
- Maintaining an acceptable **gearing ratio**

3.17 You will have encountered many of the financial ratios before. Revise your understanding of them with the following exercise.

Question 2

ABCD plc's financial performance for the past 12 months has been reported to its board of directors as follows.

Turnover	£20 million per annum
Market share	16%
Contribution/sales ratio	50%
Operating profit/sales ratio	10%
Turnover/capital employed ratio	1.2 times
P/E ratio	11.4
Average P/E ratio for the industry	16.7

The directors are considering a new strategy of spending an extra £500,000 per annum on advertising and sales promotions, to try to boost sales, combined with more liberal price discounts to regular customers.

Required

(a)   Evaluate the possible financial implications of the proposed new strategy.

(b)   What does the P/E ratio of 11.4 imply when compared with the average P/E for the industry as a whole?

Answer

(a)   (i)

Turnover per annum	£20,000,000
Operating profit	£2,000,000
ROCE (10% × 1.2)	12%
Capital employed	£16,666,667
Market capitalisation*	£22,800,000

*Earnings × P/E ratio, here assumed to be operating profit × P/E

(ii)   Extra advertising expenditure will reduce profit by £500,000 per annum (tax is ignored here, for simplicity). Higher price discounts to regular customers will reduce the C/S ratio and so will reduce profitability too. If we suppose that 25% of customers are given a further 5% price discount, the cost of this would be 25% × £20,000,000 × 5% = £250,000 per annum.

(iii)   To justify this strategy, the extra sales from greater advertising and higher price discounts must yield extra contribution of at least £750,000 per annum which, given a C/S ratio of 50%, implies extra sales of £1.5 million per annum, which is 1.2% of the market. This might be a reasonable target which the company could hope to achieve.

(iv)   If higher sales and higher profits can be achieved, the sales/capital employed ratio would improve and the sales ratio might also improve. The end result will be a higher ROCE. If there is no change in the P/E ratio, the market capitalisation of the company will improve by £11,400 for each £1,000 increase in the annual profit.

(b)   The current P/E ratio is substantially lower than the industry average, which suggests that the market has made the following judgements about ABCD.

(i)   ABCD is 'under-performing' when compared with its rivals.

(ii)   ABCD's earnings growth potential is less than the growth potential of other firms in the industry.

(iii)   The 'quality' of ABCD's earnings are not as good - ie there is some risk that profits might decline in the future.

Subsidiary or secondary objectives

3.18   Whatever primary objective or objectives are set, **subsidiary objectives** will then be developed beneath them.

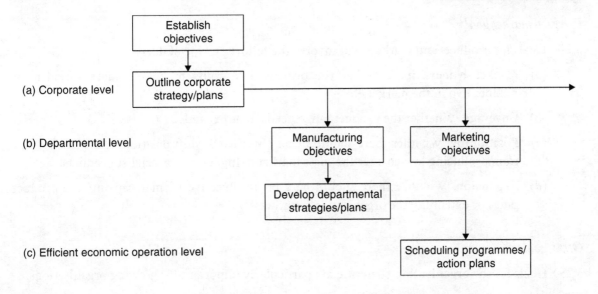

3.19 The overall objectives of the organisation will indicate different requirements for different functions.

Corporate objectives and unit objectives

3.20 Here are some examples of corporate and unit objectives.

(a) **Corporate objectives**. These objectives should relate to the key factors for business success.

- Profitability
- Market share
- Growth
- Cash flow

- Customer satisfaction
- The quality of the firm's products
- Human resources

(b) **Unit objectives**. Examples are as follows.

(i) From the business world:

- Increasing the number of customers by 10%

- Reducing the number of rejects by 50%

- Producing monthly reports more quickly, within five working days of the end of each month

(ii) From the public sector:

- Responding more quickly to emergency calls
- Reducing the length of time a patient has to wait for an operation

Technological goals

3.21 Technological goals might be stated as follows.

(a) A commitment to **product design and production methods** using current and new technology.

(b) A commitment to improve current products through research and development work.

(c) A commitment to a particular level of quality.

Product-market goals

3.22   Goals for products and markets will involve the following type of decisions.

(a)   **Market leadership.** Whether the organisation wants to be the market leader, or number two in the market etc.

(b)   **Coverage.** Whether the product range needs to be expanded.

(c)   **Positioning.** Whether there should be an objective to shift position in the market - eg from producing low-cost for the mass market to higher-cost specialist products.

(d)   **Expansion.** Whether there should be a broad objective of 'modernising' the product range or extending the organisation's markets.

Other goals

3.23   Goals for the **organisation structure** are particularly important for growing organisations.

3.24   **Productivity objectives.** When an organisation is keenly aware of a poor profit record, cost reduction will be a primary consideration. Productivity objectives are often quantified as targets to reduce unit costs **and increase output per employee** by a certain percentage each year.

3.25   **Expansion or consolidation** objectives are concerned with the question of whether there is a need to expand, or whether there is a need to consolidate for a while.

Ranking objectives and trade-offs

3.26   Where there are multiple objectives a problem of ranking can arise.

(a)   **There is never enough time or resources** to achieve all of the desired objectives.

(b)   **There are degrees of accomplishment.** For example, if there is an objective to achieve a 10% annual growth in earnings per share, an achievement of 9% could be described as a near-success. When it comes to ranking objectives, a target ROI of, say, 25% might be given greater priority than an EPS growth of 10%, but a lower priority than an EPS growth of, say, 15%.

3.27   When there are several key objectives, some might be achieved only at the expense of others. For example, attempts to achieve a good cash flow or good product quality, or to improve market share, might call for some sacrifice of short term profits.

3.28   For example, there might be a choice between the following two options.

Option A   15% sales growth, 10% profit growth, a £2 million negative cash flow and reduced product quality and customer satisfaction.

Option B   8% sales growth, 5% profit growth, a £500,000 surplus cash flow, and maintenance of high product quality/customer satisfaction.

If the firm chose option B in preference to option A, it would be trading off sales growth and profit growth for better cash flow, product quality and customer satisfaction. It may feel that the long-term effect of reduced quality would negate the benefits under Option A.

3.29   One of the tasks of strategic management is to ensure **goal congruence**. Some objectives may not be in line with each other, and different **stakeholders** have different sets of priorities.

4   STAKEHOLDER GOALS AND OBJECTIVES

Case example

Shiseido

(From the *Financial Times*).

Akira Gemma, head of Shiseido, one of the world's largest cosmetics companies, follows an un-Japanese, investor friendly strategy: setting rising targets for return on equity, stressing high standards of disclosure and planning a share buy back. About 24 per cent of its stock is held outside Japan and the company maintains investor relations offices in the US, UK and Switzerland.

The company is pushing for globalisation, aiming to be the world's number one cosmetics company and to generate a quarter of its sales outside Japan.

Shareholder's expectations are seen as very important by Gemma: 'I think that on the whole international shareholders seem to be somewhat more intent on getting information in line with global standards – return on assets and equity, efficiency of management of assets, and so on. They are also more persistent about questioning us about investments that do not seem to be paying their way.'

KEY TERM

Stakeholders are 'groups or individuals having a legitimate interest in the activities of an organisation, generally comprising customers, employees, the community, shareholders, suppliers and lenders'.

(CIMA *Official Terminology*)

4.1   There are three broad types of stakeholder in an organisation, as follows.

- **Internal** stakeholders (employees, management)
- **Connected** stakeholders (shareholders, customers, suppliers, financiers)
- **External** stakeholders (the community, government, pressure groups)

Internal stakeholders: employees and management

4.2   Because **employees and management** are so intimately connected with the company, their objectives are likely to have a strong influence on how it is run. They are interested in the following issues.

(a)   The **organisation's continuation and growth**. Management and employees have a special interest in the organisation's continued existence.

(b)   Managers and employees have **individual interests** and goals which can be harnessed to the goals of the organisation.

Internal stakeholder	Interests to defend	Response risk
Managers and employees	• Jobs/careers • Money • Promotion • Benefits • Satisfaction	• Pursuit of 'systems goals' rather than shareholder interests • Industrial action • Negative power to impede implementation • Refusal to relocate • Resignation

Connected stakeholders

4.3   Writing in *Management Accounting* (November 1997) Malcolm Smith stated that increasing shareholder value should assume a core role in the strategic management of a business. If management performance is measured and rewarded by reference to changes in **shareholder value** then shareholders will be happy, because managers are likely to encourage long-term share price growth.

Connected stakeholder	Interests to defend	Response risk
Shareholders (corporate strategy)	• Increase in shareholder wealth, measured by profitability, P/E ratios, market capitalisation, dividends and yield • Risk	• Sell shares (eg to predator) or boot out management
Bankers (cash flows)	• Security of loan • Adherence to loan agreements	• Denial of credit • Higher interest charges • Receivership
Suppliers (purchase strategy)	• Profitable sales • Payment for goods • Long-term relationship	• Refusal of credit • Court action • Wind down relationships
Customers (product market strategy)	• Goods as promised • Future benefits	• Buy elsewhere • Sue

Case example

A survey of FTSE 100 companies conducted by the *Financial Times* asked what part leading shareholders play in the running of companies and what top directors think of their investors.

Almost half of those surveyed felt that their main shareholders 'rarely or never' offered any useful comments about their business. 69% of respondents however felt that their major investors understood their business well or very well. 89% did not feel hampered by shareholders in taking the correct long term strategy.

Almost all directors felt their biggest shareholders were in it for the long term. This latter point probably reflects the fact that the top ten fund managers own 36 per cent of the FTSE 100 – few fund managers can afford to move out of a FTSE 100 company altogether and therefore remain long term shareholders whether the investment is liked or not.

There is a perceived trend towards greater involvement and communication. To quote one director: 'Investors are much more sensitive to their responsibilities than in the past because they are looked on as the guardians of the corporate conscience.'

External stakeholders

4.4   External stakeholder groups - the government, local authorities, pressure groups, the community at large, professional bodies - are likely to have quite diverse objectives.

External stakeholder	Interests to defend	Response risk
Government	• Jobs, training, tax	• Tax increases
		• Regulation
		• Legal action
Interest/pressure groups	• Pollution	• Publicity
	• Rights	• Direct action
	• Other	• Sabotage
		• Pressure on government

Dependency

4.5 A firm might depend on a stakeholder group at any particular time.

    (a) A firm with persistent cash flow problems might depend on its bankers to provide it with money to stay in business at all.

    (b) In the long term, any firm depends on its customers.

4.6 The degree of dependence or reliance can be analysed according to these criteria.

    (a) **Disruption**. Can the stakeholder disrupt the organisation's plans (eg a bank withdrawing overdraft facilities)?

    (b) **Replacement**. Can the firm replace the relationship?

    (c) **Uncertainty**. Does the stakeholder cause uncertainty in the firm's plans? A firm with healthy positive cash flows and large cash balances need not worry about its bank's attitude to a proposed investment.

Exam focus point

In an exam question, you will usually have to:

• Identify the stakeholders in the situation
• Identify what their particular interests are
• Explain the importance of developing and maintaining relationships with them

A question on the May 2002 paper asked how setting corporate objectives can help/obstruct when satisfying shareholder demands.

5 THE SHORT AND LONG TERM

KEY TERM

Short-termism is 'bias towards paying particular attention to short-term performance, with a corresponding relative disregard to the long run'.

(CIMA Official Terminology)

5.1 'Short-termism' appears in the syllabus as a factor which can affect objectives.

Long-term and short-term objectives

5.2 **Objectives may be long-term and short-term.**

(a) For example, a company's primary objective might be to increase its earnings per share from 30p to 50p in the next five years. Strategies for achieving the objective might be selected to include the following.

(i) Increasing profitability in the next twelve months by cutting expenditure.

(ii) Increasing export sales over the next three years.

(iii) Developing a successful new product for the domestic market within five years.

(b) Secondary objectives might then be re-assessed to include the following.

(i) The objective of improving manpower productivity by 10% within twelve months.

(ii) Improving customer service in export markets with the objective of doubling the number of overseas sales outlets in selected countries within the next three years.

(iii) Investing more in product-market research and development, with the objective of bringing at least three new products to the market within five years.

5.3 Targets cannot be set without an awareness of what is realistic. Quantified targets for achieving the primary objective, and targets for secondary objectives, must therefore emerge from a realistic 'position audit'.

Trade-offs between short-term and long-term objectives

5.4 Just as there may have to be a trade-off between different objectives, so too might there be a need to make trade offs between short-term objectives and long-term objectives. This is referred to as **S/L trade-off**.

KEY TERM

The **S/L trade-off** refers to the balance of organisational activities aiming to achieve long term and short-term objectives when they are in conflict or where resources are scarce.

5.5 Decisions which involve the **sacrifice of longer term objectives** include the following.

(a) Postponing or abandoning capital expenditure projects, which would eventually contribute to growth and profits, in order to protect short term cash flow and profits.

(b) Cutting R&D expenditure to save operating costs, and so reducing the prospects for future product development.

(c) Reducing quality control, to save operating costs (but also adversely affecting reputation and goodwill).

(d) Reducing the level of customer service, to save operating costs (but sacrificing goodwill).

(e) Cutting training costs or recruitment (so the company might be faced with skills shortages).

5.6 We come back to short and long-termism in Chapter 14 in the context of performance measurement.

6 SOCIAL RESPONSIBILITY AND SUSTAINABILITY

Social responsibility

6.1 If it is accepted that businesses do not bear the total **social cost** of their activities, it could be suggested that **social responsibility** might be a way of recognising this.

> **KEY TERMS**
>
> **Social cost.** 'Tangible and intangible costs and losses sustained by third parties or the general public as a result of economic activity, eg pollution by industrial effluent'.
>
> **Social responsibility accounting** 'The identification, measurement and reporting of the social costs and benefits resulting from economic activities.'
>
> *(CIMA Official Terminology)*

6.2 However, is there any justification for 'social responsibility' outside a business's normal operations?

(a) 'The public' is a stakeholder in the business. A business only succeeds because it is part of a wider society. Giving to charity is one way of enhancing the reputation of the business.

(b) Charitable donations and artistic sponsorship are a useful medium of public relations and can reflect well on the business.

(c) Involving managers and staff in community activities is good work experience.

(d) It helps create a value culture in the organisation and a sense of mission, which is good for motivation.

(e) In the long-term, upholding the community's values, responding constructively to criticism, contributing towards community well-being might be good for business, as it promotes the wider environment in which businesses flourish.

The social audit

6.3 **Social audits** involve these elements.

• Recognising a firm's rationale for engaging in socially responsible activity
• Identification of programmes which are congruent with the mission of the company
• Determination of objectives and priorities related to this programme
• Specification of the nature and range of resources required
• Evaluation of company involvement in such programmes past, present and future

6.4 Whether or not a social audit is used depends on the degree to which social responsibility is part of the **corporate philosophy**. A cultural awareness must be achieved within an organisation in order to implement environmental policy, which requires Board and staff support.

6.5   In the USA, social audits on environmental issues have increased since the Exxon Valdez catastrophe in which millions of gallons of crude oil were released into Alaskan waters. The Valdez principles were drafted by the Coalition for Environmentally Responsible Economics to focus attention on environmental concerns and corporate responsibility.

*   Eliminate pollutants and hazardous waste

*   Conserve non-renewable resources

*   Market environmentally safe products and services

*   Prepare for accidents and restore damaged environments

*   Provide protection for employees who report environmental hazards

*   Companies should appoint an environmentalist to the board of directors, name an executive for environmental affairs and develop an environmental audit of global operations.

6.6   There are three contrasting views about the responsibilities of the corporation.

(a) If the company creates a social problem, it must fix it (eg Exxon).

(b) The multinational corporation has the resources to fight poverty, illiteracy, malnutrition, illness, etc. This approach disregards who actually creates the problems.

Case example

This school of communitarian thought may date back to Henry Ford, who said, 'I do not believe that we should make such an awful profit on our cars. A reasonable profit is right, but not too much. So it has been my policy to force the price of the car down as fast as production would permit, and give the benefits to the users and the labourers, with surprisingly enormous benefits to ourselves.'

(c) The third perspective says that companies already discharge their social responsibility, simply by increasing their profits and thereby contributing more in taxes. If a company was expected to divert more resources to solve society's problems, this would represent a double tax.

Strategies for social responsibility

Proactive strategy

6.7   A proactive strategy is a strategy which a business follows where it is prepared to take full responsibility for its actions. A company which discovers a fault in a product and recalls the product without being forced to, before any injury or damage is caused, acts in a proactive way.

Reactive strategy

6.8   This involves allowing a situation to continue unresolved until the public, government or consumer groups find out about it.

Defence strategy

6.9 This involves minimising or attempting to avoid additional obligations arising from a particular problem.

Accommodation strategy

6.10 This approach involves taking responsibility for actions, probably when one of the following happens.

- Encouragement from special interest groups
- Perception that a failure to act will result in government intervention

Green concerns

6.11 Business activities in general were formerly regarded as problems for the environmental movement, but the two are now increasingly complementary. There has been an increase in the use of the 'green' approach to market products. 'Dolphin friendly' tuna and paper products from 'managed forests' are examples.

The impact of green issues on business practice

6.12 **Environmental impacts** on business may be **direct**.

- Changes affecting costs or resource availability
- Impact on demand
- Effect on power balances between competitors in a market

6.13 They may also be **indirect,** as legislative change may affect the environment within which businesses operate. Finally, pressure may come from customers or staff as a consequence of concern over environmental problems.

Green pressures on business

6.14 Pressure for better environmental performance is coming from many quarters.

(a) **Green pressure groups** have increased their membership and influence dramatically.

(b) **Employees** are increasing pressure on the businesses in which they work for a number of reasons - partly for their own safety, partly in order to improve the public image of the company.

(c) **Legislation** is increasing almost by the day. Growing pressure from the 'green' or green-influenced vote has led to mainstream political parties taking these issues into their programmes, and most countries now have laws to cover land use planning, smoke emission, water pollution and the destruction of animals and natural habitats.

(d) **Environmental risk screening** has become increasingly important. Companies in the future will become responsible for the environmental impact of their activities.

Social responsibility and sustainability

6.15 Green concerns are founded on two main ideas. One is a response to and **responsibility for the community.** The other is **sustainability**.

> **KEY TERM**
>
> **Sustainability** involves developing strategies so that the company only uses resources at a rate which allows them to be replenished. At the same time, emissions of waste are confined to levels which do not exceed the capacity of the environment to absorb them.

Ecology and strategic planning

6.16 Physical environmental conditions are important.

(a) **Resource inputs**. Managing physical resources successfully (eg oil companies, mining companies) is a good source of profits.

(b) **Logistics.** The physical environment presents logistical problems or opportunities to organisations. Proximity to road and rail links can be a reason for siting a warehouse in a particular area.

(c) **Government.** The physical environment is under the control of other organisations.

(i) Local authority town planning departments can influence where a building and necessary infrastructure can be sited.

(ii) Governments can set regulations about some of the organisation's environmental interactions.

(d) **Disasters.** In some countries, the physical environment can pose a major 'threat' to organisations.

6.17 Issues relating to the effect of an organisation's activities on the physical environment (which, to avoid confusion, we shall refer to as 'ecology'), have come to the fore in recent years.

How issues of ecology will impinge on business

6.18 Possible issues to consider are these.

- **Consumer demand** for products which appear to be ecologically friendly
- Demand for **less pollution** from industry
- Greater **regulation** by government and the EU (eg recycling targets)
- Demand that **businesses be charged** with the external cost of their activities
- Possible requirements to conduct **ecology audits**
- Opportunities to develop **products and technologies** which are ecologically friendly
- Taxes (eg landfill tax)

6.19 The consumer demand for products which claim ecological soundness has waxed and waned, with initial enthusiasm replaced by cynicism as to 'green' claims.

(a) **Marketing.** Companies such as Body Shop have exploited ecological friendliness as a marketing tool.

(b) **Publicity.** Perhaps companies have more to fear from the impact of bad publicity (relating to their environmental practices) than they have to benefit from positive ecological messages as such. Public relations is a vital competitive weapon.

(c) **Lifestyles.** There may be a limit to which consumers are prepared to alter their lifestyles for the sake of ecological correctness.

(d) Consumers may be **imperfectly educated** about ecological issues. (For example, much recycled paper has simply replaced paper produced from trees from properly managed (ie sustainably developed) forests.) In short, some companies may have to 'educate' consumers as to the relative ecological impact of their products.

Ecology and the management accountant

6.20 One of the ways in which governments have tried to make pollution control palatable is by claiming that business will benefit by good environmental practices. There are sadly some doubts about this, largely explained by the law of diminishing returns.

(a) Measures to control pollution have had the effect of reducing waste in other ways. TQM principles, such as zero defects production, save money by reducing waste.

(b) The earliest and easiest savings are the cheapest to make. Savings at the margin become more and more expensive.

(c) The annual costs of pollution control are rising each year.

6.21 Firms need a suitable policy to identify which investments in environmentally friendly activities yield the best ecological payoff for the money spent.

Environmental accounting

6.22 In their capacity as information providers, management accountants may be required to report on a firm's environmental impact and possible consequences. Environmental management accounting according to Frank Kirken in *Management Accounting*, February 1996) is more advanced in Germany or Scandinavia than in the UK.

6.23 Environmental management accounting (EMA) information is:

- Future-orientated, reflecting environmental as well as economic realities
- A natural development from management accounting

It may be necessary, for example, for a management accountant to play a role in distributing information focusing on the implications of the misuse of scarce resources.

6.24 According to BS 7750, EMA systems should be integrated with other control systems within the company, so that the two desirable goals of economic and environmental efficiency coincide at company operation levels. Examples of EMA are as follows.

(a) **Eco-balance.** The firm identifies the raw materials it uses and outputs such as waste, noise etc, which it gives a notional value. The firm can identify these outputs as a social 'cost'.

(b) **Cleaner technology,** in the manufacturing process to avoid waste. Simple waste-minimisation measures can increase profit on purely economic grounds.

(c) **Corporate liabilities.** Firms are being sued for environmental damage, and this might need to be recorded as a liability, with a suitable risk assessment. This might have to be factored into the project appraisal and risk.

(d) **Performance appraisal** can include reducing pollution.

(e) **Life cycle assessments.** The total environmental impact of a product is measured, from the resources it consumes, the energy it requires in use, and how it is disposed of, if not recycled. It may be that a product's poor ecological impact (and consequent liability or poor publicity) can be traced back to one component or material, which can be replaced.

(f) **Budgetary planning** and control systems can be used to develop variances analysing environmental issues.

Renewable and non-renewable resources

6.25 As we have seen, **sustainability** means that resources consumed are replaced in some way: for every tree cut down another is planted. Some resources, however, are inherently non-renewable. For example, oil will eventually run out, even though governments and oil firms have consistently underestimated reserves.

(a) Metals can be recycled. Some car manufacturers are building cars with recyclable components.

(b) An argument is that as the price of resources rise, market forces will operate to make more efficient use of them or to develop alternatives. When oil becomes too expensive, solar power will become economic.

6.26 John Elkington, chairman of the think-tank SustainAbility Ltd, has said that **sustainability** now embraces not only environmental and economic questions, but also social and ethical dimensions. He writes about the **triple bottom line**, which means 'business people must increasingly recognise that the challenge now is to help deliver simultaneously:

* Economic prosperity
* Environmental quality
* Social equity'

Case example

Elkington quotes the example of Kvaerner, the Norwegian construction company. An environmental report compiled by the company listed the following.

* A 1% reduction in absence due to sick leave is worth $30 million
* A 1% reduction in material and energy consumption is worth $60 million
* A 20% cut in insurance premiums would be worth $15 million

6.27 A full consideration of sustainability in company reports is hampered by several difficulties.

* Lack of a standard methodology
* Accountants/auditors lack environmental expertise
* Difficulties in determining environmental costs
* Identification and valuation of potential liabilities is problematic

6.28 Elkington considers there to be three main forms of capital that businesses need to value

* **Economic capital** (physical, financial and human skills and knowledge)
* **Natural capital** (replaceable and irreplaceable)
* **Social capital** (the ability of people to work together)

6.29 Environmental and social accounting is still embryonic, but Elkington believes that it will eventually develop our ability to see whether or not a particular company or industry is 'moving in the right direction'.

Case example

Some business leaders have made a case for becoming ecologically and socially sustainable:

- 'Institutions that operate so as to capitalise all gain in the interests of the few, while socialising all loss to the detriment of the many, are ethically, socially and operationally unsound ... This must change.' – Dee Hock, Founder, President and CEO Emeritus of Visa International, the credit card organisation.

- 'Far from being a soft issue grounded in emotion and ethics, sustainable development involves cold, rational business logic'. – Robert B. Shapiro, Chairman of Monsanto, the US multinational.

- 'The gap between rhetoric and reality is increasing. I would tell multinationals they have to watch out ... they are much more vulnerable because they have to be accountable to the public everyday.' – Thilo Bode, Executive Director of Greenpeace.

- Explaining his company's forays into renewable energy and enhanced support for the communities where it does business: 'These efforts have nothing to do with charity, and everything to do with our long-term self interests ... our shareholders want performance today, and tomorrow, and the day after.' – Sir John Browne, CEO of British Petroleum/Amoco.

Exam focus point

A number of articles have appeared in *Management Accounting* (now *Financial Management)* on the topic of ecology, which all conclude that the management accountant has a lot to contribute. It ties neatly in with this examiner's preoccupation with short- and long -termism, in that some decisions that could be taken from an 'ecological sustainability' standpoint may impact short-term performance.

7   NOT FOR PROFIT ORGANISATIONS   5/01

Voluntary and not-for-profit sectors

7.1   Although most people would 'know one if they saw it', there is a surprising problem in clearly defining what counts as a **not-for-profit (NFP) organisation**. Local authority services, for example, would not be setting objectives in order to arrive at a profit for shareholders, but nowadays they are being increasingly required to apply the same disciplines and processes as companies which are oriented towards straightforward profit goals.

Case example

Oxfam operates more shops than any commercial organisation in Britain, and these operate at a profit. The Royal Society for the Protection of Birds operates a mail order trading company which provides a 25% return on capital, operating very profitably and effectively.

> **KEY TERM**
>
> Bois proposes that a **not-for-profit organisation** be defined as:' ... an organisation whose attainment of its prime goal is not assessed by economic measures. However, in pursuit of that goal it may undertake profit-making activities.'
>
> This may involve a number of different kinds of organisation with, for example, differing legal status - charities, statutory bodies offering public transport or the provision of services such as leisure, health or public utilities such as water or road maintenance.

7.2 Business strategy issues are just as relevant to a not-for-profit organisation as they are to a business operating with a profit motive. The tasks of setting objectives, developing strategies and controls for their implementation can all help in improving the performance of charities and NFP organisations. Whilst the basic principles are appropriate for this sector, differences in how they can be applied should not be forgotten.

Objectives

7.3 Objectives will not be based on profit achievement but rather on achieving a **particular response** from various target markets. This has implications for reporting of results. The organisation will need to be open and honest in showing how it has managed its budget and allocated funds raised. **Efficiency and effectiveness** are particularly important in the use of donated funds, but there is a danger that resource efficiency becomes more important than the service effectiveness.

7.4 Here are some possible objectives for a NFP organisation.

- Surplus maximisation (equivalent to profit maximisation)
- Revenue maximisation (as for a commercial business)
- Usage maximisation (as in leisure centre swimming pool usage)
- Usage targeting (matching the capacity available, as in the NHS)
- Full/partial cost recovery (minimising subsidy)
- Budget maximisation (maximising what is offered)
- Producer satisfaction maximisation (satisfying the wants of staff and volunteers)
- Client satisfaction maximisation (the police generating the support of the public)

7.5 There are no buyers in the NFP sector, but rather a number of different **audiences**.

(a) A **target public** is a group of individuals who have an interest or concern about the charity.

(b) Those benefiting from the organisation's activities are known as the **client public**.

(c) Relationships are also vital with **donors and volunteers** from the general public.

(d) There may also be a need to lobby **local and national government** and businesses for support.

7.6 Charities and NFP organisations often deal more with **services and ideas** than products.

(a) **Appearance** needs to be business-like rather than appearing extravagant.

(b) **Process** is increasingly important, for example, the use of direct debit to pay for council tax, reduces administration costs leaving more budget for community services.

(c)   **People** need to offer good service and be caring in their dealings with their clients.

(d)   **Distribution channels** are often shorter with fewer intermediaries than in the profit making sector. Wholesalers and distributors available to a business organisations do not exist in most non-business contexts.

(e)   **Promotion is usually dominated by personal selling**. Advertising is often limited to public service announcements due to limited budgets. Direct marketing is growing due to the ease of developing databases. Sponsorship, competitions and special events are also widely used.

(f)   **Pricing** is probably the most different element in this sector. Financial price is often not a relevant concept. Rather, opportunity cost, where an individual is persuaded of the value of donating time or funds, is more relevant.

7.7   Controlling activities is complicated by the difficulty of judging whether **non-quantitative objectives** have been met. For example assessing whether the charity has improved the situation of client publics is difficult to research. Statistics related to product mix, financial resources, size of budgets, number of employees, number of volunteers, number of customers serviced and number and location of facilities, are all useful for this task.

8   **THE PUBLIC SECTOR**   Pilot paper, 5/01

Exam focus point

The syllabus content specifically indicates that the objectives of not for profit organisations should be considered. Below are some examples to get you thinking about the requirements of the public sector. The May 2001 paper contained a question about the differing objectives of public sector organisations, concentrating on the way they are set and how performance towards achieving them is measured.

8.1   In a business, the level of sales often indicates the level of activity (number of goods produced). Effectively, sales are a limiting factor, and once the level of activity has been determined, resources are obtained to satisfy this demand.

8.2   While sales of services can be used in some public sector organisations as the starting point of the budgeting process, this cannot be the case when the services are not 'sold' but are provided to meet social needs. Instead **resources are the limiting factor,** since demand is potentially limitless. Many of the concerns about 'rationing' health care suggest precisely this problem.

'Care in the Community'

8.3   The Audit Commission published some guidelines for budgeting, in situations where levels of service provision must be matched to available resources. An example is a guideline for budgeting for local authority support for community care. Rather than look after the elderly, disabled or mentally ill in institutions, care is delivered at the patient's home. How do authorities deal with the delivery of services to dependent elderly people?

8.4   A basic problem with this sort of budget in the public sector is to find the starting point.

(a)   Planners can **budget for a set level of service provision**. The budget is based upon the number of home helps currently available and the number of day care centres to be run.

(b) Planners can identify the **needs of service recipients**. These can be classified and ranked to establish various levels of possible demand for the service.

8.5 Relevant factors need to be identified.

- The **needs** of the local dependent elderly population
- The various **alternative policies** by which these needs can be met
- The **resources actually available**
- The amount of those resources which are already **committed**

8.6 Identifying the needs means that the level of service can be tailored more accurately to the requirements of the clients. The Commission recommends three stages.

Stage 1: identify the care needs of the local dependent elderly population

8.7 Developing budgets for different levels of care needed by the dependent elderly might involve the following process.

(a) **What is the demand?**

(i) **Identify categories of needs**. An example is given below.

Guide for categorising the needs of dependent elderly people	
Level of need	Detailed criteria
High	Unable to do one or more of the following without help: ° get in and out of bed ° eat and drink ° get to and use WC/commode ° get dressed ° wash hands and face and/or ° are incontinent ° are mentally infirm
Moderate	Unable to: ° bath/strip wash themselves ° do shopping ° do light household cleaning ° cook meals and/or ° are mildly confused
Low	Some disability but do not need help more than once a week.

(ii) **Identify the number of people in each category of need.** There is a variety of data sources, including data collected in the Census and other exercises.

(b) **Estimate the type of package of care required** to satisfy people in each need category (high, moderate, low).

(i) Seek the **professional judgement** of relevant personnel in the social services department.

(ii) These 'packages' are then costed. It may mean an assessment of the likely fees to be paid to private sector contractors.

(c) So, the final budgeted cost of meeting identified needs is:
Cost of a typical care package × **Estimated numbers needing care package**

Stage 2: suggest options for satisfying needs and budget for them

8.8   It is possible that Stage 1 above will reveal:

- A demand pattern for services that is not matched by existing provision
- A **shortage of available resources**, leading to a requirement for **rationing**

8.9   The budgeting process should therefore take mismatches and shortages into account.

(a)   It may be difficult to alter existing patterns of services in the short term, so there will be excessive or deficient levels of capacity in some areas.

(b)   The authority will have to make a judgement of how much it will be able to spend on Community Care.

(i)   For example, it may only be possible to provide a 'full' service to those with high needs.

(ii)   Alternatively they might provide a wider, but less intensive, level of service. The number of people receiving the service can be reduced by changing criteria of eligibility.

Stage 3: implementation

8.10   In practice resources are almost certain to be limited, and the services will be rationed according to the eligibility criteria for individuals, or in changes to the package of services offered.

Integration with the total budget

8.11   It is possible that a similar budgeting process can be implemented for other services (eg services to the mentally disabled, those with learning disabilities).

8.12   If total social services are delivered on an area basis, it might be necessary to use these service budgets as the building blocks of an area budget.

Responsibility accounting in health care

8.13   An example of the problems in introducing management accounting techniques to achieve the objectives of public sector stakeholders is offered by the extension since the 1970s of **responsibility accounting** to the National Health Service (outlined by Irvine Lapsey in an article in *Management Accounting Research*). Responsibility accounting aims to devolve budget and expenditure control to decision-makers, such as doctors.

8.14   The NHS 'internal market' is now in place with 'purchasers' (eg regional health authorities, fundholding general practitioners) arranging contracts with hospitals. Trust hospitals now work autonomously.

8.15   In the NHS, the introduction of management accounting techniques based on private sector practice is problematic for the following reasons.

(a)   Although NHS self-governing hospital trusts are financially autonomous, they are not profit-making businesses. The purpose of the internal market is to **allocate resources efficiently**, not to make a profit.

(b) Many doctors resent managerial and financial involvement in medical decisions. NHS managers may seek the 'cheapest' option rather than what the doctor considers most effective.

(c) The level of paperwork involved in implementing the system causes a lot of resentment.

(d) The budgetary system is often conducted on an annual basis. Strategic planning, as we have seen, should be a long-term process.

(e) There is political interference - after all, the NHS survives on tax-payers' money and NHS funding decisions are a matter of public policy.

8.16 What is undeniably true is that there is an increased emphasis on **performance**. Schools and hospitals publicise **league tables** on certain key criteria.

(a) Critics argue these ignore the real differences in the schools' environments (eg a school's exam success might depend on the 'quality' of its pupils and the relative social deprivation of its catchment area).

(b) Supporters argue that league tables give clients of services a better choice and concentrate managers' minds on improving performance.

Unity Bicycles plc

(1) Draft a brief mission statement for UB.

(2) What do you consider to be the strategic significance of UB's decision to outsource its components?

(3) Suggest some critical success factors for UB's Mexican factory.

(4) Why might UB's external shareholders welcome the fact that UB's management are shareholders too?

(5) What other stakeholders might influence UB's decisions significantly?

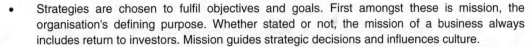

Chapter roundup

- Strategies are chosen to fulfil objectives and goals. First amongst these is mission, the organisation's defining purpose. Whether stated or not, the mission of a business always includes return to investors. Mission guides strategic decisions and influences culture.

  If there is no fit between existing resources and required resources then either the strategy will have to be changed, or resources somehow obtained. Sometimes, when resources are scarce, departments will have to compete for them. Resource requirements can be determined by developing **critical success factors** and the key tasks to achieve them

- Objectives and goals relate to how the firm can fulfil its mission. For a business, objectives will be set for the return offered to shareholders. These will be achieved by the commercial objectives for growth, technology etc.

- Many different groups have an interest in what the organisation does.

- A key factor which can affect objectives is **short termism**. There is a **trade-off** between long and short term objectives when they are in conflict or resources are scarce. For example, capital expenditure projects may be postponed or abandoned in order to protect short term cash flow and profits.

- Some argue that a business has a **social responsibility** for the cost of its activities, while others argue that businesses already contribute enough to society via the taxes on their profits.

- The **sustainability** of business activity is becoming a major concern as business moves into the 21st century. This considers both environmental and social pressures. The '**triple bottom line**' refers to a whole new way of measuring business performance using not only economic prosperity, but environmental quality and social equality.

- Not-for-profit and public sector organisations have their own objectives, generally concerned with **efficient use of resources**.

Quick quiz

1   What are the four elements in a definition of 'mission'?

  P ....

  S ....

  P ....

  V ....

2   Mission statements have a standard format

  ☐ True
  ☐ False

3   Distinguish between critical success factors, key tasks and priorities.

4   Fill in the gaps: 'Most organisations set themselves quantified (1) .... in order to enact the corporate (2) .... Many objectives are:

  (3) S ....

  (4) M ....

  (5) A ....

  (6) R ....

  (7) T ....

5   Some objectives are more important than others. These are called .... corporate objectives.

6   (a) 'Increase the number of customers by 15%'

    (b) 'Produce reports within three days of month end'

    (c) 'Achieve 35% market share'

    Are each of the above examples of unit objectives or corporate objectives?

7   There are three broad types of stakeholder

    (1) ....

    (2) ....

    (3) ....

8   How do questions of sustainability tie in with the long/short term debate?

9   Define an NFP organisation.

10   What is usually the limiting factor for a public sector organisation?

Answers to quick quiz

1   Purpose

    Strategy

    Policies and standards of behaviour

    Values

2   False

3   Critical success factors (CSFs) 'are those factors on which the strategy is fundamentally dependent for its success'.

    Key tasks are what must be done to ensure each critical success factor is achieved.

    Priorities indicate the order in which tasks are achieved.

4   (1) objectives (2) mission (3) specific (4) measurable (5) attainable (6) results-orientated (7) time bounded

5   Primary

6   (a)   unit
    (b)   unit
    (c)   corporate

7   (1)   internal
    (2)   connected
    (3)   external

8   For example, some decisions that are taken from an ecological sustainability standpoint may impact short term performance, such as the decision to invest in a new recycling process.

9   An organisation whose attainment of its prime goal is not assessed by economic measures. Their first objective is to be a non-loss operation in order to cover costs. Profits are made only as a means to an end, such as providing a service.

10   Availability/supply of resources

Unity Bicycles plc review

Question 1. There are several examples in this chapter.

Question 2. Outsourcing can be either an operational or strategic decision, of course. But what did you jot down for its *strategic* importance to UB? To save money? True enough, but this is just an accountant's view. The point is that outsourcing enables UB to compete with Chinese manufacturers. In other words the *relative* costs are important.

Question 3. The Tijuana factory will have a more important role in extending UB's influence in the Americas. In the short term, CSFs relate to improving quality at least to competitor standards and to UB's own standards in the long-term. *Key tasks* might involve introducing new equipment, training the work force and sending them on quality programmes.

Question 4. In theory, UB's management and external shareholders enjoy goal congruence, because managers are shareholders too.

Question 5. UB is financing more of its activities by borrowing. UB's bank might become more interested.

Now try the question below from the Exam Question Bank

Question to try	Level	Marks	Time
16	Exam	25	45 mins

As this is the first exam-level question you have encountered so far in the text, and because it is fairly tricky, we have analysed the question and its requirements in detail.

BPP PUBLISHING

Part B
Appraising the environment

Chapter 4

THE CHANGING ENVIRONMENT

Topic list	Syllabus reference	Ability required
1　Relating the organisation to its environment	(ii)	Evaluation
2　The political and legal environment	(ii), (v)	Evaluation
3　The economic environment	(ii), (v)	Evaluation
4　The social and cultural environment	(ii), (v)	Evaluation
5　The technological environment	(ii), (v)	Comprehension
6　Interest and pressure groups	(ii), (v)	Evaluation
7　Environmental information and analysis	(ii), (v)	Evaluation

Introduction

'**Appraising the environment**' makes up 25% of the syllabus for this paper.

(a) You should note the **influences of the environment** on an organisation. Some factors are more directly relevant than others. You should remember that information about the environment is often uncertain, incomplete and even ambiguous. This makes some of the tasks of business strategy quite difficult for the management accountant.

(b) You should appreciate how **environmental changes**, in any given situation, might have an impact on **corporate appraisal**, particularly in terms of opportunities and threats.

Gathering **strategic intelligence** is an important task. The **internet** and **databases** are increasingly being used as sources of strategic intelligence.

Learning outcomes covered in this chapter

- **Evaluate** the importance of international issues including competition, management and regulation

- **Explain** the role and activities of pressure groups

- **Evaluate** the availability and quality of data for environmental analysis

Syllabus content covered in this chapter

- The importance of relating the organisation to its environment when assessing its competitive position and consideration of the level of uncertainty and risks that the organisation faces

- Classifying and assessing the changing national and international influences on the organisation carefully using appropriate models and techniques (eg PEST). This would include such issues as EU regulation, GATT agreements and trade cycles

- The role and activities of interest groups and pressure groups (eg self interest groups, such as industry associations, as well as environmental and ethical pressure groups). This topic is concerned with the recognition of additional stakeholders

- The availability and quality of data and information for environmental analysis. This includes the need for Internet and database interrogation

- The effect of regulation, both voluntary and legal, on corporate performance

1 RELATING THE ORGANISATION TO ITS ENVIRONMENT

Pilot paper, 5/01

1.1 Organisations exist within an environment which strongly influences what they do and whether they survive and develop. Strategic planners must take account of environmental influences in order to produce plans that are realistic and achievable.

The environment of an organisation is everything outside its boundaries.

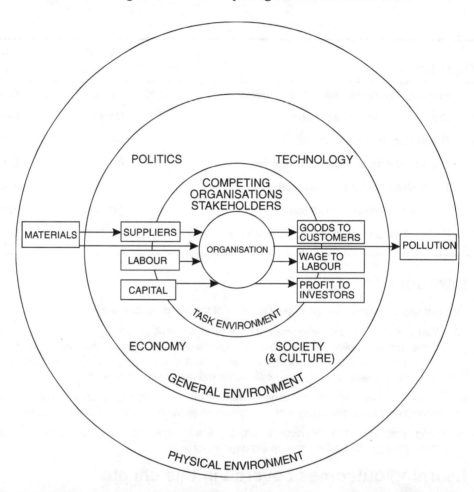

KEY TERMS

The **general environment** covers all the political/legal, economic, social/cultural and technological (PEST) influences in the countries an organisation operates in.

The **task environment** relates to factors of particular relevance to a firm, such as its competitors, customers and suppliers of resources.

Exam focus point

The PEST model is a useful checklist for general environmental factors - remember that in the real world they are interlinked and form an overall picture of the environment that a business is faced with. The influence of the environment on its strategic choices is a key theme of many questions.

Environmental fit

1.2 One purpose of a strategy is to ensure **environmental fit**, relating a company to its environment.

1.3 Any strategy is made in conditions of **partial ignorance**. The environment is a major cause of such 'ignorance'.

(a) It contains **opportunities and threats** which may influence the organisation's activities and may even threaten its existence.

(b) The environment is so **varied** that many organisations will find it difficult to discern its effects on them.

(c) Firms can conduct **audits** to identify which of the many different sorts of environmental factors have had a significant influence.

Complexity and dynamism

1.4 Johnson and Scholes contrast the concepts of **environmental complexity** and **environmental dynamism**.

(a) **Complexity** arises from three factors.

- The **variety** of influences faced by an organisation
- The amount of **knowledge** necessary
- The **interconnectedness** of environmental influences

(b) **Dynamic** environments are in a state of change. The market for computers is a dynamic market because of the rate of technological development.

Time horizon

1.5 Finally, you should bear in mind which environmental issues are of:

- **Long-term impact,** which can be dealt with in advance
- **Short-term impact,** which require crisis management

Question 1

How do you consider that the Johnson and Scholes model can be applied to the BSE scare by a hamburger retailer?

Answer

Complexity. Although we can concentrate at length on the disease, an important 'environmental' factor is the media. Many measures are taken to increase public 'confidence', even if not strictly necessary, hence McDonald's use of imported beef. Other influences include the EU, animal rights campaigners. Uncertainty is caused by inadequate knowledge as to the link, if any, between BSE and CJD. Clearly, there has been insufficient knowledge as to risk. The variety of influences include technological factors, the animal feed industry etc.

2 THE POLITICAL AND LEGAL ENVIRONMENT

2.1 The **political environment** affects the firm in a number of ways.

- A basic legal framework generally exists

- The government can take a particular stance on an issue of direct relevance to a business or industry

- The government's overall conduct of its economic policy is relevant to business

---

Case study link

PEST analysis is a useful tool to employ in the case study as an initial survey of conditions and options. In May 2002, the environment surrounding Global Inc did not favour further acquisitions at home. The political and regulatory environment was generally unfavourable.

The political and legal environment

2.2 Laws come from common law, parliamentary legislation and government regulations derived from it, and obligations under EU membership and other treaties.

2.3 **Legal factors affecting all companies**

Factor	Example
General legal framework: contract, tort, agency	Basic ways of doing business, negligence proceedings
Criminal law	Theft (eg of documents in Lanica's failed bid for the Co-op), insider dealing, bribery, deception
Company law	Directors and their duties, reporting requirements, takeover proceedings, shareholders' rights, insolvency
Employment law	Trade Union recognition, Social Chapter provisions, minimum wage, unfair dismissal, redundancy, maternity, Equal Opportunities
Health and Safety	Fire precautions, safety procedures
Data protection	Use of information about employees and customers
Marketing and sales	Laws to protect consumers (eg refunds and replacement, 'cooling off' period after credit agreements), what is or isn't allowed in advertising
Environment	Pollution control, waste disposal
Tax law	Corporation tax payment, Collection of income tax (PAYE) and National Insurance contributions, VAT

2.4 Some legal and regulatory factors affect **particular industries,** if the public interest is served. For example, electricity, gas, telecommunications, water and rail transport are subject to **regulators** (Offer, Ofgas, Oftel, Ofwat, Ofrail) who have influence over market access, competition and pricing policy (can restrict price increase)

2.5 This is because either:

- The industries are, effectively, monopolies
- Large sums of public money are involved (eg in subsidies to rail companies)

Case example

The National Lottery (or 'Lotto') in the UK is one of the most highly regulated lotteries in the world. Under the terms of its licence, Camelot (the operator) is required to operate the lottery in an efficient and socially responsible way, protecting players and the integrity of the lottery, and to ensure that it generates the maximum amount of money for the 'Good Causes' which are designated by Parliament:

- The Community Fund
- The Millennium Commission
- The Sports Council
- The Heritage Lottery Fund
- The Arts Council
- New Opportunities Fund

The National Lottery Commission regulates the operation of the lottery. It has the right to award and revoke the operating licence, determine the number of games that can be offered and to carry out compliance audits (such as making sure there are no sales to under 16s).

Camelot's strategic objectives are clear:

(i)   Deliver target returns to Good Causes in a socially responsible way
(ii)   Increase the number of players and total sales
(iii)   Maximise player and retailer satisfaction
(iv)   Retain the trust and support of the general public
(v)   Deliver healthy returns for shareholders

However, it sees the regulatory regime in which it operates (there are over 2,000 regulations) as a barrier to a rapid response to an increasingly competitive market. Unequal tax regimes are a prime concern. The tax on bingo has been abolished, and it seems likely that regulation over competitors to the Lottery will be further reduced. Camelot believes that the only way to achieve a more effective balance between its own commercial requirements and the needs of customers is to allow it greater self regulation. It believes that its 8 years of running the Lottery are testament to its integrity and ability.

2.6   **Porter** notes several ways whereby the government can directly affect the **economic structure** of an industry. They are explained below.

2.7   **Capacity expansion.** Government policy can encourage firms to increase or cut their capacity.

(a)   The UK tax system offers 'capital allowances' to encourage investment in equipment

(b)   A variety of incentives, funded by the EU and national governments, exist for locating capacity in a particular area

(c)   **Incentives** are used to encourage investment by overseas firms. Different countries in the EU have 'competed' for investment from Japan, for example

2.8   **Demand**

- The government is a major customer
- Government can also influence demand by legislation, tax reliefs or subsidies

2.9   **Divestment and rationalisation.** In some European countries, the state takes many decisions regarding the selling off or closure of businesses, especially in sensitive areas such as defence.

2.10   **Emerging industries** can be promoted by the government or damaged by it.

2.11   **Entry barriers.** Government policy can discourage firms from entering an industry, by restricting investment or competition or by making it harder, by use of quotas and tariffs, for overseas firms to compete in the domestic market.

2.12 **Competition**.

   (a) The government's **purchasing decisions** will have a strong influence on the strength of one firm relative to another in the market (eg armaments).

   (b) **Regulations and controls** in an industry will affect the growth and profits of the industry - eg minimum product quality standards.

   (c) As a supplier of **infrastructure** (eg roads), the government is also in a position to influence competition in an industry.

   (d) Governments and supra-national institutions such as the EU might impose policies which keep an industry **fragmented**, and prevent the concentration of too much market share in the hands of one or two producers.

2.13 In some industries, governments regulate the adoption of **new products**. This is well illustrated by the pharmaceuticals industry, where new drugs or medicines must in many countries undergo stringent testing and obtain government approval before they can be marketed.

Operations

2.14 National and EU institutions also affect the detailed operations of some organisations.

   • Anti-discrimination legislation
   • Health and safety legislation
   • Product safety and standardisation (especially EU standards)
   • Workers' rights (eg unfair dismissal, maternity leave)
   • Training and education policies can determine the 'standard' of recruits

Question 2

How do you think UK government policy affects the UK pharmaceutical industry?

Answer

(a) The government must authorise most new drugs (eg for safety before they can be sold).
(b) In case of the UK, the government is a major purchaser of pharmaceuticals.
(c) Health education policies affect consumer demand.

Influencing government and EU policy

2.15 Businesses are able to influence government policies in a number of ways.

   (a) They can employ **lobbyists** to put their case to individual ministers or civil servants.

   (b) They can give MPs **non-executive directorships**, in the hope that the MP will take an interest in all legislation that affects them.

   (c) They can try to **influence public opinion**, and hence the legislative agenda, by advertising.

2.16 The EU will have an increasing role in the conduct of **European businesses** in:

   • Product standards
   • Environmental protection
   • Monetary policy (a European Central Bank might set interest rates)
   • Research and development

- Regional policy
- Labour costs (wages, pensions)

2.17 The following approach can be recommended to influencing EU decision making.

(a) **Get in early**. A business should make its views known in the drafting stage.

(b) **Work with others**. 'A spread of opinion carries more weight than a lone voice'.

(c) **Think European**. Show that the issue is relevant to the single market program or the EU's other aims.

(d) **Be prepared**. Firms should monitor the issues that are being dealt with by the Commission.

(e) **Think long-term**. A long term presence in Brussels can be of immense benefit.

2.18 Changes in UK law are often predictable. A government will publish a **green paper** discussing a proposed change in the law, before issuing a **white paper** and passing a bill through Parliament. Plans should be formulated about what to do if the change takes place.

Politics

2.19 Many economic forecasts ignore the implications of a change in government policy.

(a) At **national level,** political influence is significant and includes legislation on trading, pricing, dividends, tax, employment as well as health and safety (to list but a few).

(b) Politics at **international level** also has a direct bearing on organisations. EU directives affect all countries in the EU.

Political risk and political change

2.20 The political environment is not simply limited to legal factors. Government policy affects the whole **economy,** and governments are responsible for enforcing and creating a **stable framework** in which business can be done. A report by the World Bank indicated that the quality of **government policy is important in providing the right**:

- Physical infrastructure (eg transport)
- Social infrastructure (education, a welfare safety net, law enforcement)
- Market infrastructure (enforceable contracts, policing corruption)

2.21 However, it is **political change** which complicates the planning activities of many firms.

Political risk

2.22 The political risk in a decision is the risk that political factors will invalidate the strategy and perhaps severely damage the firm. Examples are wars, political chaos, corruption and nationalisation.

2.23 A **political risk checklist** was outlined by Jeannet and Hennessey. Companies should ask the following six questions.

1   How **stable** is the host country's political system?

2   How **strong** is the host government's commitment to specific rules of the game, such as ownership or contractual rights, given its ideology and power position?

3   How **long** is the government likely to remain in **power**?

4   If the present government is **succeeded**, how would the specific rules of the game change?

5   What would be the effects of any expected **changes** in the specific rules of the game?

6   In light of those effects, what **decisions and actions should be taken now**?

Question 3

For a business of your choice, identify the most significant areas of political risk.

3   THE ECONOMIC ENVIRONMENT

3.1   The economic environment is an important influence at local and national level.

Factor	Impact
Overall growth or fall in Gross Domestic Product	Increased/decreased demand for goods (eg dishwashers) and services (holidays).
Local economic trends	Type of industry in the area. Office/factory rents. Labour rates House prices.

National economic trends:

• Inflation	Low in most countries; distorts business decisions; wage inflation compensates for price inflation
• Interest rates	How much it costs to borrow money affects **cash flow**. Some businesses carry a high level of debt. How much customers can afford to spend is also affected as rises in interest rates affect people's mortgage payments.
• Tax levels	Corporation tax affects how much firms can invest or return to shareholders. Income tax and VAT affect how much consumers have to spend, hence demand.
• Government spending	Suppliers to the government (eg construction firms) are affected by spending.
• The business cycle	Economic activity is always punctuated by periods of growth followed by decline, simply because of the nature of trade. The UK economy has been characterised by periods of 'boom' and 'bust'. Government policy can cause, exacerbate or mitigate such trends, but cannot abolish the business cycle. (Industries which prosper when others are declining are called counter-cyclical industries.)

3.2   The **forecast state of the economy** will influence the planning process for organisations which operate within it. In times of boom and increased demand and consumption, the overall planning problem will be to **identify** the demand. Conversely, in times of recession, the emphasis will be on cost-effectiveness, continuing profitability, survival and competition.

3.3 Key issues for the UK economy

(a) The **service sector** accounts for most output. Services include activities such as restaurants, tourism, nursing, education, management consultancy, computer consulting, banking and finance. Manufacturing is still important, especially in exports, but it employs fewer and fewer people.

KEY TERM

Services are defined by the CIMA as 'value creating activities which in themselves do not involve the supply of physical product. Service provision may be subdivided into:

(i) *Pure services*, where there is no physical product, such as consultancy

(ii) *Service with a product attached*, such as the design and installation of a computer network

(iii) *Products with services attached*, such as the purchase of a computer with a maintenance contract.'

(b) The **housing market** is a key factor for people in the UK. Most houses are owner-occupied, and most people's wealth is tied up in their homes. UK borrowers generally borrow at variable rates of interest, so are vulnerable to changes in interest rates.

(c) **Tax and welfare.** Although headline rates of tax have fallen, people have to spend more on private insurance schemes for health or pensions. The government aims to target welfare provision on the needy and to reduce overall welfare spending by getting people into work.

(d) **Productivity.** An economy cannot grow faster than the underlying growth in productivity, without risking inflation. UK manufacturing productivity is still lower than that of its main competitors, but in services, the UK is relatively efficient.

3.4 Impact of international factors

Factor	Impact
Exchange rates	Cost of imports, selling prices and value of exports; cost of hedging against fluctuations
Characteristics of overseas markets. Different rates of economic growth and prosperity, tax etc.	Desirable overseas markets (demand) or sources of supply.
Capital, flows and trade	Investment opportunities, free trade, cost of exporting

Government economic policy

3.5 The government uses various policy tools as follows.

(a) **Fiscal policy**

- Taxation and other sources of income
- Government spending
- Borrowing whenever spending exceeds income
- Repaying debt when income exceeds expenditure

(b) **Monetary policy**

- Interest rates
- Exchange rates
- Control of the money supply
- Controls over bank lending and credit (rarely used) nowadays

3.6 Businesses are affected by a government's tax policy (eg corporation tax rates), and monetary policy (high interest rates increase the cost of investment, or depress consumer demand).

Government spending

3.7 Governments nationally and locally spend money on the following.

- Payments of wages and salaries to employees, and of pensions to old age pensioners
- Payments for materials, supplies and services
- Purchases of capital equipment
- Payments of interest on borrowings and repayments of capital

3.8 Tax and spending decisions have the effect of increasing or decreasing the amount that consumers have to spend generally and **re-allocating resources** in the economy to the public sector activities.

Privatisation of the public sector

3.9 Since 1979 various areas of the public sector have been delivered to the private sector in a process of **privatisation**. Where these were utilities, these organisations are regulated by bodies such as Oftel and Ofwat. This process had a number of sometimes conflicting objectives.

(a) **Reductions in public sector borrowing** and expenditure to finance tax cuts and/or spending.

(b) **Greater investment** which the government is unwilling to fund from taxation.

(c) Privatised utilities are then **free to borrow**.

(d) **New management practices** are introduced.

(e) Privatisation was held to encourage **competition**, but some were sold off as **monopolies**.

3.10 (a) **Contracting out**. Some work which was previously done by government employees has been contracted out to firms in the private sector.

(b) **Welfare spending**. Government policy has been to shift welfare spending to individuals, such as in personal pensions.

(c) **Private finance initiative**. The private sector is involved in financing public projects, such as roads and hospitals.

Inflation and interest rates

3.11 **Inflation** can be a deterrent to real economic growth, creating expectations of further inflation and undermining business confidence. The consequences include the following.

(a) A demand for **higher money wages** to be paid to employees to compensate for the fall in value of their wages.

(b) A demand for **high interest rates**, so that investors can be compensated for inflation and borrowers are deterred.

The housing market

3.12 An important feature of the UK economy is the **housing market**.

(a) The UK has a very high proportion of home ownership compared to most European countries.

(b) **Rising prices** encourage people to take out extra loans to spend on other things. This was held to lead to inflation.

(c) Most of the debt is at **variable rate**. Changes in interest rates have an immediate effect on people's pockets.

Exam focus point

Although you should be aware of the relationship between the organisation and the environment, the examiner will not expect candidates to demonstrate detailed understanding of cultural or economic factors that affect only the UK. We use the UK as an example in this Study Text, although the environmental conditions in your own country might be different. Questions will often have an international context and might concern large multinational enterprises, so an understanding of international influences is important.

International trade and exchange rates

3.13 International trade and finance consists of the following.

- Trade in goods and services, forming the **balance of trade**
- Long-term and short-term **investments** from other countries and into other countries
- Movements in a government's **official reserves** of foreign currency, gold etc

3.14 Faced with a **trade deficit**, a government might once have considered **protectionist measures** and, in the case of developing countries, **exchange controls**.

3.15 However, a government's long-term strategy for a balance of trade deficit should be to improve conditions in the domestic economy.

(a) The improvements required could include bringing inflation under control, encouraging investment in domestic industries and depressing consumer demand.

(b) The **quality** of the deficit is an important consideration. If capital goods are imported, this might mean only a short-term deficit, as the machinery enhances the productivity and export capacity of domestic firms in the long term. If consumer goods are imported, this might not be as sustainable in the long run.

Exchange rate policy

> **KEY TERM**
>
> **Exchange rate.** The rate at which a national currency exchanges for other national currencies, being set by the interaction of demand and supply of the various currencies in the foreign exchange markets (floating exchange rate), or by government intervention in order to maintain a constant rate of exchange (fixed exchange rate).
>
> - *Closing rate:* the exchange rate for spot transactions ruling at the balance sheet date, being the mean of the buying and selling rates at the close of business on the day for which the rate is to be ascertained.
>
> - *Forward exchange rate:* an exchange rate set for the exchange of currencies at some future date
>
> - *Spot exchange rate:* an exchange rate set for the immediate delivery of a currency
>
> (CIMA *Official Terminology*)

3.16 When there is a fall in the exchange rate, the price of imports rises. If the exchange rate between sterling and the Japanese Yen changed, say, so that sterling weakened from 225 Yen = £1 to 200 Yen = £1, the cost of imports costing 225,000 Yen would rise from £1,000 to £1,125. The effect of this imports price rise on the total cost of imports would depend on the **price elasticity** of demand for imported goods. If demand is **inelastic**, the total spending on imports would rise, whereas if demand is **elastic**, total spending on imports would fall (as consumers would buy goods made at home). In the UK, the price elasticity of demand for imported goods tends to be inelastic.

Managed exchange rates

3.17 **Exchange rate stability** has been, at various times, a feature of government policy. It is useful as it also allows enterprises to plan ahead, and institute coherent strategies for exports and imports.

(a) The **Exchange Rate Mechanism** of the European Monetary System was supposed to co-ordinate exchange rates of European currencies. Some members had to withdraw, because the economic policies of member states were not synchronised.

(b) Many states joined the European economic and monetary union (EMU) in 1999, with the single currency, the **Euro**. Monetary policy is managed by the European Central Bank. This is felt to be a necessary adjunct to the single European market.

Question 4

What might be the implications of European economic and monetary union (EMU), and a single European currency, for the following UK businesses?

(a) A package holiday firm, mainly selling holidays to France and Germany.
(b) An exporter of power station generating equipment to developing countries in Asia.
(c) An importer of wine from Australia.

Do this exercise twice, firstly on the assumption that the UK participates in EMU, swapping sterling for the Euro, and secondly on the assumption that it stays outside of EMU.

Answer

We can offer no definitive solution, but here are some points to consider.

(a) For companies trading primarily within the EU, such as the package holiday firm, participation in EMU will mean a reduction in exchange rate volatility - businesses will be able to compete on the essentials of cost and productivity. An analogy is the USA - although there are many 'states' there is only one currency. Most of British trade is with EU countries.

(b) and (c)

Companies trading outside the EU would remain subject to exchange rate risk, based on the Euro rather than sterling. It all depends on how the European Central Bank manages the currency - if the Euro becomes a 'hard' currency, like the Deutschmark, then exports will cost more to overseas customers, but imports from overseas suppliers might be cheaper. Many internationally traded goods, such as oil or aircraft, are priced in US dollars anyhow, so the impact will be indirect.

Of course, if the UK stays out of EMU it will not be in a position to influence the monetary policies of countries which use the Euro, although these policies will undoubtedly affect the UK economy and British businesses.

Effect on the firm

3.18 The management accountant may be asked to estimate the effect of particular economic factors on the firm's operations.

(a) **Interest rates**

(i) A rise might increase the cost of any borrowing the company has undertaken, thereby reducing its profitability. It also has the possible effect of raising a firm's cost of capital. An investment project therefore has a higher hurdle to overcome to be accepted. If, on the other hand, a firm has surplus cash, this can be invested for a higher return.

(ii) Interest rates also have a general effect on consumer confidence and liquidity, and hence demand, especially in relation to the housing markets

(b) **Inflation**. For an economy has a whole, inflation works as a 'tax on savers' given that it reduces the value of financial assets and the income of those on fixed incomes.

(i) It requires high **nominal interest rates** to offer investors a real return.

(ii) Inflation makes it hard for businesses to plan, owing to the uncertainty of future financial returns. Inflation and expectations of it help explain 'short-termism'.

(iii) Inflation has a number of effects on how firms report their performance and how they plan.

3.19 **Exchange rate** volatility affects the cost of imports from overseas, and the prices that can be charged to overseas customers. A high value to the pound means that customers must be charged more in their local currencies - and imports are cheaper.

3.20 Exchange rates do not only affect imports and exports. Many firms invest large sums of money in factories in overseas markets.

(a) The **purchasing power parity** theory of exchange rate suggests that, in the long term, differences in exchange rates caused by inflation or higher interest rates will even out. For example, in the 1960s, £1 = 8 DM, whereas now the rate is around £1 = DM 2.30. This is mainly explained by the UK's higher inflation rates. The fall in the exchange rate has compensated for the higher inflation. Over the long term, therefore, the underlying economic reality will assert itself. So, if UK labour costs are cheaper than German ones and UK workers are as productive, all other things being equal, the UK will be an attractive site for investment.

(b) On the other hand, firms are very vulnerable to changes in exchange rates over the short to medium term, especially as a subsidiary's reported profit can affect the reported profit of the holding company and hence, by implication, its share price. Firms can guard against the risk of exchange rates by a number of financial instruments such as **hedges**.

4 THE SOCIAL AND CULTURAL ENVIRONMENT

Social change and social trends

4.1 Social change involves changes in the nature, attitudes and habits of society. Social changes are continually happening, and trends can be identified, which may or may not be relevant to a business.

Demography

> **KEY TERM**
>
> **Demography** is the analysis of statistics on birth and death rates, age structures of populations, ethnic groups within communities etc.

4.2 Demography is important for these reasons.

- Labour is a factor of production
- People create demand for goods, services and resources
- It has a long-term impact on government policies
- There is a relationship between population growth and living standards

4.3 Here are some statistics, which might help to explain the importance many businesses are placing on overseas markets. The figures are taken from *Social Trends*.

	1994 Population (millions)	*2025 Population (millions)*	*% increase 1994-2025*
World population	5,665.5	8,472.4	49%
Europe (including Baltic states)	512.0	541.9	5%
Former USSR (excluding Baltic states)	284.5	344.5	21%
Canada and USA	282.7	360.5	27%
Africa	681.7	1,582.5	32%
Asia	3,233.0	4,900.3	65%
Latin America	457.7	701.6	53%
Oceania (including Australia)	27.5	41.3	50%

4.4 The following demographic factors are important to organisational planners.

Factor	Comment
Growth	The rate of growth or decline in a national population and in regional populations.
Age	Changes in the age distribution of the population. In the UK, there will be an increasing proportion of the national population over retirement age. In developing countries there are very large numbers of young people.
Geography	The concentration of population into certain geographical areas.

Factor	Comment
Ethnicity	A population might contain groups with different ethnic origins from the majority. In the UK, about 5% come from ethnic minorities, although most of these live in London and the South East.
Household and family structure	A household is the basic social unit and its size might be determined by the number of children, whether elderly parents live at home etc. In the UK, there has been an increase in single-person households and lone parent families.
Social structure	The population of a society can be broken down into a number of subgroups, with different attitudes and access to economic resources. Social class, however, is hard to measure (as people's subjective perceptions vary).
Employment	In part, this is related to changes in the workplace. Many people believe that there is a move to a casual flexible workforce; factories will have a group of **core employees**, supplemented by a group of insecure **peripheral employees**, on part time or temporary contracts, working as and when required. Some research indicates a 'two-tier' society split between '**work-rich**' (with two wage-earners) and '**work-poor**'. However, despite some claims, **most employees are in permanent, full-time employment.**
Wealth	Rising standards of living lead to increased demand for certain types of consumer good. This is why developing countries are attractive as markets.

4.5 **Implications of demographic change**

(a) **Changes in patterns of demand**: an ageing population suggests increased demand for health care services: a 'young' growing population has a growing demand for schools, housing and work.

(b) **Location of demand**: people are moving to the suburbs and small towns.

(c) **Recruitment policies**: there are relatively fewer young people so firms will have to recruit from less familiar sources of labour.

(d) **Wealth and tax**.

Culture

> **KEY TERM**
>
> **Culture** is used by sociologists and anthropologists to encompass 'the sum total of the beliefs, knowledge, attitudes of mind and customs to which people are exposed in their social conditioning.'

4.6 Through contact with a particular culture, individuals learn a language, acquire values and learn habits of behaviour and thought.

(a) **Beliefs and values**. Beliefs are what we feel to be the case on the basis of objective and subjective information (eg people can believe the world is round or flat). Values are beliefs which are relatively enduring, relatively general and fairly widely accepted as a guide to culturally appropriate behaviour.

    (b) **Customs:** modes of behaviour which represent culturally accepted ways of behaving in response to given situations.

    (c) **Artefacts:** all the physical tools designed by human beings for their physical and psychological well-being: works of art, technology, products.

    (d) **Rituals.** A ritual is a type of activity which takes on symbolic meaning, consisting of a fixed sequence of behaviour repeated over time.

The learning and sharing of culture is made possible by language (both written and spoken, verbal and non-verbal).

4.7 Underlying characteristics of culture

    (a) **Purposeful.** Culture offers order, direction and guidance in all phases of human problem solving.

    (b) **Learned.** Cultural values are 'transferred' in institutions (the family, school and church) and through on-going social interaction and mass media exposure in adulthood.

    (c) **Shared.** A belief or practice must be common to a significant proportion of a society or group before it can be defined as a cultural characteristic.

    (d) **Cumulative.** Culture is 'handed down' to each new generation. There is a strong traditional/historical element to many aspects of culture (eg classical music).

    (e) **Dynamic.** Cultures adapt to changes in society: eg technological breakthrough, population shifts, exposure to other cultures.

Case example

Islamic banking

Islamic banking is a powerful example of the importance of culture in an economy. The Koran abjures the charging of interest, which is usury. However whilst interest is banned, profits are allowed. A problem is that there is no standard interpretation of the sharia law regarding this. Products promoted by Islamic banks include:

(a)   Leasing (the Islamic Bank TII arranged leases for seven Kuwait Airways aircraft)
(b)   Trade finance
(c)   Commodities trading

The earlier Islamic banks offered current accounts only, but depositors now ask for shares in the bank profits. To tap this market, Citibank, the US bank, opened an Islamic banking subsidiary in Bahrain.

4.8 Knowledge of the culture of a society is clearly of value to businesses in a number of ways.

    (a) **Marketers** can adapt their products accordingly, and be fairly sure of a sizeable market. This is particularly important in export markets.

    (b) **Human resource managers** may need to tackle cultural differences in recruitment. For example, some ethnic minorities have a different body language from the majority, which may be hard for some interviewers to interpret.

4.9 Culture in a society can be divided into **subcultures** reflecting social differences. Most people participate in several of them.

Subculture	Comment
Class	People from different social classes might have different values reflecting their position of society.
Ethnic background	Some ethnic groups can still be considered a distinct cultural group.
Religion	Religion and ethnicity are related.
Geography or region	Distinct regional differences might be brought about by the past effects of physical geography (socio-economic differences etc). Speech accents most noticeably differ.
Age	Age subcultures vary according to the period in which individuals were socialised to an extent, because of the great shifts in social values and customs in this century. ('Youth culture'; the 'generation gap' etc).
Sex	Some products are targeted directly to women or to men.
Work	Different organisations have different corporate cultures, in that the shared values of one workplace may be different from another.

Case example

Consider the case of a young French employee of Eurodisney.

(a)   The employee speaks the French language - part of the national culture - and has participated in the French education system etc.

(b)   As a youth, the employee might, in his or her spare time, participate in various 'youth culture' activities. Music and fashion are emblematic of youth culture.

(c)   As an employee of Eurodisney, the employee will have to participate in the corporate culture, which is based on American standards of service with a high priority put on friendliness to customers.

4.10   Cultural change might have to be planned for. There has been a revolution in attitudes to female employment, despite the well-publicised problems of discrimination that still remain.

Question 5

Club Fun is a UK company which sells packaged holidays. Founded in the 1960s, it offered a standard 'cheap and cheerful' package to resorts in Spain and, more recently, to some of the Greek islands. It was particularly successful at providing holidays for the 18-30 age group.

What do you think the implications are for Club Fun of the following developments?

- A fall in the number of school leavers
- The fact that young people are more likely now than in the 1960s to go into higher education
- Holiday programmes on TV which feature a much greater variety of locations
- Greater disposable income among the 18-30 age group

Answer

The firm's market is shrinking. There is an absolute fall in the number of school leavers. Moreover, it is possible that the increasing proportion of school leavers going to higher education will mean there will be fewer who can afford Club Fun's packages. That said, a higher disposable income in the population

BPP PUBLISHING

at large might compensate for this trend. People might be encouraged to try destinations other than Club Fun's traditional resorts if these other destinations are publicised on television.

5 THE TECHNOLOGICAL ENVIRONMENT

5.1 The strategic importance of technology relates to all these aspects. In the most general senses, technology contributes to overall **economic growth**. Consider the **production possibility curve** which describes the total production in an economy. Technology can shift this curve, increasing total output, by enabling:

- gains in productivity (more output per units of input)
- reduced costs (eg transportation technology, preservatives)
- new types of product

5.2 Technological change is rapid, and organisations must adapt themselves to it. Technological change can affect the activities of organisations as follows.

(a) **The type of products or services that are made and sold.** For example, consumer markets have seen the emergence of home computers, compact discs and satellite dishes for receiving satellite TV; industrial markets have seen the emergence of custom-built microchips, robots and local area networks for office information systems.

Case example

The development of the transistor made valve radios obsolete. Japanese firms were thus able easily to enter the consumer electronics market, where they are now key competitors. Japanese firms had no previous investment in valve radio production.

(b) **The way in which products are made.**

(i) There is a continuing trend towards the use of modern labour-saving production equipment, such as robots.

(ii) Technology can also develop new raw materials.

(c) **The way in which services are provided.**

(d) **The way in which markets are identified.** Database systems make it much easier to analyse the market place.

(e) **The way in which firms are managed.** There is some concern that computerisation encourages 'delayering' of organisational hierarchies (in other words, the reduction of management layers between the senior managers and the workforce), but requires greater workforce skills. Using technology often requires changes in working methods. Information technology, in particular, requires skills at manipulating and interpreting abstract data.

(f) The means and extent of **communications** with external clients.

5.3 The impact of technological change also has potentially important social consequences.

(a) Whereas people were once collected together to work in factories, **home working** will become more important.

(b) Certain sorts of skill, related to **interpretation** of data and information processes, are likely to become more valued than manual or physical skills.

(c) Technology increases manufacturing productivity, so that more people will be involved in **service** jobs.

Technological forecasting

5.4 It is extremely difficult to forecast developments beyond more than a few years. For example, many of the current developments in information technology would have seemed almost impossible not much more than a decade ago.

(a) **Futurology** is the science and study of sociological and technological developments, values and trends with a view to planning for the future.

(b) The **Delphi model** involves a panel of experts providing views on various events to be forecast such as inventions and breakthroughs, or even regulations or changes over a time period in to the future.

(c) In some cases, instead of technical developments being used to predict future technologies, future social developments can be predicted, in order to predict future **customer needs**.

5.5 It is also possible that one particular invention or technique will have wide ranging applications. Such a technology might be called a **meta-technology**.

Case example

An example of a meta-technology might be the technology behind lasers which are used for a huge variety of jobs.

- Eye surgery (eg on the cornea, as it is more precise than a scalpel, and the heat effectively seals the wound)
- Industrial cutting
- Illuminating public monuments at night
- Reading data from compact disks (for recorded music, interactive video games, interactive encyclopaedias, publishing)
- Discotheques

---

6 INTEREST AND PRESSURE GROUPS

6.1 In the past 30 years, hundreds of pressure groups, representing interests - from pedestrians to civil liberties - are competing for the attention of the public, civil servants politicians and business people. They are relevant to business in one of two ways.

(a) **Indirectly,** if they aim to change government policy as insiders (if consulted) or as outsiders (if they rely on public pressure)

(b) **Directly,** if their activities are devoted to influencing a particular business - a good example of this was the campaign against Barclays' involvement in apartheid South Africa, in which activists dissuaded people from opening bank accounts.

6.2 A distinction is sometimes drawn between two types of group.

(a) **Cause groups** which espouse a distinct cause (eg Friends of the Earth)

(b) **Interest groups** which promote a particular interest, such as businesses (CBI), doctors (British Medical Association), or people working in a particular industry (trade unions).

6.3 A business might therefore be a member of an interest group or might promote one. For example, the Portman Group has been set up by the drinks industry to discourage irresponsible consumption of alcohol.

6.4 The effectiveness of pressure groups varies. Some are run by a core of highly professional activists.

Case example

Greenpeace mobilised consumer opinion in Germany to dissuade Shell, the oil firm, from dumping one of its old oil platforms in the North Sea, despite the fact that the firm had asked for, and received, support from the UK government.

Greenpeace works with industry to find solutions to problems and invites captains of industry to speak at its conferences. It is keen to get away from the label of 'environmental terrorist'.

Shell also became the focus of criticisms of oil industry practice in Nigeria, but is now, thanks mainly to external pressure rather than corporate initiative, one of only three companies highlighted by Amnesty International for having 'explicitly committed themselves to human rights in their codes of conduct.'

Economic interests

6.5 The main interest groups reflecting **economic interests** are as follows.

(a) **Businesses***:* CBI, Institute of Directors. These can be supplemented by smaller more specialist trade associations in particular industries, which gang together to promote common interests (eg newspapers to oppose VAT on the newspapers).

(b) **Professional associations** are groups of people who do the same job or practise the same skill. Examples include the following.

- Accountants (eg CIMA)
- Doctors (British Medical Association)

Professional associations are generally involved in setting standards of skill and enforcing adherence to good practice (eg through disciplinary schemes).

(c) **Trades Unions** are similar to professional associations, in that they represent people who work. A trade union may represent people in a variety of jobs, or it may be concentrated in a particular sector of the economy.

(d) Consumers' associations.

Exam focus point

Dealing with pressure groups might be a challenge in your exam. A plan might identify the following.

(a) Which pressure groups are likely to have an impact or an interest
(b) How these impacts can be addressed:

- Provide information to correct misapprehensions
- Use public relations in crisis management.

7   **ENVIRONMENTAL INFORMATION AND ANALYSIS**   **Pilot paper, 5/01**

Environmental analysis

7.1   Johnson and Scholes suggest that a firm should conduct an **audit of environmental influences**. This will identify the environmental factors which have had a significant influence on the organisation's development or performance in the past.

7.2   Strategic decisions are made in partial ignorance, as we have seen, because the environment is uncertain. Uncertainty relates to the **complexity and dynamism** of the environment.

(a)   **Complexity** arises from:

(i)   The **variety of influences** faced by the organisation. The more open an organisation is, the greater the variety of influences. The greater the number of markets the organisation operates in, the greater the number of influences to which it is subject.

(ii)   The amount of **knowledge** necessary. All businesses need to have knowledge of the tax system, for example, but only pharmaceuticals businesses need to know about mandatory testing procedures for new drugs.

(iii) The **interconnectedness** of environmental influences. Importing and exporting companies are sensitive to exchange rates, which themselves are sensitive to interest rates. Interest rates then influence a company's borrowing costs.

(b)   **Dynamism**. Stable environments are unchanging. Dynamic environments are in a state of change. The computer market is a dynamic market because of the rate of technological change.

Question 6

Analyse the environments of the two situations below according to the criteria in paragraph 7.2.

(a)   A new product has just been introduced to a market segment. It is proving popular. As it is based on a unique technology, barriers to entry are high. The product will not be sold outside this market segment.

(b)   A group of scientists has recently been guaranteed, by an EU research sponsoring body, funds for the next ten years to investigate new technologies in the construction industry, such as 'smart materials' (which respond automatically to weather and light conditions). This is a multi-disciplinary project with possible benefits for the construction industry. A number of building firms have also guaranteed funds.

Answer

(a)   The environment is simple, as the product is only being sold in one market. The environment is dynamic, as the product is still at the introduction stage and demand might be predicted to increase dramatically.

(b)   The environment is complex, but stable. The knowledge required is uncertain, but funds are guaranteed for ten years.

Forecasts

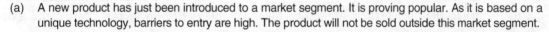

KEY TERM

The CIMA defines a **forecast** as 'a prediction of future events and their quantification for planning purposes'

7.3 Forecasting attempts to reduce the uncertainty managers face. In **simple/static conditions the past is a relatively good guide** to the future. Techniques are:

(a) **Time series analysis.** Data for a number of months/years is obtained and analysed. The aim of time series analysis is to identify:

- Seasonal and other cyclical fluctuations
- Long term underlying trends

An example of the use of this approach is the UK's monthly unemployment statistics which show a 'headline figure' and the 'underlying trend'.

(b) **Regression analysis** is a quantitative technique to check any underlying correlations between two variables (eg sales of ice cream and the weather). Remember that the relationship between two variables may only hold between certain values.

7.4 **Dynamic/complex conditions**

- **Future developments:** the past is not a reliable guide.

- Techniques such as **scenario building** are useful as they can propose a number of possible futures.

- **Complex environments** require techniques to reduce the effects of complexity on organisational structure and decision-making.

Econometric models for medium-term forecasting

7.5 Econometrics is the study of economic variables and their interrelationships.

(a) **Leading indicators** are indicators which change before market demand changes. For example, a sudden increase in the birth rate would be an indicator of future demand for children's clothes.

(b) The ability to predict the span of time between a change in the indicator and a change in market demand. Change in an indicator is especially useful for demand forecasting when they reach their highest or lowest points (when an increase turns into a decline or vice versa).

Strategic intelligence

7.6 If a key task of strategic management is to ensure environmental fit, managers need a willingness and an ability to understand the environment and to anticipate future trends.

- A separate strategic planning department collects data on trends
- The marketing department identifies customer needs
- The R&D department identifies new technology
- The production department suggests process innovation

7.7 Arguably, as strategy is about the whole organisation, there are dangers in restricting the gathering of strategic information to functional departments. The whole firm needs to be aware of **strategic intelligence**.

KEY TERM

Strategic intelligence, according to Donald Marchand, is defined as 'what a company needs to know about its business environment to enable it to anticipate change and design appropriate strategies that will create business value for customers and be profitable in new markets and new industries in the future'.

7.8 A model of the process of creating strategic intelligence is outlined below.

Sensing	Identify appropriate external indicators of change
↓	↓
Collecting	Gather information in ways that ensure it is relevant and meaningful
↓	↓
Organising	Structure the information in the right format
↓	↓
Processing	Analyse information for implications
↓	↓
Communicating	Package and simplify information for users
↓	↓
Using	Apply strategic intelligence

7.9 Key dimensions in strategic intelligence are these.

(a) **Information culture**. What is the role of information in the organisation? Is it only distributed on a 'need to know basis' or do people have to give specific reasons for secrecy?

(b) **Future orientation**. Is the focus on specific decisions and trade-offs, or a general attitude of enquiry?

(c) The **structure** of information flows. Is communication vertical, up and down the hierarchy, or lateral?

(d) **Processing strategic intelligence**. Are 'professional' strategists delegated to this task or is it everybody's concern?

(e) **Scope**. Is strategic intelligence dealt with by senior management only, or is intelligence built throughout the organisation?

(f) **Time horizon**. Short-termist or orientated towards the long term?

(g) **The role of IT**.

(h) **Organisational 'memory'**. In other words, do managers keep in mind the lessons of past successes or failures?

Sources of strategic intelligence

7.10 There are many sources of environmental information.

(a) **Internal sources** or sources relatively close to the company.

(i) The **sales force** deals with customers, and so is in a position to obtain customer and competitor information.

(ii) Many companies conduct **market research**. Although generally this deals with specific issues, it can indicate general environmental concerns (eg consumers' worries).

(iii) The management information system may generate information about the environment, although its main focus is internal.

(b) External sources of environmental data are various.

(i) **Media**. Newspapers, periodicals and television offer environmental information.

(ii) Sometimes, more detailed country information is needed than that supplied by the press. **Export consultants** might specialise in dealing with particular countries, and so can be a valuable source of information. The **Economist Intelligence Unit** offers reports into particular countries.

BPP
PUBLISHING

(iii) Academic or **trade journals** might give information about a wide variety of relevant issues to a particular industry.

(iv) **Trade associations** also offer industry information.

(v) The government can be a source of statistical data relating to money supply, the trade balance and so forth, which is often summarised in newspapers. The DTI also publishes **Overseas Trade,** concentrating on export opportunities for UK firms.

(vi) Sources of technological environmental information can include the Patent Office.

(vii) Stockbrokers produce investment reports for the clients which involve analysis into particular industries.

(viii) Specialist consultancy firms (eg CACI census data) provide information.

The Internet

> **KEY TERM**
>
> The **internet** is the sum of all the separate networks (or stand-alone computers) run by organisations and individuals alike. (It has been described as an international telephone service for computers.)
>
> The internet offers efficient, fast and cost effective email, and massive information search and retrieval facilities. There is a great deal of financial information available and users can also access publications and news releases issued by the Treasury and other Government departments.
>
> To access the internet you require a microcomputer, a modem and the services of an internet provider.

7.11 The **Internet** allows any computer with a telecommunications link to send and receive information from any other suitably equipped computer. Terms such as 'the net', 'the information superhighway', 'cyberspace', and the 'World Wide Web (www)' are used fairly interchangeably.

7.12 Most people use the Net through interface programs called **browsers** that make it more user-friendly and accessible. These guide users to destinations throughout the world: the user simply types in a word or phrase like 'beer' to find a list of thousands of websites that contain something connected with beer.

7.13 Companies like Yahoo! make money by selling advertising space. For instance if you type in 'beer', an advertisement for Miller Genuine Draft may appear, as well as your list of beer-related sites. Thus the Web is increasingly being used for marketing research purposes. At the very least advertisers know exactly how many people have viewed their message and how many were interested enough in it to click on it to find out more.

7.14 Besides its usefulness for tapping into worldwide information resources businesses are also using it to provide information about their own products and services and to conduct research into their competitors' activities.

Database information

7.15 A **management information system** or **database** should provide managers with a useful flow of relevant information which is easy to use and easy to access. Information is an important corporate resource. Managed and used effectively it can provide considerable competitive advantage and so it is a worthwhile investment.

7.16 It is now possible to access large volumes of generally available information through databases held by public bodies and businesses.

(a) Some **newspapers** offer computerised access to old editions, with search facilities looking for information on particular companies or issues. FTPROFILE, for example, provides on-line business information.

(b) Public databases are also available for inspection.

Dun and Bradstreet provide general business information. **AC Nielsen** operate on-line information regarding products and market share.

7.17 In theory, a database is simply a coherent structure for the storage and use of data. It involves the centralised storage of information.

- **Common data** for all users to share

- Avoidance of **data duplication** in files kept by different users

- **Consistency** in the organisation's use of data, and in the accuracy and up-to-dateness of data accessed by different users, because all records are centrally maintained and updated

- **Flexibility** in the way in which shared data can be queried, analysed and formatted by individual users for specific purposes, without altering the store of data itself

7.18 Such structure could be fulfilled by a centralised file registry or library, or a self-contained data record like a master index card file. In practice, however, large scale databases are created and stored on **computer systems,** using **database application packages** such as **Microsoft Access.**

7.19 Developments in information technology allow businesses to have access to the databases of **external organisations**. Reuters, for example, provides an on-line information system about money market interest rates and foreign exchange rates to firms involved in money market and foreign exchange dealings, and to the treasury departments of a large number of companies. The growing adoption of technology at **point of sale** provides a potentially invaluable source of data to both retailer and manufacturer.

Case example

CACI is a company which provides market analysis, information systems and other data products to clients. It advertises itself as 'the winning combination of marketing and technology".

As an illustration of the information available to the marketing manager through today's technology, here is an overview of some of their products.

Paycheck: this provides income data for all 1.6 million individual post codes across the UK. This enables companies to see how mean income distribution varies from area to area.

People UK: this is a mix of geodemographics, life stage and lifestyle data. It is person rather than household specific and is designed for those companies requiring highly targeted campaigns.

InSite:	this is a geographic information system (GIS). It is designed to assist with local market planning, customers and product segmentation, direct marketing and service distribution.
Acorn:	this stands for A Classification of Residential Neighbourhoods, and has been used to profile residential neighbourhoods by post code since 1976. ACORN classifies people in any trading area or on any customer database into 54 types.
Lifestyles UK:	this database offers over 300 lifestyle selections on 44 million consumers in the UK. It helps with cross selling and customer retention strategies.
Monica:	this can help a company to identify the age of people on its database by giving the likely age profile of their first names. It uses a combination of census data and real birth registrations.

7.20 Legislation and regulation exists to protect consumers form misuse of personal details held on computer, unsolicited mail and invasion of privacy.

(a) There are now stringent trading practices and regulations in the direct mail industry, administered by the Direct Mail Services Standards Board (DMSSB) and Mail Order Protection Scheme (for display advertisements in national newspapers that ask for money in advance).

(b) The **Mailing Preference Service** allows customers to state whether they would - and more often, would not - be willing to receive direct mail on a range of specific areas.

(c) The **Data Protection Acts 1984 and 1998** provide that data users (organisations or individuals who control the contents of files of personal data and the use of personal data) must register with the Data Protection Registrar. They must limit their use of personal data (defined as any information about an identifiable living individual) to the uses registered.

Case example

Even organisations in the FMCG field, such as Nestlé, Pedigree Petfoods and Kraft General Foods, are consolidating data that they accumulate about their customers and in the USA, Sears Roebuck uses the computerised database information on its 40 million customers to promote special offers to specific target segments. MCI, the US phone company, has a database of 120 million subscribers.

Environmental data

7.21 McNamee lists nine areas of environmental data that ought to be included in a database for strategic planners. These are as follows.

(a) **Competitive data.** This would include information derived from an application of Porter's Five Forces analysis (see Chapter 5)

(b) **Economic data.** Details of past growth and predictions of future growth in GDP and disposable income, the pattern of interest rates, predictions of the rate of inflation, unemployment levels and tax rates, developments in international trade and so on

(c) **Political data.** The influence that the government is having on the industry

(d) **Legal data.** The likely implications of recent legislation, legislation likely to be introduced in the future and its implications

(e) **Social data.** Changing habits, attitudes, cultures and educational standards of the population as a whole, and customers in particular

(f)   **Technological data.** Technological changes that have occurred or will occur, and the implications that these will have for the organisation

(g)   **Geographical data.** Data about individual regions or countries, each of them potentially segments of the market with their own unique characteristics

(h)   **Energy suppliers data.** Energy sources, availability and price of sources of supply generally

(i)   **Data about stakeholders in the business.** Employees, management and shareholders, the influence of each group, and what each group wants from the organisation

In other words data which covers the key elements of the general and market environment should be included in a database for strategic and marketing planners.

7.22   As well as obtaining data from its own internal database system an organisation can obtain it from an **external database** operated by another organisation.

On-line databases

7.23   Most external databases are on-line databases, which are very large computer files of information, supplied by **database providers** and managed by 'host' companies whose business revenue is generated through charges made to **users**. Access to such databases is open to anyone prepared to pay, and who is equipped with a PC plus a modem (to provide a phone link to the database) and communication software. These days there are an increasing number of companies offering free internet access. Most databases can be accessed around the clock.

7.24   Providers of **database information** include the following.

- Directory publishers such as Kompass
- Market research publishers such as Mintel, Keynote and Front & Sullivan
- Producers of statistical data, including the UK government and Eurostat
- Reuters Business Briefing
- FT Profile

7.25   External databases are becoming increasingly specialised, but they have to be used with caution.

- How up-to-date are they?
- Is the information accurate?
- Security?
- Legality?

Case example

(a)   Companies can now subscribe to appropriate "knowledge brokers" which can provide industry-specific information, such as regional reports or statistics.

(b)   Courier providers are now offering systems advice to companies with logistics problems.

(c)   BT has launched BT Workstyle Consultancy so that it can use the knowledge gained from its homeworking and teleworking experience.

Such examples indicate how some companies are now seeking to exploit their knowledge.

Unity Bicycles plc

(1)   How complex is UB's environment?

(2)   Identify the political risks to which UB might be subjected.

(3)   What might be the implications for UB of population growth in China and India and the changing age structure of the populations of Europe and the USA?

(4)   What ecological concerns affect UB?

Chapter roundup

- To secure **environmental fit**, an analysis of the environment therefore is required.

- The environment of a firm can be assessed as to its **complexity** and its **dynamism** (rate of change).

- A framework for considering general environmental factors in PEST: political (and legal). economic, social (and cultural) and technological. (Some factors are not always easy to classify in this framework.)

- Political and legal factors relate to the general framework of laws, specific government policies, the sources of power and the institutions of government. Political instability is a cause of risk. Different approaches to the political environment apply in different countries.

- Economic factors include the rate of growth in the economy, inflation, interest rates and so forth. They are influenced by government fiscal policy (tax and spending) and monetary policy (interest rates). Economic factors are relevant in domestic markets and overseas markets.

- Social and cultural factors relate to two main issues. **Demography** is the study of the population as a whole: its overall size, whether it is growing, stable, or falling; the proportion of people of different age groups - in industrial countries the proportion of elderly people is increasing; where people live and work; ethnic origin. **Culture** refers to characteristic ways of viewing the world and behaviour: most countries contain several subcultures.

- Technological factors have implications for economic growth overall, and offer opportunities and threats to many businesses. Meta-technologies are technologies which are applicable to many applications.

- As well PEST factors, businesses should consider the **physical** environment: it is an operational issue for them, and also of a wide political and cultural significance. The management accountant can assist by providing cost information in an environmental management system.

- An organisation should have in place an appropriate process for gaining strategic **intelligence**, and communicating it throughout the organisation.

Quick quiz

1   Distinguish between the general environment and the task environment.

2   Environmental complexity arises from three factors

   (1) ....

   (2) ....

   (3) ....

3   What is political risk?

4   Are the following related to government fiscal or monetary policy?

   (a)   taxation

   (b)   borrowing

(c)   interest rates

(d)   control of the money supply

(e)   exchange rates

(f)   government spending

5   **Fill in the blanks**

When there is a fall in the exchange rate, the price of imports (1) .... If the exchange rate between sterling and the US$ changed so that sterling (2) .... from $1.60 = £1 to $1.50 = £1, the cost of imports costing $160,000 would (3) .... from (4) .... to (5) ....

6   What is the purchasing power parity theory?

7   What is the Delphi model?

8   Outline the process of creating strategic intelligence.

    S ....

    C ....

    O ....

    P ....

    C ....

    U ....

9   A database involves the centralised storage of information.

    ☐   True

    ☐   False

10   Give an example showing why knowledge of culture is useful.

Answers to quick quiz

1   The general environment covers all the political/legal, economic, social/cultural and technological (PEST) influences in the countries an organisation operates in.

    The task environment relates to factors of particular relevance to a firm, such as its competitors, customers and suppliers of resources.

2   (1)   Variety of influences faced by an organisation

    (2)   The amount of knowledge necessary

    (3)   The interconnectedness of environmental influences

3   The political risk in a decision is the risk that political factors will invalidate the strategy and perhaps severely damage the firm. Examples are wars, political chaos, corruption and nationalisation.

4   (a)   fiscal
    (b)   fiscal
    (c)   monetary
    (d)   monetary
    (e)   monetary
    (f)   fiscal

5   (1)   rises
    (2)   weakened
    (3)   rise
    (4)   £100,000
    (5)   £106,667

6   The purchasing power parity theory of exchange rate suggests that, in the long term, differences in exchange rates caused by inflation of higher-interests rates will even out.

7   The Delphi model involves a panel of experts providing views on various events to be forecast such as inventions and breakthroughs, or even regulations or changes over a time period in to the future.

8   Sensing
        Collecting
        Organising
        Processing
        Communicating
        Using

9   True

10   Marketers can adapt their products accordingly, and be fairly sure of a sizeable market. This is particularly important in export markets. Human resource managers may need to tackle cultural differences in recruitment. For example, some ethnic minorities have a different body language from the majority, which may be hard for some interviewers to interpret.

Unity Bicycles plc review

Question 1. UB's environment is fairly complex, because it operates in so many different countries, but the basic technology is fairly simple - a bicycle is not a complex product.

Question 2. To identify the political risks in any of the areas mentioned in the case study, read a newspaper! Hong Kong reverted to Chinese sovereignty in 1997: but this is unlikely to raise the risk profile of the business, since it already has substantial operations in China, and there is no evidence that the Chinese government is going to nationalise profitable businesses.

Question 3. The implication of population growth is an increased market. However, if accompanied by increases in prosperity, customers may be able to afford other means of transport for commuting (eg motor scooters and cars). The new battery technology may be useful in developing countries, rather than in Europe. In Europe, the changing age structure may affect the use of bikes: fewer young people will buy them, so the aim might be to promote them on the grounds that they offer health-giving exercise.

Question 4. In ecological terms, the push-bike is energy-efficient, and so is a prime example of an ecologically friendly product. Other issues include energy efficiency in its factories, and how hazardous materials are dealt with.

Now try the question below from the Exam Question Bank

Question to try	Level	Marks	Time
3	Exam	25	45 mins

Chapter 5

THE GLOBAL COMPETITIVE ENVIRONMENT

Topic list	Syllabus reference	Ability required
1 The competitive environment: the five forces	(ii)	Evaluation
2 The impact of globalisation on competition	(ii)	Evaluation
3 The competitive advantage of a nation's industries	(ii)	Evaluation
4 Competitor analysis	(ii)	Evaluation

Introduction

Chapter 4 dealt with **general environmental factors**, in what is called the '**macro**' **environment**, identifying some trends which affect most organisations to a greater or lesser degree. In this chapter we narrow the focus significantly, and deal with a number of aspects of the **micro environment**.

(a) Most businesses compete with other firms, but they do not compete with every firm. **Competitors** are a vital influence on decision-making. So Section 1 discusses the **five competitive forces** underlying a particular industry.

(b) Section 2, on **globalisation**, indicates how the competitive environment of many industries might be fundamentally changed by much freer international trade - but we also warn against some of the hype surrounding notions of a 'borderless world'. Section 3, on the **competitive advantage of nations**, indicates how the domestic origins of an industry can affect its competitive success.

Finally, we narrow the focus still further, and analyse individual competitors. It is here that you might find your management accounting techniques most useful.

Learning outcomes covered in this chapter

*   **Evaluate** the importance of international issues including competition, management and regulation

*   **Evaluate** the competitive forces in the market place

*   **Prepare** and **evaluate** competitor analysis

Syllabus content covered in this chapter

*   Classifying and assessing the changing national and international influences on the organisation carefully using appropriate models and techniques (eg PEST). This would include such issues as EU regulation, GATT agreements and trade cycles

*   The influence of industry forces on the market place (eg Porter's five forces model)

*   International factors affecting the market place: country advantages and global factors

*   The implications of the above for the Chartered Management Accountant and the management accounting information system

1   THE COMPETITIVE ENVIRONMENT: THE FIVE FORCES   5/02

1.1   Before we start we must make a basic distinction between the **market** and the **industry**.

> ### KEY TERMS
>
> The **market** comprises the customers or potential customers who have needs which are satisfied by a product or service.
>
> The **industry** comprises those firms which use a particular competence, technology, product or service to satisfy customer needs.

Question 1

Assume that you are based in London and that you need to attend a conference in Glasgow. Which industries can satisfy your needs to attend the conference?

Answer

(a)   The airline industry: a number of airlines will compete to fly you from London to Glasgow.

(b)   The railways: it is possible that two railway companies will compete to take you there.

(c)   The car industry, if you have purchased a car.

(d)   The bus industry: several bus firms will compete to drive you to Glasgow.

(e)   The telecommunications industry. You may not need to travel at all, if the conference can be held via a video-conferencing system. BT and Mercury might compete to provide this service.

> ### KEY TERM
>
> **Competitive forces/five forces.** CIMA defines these as 'external influences upon the extent of actual and potential competition within any industry which in aggregate determine the ability of firms within that industry to earn a profit'. Porter argues that a firm must adopt a strategy that combats these forces better than its rivals' strategies if it is to enhance shareholder value.

1.2   In discussing competition Porter (*Competitive Strategy*) distinguishes between factors which characterise the nature of competition:

(a)   **In one industry compared with another** (eg in the chemicals industry compared with the clothing retail industry) and make one industry as a whole potentially more profitable than another (ie yielding a bigger return on investment).

(b)   **Within a particular industry.** These relate to the competitive strategies that individual firms might select.

1.3   Five **competitive forces** influence the state of competition in an industry, which collectively determine the profit (ie long-run return on capital) potential of the industry as a whole. **Learn them.**

- The threat of **new entrants** to the industry
- The threat of **substitute** products or services
- The bargaining power of **customers**
- The bargaining power of **suppliers**

110

- The **rivalry** amongst current competitors in the industry

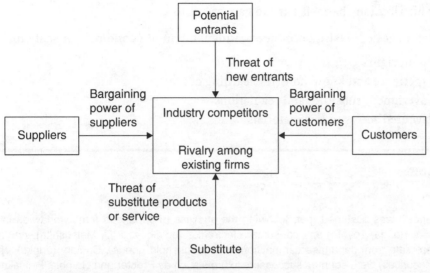

Source: adapted from Porter *(Competitive Strategy)*

Exam focus point

This model is fundamental to this subject. You must know it and be able to apply it to circumstances as set out in questions. The May 2002 paper contained an unusual question linking the five forces to performance indicators that could be used to judge their strength.

The threat of new entrants (and barriers to entry to keep them out)

1.4 A new entrant into an industry will bring extra capacity and more competition. The strength of this threat is likely to vary from industry to industry, depending on:

- The strength of the **barriers to entry**. Barriers to entry discourage new entrants.
- The likely **response of existing competitors** to the new entrant.

1.5 **Barriers to entry**

(a) **Scale economies.** High fixed costs often imply a high breakeven point, and a high breakeven point depends on a large volume of sales. If the market as a whole is not growing, the new entrant has to capture a large slice of the market from existing competitors

(b) **Product differentiation.** Existing firms in an industry may have built up a good brand image and strong customer loyalty over a long period of time. A few firms may promote a large number of brands to crowd out the competition.

(c) **Capital requirements.** When capital investment requirements are high, the barrier against new entrants will be strong, particularly when the investment would possibly be high-risk.

(d) **Switching costs.** Switching costs refer to the costs (time, money, convenience) that a customer would have to incur by switching from one supplier's products to another's. Although it might cost a **consumer** nothing to switch from one brand of frozen peas to another, the potential costs for the **retailer or distributor** might be high.

(e) **Access to distribution channels**. Distribution channels carry a manufacturer's products to the end-buyer. New distribution channels are difficult to establish, and existing distribution channels hard to gain access to.

(f) **Cost advantages of existing producers, independent of economies of scale** include:

- Patent rights
- Experience and know-how (the learning curve)
- Government subsidies and regulations
- Favoured access to raw materials

Case example

Japanese firms

A little while ago, it was assumed that, following the success of Japanese firms worldwide in motor vehicles (Nissan, Honda, Toyota) and consumer electronics (eg Sony, JVC, Matsushita), *no* Western companies were safe from Japanese competition. Kao (household goods), Suntory (drinks), Nomura (banking and securities) were seen as successors to firms such as Procter and Gamble, Heineken etc.

This has not happened: for example, Japanese pharmaceutical firms, such as Green Cross, have not achieved world domination. US and European firms are still dominant in this industry.

Perhaps cars and consumer electronics are the exception rather than the rule. The reason for this might be distribution. Normally, outsiders do not find it easy to break into established distribution patterns. However, distribution channels in cars and consumer electronics offered outsiders an easy way in.

(a) The car industry is vertically integrated, with a network of exclusive dealerships. Given time and money, the Japanese firms could simply build their own dealerships and run them as they liked, with the help of local partners. This barrier to entry was not inherently complex.

(b) *Consumer electronics*

 (i) In the early years, the consumer electronics market was driven by technology, so innovative firms such as Sony and Matsushita could overcome distribution weaknesses with innovative products, as they had plenty to invest. This lowered entry barriers.

 (ii) Falling prices changed the distribution of hifi goods from small specialist shops to large cut-price outlets, such as Comet. Newcomers to a market are the natural allies of such new outlets: existing suppliers prefer to shun 'discount' retailers to protect margins in their current distribution networks.

Japanese firms have *not* established dominant positions in:

(a) Healthcare, where national pharmaceuticals wholesalers are active as 'gatekeepers'
(b) Household products, where there are strong supermarket chains
(c) Cosmetics, where department stores and specialist shops offer a wide choice.

1.6 Entry barriers might be **lowered** by:

- Changes in the environment
- Technological changes
- Novel distribution channels for products or services

The threat from substitute products

1.7 A **substitute product** is a good/service produced by **another industry** which satisfies the same customer needs.

Case example

The Channel Tunnel

Passengers have several ways of getting from London to Paris, and the pricing policies of the various industries transporting them there reflects this.

(a) 'Le Shuttle' carries cars in the Channel Tunnel. Its main competitors come from the *ferry* companies, offering a substitute service. Therefore, you will find that Le Shuttle sets its prices with reference to ferry company prices, and vice versa.

(b) Eurostar is the rail service from London to Paris/Brussels. Its main competitors are not the ferry companies but the airlines. Prices on the London-Paris air routes fell with the commencement of Eurostar services, and some airlines have curtailed the number of flights they offer.

The bargaining power of customers

1.8 Customers want better quality products and services at a lower price. Satisfying this want might force down the profitability of suppliers in the industry. Just how strong the position of customers is dependent on several factors.

- How much the **customer buys**
- How **critical** the product is to the customer's own business
- **Switching costs (ie the cost of switching supplier)**
- Whether the products are **standard items** (hence easily copied) or specialised
- The **customer's own profitability**
- Customer's **ability to bypass** the supplier or might take over the supplier
- The **skills** of the customer **purchasing staff,** or the price-awareness of consumers
- The importance of **product quality** to the customer

Case example

Although the Ministry of Defence may wish to keep control over defence spending, it is likely as a customer to be more concerned that the products it purchases perform satisfactorily than with getting the lowest price possible for everything it buys.

The bargaining power of suppliers

1.9 Suppliers can exert pressure for higher prices but this is dependent on several factors.

(a) Whether there are just **one or two dominant suppliers** to the industry, able to charge monopoly or oligopoly prices

(b) The threat of **new entrants** or substitute products to the **supplier's industry**

(c) Whether the suppliers have **other customers** outside the industry, and do not rely on the industry for the majority of their sales

(d) The **importance of the supplier's product** to the customer's business

(e) Whether the supplier has a **differentiated product** which buyers need to obtain

(f) Whether **switching costs** for customers would be high

 BPP PUBLISHING

The rivalry amongst current competitors in the industry

1.10 The **intensity of competitive rivalry** within an industry will affect the profitability of the industry as a whole. Competitive actions might take the form of price competition, advertising battles, sales promotion campaigns, introducing new products for the market, improving after sales service or providing guarantees or warranties.

Case study link

A five forces analysis for Global Inc in the May 2002 case study would have shown that the major force affecting industry profitability was the level of competitive rivalry. The company was under extreme pressure from fast-growing competitors.

1.11 The intensity of competition will depend on the following factors.

(a) **Market growth.** Rivalry is intensified when firms are competing for a greater market share in a total market where growth is slow or stagnant.

(b) **Cost structure.** High fixed costs are a tempt for to compete on price, as in the short run any contribution from sales is better than none at all.

(c) **Switching.** Suppliers will compete if buyers switch easily (eg Coke vs Pepsi).

(d) **Capacity.** A supplier might need to achieve a substantial increase in output *capacity*, in order to obtain reductions in unit costs.

(e) **Uncertainty.** When one firm is not sure what another is up to, there is a tendency to respond to the uncertainty by formulating a more competitive strategy.

(f) **Strategic importance.** If success is a prime strategic objective, firms will be likely to act very competitively to meet their targets.

(g) **Exit barriers** make it difficult for an existing supplier to leave the industry.

   (i) Fixed assets with a low **break-up value** (eg there may be no other use for them, or they may be old).

   (ii) The cost of **redundancy payments** to employees.

   (iii) If the firm is a division or subsidiary of a larger enterprise, the **effect of withdrawal on the other operations** within the group.

Case example

EasyJet's merger with Go in the budget airline sector has led to concerns that fares will now rise. According to its rival Ryanair: '... the new combine will offer significantly higher fares and will have a significantly higher cost structure.'

A brief analysis of the competitive forces at work could indicate that a price rise is likely to capitalise on high potential profitability:

(i) *Bargaining power of customers* – not high. They are fragmented.

(ii) *Bargaining power of suppliers* – again, not likely to be high against a large airline.

(iii) *Threat of new entrants* – always a possibility, but the set-up costs involved make this unlikely in the short term.

(iv) *Availability of substitutes* – other forms of transport are available, but without the speed, frequency or choice of destination.

(v) *Rivalry amongst competition* – this is keen in the airline sector, but more especially against the national carriers, and is probably the factor that mitigates most against short-term fare increases.

According to an article in *The Observer* (May 2002), there is still everything to play for in Europe for the low-cost airlines. The sector is still embryonic there, accounting for just 5% of the market. That figure is expected to move up to 30%.

Another factor mitigating against a price war is that the 'no-frills' operators tend to fly different routes. Direct confrontation between them is rare. However, the EasyJet/Go merger has removed one potential for confrontation, and analysts believe that prices will be hiked on the seven routes where it is now the only operator.

The impact of information technology on the competitive forces

Case example

The Internet has had a variety of impacts.

The Financial Times reported that German companies were losing lucrative niche markets because the Internet made it easier for customers to compare prices from other suppliers by obtaining other information over the Internet. High prices made German retailers vulnerable in an age when 'a shopper with a credit card and computer could sit at home and could order from around the world'.

The Internet has increased competition. The Internet is a competitive weapon. Supermarket home shopping service are supported by Internet technology.

1.12 **Barriers to entry and IT**

(a) **IT can raise entry barriers** by increasing economies of scale, raising the capital cost of entry or effectively colonising distribution channels by tying customers and suppliers into the supply chain or distribution chain.

(b) **IT can surmount entry barriers.** An example is the use of telephone banking.

1.13 **Bargaining power of suppliers and IT**

(a) **Increasing the number of** accessible **suppliers.** IT enhances supplier information available to customers.

(b) **Closer supplier relationships.** Suppliers' power can be shared. CAD can be used to design components in tandem with suppliers. Such relationships might be developed with a few key suppliers.

(c) **Switching costs.** Suppliers can be integrated with the firm's administrative operations, by a system of electronic data interchange.

1.14 **Bargaining power of customers.** IT can 'lock customers in'.

(a) **IT can raise switching costs**

(b) **Customer information systems** can enable a thorough analysis of marketing information so that products and services can be tailored to the needs of certain segments.

1.15 **Substitutes.** In many respects, **IT itself is 'the substitute product'.** Here are some examples.

(a) Video-conferencing systems might substitute for air transport in providing a means by which managers from all over the world can get together in a meeting.

(b) IT is the basis for new leisure activities (eg computer games) which substitute for TV or other pursuits.

(c) E-mail might substitute for some postal deliveries.

1.16 **IT and the state of competitive rivalry**

(a) IT can be used in support of a firm's **competitive** strategy of cost leadership, differentiation or focus. These are discussed later in this text.

(b) IT can be used in a **collaborative** venture, perhaps to set up new communications networks. Some competitors in the financial services industry share the same ATM network.

Criticism of the five forces model

1.17 Porter's five forces model has come in for criticism. Writing in *Management Accounting* (January 1998) Alan Marsden notes the following.

(a) The model relies on a **static picture of the competition** and therefore plays down the role of innovation.

Case example

Innovation can revolutionise industry structure. The computer industry is one of the more dramatic recent examples. Fifteen years ago the industry was dominated by IBM, but the PC revolution started by Apple has transformed the structure of the industry.

As a result, a five forces analysis conducted in 1980 would look completely different from one done today.

(b) It overemphasises the importance of the **wider environment** and therefore ignores the significance of possible individual company advantages with regard to resources, capabilities and competence.

Exam focus point

It is still important to learn Porter's five forces; the examiner has sometimes expressed surprise at candidates' lack of familiarity with them.

2 THE IMPACT OF GLOBALISATION ON COMPETITION

2.1 Harvard Business School professor Ted Levitt predicted the development of a 'global village' in which consumers around the world would have the same needs and attitudes and use the same products.

KEY TERM

'**Globalisation** of markets' (Levitt 1983) is an expression which relates first to demand: tastes, preferences and price-mindedness are becoming increasingly universal.

Second, it relates to the supply side: profits and services tend to become more standardised and competition within industries reaches a world-wide scale.

Third, it relates to the way firms, mainly multinational corporations (ie those with operations in more than one country), try to design their marketing policies and control systems appropriately so as to remain winners in the global competition of global products for global consumers.

2.2 Other writers have developed the globalisation debate and the factors defining **global competitiveness**. They include Michael Porter (see Section 3).

2.3 Some would say that **global organisations** are rare. Industry structures change, foreign markets are culturally diverse, and the transformations brought about by developments in information technology mean that the world market is in a state of **turbulence**.

2.4 Here are some of the changes that have happened in the world market place.

- **Globalisation of business** - increased competition and global customers

- **Science and technology** developments

- Mergers, acquisitions and **strategic alliances**

- Changing **customer values** and behaviour

- Increased **scrutiny** of business decisions by government and the public

- Increased **deregulation** and co-operation between business and government

- Changes in **business practices** - downsizing, outsourcing and re-engineering

- Changes in the **social and business** relationships between companies and their employees, customers and other stakeholders

2.5 While more and more companies are competing in the world market place, most of them tend to focus on the developed markets of North America, Europe and Japan. A vast majority of the world's population resides in countries where GDP is less than $10,000 per head. Such countries offer tremendous marketing opportunities.

2.6 This leads on to the question of **market convergence** - how likely is it that consumers' tastes and preferences may converge? On the face of it, there is no reason why they should not, and **convergence theories** do have strong anecdotal support. The average French high school student appears very similar to American students of the same age (clothing, eating and entertainment preferences). Take a student from Nigeria and compare him to one from Finland, however, and the story is likely to be different.

2.7 **Global drivers** (factors encouraging the globalisation of world trade) include the following.

(a) **Financial factors** eg Third world debt. Often the lenders require the initiation of economic reforms as a condition of the loan.

(b) **Country/continent** alliances, such as that between the UK and USA, which fosters trade and tourism.

(c) **Legal factors** such as patents and trade marks, which encourage the development of technology and design.

(d) **Stock markets** trading in international commodities.

(e) The level of **protectionist** measures.

2.8 Despite the real gains in liberalisation 'globalisation' in its full-blooded form is **not an accurate description** of the reality facing most businesses.

BPP PUBLISHING

(a) **Depends on the industry.** Some services are still subject to **managed trade** (eg some countries prohibit firms from other countries from selling insurance) and there are some services which by their very nature can never be exported (eg haircuts are resolutely 'local').

(b) There is **unlikely ever to be a global market for labour,** given the disparity in skills between different countries, and restrictions on immigration.

(c) **Depends on the market**

    (i) **Upmarket luxury goods** may not be required or afforded by people in developing nations: whilst there is competition, it is limited to certain locations.

    (ii) Some goods can be sold almost anywhere, but to limited degrees. Television sets are consumer durables in some countries, but still luxury or relatively expensive items in other ones. Goods, such as oil, are needed almost everywhere: arguably, the oil industry is truly global.

2.9 **Effect of 'globalisation' on the firm**
- Opportunities to compete abroad via exports
- Opportunities to invest abroad
- Opportunities to raise finance from overseas sources of capital

Global or boundary-less corporations

2.10 Some argue there is an increasing number of 'stateless corporations', whose activities transcend national boundaries, and whose personnel come from any country.

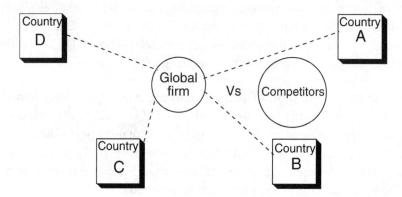

2.11 Many firms are setting up global alliances and firms such as BT see their ambitions as being worldwide.

2.12 **Do these stateless corporations really exist?** The following objections have been raised.

(a) **Workforce.** Most multinationals, other than those based in small nations, have less than half of their employees abroad.

(b) **Ownership and control of multinationals remain restricted.** Few so-called global companies are currently quoted on more than two stock markets, but more and more are seeking a listing in a number of financial markets.

(c) **Top management is rarely as multinational in composition** as the firm's activities. (A foreigner is rarely seen on the Tokyo-based board of a Japanese multinational.)

(d) National residence and status is important for **tax reasons.**

(e) **R&D.** The bulk of a typical multinational's research and development is generally done in the home country, where strategic decisions are made. But this is changing, especially as R & D is sometimes subcontracted.

(f) Where **capital is limited**, 'global' companies stick to the home market rather than developing overseas ones.

(g) Profits from a global company must be **remitted somewhere.**

2.13 International business conditions affect:

(a) The nature of the industry.

(b) The various positions of different countries, the size and wealth of their markets and the prosperity and efficiency of their productive bases.

(c) The management, by governments or international institutions, of the framework in which business is done.

2.14 Before getting carried away by notions that the world is splitting into trading blocks, remember that:

- There is increasingly free movement of capital

- Global trade is becoming liberalised

- Some of the world's markets offering the greatest potential for growth (eg India and China) are not part of a 'trading block'

- New technology, such as the Internet, makes it harder to police trade barriers in some areas

2.15 The theory of **comparative advantage** suggests that **free trade** is the best way to promote global economic growth and, by implication, domestic prosperity. In other words, people should be free to buy and sell goods and services anywhere in the world.

2.16 Many countries have limited or controlled their trading activities, with varying success. **Protectionist measures to restrict competition** from overseas include:

- **Quotas** on the number of items that can be imported (eg Japanese cars)
- **Import bans** (eg Brazil prohibited the import of cheap US-made computers)
- **Restrictions** on foreign ownership of certain industries (eg defence)
- **Tariffs**

2.17 Business people and politicians have had an ambivalent attitude in the past towards this issue. Free trade is favoured by importers or multinationals, but protectionism gives businesses the benefit of a cosy domestic market. Their inefficiencies are not penalised and customers pay higher prices.

POINT TO NOTE

Bear in mind that 'protectionist' measures are not the only barrier to entry. Differences in:

- Tax regimes   • Language and culture
- Wage levels   • Skills levels
- Infrastructure   • Prosperity

still exist.

Regional trading organisations

2.18 Countries in various regions have entered into closer economic arrangements such as NAFTA (USA, Canada, Mexico), the EU, Mercosur (Brazil, Argentina, Uruguay, Paraguay and now Chile). The **EU** is the world's largest single market, but is unusual in that it features a common political decision-making process (Council of Ministers, Commission, Parliament) and a single currency.

2.19 The EU single market programme has involved areas as diverse as harmonising technical standards, opening up areas such as telecommunications to competition, consumer protection, mutual recognition of professional qualifications and so on. Much work remains to be done.

Case example

Aviation in the EU

On April 2 1997, the European Union completed the liberalisation of its aviation market. From that day, European airlines saw the removal of the last restrictions on their operations, leaving them free to operate domestic services in countries other than their own. In the past, air transport (including level of fares and services) had been heavily regulated, as many governments chose to support the 'national' airline. The UK was one of the first to privatise air transport. The final stage allows airlines to set their own fares or services within the EU, subject to predatory pricing restrictions.

Small airlines such as Ryanair and EasyJet have proliferated, and have introduced low cost flights between a range of EU countries. However, fares for many European routes are still higher than the equivalent distances in the US. In part this is because airports are still publicly owned, in the main, and landing 'slots' (periods of time available for take off and landing) are hard to come by.

International trade liberalisation: the World Trade Organisation (WTO)

2.20 Since 1945, the major industrial, and now the developing, countries have sought to increase trade. Efforts to liberalise trade culminated in the founding of the WTO in 1995 as successor to the former General Agreement on Tariffs and Trade (GATT).

2.21 Most countries in the developed world are signatories and the WTO is an important influence over the trading environment, although it also attracts a lot of criticism from activists and commentators who claim that it can have too much power (and too little accountability) over the lives of people in economically disadvantaged countries. Important facts to keep in mind about the WTO are these.

(a) **The WTO has dispute resolution powers**. Aggrieved countries can take matters up with the WTO if they cannot be resolved bilaterally.

(b) **Membership** of the WTO requires **adherence to certain conditions** regarding competition in the home market etc. Consequently, certain countries such as China have yet to be admitted, despite intense political pressure.

(c) **Membership rules are slightly less onerous for 'developing countries'**, which can maintain some protectionist measures.

The single European market

2.22 Most of Britain's trade is within the European Union. Since 31 December 1992 there has been a single European market, allowing for the free movement of labour, goods and services, and free competition.

- **Physical barriers** (eg customs inspection) on goods and service have been removed for most products.

- **Technical standards** (eg for quality and safety) should be harmonised.

- Governments should not discriminate between EU companies in awarding public works contracts.

- Telecommunications should be subject to **greater competition**.

- It should be possible to provide **financial services** in any country.

- Measures are being taken to rationalise **transport services**.

- There should be **free movement of capital** within the community.

- **Professional qualifications** awarded in one member state should be recognised in the others.

- The EU is taking a co-ordinated stand on matters related to **consumer protection**.

2.23 There are many areas where harmonisation is some way from being achieved. Here are some examples.

(a) **Company taxation**. Tax rates, which can affect the viability of investment plans, vary from country to country within the EU.

(b) **Indirect taxation (VAT)**. Whilst there have been moves to harmonisation, there are still differences between rates imposed by member states.

(c) **Differences in prosperity**. There are considerable differences in prosperity between the wealthiest EU economy (Germany), and the poorest (eg Greece). The UK comes somewhere in the middle.

    (i) Grants are sometimes available to depressed regions, which might affect investment decisions

    (ii) Different marketing strategies are appropriate for different markets

(d) **Differences in workforce skills**. Again, this can have a significant effect on investment decisions. The workforce in Germany is perhaps the most highly trained, but also the most highly paid, and so might be suitable for products of a high added value.

(e) **Infrastructure**. Some countries are better provided with road and rail than others. Where accessibility to a market is an important issue, infrastructure can mean significant variations in distribution costs.

3 THE COMPETITIVE ADVANTAGE OF A NATION'S INDUSTRIES
5/01, 11/01

3.1 Michael Porter's *The Competitive Advantage s*, suggests that some nations' industries succeed more than others in terms of international competition. UK leadership in some industries (eg ship-building) has been overtaken (by Japan and Korea).

3.2 Porter does not believe that countries or nations as such are competitive, but he asks:

(a) 'Why does a **nation become the home base** for successful international competitors in an industry?'

(b) 'Why are firms based in a particular nation able to create and **sustain competitive advantage** against the world's best competitors in a particular field?'

(c) 'Why is **one nation** often the home for **so many of an industry's world leaders?**'

3.3   The original explanation for **national** success was the theory of **comparative advantage.** This held that relative **factor costs** in countries (eg the fact that some raw materials are cheaper in country A than in country B, but others are cheaper in B than A) determined the appropriateness of particular economic activities in relation to other countries. (In other words, countries should monopolise in what they are best at in relation to other countries.)

3.4   Porter argues that **industries which require high technology and highly skilled employees are less affected** than low technology industries by the relative costs of their inputs of raw materials and basic labour as determined by the national endowment of factors.

3.5   **Comparative advantage** is too **general a concept** to explain the success of **individual companies and industries.** If high technology and global markets allow firms to circumvent (or ignore) the constraints (or advantages) of their home country's endowment of raw materials, cheap labour, access to capital and so forth, how can they be successful internationally?

3.6   Porter identifies determinants of national competitive advantage which are outlined in the diagram below. Porter refers to this as the **diamond.**

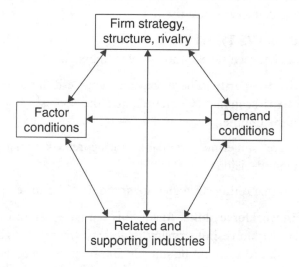

Analysing the 'diamond'

Exam focus point

The May 2001 paper contained a question asking how the diamond could be used by the subject company in deciding whether to market its products internationally. A similar slant was examined in November 2001 as part of the scenario question. The examiner has since noted that many candidates did not seem to know enough about the diamond.

Factor conditions

3.7   **Factor conditions** are a country's endowment of inputs to production.

- Human resources (skills, price, motivation, industrial relations)
- Physical resources (land, minerals, climate, location relative to other nations)
- Knowledge (scientific and technical know-how, educational institutions)
- Capital (ie amounts available for investment, how it is deployed)
- Infrastructure (transport, communications, housing)

3.8 Porter distinguishes between:

(a) **Basic factors:** natural resources, climate, semiskilled and unskilled labour. Basic factors are inherited, or at best their creation involves little investment.

(b) **Advanced factors** include modern digital communications, highly educated personnel research laboratories and so forth. They are necessary to achieve high order competitive advantages such as differentiated products and proprietary production technology.

POINT TO NOTE

An abundance of factors is not enough. It is the efficiency with which they are deployed that matters. The former USSR has an abundance of natural resources and a fairly well educated workforce, but was an economic catastrophe.

Demand conditions: the home market

3.9 The **home market determines how firms perceive, interpret and respond to buyer needs.** This information puts pressure on firms to innovate and provides a launch pad for global ambitions.

(a) There are **no 'cultural' impediments** to communication.

(b) The **segmentation** of the home market shapes a firm's priorities: companies will be successful globally in segments which are similar to the home market.

(c) **Sophisticated and demanding buyers** set standards. ('The British are known for gardening, and British firms are world class in garden tools'.)

(d) **Anticipatory buyer needs:** if consumer needs are expressed in the home market earlier than in the world market, the firm benefits from 'experience'.

(e) The **rate of growth**. Slow growing home markets do not encourage the adoption of 'state of the art' technology.

(f) **Early saturation** of the home market will encourage a firm to export.

Related and supporting industries

3.10 **Competitive success in one industry is linked to success in related industries.** Domestic suppliers are preferable to foreign suppliers, as 'proximity of managerial and technical personnel, along with cultural similarity, tends to facilitate free and open information flow' at an early stage.

Firm strategy, structure and rivalry

3.11 **Structure**. National cultural factors create certain tendencies to orientate business-people to certain industries. German firms, according to Porter, have a strong showing in 'industries with a high technical content.'

3.12 **Strategy.** Industries in different countries have different **time horizons,** funding needs and so forth.

(a) **National capital markets** set different goals for performance. In some countries, banks are the main source of capital, not equity shareholders.

(b) When an industry faces difficult times, it **can either innovate within the industry**, to sustain competitive position or **shift resources from one industry to another** (eg diversification).

3.13 Domestic rivalry is important because:

- With little domestic rivalry, firms are happy to rely on the home market
- Tough domestic rivals teach a firm about competitive success
- Each rival can try a different strategic approach

Influencing the 'diamond'

Interactions between the determinants

3.14 The factors in the 'diamond' are interrelated. Competitive advantage rarely rests on only one element of the diamond.

(a) **Related industries** affect **demand conditions** for an industry. An example from the context of international marketing is 'piggy-back' exporting in which an exporting company also exports some of the products of related industries.

(b) **Domestic rivalry** can encourage the **creation of more specialised supplier industries.**

3.15 Porter says that a nation's competitive industries are **clustered**. Porter believes clustering to be a key to national competitive advantage. A cluster is a linking of industries through relationships which are either vertical (buyer-supplier) or horizontal (common customers, technology, skills). For example, the UK financial services industry is clustered in London.

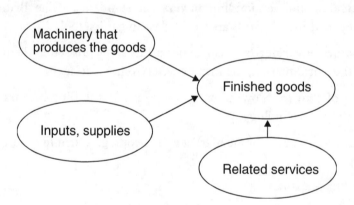

3.16 The **individual** firm will be more likely to succeed internationally if there is a **supporting cluster.**

3.17 However, if, say a UK firm wishes to compete in an industry in which there is no national competitive advantage, it can take a number of steps to succeed.

(a) **Compete in the most challenging market,** to emulate domestic rivalry and to obtain information.

(b) **Spread research and development** activities to countries where there is an established research base or industry cluster already.

(c) Be prepared to **invest heavily in innovation**.

(d) **Invest in human resources,** both in the firm and the industry as a whole.

(e) **Look out for new technologies** which will change the rules of the industry.

(f) **Collaborate with foreign companies.** American motor companies successfully learned 'Japanese' production techniques.

(g) **Supply overseas companies.** Japanese car plants in the UK have encouraged greater quality in UK components suppliers.

(h) **Source components from overseas.** In the UK crystal glass industry, many firms buy crystal glass from the Czech Republic, and do the cutting and design work themselves.

(i) **Exert pressure on politicians** and opinion formers to create better conditions for the 'diamond' to develop (eg in education).

Question 2

The Republic of Albion, an island in the North East Atlantic inhabited by about 40m people, has a climate which is plagued by fog, damp and rain. Life is a battle to keep dry. In this battle, the Republic has set up 20 research institutes into 'Water and Aridity Studies'. A variety of companies compete in devising new ways of keeping houses (and their owners!) dry, involving advanced technology. A recent innovation is the ionising umbrella, with an electric field that drives away water particles. The country imports most of its raw materials. The water problem is so bad that the country has a network of canals taking surplus water to the sea, through a network of hydroelectric turbines.

What do you think are the possible competitive advantages of the industries of the Republic of Albion?

Answer

The only basic factor endowment appears to be rain! Advanced factors include the research institutes. The country also has very sophisticated demand conditions for umbrellas and water-proof items. There seems to be domestic competition in the industry. In addition to umbrellas, you would expect related industries (such as high-technology waterproof raincoats) to appear. The country's firms could compete successfully in global markets for waterproof materials.

It is possible that the country's inhabitants would also have certain expertise in building technologies (eg damp proofing) which could be exported to the construction industry. Finally hydro-electric turbines *might* be a source of advantage: but the amount of water-for-energy is so plentiful that only the simplest technology need be used to harness it.

4 COMPETITOR ANALYSIS

Who are competitors?

> ### KEY TERM
>
> A firm must consider its **competitive position** which is defined in CIMA's Official Terminology as 'the market share, costs, prices, quality and accumulated experience of an entity or a product relative to competition.'

4.1 In any market where there is one or more significant competitors, the strategic decisions and marketing decisions by a firm will often be partly a response to what a competitor has done .

4.2 Firms must also be on the lookout for **potential competitors**.

Case examples

(a) Ward quotes the example of the UK financial services sector. The 'big four' clearing banks regarded each other as 'the competition', not the building societies. However, the building societies, having invested heavily in automation, now rival the banks and have forced the banks to offer service improvements,

(b) In the UK, petrol companies have been wrong-footed by supermarkets, who now sell petrol.

4.3 Finally a firm can **define who its competitors actually are**. Coca-Cola, for example, competes against the following.

- Pepsi in the Cola market
- All other soft drinks
- Tea and coffee
- Coca-Cola's chief executive has declared that 'the main competitor is tap water: any other definition is too narrow'.

Analysing competitors: main issues

KEY TERM

The CIMA defines **competitor analysis** as 'the systematic review of all available information (marketing, production, financial etc) on the activities of competitors in order to gain a competitive advantage'.

Future goals

4.4 An analysis of competitors' goals should include the firm as a whole and the business unit.

(a) What are the business's **stated financial goals**? What trade-offs are made between long-term and short-term objectives?

(b) What is the competitor's attitude to **risk**?

(c) Do **managerial beliefs** (eg that the firm should be a market leader) affect its goals?

(d) **Organisation structure**: what is the relative status of functional areas?

(e) What **incentive systems** are in place?

(f) What are the **managers** like? Do they favour one particular type of strategy?

(g) To what extent does the business **cross-subsidise** others in the group if the business is part of a group? What is the purpose of the business: to raise money for the group?

Competitor assumptions

4.5 Competitor assumptions may not be accurate but they do indicate the way in which the competitor might react.

(a) What does a competitor believe to be its **relative position** in the industry (in terms of cost, product quality etc)?

(b) Are there any **cultural or regional differences** that indicate the way managers are likely to respond?

(c) What does the competitor believe about the future for the industry?

(d) Does the competitor accept the industry's '**conventional wisdom**'?

Competitor's current situation and strategy

4.6 The competitor's current situation and strategy can be analysed in the following areas.

- Distribution
- Operations
- Overall costs
- Marketing and selling
- Financial strengths

- Organisation
- Research and engineering
- Managerial ability
- Products

Competitor's capability

4.7 This analysis should also identify two issues.

(a) The **competitor's core competences**. In other words, what does the competitor do distinctively well?

(b) Does the competitor have the **ability to expand** in a particular market?

Competitor response profiles

4.8 All these are combined in a **competitor response profile**. This indicates the competitor's vulnerability and the right 'battleground' on which to fight.

4.9 The **strategic intelligence system** can collect information from the following sources.

- Financial statements
- Information from common customers and suppliers
- Inspection of a competitor's products
- Information from former employees
- Job advertisements

Question 3

Jot down a list of items of information that might be obtained from an environmental analysis of competitors. The list can be a long one!

Answer

(a) Who are the existing competitors? How much of the market do they hold in each segment of the markets (eg in each particular region or country?)

(b) Who are potential competitors? How soon might they enter the market?

(c) How profitable are existing competitors? What is their EPS, dividend yield, ROCE etc?

(d) What do the goals of each competitor appear to be, and what strategies have they adopted so far?

(e) What products/services do they sell? How do they compare with the organisation's own products or services?

(f) How broad is their product line? (eg Are they 'up-market high quality, or down-market low quality, low price and high volume producers?)

(g) What is their distribution network?

(h) What are their skills and weakness in direct selling, advertising, sales promotions, product design etc.

(i) What are their design skills or R & D skills? do they innovate or follow the market leader with new product ideas?

(j) What are their costs of sale and operational capabilities? With respect to equipment, technology, intellectual property etc?

(k) What are their general managerial capabilities? How do these compare with those of the organisation?

(l) Financial strengths and weaknesses. What is the debt position and financial gearing of each competitor? Do they have easy access to sources of new finance? What proportion of profits do they return in the business in order to finance growth?

(m) How is each competitor organised? How much decentralisation of authority do they allow to operating divisions, and so how flexible or independent can each of the operating divisions be?

(n) Does the competitor have a good spread or portfolio of activities? What is the risk profile of each competitor?

(o) Does any competitor have a special competitive advantage - eg a unique government contract or special access to government authorities?

(p) Does any competitor show signs of changing strategy to increase competition to the market?

Competitor response

4.10 In practice, anticipated **competitor actions** are dealt with indirectly in the planning process. The management accounting system may not be able to identify those deficiencies in performance arising from competitors' activities **after** the plan has been implemented.

Opportunity costs: market share and deterrence

4.11 A few detergent companies own many of the brands offered to the market. This deters competitors. How do you evaluate, financially, a strategy such as this?

(a) The expenditure to **maintain market share** and sustain brands is a known cost. However the benefit is not known exactly.

(b) There might be a variety of assumptions about market size, market shares and the profit assumptions of a number of the scenarios identified.

(c) There are problems with forecasting the future cash flows of market share estimates.

4.12 A useful approach to take is to analyse the anticipated loss caused by not undertaking a particular course of action: the present value of this loss becomes, effectively, the maximum size of the investment. For example, A Ltd is worried that a competitor will shift the market dynamics from I to II.

	Market state	
	I	*II*
A Ltd's market share	20%	15%
Present value of future cash flows	£1m	£800,000

(a) There is a present value loss of £200,000. If a marketing manager suggested that an expenditure of £100,000 would see off the competitor, this would be worth doing.

(b) There is still the problem of estimating the difference between market states I and II: after all the marketing campaign might deter other competitors, too, or create an increase in demand. It is also impossible to be certain that the competitor will in fact be deterred by an advertising campaign.

Exit

4.13 **Exit barriers** are those which prevent a firm from leaving an industry, or increase the cost of so doing. Cost-related exit barriers include the following.

(a) **Vertically integrated companies** producing products for many markets. Exiting one market would not significantly alter its cost structure.

(b) **Common administrative costs** might be shared over a number of different businesses. This might result in a high overhead charge, but whilst the apportionment might turn one of the businesses into a loss, closing the business down might save little of the overhead expenditure.

Competitor modelling

4.14 Data sources include published accounts, suppliers, shared customers, the competitor's marketing strategy, public communications and history.

4.15 A great deal can be gleaned from using one's own company as a model, and adjusting it for significant differences in competitors' businesses. For example, a firm might make some sub-components in-house, whereas a competitor might buy them on the open market.

4.16 Important differences between firms include the following.

- Absolute cost levels
- The proportion of fixed to variable costs
- The strategic impact of outsourcing decisions on competitive flexibility
- The sales price in relation to costs
- Not all businesses require the same rate of return

Example

4.17 A simple numerical example will demonstrate the relationship between cost structure and competitive strategy. No new management accounting techniques are required - just the adaptation of simple DCF/NPV analysis to a competitive situation.

The situation in 2002

4.18 **Orange plc** is a conglomerate listed on the Stock Exchange. It has developed a new product idea. The new product idea requires investment in new capacity (100,000 units pa) of £1m in 2002 and £200,000 of maintenance expenditure in 2007. If Orange does not maintain the equipment in 2007 it will no longer be functioning at the end of 2009. The capacity of 100,000 units pa is where profit can be maximised, setting demand at 100,000 units pa and a selling price of £9.50 per unit. The new product involves no technological breakthrough. The investment in new capacity will take place at Orange's existing sites. The plant will be fully depreciated after 8 years. The firm has a cost of capital of 15%.

		£	Units	£ pa
Sales price		9.50	100,000	950,000
Variable costs		4.75		475,000
Contribution		4.75		475,000
Fixed costs	assuming 100,000	.75		75,000
Depreciation	pa capacity	1.25		125,000
Profit		2.75		275,000

Net annual cash inflows are £400,000 (ie £475,000 less £75,000) other than investment and maintenance.

4.19 We can convert this into discounted cash flows.

		£	Discount factor at 15%	£
Initial investment	Year 0 (2002)	1,000,000	1	(1,000,000)
Extra investment to upgrade equipment	Year 5 (2007)	200,000	0.497	(99,400)
Net annual cash flows	Years 1 - 8 (2003-10)	400,000	4.487	1,794,800
Net present value				695,400

But note the key assumption. Capacity in the industry is fixed at 100,000 units pa. This effectively underpins the selling price at £9.50.

4.20 **Apple Ltd** decides to enter the market. Apple Ltd sources the products overseas where variable costs are higher but fixed costs are lower. It only invests £400,000 in 2006. Apple Ltd's investors are a private firm, more concerned with building market share than maximising returns in the short term. They use a discount rate of only 8%.

4.21 Apple Ltd has capacity of 50,000 units pa. Apple's and Orange's directors know that reducing prices to £8 per unit will mean that 150,000 units will be sold in the market: 100,000 by Orange and 50,000 by Apple.

	£	Units	£
Sales revenue	8.00	50,000	400,000
Variable costs	5.00		250,000
Contribution	3.00		150,000
Fixed costs			25,000
Depreciation			70,000
Profit			£55,000

For Apple, the discount rate is 8%.

	Discount factor at 8%	£
Year 0 for Apple (2006)	1	400,000
£125,000 (£55,000 + £70,000) for 5 years (2007-2011)	3.993	499,125
Positive NPV at 8%		£99,125

4.22 Orange's directors may be confused - after all, their discount rate is 15%. Applying Orange's discount rate to Apple's cash flow would reveal £400,000 − (125,000 × 3.352) a positive NPV of only £19,000. This is why it is crucial to understand competitors' assumptions.

What should Orange do?

4.23 Orange Ltd's directors have a higher cost of capital. However in Year 5 (2007), in their original calculation they have to make a cash investment of £200,000 to keep going to the end of 2010 - otherwise they will have to shut down at the end of year 2009. Should they go ahead with the new investment? In 2007, the consequence of Apple's new capacity has meant that prices will fall.

	£	Units	£pa
Sales revenue	8.00	100,000	800,000
Variable costs (except depreciation)	4.75		475,000
			325,000
Fixed costs			75,000
Net annual cash flows			250,000

4.24

	Discount factor at 15%	£
Cash investment 2007 (Year 0)	1	200,000
Cash flows (£250,000) × 2007 to 2010 (4 years)	2.855	713,750
Positive NPV		513,750

The alternative however is simple.

Cash investment in 2007	NIL
Cash flows £250,000 × 2007-09 (3 years @ 15%) 2.283	570,750

In 2007, the decision would be to abandon the upgrade and pull out of the market, even though this would leave Apple the prospect of significantly increasing prices.

Summary

4.25 Apple's entry to the market had the effect of changing Orange's strategy: Orange has forgone the chance of carrying on to the end of Year 8 and is sacrificing one year's sales.

If Orange had predicted Apple would compete, would this have altered its original investment decision?

4.26 Going back to 2002

		£
Initial investment 2002		1,000,000
Sales revenue 2003-06	400,000 @ 15% × 2.855	1,142,000
2007-09	250,000 @ 15% (4.160 – 2.855)	326,250
Positive NPV		468,250

Yes, the firm would still have gone ahead with the project, but only for seven years.

	£
NPV in initial estimate, assuming no competition	695,400
NPV assuming Apple entered market	468,250
Cash flows 'lost' as a result of competitor action	227,150

In the above example, we have used a number of viewpoints.

(a) Orange's outlook in 2002, when it didn't know about Apple.

(b) Apple's own projections - and lower cost of capital.

(c) Orange's perspective at the beginning of 2007, when it knew it had to make a choice.

(d) Orange's 2002 perspective if it had been able to forecast that Apple would enter the market, increase capacity and drive down selling prices.

4.27 Item (d) above is interesting. Orange **could** have predicted the fall in NPV of £227,150 because of competitor action. This suggests the following.

(a) Orange should have expected other competitors to be interested in a market if Orange made a success of it. This is the heart of the product life cycle model.

Case example

Dyson revolutionised the design of vacuum cleaners - other manufacturers have followed suit. Dyson has now turned its attention to washing machines.

(b) Apple had **different objectives** - a lower return was required. Why?

    (i)   A **different perception of risk**? Apple's risk/return profile might have been different from Orange's and investors might have had different expectations. Moreover, Orange took the original risk of launching the product and building a market for it - Orange had some early mover advantages, but these were not overwhelming.

   (ii)   **Different objectives and perceptions.** Apple was a private company whose shareholders are less demanding, for whatever reason. Orange should not assume that Apple has the same objectives as itself. Orange's directors might have **wrongly assumed** that Apple had the same cost of capital as Orange - this is why they were surprised that Apple would go ahead with an NPV of only £19,000. Apple's perceptions were quite different.

(c)   Orange could have protected its market by building **barriers to entry** or engaging in **competitor deterrence**, costing up to £227,150 in 2002 prices.

Examples

- Heavy advertising on branding - Apple would have to follow suit.

- Exclusive distribution arrangements.

- Invest in extra capacity early on, so that the market is less attractive to Apple. Orange could have increased its **own** capacity to 150,000.

(d)   Orange could have sold capacity to Apple, thereby making exit in 2009 even more palatable. Apple would use a different discount rate and so might find the investment more attractive.

4.28   This example has been deliberately simplified, and you can probably think of many other factors we have left out.

(a)   Ever more competitors will enter the market, further driving down prices.

(b)   Lowering the selling price by £1.50 increased demand by 50,000 units. This has two implications.

   (i)   A firm with better economies of scale might produce in bulk to sell cheaply.

   (ii)   New technology can massively alter the cost profiles and a new competitor may change the cost profile of the business completely.

(c)   Taxation and inflation implications have been ignored.

(d)   Most firms do **not** enter a market for only eight years. Product-markets have a different life to plant and investment decisions - the eight and five year time horizons are relevant to **equipment purchases**, but not to markets. **Consequently,** there will be a series of decisions to upgrade equipment and improve production processes.

(e)   **Learning curve effects** have been ignored.

Unity Bicycles plc

(1)   Briefly assess the competitive forces in UB's environment.

(2)   To what extent do you think there is global competition in UB's industry?

(3)   Do you think Porter's theory of the competitive advantages of nations is relevant to UB?

(4)   How do you think UB is placed in regard to its various competitors?

Chapter roundup

- The **competitive environment** (according to Porter) consists of **five forces**: the threat of new entrants, the threat of substitute products, the bargaining power of customers, the bargaining power of suppliers and the competitive rivalry within the industry.

- Although international trade is nothing new, some thinkers argue that advances in transportation and communications mean that the market for goods and services is necessarily '**global**'. Certainly, there is a movement towards free trade.

- The global market, in some industries, means that firms face more competition but there are greater opportunities also.

- A variety of factors support **competitive success** in a particular industry. These can be related to national origin to the extent that a firm's success is determined by factor conditions, demand conditions, related and supporting industries, and firm strategy, structure and rivalry.

- A key to success in an industry is by adopting strategies superior to or different from competitors. **Analysing competitors** is an important task of strategic management.

- Competitor analysis involves analysing competitors' goals, assumptions about the industry and their position in it, their current strategies and likely response.

- The management accountant's **analytical techniques** are useful in this context. Analysis of a competitor's cost structures indicates the choices available to it and perhaps its likely response; it is possible to use your own firm as a model and adjust accordingly.

Quick quiz

1 Distinguish the 'market' and the 'industry'

2 **Fill in the blanks** in the statement below, using the words in the box.

(1) .... competitive (2) .... influence the state of (3) .... in an (4) .... , which collectively determine the (5) .... of the industry as a whole:

- the threat of (6) .... to the industry
- the threat of (7) ....
- the (8) .... power of (9) ....
- the bargaining power of (10) ....
- the (11) .... amongst current (12) ....

industry	five	profit	new entrants
competition	bargaining	forces	competitors
substitutes	rivalry	customers	suppliers

3 Define a 'switching cost'.

4 List three factors encouraging the globalisation of world trade

   ....

   ....

   ....

5 The theory of .... suggests that .... is the best way to promote global economic growth and domestic prosperity.

6   Fill in the diagram of Porter's diamond

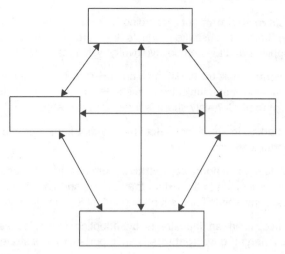

7   Define 'competitive position'

8   What would you find in a competitor response profile?

9   How can IT raise entry barriers?

10   Protectionist measures include:

Q ....

I ....

R ....

T ....

6

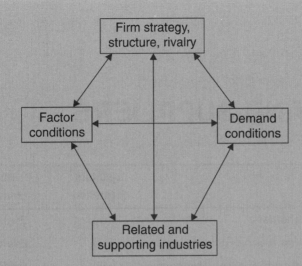

7   This is defined by CIMA as 'the market share, costs, prices, quality and accumulated experience of an entity or a product relative to competition'.

8   An analysis of competitors' goals, assumptions, current situation, strategy and capabilities. This indicates the competitors' vulnerability and the right battleground on which to fight

9   IT can raise entry barriers by increasing economies of scale, raising the capital cost of entry (by requiring a similar investment in IT) or effectively colonising distribution channels by tying customers and suppliers into the supply chain or distribution chain.

10   Quotas
      Import bans
      Restrictions on foreign ownership
      Tariffs

Unity Bicycles plc review

Question 1. The threat of *new* entrants might be more apparent than real. The industry is complex, and UB has invested heavily in distribution. UB is dealing with the threat by licensing. Substitute products include motorscooters or any other means of personal transport - but a car or even a motor bike is a lot more expensive than a bike. Suppliers and customer bargaining power are low. These factors make the industry very attractive which is why competition is intense.

Question 2. Global competition appears to exist, and UB is one of the major global competitors.

Question 3. Bikes are not hi-tech products, although UB might use sophisticated machines to make them and, at the specialist end, some bikes require the use of expensive metals. However, the need for *advanced factors* is sufficient to give UB an advantage and something to sell to the Chinese. The UK is not uniquely well or ill suited to cycling, but cycling enthusiasts and the sponsorship arrangement with the Cyclists Tourist Clubs gives it some information about customer demands.

UB has less knowledge about how bikes are used for commuting in India and China and what potential customers require. The fact that there exists no cluster of bike-makers in the UK is insignificant. There is enough competition in Europe.

Question 4. We are given little information about competitors. In Europe, they are owned by other firms and perhaps not of key importance for their holding companies. However, the Chinese firms are low-cost competitors, held at bay by anti-dumping duties: a ferocious onslaught might be expected. UB recognises the need to analyse competitors' costs.

Now try the question below from the Exam Question Bank

Question to try	Level	Marks	Time
4	Exam	25	45 mins

BPP PUBLISHING

Chapter 6

CUSTOMERS AND SUPPLIERS

Topic list	Syllabus reference	Ability required
1　The strategic value of stakeholders	(ii)	Evaluation
2　Marketing: products, customers and segmentation	(ii)	Evaluation
3　Marketing: the marketing mix, life cycle and brands	(ii)	Evaluation
4　Reviewing the customer portfolio	(ii)	Analysis/Evaluation
5　Relationship marketing: customer care and customer loyalty	(ii)	Evaluation
6　Distribution channels and the supply chain	(ii)	Evaluation

Introduction

In order to fulfil the company's mission and maximise long-term owner value, management activities will be influenced to a greater or lesser extent by **customers** and **suppliers**, some of the key **stakeholders** in the organisation.

Customer's demands will dictate decisions for investment in new products, development of existing ones and setting-up of new outlets. They will also affect the standards adopted for quality control, and the extent to which they can be enticed away by competitors' products will affect the planned advertising spend.

Suppliers' and distributors' demands will affect the timing and amount of production.

In this chapter we have included an overview of some key **marketing** issues. Detailed knowledge of marketing concepts and techniques is not required by the *Business Strategy* syllabus, but it is worth presenting some background to the syllabus material.

Learning outcomes covered in this chapter

- **Analyse** and **evaluate** the organisation's customer portfolio

- **Evaluate** relationships with customers and suppliers and recommend appropriate changes or improvements

Syllabus content covered in this chapter

- The customer portfolio: customer analysis and behaviour, including the marketing audit and customer profitability analysis as well as customer retention and loyalty. The concept of relationship marketing

- The importance of relationships with customers and suppliers, adversarial relationships or partnerships in the supply chain

- The implications of the above for the Chartered Management Accountant and the management accounting information system

1 THE STRATEGIC VALUE OF STAKEHOLDERS

1.1 The firm can make strategic gains from managing stakeholder relationships. This was highlighted by a recent report by the Royal Society of Arts on *Tomorrow's Company*. Studies have revealed the following correlations.

(a) A correlation between **employee** and **customer loyalty** (eg reduced staff turnover in service firms generally results in more repeat business).

(b) **Continuity** and **stability** in relationships with employees, customers and suppliers is important in enabling organisations to respond to certain types of change, necessary for business as a sustained activity.

1.2 **Responsibilities towards customers** are mainly those of providing a product or service of a quality that customers expect, and of dealing honestly and fairly with customers.

1.3 **Responsibilities towards suppliers** are expressed mainly in terms of trading relationships.

(a) The organisation's size could give it considerable power as a buyer. One ethical guideline might be that the organisation should not use its power unscrupulously.

(b) Suppliers might rely on getting prompt payment in accordance with the terms of trade negotiated with its customers.

(c) All information obtained from suppliers and potential suppliers should be kept confidential.

2 MARKETING: PRODUCTS, CUSTOMERS AND SEGMENTATION

2.1 **What is marketing?**

> **KEY TERM**
>
> 'Marketing is the management process which identifies, anticipates and supplies customer requirements efficiently and profitably.' (The *Chartered Institute of Marketing*)
>
> 'Marketing is concerned with meeting organisation objectives by providing customer satisfactions'. When people buy products or services they do not simply want the products, they also want the benefits from using the products or services. Products and services help to solve a customer's problems. It is the solution to these problems that customers are buying.

2.2 The marketing task is as follows.

- Identify who the **customers** are, or will be in future
- Identify what their **needs and wants** are or will be in future
- Anticipate any **changes** in their needs and wants
- Make products/services which **satisfy** their needs
- Ensure customers **know** about the **products** (eg advertising)
- Ensure customers are able to **get hold** of the product
- Ensure the firm makes a **profit** when charging a price that customers are able to pay

2.3 The **marketing concept** is an outlook that accepts that the key task of the organisation is to determine the needs, wants and values of a target market and to adapt the organisation to delivering the desired satisfaction more effectively and efficiently than its competitors.

Since technology, markets, the economy, social attitudes, fashions, the law etc are all constantly changing, customer needs are likely to change too.

> ### KEY TERM
>
> A **product** (goods or services) is anything that satisfies a need or want. It is not a 'thing' with 'features' but a package of benefits. For example a CD and hifi system provide recorded music, and other benefits. From most customers' point of view, the electronics inside are not important as long as they are reliable and deliver a certain quality of sound.

2.4 The immediate task of a marketing manager with respect to the **products** of the organisation may be any of the following.

- To create demand (where none exists)
- To develop a latent demand
- To revitalise a sagging demand
- To attempt to smooth out (synchronise) uneven demand
- To sustain a buoyant demand (maintenance marketing)
- To reduce excess demand

Products and customers

2.5 Many products might satisfy the same customer need. On what basis might a customer choose?

(a) **Customer value** is the customer's estimate of how far a product or service goes towards satisfying his or her need(s).

(b) Every product has a cost, and so the customer makes a trade-off between the expenditure and the value offered.

(c) According to Kotler a customer must feel he or she gets a better deal from buying an item than by any of the alternatives.

2.6 Companies must make a distinction between the **customer** and the **consumer**.

(a) The **customer** is the person or organisation buying the product or service. For example, a cat's owner will buy food for the cat.

(b) The **consumer** is the person who uses the product or receives the benefit of the service. In the case of cat food, the cat is the consumer, not the purchaser.

2.7 Marketing has a role in the organisation's **value chain**. The end result of a value chain is a product or service, whose price must in some way equate with the **customer's perception of value**, but whose cost allows the producer a **margin or profit**.

The importance of developing a market orientation in strategic planning

2.8 The importance of developing a market orientation to strategic planning is implicit in the marketing concept. An organisation commits itself to supplying what customers need. As those needs change, so too must the goods or services which are produced. In other words, **marketing orientation enables a firm to adapt to the environment**.

(a) By applying the marketing concept to product design the company might hope to make more attractive products, hence to achieve sustained sales growth and so make higher profits.

(b) Profits do not only come from individual transactions with customers, but also from the customer's propensity to deal with the firm rather than its competitors.

2.9 Strategic planning involves making decisions about the choice of **product-market strategies** - developing new products and new markets that will fill the **'profit gap'**. A marketing orientation should help planners to identify more successfully what products or markets would earn good profits for the organisation.

2.10 Having decided on a competitive strategy a firm must then decide on the following.

- Which target markets should be selected for development

- How the firm should offer its product or service in comparison with the offerings of competitors.

- How to establish a **marketing system** and organisation for the firm.

- How to develop a **marketing plan** and then implement and control it.

Case study link

Consumer buying behaviour featured in the May 2002 case study scenario. Market Stores, Global Inc.'s rival, had stepped up its customer service levels and contributed to the development of out of town stores with cheap parking – the 'one stop shop'.

Buyer behaviour

2.11 In marketing, a market is defined in terms of its **buyers** or **potential buyers**.

- **Consumer markets** (eg for soap powder, washing machines, TV sets, clothes)
- **Industrial markets** (eg for machine tools, construction equipment)
- **Government markets** (eg for armaments, and, in the UK, medical equipment)
- **Reseller markets**
- **Export markets**

Consumer goods

2.12 Consumer goods are in such a form that they can be used by the consumer without the need for any further commercial processing. Consumer goods are further classified according to the method by which they are purchased.

- **Convenience goods**
- **Shopping goods**
- **Speciality goods**

2.13 If an article has close substitutes, is purchased regularly in small amounts of low unit value, and the customer insists on buying it with the minimum of inconvenience, the article is called a **convenience good**. Convenience goods are everyday purchases such as toothpaste, bread, coffee, chocolate etc, and are likely to be produced by several manufacturers. Promoting a unique image for the product, for example by **branding**, is therefore important.

BPP PUBLISHING

2.14 **Shopping goods** are goods for which customers are more discriminating. They usually have a higher unit value than convenience goods and are bought less frequently, usually from a specialist outlet with a wider range on offer. **Examples** of shopping goods are cars, furniture, hi-fi equipment, many clothes, household appliances such as washing machines and cookers.

2.15 When a manufacturer, either by product design or advertising, has become associated in the public mind with a particular product (eg Rolls Royce cars, Wedgwood pottery) the article produced is no longer a shopping good, but a **speciality good**, possessing a unique character which will make a customer go out of his way to ask for it by name and find a dealer who sells it.

The buying decision

2.16 A **buying decision** might be taken entirely by one person. However, the buying process might be influenced by several different individuals.

(a) **Indicators or initiators**. These are the individuals who first suggest the idea of buying a particular product.

(b) **Influencers**. These are people who stimulate, inform or persuade at any stage of the buying process. (An influencer could be a character in a TV advertisement.)

(c) **Deciders**. These are the people who make the decision that a product should be bought.

(d) **Buyers**. The person who actually goes out and buys the product might not be the person who originally decided that it ought to be bought.

(e) **Users**. The ultimate user of the product might be neither the decider nor the buyer, although their perceptions of what the user needs is likely to influence the buying decision/purchase action.

Industrial or business-to-business markets

2.17 In industrial markets, the customer is another firm, such as for the sale of machine tools or consultancy advice. The industrial market, more than the consumer market, is influenced by the general state of the economy and the government's economic policy (see Chapter 4).

2.18 The demand for industrial goods and services is derived from the demand for the product or service to which they contribute. For example, the demand for aluminium is in part derived from the demand for cans, which might itself be derived from demand for the beer with which the cans will be filled.

2.19 **Industrial buyers** are more **rationally motivated** than consumers in deciding which goods to buy. Sales policy decisions by a supplier are therefore more important than sales promotion activities in an industrial market. Special attention should be given in selling to quality, price, credit, delivery dates, after-sales service, etc, and it is the importance of these rational motivations which make it difficult for an untried newcomer to break into an industrial goods market.

Organisational buying behaviour

2.20 The organisational buying behaviour process has some similarities with consumer buyer behaviour, but is supposedly more rational.

- How are needs recognised in a company?
- What is the type of buying situation?
- How is a supplier selected?
- How will performance be reviewed after purchase?

The decision-making unit

2.21 The **decision-making unit (DMU)** is a term used to describe the person or people who actually take the decision to buy a good or service. The marketing manager needs to know who in each organisation makes the effective buying decisions and how decisions are made: the DMU might act with formal authority, or as an informal group reaching a joint decision. Many large organisations employ specialist purchasing departments or 'buyers' - but the independence of the buyers will vary from situation to situation. Webster and Wind identified the following categories of employees who have an interest in an industrial buying decision:

(a) The **gatekeeper** controls the flow of information about the purchase. This role can be senior or junior but is important because it influences the communication flow within the organisation.

(b) **Influencers**. In this environment the salesperson can be a respected technical link with the buyer able to influence the purchasing process.

(c) **Users**, employees or managers in sales and production etc might make recommendations about what type of supplies should be purchased.

(d) Recommendations might have to be submitted to a superior for approval, ultimately at board level.

(e) Other experts in the organisation (such as engineers for technical specifications, or accountants for budget considerations) may provide input to the buying decision.

Factors in the motivation mix of business or government buyers

2.22 Business or government buyers are motivated as follows.

(a) **Quality**.

(b) **Price**. Where profit margins in the final market are under pressure, the buyer of industrial goods will probably make price the main purchasing motivation.

(c) **Budgetary control** may encourage the buying department to look further afield for potential suppliers to obtain a better price or quality of goods.

(d) **Fear of breakdown**. Where a customer has a highly organised and costly production system, he will clearly want to avoid a breakdown in the system, due to a faulty machine or running out of stocks of materials.

(e) **Credit**. The importance of credit could vary with the financial size of the buyer.

Market segmentation

2.23 Much marketing planning is based on the concepts of **segmentation and product positioning.** The purpose of segmentation is to identify target markets in which the firm can take a position. A market is not a mass, homogeneous group of customers, each wanting an identical product. Market segmentation is based on the recognition that every market consists of potential buyers with different needs, and different buying behaviour. It is relevant to a **focus strategy**.

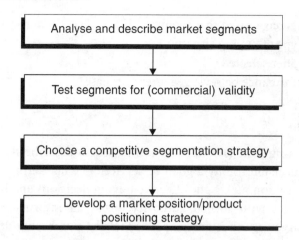

```
┌─────────────────────────────────────────┐
│  Analyse and describe market segments    │
└─────────────────────────────────────────┘
                    │
                    ▼
┌─────────────────────────────────────────┐
│  Test segments for (commercial) validity │
└─────────────────────────────────────────┘
                    │
                    ▼
┌─────────────────────────────────────────┐
│ Choose a competitive segmentation strategy│
└─────────────────────────────────────────┘
                    │
                    ▼
┌─────────────────────────────────────────┐
│  Develop a market position/product       │
│  positioning strategy                    │
└─────────────────────────────────────────┘
```

KEY TERM

Market segmentation may be defined as 'the subdividing of a market into distinct and increasingly homogeneous subgroups of customers, where any subgroup can conceivably be selected as a target market to be met with a distinct marketing mix'. (Kotler)

2.24 There are two important elements in this definition of market segmentation.

(a) Although the total market consists of widely different groups of consumers, each group consists of people (or organisations) with **common needs and preferences**, who perhaps react to 'market stimuli' in much the same way.

(b) Each market segment can become a **target market for a firm**, and would require a unique marketing mix if the firm is to exploit it successfully.

2.25 **Reasons for segmenting markets**

Reason	Comment
Better satisfaction of customer needs	One solution won't satisfy **all** customers
Growth in profits	Some customers will pay more for certain benefits
Revenue growth	Segmentation means that more customers may be attracted by what is on offer, in preference to competing products
Customer retention	By targeting customers, a number of different products can be offered to them
Targeted communications	Segmentation enables clear communications as people in the target audience share common needs
Innovation	By identifying unmet needs, companies can innovate to satisfy them
Segment share	Segmentation enables a firm to implement a focus strategy successfully

2.26 **Steps in segmentation, targeting and positioning identified by Kotler**

Step 1.	Identify **segmentation** variables and segment the market	Segmentation
Step 2.	Develop segment profiles	
Step 3.	Evaluate the attractiveness of each segment	Targeting
Step 4.	Select the **target** segment(s)	
Step 5.	Identify **positioning** concepts for each target segment	Positioning
Step 6.	Select, develop and communicate the chosen concept	

Identifying segments

2.27 An important initial marketing task is the **identification of segments** within the market. Segmentation applies more obviously to the consumer market, but it can also be applied to an **industrial market**. An important basis for segmentation is the nature of the customer's business.

2.28 (a) One basis will not be appropriate in every market, and sometimes two or more bases might be valid at the same time.

(b) One basis or 'segmentation variable' might be 'superior' to another in a hierarchy of variables. Here are thus **primary and secondary segmentation variables.**

Case example

An airport cafe conducted a segmentation exercise of its customers. It identified a number of possible segments.

- Business travellers
- Airport employees
- Groups
- Single tourists

However, further analysis revealed that running through each of these categories was the same fault line.

- Those 'in a hurry'
- Those with time to spare

For marketing purposes, this latter segmentation exercise was more useful, and the firm was able to develop an 'express menu' for those in a hurry.

Geography

2.29 At its simplest, this involves dividing the market into regions and tailoring the marketing mix accordingly.

(a) An example is **commercial radio stations,** which broadcast local news.

(b) The market for educational material in the UK segments geographically: Scotland has a different system to England.

Case examples

The Australian Tourist Commission (ATC) was established in 1967 to promote Australia as an international tourism destination. Two of its principal objectives are to increase the number of visitors to Australia from overseas, and to maximise the benefits to Australia from overseas visitors. ATC has maximised the efficiency of its marketing by breaking up the travel market into the following segments:

- Independent adventurers aged 25-34
- Young independent travellers aged 18-24
- Independent travellers aged 45-65

With young travellers, the marketing approach was to communicate the aspects of Australia that would most appeal to them:

- Young, vibrant, dynamic (city life)
- Innovative (lifestyle, food and wine, culture)
- Active and sporty (beaches and sport facilities)
- Fun loving (parties, festivals, events)

Geodemographic segmentation

2.31 The ACORN system divides the UK into 17 groups which together comprise a total of 54 different types of areas, which share common socio-economic characteristics. Unlike geographical segmentation, which is fairly crude by area, geodemographics enables similar groups of people to be targeted, even though they might exist in different areas of the country. These various classifications share certain characteristics, including:

- Car ownership
- Unemployment rates
- Purchase of financial service products
- Number of holidays
- Age profile

Psychographic segmentation

2.32 Psychographic segmentation is not based on 'objective' data so much as how people see themselves and their **subjective** feelings and attitudes towards a particular product or service, or towards life in general.

Social class

2.33 Age and sex present few problems but social class has always been one of the most dubious areas of marketing research investigation. 'Class' is a highly personal and subjective phenomenon, to the extent that some people are 'class conscious' or class aware and have a sense of belonging to a particular group.

2.34 From 2001 the UK Office for National Statistics used a new categorisation system, which reflects recent changes in the UK population.

New social class	Occupations	Example
1	Higher managerial and professional occupations	
1.1	Employers and managers in larger organisations	Bank managers, company directors

1.2	Higher professional	Doctors, lawyers
2	Lower managerial and professional occupations	Police officers
3	Intermediate occupations	Secretaries, clerical workers
4	Small employers and own-account workers	
5	Lower supervisory, craft and related occupations	Electricians
6	Semi-routine occupations	Drivers, hairdressers, bricklayers
7	Routine occupations	Car park attendants, cleaners

Behavioural segmentation

2.35 Behavioural segmentation segments buyers into groups based on their attitudes to and use of the product, and the **benefits** they expect to receive.

Benefit segmentation of the toothpaste market

Segment Name	Principal benefit sought	Demographic Strengths	Special behavioural characteristics	Brands disproportion-ately favoured	Personality character-istics	Lifestyle character-istics
The sensory segment	Flavour, product appearance	Children	Users of spearmint flavoured toothpaste	Colgate, Stripe	High self-involvement	Hedonistic
The Sociables	Brightness of teeth	Teens, young people	Smokers	Macleans, Ultra-Brite	High sociability	Active
The Worriers	Decay prevention	Large families	Heavy users	Crest	High hypochon-driasis	Conserva-tive
The Independent Segment	Price	Men	Heavy users	Brands on sale	High autonomy	Value-oriented

Segmentation of the industrial market

2.36 Industrial markets can be segmented with many of the bases used in consumer markets such as geography, usage rate and benefits sought. Additional, more traditional bases include customer type, product/technology, customer size and purchasing procedures.

(a) **Geographic location.** Some industries and related industries are clustered in particular areas. Firms selling services to the banking sector might be interested in the City of London.

(b) **Type of business** (eg service, manufacturing)

(i) **Nature of the customers' business.** Accountants or lawyers, for example, might choose to specialise in serving customers in a particular type of business. An accountant may choose to specialise in the accounts of retail businesses, and a firm of solicitors may specialise in conveyancing work for property development companies.

(ii) **Components manufacturers specialise in the industries of the firms to which they supply components.**

(c) **Use of the product.** In the UK, many new cars are sold to businesses, as benefit cars. Although this practice is changing with the viability of a 'cash alternative' to a company car, the varying levels of specification are developed with the business buyer in mind (eg junior salesperson gets an Escort, Regional Manager gets a Ford Mondeo).

(d) **Type of organisation.** Organisations in an industry as a whole may have certain needs in common. Employment agencies offering business services to publishers, say, must offer their clients personnel with experience in particular desk top publishing packages. Suitable temporary staff offered to legal firms can be more effective if used to legal jargon. Each different type of firm can be offered a tailored product or service.

(e) **Size of organisation**. Large organisations may have elaborate purchasing procedures, and may do many things in-house. Small organisations may be more likely to subcontract certain specialist services.

Segment validity

2.37 A market segment will only **be valid if it is worth designing and developing a unique** marketing mix for that specific segment. The following questions are commonly asked to decide whether or not the segment can be used for developing marketing plans.

Criteria	Comment
Can the segment be measured?	It might be possible to conceive of a market segment, but it is not necessarily easy to measure it. For example for a segment based on people with a conservative outlook to life, can conservatism of outlook be measured by market research?
Is the segment big enough?	There has to be a large enough potential market to be profitable.
Can the segment be reached?	There has to be a way of getting to the potential customers via the organisation's promotion and distribution channels.
Do segments respond differently?	If two or more segments are identified by marketing planners but each segment responds in the same way to a marketing mix, the segments are effectively one and the same and there is no point in distinguishing them from each other.
Can the segment be reached profitably?	Do the identified customer needs, cost less to satisfy than the revenue they earn?
Is the segment suitably stable?	The stability of the segment is important, if the organisation is to commit huge production and marketing resources to serve it. The firm does not want the segment to 'disappear' next year. Of course, this may not matter in some industries.

Steps in the analysis of segmentation

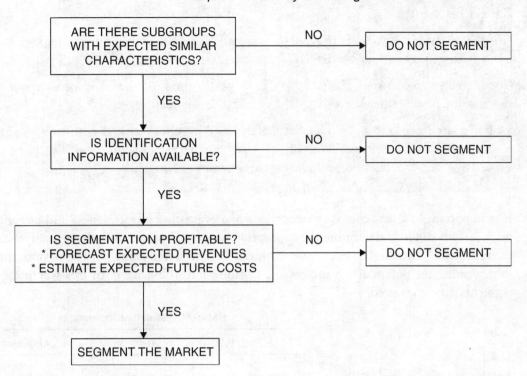

Segment attractiveness

2.38 A segment might be valid and potentially profitable, but is it potentially **attractive?**

(a) A segment which has **high barriers to entry** might cost more to enter but will be less **vulnerable to competitors.**

(b) For firms involved in **relationship marketing,** the segment should be one in which **viable relationship** between the firm and the customer can be established.

2.39 Segments which are most attractive will be those whose needs can be met by building on the company's strengths and where forecasts for demand, sales profitability and **growth** are favourable.

Target markets

2.40 Because of limited resources, competition and large markets, organisations are not usually able to sell with equal efficiency and success to the entire market, ie to every market segment. It is necessary for the sake of efficiency to select **target markets.** A target market is a market or segment selected for special attention by an organisation, possibly to be served with a distinct marketing mix. The marketing management of a company may choose one of the following policy options.

BPP
PUBLISHING

2.41 It is important to assess company strengths when evaluating attractiveness and targeting a market. This can help determine the appropriate strategy, because once the attractiveness of each identified segment has been assessed it can be considered along with relative strengths to determine the potential advantages the organisation would have. In this way preferred segments can be targeted.

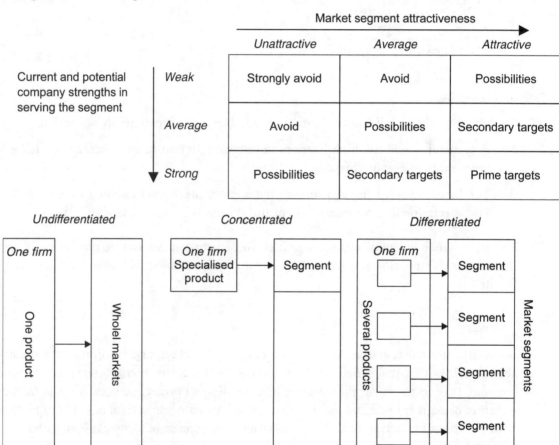

2.42 The major **disadvantage of differentiated marketing** is the additional costs of marketing and production (more product design and development costs, the loss of economies of scale in production and storage, additional promotion costs and administrative costs etc). When the **costs of further differentiation of the market exceed the benefits** from further segmentation and **target marketing**, a firm is said to have **'over-differentiated'**.

2.43 The major **disadvantage of concentrated marketing** is the business risk of relying on a single segment of a single market. On the other hand, specialisation in a particular market segment can give a firm a profitable, although perhaps temporary, competitive edge over rival firms.

2.44 The choice between undifferentiated, differentiated or concentrated marketing as a marketing strategy will depend on the following factors.

(a) The extent to which the product and/or the market may be considered **homogeneous**. **Mass marketing** may be 'sufficient' if the market is largely homogeneous (for example, for safety matches).

(b) The **company's resources** must not be over extended by differentiated marketing. Small firms may succeed better by concentrating on one segment only.

(c) The product must be sufficiently **advanced in its life cycle** to have attracted a substantial total market; otherwise segmentation and target marketing is unlikely to be profitable, because each segment would be too small in size.

3 MARKETING: THE MARKETING MIX, LIFE CYCLE AND BRANDS

3.1 The aim of marketing is, generally speaking, to **maximise profits**. There is a wide variety of possible combinations of marketing methods which management can select, and some combinations will earn a greater profit than others. This combination of factors is the **marketing mix**.

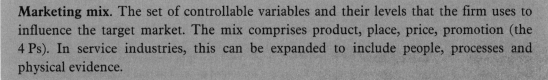

KEY TERM

Marketing mix. The set of controllable variables and their levels that the firm uses to influence the target market. The mix comprises product, place, price, promotion (the 4 Ps). In service industries, this can be expanded to include people, processes and physical evidence.

3.2 The marketing mix has four Ps.

(a) **Product.** A product is a package of benefits, but we tend to think of it as a 'thing' with 'features'.

(b) **Place.** The producer must plan for the availability of the product, and the distribution channels to be used. The product must be readily available where consumers would expect to find it.

(c) **Price.** If the consumer's buying decisions are strongly influenced by price factors, a product should be made available:

• At an attractive price
• Where appropriate with suitable available credit facilities.

(d) **Promotion.** Advertising and sales promotion maintain customer awareness.

3.3 In addition, for services we have three extra Ps.

(a) **People,** who give the service. How well are they trained?

(b) **Processes** by which the service is delivered (eg IT systems).

(c) **Physical evidence.** The environment of the service encounter (eg the cleanliness of Disneyland).

Case example

Abbey National won the 2001 Retail Innovation of the Year award for the way it has adapted its local branches to meet its customers' needs. Costa now provides coffee for customers in several outlets across the UK, while other branches provide toys, web access, books and meeting rooms with videos to keep children occupied.

It is the first time a bank has been shortlisted for this award and may reflect the fact that Abbey began to research what its customers wanted in 1997.

Ron D'Mello, head of local communications, believes that the investment is paying off. 'Footfall is up by 20 per cent at the new-style branches and we have clear evidence that results in all areas, particularly banking products, are significantly up,' he says.

Abbey National has now approved funding for another 60 branches to be converted. 'Staff and customer satisfaction levels have improved. It is a great staff retention tool and research has shown that when staff satisfaction drops so do sales. We wouldn't be investing this much if we weren't seeing very good results,' D'Mello says.

Adapted from Financial Management

Question 1

How might a manufacturer of chairs market to both the consumer market and the industrial market for office furniture?

Answer

The marketing mix selected for the consumer market might be low prices with attractive dealer discounts, sales largely through discount warehouses, modern design but fairly low quality and sales promotion relying on advertising by the retail outlets, together with personal selling by the manufacturing firm to the reseller. For the industrial market, the firm might develop a durable, robust product which sells at a higher price; selling may be by means of direct mail-shots, backed by personal visits from salespeople

Deciding the marketing mix

3.4   The 'design' of the marketing mix will be decided on the basis of management intuition and judgement, together with information provided by marketing research. It is particularly important that management should be able to understand the image of the product in the eyes of the customer, and the product's **positioning**.

3.5   Kotler notes that every marketing mix strategy will lead to a certain level of profit as indicated in the equation below.

$$Z = [(P - k) - c] Q - F - M$$

where Z = total profits
P = list price (per unit)
k = commissions, discounts etc (per unit)
c = production and distribution variable costs
Q = number of units sold
F = fixed costs
M = discretionary marketing costs.

3.6   The stages in the formulation of a marketing mix might be as follows.

3.7 The ideal marketing mix is one which holds a **proper balance** between each of these elements.

(a) One marketing activity in the mix will not be fully effective unless proper attention is given to all the other activities. For example, if a company launches a costly promotion campaign which emphasises the superior quality of a product, the outlay on advertising, packaging and personal selling will be wasted if the quality does not live up to customer expectations.

(b) A company might also place too much emphasis on one aspect of the marketing mix, and much of the effort and expenditure might not be justified for the additional returns it obtains. It might for example, place too much importance on price reductions to earn higher profits, when in fact a smaller price reduction and greater spending on sales promotion or product design might have a more profitable effect.

REMEMBER

The ideal mix for a convenience good (requiring a heavy emphasis on distribution and sales promotion) will be different from that for an industrial good (where price, design, quality and after-sales service are more important).

Life cycle and segmentation issues

3.8 The **product life cycle** is relevant to overall corporate planning. Reviewing the position regarding current products is necessary in order to identify the need for new products to fill the 'gap'. Different marketing tactics are appropriate to different stages of the life cycle.

The diffusion process and the life cycle

3.9 An important issue to planners is how quickly a new product will be adopted by the market. A number of factors influence the speed at which new ideas and product innovations will spread or be diffused through the marketplace.

- The **complexity** of the new product

- The relative **advantages** it offers

- The degree to which the innovation fits into **existing patterns** of behaviour or needs

- The **ability to try** the new product, such as samples, test drives or low value purchases entailing little risk

- The ease with which the products benefits can be **communicated** to the potential customer

3.10 The **adoption process** refers to the stages a customer goes through before making a purchase decision. The five stages identifiable in most models of this process are these.

| Awareness | Interest | Evaluation | Trial | Adoption |

There can be a considerable time lag between awareness and adoption.

3.11 In *Consumer Behaviour* Schiffmann and Kanuk offer the following analysis.

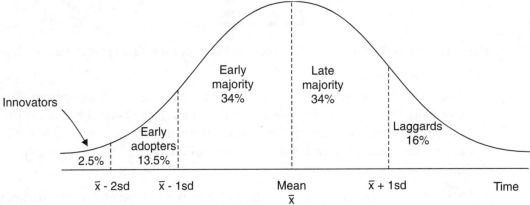

3.12 The characteristics of consumers in these adopter categories vary.

Innovators	Eager to try new ideas and products and often in close contact with agents like sales staff.
Early adopters	Willing to change and often opinion leaders.
Early majority	More conservative segment which tends to purchase a new product just ahead of the average time, but who will have given it some thought.
Late majority	Slower than the average and sceptical.
Laggards	Traditionalists actually unwilling to change.

Diffusion and marketing strategy

3.13 Marketers usually want to ensure a rapid diffusion or rate of adoption for a new product. This allows them to gain a large share of the market prior to competitors responding. A **penetration policy** of low introductory pricing and promotions designed to facilitate trial is associated with such a strategy.

3.14 In some markets, particularly where R & D cost has been high, where the product involves 'new' technology or where it is protected from competition perhaps by patent, a **skimming policy** may be adopted. Here price is high representing very high unit profits. Sales can be increased in steps with price reductions, in line with available capacity or competitors responses.

Segmentation and the life cycle

3.15 Segmentation issues are relevant to the product life cycle.

(a)	At the introduction and growth stage, it may not be possible to segment the market as sales volumes are so small.

(b)	Rather more difficult decisions occur at the maturity and decline stages.

- Do you find new segments in the market?
- Do you let the product die?
- Do you re-position the product, by technical modifications or other changes in the marketing mix to extend the life cycle?

3.16	Traditionally many firms have tended only to operate at home as long as performance there was satisfactory. Then, when domestic performance declined, they tried to close the gap by exporting. But this is possible only if the product is at different stages in its life cycle in different countries.

3.17	This type of strategy is now far less feasible, although not entirely impossible. The revolution in communications among countries during recent years has narrowed the time gap. As a result of these developments, **international marketing must consider many markets simultaneously**, with a view to implementing a global introduction.

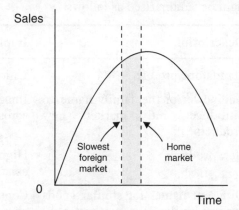

3.18	Where overseas markets or alternative market segments are similar, simultaneous product launches in different markets are necessary to ensure that the product is launched in all potential markets before rivals have time to pre-empt the firm.

Brands

3.19	**Branding** removes anonymity and gives identification to a company and its goods and services.

> **KEY TERM**
>
> According to Kotler a **brand** is 'a name, term, sign, symbol or design or combination of them, intended to identify the goods or services of one seller or group of sellers and to differentiate them from those of competitors'.

3.20	Another way of considering this issue is the concept of **brand equity**. This is the asset that the marketer builds to ensure continuity of satisfaction for the customer and profit for the supplier. The 'asset' consists of consumer attitudes, distribution channels and other relationships.

3.21	The reasons for branding are as follows.

(a) It is a form of **product differentiation**, which makes customers readily identify the goods or services and thereby helps to create a customer loyalty to the brand.

(b) The more a product is similar to competing goods, the more branding is necessary to create a separate **product identity**.

(c) Branding leads to a more ready **acceptance** of a manufacturer's goods by wholesalers and retailers.

(d) It facilitates **self-selection** of goods in self-service stores and also makes it easier for a manufacturer to obtain the optimum **display space** in shops and stores.

(e) It reduces the importance of **price differentials** between goods.

(f) **Brand loyalty** in customers gives a manufacturer more control over marketing strategy and his choice of channels of distribution.

(g) Other products can be introduced into a brand range through 'piggy-back' on the articles already known to the customer. Adding products to an existing brand range is known as a **brand extension strategy**.

3.22 Branding strategies might be summarised as follows.

Branding strategy	Description	Implies
Individual name	Standalone product	Unique
Family branding	The power of the 'family name' to introduce and market new products	Image of the family brand across a range of products
Brand extension	New products	High consumer loyalty to existing brand
Multi-branding	Different names for similar goods serving similar consumer tastes	Consumers make random purchases across brands

3.23 The decision as to whether a brand name should be given to a range of products or whether products should be branded individually depends on quality factors.

(a) If the brand name is associated with quality, all goods in the range must be of that standard.

(b) If a company produces different quality (and price) goods for different market segments, it would be unwise to give the same brand name to the higher and the lower quality goods because this could deter buyers in the high quality/price market segment.

To brand or not to brand?

3.24 The advantages of branding include the following.

(a) Branding facilitates **memory recall**, thus contributing to self-selection and improving customer loyalty.

(b) In many **cultures** branding is preferred, particularly in the distribution channel.

(c) Branding is a way of obtaining **legal protection** for product features.

(d) It helps with **market segmentation**.

(e) It helps build a strong and positive **corporate image**, especially if the brand name used is the company name (eg Kelloggs, Heinz).

(f)   Branding makes it easier to link **advertising** to other marketing communications programmes.

(g)   **Display space** is more easily obtained and point-of-sale promotions are more practicable.

(h)   If branding is successful, other **associated products** can be introduced.

(i)   The need for expensive **personal selling**/persuasion may be reduced.

Brand valuation

3.25   In the late 1980s a number of high profile firms such as Rank Hovis McDougall started putting brand valuations on their balance sheets, as valuable assets meriting inclusion. There is a distinction to be drawn, however, between two types of brand.

- Purchased when another business is acquired
- 'Home grown'

3.26   In the first case, the transaction can be identified and the cost capitalised and amortised over time. In the second case, FRS 10 says that home-grown brands should not be included. This is an area for controversy, as brands are now seen as a key form of intellectual capital, and part of the growing gap between market and asset values in many companies.

Case examples

(a)   'Brand value' was pushed to the forefront when Nestle mounted its hostile takeover bid for Rowntree. Rowntree rejected the initial offer because it felt that its stable of brands (including Polo, Fruit Pastilles and many others) was not being recognised sufficiently in the price. Nestle had to increase its offer.

(b)   The Coca-Cola brand is valued at £50 billion.

Brand management accounting

3.27   In an article in the February 2002 issue of *Financial Management*, Hart and Roslender link the tasks of brand management and marketing firmly with the accountant's role, as a new step in strategic management accounting.

3.28   Their research found a range of brand management accounting techniques in the companies they studied.

- Brand profit and loss accounts

- Brand contribution analyses

- Brand net cash flow projections and market valuations

- Brand marketing expenditure plans

- Brand performance information (such as measures of market share, brand awareness and customer loyalty)

3.29   Other approaches to valuing brands include the following.

(a)   **How much the brand cost to create.** This can be inaccurate, as current values may not reflect historic cost.

(b) **How much would be expected to be received in royalties** from any franchise of the brand. Calculation of this can be difficult.

(c) **Calculate the NPV of net earnings** attributable to the brand – a standard shareholder value approach (as discussed later in Chapter 15).

4 REVIEWING THE CUSTOMER PORTFOLIO

4.1 It will help you in evaluating the customer portfolio if you consider the customer base as an asset worth 'investing' in.

Case examples

(a) Coca-Cola paid $200m to Pernod of France, which, under contract, had effectively built a customer base for Coca-Cola, as well as building up a distribution network. Coca-Cola wanted to take charge of the marketing of Coke in France.

(b) Supermarket 'loyalty cards' reward customers with bonus points, saving them money, or allowing them to redeem points for products according to how much they spend.

(c) Many banks lose money on student accounts, in the hope that they will earn it back over the customer's life cycle later.

4.2 A **marketing audit** involves a review of an organisation's products and markets, the marketing environment, and its marketing system and operations. The profitability of each product and each market should be assessed, and the costs of different marketing activities established.

4.3 **Information obtained about markets**

(a) **Size of the customer base.** Does the organisation sell to a large number of small customers or a small number of big customers?

(b) **Size of individual orders.** The organisation might sell its products in many small orders, or it might have large individual orders. Delivery costs can be compared with order sizes.

(c) **Sales revenue and profitability.** The performance of individual products can be compared, perhaps as follows:

Product group	Sales revenue £'000	% of total	Contribution to profits £'000	% of total
B	7,500	35.7	2,500	55.6
E	2,000	9.5	1,200	26.7
C	4,500	21.4	450	10.0
A	5,000	23.8	250	5.6
D	2,000	9.5	100	2.2
	21,000	100.0%	4,500	100.0%

An imbalance between sales and profits over various product ranges can be potentially dangerous. In the figures above, product group A accounts for 23.8% of turnover but only 5.6% of total contribution, and product group D accounts for 9.5% of turnover but only 2.2% of total contribution.

(d) **Segments.** An analysis of sales and profitability into export markets and domestic markets.

(e) **Market share.** Estimated share of the market obtained by each product group.

(f) **Growth.** Sales growth and contribution growth over the previous four years or so, for each product group.

(g) Whether the **demand** for certain products is **growing, stable or likely to decline.**

(h) Whether **demand is price sensitive** or not.

(i) Whether there is a growing tendency for the market to become **fragmented,** with more specialist and 'custom-made' products.

4.4 Information about current marketing activities

- Comparative pricing
- Advertising effectiveness
- Effectiveness of distribution network
- Attitudes to the product, in comparison with competitors

Customers

4.5 Many firms - especially in business-to-business markets - sell to a relatively small number of customers. **Not all customers are as important as others.** The checklist below can help identify the most important.

Strategic importance evaluation guide	High	Medium	Low	N/A
1 Fit between customer's needs and our capabilities, at present and potentially.				
2 Ability to serve customer compared with our major competitors, at present and potentially.				
3 'Health' of customer's industry, current and forecast.				
4 'Health' of the customer, current and forecast.				
5 Customer's growth prospects, current and forecast.				
6 What can we learn from this customer?				
7 Can the customer help us attract others?				
8 Relative *significance:* how important is the customer compared *with other* customers?				
9 What is the *profitability* of serving the customer?				

Customer analysis

4.6 **Key customer analysis** calls for six main areas of investigation into customers. A firm might wish to identify which customers offer most profit. Small businesses are especially prone.

(a) **Key customer identity.**

- Name of each key customer
- Location
- Status in market

- Products they make and sell
- Size of firm (capital employed, turnover, number of employees)

(b) **Customer history**

- First purchase date.
- Who makes the buying decision in the customer's organisation?
- What is the average order size, by product?
- What is the regularity/ periodicity of the order, by product?
- What is the trend in size of orders?
- What is the motive in purchasing?
- What does the customer know about the firm's and competitors' products?
- On what basis does the customer reorder?
- How is the useful life of the product judged?
- Were there any lost or cancelled orders? For what reason?

(c) **Relationship of customer to product**

- What does the customer use the product for?
- Do the products form part of the customer's own service/product?

(d) **Relationship of customer to potential market**

- What is the size of the customer in relation to the total end-market?
- Is the customer likely to expand, or not? Diversify? Integrate?

(e) **Customer attitudes and behaviour**

- What interpersonal factors exist which could affect sales by the firm and by competitors?
- Does the customer also buy competitors' products?
- To what extent may purchases be postponed?

(f) **The financial performance of the customer.** How successful is the customer?

Customer profitability analysis (customer account profitability)

> **KEY TERM**
>
> **Customer profitability analysis (CPA).** 'Analysis of the revenue streams and service costs associated with specific customers or customer groups'.
>
> (CIMA *Official Terminology*)

4.7 'An immediate impact of introducing any level of strategic management accounting into virtually every organisation is to destroy totally any illusion that the same level of profit is derived from all customers'. (Ward, *Strategic Management Accounting*)

4.8 The total costs of servicing customers can vary depending on how customers are serviced.

(a) **Volume discounts.** A customer who places one large order is given a discount, presumably because it benefits the supplier to do so (eg savings on administrative overhead is processing the orders - as identified by an ABC system).

(b) **Different rates** charged by power companies to domestic as opposed to business users. This in part reflects the administrative overhead of dealing with individual customers. In practice, many domestic consumers benefit from cross-subsidy.

REMEMBER

Customer profitability is the 'total sales revenue generated from a customer or customer group, less all the costs that are incurred in servicing that customer or customer group.'

Case example

In the mobile phone business, high customer acquisition costs mean that it can take up to two years to break even on a new customer. When this factor is added to the worldwide downturn in demand for mobile phones, it is easy to see why some of the big names have announced staff cuts recently.

Question 2

Seth Ltd supplies shoes to Narayan Ltd and Kipling Ltd. Each pair of shoes has a list price of £50 each; as Kipling buys in bulk, Kipling receives a 10% trade discount for every order over 100 shoes. it costs £1,000 to deliver each order. In the year so far, Kipling has made five orders of 100 shoes each. Narayan Ltd receives a 15% discount irrespective of order size, because Narayan Ltd collects the shoes, thereby saving Seth Ltd any distribution costs. The cost of administering each order is £50. Narayan makes ten orders in the year, totalling 420 pairs of shoes. Which relationship is the most profitable for Seth?

Answer

You can see below that the profit earned by Seth in servicing Narayan is greater, despite the increased discount.

	Kipling	Narayan
Number of shoes	500	420
	£	£
Revenue (after discount)	22,500	17,850
Transport	(5,000)	-
Administration	(250)	(500)
Net profit	17,250	17,350

4.9 Customer profitability analysis (CPA) focuses on profits generated by customers and suggests that **profit does not automatically increase with sales revenue**. CPA can benefit a company in the following ways.

- It enables a company to **focus resources** on the most profitable areas
- It identifies unexpected **differences in profitability** between customers
- It helps quantify the **financial impact** of proposed changes
- It helps highlight the **cost** of obtaining **new** customers and the **benefit** of retaining existing customers
- It helps to highlight whether **product** development or **market** development is to be preferred
- An appreciation of the costs of servicing clients assists in **negotiations** with customers

Identifying profitable customers/segments

4.10 An important area in marketing strategy is **retaining** customers, so as to generate new business from them. But how do you identify which customers, or customer groups generate the most profit?

Question 3

Busqueros Ltd has 1,000 business customers spread fairly evenly over the UK. The sales force is organised into ten regions, each with 100 customers to be serviced. There are sales force offices at the heart of each region. Information is collected on a regional basis. The marketing director has recently carried out an analysis of the major customers by sales revenue. There are five significant customers, who between them account for 20% of the sales revenue of the firm. They do not get special treatment. What does this say about customer profitability analysis in Busqueros Ltd?

Answer

The information reflects sales force administration and convenience. However, it might obscure an analysis of customer profitability, in which case presenting information by customer size might be more important than geography.

4.11 To analyse customer profitability successfully it may be necessary to structure accounting information systems to take account of the many factors by which customers can be analysed. A **relational database**, whereby information can be structured in many different ways, offers a useful approach.

4.12 How do you apportion costs to customer segments? Assume you have a customer base of 15,000 people. You have just spent £20,000 on an advertising campaign and 5,000 new customers have been found. How do you allocate the cost of the campaign? You do not know whether each new customer was attracted by the campaign, or by word-of-mouth.

4.13 Different customer costs can arise out of the following.

- Order size
- Sales mix
- Order processing
- Transport costs (eg if JIT requires frequent deliveries)
- Management time
- Cash flow problems (eg increased overdraft interest) caused by slow payers
- Order complexity (eg if the order has to be sent out in several stages)
- Stockholding costs can relate to specify customers
- The customer's negotiating strength.

4.14 Here is a possible layout for a **customer profitability analysis.**

	£'000
Gross sales	1,072
less discounts	45
Net sales	1,027
Production	
less production costs	510
	517
Marketing	
less specific marketing costs:	
sales calls	10
in-store promotions	5
customer bonuses	5
less share of other marketing costs:	
sales force management	10
customer service	10
	477

	£'000
Distribution	
less specific distribution costs:	
transportation	5
packaging	17
refusals	2
outstanding debts	30
	423
less shares of distribution costs:	
order processing	4
stock holding	24
warehousing	20
collecting debts	10
Customer Contribution	365

4.15 Such a report can highlight the differences between the cost of servicing different individuals or firms which can then be applied as follows.

(a) **Directing effort to cutting customer specific costs.** Installing an electric data interchange system (EDI) can save the costs of paperwork and data input.

(b) **Identifying those customers who are expensive to service,** thereby suggesting action to increase profitability.

(c) **Using CPA as part of a comparison with competitors' costs.** A firm which services a customer more cheaply than a competitor can use this cost advantage to offer extra benefits to the customer.

(d) Indicating cases where **profitability might be endangered,** for example by servicing customers for whom the firm's core competence is not especially relevant.

4.16 CPA might provide answers to the following questions. Obviously a firm doing work for one major customer will find it easier to answer these questions than one which works for many customers.

- What **profit/contribution** is the organisation making on sales to the customer, after discounts and selling and delivery costs?

- What would be the **financial consequences** of losing the customer?

- Is the customer buying in order sizes that are **unprofitable** to supply?

- What is **return on investment** on plant used?

- What is the level of **inventory** required specifically to supply these customers?

- Are there any other **specific costs** involved in supplying this customer, eg technical and test facilities, R & D facilities, special design staff?

- What is the ratio of net **contribution per customer to total investment**?

4.17 Questions 4 and 5 below explore these issues.

Question 4

Pear Ltd supplies components to the motor trade. It has the possibility of a long-term contract with a Japanese firm, *Kabuki* who guarantees purchases of £200,000 pa for 15 years. Against this, direct annual product costs for the Kabuki contract are £120,000, distribution is £20,000 and customer specific inventory £1,000.

Taking the Kabuki contract would involve shedding some other customers.

	Turnover	Direct product costs
Abandon Kabuki contract	£1,100,000	£700,000
Value of Kabuki contract in isolation	£200,000	£120,000
Continue Kabuki contract, but lose some business	£1,200,000	£850,000

Without Kabuki, distribution costs will be £40,000. With Kabuki, *total* distribution costs will only rise to £50,000.

Without Kabuki, financing costs would be £11,000 for credit taken; with the Kabuki contract, this will be £10,000 but there will be £1,000 of customer specific inventory. In either case, sales force and customer service each amount to £60,000 pa and management costs £70,000.

Rebates, discounts and promotion are £15,000 and £100,000 without the Kabuki contract. In itself, the Kabuki contract will involve no rebates/discounts or promotion. However, given the knock on effect elsewhere, Pear will still spend £50,000 on promotion, and £10,000 on rebates and discounts.

Is it worth going ahead with the Kabuki contract?

Answer

	(A) Results if Kabuki contract is rejected	(B) Kabuki contract in isolation	(C) Go ahead with Kabuki contract	(D) Differential effect of Kabuki contract (C) – (A)
	£	£	£	£
Sales	1,100,000	200,000	1,200,000	100,000
Direct product costs	(700,000)	(120,000)	(850,000)	(150,000)
	400,000	80,000	350,000	(50,000)
Distribution	(40,000)	(20,000)	(50,000)	(10,000)
Rebates/discounts	(15,000)	-	(10,000)	5,000
Promotion	(100,000)		(50,000)	50,000
	245,000	60,000	240,000	(5,000)
Sales force	(60,000)		(60,000)	-
Customer service	(60,000)		(60,000)	-
Management	(70,000)		(70,000)	-
	55,000	60,000	50,000	(5,000)
Financing costs				
Credit period costs	(11,000)	-	(10,000)	1,000
Customer specific inventory	-	(1,000)	(1,000)	(1,000)
	44,000	59,000	39,000	(5,000)

Although the Kabuki contract brings in £59,000 each year when viewed in isolation, it is not an unmixed blessing. On the figures given Pear would be £5,000 pa better off if it *rejected* the contract. Whilst it would double its advertising spend, distribution management would be simpler, direct product costs would be lower, more than compensating for the fall in sales revenues.

Pear is probably being unrealistic. A change in marketing strategy would certainly have implications for sales force and customer service costs. And finally, Kabuki's revenue is *guaranteed*.

4.18 We can extend DCF techniques into the evaluating customer profitably especially if DCF is adjusted for risk. No new techniques are involved, just applying what you already know.

Question 5

(Pear and Kabuki continued)

Forecast annual profits are £44,000 without the Kabuki contract, or £39,000 with the contract. For the purposes of this exercise, these figures equate to cash flows.

The Kabuki contract has 15 years to run, but Pear's sales to Kabuki are guaranteed. Abandoning the Kabuki contract would mean that Pear Ltd would not be guaranteed this profit - the directors therefore consider that the risk has to be taken into account which they estimate will add 3% to Pear's cost of capital, which with the Kabuki contract, is 10%. The perceived risk therefore increases.

	Reject Kabuki	*Accept Kabuki*
Annual cash inflows	£44,000	£39,000
Discount rate	13%	10%
Cumulative years 1-15	6.462	7.606
NPV	£284,328	£296,634

Continuing with Kabuki, even though it involves lower revenue, conceivably could give a better return for the level of risk.

Of course, this is not realistic, but it shows how you can use DCF creatively.

5 RELATIONSHIP MARKETING: CUSTOMER CARE AND CUSTOMER LOYALTY

5.1 The twentieth century was characterised by **mass media** (television, newspapers, radio) creating **mass marketing** and **mass consumption,** aided by production efficiencies. Products became nationally recognisable via distribution and advertising. Technology impacted dramatically on transportation, travel and communications. Individual customer attention was diluted.

5.2 This situation is now changing. For example, long-standardised products such as Coca Cola now have different variants (Diet, Cherry) to appeal to different customer segments. Now that there are more products to promote, companies need to **target the market** more carefully.

5.3 **Relationship marketing** helps them to do this. Technology is the key factor. Software developments have made **databases** flexible and powerful enough to hold large amounts of **customer specific data**. Companies today can recognise customers electronically.

KEY TERM

Relationship marketing can be seen as the successor to mass marketing, and is the process by which information about the customer is consistently applied by the company when developing and delivering products and services. Developments are communicated to the customer, for example via specially targeted promotions and product launches, in order to build a 'partnership' with him and encourage a long term relationship by paying attention to his specific needs. A sale is not the end of a process, but the beginning of a relationship.

5.4 The rewards from effective relationship marketing are potentially impressive (and are linked to the whole exercise of **customer retention**).

(a) One credit card company calculated that a 5% increase in customer retention would create a 125% increase in profits.

(b) American Express believes that by extending customer lifecycles by five years, it could treble its profits per customer.

(c) According to Coca-Cola, a 10% increase in retailer retention should translate to a 20% increase in sales.

5.5 Existing, loyal customers are valuable because:

- They do not have to be acquired
- They buy a broader range of products
- They cost less to service as they are familiar with the company's ways of doing business
- They become less sensitive to price over time
- They can recommend by word of mouth

5.6 The justification for relationship marketing comes from the **need to retain customers**. There are five different levels of customer relationship.

(a) **Basic.** The salesperson sells the product without any further contact with the customer.

(b) **Reactive.** The customer is encouraged to call the salesperson if there are any problems.

(c) **Accountable.** The salesperson phones the customer to see if there are any problems and to elicit ideas for product improvements.

(d) **Proactive.** The salesperson contacts the customer on a regular basis.

(e) **Partnership.** The salesperson and customer work together to effect customer savings. Partnership sourcing implies that the commercial buyer works more closely with the supplier to ensure that all aspects of the deal suit the needs of both parties, not just for this deal, but those which can be expected in the future.

5.7 Broadly speaking, the greater the number of customers and the smaller the profit per unit sold, the greater the likelihood that the type of marketing will be **basic**. At the other extreme, where a firm has few customers, but where profits are high, the **partnership** approach is most likely.

(a) Customers are in long-term relationship with their banks. Banks try and satisfy many of customers' financial needs over a customer's lifetime (eg current accounts, overdrafts, secured lending, pensions advice, investment advice, insurance).

(b) On the other hand, there is no-long term relationship between a consumer of chocolate bars and the chocolate manufacturer.

5.8 Some firms are trying to **convert** a basic approach into relationship marketing. Many car dealerships, for example, seek to generate additional profits by servicing the cars they sell, and by keeping in touch with their customers so that they can earn repeat business.

5.9 Another way of looking at this is to understand that building up customer relationships requires a change of focus from the 'transaction-based approach' to the relationship approach. The contrast is shown in the table below.

TRANSACTION MARKETING (mainly one-way communication)	RELATIONSHIP MARKETING (mainly two-way communication)
• Focus on single sale	• Focus on customer retention
• Orientation on product features	• Orientation on product benefits
• Short time-scale	• Long time-scale
• Little customer service	• High customer service
• Limited customer commitment	• High customer commitment
• Moderate customer contact	• High customer contact
• Quality is the concern of production	• Quality is the concern of all

5.10 The process of retaining customers for a lifetime is an important one. Instead of one-way communication aimed solely at gaining a sale, it is necessary to develop an effective two-way process to turn a **prospect** into an **advocate**. This is shown in the following ladder of customer loyalty.

Ladder of customer loyalty

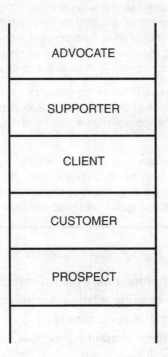

5.11 In terms of the competitive forces, relationship marketing attempts to make it harder, or less desirable, for a customer to switch. It raises **switching costs** (emotional, if not financial). The advantages to the supplier can be made more apparent if we estimate the potential profit made from a customer over the customer's lifetime. For example, when a

Relationship marketing and competition

customer changes bank, the deserted bank loses potential commission on products such as pensions, as well as loss of profits on loans the customer will need in future.

5.12 To work, relationship marketing has to operate in three ways.

(a) **Borrow the idea of customer/supplier partnerships from industry**: by sharing information and supporting each other's shared objectives, marketers and their customers can create real mutual benefit.

(b) **Recreate the personal feel** that characterised the old-fashioned store: make customers feel valued as individuals, and (using modern IT systems) convince them that their individual needs are being recognised and catered for.

(c) **Continually deepen and improve the relationship** by making sure that everything which impinges on the customer's experience of the brand delights them.

5.13 The value of relationship marketing lies in the fact that customers, consumers, retailers, distributors and agents may be spread all over the world, but they will still look for the familiar features when deciding whether or not to do business: product or service performance, enhancements and reliability of supply. If these business partners are looked after, market share will be of better quality because a greater proportion of sales will be derived from **repeat business**.

Case example

From Computer Business Review, March 1999:

Customer relationship management (CRM) software is an industry in its own right. California-based Siebel Systems is market leader and its chief executive, Tom Siebel, says: 'I think now we have entered an era where the most precious resource is being recognised as the customer relationship. 'A customer in Paris, London or New York ordering on the Internet or by telephone does not care where the supplier is based, he just wants good service and quick delivery. 'There is a huge feeling, even in formerly not-so-service-oriented economies, that companies need to reach, serve and embrace customers. And the game they are playing is absolutely economic survival'.

Another CRM company boss says 'Think of any industry - telecoms, high tech, consumer packaged goods, financial services. There is no time for building relationships ... a system has to be implemented immediately. Loyalty and retention equal revenue ... [and] ... it is the level of service that will keep customers coming back'.

In many industries, mass globalisation has diluted the significance of product features and functionality. Customers are clamouring for a more personalised service, and companies have to satisfy highly individualised markets - ultimately a target market of one customer. Companies like One 2 One, BAT and the Prudential are all using CRM software to build databases and customer information profiles.

5.14 To summarise, these are the distinguishing characteristics of relationship marketing.

- A focus on **customer retention** rather than attraction
- The development of an **on-going relationship** as opposed to a one-off transaction
- A **long time scale** rather than short time scale
- Direct and **regular customer contact** rather than impersonal, discrete sales
- **Multiple employee/customer contacts**
- **Quality and customer satisfaction** being the concern of all employees
- Emphasis on **key account relationship management**
- Importance of **trust** and keeping promises
- **Multiple exchanges** with a number of parties

5.15 Recently there has been a **backlash** against relationship marketing especially as applied to the consumer sector. Not all 'customers' want a relationship and resent the potential for intrusion. Furthermore, many firms practise relationship marketing purely as an information gathering exercise. Does the **customer** benefit from the relationship?

6 DISTRIBUTION CHANNELS AND THE SUPPLY CHAIN

The distribution channel

> **KEY TERM**
>
> The **distribution channel** is the means of getting the goods to the customer.

6.1 The distribution channel is of strategic importance.

(a) It is **hard to change** in the short term, unlike the price or promotion elements in the marketing mix.

    (i) A distribution channel often involves **contractual arrangements** with the distributor which cannot be changed easily.

    (ii) There is a substantial **physical infrastructure** involved, of warehouses, lorry fleets, containers etc.

    (iii) In many respects, **distributors are** 'customers' whose needs should be considered, and with whom a **long-term relationship** should be built.

(b) A firm's **marketing communications** will be strongly influenced by the extent to which the firm is able to obtain wide distribution.

(c) In overseas markets most new managers will be inexperienced. At home, the distribution channel will exist already, whereas abroad a new channel will have to be built up from scratch, in very different conditions. Distribution is often **outsourced.** The firm obtains services from logistics firms, banks and insurance companies.

(d) Distribution is a competitive battlefield.

(e) Distribution can offer competitive advantage.

6.2 Key issues in distribution are these.

(a) **Coverage and density,** in other words the number of sales outlets.

    (i) Countries like the UK and US allow large stores.

    (ii) In Japan, there have been restrictions on store size, to protect the livelihoods of small retailers.

(b) **Channel length** - the number of intermediaries between producer and consumer.

(c) **Power and alignment.** The international marketer has to realise that distribution channel power is not equal in each country. Different roles are played by retailers, wholesalers and agents in each country. For example, wholesalers are most important where retailing is fragmented. In the UK, where, in groceries, concentration of retail power has gone furthest, the major supermarket chains are powerful.

(d) **Logistics** and physical distribution.

Distribution costs

6.3 The company should remember its basic distribution and logistics strategy is constrained by the distribution cost structure which may be represented by the following function:

$$D = T + W + I + O + P + S$$

where D = total distribution cost
T = total transport costs
W = warehousing costs
I = inventory costs
O = order processing and documentation cost
P = packaging cost
S = total cost of lost sales for not meeting standards set

6.4 In international distribution many of these costs will rise.

- Transport: longer distances and the use of several modes will raise costs
- Warehousing: the firm might have a warehouse system for each country
- Stock and inventory will be higher
- Packaging might need to be able to handle long journeys
- Order processing and documentation: customs forms, taxes and excise, insurance etc

6.5 The key here is to remember that as some of these cost functions increase others will decrease. So, for example, larger deliveries to a holding warehouse in the main market may reduce total transport costs through efficiencies or discounts with the freight forwarders or shipping companies, but this may be achieved at the expense of increased warehousing and inventory costs.

The supply chain

6.6 Many multinational enterprises (MNEs) have been getting larger. Some writers are arguing that the trend will continue - so that for many sectors there will be fewer players of world class. We have seen this in the automobile industry for example, with many European companies merging to be able to compete effectively with US giants and the Japanese.

6.7 There have been, at the same time, much **closer links** with companies in the supply chain in order to extract best value for money and reduce stockholdings. This has had major consequences on the distribution methods of companies in these supply chains, delivering to their customers on a **just in time** (JIT) basis. The **adversarial,** arms length relationship with a supplier has been replaced by one which is characterised by closer co-operation.

6.8 The change in supply chain linkage is demonstrated in the following model (taken from Monczka).

Supply chain model

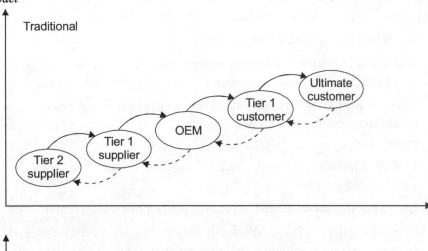

Traditional

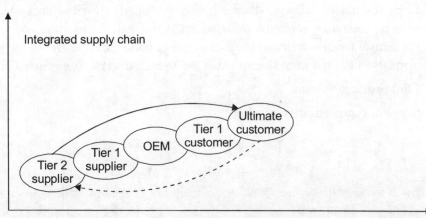

Integrated supply chain

6.9 Historically, businesses in the supply chain operated relatively independently of one another to create value for an ultimate customer. Independence was maintained by buffers of material, capacity and lead-times. This is represented in the 'Traditional' model shown above.

6.10 Market and competitive demands are now, however, **compressing lead times** and businesses are reducing inventories and excess capacity. Linkages between businesses in the supply chain must therefore become much tighter. This new condition is shown in the 'Integrated supply chain' model.

Case study link

Maintaining relationships with suppliers featured in the May 2002 case study. Loyalty and support for long term suppliers contrasted sharply with the view that the number of product lines and suppliers should be reduced, with suppliers being made to compete for their place in the value chain.

6.11 Monczka further claims that there seems to be increasing recognition that, in the future, it will be **whole supply chains** which will compete and not just individual firms. This will continue to have a great impact upon distribution methods.

KEY TERM

Supply chain management is about optimising the activities of companies working together to produce goods and services.

6.12 **Supply chain management (SCM)** is a means by which the firm aims to manage the chain from input resources to the consumer. It involves the following.

(a) **Reduction in the number of suppliers**

(b) **Reduction in customers served,** in some cases, for the sake of focus, and concentration of the company's resources on customers of high potential value

(c) **Price and stock co-ordination.** Firms co-ordinate their price and stock policies to avoid problems and bottlenecks caused by short-term surges in demand, such as promotions

(d) **Linked computer systems** - electronic data interchange saves on paperwork and warehousing expense

(e) **Early supplier involvement** in product development and component design

(f) **Logistics design.** Hewlett-Packard restructured its distribution system by enabling certain product components to be added at the distribution warehouse rather than at the central factory, for example user-manuals which are specific to the market (ie user manuals in French would be added at the French distribution centre)

(g) **Joint problem solving**

(h) **Supplier representative on site**

POINT TO NOTE

The aim is to co-ordinate the whole chain, from raw material suppliers to end customers. The chain should be considered as a **network** rather than a **pipeline** - a network of vendors support a network of customers, with third parties such as transport firms helping to link the companies. We look at networks again in Chapter 12.

Case example

The Hong Kong based export trading company, Li and Fung, takes the following approach to its manufacturing supply chain.

'Say we get an order from a European retailer to produce 10,000 garments. It's not a simple matter of our Korean office sourcing Korean products or our Indonesian office sourcing Indonesian products. For the customer we might decide to buy yarn from a Korean producer but have it woven and dyed in Taiwan. So we pick the yarn and ship it to Taiwan. The Japanese have the best zippers and buttons, but they manufacture them mostly in China. Okay, so we go to YKK, a big Japanese zipper manufacturer and we order the right zippers from their Chinese plants. Then we determine that, because of quotas and labour conditions, the best place to make the garments is Thailand. So we ship everything there. And because the customer needs quick delivery, we may divide the order across five factories in Thailand. Effectively, we are customising the value chain to best meet the customer's needs.

'Five weeks after we have received the order, 10,000 garments arrive on the shelves in Europe, all looking like they came from one factory with colours, for example, perfectly matched. Just think about the logistics and the co-ordination.

'This is a new type of value added, a truly global product that has never been seen before. The label may say "Made in Thailand", but it's not a Thai product. We dissect the manufacturing process and look for the best solution to each step. We're not asking which country can do the best job overall. Instead, we're pulling apart the value chain and optimising each step - and we're doing it globally... . The classic supply-chain manager in retailing is Marks & Spencer. They don't own any factories, but they have a huge team that goes into the factories and works with the management.'

(Harvard Business Review)

6.13 Managing the supply chain **varies from company to company**. A company such as Unilever will provide the same margarine to both Tesco and Sainsbury. The way in which the product is delivered, transactions are processed and other parts of the relationship are managed will be different since these competing supermarket chains have their own ways of operating. The focus will need to be on customer interaction, account management, after sales service and order processing.

6.14 A supplier that 'knows' what his customers want does not have to guess or wait until the customer places an order. It will be able to better plan its own delivery systems. The potential for using the **Internet** to allow customers and suppliers to acquire up to date information about forecast needs and delivery schedules is a very recent development, but one which is being used by an increasing number of companies.

6.15 The greatest changes in supply chain management have taken place in the implementation of **software applications**. Managers today have a wider choice of systems with quick implementation times - important in a competitive market where a new supply chain system is required. Supply chains at local, regional and global level are often managed simultaneously, via a standardised infrastructure that nevertheless allows for local adaptation where this is important.

Case example

- A leading European manufacturer has said: 'We must localise those part of our supply chain that face the customer and regionalise all other parts of our supply chain to lower costs and improve speed of operations'.

- PricewaterhouseCoopers ran full page newspaper advertisements promoting its supply chain consultancy services, which indicates the importance of supply chain management to most companies. The text of one such advertisement reads: 'When it comes to supply chain management, there's one universal truth: every customer is unique. What may be right for one, may not be for another.... We're working on some of the toughest supply chain problems all around the world. Reinventing strategy, optimising processes and applying new technologies intelligently. All to help companies improve their ability to operate globally and serve customers locally. With 150,000 people working in 50 different countries, we can make the world seem like a pretty small place'.

  This may contain more than its fair share of buzzwords, but it does illustrate the issues involved: the importance of individual customers, strategy and technology, and the ability of a large company to deliver services on a global basis because it has the resources.

6.16 As well as tactical issues, what might be the underlying strategic concerns?

(a) Close partnerships are needed with suppliers whose components are essential for the business unit.

(b) A firm should choose suppliers with a distinctive competence similar to its own. A firm selling 'cheap and cheerful' goods will want suppliers who are able to supply 'cheap and cheerful' subcomponents.

6.17 Problems with the **partnership approach** to supply chain management are these.

- Each partner needs to remain competitive in the long term
- There is a possible **loss of flexibility**
- The **relative bargaining power** may make partnership unnecessary
- Arguments about sharing profits

171 **BPP**
PUBLISHING

Unity Bicycles plc

(1) What do you think are UB's distinctive competences?

(2) How would you go about preparing a key customer analysis for UB?

(3) Comment on UB's distribution arrangements.

(4) Should UB build up a supply chain partnership with its former owner, MT?

(5) Does UB have a marketing orientation?

(6) How important is branding to UB in its various markets?

Chapter roundup

- A firm can make strategic gains from managing **stakeholder relationships**, such as those with customers and suppliers.

- To understand the importance of customers, it is necessary to have knowledge of some basic **marketing** ideas.

- This chapter looked at:
  ° definition of marketing
  ° the marketing concept
  ° products
  ° customers and buyer behaviour
  ° market segmentation
  ° the marketing mix
  ° product life cycle
  ° brands and brand management accounting

- The **customer base** is an asset to be invested in, as future benefits will come from existing customers, but not all customers are as important as others.

- **Key customer analysis** calls for six main areas of investigation in to customers, in order to identify which customers offer most profit.

- **Customer profitability analysis** is an analysis of the total sales revenue generated from a customer or customer group, less all the costs that are incurred in servicing that customer group.

- To analyse customer profitability successfully it may be necessary to structure **accounting information systems** to take account of the many factors by which customers can be analysed.

- **Relationship marketing** can be seen as the successor to mass marketing, and is the process by which information about the customer is consistently applied by the company when developing and delivering products and services. It contrasts with transaction marketing which is more one-way and focused upon a single sale.

- The **distribution channel**, the means of getting the goods to the customer, is of strategic importance. It often involves **contractual relationships** and **investment** in physical infrastructure.

- **Supply chain management** is about optimising the activities of companies working together to produce goods and services. Supply chain relationships are becoming increasingly more co-operative rather than adversarial.

Quick quiz

1 Give an example showing why there should be a correlation between employee and customer loyalty.

2 A (1) .... is anything that satisfies a (2) .... It is not a thing with (3) .... but a package of (4) ....

3 How does the Chartered Institute of Marketing define 'marketing'?

4   List the 7 Ps of the extended marketing mix.

5   Which of the statements below describes differentiated marketing?

    (a)   The company attempts to produce the ideal product for a single segment of the market (eg Rolls Royce cars for the wealthy).

    (b)   This policy is to produce a single product and hope to get as many customers as possible to buy it, ignoring segmentation entirely.

    (c)   The company attempts to introduce several product versions, each aimed at a different market segment. For example, manufacturers of soap powder make a number of different brands, marketed to different segments.

6   'Family branding' describes the use of different names for similar goods serving similar consumer tastes.

    ☐ True
    ☐ False

7   What does a marketing audit involve?

8   How can different costs arise with different customers? Give five examples.

9   Relationship marketing focuses on retention rather than attraction of customers.

    ☐ True
    ☐ False

10   What is the difference between the 'traditional' and the 'integrated' supply chain?

Answers to quick quiz

1   Reduced staff turnover in service firms can result in more repeat business because of improved service quality due to more knowledgeable staff.

2   (1) product (2) need/want (3) features (4) benefits

3   Marketing is the management process which identifies, anticipates and supplies customer requirements efficiently and profitably.

4   Product
    Price
    Place
    Promotion
    Physical evidence
    People
    Process

5   (c)

6   False. The definition given describes multi-branding.

7   A marketing audit involves a review of an organisation's products and markets, the marketing environment, and its marketing system and operations.

8   • Order size
    • Sales mix
    • Order processing
    • Transport costs (eg if JIT requires frequent deliveries)
    • Management time
    • Cash flow problems (eg increased overdraft interest) caused by slow payers
    • Order complexity (eg if the order has to be sent out in several stages)
    • Stockholding costs can relate to specify customers
    • The customer's negotiating strength.

9   True

10   With the 'traditional' model, businesses in the supply chain operated relatively independently of one another, with independence maintained by factors such as capacity limitations and lead times. Linkages are now much tighter, business pressures have compressed lead times and reduced stock holding and excess capacity. This new situation is shown by the 'integrated' model.

BPP PUBLISHING

Unity Bicycles plc review

Question 1. UB is good at several things. Obviously it shares the basic bike technology and it can manufacture cost-effectively, as can its competitors. UB is good at identifying new markets. UB also is good at high technology - if it can transfer its discoveries into commercially saleable products, that is a competence.

Question 2. A key customer analysis would be hard to glean from the data.

(a)   We could do an analysis of distributors and similar retail chains.

(b)   We could do an analysis of each market, to assess costs of transport distribution, exchange risk, the cost of consignment stock at dealers, credit etc.

Question 3. As for distribution, UB has paid some attention to infrastructure, but the whole spectrum of issues from warehouse siting to the credit given to retailers has not been addressed. Does UB need its dedicated fleet of lorries in the UK? There is no evidence of coherent planning.

Question 4. Any partnership with MT is likely, on the face of it, to be one-sided, as MT has many more customers. However, MT seems to be interested, so a closer relationship might be valuable. The fact that the personnel in the business are acquainted already might make such a relationship easy to establish.

Question 5. UB is fairly well focused on its customers' needs, hence the variety of products it makes and sells. UB recognises that customers have different needs in different markets.

Question 6. Branding is very important to UB, especially in Europe and the USA, where it positions itself on the basis of quality. It may become important in Russia, if there is a continued demand for Western goods.

Now try the question below from the Exam Question Bank

Question to try	Level	Marks	Time
5	Exam	25	45 mins

Part C
Position appraisal and analysis

Chapter 7

RESOURCE ANALYSIS

Topic list	Syllabus reference	Ability required
1 The position audit	(iii)	Evaluation/analysis
2 Resources and limiting factors	(iii)	Evaluation/analysis
3 Converting resources: the value chain	(iii)	Comprehension/evaluation
4 Outputs: the product portfolio	(iii)	Evaluation/analysis
5 New products	(iii)	Evaluation/analysis
6 Competences and critical success factors	(iii)	Evaluation/analysis
7 Benchmarking	(iii)	Analysis/evaluation

Introduction

In earlier chapters we reviewed both the general and competitive environments. In this chapter we examine some of the key aspects of the organisation's current **position**.

A **resource audit** (sections 1 and 2) identifies any gaps in resources and limiting factors on organisational activity.

Value chain analysis (section 3) identifies how the business adds value to the resources it obtains, and how it deploys these resources to satisfy customers.

We then review the organisation's current outputs, its **product portfolio**, in sections 4 and 5.

A **competence** (section 6) is a skill which the organisation has which can ensure a 'fit' between the environment and the organisation's capability.

Competences are difficult to assess in isolation, so some form of comparison is needed. **Benchmarking** (section 7) is now common, and involves comparing an organisation's processes with those of best practice, such as those employed by an exemplar organisation, which may be an organisation in a different industry. Such an exercise will highlight areas where improvements can be made, notably in the value chain.

Learning outcomes covered in this chapter

- **Evaluate** and **produce** a comprehensive review of performance, resources and capabilities
- **Evaluate** the product portfolio of the organisation and **advise** on appropriate action
- **Produce** a benchmarking exercise and **evaluate** the outcomes
- **Identify** and **evaluate** an organisation's value chain and the accounting implications thereof

Syllabus content covered in this chapter

- Auditing an organisation's resources; considering intangible resources, products, services, people, structure, finance, stakeholder relations and systems
- The product portfolio, product life cycle and BCG analysis
- Benchmarking performance with best practice organisations
- Value chain analysis and the implications for the organisation and the accounting system

1 THE POSITION AUDIT 5/02

KEY TERM

Position audit is 'part of the planning process which examines the current state of the entity in respect of:

- Resources of tangible and intangible assets and finance
- Products, brands and markets
- Operating systems (such as production and distribution)
- Internal organisation
- Current results
- Returns to stockholders'. *(CIMA Official Terminology)*

It is worth learning this list by heart.

2 RESOURCES AND LIMITING FACTORS 5/02

2.1 A resource audit is an internal review. The Ms model categorises the factors as follows.

Resource	Example
Machinery	Age. Condition. Utilisation rate. Value. Replacement. Technologically up-to-date? Cost. Patents. Goodwill. Brands.
Make-up	Culture and structure.
Management	Size. Skills. Loyalty. Career progression. Structure.
Management information	Ability to generate and disseminate ideas. Innovation. Information systems.
Markets	Products and customers
Materials	Source. Suppliers and partnering. Waste. New materials. Cost. Availability. Future provision
Men	Number. Skills. Wage costs. Proportion of total costs. Efficiency. Labour turnover. Industrial relations
Methods	How are activities carried out? Outsourcing, JIT.
Money	Credit and turnover periods. Cash surpluses/ deficits. Short term and long term finance. Gearing levels.

2.2 **Resources are of no value unless they are organised into systems,** and so a resource audit should go on to consider how well or how badly resources have been utilised, and whether the organisation's systems are effective and efficient. This includes the quality and timeliness of information available to managers

Exam focus point

The Ms model was specifically examined in May 2002 as it applied to a homecare support service company.

Limiting factors

2.3 Every organisation operates under resource **constraints**.

> **KEY TERM**
>
> A **limiting factor** or **key factor** is 'anything which limits the activity of an entity. An entity seeks to optimise the benefit it obtains from the limiting factor.
>
> Examples are a shortage of supply of a resource or a restriction on sales demand at a particular price. *(CIMA Official Terminology)*

Examples

- A shortage of production capacity
- A limited number of key personnel, such as salespeople with technical knowledge
- A restricted distribution network
- Too few managers with knowledge about finance, or overseas markets
- Inadequate research design resources to develop new products or services
- A poor system of strategic intelligence
- Lack of money
- A lack of staff who are adequately trained

2.4 Once the limiting factor has been identified, the planners should:

- In the short term, make best use of the resources available.
- Try to reduce the limitation in the long term.

Resource use

2.5 Resource use is concerned with the **efficiency** with which resources are used, and the **effectiveness** of their use in achieving the planning objectives of the business.

> **KEY TERMS**
>
> (a) **Efficiency** is 'how well the resources have been utilised irrespective of the purpose for which they have been employed'.
>
> (b) **Effectiveness** is: 'whether the resources have been deployed in the best possible way'.

Case example

A key resource is 'capital'. British and US firms have been accused of not making enough capital investment, in comparison with businesses in the Tiger economies. But investment has to be productive: much of the late 1980s investment boom in Japan resulted in massive over-capacity. Other investment capital was wasted in speculative property development.

American firms score highly on capital productivity. In other words, they get the best return from the capital invested.

BPP PUBLISHING

3 CONVERTING RESOURCES: THE VALUE CHAIN 11/01

3.1 The **value chain** model of corporate activities, developed by Michael Porter, offers a bird's eye view of the firm and what it does. Competitive advantage, says Porter, arises out of the way in which firms organise and perform **activities**.

Activities

> **KEY TERM**
>
> **Activities** are the means by which a firm creates value in its products. (They are sometimes referred to as **value activities**.)

3.2 Activities incur costs, and, in combination with other activities, provide a product or service which earns revenue.

3.3 EXAMPLE

Let us explain this point by using the example of a **restaurant**. A restaurant's activities can be divided into buying food, cooking it, and serving it (to customers). There is no reason, in theory, why the customers should not do all these things themselves, at home. The customer however, is not only prepared to **pay for someone else** to do all this but also **pays more than the cost of** the resources (food, wages etc). The ultimate value a firm creates is measured by the amount customers are willing to pay for its products or services above the cost of carrying out value activities. A firm is profitable if the realised value to customers exceeds the collective cost of performing the activities.

(a) Customers '**purchase**' value, which they measure by comparing a firm's products and services with similar offerings by competitors.

(b) The business '**creates**' value by carrying out its activities either more efficiently than other businesses, or combine them in such a way as to provide a unique product or service.

Question 1

Outline different ways in which the restaurant can 'create' value.

Answer

Here are some ideas. Each of these options is a way of organising the activities of buying, cooking and serving food in a way that customers will value.

(a) It can become more efficient, by automating the production of food, as in a fast food chain.

(b) The chef can develop commercial relationships with growers, so he or she can obtain the best quality fresh produce.

(c) The chef can specialise in a particular type of cuisine (eg Nepalese, Korean).

(d) The restaurant can be sumptuously decorated for those customers who value 'atmosphere' and a sense of occasion, in addition to a restaurant's purely gastronomic pleasures.

(e) The restaurant can serve a particular type of customer (eg celebrities).

3.4 Porter (in *Competitive Advantage*) grouped the various activities of an organisation into a value chain.

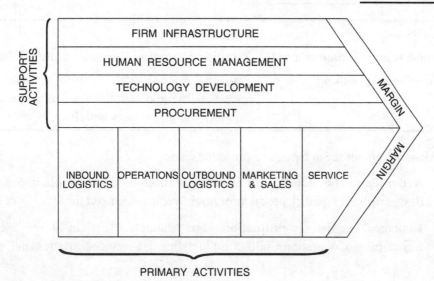

PRIMARY ACTIVITIES

The **margin** is the excess the customer is prepared to **pay** over the **cost** to the firm of obtaining resource inputs and providing value activities.

> **KEY TERM**
>
> The **value chain** is 'the sequence of business activities by which, in the perspective of the end user, value is added to the products or services produced by an organisation'.
>
> (CIMA *Official Terminology*)

Activity

3.5 **Primary activities** are directly related to production, sales, marketing, delivery and service.

	Comment
Inbound logistics	Receiving, handling and storing inputs to the production system (ie warehousing, transport, stock control etc).
Operations	Convert resource inputs into a final product. Resource inputs are not only materials. 'People' are a 'resource' especially in service industries.
Outbound logistics	Storing the product and its distribution to customers: packaging, warehousing, testing etc.
Marketing and sales	Informing customers about the product, persuading them to buy it, and enabling them to do so: advertising, promotion etc.
After sales service	Installing products, repairing them, upgrading them, providing spare parts and so forth.

3.6 **Support activities** provide purchased inputs, human resources, technology and infrastructural functions to support the primary activities.

Activity	Comment
Procurement	Acquire the resource inputs to the primary activities (eg purchase of materials, subcomponents equipment).
Technology development	Product design, improving processes and/or resource utilisation.

Activity	Comment
Human resource management	Recruiting, training, developing and rewarding people.
Management planning	Planning, finance, quality control: Porter believes they are crucially important to an organisation's strategic capability in all primary activities.

3.7 **Linkages** connect the activities of the value chain.

(a) **Activities in the value chain affect one another**. For example, more costly product design or better quality production might reduce the need for after-sales service.

(b) **Linkages require co-ordination**. For example, Just In Time requires smooth functioning of operations, outbound logistics and service activities such as installation.

Value system

3.8 Activities that add value do not stop at the organisation's **boundaries**. For example, when a restaurant serves a meal, the quality of the ingredients - although they are chosen by the cook - is determined by the grower. The grower has added value, and the grower's success in growing produce of good quality is as important to the customer's ultimate satisfaction as the skills of the chef. A firm's value chain is connected to what Porter calls a **value system**.

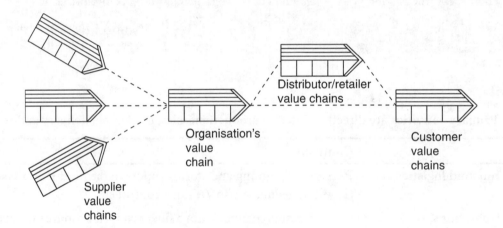

3.9 **Using the value chain.** A firm can secure competitive advantage by:

- Inventing new or better ways to do activities
- Combining activities in new or better ways
- Managing the linkages in its own value chain
- Managing the linkages in the value system

Question 2

Sana Sounds is a small record company. Representatives from Sana Sounds scour music clubs for new bands to promote. Once a band has signed a contract (with Sana Sounds) it makes a recording. The recording process is subcontracted to one of a number of recording studio firms which Sana Sounds uses regularly. (At the moment Sana Sounds is not large enough to invest in its own equipment and studios.) Sana Sounds also subcontracts the production of records and CDs to a number of manufacturing companies. Sana Sounds then distributes the disks to selected stores, and engages in any promotional activities required.

What would you say were the activities in Sana Sounds' value chain?

Answer

Sana Sounds is involved in the record industry from start to finish. Although recording and CD manufacture are contracted out to external suppliers, this makes no difference to the fact that these activities are part of Sana Sounds' own value chain. Sana Sounds earns its money by managing the whole set of activities. If the company grows then perhaps it will acquire its own recording studios.

3.10 The value chain is an important analytical tool because it helps management:

- To see the business as a whole
- To identify potential sources of competitive advantage
- To suggest strategies
- To analyse competitors

Exam focus point

A question on the November 2001 paper required students to apply value chain analysis to the activities of a university.

3.11 **The value chain models the process by which organisations convert inputs into outputs.** If the purpose of this process is the creation of value, then the accountant should be able to contribute to the **strategic analysis of costs**.

Case example

The Department of Trade and Industry in the UK produced a 'Value Added Scoreboard' in May 2002, focusing on a particular measure of company output. A company's basic 'value added' is calculated by taking its sales and subtracting the cost of buying materials, components and services. When this is divided by the number of employees (or their hours worked), this indicates how good a company is at turning ideas and goods into services and products that customers will buy.

The 300 businesses in the report have an average annual added value per employee of £49,900, but value added ratios differ widely between different sectors. Oil and gas, for example, score very highly (average value added per employee of £191,500) for the following reasons.

- Cheap raw materials
- Uses more capital equipment than labour
- Workers are highly skilled
- Tight control over distribution, and therefore pricing

Retailing, by contrast, is a low scorer, with £21,300 per employee.

- Virtually all goods sold are bought-in from suppliers
- Employees are numerous but low-skilled
- Little intellectual capital

Failure of traditional costing

3.12 A summary of the failure of traditional costing systems is outlined in the table below.

	Traditional costing systems	*Value chain cost analysis*
Focus (	Manufacturing operations	Customers Value perceptions
Cost objects	Products Functions Expense heads	Value-creating activities Product attributes
Organisational focus	Cost and responsibility centres	Strategic business units (SBUs) Value-creating activities
Linkages	1 Largely ignored 2 Cost allocations and transfer prices used to reflect interdependencies	Recognised and maximised
Cost drivers	Simple volume measures	Strategic decisions
Accuracy	High apparent precision	Low precision Indicative answers

Case example

The practical application of value chain cost analysis can be seen with the following illustration which relates each element to the example of a supermarket's operations.

	Value chain cost analysis	*Practical example*
Focus	Customers	The supermarket is keenly focused on the customers as the key source of value. Specific customers are targeted through marketing campaigns and 'customer delight' is sought. All retailers are being forced by competition to invest more in customer service, systems and price.
Cost objects	Value-creating activities and profit attributes	Activities which promote customer loyalty and bigger spend are investigated and developed. For example, giving a 10% discount to new mothers could increase sales and profit margin above the cost of the discounts given. Self-scanning technology increases sales in the stores where it is introduced.
Organisation focus	SBUs	Supermarkets are organised into trading units corresponding with commodities sold eg meat and dairy, grocery, beers, wines and spirits, non-foods etc. These, along with other departments such as marketing, distribution, finance, PR etc have their own performance targets. Cont...
Linkages	Recognised and maximised	Supplier and customer relationships are nurtured. Suppliers are ranked for their ability to meet the supermarket's demand and customers are constantly reminded via instore promotions of the supermarket's commitment to giving them value.
Cost drivers	Strategic decisions	These are prompted either by competitor activity (eg price cuts) or new business initiatives such as investment in new technology or development of overseas markets. Target rates of return are required, often also measured in terms of the required sales uplift and related margin to justify an activity.

	Value chain cost analysis	Practical example
Accuracy	Indicative answers	A wealth of detail on sales and margin by product is collected and individual customer spends are analysed.
		Much importance is also attached to less quantifiable measures such as customer surveys, and level of customer complaints. They may highlight areas where the business is falling down and losing customers to rivals.

How the value chain drives costs

3.13 What might influence the costs of the value chain?

(a) **Structural cost drivers** are major 'strategic choices made by the firm which determine its underlying cost base'.

- **Scale** of operations, capacity etc, giving rise to economies or diseconomies of scale

- **Scope**: to what extent is the firm vertically integrated?

- **Experience**: has the firm climbed the learning curve?

- **Technology** used in the value chain

- **Complexity** and breadth of product range

(b) Management issues influence how well a firm manages the value chain in operation terms.

- Capacity utilisation
- Product and process design
- Learning opportunities offered by continuous improvement programmes
- How well external linkages (eg liaison with suppliers) are exploited

Concentrating on value

3.14 Firms might create a more **outward-looking focus** in their costing systems as follows.

(a) Most products are a collection of benefits, which is why customers buy them. Ultimately, the provision of customer benefits is the real cost driver of the business, and it should be possible to work backwards, as it were, from these customer benefits to the underlying costs.

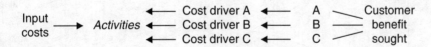

(b) For different products, it should be possible to identify the customer's perception of the value of the benefit and the cost of providing it.

3.15 For the accountant, a problem with this approach is:

- A lack of precision in the data
- The inevitable subjectivity in deciding what customers value as a benefit

BPP
PUBLISHING

4   OUTPUTS: THE PRODUCT PORTFOLIO   Pilot paper

The product life cycle

4.1   Many firms make a number of different products or services. Each product or service has its own financial, marketing and risk characteristics. The combination of products or services influences the attractiveness and profitability of the firm.

> **KEY TERM**
>
> **Product life cycle.** The period which begins with the initial product specification, and ends with the withdrawal from the market of both the product and its support. It is characterised by defined stages including research, development, introduction, maturity, decline and abandonment.   (CIMA *Official Terminology*)

4.2   The profitability and sales of a product can be expected to change over time. The **product life cycle** is an attempt to recognise distinct stages in a product's sales history. Marketing managers distinguish between the following.

(a) **Product class:** this is a broad category of product, such as cars, washing machines, newspapers, also referred to as the generic product.

(b) **Product form:** within a product class there are different forms that the product can take, for example five-door hatchback cars or two-seater sports cars, twin tub or front loading automatic washing machines, national daily newspapers or weekly local papers etc.

(c) **Brand:** the particular type of the product form (for example Ford Escort, Vauxhall Astra; Financial Times, Daily Mail, Sun etc).

4.3   The product life cycle applies in differing degrees to each of the three cases. A product-class (eg cars) may have a long maturity stage, and a particular make or brand might have an erratic life cycle (eg Rolls Royce) or not. Product forms however tend to conform to the 'classic' life cycle pattern, commonly described by a curve as follows.

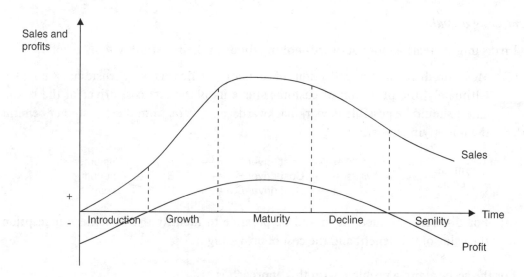

4.4   **Introduction**

- A new product takes time to find acceptance by would-be purchasers and there is a slow growth in sales. Unit costs are high because of low output and expensive sales promotion.

- There may be early teething troubles with production technology.

- The product for the time being is a loss-maker.

4.5 Growth

- If the new product gains market acceptance, sales will eventually rise more sharply and the product will start to make profits.

- Competitors are attracted. As sales and production rise, unit costs fall.

4.6 Maturity. The rate of sales growth slows down and the product reaches a period of maturity which is probably the longest period of a successful product's life. Most products on the market will be at the mature stage of their life. Profits are good.

4.7 Decline. Eventually, sales will begin to decline so that there is over-capacity of production in the industry. Severe competition occurs, profits fall and some producers leave the market. The remaining producers seek means of prolonging the product life by modifying it and searching for new market segments. Many producers are reluctant to leave the market, although some inevitably do because of falling profits.

Exam focus point

The life cycle concept can also be applied to an entire industry, not merely confined to products within it. This forms a question on the pilot paper.

The relevance of the product life cycle to strategic planning

4.8 In reviewing outputs, planners should assess, if possible:

(a) The **stage of its life cycle** that any product has reached.

(b) The **product's remaining life**, ie how much longer the product will contribute to profits.

(c) How **urgent is the need to innovate,** to develop new and improved products? New and innovative products can lower entry barriers to existing industries and markets, especially if new technology is involved.

(d) The interests of the company are best met with a balanced product portfolio. Managers therefore must plan when to introduce new products, how best to extend the life of mature ones and when to abandon those in decline.

Difficulties of the product life cycle concept

4.9 (a) **Recognition.** How can managers recognise where a product stands in its life cycle?

(b) **Not always true.** The S-shaped curve of a product life cycle does not always occur in practice. Some products have no maturity phase, and go straight from growth to decline. Some never decline if they are marketed competitively.

(c) **Changeable.** Strategic decisions can change or extend a product's life cycle.

(d) **Competition varies** in different industries. The financial markets are an example of markets where there is a tendency for competitors to copy the leader very quickly, so that competition has built up well ahead of demand.

Portfolio planning: the Boston Matrix

4.10 **Portfolio planning** analyses the current position of an organisation's products in their markets, and the state of growth or decline in each of those markets.

Market share, market growth and cash generation: the Boston classification

> ### KEY TERM
>
> **Market share:** 'One entity's sale of a product or service in a specified market expressed as a percentage of total sales by all entities offering that product or service to the market. A planning tool and a performance assessment ratio'. *(CIMA Official Terminology)*

4.11 The **Boston Consulting Group** (BCG) developed a matrix (The Boston Matrix), based on empirical research, which classifies a company's products in terms of potential cash generation and cash expenditure requirements.

> ### KEY TERM
>
> **Boston Consulting Group matrix.** 'A representation of an organisation's product or service offerings which shows the value of each product sales expressed in relation to the growth rate of the market served and the market share held. The objective of the matrix is to assist in the allocation of funds to projects.' *(CIMA Official Terminology)*

		Market share	
		High	*Low*
Market growth	*High*	Stars	Question marks
	Low	Cash cows	Dogs

4.12 The **Boston Matrix**

(a) **Stars.** In the short term, these require capital expenditure in excess of the cash they generate, in order to maintain their market position, but promise high returns in the future.

(b) In due course, stars will become **cash cows**. Cash cows need very little capital expenditure and generate high levels of cash income. Cash cows can be used to finance the stars.

(c) **Question marks.** Do the products justify considerable capital expenditure in the hope of increasing their market share, or should they be allowed to 'die' quietly as they are squeezed out of the expanding market by rival products?

(d) **Dogs.** They may be ex-cash cows that have now fallen on hard times. Dogs should be allowed to die or should be killed off. Although they will show only a modest net cash outflow, or even a modest net cash inflow, they are 'cash traps' which tie up funds and provide a poor return on investment.

Question 3

The marketing manager of Juicy Drinks Ltd has invited you in for a chat. Juicy Drinks Ltd provides fruit juices to a number of supermarket chains, which sell them under their own label. 'We've got a large number of products, of course. Our freshly squeezed orange juice is doing fine - it sells in huge quantities. Although margins are low, we have sufficient economies of scale to do very nicely in this market. We've got advanced production and bottling equipment and long term contracts with some major growers. No problems there. We also sell freshly squeezed pomegranate juice: customers loved it in the tests, but producing the stuff at the right price is a major hassle: all the seeds get in the way. We hope it will be a winner, once we get the production right and start converting customers to it. After all the market for exotic fruit juices generally is expanding fast.'

What sort of products, according to the Boston classification, are described here?

Answer

(a) Orange juice is a cash cow

(b) Pomegranate juice is a question mark, which the company wants to turn into a star.

Exam focus point

It is possible to apply the portfolio approach to a firm in several different businesses. A firm may operate in a low-tech industry but be considering entering a high-tech business. In a diversified business, each industry has different cash characteristics, in a similar way to products in a portfolio.

4.13 The product life cycle concept can be added to a market share/market growth classification of products, as follows.

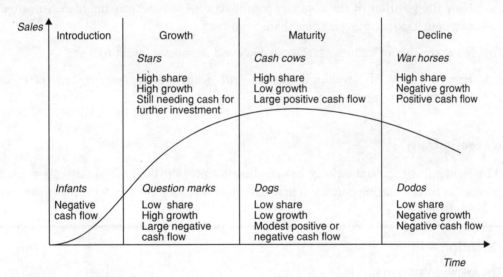

Competitiveness of products

4.14 Johnson and Scholes cite a variation on the Boston matrix. **General Electric's Business Screen** compares the following.

(a) The **competitive position** of products compared with rival products in the market.

(b) The **strength of attraction** that the product has in general for customers (for whatever reasons).

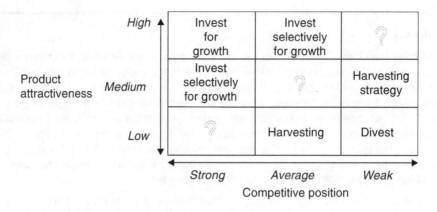

4.15 In the matrix above 'invest for growth' is self-explanatory. 'Harvest' means that the firm should invest no more, but earn what profits it can before quitting.

Problems with portfolio planning

Exam focus point

Portfolio planning, whether by means of market growth/market share analysis or product life cycle analysis, is something that you might be called on to apply yourself in an examination question. It is a useful approach to the analysis of a firm's product-market mix.

4.16 It is difficult to convert these analyses into a planning technique for deciding the following:

(a) How the position of the company's products in its markets should be **improved** - ie how much extra or less market share to go for.

(b) What the **mix** of infants, stars, cash cows and warhorses ought to be.

(c) How a policy of developing infants into stars and stars into cash cows can be implemented in **practice**.

Product profitability

4.17 The management accountant may be called upon to review the profitability of a product or a product line. As a starting point, you may have to produce forecasts. Try the following exercise.

Question 4

The following data relates to Product X

	Year	1996/97	1997/98	1998/99	1999/2000
(a)	Total market (units)	100,000,000	140,000,000	170,000,000	180,000,000
(b)	Market share	5%	8%	10%	9%
(c)	Sales volume (units)	5,000,000	11,200,000	17,000,000	16,200,000
(d)	Average sales price	£4.0	£4.4	£5.0	£6.0
(e)	Average variable cost	£2.0	£2.3	£3.0	£3.6
(f)	Unit contribution	£2.0	£2.1	£2.0	£2.4
(g)	Total sales revenue	20,000	49,280	85,000	97,200
(h)	Total contribution	10,000	23,520	34,000	38,880
(i)	Production overhead	1,000	3,500	6,000	7,500
(j)	Selling costs	2,000	2,500	5,000	6,000
(k)	Advertising	1,500	3,000	5,000	6,000

Year	1996/97	1997/98	1998/99	1999/2000
(l) Distribution	1,500	3,000	5,000	6,500
(m) Other marketing costs	1,000	2,000	4,000	5,000
(n) Profit	3,000	9,520	9,000	7,880

From information about the product background, it might be possible to estimate the future trend of the total market and the market share of the company's own product, and to relate the trend in profitability to turnover, contribution and overhead allocation. You might be required to model a number of possible outcomes.

If there is no change in the marketing strategy for a particular product it ought to be possible to project future sales and profits using linear or multiple regression analysis techniques, or possibly simpler analysis techniques projecting future trends. In 2000/2001, the following assumptions could be made.

(a) Total market. Might increase to, say 190,000,000 units, at most. Little further growth is expected. Market share will remain 9%. (The firm with the biggest market share has 12% - there are many small firms in the industry).

(b) Price inflation of sales revenues and variable costs is anticipated to be 5%, leading to a unit contribution of £2.52.

(c) Profit after overheads, advertising etc is expected to be about £9,000.

What conclusions might you draw?

Answer

If this analysis were realistic, you might well conclude that the product is a cash cow in a maturing market, and plans would presumably be formulated for the product to try to ensure that the sales target of 17.1m units, and the sales price and marketing costs targets are achievable. However, in 1996/97 it looks as if it might have been hovering between being a question mark and a star. 5% is high, but the product has increased its share by higher expenditure on advertising.

Direct product profitability (DPP)

4.18 An example of how management accounting techniques are used in practice is **direct product profitability**. This is a technique to analyse the profit on each individual product line, to arrive at relative profitabilities of different products.

> **KEY TERM**
>
> **Direct product profitability** (DPP). Technique used mainly by retailers to assess the profitability of a product or product line taking into account purchase cost, delivery cost, stock turnover, shelf space etc.

4.19 DPP has grown primarily from the need for manufacturers to encourage retailers to place new products onto their shelves. Supermarkets analyse the direct profitability of every branded and non-branded product they sell. This helps them decide on what ranges to present in store and also provides a focus for individual marketing initiatives. The profitability of entire commodity groups is presented after taking account of factors in addition to cost, such as supplier discounts and wastage levels.

4.20 It is useful to analyse how DPP can be used in practice. We can take the limiting factor to be shelf space in this example.

	Product		
	X	Y	Z
Selling price	£1.50	£1.25	£1.30
Purchase cost	£1.00	£0.80	£1.00
Contribution	£0.50	£0.45	£0.30

	Product		
	X	*Y*	*Z*
Contribution % of sales price	33%	36%	23%
Shelf space per unit	15 cm^2	9 cm^2	12 cm^2
Contribution per cm^2	3.3p	5p	2.5p

4.21 This would imply that Y was the most profitable for the retailer: however this ignores stock turnover. In other words, if sales volumes of Y are higher than for X or Z, the product makes a higher contribution in total. Let us add sales volumes into the calculation and estimate as to how much shelf space the product takes up.

	Product		
	X	*Y*	*Z*
Contribution per product	£0.50	£0.45	£0.30
Total shelf space	750 cm^2	600 cm^2	$1,200 \text{ cm}^2$
Weekly sales volume	30	20	60
Contribution per cm^2 per week	$\dfrac{50\text{p} \times 30}{750} = 2\text{p}$	$\dfrac{45\text{p} \times 20}{600} = 1.5\text{p}$	$\dfrac{30\text{p} \times 60}{1,200} = 1.5\text{p}$

4.22 This analysis, based on sales volume suggests that for the retailer X is the better bet. Why might this be so?

(a) **Stock turnover.** The manufacturer of X might offer to replenish the shelves twice a week, thereby halving the amount of space needed to support the same sales volume. This increases the contribution per unit of scarce resource.

(b) **Product size,** as indicated, is a reason why the unit contribution might differ. This is why packaging decisions can, from the retailer's viewpoint, affect a product's attractiveness.

4.23 This example demonstrates how it is necessary for the management accountant to obtain sufficient information before a meaningful analysis can be carried out. Simple information on cm^2 occupied per unit was insufficient. Sales volumes, total shelf space required and probably in some cases additional direct costs (such as handling, administration) all need to be taken into account.

4.24 The problems with DPP are these.

(a) Expenditure supporting a brand can be spread over a number of different individual products, and from the **manufacturer's** point of view it might not be a simple matter to allocate this expenditure properly.

(b) **Cross-subsidisation** is a feature of many product strategies. An example is provided by computer games.

  (i) The hardware (eg the games console) may be priced relatively cheaply:

  - To deter competitors (raising entry barriers)
  - To encourage customers to buy

  (ii) The software, or games which are run, will be priced relatively expensively, to recoup some of the cost. Also, barriers to entry will exist as the manufacturer will own patents, have exclusive distribution deals etc, and there will be a switching cost, of course.

5 NEW PRODUCTS

5.1 The development of new products might be considered an important aspect of a firm's competitive and marketing strategies.

(a) New and innovative products can lower entry barriers to existing industries and markets, if new technology is involved.

(b) The interests of the company are best met with a balanced product portfolio. Managers therefore must plan when to introduce new products, how best to extend the life of mature ones and when to abandon those in decline.

5.2 A strategic issue managers must consider is their approach to new product development.

(a) **Leader strategy.** Do they intend to gain competitive advantage by operating at the leading edge of new developments - in which case there are significant implications for the R&D activity and the likely length of products life cycles within the portfolio.

(b) **Follower strategy.** Alternatively they can be more pro-active, adopt a follower strategy, which involves lower costs and less emphasis on the R & D activity. It sacrifices early rewards of innovation, but avoids its risks. A follower might have to license certain technologies from a leader (as is the case with many consumer electronics companies).

5.3 A matrix of new product strategies and new market strategies can be set out as follows.

	Product		
	No technological change	*Improved technology*	*New technology*
Market unchanged	-	*Reformulation* A new balance between price/quality has to be formulated	*Replacement* The new technology replaces the old
Market strengthened (ie new demand from same customers)	*Remerchandising* The product is sold in a new way - eg by re-packaging	*Improved product* Sales growth to existing customers sought on the strength of product improvements	*Product line extension* The new product is added to the existing product line to increase total demand
New market	*New use* By finding a new use for the existing product, new customers are found	*Market extension* New customers sought on the strength of product improvements	*Diversification*

What are new products?

5.4 Booz, Allen and Hamilton identified the following categories in a survey of 700 firms.

- New to the world   10%
- New product lines   20%
- Additions to product line   26%
- Repositionings   7%
- Improvements/revisions   26%
- Cost reductions   11%

BPP PUBLISHING

5.5 The **failure rate of new products** is very high. The *Economist Pocket Marketing* describes a museum (in New York) of failed products. These include yoghurt shampoo, deodorant tablets, and egg coffee.

New product development plan

5.6 New products should only be taken to an advanced development stage if they fit the criteria of:

- Adequate demand
- Compatibility with existing marketing ability
- Compatibility with existing production ability.

Initial assessment

5.7 The concept for the new product could be tested on potential customers to obtain their reactions. Here are some examples.

(a) New designs for wallpaper. When innovative new designs are tested on potential customers it is often found that they are conditioned by traditional designs and are dismissive of new design ideas.

(b) New ideas for chocolate confectionery have the opposite problem. Potential customers typically say they like the new concept (because most people like chocolate bars) but when the new product is launched it is not successful because people continue to buy old favourites.

Business analysis

5.8 A thorough **business analysis** is made for each product idea, projecting future sales and revenues, giving a description of the product so as to provide costs of production, providing estimates of sales promotion and advertising costs, the resources required, profits and ROI.

Development

5.9 Here, money is invested to produce a working **prototype** of the product which can be tried by customers. This stage is also very useful to ensure that the product could be produced in sufficient quantities at the right price if it were to be launched.

5.10 Quality is an important policy consideration. Customers do not necessarily want the best quality of goods, and there may be potential in a market dominated by established brand names for a lower quality article.

Testing, launch

5.11 The purpose of test marketing is to obtain information about how consumers react to the product - will they buy it, and if so, will they buy it again and again?

5.12 A **test market** involves testing a new consumer product in selected areas which are thought to be 'representative' of the total market. In the selected areas, the firm will attempt to distribute the product through the same types of sales outlets it plans to use in the full market launch, and also to use the advertising and promotion plans it intends to use in the full market.

Commercialisation

5.13 Finally the product is developed for full launch. This involves ensuring that the product is in the right place at the right time, and that customers know about it.

The management accountant's role

5.14 There are two techniques which the management accountant can use in new product design.

(a) **Functional cost analysis** involves analysing what a product is supposed to do: its function. These functions become the focus of the design and also of the costing exercise.

(b) **Value analysis** is similar to functional cost analysis but is devoted to cost reduction, by establishing exactly what the customer wants and removing superfluous features.

6 COMPETENCES AND CRITICAL SUCCESS FACTORS

6.1 A strategic approach involves identifying a firm's **competences**. 'Members of organisations develop judgements about what they think the company can do well - its core competence.' These competences may derive from:

- **Experience** in making and marketing a product or service
- The talents and potential of individuals in the organisation
- The **quality of co-ordination**

6.2 The **distinctive competence** of an organisation is what it does well, or better, than its rivals. Andrews says that, for a relatively undifferentiated product like cement, the ability of a maker to 'run a truck fleet more effectively' than its competitors will give it competitive strengths (if, for example, it can satisfy orders quickly).

6.3 Some competences are necessary to stay in business at all. For a restaurant, catering is a core competence; for a manufacturing firm it is not.

6.4 **Tests for identifying a core competence.**

(a) **It provides potential access to a wide variety of markets**. GPS of France developed a 'core competence' in 'one-hour' processing, enabling it to process films and build reading glasses in one hour.

(b) **It contributes significantly to the value enjoyed by the customer.** For example, in GPS in (a) above, the waiting time restriction was very important.

(c) **It should be hard for a competitor to copy,** if it is technically complex, involves specialised processes, involves complex interrelationships between different people in the organisation or is hard to define.

Preparing resource plans

Planning issues: critical success factors

6.5 Competences can be related to critical success factors. The relationship between competences and CSFs is this.

- A **competence** is what an organisation has or is able to do
- A **CSF** is what is necessary to achieve an objective

7 **BENCHMARKING**

> **KEY TERM**
>
> **Benchmarking.** 'The establishment, through data gathering, of targets and comparators, through whose use relative levels of performance (and particularly areas of underperformance) can be identified. By the adoption of identified best practices it is hoped that performance will improve. Types of benchmarking include:
>
> - *Internal benchmarking.* A method of comparing one operating unit or function with another within the same industry.
>
> - *Functional benchmarking.* Internal functions are compared with those of the best external practitioners of those functions, regardless of the industry they are in (also known as operational benchmarking or generic benchmarking).
>
> - *Competitive benchmarking.* Information is gathered about direct competitors, through techniques such as reverse engineering
>
> - *Strategic benchmarking.* A type of competitive benchmarking aimed at strategic action and organisational change. (CIMA *Official Terminology*)

7.1 Benchmarking can be divided into stages.

- **Set objectives** and determine the areas to benchmark
- Establish **key performance measures**
- **Select organisations** to study
- **Measure** own and others' performance
- **Compare** performances
- Design and implement **improvement programme**
- **Monitor** improvements

7.2 Johnson and Scholes set out questions that should be asked when carrrying out a benchmarking exercise as part of a wider strategic review.

- **Why** are these products or services provided at all?
- Why are they provided **in that particular way**?
- What are the examples of **best practice** elsewhere?
- How should activities be **reshaped** in the light of these comparisons?

7.3 They see three levels of benchmarking.

Level of benchmarking	Through	Examples of measures
Resources	Resource audit	Quantity of resources • revenue/employee • capital intensity Quality of resources • Qualifications of employees • Age of machinery • Uniqueness (eg patents)

Level of benchmarking	Through	Examples of measures
Competences in separate activities	Analysing activities	Sales calls per salesperson Output per employee Materials wastage
Competences in linked activities	Analysing overall performances	Market share Profitability Productivity

Exam focus point

You could use the information in paragraphs 7.1 - 7.3 as the framework for an answer to a question about carrying out a benchmarking exercise. Such a question appeared in the May 2001 paper.

7.4 When selecting an appropriate **benchmark basis,** companies should ask themselves the following questions.

(a) Is it possible and easy to obtain reliable competitor information?

(b) Is there any wide discrepancy between different internal divisions?

(c) Can similar processes be identified in non-competing environments and are these non competing companies willing to co-operate?

(d) Is best practice operating in a similar environmental setting?

(e) What is our timescale?

(f) Do the chosen companies have similar objectives and strategies?

7.5 Benchmarking has the following advantages.

(a) **Position audit**. Benchmarking can assess a firm's existing position, and provide a basis for establishing standards of performance.

(b) The comparisons are **carried out by the managers** who have to live with any changes implemented as a result of the exercise.

(c) Benchmarking **focuses** on improvement in key areas and sets targets which are challenging but evidently 'achievable'.

(d) The sharing of information can be a **spur to innovation**.

7.6 Many companies have gained significant benefits from benchmarking but it is worth pointing out a number of possible dangers.

(a) It implies there is **one best way** of doing business - arguably this boils down to the difference between efficiency and effectiveness. A process can be efficient but its output may not be useful. Other measures (such as amending the value chain) may be a better way of securing competitive advantage.

(b) The benchmark may be **yesterday's solution to tomorrow's problem**. For example, a cross-channel ferry company might benchmark its activities (eg speed of turnround at Dover and Calais, cleanliness on ship) against another ferry company, whereas the real competitor is the Channel Tunnel.

(c) It is a **catching-up exercise** rather than the development of anything distinctive. After the benchmarking exercise, the competitor might improve performance in a different way.

(d) It depends on **accurate** information about comparator companies.

Case example

A recent five year research programme by Insead business school identified the following five companies as likely to still be successful 10 or 20 years from now.

- American International Group (AIG), the US insurer

- Heineken, the Dutch brewer

- Hewlett-Packard, the US electronics manufacturer

- JP Morgan, the US bank

- SGS Thomson, the Franco-Italian semiconductor maker

The underlying premise of the study , as reported in the *Financial Times*, is that success or failure depends on a complex series of actions. Companies were compared on 12 capabilities - customer orientation, technical resources, market strategy and so forth. An overall score for effectiveness was calculated.

The study showed how the best companies go about their business, and allowed others to diagnose their shortcomings. To quote the project leader when talking about IBM: 'There was a time when it was the best at customer orientation. If we had had this tool 20 years ago, we could have seen it going wrong.'

Unity Bicycles plc

(1) What are the implications of the product life cycle of UB?

Chapter roundup

- To develop a strategic plan, an organisation's management must be aware of the current position of the organisation.

- A position audit is a review of:

  ° resources
  ° products brands markets
  ° operating systems
  ° internal organisation
  ° current results
  ° shareholders' expectations.

- For many companies this might involve a broader review of the firm's:

  ° effectiveness in meeting the needs of its chosen client or stakeholder groups;
  ° efficiency in the use of resources (the maximum output for a given level of input).

- A firm should be aware of its distinctive competence - what it does uniquely well. This can be applied to the business areas it wishes to enter.

- A resource audit covers the inputs of resources a business has access to, including materials, machines, human resources and knowledge.

- Value chain analysis offers a model of what a firm does with its resource inputs, by identifying activities, the ways in which activities add value and the linkages between activities.

- Reviewing present position also involves an analysis of the current products and markets.

  ° At what stage in the product life cycle (introduction, growth, maturity, decline) does a product occupy? (Remember that the product life cycle does not always apply.) Are new products needed to compensate for products in decline?

  ° What is the relationship between products and their markets? The BCG matrix identifies market growth and market share as key variables.

  ° The management accountant should be able to identify the profitability of a product line. An example of the use of management accounting techniques is direct product profitability.

  ° The development of **new products might** be considered an important aspect of a firm's strategy where the management accountant has a role to play.

- A firm's competences may derive from:

  ° **Experience** in making and marketing a product or service
  ° The talents and potential of **individuals** in the organisation
  ° The **quality of co-ordination**

- Benchmarking is a technique by which a company tries to emulate or exceed standards achieved or processes adopted by another company, generally an exemplar organisation.

Quick quiz

1. Position audit is part of the planning process which examines the current state of the entity in respect of:

   R ....
   P ....
   O ....
   I ....
   C ....
   R ....

2. 'A resource audit is an external/internal review.' Which?

3   What is a limiting or key factor? Give an example.

4   Which of these describes 'efficiency', and which 'effectiveness'?

(a)   Whether the resources have been deployed in the best possible way.

(b)   How well the resources have been utilised irrespective of the purpose for which they have been employed.

5   Is logistics a primary or secondary activity in the value chain?

6   The value chain models the process by which organisations convert .... into ....

7   Complete the BCG matrix below

Market ....

	High	Low
High	....	....
Low	....	....

Market .... (left axis label)

8   Who are the chief users of direct product profitability?

9   Distinguish a competence from a CSF.

10   What are the Johnson and Scholes three levels of benchmarking?

Answer to quick quiz

1   • Resources of tangible and intangible assets and finance
     • Products, brands and markets
     • Operating systems (such as production and distribution)
     • Internal organisation
     • Current results
     • Returns to stockholders

2   Internal

3   A limiting factor or key factor is 'a factor which at any time or over a period may limit the activity of an entity, often one where there is shortage or difficulty of supply.' An example would be a shortage of production capacity.

4   (a)   effectiveness

     (b)   efficiency

5   Primary

6   inputs, outputs

7   Market share

		High	Low
Market growth	High	Stars	Question marks
	Low	Cash cows	Dogs

8   Retailers, because it takes into account factors such as stock turnover and shelf space.

9   • A competence is what an organisation has or is able to do

    • A CSF is what is necessary to achieve an objective

10 Resources, competences in separate activities, competences in linked activities.

Unity Bicycles plc review

Question 1. Bicycles as a product class are unlikely to decline. However, product forms such as mountain bikes may well go in and out of fashion - after all, sports enthusiasts are always wanting improvements. Finally, the basic commuter bikes in China and India might eventually go out of fashion.

Now try the question below from the Exam Question Bank

Question to try	Level	Marks	Time
6	Intermediate	n/a	30 mins

BPP
PUBLISHING

Chapter 8

SWOT ANALYSIS AND GAP ANALYSIS

Topic list	Syllabus reference	Ability required
1 Corporate appraisal: SWOT analysis	(iii)	Evaluation
2 Strengths and weaknesses	(iii)	Evaluation
3 Opportunities and threats	(iii)	Evaluation
4 Combining the elements of the SWOT analysis	(iii)	Evaluation
5 Flexibility: strength or weakness?	(iii)	Evaluation
6 Analysing the planning gap	(iv)	Comprehension/evaluation
7 Scenario planning	(iv)	Application/evaluation

Introduction

In SWOT analysis (Section 1) we combine the results of the **environmental analysis** we covered in Chapters 4 and 5 with the internal appraisal covered in Chapter 6, to see how the organisation's strategy (specifically its strengths and weaknesses) is able to deal with changes in the environment.

The position audit identifies **strengths and weaknesses** (Section 2). The environmental analysis identifies **opportunities and threats** (Section 3). These are combined (Section 4) so that appropriate strategies can be suggested which will exploit core competences. A separate section is provided on the need to be flexible (Section 5).

Gap analysis (section 6) indicates the scale of the task to be achieved to reach the organisation's financial objectives, and **scenario planning** (section 7) is undertaken by firms to try and predict what the future will be.

These analyses indicate the type of strategic decisions that need to be addressed.

Learning outcomes covered in this chapter

- **Evaluate** the strengths, weaknesses, opportunities and threats of an organisation

- **Evaluate** the impact of the external environment and the strategic objectives on an organisation

- **Identify** and **evaluate** an organisation's planning gap

- **Prepare** and **evaluate** strategic scenario plans

Syllabus content covered in this chapter

- The current state of the organisation and its advantages and disadvantages (eg SWOT analysis)

- The importance of the planning gap and the use of scenario planning

1 CORPORATE APPRAISAL: SWOT ANALYSIS   5/02

1.1 Having gathered information about itself and its environment from a **position audit** and an **environmental analysis**, strategic planners can go on to make a **corporate appraisal**.

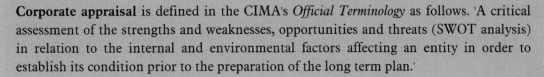

> **KEY TERM**
>
> **Corporate appraisal** is defined in the CIMA's *Official Terminology* as follows. 'A critical assessment of the strengths and weaknesses, opportunities and threats (SWOT analysis) in relation to the internal and environmental factors affecting an entity in order to establish its condition prior to the preparation of the long term plan.'

(a) **Strengths and weaknesses** analysis involves looking at the particular strengths and weaknesses of the organisation itself and its product/service range. It is an **internal appraisal**.

(b) An analysis of **opportunities and threats** is concerned with profit-making opportunities in the business environment, and with identifiable threats. It is therefore an **external appraisal**.

2 STRENGTHS AND WEAKNESSES

2.1 In essence, an internal appraisal seeks to identify the following.

- **Shortcomings** in the company's present skills and resources
- **Strengths** which the company should seek to exploit

2.2 The precise content of the SWOT analysis will depend on the company.

Area	Issues
Marketing	Fate of new product launches
	Use of advertising
	Market shares and market sizes
	Growth markets
	Success rate of the sales team
	Level of customer/client service
Products and brands	Analysis of sales
	Margin and contribution
	Product quality
	Reputation of brands
	Age and future life of products
	Price elasticity of demand
Distribution	Service standards
	Delivery fleet facilities
	Geographical availability
Research and development	Relevance
	Costs
	Benefits
	Workload
Finance	Availability of funds
	Contribution
	Returns on investment
	Accounting ratios

Area	Issues
Plant and equipment/ production	Production capacity
	Value of assets
	Land and buildings
	Economies of scale
Management and staff	Age
	Skills
	Industrial relations
	Training
	Recruitment
	Communications
Business management: organisation	Organisation structure
	Management style
	Communication links
	Information systems
	Strategic intelligence
Raw material and finished goods stocks	Sources of supply
	Turnover periods
	Storage capacity
	Obsolescence and deterioration

2.3 The appraisal should give particular attention to the following.

(a) **A study of past accounts and the use of ratios**. By looking at trends, or by comparing ratios with those of other firms in a similar industry, it might be possible to identify strengths and weaknesses.

(b) **Product position** and product-market portfolio.

(c) **Cash and financial structure**. If a company intends to expand or diversify, it will need cash or sufficient financial standing in order to acquire subsidiaries by issuing shares.

(d) **Cost structure**. If a company operates with high fixed costs and relatively low variable costs, it might be in a relatively weak position with regards to production capacity as this implies a high breakeven point.

(e) **Managerial ability**. Objective measurements should be sought.

The role of the management accountant in strengths and weaknesses analysis

2.4 The role of the management accountant will be to supply relevant information for this appraisal to be carried out successfully. Improving results within the existing business can take the form of cutting costs and/or improving product appeal.

(a) **Cost effectiveness programme**

- Improvements to labour utilisation
- Reduction in systems costs and delays
- Implementation of a value analysis programme

(b) **Product analysis**

- An analysis of competing products to see what features might be 'copied'
- Marketing appeal of competing products to see if improved products can be developed cost effectively

- An analysis of what customers require, and if these requirements can be supplied cheaply

(c) **Product attitude survey**

- How do the customers see our products?
- Sales staff opinions
- Brand image in comparison with competitors

2.5 Specific areas of finance or accounting where weaknesses may exist include the following.

- The average debtors' payment period and credit taken from suppliers
- Liquidity
- Investments in stock
- Interest rates on current loans
- Earning interest on cash in hand
- Tax liability arrangements
- Under-utilised assets
- Overall utilisation of assets
- The interest burden and the gearing level

2.6 However, it is in the area of **product profitability** that the greatest opportunities are likely to exist.

- Changes in pricing policy, and the potential response from the competition or risks of a potential price war

- Increasing sales in existing markets

- Entering new markets with existing products

- Improving product sales appeal by, for example, market segmentation

- Improving distribution services

- Reducing overhead costs

- Reducing labour and material costs

- Rationalising the product range

- Standardising parts of a product or methods of manufacture

3 OPPORTUNITIES AND THREATS

3.1 An **external appraisal** is required to identify profit-making opportunities which can be exploited by the company's strengths and also to anticipate environmental threats (a declining economy, competitors' actions, government legislation, industrial unrest etc) against which the company must protect itself.

3.2 For **opportunities**, it is necessary to decide the following.

- What opportunities exist in the business environment?

- What is the capability profile of competitors? Are they better placed to exploit these opportunities?

- What is the company's comparative performance potential in this field of opportunity?

3.3 For **threats**, it is necessary to decide the following.

- What threats might arise, to the company or its business environment?
- How will market players be affected?

3.4 Opportunities and threats might relate to any or all of the items covered in Chapters 4 and 5.

(a) **Economic**: a recession might imply poor sales.

(b) **Political**: legislation may affect a company's prospects through the threats/opportunities of pollution control or a ban on certain products, for example.

(c) **Competitors** can threaten to 'steal' customers with better and/or cheaper products or services.

(d) **Technology**: if technological changes are anticipated, there is a possibility of new products appearing, or cheaper means of production or distribution being introduced.

(e) **Social** attitudes can be a threat.

Exam focus point

The compulsory case study question may ask you for a corporate appraisal of the company outlined in the scenario.

As a more straightforward question, the May 2002 paper asked candidates to evaluate the usefulness of SWOT as a position appraisal tool.

4 COMBINING THE ELEMENTS OF THE SWOT ANALYSIS

4.1 The internal and external appraisals of SWOT analysis will be brought together. It is likely that **alternative strategies** will emerge from the identification of strengths, weaknesses, opportunities and threats.

(a) Major strengths and profitable opportunities can be exploited especially if strengths and opportunities are matched with each other.

(b) Major weaknesses and threats should be countered, or a contingency strategy or corrective strategy developed.

4.2 A **cruciform chart** is a table summarising significant strengths, weaknesses, opportunities and threats. In the example below, the development of potential strategies from an analysis is illustrated.

Strengths	*Weaknesses*
£10 million of capital available.	Heavy reliance on a small number of customers.
Production expertise and appropriate marketing skills.	Limited product range, with no new products and expected market decline. Small marketing organisation.
Threats	*Opportunities*
Major competitor has already entered the new market.	Government tax incentives for new investment. Growing demand in a new market, although customers so far relatively small in number.

4.3 In this simple example, it might be possible to identify that the company is in imminent danger of losing its existing markets and must diversify. The new market opportunity exists to be exploited and since the number of customers is currently few, the relatively small size of the existing marketing force would not be an immediate hindrance.

4.4 In practice, **a combination of individual strategies** will be required with regard to product development, market development, diversification, resource planning, risk reduction etc. The following three steps are taken.

- The gap between the current position of the firm and its planned targets is estimated
- One or more courses of action are proposed
- These are tested for their 'gap-reducing properties'

4.5 It will help you to get used to the basic thinking that underlies strategic planning if you try a short exercise in SWOT analysis.

Question 1

Hall Faull Downes Ltd has been in business for 25 years, during which time profits have risen by an average of 3% per annum, although there have been peaks and troughs in profitability due to the ups and downs of trade in the customers' industry. The increase in profits until five years ago was the result of increasing sales in a buoyant market, but more recently, the total market has become somewhat smaller and Hall Faull Downes has only increased sales and profits as a result of improving its market share.

The company produces components for manufacturers in the engineering industry.

In recent years, the company has developed many new products and currently has 40 items in its range compared to 24 only five years ago. Over the same five year period, the number of customers has fallen from 20 to nine, two of whom together account for 60% of the company's sales.

Give your appraisal of the company's future, and suggest what it is probably doing wrong.

Answer

A general interpretation of the facts as given might be sketched as follows.

(a) Objectives: the company has no declared objectives. Profits have risen by 3% per annum in the past, which has failed to keep pace with inflation but may have been a satisfactory rate of increase in the current conditions of the industry. Even so, stronger growth is indicated in the future.

(b)

Strengths	Weaknesses
Many new products developed. Marketing success in increasing market share	Products may be reaching the end of their life and entering decline. New product life cycles may be shorter. Reduction in customers. Excessive reliance on a few customers. Doubtful whether profit record is satisfactory.
Threats Possible decline in the end-product. Smaller end-product market will restrict future sales prospects for Hall Faull Downes.	Opportunities None identified.

(c) Strengths: the growth in company sales in the last five years has been as a result of increasing the market share in a declining market. This success may be the result of the following.

- Research and development spending.
- Good product development programmes.
- Extending the product range to suit changing customer needs.
- Marketing skills.
- Long-term supply contracts with customers.
- Cheap pricing policy.

- Product quality and reliable service.

(d) Weaknesses:

(i) The products may be custom-made for customers so that they provide little or no opportunity for market development.

(ii) Products might have a shorter life cycle than in the past, in view of the declining total market demand.

(iii) Excessive reliance on two major customers leaves the company exposed to the dangers of losing their custom.

(e) Threats: there may be a decline in the end-market for the customers' product so that the customer demands for the company's own products will also fall.

(f) Opportunities: no opportunities have been identified, but in view of the situation as described, new strategies for the longer term would appear to be essential.

(g) Conclusions: the company does not appear to be planning beyond the short-term, or is reacting to the business environment in a piecemeal fashion. A strategic planning programme should be introduced.

(h) Recommendations: the company must look for new opportunities in the longer-term.

(i) In the short term, current strengths must be exploited to continue to increase market share in existing markets and product development programmes should also continue.

(ii) In the longer term, the company must diversify into new markets or into new products and new markets. Diversification opportunities should be sought with a view to exploiting any competitive advantage or synergy that might be achievable.

(iii) The company should use its strengths (whether in R & D, production skills or marketing expertise) in exploiting any identifiable opportunities.

(iv) Objectives need to be quantified in order to assess the extent to which new long-term strategies are required.

4.6 Having constructed a matrix of strengths, weaknesses, opportunities and threats with some evaluation attached to them, it then becomes feasible to make use of that matrix in guiding strategy formulation. The two major options are as follows.

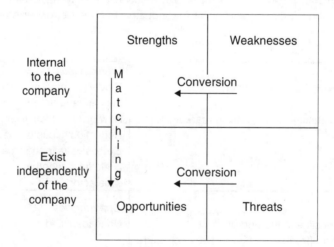

(a) **Matching**

This entails finding, where possible, a match between the strengths of the organisation and the opportunities presented by the market.

(b) **Conversion**

This requires the development of strategies which will convert weaknesses into strengths in order to take advantage of some particular opportunity.

5 FLEXIBILITY: STRENGTH OR WEAKNESS?

Flexibility as a strength

5.1 An organisation should have the flexibility to cope with unforeseen disasters, and such flexibility can be offered by **contingency planning**. Contingencies can be included in a scenario building exercise.

5.2 Flexibility also implies an ability to **deploy resources quickly**, efficiently and effectively to cope with changes.

(a) In many respects, flexibility can be provided by a **suitable information system**.

(b) Certain industries, such as the music and entertainment industry, depend on flexibility, as they are driven by **fashion**.

(c) In manufacturing, flexibility includes the ability to retool equipment, produce small orders, identify target markets etc.

(d) Workers in a team are expected to turn their hands to any job.

Flexibility as a weakness

5.3 Ansoff identified flexibility as a separate corporate goal, and like any goal, flexibility requires resources if it is to be achieved.

5.4 **External flexibility** can be described as 'not putting all one's eggs in one basket'. Firms can protect themselves against catastrophe by taking the following steps.

- Increasing the number of independent customers they have.
- Operating in as many different markets as possible
- Using different kinds of technology in their products

5.5 These policies offer their own drawbacks.

- Managers and shareholders might have different attitudes.

- Moreover, Porter argues that flexibility as a corporate objective can lead to a **misallocation of resources**: ensuring that every option is covered can result in insufficient resources being available to exploit the best option.

> **POINT TO NOTE**
>
> To summarise, flexibility in itself can be a strength or a weakness, depending on the circumstances.
> - As a strength, it can enhance the organisation's responsiveness
> - As a weakness, it can lead to lack of focus and a waste of resources

SWOT and critical success factors

> **KEY TERM**
>
> As we saw in Chapter 3, **critical success factors** are those factors that are fundamental to strategic success. Johnson and Scholes define them as 'those components of strategy in which the organisation must excel to outperform competition'.

BPP PUBLISHING

5.6 There is no such thing as an ideal set of resources and competences. Each resource and competence can only be assessed in relation to the strategic choices of the organisation. Critical success factors may change over time, so the SWOT analysis of strategic capability will evolve and different strengths and weaknesses will be highlighted.

6 ANALYSING THE PLANNING GAP

6.1 Having carried out a SWOT analysis, strategic planners must next think about the extent to which new strategies are needed to enable the organisation to achieve its objectives. One technique whereby this can be done is **gap analysis**.

KEY TERM

Gap analysis. 'A comparison between an entity's ultimate objective (most commonly expressed in terms of demand, but may be reported in terms of profit, ROCE etc) and the expected performance of projects both planned and underway.'

(CIMA Official Terminology)

POINT TO NOTE

The planning gap is **not** the gap between the current position of the organisation and the forecast desired position.

Rather, it's the gap between the forecast position from continuing with current activities, and the forecast of the desired position.

6.2 The purpose of gap analysis is to establish the following.

(a) What are the organisation's targets for achievement over the planning period?

(b) What would the organisation be expected to achieve if it 'did nothing' - ie did not develop any new strategies, but simply carried on in the current way with the same products and selling to the same markets?

REMEMBER

This difference is the 'gap'. New strategies will then have to be developed which will close this gap, so that the organisation can expect to achieve its targets over the planning period.

6.3 Some definitions can usefully be outlined at this stage.

> **KEY TERMS**
>
> **Forecasting** is the identification of factors and quantification of their effect on an entity as a basis for planning.
>
> **Projection.** A projection is 'an expected future trend pattern obtained by extrapolation. It is principally concerned with quantitative factors whereas a forecast includes judgements.' *(CIMA Official Terminology)*
>
> **Extrapolation** is the technique of determining a projection by statistical means.

A forecast or projection based on existing performance: F_0 forecasts

6.4 This is a **forecast** of the company's future results assuming that it does nothing. For example, if the company sells ten products in eight markets, produces them on a certain quantity and type of machinery in one factory, has a gearing structure of 30% etc, a forecast will be prepared, covering the corporate planning period, on the assumption that none of these items are changed.

6.5 Argenti identified four stages in the preparation of such a forecast.

(a) **Review past results** and analyse

- revenues into units of sale and price
- costs into variable, fixed, and semi-variable

(b) A **projection** into the future for each major item of revenue and cost should be made up to the end of the planning period.

(c) **Consider any other factors** which might significantly affect the projections. Examples are as follows.

- Internal factors such as machine breakdown, strikes etc
- External PEST factors, such as new technology or changes in the law

(d) The forecast is then **finalised**. The forecast allows the company no new products or markets and no other new strategies: but the purpose of the forecast and gap analysis is to determine the size of the task facing the company if it wishes to achieve its target profits.

Errors in the forecast

6.6 A forecast cannot be expected to guarantee **accuracy** and there must inevitably be some **latitude for error**.

(a) By estimating **likely variations**. For example, 'in 2001 the forecast profit is £5 million with possible variations of plus or minus £2 million'.

(b) By providing a **probability distribution** for profits. For example, 'in 2001 there is a 20% chance that profits will exceed £7 million, a 50% chance that they will exceed £5 million and an 80% chance that they will exceed £2½ million. Minimum profits in 2001 will be £2 million.'

The profit gap

6.7 The **profit gap** is the difference between the target profits and the profits on the forecast.

(a) First of all the firm can estimate the effects on the gap of any projects or strategies in the pipeline. Some of the gap might be filled by a new project.

(b) Then, if a gap remains, new strategies have to be considered to close the gap.

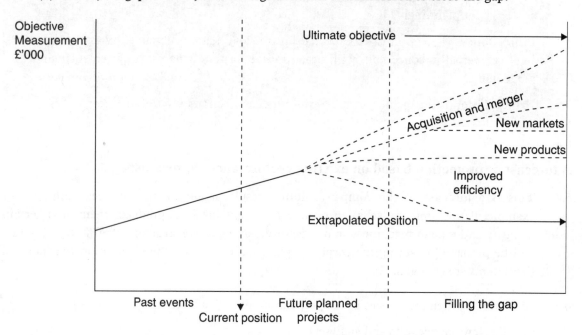

6.8 Some possible problems are these.

(a) The financial propositions may be susceptible to **inflation** - there is no easy way of dealing with this problem.

(b) More serious, however, is risk: remember that in many cases a higher return can equate to a higher risk. In seeking to develop strategies to give a higher return, the firm may, unwittingly, be raising its **risk profile**.

Other forms of gap analysis

6.9 The same basic technique can be used as a starting point for formulating any particular strategy.

(a) In planning for **manpower**, gap analysis would be used to assess the difference over time between the following.

- What the organisation **needs** to have in terms of differing skills and seniority
- What the organisation **is likely** to have

(b) In planning facilities, a similar analysis can be made of the gap between the facilities which the organisation needs to have, and what it is likely to have if nothing is done about the situation.

(c) A sales gap can be filled by diversification, product development etc.

Continuous gap analysis

6.10 A gap analysis can be used as a means of strategic control. This means that the gap analysis is regularly updated.

(a) Were the assumptions in the F_0 forecast justified?

(b) A similar question can be asked of the other strategies which are supposed to fill the gap.

- Have they been implemented as planned?
- Have they generated the expected level of sales and/or profit?

6.11 This **continuing gap analysis** can be allied to forecasting as it can be used to measure the extent to which it is likely a firm can fulfil its objectives.

7 SCENARIO PLANNING

7.1 Because the environment is so complex, it is easy to become overwhelmed by the many factors. Firms therefore try to model the future and the technique is **scenario planning**.

> ## KEY TERM
>
> A **scenario** is 'an internally consistent view of what the future might turn out to be'.

Macro scenarios

7.2 **Macro scenarios** use macro-economic or political factors, creating alternative views of the future environment (eg global economic growth, political changes, interest rates). Macro scenarios developed because the activities of oil and resource companies (which are global and at one time were heavily influenced by political factors) needed techniques to deal with uncertainties.

7.3 **Steps in scenario planning (Mercer).**

Step 1 **Decide on the drivers for change**

- Environmental analysis helps determine key factors
- **At least** a ten year time horizon is needed, to avoid simply extrapolating from the present
- Identify and select the **important** issues and degree of certainty

Step 2 **Bring drivers together into a viable framework**

- This relies almost on an intuitive ability to make patterns out of 'soft' data, so is the hardest
- Items identified can be brought together as mini-scenarios
- There might be many trends, but these can be grouped together

Step 3 - Produce seven to nine mini-scenarios

Step 4 Group mini-scenarios into two or three larger scenarios containing all topics.

- This generates most debate and is likely to highlight fundamental issues
- More than three scenarios will confuse people
- The scenarios should be complementary and equally likely
- The scenarios should be tested to ensure they hang together

Step 5 **Write the scenarios**

- The scenarios should be written up in the form most suitable for managers
- Most scenarios are qualitative rather than quantitative in nature

Step 6   **Identify issues arising**

- Determine the most critical outcomes
- Role play can be used to test what the scenarios mean to key staff involved

Industry scenarios

7.4   Porter believes that the most appropriate use for scenario analysis is if it is restricted to an industry. An **industry scenario** is an internally consistent view of an **industry's** future structure. Different competitive strategies may be appropriate to different scenarios.

7.5   **Using scenarios to formulate competitive strategy**

(a)   A strategy built in response to only **one scenario is risky**, whereas one supposed to cope with them **all might be expensive**.

(b)   Choosing scenarios as a basis for decisions about competitive strategy.

Approach	Comment
Assume the most probable	This choice puts too much faith in the scenario process and guesswork. A less probable scenario may be one whose **failure** to occur would have the **worst** consequences for the firm.
Hope for the best	A firm designs a strategy based on the scenario most attractive to the firm: wishful thinking.
Hedge	The firm chooses the strategy that produces **satisfactory** results under **all** scenarios. **Hedging, however, is not optimal**. The **low risk** is paid for by a **low reward**.
Flexibility	A firm taking this approach plays a 'wait and see' game. It is safer, but sacrifices first-mover advantages.
Influence	A firm will try and influence the future, for example by influencing demand for related products in order that its favoured scenario will be realised in events as they unfold.

Unity Bicycle plc

(1)   Conduct a brief SWOT analysis of UB. Identify the issues you think are most important.

Chapter roundup

- **SWOT analysis** or **corporate appraisal** is a quantitative and qualitative review of internal **strengths** and **weaknesses** and their relationship with external **threats** and **opportunities**.

- Strategies should be developed which **fill gaps** in any area - ie remove weaknesses or develop strengths, and exploit opportunities and counter threats.

- SWOT analysis indicates the **types of strategies** that appear to be available, both to exploit strengths and opportunities and to deal with weaknesses and take defence against threats.

- **Gap analysis** quantifies the size of the gap between the objective/targets for the planning period and the forecast based on the extrapolation of the current situation, and current prospects in the pipeline.

- **Industry scenarios** can be used to analyse the industry environment. They are more local than the global scenarios which analyse the effects of general environmental trends.

- Successful scenario building requires that the likely responses of **competitors** can be input into the model. **Competitor analysis** makes this possible.

Quick quiz

1   A SWOT analysis is also known as a ....

2   (a)   Strengths and weaknesses analysis offers an internal/external appraisal

    (b)   Opportunities and threats analysis offers an internal/external appraisal

3   List some areas of finance or accounting where weaknesses may exist.

4   **Fill in the gaps** in the statements below, using the words in the box.

- For opportunities, it is necessary to decide the following.
  - What opportunities exist in the (1) ....?
  - What is the (2)............... of competitors? Are they better placed to (3) .... these opportunities?
  - What is the company's (4) .... performance potential in this field?

• comparative	◉ business environment
• capability profile	• exploit

5   What is a cruciform chart?

6   Show how flexibility can be both a strength and a weakness.

7   The planning gap is the gap between the current position of the organisation and the forecast desired position.

    ☐   True
    ☐   False

8   The profit gap is the difference between (1) .... and (2) ....

9   Distinguish a 'forecast' from a 'projection'.

10   What are the six steps in scenario planning?

Answers to quick quiz

1   Corporate appraisal

2   (a)   internal
    (b)   external

3   •   The average debtors' payment period and credit taken from suppliers
    •   Liquidity
    •   Investments in stock
    •   Interest rates on current loans
    •   Earning interest on cash in hand
    •   Tax liability arrangements
    •   Under-utilised assets
    •   Overall utilisation of assets
    •   The interest burden and the gearing level

4   (1) business environment (2) capability profile (3) exploit (4) comparative

5   A cruciform chart is a table summarising the significant strengths, weaknesses, opportunities and threats.

6   As a strength, it can enhance the organisation's responsiveness.
    As a weakness, it can lead to lack of focus and a waste of resources.

7   False

8   (1) Target profits (2) profits on the forecast

9   Forecasting is 'the identification of factors and quantification of their effect on an entity as a basis for planning.' (CIMA)

    A projection is 'an expected future trend pattern obtained by extrapolation. It is principally concerned with quantitative factors whereas a forecast includes judgements.' (CIMA)

10 Step 1   Decide on the key drivers of change
    Step 2   Bring the drivers together into a viable framework
    Step 3   Produce mini-scenarios
    Step 4   Group them into larger scenarios
    Step 5   Write the scenarios
    Step 6   Identify issues arising

Unity Bicycles plc review

Question 1. In your SWOT analysis you might have mentioned the following.

(a)   *Strengths:* managerial focus; good reputation; ties with MT on materials.

(b)   *Weaknesses:* quality at Mexican and Romanian plants; the dealer network is a cost; may not be reaching some customers; poor management information; reliance on bank finance.

(c)   *Opportunities:* Chinese and Indian markets - customers might want to 'trade up' to better bikes. Ecology and discouragement of motor transport.

(d)   *Threats:* licencees can pull out of the agreement. Russian competitors. Chinese competitors.

Now try the question below from the Exam Question Bank

Question to try	Level	Marks	Time
7	Exam	25	45 mins

Part D
Evaluating strategic options

Chapter 9

STRATEGIC OPTIONS: COMPETITION, PRODUCTS AND MARKETS

Topic list	Syllabus reference	Ability required
1 Strategic options and marketing issues	(iv)	Evaluation
2 Generic competitive strategies	(iv)	Evaluation
3 Using the value chain in competitive strategy	(iv)	Evaluation
4 Pricing and competition	(iv)	Evaluation
5 Product-market strategy: direction of growth	(iv)	Evaluation

Introduction

After the corporate appraisal, we come to **strategic choices** that firms make, the subject of Chapters 9 and 10.

Section 1 offers a brief overview of some strategic options, and includes a discussion of what firms consider to be their **core activity.** We need some understanding of what a firm competes with: what products and services does it offer? So we also discuss some key issues relating to **marketing**.

To respond to the environment, business have three choices.

(a) **How to compete.** Competitive strategies include cost leadership, differentiation or focus (section 2). You should be aware of some of the problems with this approach.

(b) **Direction of growth.** Product/market strategy refers to the mix of product and markets (new or existing) and what the firm should do. This includes pricing strategy and is covered in section 3, 4 and 5.

(c) **Method of growth** (acquisition or organic growth) is covered in Chapter 10.

These decisions are not necessarily taken at the same time, of course, nor are they taken in the same way. The basic competitive strategy cannot be changed every year – but the decision to acquire a business is often taken suddenly.

Learning outcomes covered in this chapter

- **Evaluate** and **recommend** response strategies to competitors' actions
- **Identify** the position of organisational boundaries

Syllabus content covered in this chapter

- Competitor analysis including generic competitive strategies, product-market strategies (Ansoff) and competitor response profiles

- The development and evaluation of response strategies to the actions of competitive forces (eg competitor price changes)

- Branding and brand switching strategies

BPP PUBLISHING

1 STRATEGIC OPTIONS AND MARKETING ISSUES

1.1 An organisation, having identified its strengths and weaknesses, and its opportunities and threats, must make choices about what **strategies** to pursue in order to achieve its targets and objectives.

Core businesses

1.2 A business should have a **common thread** running through all of its activities, which gives them a purpose or logic.

(a) The aim of some businesses is to pursue **diversified activities**. The common thread in such businesses will usually be to earn a high return on investments, largely through acquisitions and disposals.

(b) Many organisations, however, identify themselves with **certain products or markets**, to which most of their activities are devoted. These are the organisation's **core businesses**.

1.3 In seeking to define their core businesses, firms should not confuse the **market** with the **industry**.

(a) **The market** is defined by consumer needs and reflects consumer demands.

(b) **The industry** is defined by related firm capabilities and industries are based on supply technologies. Washing machines and refrigerators are products of the same industry, despite their wholly different purposes.

1.4 If a company recognises that it is in a declining business, or in one where future growth will be restricted, it should seek to expand in other areas or to exploit the remaining competitive advantages it has.

Case example

Tobacco companies, for example, recognising that their markets in the West are declining because of the trend away from smoking, have opened up new markets for tobacco products in the Third World and have also diversified into paper, retailing and hotels.

Strategic choices

1.5 In chapter 2 we identified three categories of strategic choice, as follows.

(a) Competitive strategies are the strategies an organisation will pursue for competitive advantage. They determine **how you compete**.

(b) Product-market strategies determine **where you compete** and the direction of growth.

(c) Institutional strategies determine the **method of growth**.

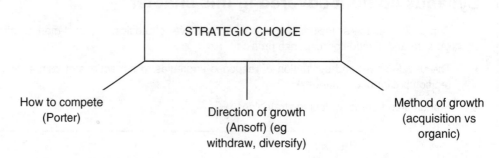

Horizontal boundaries

1.6 A firm's **horizontal boundaries** define the variety of products and services that it produces. The optimum horizontal boundary for a firm depends on **economies of scale**. In some industries, such as pharmaceuticals, company size is influenced by a preference for mergers ('bigger is better') and corporate giants, such as Du Pont. A few large firms account for the vast proportion of industry sales.

1.7 **Economies of scale** occur when large scale processes (production, distribution, etc) have cost advantages over smaller processes. Economies of scale affect both the size of firms and the structure of markets, and so consideration of them, and therefore where organisational boundaries should be, is vital in any business strategy decision about possible merger or expansion. One source of economies of scale is the **experience curve**.

Use of experience curves

1.8 The **experience curve** can be used in strategic control of costs. It suggests that as output increases, the cost per unit of output falls. This results from the following.

(a) **Economies of scale** - in other words an increased volume of production leads to lower unit costs, as the firm approaches full capacity.

(b) A genuine '**learning effect**' as the workforce becomes familiar with the job and learns to carry out the task more efficiently. As a process is repeated, it is likely that costs will reduce due to **efficiency, discounts** and **reduced waste**.

(c) **Technological improvements**.

1.9 The effects can be shown in a diagram as follows.

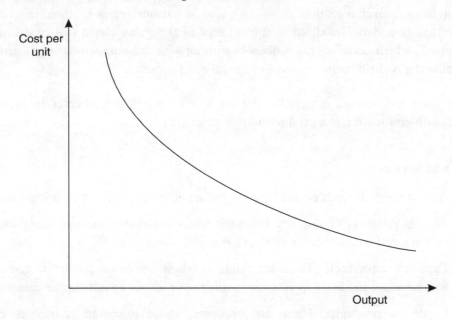

1.10 The **strategic importance** of experience curves are these.

(a) Businesses **can predict their likely future costs**, and plan more effectively in the project appraisal process.

(b) **Early mover advantages/disadvantages**. They can indicate the advantages of either being first in a market or following another firm. Being the first to enter a market is no guarantee of long-term success, of course, but if there is a very steep learning curve (ie learning benefits are obtained quickly), the first into the market may reap all the advantages and build up a commanding position by obtaining an early leadership in market share.

(c) **Life cycle.** On the other hand, a firm might be prepared to make losses in the short term, in order to build up volume and experience, so that the product is profitable over its life cycle.

(d) A policy of **reducing prices** as process costs fall can help a company to win a dominant market share. As costs fall, the company may find itself in a **cost leadership** position in terms of Porter's generic strategy model.

(e) Greater experience can also be used to **differentiate** a product, either via greater experience of the market or the ability to utilise technology in a unique way. Products may be **redesigned** to boost production efficiency.

1.11 **Price/quantity.** An experience curve which models production costs can be related to customer demand schedules.

(a) If the experience curve suggests increased quantities of production, then it is possible that the increased volume will have to be sold at a lower price.

(b) The management accountant might usefully relate experience curves to demand schedules, in particular price elasticity, to establish likely profitability of the product.

(c) Furthermore, the 'quantity sold' to the market as a whole needs to take the entry of competitors into account.

Vertical boundaries

1.12 The **vertical boundaries** of a firm define which activities the firm performs itself and which it purchases from independent firms. (We look at outsourcing in Chapter 12.) The concept of vertical boundaries is allied to the concept of the **value chain** (discussed in detail in Chapter 7) which describes the process beginning with the acquisition of raw materials and culminating in distribution and sale of the finished goods.

1.13 Horizontal and vertical integration are discussed later in this chapter in the context of **related diversification** as a product-market strategy.

Products and services

1.14 The right strategy depends on the type of product or service that the firm is producing.

(a) **Search products.** These are products whose attributes the consumer can discern, evaluate and compare fairly easily, eg size and colour.

(b) **Experience products.** These are products whose attributes cannot be discerned until the consumer has had experience of using the product - eg taste in the case of food.

(c) **Credence products.** These are products whose important attributes cannot be evaluated by the consumer either because the product's attributes might vary the next time (eg quality of service in a restaurant) or because the product's attributes cannot easily be evaluated (eg pet food).

1.15 Products may be categorised as follows.

   (a) **Breakthrough products** offer either a radical performance advantage over competition, drastically lower price, or ideally, may offer both.

   (b) **Improved products** are not radically different to their competition but are obviously superior in terms of better performance at a competitive price.

   (c) **Competitive products** show no obvious advantage over others, but derive their appeal from a particular compromise of cost and performance.

Services

1.16 It will also be useful to identify the extent to which a product has a **service element**. Kotler defines services as follows.

> **KEY TERM**
>
> '**Services** are any activity of benefit that one party can offer to another that is essentially intangible and does not result in the ownership of anything. Its production may or may not be tied to a physical product.'
> (P Kotler, *Social Marketing*)

1.17 There are five major characteristics of services.

   (a) **Intangibility** refers to the lack of substance which is involved with service delivery. Unlike goods (physical products such as confectionery), there is no substantial material or physical aspects to a service: no taste, feel, visible presence and so on. Most 'offers' to customers combine product and service elements on a 'service continuum' as we show below.

   (b) **Inseparability.** Many services are created at the same time as they are consumed. No service exists until it is actually being experienced/consumed by the person who has bought it.

   (c) **Variability.** Many services face the problem of maintaining consistency in the standard of output. It may be hard to attain precise standardisation of the service offered.

   (d) **Perishability.** Services are innately perishable.

   (e) **Lack of ownership.** Services do not result in the transfer of property. The purchase of a service only confers on the customer access to or a right to use a facility.

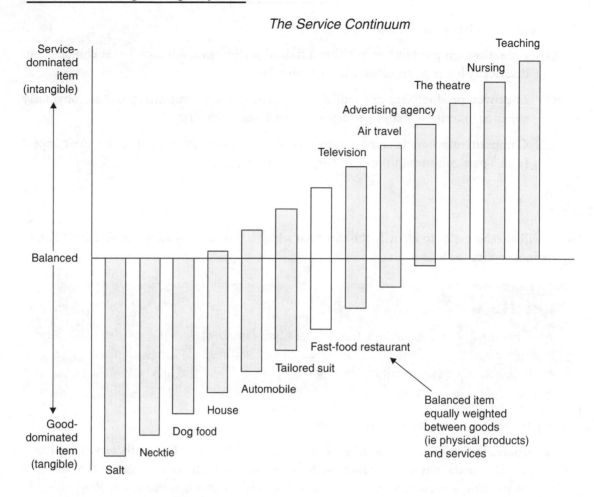

The Service Continuum

Strategic marketing issues

1.18 A **standard** product might satisfy the needs of all customers in the market. On the other hand, **variations** in a product's design might appeal more strongly to some prospective customers than others.

1.19 Customers differ in various respects - according to age, sex, income, geographical area, buying attitudes, buying habits etc. Each of these differences can be used to **segment** a market.

> ### KEY TERM
>
> '**Market segmentation** is the sub-dividing of a market into distinct subsets of customers, where any subset may conceivably be selected as a target market to be reached with a distinct marketing mix.' (Kotler)

1.20 By creating a new market segment or entering a growing market segment a company can hope to achieve the following.

- **Increase sales and profits,** by meeting customer needs in a number of different ways
- **Extend the life cycle** of the product
- Capture some of the overall **market share** from competitors
- **Survive** in the face of competition

Market share

KEY TERM

Market share is 'one entity's sales of a product or service in a specified market expressed as a proportion of total sales by all entities offering that product or service to the market. It is both a planning tool and a performance assessment ratio'.

(CIMA *Official Terminology*).

1.21   The evaluation of market share has two purposes.

- It helps to identify who the **true competitor** is
- It serves as a **basis for marketing strategy**

Developing a strategy for market share

1.22   There are four strategic options for market share.

(a) **Building market share**. This is usually easiest when the product is in the early stages of its life, and the market is growing (a rising star, or question mark in BCG terminology).

(b) **Holding market share**. This strategy is appropriate in a situation where the products are mature, and in a mature market (cash cows). Competition will come from innovators, and competitive promotions.

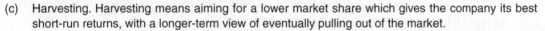

Case example

Xerox lost out, for example, by ignoring the lower end of the photocopier market, as Japanese competitors entered this part of the market and took most of Xerox's market share.

(c) Harvesting. Harvesting means aiming for a lower market share which gives the company its best short-run returns, with a longer-term view of eventually pulling out of the market.

(d) Divestment/withdrawal. In such circumstances, the market share is so low that the product is no longer viable.

1.23   Market share strategies for declining industries would include harvesting or divestment options.

Profit Impact of Marketing Strategies (PIMS)

1.24   **PIMS analysis** attempts to establish the profitability of various marketing strategies. PIMS researchers believe that 70% of the relative profit performance of an organisation derives from the areas of **competitive strength**, **market attractiveness** and **productivity**.

High market share

1.25   A 1973 research study in the USA found that there was a positive correlation between **market share** and **return on investment,** so that companies with higher market share (and likely economies of scale, bargaining power and quality management) earned high returns.

Low market share

1.26 Low market share does not inevitably mean poor returns. Company strategy and/or market characteristics may lead to prosperity even with a low market share.

(a) **Company strategy**

- **Market segmentation.** New market segments might be a small proportion of the total market, but profitable.

- **Premium products.** Emphasising product quality, and charging higher prices.

- Wanting to stay small, and consciously avoiding growth

- Cost control

(b) **Market characteristics**

- The market is stable
- Product innovations are rare
- Most products are standardised
- Companies produce supplies or components for industrial customers
- Repeat-buying is frequent
- The value added is high

Trade-offs

1.27 Some firms are prepared to **sacrifice profitability for market share** over a period of time. Some Japanese firms were willing to charge low prices to buy market share and fatally weaken competitors.

2 GENERIC COMPETITIVE STRATEGIES

2.1 In any market where there are competitors, strategic and marketing decisions will often be in response to what a competitor has done.

2.2 **Competitive advantage** is anything which gives one organisation an edge over its rivals. Porter argues that a firm should adopt a competitive strategy which is intended to achieve some form of competitive advantage for the firm.

KEY TERM

Competitive strategy means 'taking offensive or defensive actions to create a dependable position in an industry, to cope successfully with ... competitive forces and thereby yield a superior return on investment for the firm. Firms have discovered many different approaches to this end, and the best strategy for a given firm is ultimately a unique construction reflecting its particular circumstances'. (Porter)

The choice of competitive strategy

2.3 Porter believes there are three **generic strategies** for competitive advantage.

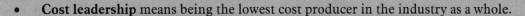

KEY TERMS

- **Cost leadership** means being the lowest cost producer in the industry as a whole.

- **Differentiation** is the exploitation of a product or service which the **industry as a whole** believes to be unique.

- **Focus** involves a restriction of activities to only part of the market (a segment) through:

  ° Providing goods and/or services at lower cost to that segment (**cost-focus**)

  ° Providing a differentiated product or service to that segment (**differentiation-focus**)

2.4 **Cost leadership and differentiation are industry-wide strategies. Focus involves segmentation** but involves pursuing, **within the segment only,** a strategy of cost leadership or differentiation.

Cost leadership

2.5 A cost leadership strategy seeks to achieve the position of lowest-cost producer in the **industry as a whole.** By producing at the lowest cost, the manufacturer can compete on price with every other producer in the industry, and earn the higher unit profits, if the manufacturer so chooses.

2.6 **How to achieve overall cost leadership**

- Set up production facilities to obtain **economies of scale**

- Use the **latest technology** to reduce costs and/or enhance productivity (or use cheap labour if available)

- Exploit the **learning curve effect**

- Concentrate on **improving productivity**

- **Minimise overhead costs**

- **Get favourable access to sources of supply**

- **Relocate to cheaper areas**

Case study link

In the May 2002 case study, Market Stores is able to follow a cost leadership strategy by using its large purchasing power to buy cheaply, and then sell cheaply without damaging margins. Other competitors focus on other customers, either in the regions or in the more affluent segments.

Differentiation

2.7 A differentiation strategy assumes that competitive advantage can be gained through **particular characteristics** of a firm's products. Products may be categorised as:

(a) **Breakthrough products** offer a radical performance advantage over competition, perhaps at a drastically lower price (eg float glass, developed by Pilkington).

(b) **Improved products** are not radically different from their competition but are obviously superior in terms of better performance at a competitive price (eg microchips).

(c) **Competitive products** derive their appeal from a particular compromise of cost and performance. For example, cars are not all sold at rock-bottom prices, nor do they all provide immaculate comfort and performance. They compete with each other by trying to offer a more attractive compromise than rival models.

2.8 How to differentiate

- **Build up a brand image**
- **Give the product special features** to make it stand out
- **Exploit other activities of the value chain**

2.9 Advantages and disadvantages of industry-wide strategies

Advantages	Cost leadership	Differentiation
New entrants	Economies of scale raise entry barriers	Brand loyalty and perceived uniqueness are entry barriers
Substitutes	Firm is not so vulnerable as its less cost-effective competitors to the threat of substitutes	Customer loyalty is a weapon against substitutes
Customers	Customers cannot drive down prices further than the next most efficient competitor	Customers have no comparable alternative
Suppliers	Flexibility to deal with cost increases	Higher margins can offset vulnerability to supplier price rises
Industry rivalry	Firm remains profitable when rivals go under through excessive price competition	Brand loyalty should lower price sensitivity

Disadvantages

Cost leadership	Differentiation
Technological change will require capital investment, or make production cheaper for competitors	Sooner or later, customers become price sensitive
Competitors can learn via imitation	Customers may no longer need the differentiating factor
Cost concerns ignore product design or marketing issues	
Increase in input costs can reduce price advantages	Imitation narrows differentiation

Focus (or niche) strategy

2.10 In a focus strategy, a firm concentrates its attention on one or more particular segments or niches of the market, and does not try to serve the entire market with a single product.

(a) A **cost-focus strategy:** aim to be a cost leader for a particular segment. This type of strategy is often found in the printing, clothes manufacture and car repair industries.

(b) A **differentiation-focus strategy:** pursue differentiation for a chosen segment. Luxury goods are the prime example of such a strategy.

2.11 Advantages

- A niche is more secure and a firm can insulate itself from competition.
- The firm does not spread itself too thinly.

2.12 Drawbacks of a focus strategy

(a) The firm sacrifices economies of scale which would be gained by serving a wider market.

(b) Competitors can move into the segment, with increased resources (eg the Japanese moved into the US luxury car market, to compete with Mercedes and BMW).

(c) The segment's needs may eventually become less distinct from the main market.

Which strategy?

2.13 Although there is a risk with any of the generic strategies, Porter argues that a firm must pursue one of them. A **stuck-in-the-middle** strategy is almost certain to make only low profits. 'This firm lacks the market share, capital investment and resolve to play the low-cost game, the industry-wide differentiation necessary to obviate the need for a low-cost position, or the focus to create differentiation or a low-cost position in a more limited sphere.'

Question 1

The managing director of Hermes Telecommunications plc is interested in corporate strategy. Hermes has invested a great deal of money in establishing a network which competes with that of Telecom UK, a recently privatised utility. Initially Hermes concentrated its efforts on business customers in the South East of England, especially the City of London, where it offered a lower cost service to that supplied by Telecom UK. Recently, Hermes has approached the residential market (ie domestic telephone users) offering a lower cost service on long-distance calls. Technological developments have resulted in the possibility of a cheap mobile telecommunication network, using microwave radio links. The franchise for this service has been awarded to Gerbil phone, which is installing transmitters in town centres and stations etc.

What issues of competitive strategy have been raised in the above scenario, particularly in relation to Hermes Telecommunications plc?

Answer

(a) Arguably, Hermes initially pursued a cost-focus strategy, by targeting the business segment.

(b) It seems to be moving into a cost leadership strategy over the whole market although its competitive offer, in terms of lower costs for local calls, is incomplete.

(c) The barriers to entry to the market have been lowered by the new technology. Gerbil phone might pick up a significant amount of business.

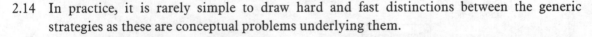

2.14 In practice, it is rarely simple to draw hard and fast distinctions between the generic strategies as these are conceptual problems underlying them.

(a) **Problems with 'cost leadership'**

    (i) **Internal focus.** Cost refers to internal measures, rather than the market demand. It can be used to gain market share: but it is the **market share which is important,** not cost leadership as such.

    (ii) **Only one firm.** If cost leadership applies cross the whole industry, only one firm will pursue this strategy successfully.

    (iii) **Higher margins can be used for differentiation.** Having low costs does not mean you have to charge lower prices or compete on price. A cost leader can choose to 'invest higher margins in R & D or marketing'. Being a cost leader arguably gives producers more freedom to choose other competitive strategies.

(b) **Problems with differentiation**. Porter assumes that a differentiated product will always be sold at a higher price.

(i) However, a **differentiated product** may be sold at the same price as competing products in order to **increase market share.**

(ii) **Choice of competitor.** Differentiation from whom? Who are the competitors? Do they serve other market segments? Do they compete on the same basis?

(iii) **Source of differentiation**. This can include **all** aspects of the firm's offer, not only the product. Restaurants aim to create an atmosphere or 'ambience', as well as serving food of good quality.

2.15 **Focus** probably has fewer conceptual difficulties, as it ties in very neatly with ideas of market segmentation. In practice most companies pursue this strategy to some extent, by designing products/services to meet the needs of particular target markets.

2.16 'Stuck-in-the-middle' is therefore what many companies actually pursue quite successfully. Any number of strategies can be pursued, with different approaches to **price** and the **perceived added value** (ie the differentiation factor) in the eyes of the customer.

Case example

Petrol is a commodity product, so competitors in the market cannot rely on stressing factors such as brand image and product characteristics to sustain competitive advantage. Instead, they tend to concentrate on cost reduction and operational efficiencies.

Mobil took this one step further in the late 1990s. Because some competitors had access to low cost crude, it realised that a cost leadership strategy was unlikely to be sustainable in the long run. Mobil's strategy for growth therefore aimed to attract customers who bought more petrol than average, were willing to pay higher prices for Mobil petrol, and who would also provide non-petrol revenue (eg from the forecourt's convenience store). To help in this, they identified five distinct consumer segments in the gasoline buying public and targeted the top three.

3 USING THE VALUE CHAIN IN COMPETITIVE STRATEGY

3.1 The value chain can be used to design a competitive strategy, by deploying the various activities strategically. The examples below are based on two supermarket chains, one concentrating on low prices, the other differentiated on quality and service. See if you can tell which is which.

(a)

	INBOUND LOGISTICS	OPERATIONS	OUTBOUND LOGISTICS	MARKETING & SALES	SERVICE
Firm infrastructure	Minimum corporate HQ				
Human resource management		De-skilled store-ops	Dismissal for checkout error		
Technology development	Computerised warehousing		Checkouts simple		
Procurement	Branded only purchases big discounts	Low cost sites			Use of concessions
	Bulk warehousing	1,000 lines only		Low price promotion	Nil
		Price points		Local focus	
		Basic store design			

(b)

	INBOUND LOGISTICS	OPERATIONS	OUTBOUND LOGISTICS	MARKETING & SALES	SERVICE
Firm infrastructure	Central control of operations and credit control				
Human resource management	Recruitment of mature staff	Client care training	Flexible staff to help with packing		
Technology development		Recipe research	Electronic point of sale	Consumer research & tests	Itemised bills
Procurement	Own label products	Prime retail positions		Adverts in quality magazines & poster sites	
	Dedicated refrigerated transport	In store food halls Modern store design Open front refrigerators Tight control of sell-by dates	Collect by car service	No price discounts on food past sell-by dates	No quibble refunds

3.2   The two supermarkets represented are based on the following.

(a)   The value chain in 3.1(a) is similar to that of Lidl, a 'discount' supermarket chain which sells on price, pursuing a cost leadership, or perhaps more accurately, a cost-focus strategy. This can be seen in the limited product range and its low-cost sites.

(b)   The value chain in 3.1(b) is based on Marks and Spencer, which seeks to differentiate on quality and service. Hence the 'no quibble' refunds, the use of prime retail sites, and customer care training.

3.3   You can probably think of other innovations, such as loyalty cards and Internet shopping.

4   PRICING AND COMPETITION

> **KEY TERM**
>
> **Pricing.** 'The determination of a selling price for the product or service produced. A number of methodologies may be used.
>
> *Competitive pricing*
> Setting a price by reference to the prices of competitive products.
>
> *Cost plus pricing*
> The determination of price by adding a markup, which may incorporate a desired return on investment, to a measure of the cost of the product/service.
>
> *Dual pricing*
> A form of transfer pricing in which the two parties to a common transaction use different prices.
>
> *Historical Pricing*
> Basing current prices on prior period prices, perhaps uplifted by a factor such as inflation.
>
> *Market based pricing*
> Setting a price based on the value of the product in the perception of the customer. Also known as perceived value pricing.

KEY TERM cont.

Penetration pricing
Setting a low selling price in order to gain market share.

Predatory pricing
Setting a low selling price in order to damage competitors. This may involve dumping, which is selling a product in a foreign market at below cost, or below the domestic market price.

Price skimming
Setting a high price in order to maximise short-term profitability, often on the introduction of a novel product.

Range pricing
The pricing of individual products such that their prices fit logically within a range of connected products offered by one supplier, and differentiated by a factor such as weight of pack or number of product attributes offered.

Selective pricing
Setting different prices for the same product or service in different markets. This practise can be broken down as follows:

- *Category pricing.* Cosmetically modifying a product such that the variations allow it to sell in a number of price categories, as where a range of 'brands' are based on a common product.

- *Customer group pricing.* Modifying the price of a product or service so that different groups of consumers pay different prices.

- *Peak pricing.* Setting a price which varies according to level of demand.

- *Service level pricing.* Setting a price based on the particular level of service chosen from a range.

Time and material pricing
A form of cost plus pricing in which price is determined by reference to the cost of the labour and material inputs to the product/service.'

(CIMA *Official Terminology*)

Price in the marketing mix

4.1 All profit organisations and many non-profit organisations face the task of **setting a price** on their products or services. Price can go by many names: fares, tuitions, rent, assessments and so on.

4.2 Price can be defined as a measure of the **value exchanged by the buyer for the value offered by the seller**. It might be expected, therefore, that the price would reflect the costs to the seller of producing the product and the benefit to the buyer of consuming it.

4.3 Unlike the other marketing mix elements, pricing decisions affect profits through their impact on **revenues** rather than costs. It also has an important role as a **competitive tool** to differentiate a product and an organisation and thereby exploit market opportunities.

4.4 Although pricing can be thought of as fulfilling a number of roles, in overall terms a price aims to produce the desired level of sales in order to meet the objectives of the business strategy.

4.5 Two broad categories of objectives may be specified for pricing decisions.

(a) **Maximising profits** is concerned with maximising the returns on assets or investments. This may be realised even with a comparatively small market share depending on the patterns of cost and demand.

(b) **Maintaining or increasing market share** involves increasing or maintaining the customer base which may require a different, more competitive approach to pricing, while the company with the largest market share may not necessarily earn the best profits.

Pricing and the customer

Elasticity of demand

4.6 Pricing policy is also crucial in matching production capacity with customer demand. The concept of price elasticity is important.

$$\frac{\% \text{ change in sales demand}}{\% \text{ change in sales price}}$$

(a) When elasticity is greater than 1 (ie **elastic**), a change in price will lead to a change in total revenue.

(i) If the price is lowered, total sales revenue would rise, because of the large increase in demand.

(ii) If the price is raised, total sales revenue would fall because of the large fall in demand.

(b) When elasticity is less than 1 (ie **inelastic**) the following will happen.

(i) If the price is lowered, total sales revenue would fall, because the increase in sales volume would be too small to compensate for the price reduction.

(ii) If the price is raised, total sales revenue would go up in spite of the small drop in sales quantities.

Price sensitivity

4.7 **Price sensitivity** will vary amongst purchasers. Those that can pass on the cost of purchases will be the least sensitive and will therefore respond more to other elements of perceived value.

(a) The family on holiday is likely to be very price sensitive when choosing an overnight stay.

(b) In industrial marketing the purchasing manager is likely to be more price sensitive than the engineer who will use the new equipment that is being sourced.

Price perception and quality connotations

4.8 **Price perception** is an important factor in the ways customers react to prices. For example, customers may react to a price increase by buying more. This could be for a variety of reasons.

(a) They expect further price increases to follow (they are 'stocking up')

(b) Many customers appear to judge quality by price

- They assume the quality has increased, if there is a price rise
- The brand takes on a 'snob appeal' because of the high price

Intermediaries' objectives

4.9 If an organisation distributes products or services to the market through independent **intermediaries,** the objectives of these intermediaries complicate the pricing decision. Such intermediaries are likely to deal with a range of suppliers and their aims concern their own profits rather than those of suppliers.

Suppliers

4.10 If an organisation's suppliers notice a price rise for the organisation's products, they may seek a rise in the price for their supplies to the organisation on the grounds that it is now able to pay a higher price.

Inflation

4.11 In periods of inflation the organisation may need to change prices to reflect increases in the prices of supplies, labour, rent and so on.

Exchange rates

4.12 Changes in the rate of exchange can lead to price rises or decreases, and are particularly relevant to importers and exporters.

Income effects

4.13 In times of rising incomes, price may become a less important marketing variable compared with product quality and convenience of access (distribution). When income levels are falling and/or unemployment levels rising, price will become a much more important marketing variable.

Multiple products and loss leaders

4.14 Most organisations sell a range of products. The management of the pricing function is likely to focus on the profit from the whole range rather than the profit on each single product. Take, for example, the use of **loss leaders***:* a very low price for one product is intended to make consumers buy additional products in the range which carry higher profit margins.

Ethics

4.15 Ethical considerations are a further factor, for example whether or not to exploit short-term shortages through higher prices. The outcry surrounding the series of petrol price rises following the outbreak of the Gulf Crisis in 1990 was a good example of public sensitivity to pricing decisions.

New product pricing: market penetration and market skimming

4.16 There are three elements in the pricing decision for a new product.

- Getting the product **accepted**
- Maintaining a **market share** in the face of competition
- Making a **profit** from the product

Penetration

4.17 **Market penetration** pricing is a policy of low prices when the product is first launched in order to gain sufficient penetration into the market. It is therefore a policy of sacrificing short-term profits in the interests of long-term profits.

(a) The firm wishes to **discourage rivals** from entering the market.

(b) The firm wishes to **shorten the initial period of the product's life cycle**, in order to enter the growth and maturity stages as quickly as possible. (This would happen if there is high elasticity of demand for the product.)

Skimming

4.18 **Market skimming**. The aim of market skimming is to gain high unit profits very early on in the product's life.

(a) The firm charges high prices when a product is first launched.

(b) The firm spends heavily on advertising and sales promotion to win customers.

(c) As the product moves into the later stages of its life cycle (growth, maturity and decline) progressively lower prices will be charged. The profitable 'cream' is thus 'skimmed' off in progressive stages until sales can only be sustained at lower prices.

(d) The firm may lower its prices in order to attract more price-elastic segments of the market; however, these price reductions will be gradual. Alternatively, the entry of competitors into the market may make price reductions inevitable.

4.19 **Introductory offers** and temporary **discounts** may be used to attract an initial customer interest.

Other pricing decisions

4.20 **Promotional prices** are short-term price reductions or price offers which are intended to attract an increase in sales volume. (The increase is usually short-term for the duration of the offer, which does not appear to create any substantial new customer loyalty). Loss leaders and 'money off' coupons are a form of promotional pricing.

4.21 A temporary **price cut** may be preferable to a permanent reduction because it can be ended without unduly offending customers and can be reinstated later to give a repeated boost to sales.

Pricing and the management accountant

4.22 The decision about pricing is one which involves both the accountant and the marketing manager.

4.23 **Short-term pricing**. Marketing management should have the responsibility for estimating the price-demand inter-relationship for their organisation's products. The accountant should become involved in short-term pricing decisions because of cost.

(a) The sales-revenue maximising price for a product and the profit-maximising price might not be the same.

(b) Simple CVP analysis can be used to estimate the breakeven point of sales, and the sales volume needed to achieve a target profit figure.

(c) Many organisations use a **cost-plus** approach to pricing. Accounting figures are needed for cost in order to establish a floor for making a cost-plus pricing decision.

4.24 By analysing **product profitability**, the accountant also provides information for pricing control, because profit statements indicate whether prices have been high enough, given the sales demand, to provide a satisfactory return.

Discount policy

4.25 The purpose of discounts is to encourage more sales (or earlier payment). The cost of discounts should not exceed the benefits from extra sales or earlier payment, and the size of discounts offered should not be excessive. After all, why offer a 15% discount for a sale if the customer would still buy if he obtained a 10% discount?

Competitive bidding and tendering

4.26 Competitive bidding calls for the preparation of cost data for the purpose of submitting a bid to a potential customer, in the hope of securing his order. There will be three factors in the customer's choice of supplier from among the tenders submitted.

   (a) The **price** itself.

   (b) **Performance**, especially if the product is new and largely untested in the open market, reliability, service etc.

   (c) **Financial matters,** such as inflation (and cost escalation clauses) and foreign exchange rates (for overseas contracts), export credit insurance.

4.27 Co-operation is needed between the accounting and marketing departments of a bidding company because a balance has to be drawn between putting in a bid which is too low to make an adequate profit, but keeping the bid low enough to stand a good chance of winning the contract.

Price and competition

4.28 In classical economic theory, price is the major determinant of demand and brings together supply and demand to form an equilibrium market price. However, economic theory can only determine the optimal price structure under the two extreme market conditions.

   (a) **Perfect competition:** many buyers and many sellers all dealing in an identical product. Neither producer nor user has any market power and both must accept the prevailing market price.

   (b) **Monopoly:** one seller who dominates many buyers. The monopolist can use his market power to set a profit maximising price.

4.29 However, in practice most of British industry can be described as an **oligopoly:** where relatively few competitive companies dominate the market.

Price leadership

4.30 Given that price competition can have disastrous consequences in conditions of oligopoly, it is not unusual to find that large corporations emerge as price leaders.

4.31 A price leader will have the dominant influence on price levels for a class of products. Price increases or decreases by the price leader provide a direction to market price patterns.

4.32 However, a danger with price leadership is that it might appear to limit the impact of competition. If firms actively collude to keep prices to a certain level, and to divide the 'spoils' between them, they are forming a cartel. Cartels are illegal under UK and European competition law.

4.33 Generally speaking, therefore, price cuts to increase market share will be matched by competitors in some way. If a rival firm cuts its prices in the expectation of increasing its market share, a firm has the following options.

(a) **Maintain its existing prices**. This would be done if the expectation is that only a small market share would be lost, so that it is more profitable to keep prices at their existing level. Eventually, the rival firm may drop out of the market or be forced to raise its prices.

(b) **Maintain prices but respond with a non-price counter-attack**. This is a more positive response, because the firm will be securing or justifying its current prices with a product change, advertising, or better back-up services, etc.

(c) **Reduce prices**. This should protect the firm's market share so that the main beneficiary from the price reduction will be the consumer.

(d) **Raise prices and respond with a non-price counter-attack**. A price increase would be based on a campaign to emphasise the quality difference between the rival products.

4.34 **Predatory pricing** is the use of price to drive a competitor out of business. It is a grey area, as competing on price is legitimate and economically efficient.

4.35 The intensely competitive supermarket sector in the UK and US provides a prime example of periodic price cutting activity, that can lead in extreme cases to all-out price 'wars' between the largest competitors. **Price competition** like this will undermine the value of the market that is being competed for.

4.36 Here are some questions that companies in such an environment might ask themselves.

- What is the minimum potential **sales loss** that justifies meeting a **lower competitive price**?

- What is the minimum potential **sales gain** that justifies **not following** a competitive price **increase**?

- What is the minimum potential **sales loss** that justifies **not following** a competitive price **decrease**?

4.37 EXAMPLE

Deere Ltd's largest competitor has reduced its prices by 15%. Deere currently enjoys a contribution margin of 45%. If Deere's customers are highly loyal there will of course be no need to respond, but what sales volume change would justify a response?

4.38 SOLUTION

	@ Reduced price £85	@ Current price £100
	£	£
Sales revenue (3,000 units)	255,000	300,000
Variable cost (£55 per unit)	165,000	165,000
Contribution	90,000	135,000
Contribution margin	35.3%	45%

Deere Ltd needs to work out the level of sales at the current price (£100) which will yield the same contribution as current sales volume at the new reduced price. If sales decrease below that level, the company should match the price change. The relevant formula is below.

$$\frac{\text{\% breakeven sales change}}{\text{for reactive price change}} = \frac{\text{Change in price}}{\text{Contribution margin}} = \frac{-15\%}{45\%} = -33^{1}/_{3}\%$$

If Deere Ltd is to generate £90,000 worth of contribution at current price levels, sales can drop by $33^{1}/_{3}$, or 1,000 units, as demonstrated below.

	£
Sales revenue (2,000 units)	200,000
Variable cost	110,000
Contribution	90,000

If sales fall any further, Deere should match the price change.

4.39 Note that in the formula, 'breakeven sales' refers to the **level of sales needed to generate the same contribution**.

4.40 For the purposes of this example, Deere Ltd has a choice between reducing its prices by 15% or maintaining them at current levels. If it does reduce its prices, contribution decreases (assuming sales volume stays the same). If it maintains it prices, it can expect sales volume to fall.

4.41 We can of course turn this on its head and, still applying the formula above, say that if Deere Ltd's competitors had **increased** their prices by 15%, a 33.3% **gain** in sales volume would have to be realised in order for 'doing nothing' to be more profitable than a reactive price increase. This is of course a simplistic analysis that assumes sales volumes will rise and fall exactly in line with any price changes, but it illustrates the issues involved.

Competitive pricing actions

4.42 Different competitive pricing actions can say a lot about a company's strategy and send signals to the market.

(a) **Reducing price below that of competitors** in order to win a contract gives certain messages.

- The company is desperate for sales volume
- It believes it is the lowest cost supplier
- The target customer is strategically important

(b) **Reducing price by the same amount as a competitor,** in order to win back business, demonstrates to that competitor that contracts cannot be won or lost on price considerations alone.

(c) **Substantial price reductions** and public announcements of new manufacturing facilities show the market that despite price reductions, sales are set to expand and revenues will not decrease in the long term.

(d) A **quick negotiation of lower prices** without alerting the competition indicates a belief that a gain can be made through the short term winning of a customer.

5   PRODUCT-MARKET STRATEGY: DIRECTION OF GROWTH

Pilot paper, 5/01

KEY TERM

Product-market mix is a short hand term for the **products/services** a firm sells (or a service which a public sector organisation provides) and the **markets** it sells them to.

Product-market mix: Ansoff's growth vector matrix

5.1   Ansoff drew up a **growth vector matrix**, describing a combination of a firm's activities in current and new markets, with existing and new products.

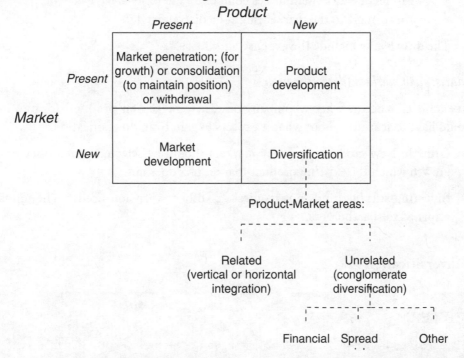

Exam focus point

Do not confuse this matrix with the BCG matrix of market growth and share! You must be familiar with core strategic planning models and be able to use them confidently in the exam. The strategy outlined by the company in the November 2001 case study (IRS Ltd) included product and market development.

Current products and current markets: market penetration

5.2   **Market penetration**. The firm seeks to:

- **Maintain or to increase its share** of current markets with current products, eg through competitive pricing, advertising, sales promotion

- Secure dominance of growth markets

- Restructure a mature market by driving out competitors

- Increase usage by existing customers (eg airmiles, loyalty cards)

Present products and new markets: market development

5.3 • New geographical areas and export markets

• Different package sizes for food and other domestic items

• New distribution channels to attract new customers

• Differential pricing policies to attract different types of customer and create new market segments.

New products and present markets: product development

5.4 Product development is the launch of new products to existing markets.

(a) Advantages

• Product development forces competitors to innovate
• Newcomers to the market might be discouraged

(b) The drawbacks include the expense and the risk.

New products: new markets (diversification)

5.5 Diversification occurs when a company decides to make new products for new markets. It should have a clear idea about what it expects to gain from diversification.

(a) Growth. New products and new markets should be selected which offer prospects for growth which the existing product-market mix does not.

(b) Investing surplus funds not required for other expansion needs. (The funds could be returned to shareholders.)

Related diversification

> **KEY TERM**
>
> Related diversification is 'development beyond the present product market, but still within the broad confines of the industry ... [it] ... therefore builds on the assets or activities which the firm has developed' (Johnson and Scholes). It takes the form of vertical or horizontal integration.

5.6 Horizontal integration refers to development into activities which are competitive with or directly complementary to a company's present activities. For example, Polygram finances film production.

5.7 Vertical integration occurs when a company becomes its own:

(a) Supplier of raw materials, components or services (backward vertical integration). For example, backward integration would occur where a milk producer acquires its own dairy farms rather than buying raw milk from independent farmers.

(b) Distributor or sales agent (forward vertical integration), for example: where a manufacturer of synthetic yarn begins to produce shirts from the yarn instead of selling it to other shirt manufacturers.

5.8 Advantages of vertical integration

- A **secure supply of components** or **materials,** thus lower supplier bargaining power
- **Stronger relationships** with the 'final consumer' of the product
- Win a share of the **higher profits** at all stages of the value chain
- Pursue a **differentiation strategy** more effectively
- Raise **barriers to entry**

5.9 **Disadvantages of vertical integration**

(a) **Overconcentration.** A company places 'more eggs in the same end-market basket' (Ansoff). Such a policy is fairly inflexible, more sensitive to instabilities and increases the firm's dependence on a particular aspect of economic demand.

(b) The firm **fails to benefit from any economies of scale or technical advances** in the industry into which it has diversified. This is why, in the publishing industry, most printing is subcontracted to specialist printing firms, who can work machinery to capacity by doing work for many firms.

(c) **Risk.** Ward regards the benefits of vertical integration as 'one of the all-time great myths of the business world'. 'In most cases, vertical integration strategies take the business away from their previous areas of competitive strength and involve managers in new products with new technologies and processes'. Ward believes that vertical integration increases the risk to shareholders, without a corresponding return, thus leading to an erosion in value.

Unrelated diversification

> **KEY TERM**
>
> **Unrelated or conglomerate diversification** 'is development beyond the present industry into products/ markets which, at face value, may bear no close relation to the present product/market.'

5.10 Conglomerate diversification is now very unfashionable. However, it has been a key strategy for companies in Asia, particularly South Korea.

5.11 **Advantages of conglomerate diversification**

- **Risk-spreading** by entering new products into new markets
- An improvement of the **overall profitability and flexibility** of the firm through acquisition
- **Escape** from the present business
- **Better access to capital** markets
- **No other way to grow**
- **Use surplus cash**
- **Exploit under-utilised resources**
- **Obtain cash,** or other financial advantages (such as accumulated tax losses)
- **Use a company's image and reputation** in one market to develop into another

5.12 **Disadvantages of conglomerate diversification**

- The **dilution of shareholders' earnings**
- **Lack of a common identity and purpose** in a conglomerate organisation
- **Failure in one of the businesses will drag down the rest**
- **Lack of management experience.**

Diversification and synergy

5.13 **Synergy** is the 2 + 2 = 5 effect, where a firm looks for **combined results** that reflect a better rate of return than would be achieved by the same resources used independently as separate operations. Synergy is used to justify diversification.

5.14 **Obtaining synergy**

(a) **Marketing synergy:** use of common marketing facilities such as distribution channels, sales staff and administration, and warehousing.

(b) **Operating synergy:** arises from the better use of operational facilities and personnel, bulk purchasing, a greater spread of fixed costs whereby the firm's competence can be transferred to making new products. For example, although there is very little in common between sausages and ice cream, both depend on a competence of refrigeration.

(c) **Investment synergy:** the joint use of plant, common raw material stocks, transfer of research and development from one product to another - ie from the wider use of a common investment in fixed assets, working capital or research.

(d) **Management synergy:** the advantage to be gained where management skills concerning current operations are easily transferred to new operations because of the similarity of problems in the two industries.

Question 2

A large organisation in road transport operates nationwide in general haulage. This field has become very competitive and with the recent down-turn in trade, has become only marginally profitable. It has been suggested that the strategic structure of the company should be widened to include other aspects of physical distribution so that the maximum synergy would be obtained from that type of diversification.

Suggest two activities which might fit into the suggested new strategic structure, explaining each one briefly. Explain how each of these activities could be incorporated into the existing structure. State the advantages and disadvantages of such diversification.

Answer

The first step in a suggested solution is to think of how a company operating nationwide in general road haulage might diversify, with some synergistic benefits. Perhaps you thought of the following.

(a) To move from nationwide to international haulage, the company might be able to use its existing contacts with customers to develop an international trade. Existing administration and depot facilities in the UK could be used. Drivers should be available who are willing to work abroad, and the scope for making reasonable profits should exist. However, international road haulage might involve the company in the purchase of new vehicles (eg road haulage in Europe often involves the carriage of containerised products on large purpose-built vehicles). Since international haulage takes longer, vehicles will be tied up in jobs for several days, and a substantial investment might be required to develop the business. In addition, in the event of breakdowns, a network of overseas garage service arrangements will have to be created. It might take some time before business builds up sufficiently to become profitable.

(b) Moving from general haulage to 'speciality' types of haulage, perhaps haulage of large items of plant and machinery, or computer equipment. The same broad considerations apply to speciality types of haulage. Existing depot facilities could be used and existing customer contacts might be developed. However, expertise in specialist work will have to be 'brought in' as well as developed within the company and special vehicles might need to be bought. Business might take some time to build up and if the initial investment is high, there could be substantial early losses.

Withdrawal

5.15 It might be the right decision to cease producing a product and/or to pull out of a market completely. This is a hard decision for managers to take if they have invested time and money or if the decision involves redundancies.

5.16 **Exit barriers** make this difficult.

- Cost barriers include redundancy costs and the difficulty of selling assets
- Managers might fail to grasp opportunity costing
- Political barriers include government attitudes
- Marketing considerations may delay withdrawal
- Managers hate to admit failure
- People might wrongly assume that carrying on is a low risk strategy

5.17 **Reasons for exit**

- The company's business may be in buying and selling firms
- Resource limitations mean that less profitable businesses have to be abandoned
- A company may be forced to quit, because of insolvency
- Change of competitive strategy
- Decline in attractiveness of the market
- Funds can earn more elsewhere

Guidelines for a product-market strategy

5.18 Johnson and Scholes suggested the following principles and guidelines for product-market planning.

(a) **The potential for improvement and growth.** It is one thing to eliminate unprofitable products but will there be sufficient growth potential among the products that remain in the product range?

(b) **Cash generation.** New products require some initial capital expenditure. Retained profits are by far the most significant source of new funds for companies. A company investing in the medium to long term which does not have enough current income from existing products, will go into liquidation, in spite of its future prospects.

(c) **The timing decision for killing off existing products.** There are some situations where existing products should be kept going for a while longer, to provide or maintain a necessary platform for launching new models.

(d) **The long-term rationale of a product or market development.**

(e) **Diversification by acquisition.** It might pay to buy product ranges or brands in a takeover deal. If the product-market strategy includes a policy of diversification, then the products or services which the expanding company should seek to acquire should provide definite benefits. We discuss acquisitions in the next chapter.

Closing the profit gap and product-market strategy

5.19 The aim of product-market strategies is to **close the profit gap** that is found by gap analysis. A mixture of strategies may be needed to do this.

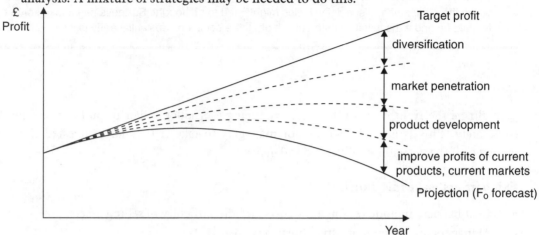

5.20 It is worth remembering that **divestment** is a product-market option to close the profit gap, if the business is creating losses.

5.21 A related question in what do you do with spare capacity - go for market penetration, or go into new markets. Many companies begin exporting into new overseas markets to use surplus capacity.

5.22 The strategies in the Ansoff matrix are not mutually exclusive. A firm can quite legitimately pursue a penetration strategy in some of its markets, while aiming to enter new markets.

Brand switching and competitive rivalry

5.23 A company may introduce measures to counteract **brand switching** by 'disloyal' customers (and consequent loss of market share). One example is provided by the 'loyalty card' schemes used by supermarkets to encourage repeat (and increased) spending by customers who may otherwise 'defect' to the opposition.

5.24 To evaluate investment in loyalty cards as an example, we could use the following analysis.

5.25 EXAMPLE

Two supermarkets currently have 50% each of the market share in their catchment area, with the same percentages of loyal and floating customers.

	Loyal customers	*Floating customers*
	%	%
Foodsmart	80	20
Valuestop	80	20

5.26 After the introduction of a loyalty card by Foodsmart, the percentages shift slightly.

	Loyal customers	*Floating customers*
	%	%
Foodsmart	90	10
Valuestop	80	20

5.27 How would this affect the respective market shares? We can use an equation.

Let F = equilibrium market share Foodsmart
Let V = equilibrium market share Valuestop

We will assume F + V = 1

$$0.9F + 0.2V = F$$
$$0.2V = 0.1F$$

If we substitute $\quad F = 1 - V$
$$0.2V = 0.1(1 - V)$$
$$0.2V = 0.1 - 0.1V$$
$$0.3V = 0.1$$
$$V = 33.3\%$$
$$\therefore \quad F = 66.7\%$$

5.28 A company such as Foodsmart or Valuestop will be able to use financial modelling to evaluate what a 1% change in the market share will do to its revenues and profitability, and decide what levels of investment in marketing spending may be required.

5.29 To improve competitive position further, Foodsmart and Valuestop may have to invest in other initiatives such as Internet shopping, in-store facilities and improved product availability.

Unity Bicycles plc

(1) What competitive strategy is UB pursuing, if you can identify one? Do you think UB is pursuing the right competitive strategy?

(2) To what extent was MT a vertically integrated company when it owned UB?

(3) Do you think UB should take over one of its Chinese licencees under direct ownership?

(4) What are the main influences on UB's pricing policy?

Chapter roundup

- There are three categories of strategic choice.

    ◦ **how** you compete
    ◦ **where** you compete
    ◦ **method** of growth

- **Strategic marketing issues** include market share, which may sometimes be correlated with return on investment, and segmentation (choosing which customers to pursue).

- A firm needs to choose a **competitive strategy**. Three suggested are **cost leadership**, **differentiation** or **focus**.

    ◦ Cost leadership - be the lowest cost purchaser
    ◦ Differentiation - a different product, higher prices
    ◦ Focus - concentrate on a segment

- However, cost leaders in practice do not compete on price, and have other uses for the cash generated.

- The **value chain** can be used to design a competitive strategy

- **Pricing strategy** is an important component, both as part of the marketing mix and as a company's competitive weapon.

- **Product-market strategy** refers to the mix of products and markets. Segmentation is important in identifying new markets, and a firm will use a marketing mix to arrive at a particular market position. The Ansoff matrix identifies various options.

    ◦ **Market penetration**: current products, current markets
    ◦ **Market development**: current products, new markets
    ◦ **Product development**: new products, current markets
    ◦ **Diversification**: new products, new markets

- All of these can secure growth. **Diversification** is often perceived to be most **risky**. Although justified by 'synergies' (common assets, expertise etc which can be applied in a number of different business areas), these are often more apparent than real.

Quick quiz

1   What are the three categories of strategic choice?

    ....

    ....

    ....

2   What is the difference between horizontal boundaries and vertical boundaries?

3   **Fill in the blanks**

    In the context of generic strategies:

    (1) .... and (2) .... are industry wide strategies

    (3) .... involves segmentation

4   A differentiation strategy assumes that competitive advantage can be gained through particular characteristics of a firm's products.

    ☐ True
    ☐ False

5   In a focus strategy a firm tries to serve the entire market with a single product

    ☐ True
    ☐ False

6   Define 'price'.

7   Give the formula for price elasticity

    $$\frac{\%}{\%}$$

8   A pricing policy that aims to gain high unit profits very early in the product's life is known as

Market penetration
Market skimming

9   What is the 'product market mix'?

10   Fill in the Ansoff matrix

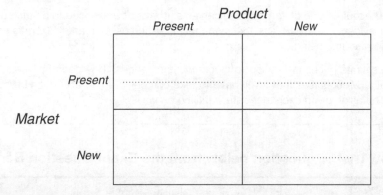

Product

	Present	New
Present	....	....
New	....	....

Market

Unity Bicycles plc review

Question 1. UB is pursuing a number of focus strategies, with different approaches to different markets. Its products include the four types of bicycles; its other 'product' is more of a service: this is the expertise in licensing to the Chinese firms. At the same time, it is not trying to be a cost leader, but is trying to prevent other firms from benefiting from that position.

Question 2. MT's purchase of UB was an example of forwards vertical integration, in that UB is in a consumer product industry, and MT hoped to reap the profit at this level.

Question 3. If UB acquired one of its Chinese licencees, it would be exposed to a much greater risk, and there is no evidence that UB has the managerial resources or market expertise to make a success of this for the time being.

Question 4. UB sets its prices in relation to its competitors' prices. This does not mean it sets the same prices, but UB recognises that it will have to take competitors into account. However, pricing in sterling might be risky, given exchange rate volatility.

Now try the question below from the Exam Question Bank

Question to try	Level	Marks	Time
8	Pilot paper	25	45 mins

This mind map demonstrates how models can be interlinked, by showing as an example the connections between the experience curve, the product life cycle and market share.

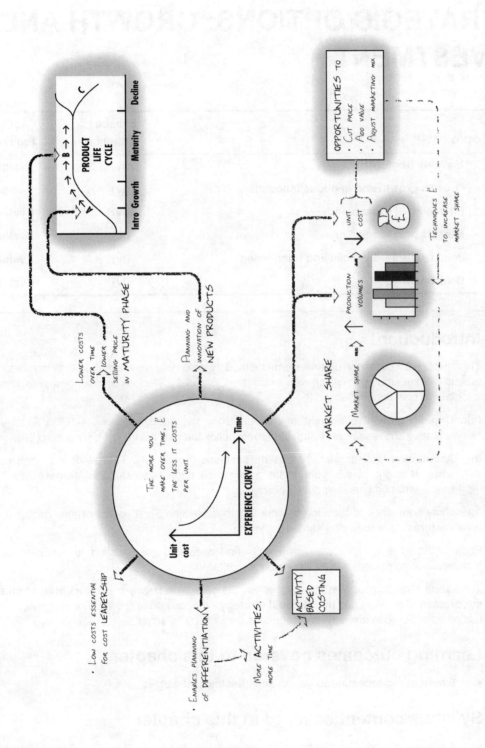

Chapter 10

STRATEGIC OPTIONS: GROWTH AND DIVESTMENT

Topic list	Syllabus reference	Ability required
1 Methods of growth	(iv)	Evaluation
2 Organic growth and in-house innovation	(iv)	Evaluation
3 International expansion	(iv)	Evaluation
4 Mergers and acquisitions	(iv)	Evaluation
5 Joint ventures, alliances and franchising	(iv)	Evaluation
6 Divestment	(iv)	Evaluation

Introduction

This chapter discusses the organisational method by which companies pursue their competitive and product-market strategies (which we identified in Chapter 9). We look at international expansion as a topic in its own right in Section 3.

(a) **Organic growth**: effectively, any expansion is managed internally, with the firm's existing expertise and resources. A firm effectively builds the new business from scratch (Section 2).

(b) **Acquisition**: buy an already existing business (Section 4). Takeovers are often headline news. It might benefit your exam answers to quote an example. **Mergers** occur when businesses combine their operations.

(c) Many firms seek to combine or work together (Section 5). A variety of arrangements - **joint ventures**, **alliances** etc - can be exploited.

Each method has its particular advantages and disadvantages, relating to a whole variety of factors, including risk, resources and corporate culture.

Try and be clear in your own mind, however, the difference between **product-market strategy** - the direction of growth - and **institutional strategy** - the method of growth. For example, a firm can use organic growth to diversify, but it can also diversify by takeover.

Learning outcomes covered in this chapter

- **Evaluate** and **recommend** growth and divestment strategies

Syllabus content covered in this chapter

- Advantages and disadvantages of different methods of growth, including international acquisitions. The evaluation of growth strategies

- Divestment strategies and demergers and the evaluation of such actions

BPP PUBLISHING

1 METHODS OF GROWTH

1.1 Once a firm has made its choice as to which strategies to pursue it needs to choose an appropriate **mechanism**.

- Develop the business from scratch
- Acquire or merge with an already existing business
- Co-operate in some way with another firm

Case study link

The May 2001 Final Level Case Study examined the strategic options faced by the subject company, Proton Quest. The options ranged from forming strategic alliances to doing nothing, and candidates were asked to make a recommendation.

1.2 The main issues involved in choosing a method of growth are these.

- A firm many not be able to go it alone, or it may have plenty of **resources** to invest
- Two different businesses might have **complementary skills**
- Does a firm need to **move fast**?
- A firm might wish to **retain control** of a product or process
- Combining businesses involves integrating **people and organisation culture**
- **Risk**. A firm may either increase or reduce the level of risk to which it is subject.

1.3 The type of relationships between two or more firms can display differing degrees of intensity.

- **Formal integration**: acquisition and merger
- **Formalised ownership/relationship,** such as a joint venture
- **Contractual relationships,** such as franchising

2 ORGANIC GROWTH AND IN-HOUSE INNOVATION

2.1 **Organic growth** is the primary method of growth for many organisations. Organic growth is achieved through the development of internal resources.

> ### KEY TERM
>
> **Organic growth**. Expansion of a firm's size, profits, activities achieved without taking over other firms.

2.2 Why might a firm pursue organic growth?

- The **process of developing** a new product gives the firm the best understanding of the market and the product

- It might be the only sensible way to pursue **genuine technological innovations**

- There is **no suitable target for acquisition**

- It can be planned and financed easily from the company's **current resources**

- The same **style of management** and corporate culture can be maintained

- **Hidden or unforeseen losses** are less likely with organic growth

2.3 If we assume that existing products have a finite life, a strategy of organic growth must include plans for **innovation**.

- It provides the organisation with a **distinctive competence**, and with the ability to maintain such a competence

- It maintains the organisation's **competitive advantage** and market share

Innovation strategy

2.4 Managers responsible for product development may be assigned the strategic objective of finding eight or so successful new products at regular intervals during the next ten years so as to achieve given sales and profit targets over that period of time. Key questions to ask will include the following.

- Who are our customers?
- What do they want now?
- What will they want next year?
- Why should they come to us rather than one of our rivals?
- How do we generate, capture and develop ideas?
- How should we set about identifying and meeting business opportunities?

2.5 Innovation strategies can be grouped into three broad categories.

(a) **Attack or leader strategies**. An organisation can try to be the first one to exploit an innovation, by marketing a new product. The new product might be aimed initially at a particular niche market, and if this is successful, other niche markets can subsequently be 'attacked' and exploited one by one. Attack strategies are usually identified as one of the following:

   (i) **Frontal**

   This is based upon a **direct attack** upon a competitor's strengths rather than its weaknesses. The outcome depends upon the competitor's **defensive capability**. A company employing this strategy would have to match or improve upon aspects of the competitor's marketing mix in all its markets.

   (ii) **Flanking**

   This strategy involves attacking a competitor's market share at the points where it is weakest. A competitor may be weak in particular **geographical areas** or in particular **market segments,** so targeting these new areas and segments could be beneficial. There may be market needs that the competitor is not meeting with its version of the product.

   (iii) **Encirclement**

   This is only possible where the aggressor has more resources. Attacking the competitor on all sides by developing the marketing mix in all areas (improved product, better distribution networks, enhanced promotion and lower price) is likely to be beyond a small company's capabilities. It is unlikely that it would be able to overwhelm a large competitor on several fronts.

   (iv) **By-pass**

   This strategy would involve concentrating on entirely **new products and markets** as a way of coping with competitor dominance in one particular segment. Techniques may include developing unrelated products, new geographical markets or, most likely, **new technologies** where the competitor is not active.

   (v)   **Guerilla**

This is another strategy suitable for smaller aggressors. Small attacks could be waged on various fronts in the marketing mix to undermine a competitor's position. **Intense promotional activity** could be an option. As a general observation, substantial promotional spending is only a good idea if a company can exhibit demonstrable superiority over competing products.

The aim of guerilla attacks is to gain a **foothold** as a prelude to a more sustained and aggressive challenge. Conducting a guerilla campaign of any duration can be expensive.

(b) **Defensive or follower strategies**. An organisation might have to respond to innovation by a competitor, either by introducing the same innovation itself, or protecting itself by taking measures to maintain customer loyalty, for example.

Case study link

The May 2002 case study (Global Incorporated) features a supermarket group that has been outstripped by its more innovative and customer-focused rival. Adopting such a 'follower' strategy has seen its previous advantages eroded.

(c) **Counter-attack strategies**. An organisation might respond to a competitor's innovation by taking measures to 'go one better', and to innovate itself. This might take the form of 'leap-frogging' - ie developing an even more technologically-advanced product than its rival. Leap-frogging has been a feature of competition in the computer manufacturing industry.

2.6   Successful innovation depends on the following.

- Responding to or anticipating **customer and market needs**

- Having people within the organisation who are innovators in **outlook,** and have sufficient **authority** to innovate

- Having a culture, leadership and organisation structure that **encourages innovation**

Case examples

Organic growth by innovation is not always the guarantee of success. The Economist reported a research study into successful innovations.

(a) Pioneers often fail to conjure up a mass market. The first video recorder was developed in 1956 by Ampex - they sold for $50,000. The firm made no attempt to expand the market. Sony, JVC and Matsushita spent 20 years turning it into a mass market product.

(b) Another reason is financial strength. Coca-Cola's Fruitopia brand was positioned against firms such as Snapple which had pioneered the market in non-cola 'alternative beverages'.

Innovative companies are not necessarily the most successful. Success is based upon other factors such as distribution capability, technical expertise and marketing skills. The anti-ulcer drug Zantac from Glaxo was an imitative product, but it overtook Tagamet from SmithKline due to Glaxo's commercial skills in exploiting it.

Capacity issues: critical mass and economies of scale

2.7   For some firms, organic growth must result in a target **critical mass** being achieved, in order to achieve economies of scale. In an industry where fixed costs are high, and variable costs relatively small, significant reductions in unit costs can be achieved by producing on a larger scale.

2.8   For example, suppose that in the widget-manufacturing industry, the following costs are applicable.

Factory capacity (output in units p.a.)	Fixed costs £	Unit variable costs £
10,000	400,000	5.00
50,000	800,000	4.80
200,000	1,600,000	4.60

Unit costs of producing at maximum capacity in each size of factory would be as follows.

Capacity units	Unit costs Fixed £	Unit costs Variable £	Total £	
10,000	40.0	5.0	45.00	Effect of
50,000	16.0	4.8	20.80	economies of
200,000	8.0	4.6	12.60	scale

2.9   If an organisation plans to achieve a certain capacity of output, it will not minimise its costs unless actual production volumes reach the capacity level. In the table above, the factory with 200,000 units capacity can achieve unit costs of £12.60 when operating at full capacity; but if actual production were only 50%, say, unit fixed costs would double to £16, and unit costs would be £20.60 (very nearly as high as in a factory with a 50,000 units capacity operating at full capacity).

3   INTERNATIONAL EXPANSION   11/01

Some key decisions for international expansion

3.1   Firms must deal with three major issues.

- Whether to market abroad at all
- Which markets to enter
- The mode(s) of entry

Why expand overseas?

3.2   An article in *Financial Management* (February 2002) highlighted some issues to consider. Driven by developments in IT, cheap travel and the emergence of giant multinationals, phrases such as 'global economy', 'global markets' and 'global trends' are now part of the language of everyday business. (We looked at issues of globalisation in Chapter 5.)

3.3   Firms may be pushed into international expansion by domestic adversity, or pulled into it by attractive opportunities abroad. More specifically, some of the reasons firms expand overseas are the following. They can be classified as either **internal** or **external** factors.

(a)   **Chance.** Firms may enter a particular country or countries by chance. A company executive may recognise an opportunity while on a foreign trip or the firm may receive chance orders or requests for information from potential foreign customers.

(b) **Life cycle.** Home sales may be in the mature or decline stages of the product life cycle. International expansion may allow sales growth since products are often in different stages of the product life cycle in different countries.

Case study link

In the November 2001 case study, IRS Ltd considered global expansion its only chance to grow sales.

(c) **Competition.** Intense competition in an overcrowded domestic market sometimes induces firms to seek markets overseas where rivalry is less keen. This was a major reason in Gillette's decision to begin marketing razor blades outside its US home markets.

(d) **Reduce dependence.** Many companies wish to diversify away from an over-dependence on a single domestic market. Increased geographic diversification can help to **spread risk**.

(e) **Economies of scale.** Technological factors may be such that a large volume is needed either to cover the high costs of plant, equipment, R&D and personnel or to exploit a large potential for economies of scale and experience. For these reasons firms in the aviation, ethical drugs, computer and automobile industries are often obliged to enter multiple countries.

(f) **Variable quality.** International expansion can facilitate the disposal of discontinued products and seconds since these can be sold abroad without spoiling the home market. Conversely, many companies, such as most UK pottery manufacturers, reserve their first quality outputs for sale in lucrative high income countries like the USA, selling only seconds in the home country.

(g) **Finance.** Many firms are attracted by favourable opportunities such as the following.

    (i)   The development of lucrative emerging markets (such as China and India)
    (ii)   Depreciation in their domestic currency values
    (iii) Corporate tax benefits offered by particular countries
    (iv) Lowering of import barriers abroad

(h) **Familial.** Many countries and companies trade because of family or cultural connections overseas. For example, the Kenyan horticultural industry exports to the UK.

(i) **Aid agencies.** Countries that benefit from bilateral or unilateral aid often purchase goods which normally they would not have the money for. Toyota vehicles have been bought for aid projects in Africa via United Nations development funds.

3.4   (a) **Reasons supporting involvement overseas**

    (i)   **Profit margins** may be higher abroad.

    (ii)   Increase in **sales volume** from foreign sales may allow large reductions in unit costs.

    (iii) The **product life cycle** may be extended if the product is at an earlier stage in the life cycle in other countries.

    (iv) **Seasonal fluctuations** may be levelled out (peak periods in some countries coinciding with troughs in others).

    (v)   It offers an opportunity of **disposing of excess production** in times of low domestic demand.

(vi) International activities **spread the risk** which exists in any single market (eg political and economic changes).

(vii) **Obsolescent products** can be sold off overseas without damage to the domestic market.

(viii) The firm's prestige may be enhanced by portraying a **global image**.

(b) **Reasons for avoiding involvement**

(i) Profits may be unduly affected by factors outside the firm's **control** (eg due to fluctuation of exchange rates and foreign government actions).

(ii) The **adaptations** to the product (or other marketing mix elements) needed for success overseas will diminish the effects of economies of scale.

(iii) Extending the product life cycle is not always **cost effective**. It may be better to develop new products for the domestic market.

(iv) The **opportunity costs** of investing abroad may be better utilised at home

(v) In the case of marginal cost pricing, **anti-dumping duties** are more quickly imposed now than in the past.

3.5 Before getting involved in overseas expansion, the company must consider both strategic and tactical issues.

(a) **Strategic issues**

(i) Does the strategic decision fit with the company's overall mission and objectives? Or will 'going international' cause a mis-match between objectives on the one hand and strategic and tactical decisions on the other?

(ii) Does the organisation have (or can it raise) the resources necessary to exploit effectively the opportunities overseas?

(b) **Tactical issues**

(i) How can the company get to understand customers' needs and preferences in foreign markets?

(ii) Does the company know how to conduct business abroad, and deal effectively with foreign nationals?

(iii) Are there foreign regulations and associated hidden costs?

(iv) Does the company have the necessary management skills and experience?

Case study link

This was an issue for IRS Ltd in the November 2001 case study, as it was not clear that they would have enough resources and staff to support the new client in the US.

3.6 In making a decision as to which market(s) to enter the firm must start by establishing its objectives. Here are some examples.

(a) What proportion of total sales will be overseas?

(b) What are the longer term objectives?

(c) Will it enter one, a few, or many markets? In most cases it is better to start by selling in countries with which there is some familiarity and then expand into other countries gradually as experience is gained. Reasons to enter fewer countries at first include the following.

- Market entry and market control costs are high
- Product and market communications modification costs are high
- There is a large market and potential growth in the initial countries chosen
- Dominant competitors can establish high barriers to entry

(d) What types of country should it enter (in terms of environmental factors, economic development, language used, cultural similarities and so on)? Three major criteria should be as follows.

- Market attractiveness
- Competitive advantage
- Risk

3.7 The matrix below can be used to bring together these three major criteria and assist managers in their decisions.

Evaluating which markets to enter

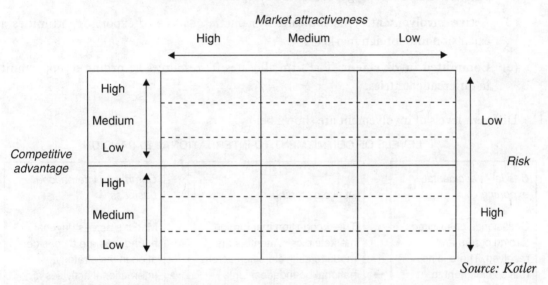

Source: Kotler

(a) **Market attractiveness**. This concerns such indicators as GNP/head and forecast demand, and market accessibility.

(b) **Competitive advantage**. This is principally dependent on prior experience in similar markets, language and cultural understanding.

(c) **Risk**. This involves an analysis of political stability, the possibility of government intervention and similar external influences.

3.8 The best markets to enter are those located at the top left of the diagram. The worst are those in the bottom right corner. Obtaining the information needed to reach this decision requires detailed and often costly international marketing research and analysis. Making these decisions is not easy, and a fairly elaborate screening process will be instituted.

3.9 In international business there are several categories of risk.

(a) **Political risk** relates to factors as diverse as wars, nationalisation, arguments between governments etc.

(b) **Business risk.** This arises from the possibility that the business idea itself might be flawed. As with political risk, it is not unique to international marketing, but firms

BPP PUBLISHING

might be exposed to more sources of risk arising from failures to understand the market.

   (c) **Currency risk.** This arises out of the volatility of foreign exchange rates. Given that there is a possibility for speculation and that capital flows are free, such risks are increasing.

   (d) **Profit repatriation risk.** Government actions may make it hard to repatriate profits.

Involvement in international markets

3.10   Firms develop through various stages of learning as commitment grows, and there are choices to be made along the way as to the extent to which a company commits itself to the international market. These stages are identified below.

   (a) **Domestic marketing.** The firm is preoccupied with home marketing.

   (b) **Pre-export stage.** A search is conducted and export opportunities are assessed.

   (c) **Experimental involvement.** There is some limited involvement in exporting: unsolicited and easy-to-get orders are accepted.

   (d) **Active involvement.** This indicates systematic analysis of export opportunities and expansion into foreign markets.

   (e) **Committed involvement.** The firm allocates its resources according to opportunities in different countries.

3.11   Different levels of involvement are shown below.

LEVELS OF COMMITMENT TO INTERNATIONAL EXPANSION

Casual or accidental exporting	*Active exporting*	*Committed international business*
Occasional, unsolicited foreign orders are received. There is no real commitment to international business.	The recognition that foreign markets exist. Attempts are made to cultivate sales across national boundaries. Little effort is made to consider foreign markets in the overall strategy. Minor adjustments may be made for foreign market product acceptance.	Markets across national boundaries are a consideration in the strategy. International activities are an integral part of the overall strategy programme. Divisions or subsidiaries may be developed to serve the foreign target market.

3.12   Another model identifies **three** stages.

   (a) **Domestic stage.** Firms are happy to concentrate on the home market. Exports are made, but without direction: overseas buyers may order products. Where domestic demand is weak, exporting is a 'second-best' means of getting rid of surplus stock. There is no particular relationship with organisation size. Many small, specialist organisations export. Many large companies do not (many of the UK's large utilities only began overseas activities after privatisation).

   (b) **International stage.** The firm's exporting activities are taken more seriously, and an export department might be set up to develop export markets. At this stage a **multi-domestic** strategy is pursued, in which each country is regarded as a separate market.

Arguably, this is sensible market segmentation. However, this relies mainly on exports; only a few activities are conducted overseas.

(c) At the **multinational** stage the company has a large number of activities in different countries, including both marketing and production facilities. However, the firm still has a recognisable 'home'.

Exam focus point

The November 2001 paper contained a question on the business case for a company's expansion overseas, along with a consideration of the strategic and operational issues involved.

4   MERGERS AND ACQUISITIONS   5/01

4.1   Many companies consider growth through acquisitions or mergers.

KEY TERMS

- A **merger** is the joining of two separate companies to form a single company.

- An **acquisition** is the purchase of a controlling interest in another company.

4.2   It is important for a company to understand its reasons for acquisition and that these reasons should be valid in terms of its strategic plan. The classic reasons for acquisition as a part of strategy are as follows.

Reason	Effect on operations
Marketing advantages	New product range Market presence Rationalise distribution and advertising Eliminate competition
Production advantages	Economies of scale Technology and skills Greater production capacity Safeguard future supplies Bulk purchase opportunities
Finance and management	Management team Cash resources Gain assets Tax advantages (eg losses bought)
Risk-spreading	Diversification
Retain independence	
Overcome barriers to entry	
Outplay rivals	

4.3   Acquisitions provide a means of entering a market, or building up a market share, more quickly and/or at a lower cost than would be incurred if the company tried to develop its own resources. Corporate planners must however consider the level of **risk** involved. Acquiring companies in overseas markets is more risky, for a number of reasons.

Case study link

Acquisitions (either domestic or international) were seen by some members of the Global Inc Board in the May 2002 case study to be the only way to grow sales.

4.4 The acquirer should attempt an evaluation of the following.

- The prospects of technological change in the industry
- The size and strength of competitors
- The reaction of competitors to an acquisition
- The likelihood of government intervention and legislation
- The state of the industry and its long-term prospects
- The amount of synergy obtainable from the merger or acquisition

Exam focus point

Whatever the reason for the merger or acquisition, it is unlikely to be successful unless it offers the company opportunities that cannot be found within the company itself and unless the new subsidiary fits closely into the strategic plan outlined for future growth. The May 2001 Section A question asked about the rationale for a proposed merger, and related this to the prevailing business environment.

Case example

Rolls-Royce has a strong business in defence aerospace, and has won an average of 30% of the civil aerospace market over the past three years.

With aerospace a maturing market, Rolls-Royce has looked for new expansion opportunities. Since its acquisition of Vickers in 1999, it has built a strong presence in marine markets, which now accounts for about 15% of the Rolls-Royce group's turnover. More than 20,000 commercial and naval vehicles use Rolls-Royce equipment, and Rolls-Royce engines power 400 ships in 30 navies. Its global presence makes this possible: Rolls-Royce Naval Marine Inc deals with the US Navy as a US-registered company. The reasons for its expansion are:

(i) The marine industry is looking to increase engine power for both passenger and freight ships
(ii) The marine industry is under pressure to meet demanding emissions regulations

The products acquired as a result of the Vickers takeover were market leading marine brands that expanded Rolls-Royce's route to market and made it a world leader in marine systems, from vessel design and control to winch manufacture and steering gear.

The mechanics of acquiring companies

4.5 As a management accountant you may be required to assess the value of an acquisition. A number of methods are available.

(a) **Price/earnings ratio:** the markets expectations of future earnings. If it is high, it indicates expectations of high growth in earnings per share and/or low risk.

(b) **Accounting rate of return,** whereby the company will be valued by estimated future profits over return on capital.

(c) **Value of net assets** (including brands).

(d) **Dividend yield**

(e) **Discounted cash flows,** if cash flows are generated by the acquisition. A suitable discount rate (eg the acquirer's cost of capital) should be applied.

(f) **Market prices.** Shareholders may prefer to hang on for a better bid.

Takeovers or mergers financed by a share exchange arrangement

4.6 Many acquisitions are paid for by **issuing new shares** in the acquiring company, which are then used to buy the shares of the company to be taken over in a 'share exchange' arrangement. An enlarged company might then have the financial 'muscle' and borrowing power to invest further so as to gain access to markets closed to either company previously because they could not individually afford the investment.

Case example

In the computer technology industry, where new business opportunities are continually presenting themselves, Sinclair proved itself to be a highly innovative company, but was restricted from greater expansion by lack of financial resources and inadequate profits, until it was eventually taken over by Amstrad.

Acquisitions and earnings per share

4.7 Growth in EPS will only occur after an acquisition in certain circumstances.

(a) When the company that is acquired is bought on a lower P/E ratio or

(b) When the company that is acquired is bought on a higher P/E ratio, but there is profit growth to offset this.

Buying companies on a lower P/E ratio

4.8 For example, suppose that Giant plc takes over Tiddler Ltd by offering two shares in Giant for one share in Tiddler. Details about each company are as follows.

	Giant plc	Tiddler Ltd
Number of shares	2,800,000	100,000
Market value per share	£4	-
Annual earnings	£560,000	£50,000
EPS	20p	50p
P/E ratio	20	-

By offering two shares in Giant worth £4 each for one share in Tiddler, the valuation placed on each Tiddler share is £8, and with Tiddler's EPS of 50p, this implies that Tiddler would be acquired on a P/E ratio of 16, which is lower than the P/E ratio of Giant, which is 20.

4.9 Now, suppose that the acquisition produces no synergy, and there is no growth in the earnings of either Giant or its new subsidiary Tiddler, the EPS of Giant would still be higher than before, because Tiddler was bought on a lower P/E ratio. The combined group's results would be as follows.

	Giant group
Number of shares (2,800,000 + 200,000)	3,000,000
Annual earnings (560,000 + 50,000)	£610,000
EPS	20.33p
If P/E ratio is still 20, the market value per share would be:	£4.07

4.10 The opposite is true as well, so that if a subsidiary is acquired on a higher P/E ratio, and there is no profit growth, then the enlarged group would suffer a fall in EPS and probably also a fall in share price.

Buying companies on a higher P/E ratio, but with profit growth

4.11 Buying companies on a higher P/E ratio will result in a fall in EPS unless there is profit growth to offset this fall. For example, suppose that Starving plc acquires Bigmeal plc, by offering two shares in Starving for three shares in Bigmeal. Details of each company are as follows.

	Starving plc	*Bigmeal plc*
Number of shares	5,000,000	3,000,000
Value per share	£6	£4
Annual earnings		
Current	£2,000,000	£600,000
Next year	£2,200,000	£950,000
EPS (current)	40p	20p
P/E ratio	15	20

4.12 Starving plc is acquiring Bigmeal on a higher P/E ratio, and it is only the profit growth in the acquired subsidiary that gives the enlarged Starving group its growth in EPS.

	Starving group
Number of shares (5,000,000 + 2,000,000)	7,000,000
Earnings	
If no profit growth (2,000,000 + 600,000)	£2,600,000 - EPS would have been 37.14p
With profit growth (2,200,000 + 950,000)	£3,150,000 - EPS will be 45p

Debt finance

4.13 Another feature of takeover activities in the USA especially, but also in the UK, has been the **debt-financed takeover**. This is a takeover bid where most or all of the purchase finance is provided by a syndicate of banks for the acquisition. The acquiring company will become very highly geared and will normally sell off parts of the target company.

4.14 A **leveraged buy-out** (LBO) is a form of debt-financed takeover where the target company is bought up by a team of managers in the company.

Acquisitions and organic growth compared

4.15 Acquisitions are probably only desirable if organic growth alone cannot achieve the targets for growth that a company has set for itself.

- Acquisitions can be made to enter new product areas, or to expand in existing markets, much more **quickly**

- Acquisitions can be made **without cash**, if share exchange transactions are acceptable

- When an acquisition is made to diversify into new product areas, the company will be buying **technical expertise, goodwill and customer contracts**

4.16 However, acquisitions and mergers do have their problems.

(a) **Cost**. They might be too expensive: some might be resisted by the directors of the target company.

(b) **Customers** of the target company might consider going to other suppliers for their goods.

(c) **Incompatibility**. In general, the problems of assimilating new products, customers, suppliers, markets, employees and different systems of operating might create 'indigestion' and management overload in the acquiring company.

(d) **Lack of information.** John Kay suggests that the 'acquisitions' market for companies is rarely efficient.

4.17 It is worth considering the **stakeholders** in the acquisition process.

(a) Some acquisitions are driven by the personal goals of the acquiring company's **managers**.

(b) **Corporate financiers and banks** also have a stake in the acquisitions process as they can charge fees for advice.

Case example

(a) A classic example of an acquisition gone wrong was the purchase, by Midland Bank, of Crocker Bank, an American bank. Midland allowed Crocker's management a fair degree of autonomy. Very shortly after the purchase, it emerged that Crocker was riddled with bad debts, largely as a result of property lending. This failed acquisition proved very expensive.

(b) A success is Rentokil, which from rat-catching and woodworm has, often by acquisition, been transformed into a £3.6bn service business 'dealing with everything from security to garden maintenance'. It has successfully transferred its management skills to its small-scale acquisitions: 'it has bought dozens of ... small fry and squeezed higher profit margins from them. It offers a career structure. It was once quoted as being Britain's 'most admired company'.

4.18 Takeovers benefit the shareholders of the acquired company often more than the acquirer. According to the Economist Intelligence Unit, there is a consensus that fewer than half all acquisitions are successful. One of the reasons for failure is that firms rarely take into account non-financial factors. A survey by London Business School examining 40 acquisitions (in the UK and USA) revealed some major flaws (supported by research by the Economist Intelligence Unit).

(a) All acquirers conducted financial audits, but only 37% conducted anything approaching a **management audit**.

(b) Some major problems of implementation relate to **human resources and personnel issues** such as morale, performance assessment and culture. If key managers or personnel leave, the business will suffer.

5 JOINT VENTURES, ALLIANCES AND FRANCHISING

5.1 Short of mergers and takeovers, there are other ways by which companies can co-operate.

5.2 **Consortia**: organisations co-operate on specific business prospects. Airbus is an example, a consortium including British Aerospace, Dasa, Aerospatiale and Casa.

5.3 **Joint ventures**: two or more organisations set up a third organisation. This is very common in entering normally closed markets. For example, Jardine Matheson (historically based in Hong Kong, from where it derives much of its profits, but now registered in Bermuda with shares traded in Singapore) has a joint venture with Robert Fleming the UK merchant bank, in the firm Jardine Fleming, which amongst other things, is involved in securities trading.

BPP PUBLISHING

KEY TERM

A **joint venture** is an arrangement where two firms (or more) join forces for manufacturing, financial and marketing purposes and each has a share in both the equity and the management of the business. A joint venture is often an alternative to seeking to buy or build a wholly owned manufacturing operation abroad.

5.4   Joint ventures are especially attractive to **smaller or risk-averse firms,** or where very expensive new technologies are being researched and developed. Other advantages are these.

*   Joint ventures permit coverage of a **larger number of countries** since each one requires less investment

*   A joint venture can reduce the risk of **government intervention**

*   Joint ventures can provide close **control** over operations

*   A joint venture with an indigenous firm provides **local knowledge**

*   Alliances offer several benefits in the **value chain**

*   Alliances can also be a **learning exercise**

*   Alliances provide funds for expensive **technology and research** projects

5.5   The major disadvantage of joint ventures is that there can be major **conflicts of interest.** Disagreements may arise over profit shares, amounts invested, the management of the joint venture, and the marketing strategy.

Alliances

5.6   Some firms enter long-term **strategic alliances** with others for a variety of reasons.

(a)   They share development costs of a particular technology.

(b)   The regulatory environment prohibits take-overs (eg most major airlines are in strategic alliances because in most countries - including the US - there are limits to the level of control an 'outsider' can have over an airline).

(c)   Complementary markets or technology.

Case study link

In the November 2001 case study, IRS Ltd sought to exploit its alliance with a US-owned equipment manufacturer to gain access to a US supermarket group.

Strategic alliances only go so far, as there may be disputes over control of strategic assets.

Choosing alliance partners

5.7 The following factors should be considered (Hooley *et al.* 1998) in choosing alliance partners.

Drivers	What benefits are offered by collaboration?
Partners	Which partners should be chosen?
Facilitators	Does the external environment favour a partnership?
Components	Activities and processes in the network
Effectiveness	Does the previous history of alliances generate good results? Is the alliance just a temporary blip? For example, in the airline industry, there are many strategic alliances, but these arise in part because there are legal barriers to cross-border ownership.
Market-orientation	Alliance partners are harder to control and may not have the same commitment to the end-user.

5.8 **Alliances have some limitations**

(a) **Core competence.** Each organisation should be able to focus on its core competence. Alliances do not enable it to create new competences.

(b) **Strategic priorities.** If a key aspect of strategic delivery is handed over to a partner, the firm loses flexibility. A core competence may not be enough to provide a comprehensive customer benefit.

Other arrangements

5.9 A **licensing agreement** is a commercial contract whereby the licenser gives something of value to the licensee in exchange for certain performances and payments.

(a) The licenser may provide any of the following.

- Rights to produce a patented product or use a patented production process
- Manufacturing know-how (unpatented)
- Technical advice and assistance
- Marketing advice and assistance
- Rights to use a trademark, brand etc

(b) The licenser receives a royalty.

(c) Production is higher with no investment.

(d) The licensee might eventually become a competitor.

(e) The supply of essential materials, components, plant.

5.10 **Subcontracting** is also a type of 'alliance'. Co-operative arrangements also feature in supply chain management.

Franchising

5.11 **Franchising** is a method of expanding the business on less capital than would otherwise be possible. Franchisers include Budget Rent-a-car, Dyno-rod, Express Dairy, Holiday Inn, Kall-Kwik Printing, KFC, Prontaprint, Sketchley Cleaners, the Body Shop and even McDonalds.

(a) Offered by the franchiser

- The franchiser's name, and any goodwill associated with it
- The franchiser's system, business methods and support services

(b) The franchisee pays the franchisers for being granted these rights.

(c) The franchisee has responsibility for the day-to-day running, and for the ultimate profitability, of his own franchise.

(d) The franchisee supplies capital, personal involvement and local market knowledge.

6 DIVESTMENT

6.1 Most strategies are designed to promote growth, but management should consider what rate of growth they want, whether they want to see any growth at all, or whether there should be a contraction of the business.

KEY TERM

Divestment means selling off a part of a firm's operations, or pulling out of certain product-market areas (ie closing down a product line). The 'divestment of non-core businesses' perhaps to a management buyout, have been quite common in recent years.

6.2 Reasons for divestment are these.

- To **rationalise** a business as a result of a strategic appraisal
- To sell off **subsidiary companies** at a profit
- To make a **profit** by buying and selling companies
- To get out while the going is good
- To **raise funds** to invest elsewhere

Case study link

The May 2001 Final Level Case Study (Proton Quest) required a report on potential implications of the sale of a division. A possible reason for such a sale was rationalisation of company activities, and concentration on more lucrative markets.

Case example

Philips, the Dutch manufacturer of consumer electronics, divested some non-core businesses in order to concentrate on core businesses as a strategy for improving profitability. It sold its production of 'white goods' (dishwashers etc) to an American firm, Whirlpool. (There was overcapacity in the market. Philips was suffering from declining profitability and did not have the resources to invest in all its product ranges).

Demergers

6.3 One term that describes divestment is **demerger**. This is sometimes referred to as **unbundling**. The main feature of a demerger is that one corporate entity becomes two or more separate entities. The newly-separated businesses might have the same shareholders, but they will usually have different people on their board of directors. In other words the supposed synergies are negative (a '2 + 2 = 3' effect, rather than a '2 + 2 = 5' effect).

Management buyouts

6.4 Typically, a better price can be obtained by selling a business as a unit, and there might well be many other firms interested in buying. In recent years there have been a large number of **management buyouts,** whereby the subsidiary is sold off to its managers. The managers put in some of their own capital, but obtain the rest from venture capital organisations and hope to make a bigger success of the business than the company which is selling it off.

> ### KEY TERM
>
> CIMA defines **management buyout** as 'the purchase of a business from its existing owners by members of the management team, generally in association with a financing institution. Where a large proportion of the new finance required to purchase the business is raised by external borrowing, the buyout is described as leveraged'.

Strategic factors in a buyout decision

6.5 Particularly important questions are as follows.

(a) Can the buyout team **raise the finance** to pay for the buyout? Buyouts are well-favoured by venture capital organisations, which regard them as less risky than new start-up businesses.

(b) Can the bought-out operation generate enough **profits** to pay for the costs of the acquisition?

Question 1

Try to identify the strategic issues facing the company in the following situation. Sharpe Bitts plc is concerned about the declining sales in one of its product ranges, industrial tools. The company's management believes that it needs to develop a new product, and it has identified a potential niche in the market for signalling equipment. One firm in the industry for manufacturing signalling equipment, Pointsduty Ltd, is a one-product firm which supplies about 20% of the market. Its cost structure, disclosed in its accounts filed at Companies House, was as follows last year.

	As a % of turnover
Cost of sales	86
Distribution costs	6
Administration costs	4
Operating profit	4
Labour (and associated) costs	15
Depreciation	0.5

It is believed that the overhead costs of Pointsduty Ltd were about 150% of its labour and associated costs. Sharpe Bitts plc believes that the market for signalling equipment could be as much as £50 million per annum. Its management have produced the following estimates of company sales, assuming that the development of signalling equipment products is undertaken.

	Previous year	Current year			
	20X0	20X1	20X2	20X3	20X4
	£m	£m	£m	£m	£m
Industrial tools	14.0	11.0	10.5	9.5	7.0
Domestic tools	4.5	5.0	5.5	7.5	8.0
Surgical instruments	15.5	16.0	17.0	17.8	19.0
Signalling equipment	-	-	-	0.2	1.0
Total sales	34.0	32.0	33.0	35.0	35.0

Required

Advise Sharpe Bitts plc in the context of the above information (and specifying what other information you would regard as appropriate) whether or not the proposed strategic development into signalling equipment should be further investigated.

Answer

There are many unknown, high-risk factors to consider. The list below tries to identify the major issues.

(a) Does the company have targets for profit growth or sales growth? If so, what are they? Does the proposed sales plan achieve these targets?

(b) We know nothing about the profitability and cash flows from the company's existing product range, nor about the costs of developing a signalling equipment product-market.

(c) What unique selling proposition would Sharpe Bitts' signalling equipment have? How would the company propose to achieve a 2% market share by 20X4? Is market share likely to get bigger in 20X5 and beyond? Are Sharpe Bitts' products likely to be sufficiently 'better' than rival products, so as to allow the company to sell them at a higher price?

(d) Can anything be done to halt or delay the decline in sales of industrial tools? For example, would price reductions or a market niche strategy be successful?

(e) Can anything be done to speed up growth in sales of domestic tools or surgical instruments. Are these rising markets or mature markets?

(f) How large would the start-up costs be? (Investment costs etc.)

(g) What synergy, if any, will be gained by diversifying into signalling equipment?

(h) The cost structure of Pointsduty Ltd can be analysed as follows.

		% of turnover
Cost of sales		86
Labour and associated costs	15.0	
Overhead (150%)	22.5	
Depreciation	0.5	
		38
Materials		48

	% of turnover
Sales	100
Materials	(48)
Added value	52
Other costs	(48)
Operating profit	4

    (i)   Sales approx 20% of £50 million pa =   £10,000,000 p.a.
    (ii) Operating profit approx 4% of £10m =   £400,000

These figures suggest the following for a company with a 20% share of the market.

(i) Unit costs are high and operating profit is low in terms of sales. High materials costs are a significant factor.

(j) It is doubtful whether a firm with just a 2% share of the market could be competitive and profitable. We need more information, however, about whether scale economies are likely to be significant, and whether Sharpe Bitts expects its market share to become much higher than 2% in the foreseeable future.

Unity Bicycles plc

(1) What do you think was the significance of MT's decision to divest itself of UB?

(2) What do you think of UB's policy of strategic alliances and joint ventures?

Chapter roundup

- To achieve their objectives firms enter into a number of different **relationships** with other firms, with varying degrees of **control** and **risk**.

- **Organic growth** is expansion by use of internal resources. The advantages are control, and the fact that managers can concentrate on product-market issues, rather than concerns of organisation structure.

- **International expansion** is a big undertaking and firms must know their reasons for it, and be sure that they have the resources to manage it, both strategically and operationally.

- The decision about which overseas market to enter should be based upon assessment of **market attractiveness**, **competitive advantage**, and **risk**.

- A **merger** is the integration of two or more businesses. An **acquisition** is where one business purchases another. This offers speedy access to new technologies and markets, but there are risks: only about half of acquisitions succeed.

- There are other types of arrangement whereby businesses pool resources.

  - **Joint ventures**, consortia and other alliances

  - **Franchising**, where the franchiser provides expertise, a brand name etc, and the franchisee offers some of the capital

- **Divestment** and **demerger** have become more common, as firms seek to reverse the diversification strategies they once pursued.

Quick quiz

1   What is the primary method of growth for most organisations?

   A   acquisitions

   B   organic growth

   C   merger

   D   franchising

2   Why is innovation important in any organic growth strategy?

3   Distinguish a merger from an acquisition.

4   What are the three broad categories of innovation strategy?

5   **Fill in the blanks** in the statement below, using the words in the box.

   (1) .... provide a means of entering a (2) .... or building up a (3) .... , more quickly and at a lower (4) .... than would be incurred if the company tried to develop its own (5) .... Corporate planners must however consider the level of (6) .... involved.

risk	cost	market
market share	resources	acquisitions

6   What is a leveraged buy-out?

7   Define a joint venture. What is their chief disadvantage?

8   **Fill in the blanks**

   Particularly important questions in a buyout decision are:

   - Can the buyout team .... to pay for the buyout?

   - Can the bought out operation generate enough ....?

9 What three broad mechanisms can be considered by a company seeking growth?

....

....

....

10 What are the classic reasons for acquisition as a part of strategy?

M ....
P ....
F ....
R ....
R ....
O ....
O ....

Answers to quick quiz

1 B

2 It provides the organisation with a distinctive competence, and with the ability to maintain such a competence. Also it maintains the organisation's competitive advantage and market share

3 A merger is the joining of two separate companies to form a single company.

An acquisition is the purchase of a controlling interest in another company.

4 Attack/leader
Defensive/follower
Counterattack

5 (1) Acquisitions (2) market (3) market share (4) cost (5) resources (6) risk

6 A leveraged buy-out (LBO) is a form of debt-financed takeover where the target company is bought up by a team of managers in the company.

7 A joint venture is an arrangement where two firms (or more) join forces for manufacturing, financial and marketing purposes and each has a share in both the equity and the management of the business. The major disadvantage of joint ventures is that there can be conflicts of interest.

8 Raise the finance
Profits

9 Develop the business from scratch
Acquire/merge with an existing business
Co-operate in some way with another firm eg joint venture

10 Marketing advantages
Production advantages
Finance and management
Risk-spreading
Retain independence
Overcome barriers to entry
Outplay rivals

Unity Bicycles plc review

Question 1. The main issue with MT's acquisition of UB was vertical integration, not acquisition as such (as opposed to organic growth). MT was unable to make a success of the business, hence the divestment.

Question 2. UB's alliance policy is sensible. UB seems to have a fairly well defined idea as to what it wants out of the various arrangements and has a realistic idea of what it can achieve.

Now try the question below from the Exam Question Bank

Question to try	Level	Marks	Time
9	Exam	25	45 mins

BPP
PUBLISHING

Chapter 11

EVALUATING STRATEGIC OPTIONS: DECISION MAKING

Topic list	Syllabus reference	Ability required
1 Strategic management accounting, DCF and investment appraisal	(iv) (iv)	Application Application
2 Risk and cost behaviour	(iv)	Application
3 Decision techniques	(iv)	Application

Introduction

This chapter describes how management accountants can apply decision techniques to strategic issues such as investment appraisal, risk and operational gearing, and uncertainty.

Learning outcomes covered in this chapter

- **Apply** investment techniques to marketing and strategy decisions

Syllabus content covered in this chapter

- The use of investment appraisal techniques in marketing and strategy selection, eg volume enhancing marketing spends and decay reducing marketing spend

1 STRATEGIC MANAGEMENT ACCOUNTING, DCF AND INVESTMENT APPRAISAL

1.1 The principles of relevant costs for decision-making and the techniques of DCF should be familiar to you already.

Exam focus point

For strategic management accounting, you must be able to apply these principles and techniques to situations where the data is either subject to uncertainty in the estimates, or else is incomplete. State your assumptions clearly. In the context of strategic management accounting, as a general guideline, the following is suggested as an approach.

(a) Recognise why the accounting information is needed - ie what are we trying to do?

(b) Assess whether the data is incomplete. If so, make any suitable assumptions that might be necessary.

(c) Recognise whether any estimated data is uncertain, and of dubious reliability. If possible, assess how variations in the estimates would affect your financial analysis and recommendation.

1.2 EXAMPLE: STRATEGIC MANAGEMENT ACCOUNTING AND DCF ANALYSIS

Booters plc is a company which specialises in purchasing and re-selling land with development potential. The following data is available.

Market value of agricultural land	£20,000 per acre
Market value of land that can be developed	£200,000 per acre
Maintenance cost of land, per acre	£2,500 pa
Booters plc's cost of capital	19%

Agricultural land that is held by Booters plc can be let to farmers on short term leases for £300 per acre per annum, but maintenance costs would be payable by Booters.

The company has now received invitations to bid for two properties.

Property 1. 1.5 acres of land near a planned major road. Some of the land is about to be made subject to a compulsory purchase order, for sale to the local authority for £25,000. The remaining land (0.8 of an acre) can be re-sold to a property developer for £190,000, but not until about five years' time.

Property 2. A country estate of 160 acres, of which 15 acres might be released for residential housing development at any time in the next four years. Development of the remaining 145 acres will not be allowed.

This land will be put up for auction, unless Booters plc agrees now to pay a price of £1,400,000 beforehand. If the land goes up for auction, it is believed that a local businessman might offer £1,600,000, but the reserve price will be only £900,000.

Required. In the case of each property, what should Booters bid for the property, if anything?

Discussion

1.3 In this example, the data is incomplete. Some of the missing items would be readily available in a real-life situation, but other data would be unobtainable, except as guesswork.

1.4 **Property 1.** Most of the data we need for a simple financial analysis exists, but the data does not state whether the land is agricultural land or not, and so whether it can be let out to a farmer.

Otherwise, we have a straightforward DCF analysis.

	Year	Value/Cost £	Discount factor at 19%	Present value £
Sale value of land, subject to compulsory purchase order	0	25,000	1.000	25,000
Sale value of remaining land	5	190,000	0.419	79,610
Maintenance cost of land, assumed to be £2,500 × 0.8 pa	1-5	(2,000)	3.058	(6,116)
Maximum purchase price				98,494

1.5 If the land sold under the compulsory purchase order takes time to sell, say one year, the value of the land would be lower, with the £25,000 sale value having to be discounted by a factor of 0.840 and a maintenance cost of land to be included (0.7 acres x £2,500, as a year 1 cost).

A maximum price of £98,000 might be indicated.

BPP PUBLISHING

1.6　**Property 2.** Here the data is incomplete and uncertain.

(a)　How likely is it that the 15 acres will be released for housing development?

(b)　When is it most likely to be released?

(c)　Is it agricultural land, and so could it be leased out to tenant farmers?

(d)　Would the unwanted 145 acres be saleable at agricultural land prices, and if so, when would Booters plc know which land it did not want? Have the 15 acres for re-development been specifically identified?

(e)　If the land goes for auction, would a bid above the reserve price be likely?

It is only by recognising what data is missing or uncertain that we can begin to carry out a sensible financial analysis.

1.7　Here the following assumptions are made.

(a)　The land is agricultural land.

(b)　The 15 acres for redevelopment have not been identified specifically. The remaining 145 acres cannot be re-sold until the planning permission has been obtained on the other 15 acres.

(c)　The 145 acres could then be resold at agricultural land prices.

1.8　Two further assumptions call for business judgement.

(a)　The 15 acres will be released for residential housing. There is a risk, of course, that it won't be.

(b)　The land will not be released for four more years. It could, of course, be sooner.

1.9　Now we can carry out a DCF analysis.

	Year	Value/cost £	Discount factor at 19%	Present value £
Sales value of 15 acres (15 × £200,000)	4	3,000,000	0.499	1,497,000
Sales value of 145 acres (145 × £20,000)	4	2,900,000	0.499	1,447,100
Sub-letting of 160 acres at £300 per acre	1-4	48,000	2.639	126,672
Maintenance cost of 160 acres at £2,500 pa	1-4	(400,000)	2.639	(1,055,600)
Maximum value of the land				2,015,172

1.10　Since Booters plc has been offered the chance to buy the property prior to auction for £1,400,000, the key questions are as follows.

(a)　Is buying the land too much of a risk? If the land is not released for development, the 15 acres would be sold for only £300,000, and the PV of this would be only around £150,000. The maximum value of the land would now be about £1,350,000 less, at approximately £671,000.

(b)　If the risk is considered to be worth accepting, should a price of £1,400,000 be accepted, or is it worth trying to get the land for something near the reserve price of £900,000 and running the risk of having to outbid a rival, by offering as much as £1,600,000 or even more?

POINT TO NOTE

There is no clear answer to either question, but a decision has to be taken. This is what strategic management is about! Now try this exercise.

Question 1

A public company responsible for the supply of domestic gas has received several requests from prospective customers in the Matsfold area to be connected to the gas supply system. Matsfold, an area consisting of about 8,000 residential dwellings, does not currently have any connection to the gas mains, and the company is now trying to reach a decision whether or not to provide gas supplies to the area.

(a) New customers are each charged £300 for being connected to the system and having a meter installed.

(b) Charges per quarter are:

　　(i) standing charge of £15 plus

　　(ii) a charge for gas consumed, at the rate of £500 per 1,000 metered units. The average domestic consumption is about 120 metered units per month.

(c) Supplies of gas cost the company £0.08 per metered unit. Wastage of 20% must be allowed for.

(d) A postal market research survey of the Matsfold area elicited a 50% response, and 90% of the respondents indicated their wish to be connected to a gas supply.

(e) The company's cost of capital is 17%.

Required. What is the maximum capital project cost that the company should be willing to incur to persuade it to provide gas supplies to the Matsfold area?

Answer

(a) The main area of uncertainty here is the number of customers who would actually wish to be connected to the gas supply.

(b) To start with, it is assumed that gas supplies can be provided fairly quickly (ie in year 0), but this assumption can be changed quite easily later on.

(c) Other assumptions

　　(i) The company might seek a payback on its investment within a specific time horizon - say ten or 15 years. However, cash flows in perpetuity will be used here to assess the project financially.

　　(ii) A cost of capital of 17% pa is equal to a cost of 4% per quarter. This quarterly cost will be used to evaluate the PV of future revenues.

　　(iii) A PV of net benefit per customer will be calculated, before an assessment is made of the maximum acceptable project cost.

(d) Workings, per customer

	£
Quarterly standing charge	15.0
Quarterly revenue for gas consumed (120 units × 3 months × £500 ÷ 1,000)	180.0
Cost of gas, including wastage (120 units × 100/80 × 3 months × £0.08)	(36.0)
Net income per quarter	159.0

(e) Financial evaluation, per customer

	Year	Discount factor at 4% per qtr	Cash flow £	Present value £
Connection charge	0	1.0	300	300
Quarterly net income	In perpetuity	1/0.04 = 25.0	159	3,975
NPV of all future net income, per customer				4,275

(f) Financial evaluation for the area

   (i) The key issue is how many customers will actually want connecting to the gas supply, and how long will it take to connect them?

   (ii) The postal survey, taking an optimistic viewpoint, might suggest demand from 90% of 8,000 dwellings - 7,200 dwellings.

   (iii) A more realistic estimate might be just 50% of this, or even less. The company's experience with similar projects in the past could provide data to help in reaching a realistic estimate about this. Without further information about the likely margin of error in the data from the postal survey, its reliability is hard to assess. After all, it is one thing to reply to a survey saying that you would like to be connected to the gas supply, but faced with a connection charge of £300, you might easily change your mind!

(g) The estimate of demand is crucial.

Possible demand (customers)		Maximum acceptable project cost £
3,000	(× £4,275)	12,825,000
5,000		21,375,000
7,000		29,925,000

As you can see, the potential variation in the figures is enormous. What would your judgement be, and how would you advise the company's senior management?

Target returns for new capital investments: the cost of capital

KEY TERM

Cost of capital. 'The minimum acceptable return on an investment, generally computed as a hurdle rate for use in investment appraisal exercises. The computation of the optimal cost of capital can be complex, and many ways of determining this opportunity cost have been suggested. ' (CIMA *Official Terminology*)

1.11 Setting target returns for new capital investments could help to ensure that the future returns for the organisation and its shareholders are sufficient to allow a company to achieve its overall target return. In practice, things are not so simple.

(a) The return on new capital investments is only one aspect of making an adequate return. For most companies, it is the **return on existing products** that is the major influence on profitability and return.

(b) The actual return on capital is measured **retrospectively**, as ROI, profits, earnings per share or dividends plus capital growth. A DCF return, in contrast, is measured by future cash flows.

1.12 Many groups of companies have a corporate treasury function within the holding company, which controls the use of the group's internally-generated funds by means of a central 'banking system.' The holding company will 'loan' capital to subsidiary operating units and charge out the funds at the corporate cost of capital. The target DCF rate of return selected by an organisation might be based on the following.

(a) The **weighted average cost of capital** (WACC of the organisation).

(b) The **marginal cost of capital** - ie the cost of the extra capital required to finance a specific project.

(c) The **opportunity cost** of the capital required to finance the project.

(d) A cost of capital that is adjusted to allow for the **risk element** in the particular capital investment.

(e) A return based on the **capital asset pricing model**.

Strategic value analysis

1.13 Ultimately, investment decisions are supposed to increase **shareholder value** (a measure of shareholders' wealth as reflected in the share price).

1.14 **Strategic value analysis** is an approach which measures the potential financial benefit or loss to shareholders from pursuing strategic options.

(a) **Shareholder value analysis** suggests the following '**value drivers**' generate a company's future cash flows.

- Sales growth rate (percentage)
- Operating profit margin
- Cash tax rate
- Incremental fixed capital investment
- Incremental working capital investment
- Planning period
- Cost of capital

The resulting free cash flows over the planning period can be discounted at the cost of capital to get an estimated shareholder value from pursuing an option

(b) **Economic value added** is a similar approach, structured in a different way. We look at these measures again in Part E of the Study Text in the context of performance measurement and control.

1.15 The model above can be used as a decision making tool. For example, moving into a new market might be associated with **sales growth**, but cash flows will be under pressure from incremental **fixed and working capital investment**.

Strategic problems in investment appraisal

KEY TERM

Strategic investment appraisal. 'Method of investment appraisal which allows the inclusion of both financial and non-financial factors. Project benefits are appraised in terms of their contribution to the strategies of the organisation.'

(CIMA *Official Terminology*)

1.16 It is not always easy, or even possible, to quantify some of the strategic issues which affect an investment decision. It is all very well to do DCF analysis on estimated future cash flows to come up with a net present value, or to work out a payback period. What is difficult to predict, however, are **trends in the industry** as a whole.

External orientation

1.17 As a firm's strategy is linked very much with its position in the market place, any investment appraisal of a project must take the broader strategic issues into account.

1.18 Two questions can be posed of a strategic investment therefore, in addition to financial evaluation.

(a) Does a project generate value to **customers,** so that the cash generated will provide a return?

(b) Will these cash flows be **sustained** in the light of the competitive environment?

POINT TO NOTE

Strategic investment decisions must be assessed with regard to their:

- Immediate **financial viability**
- Effect on **competitive advantage** in the light of environmental uncertainties

Procedure for strategic investment appraisal

1.19 The following ten steps for approaching strategic projects have been suggested.

1	Determine the investment project to be analysed.
2	Determine the strategic objectives for the project.
3	Determine alternative ways of achieving the same strategic objectives.
4	Analyse a small number of alternatives.
5	Try and determine what will happen if nothing is done (but this does not mean that you assume that competitors will do nothing).
6	Determine key internal and external assumptions.
7	Collect data on areas of greatest uncertainty.
8	Carry out sensitivity analysis tests.
9	Redefine the project on the basis of 8.
10	Expose key assumptions and debate them.

Investment decisions

1.20 There are a number of different types of spending which can be conceived as **strategic investment issues** even though not all of them are recorded as such in financial statements.

- Investing in brands and marketing
- Investing in corporate image
- R&D to create knowledge for future exploitation
- Information technology
- Acquisitions

Marketing expenditure

1.21 There is some justification for treating certain types of **marketing expenditure** as investment. Levels of marketing expenditure are often significant, and any marketing strategy will have to be evaluated accordingly. However, according to Keith Ward, 'levels of marketing expenditure...are often subjected to far less rigorous financial evaluations than smaller financial commitments on more tangible assets.'

1.22 Marketing expenditure can be evaluated using a variety of methods.

- Cash flow modelling with **NPV** (see section 1.25 below)

- Use of **non-financial measures** to benchmark spend (see Chapters 13-15 for more detail on performance measurement)

- **Modelling competitor responses**

1.23 We looked at marketing more closely in Chapter 5 when we studied the competitive environment. Here, we will consider the application of investment appraisal techniques to marketing expenditure.

1.24 EXAMPLE

(a) Consider a company that is experiencing annual 40% marketing decay, that is, its market share (and its revenues) are declining each year by 40%. Its expected cashflows over 10 years at a 20% discount rate are as follows.

Year	Cash flow	20% Discount factor	Present value
1	10,000	0.833	8,330
2	6,000	0.694	4,164
3	3,600	0.579	2,084
4	2,160	0.482	1,041
5	1,296	0.402	521
6	778	0.335	261
7	467	0.279	131
8	280	0.233	65
9	168	0.194	33
10	101	0.162	16
			16,646

The company decides to spend £1,000 on an advertising campaign, in order to **enhance volume** in year 1 by 10%. After that, marketing decay will continue to be 40%. Its expected cashflows are now as follows.

Year	Cash flow	20% Discount factor	Present value
0	(1,000)	1.000	(1,000)
1	11,000	0.833	9,163
2	6,600	0.694	4,580
3	3,960	0.579	2,293
4	2,376	0.482	1,145
5	1,426	0.402	573
6	855	0.335	286
7	513	0.279	143
8	308	0.233	72
9	185	0.194	36
10	111	0.162	18
			17,309

This investment is worthwhile because the NPV is greater than it was without the marketing spend.

(b) Suppose the company decides instead to invest £5,000 in a loyalty card scheme which will sustain existing volumes, but **reduce marketing decay** by 20%. The expected cashflows are revised again.

Year	Cash flow	20% Discount factor	Present value
0	(5,000)	1.000	(5,000)
1	10,000	0.833	8,330
2	8,000	0.694	5,552
3	6,400	0.579	3,706
4	5,120	0.482	2,468
5	4,096	0.402	1,647
6	3,277	0.335	1,098
7	2,621	0.279	731
8	2,097	0.233	489
9	1,678	0.194	326
10	1,342	0.162	217
			19,564

This spending is even more worthwhile. You have probably already noted that this analysis is simplistic, especially as it does not model competitors' responses or new entrants, and assumes constant rates of marketing decay, but it does illustrate the basic principles involved.

Exam focus point

The use of investment appraisal techniques in assessing volume enhancing marketing spends and decay reducing marketing spends is specifically identified by the examiner in the syllabus content.

2 RISK AND COST BEHAVIOUR

2.1 **Strategies deal with future events**: the future cannot be predicted. An example would be the UK's departure from the exchange rate mechanism of the European Monetary System in September 1992, in contradiction to all prior statements by the government.

2.2 We can make a distinction between risk and uncertainty, but often the terms are used interchangeably.

(a) **Risk** is sometimes used to describe situations where outcomes are not known, but their probabilities can be estimated.

(b) **Uncertainty** is present when the outcome cannot be predicted or assigned probabilities.

Types of risk

KEY TERM

Risk is taken to mean both general unquantifiable **uncertainty** (eg political risk) and **volatility**, often measured by standard deviation.

2.3 Risk can occur from many sources. Here are some examples.

(a) **Physical risk.** This has been highlighted by recent earthquakes in the US and Japan. Other physical risks include fire, flooding, and equipment breakdown.

(b) **Economic risk**. The strategy might be based on assumptions as to the economy which might turn out to be wrong.

(c) **Financial risk** relates to the type of financial arrangement in the decision. A firm which borrows heavily will suffer if interest rates are raised. Share capital gives the firm more flexibility as dividends are paid at the directors' discretion.

(d) **Business risk**. These risks relate to commercial and industry factors. In other words, there is the possibility that the strategy will fail.

Case example

In 1995, Unilever launched Persil Power, a washing powder with a new ingredient. Disaster struck. Procter and Gamble, a competitor, demonstrated that in certain conditions the ingredient damaged clothes. P&G conducted an effective public relations war. Unilever withdrew the product.

In June 1998 the Swiss pharmaceuticals company Roche announced the withdrawal of its new heart drug Posicor because of adverse side affects. Its shares suffered on the market.

(e) **Political risk**. This includes nationalisation, sanctions, civil war, political instability, if these have an impact on the business.

(f) **Exchange risk**. This is the risk that changes in exchange rates affect the value of a transaction in a currency, or how it is reported.

Who suffers risk?

2.4 **Risk and return are related**. An investor will want a higher return to compensate for the increased risk of a project.

2.5 A simple diagram of the relationship is the following.

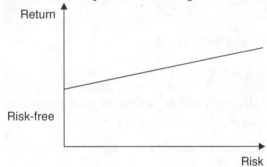

(a) For example, investors in a company in a low-risk business might be satisfied with a return of, say, 15%, whereas in a comparable high-risk business the required return might be a minimum of 25%.

Case study link

A company which operates in a high risk industry may nevertheless be risk averse, and manage the risks it faces by, for example, strong and clear contractual terms and insistence on agreed cash payments and negotiated fees. This is how Proton Quest managed its Molecular Allies division in the May 2001 Final Level Case Study.

(b) There may be a **minimum return** that shareholders will accept, allowing for the risk of the investment. Argenti's performance-risk curve for the return shareholders required would be as follows.

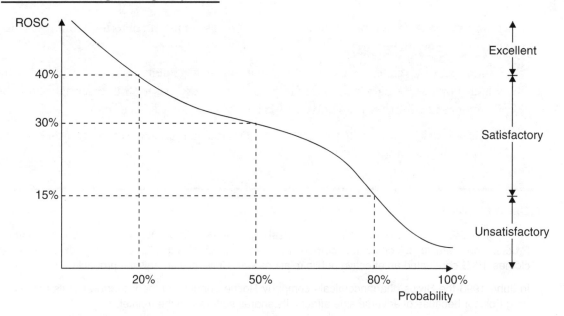

In this example, the target ROSC would be as follows.

- To have a 20% chance of achieving an ROSC of 40% or more.
- To have a 50% chance of achieving an ROSC of 30% or more.
- To have an 80% chance of achieving an ROSC of 15% or more.

2.6 **Different stakeholders** in a company or a decision have different attitudes to risk.

   (a) Shareholders are able to **diversify their portfolios,** so they can have shares in a number of firms, some offering high return for high risk, others offering a low return for a low risk.

   (b) Key decision makers are managers, and their perceptions of risk are likely to be quite different.

The management accountant and risk

Targets for risk

2.7 If the primary financial target can be converted into a target rate of return for individual capital projects, how can risk be expressed in practical terms for decision-makers?

   (a) A **premium** for risk can be added to the target DCF rate of return.

   (b) To protect cash flows, it might be made a condition of all new capital projects that the project should **pay back** within a certain period of time, say three to four years.

Risk appraisal in strategy evaluation

2.8 One of the problems arising when evaluating alternative strategies is the reliability of the data used.

   (a) Business planners frequently use various operational research techniques to measure the degree of uncertainty involved.

(b)   Also, there is the use of basic **probability theory** to express the likelihood of a forecast result occurring. This would evaluate the data given by informing the decision-maker that there is, for example, a 50% probability that an acceptable result will be achieved, a 25% chance that the worst result will occur and a 25% chance that the best possible result will occur. This evaluation of risk might help the executive to decide between alternative strategies, each with its own risk profile.

2.9   When evaluating a strategy, management should consider the following.

(a)   Whether an individual strategy involves **an unacceptable amount** of risk. If it does, it should be eliminated from further consideration in the planning process.

(b)   However, the risk of an individual strategy should also be considered in the context of the **overall portfolio** of investment strategies adopted by the company.

Risk and cost behaviour: operational gearing

2.10   **CVP analysis (breakeven analysis)** can be useful in strategic planning in order to assess what share of the market a company would need to achieve to break even or to achieve a target return with a particular strategy. For example, if a company is planning to make a new product for a particular market, and estimates of capital investment costs and fixed and variable running costs were fairly reliable, the company could assess the following for a number of different sales prices.

(a)   How many sales would be needed to break even each year, and so what market share would be needed.

(b)   How many sales would be needed over a given period (of say, three years) assuming a gradual increase in annual sales, in order to break even in DCF terms (ie achieve an NPV = 0). The required market share per year for each year of the project could then be assessed.

> **KEY TERM**
>
> **Cost-volume-profit analysis (CVP).** 'The study of the effects on future profit of changes in fixed cost, variable cost, sales price, quantity and mix.'
>
> (CIMA *Official Terminology*)

2.11   A related risk is the **cost structure** of the business.

(a)   A **high level of fixed costs** means that large losses are made if sales are less than breakeven, but that once breakeven is achieved, larger profits follow.

(b)   A **high proportion of variable product costs** means that the total costs are always sensitive to actual production volumes. Losses are lower, but so are profits.

2.12   In other words, the business's **operational gearing** (the ratio of fixed to variable costs) is an important indicator of risk. Where there is a high proportion of fixed costs, a strategy might be more risky, although it promises a higher return. A high proportion of genuinely variable costs can mean more flexibility.

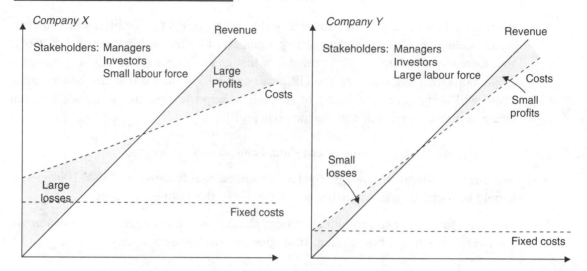

The two graphs have the same breakeven point, but X is much more sensitive to lower sales. It is more volatile. X promises higher profits, but risks higher losses than Y.

2.13 With any strategy there is a **stakeholder response risk**, an environmental factor which can intrude on the management accountant's cost behaviour diagrams. Bankers, employees and the government are all interested parties in a business. If a business pursues a particular strategy, this might antagonise the government of the country in which it is operating.

Probabilities and risk

2.14 Higher risks tend to be associated with higher returns. This is the principle underlying the Capital Asset Pricing Model, and we have already seen that the target DCF rate of return for capital expenditure projects may be varied according to the project's risk.

2.15 Some risks can be measured by probabilities.

(a) An average expected profit or NPV can be measured as an **expected value** (EV) of the different probabilities.

(b) Risk can be quantified as a **standard deviation of expected profit or NPV**.

2.16 EXAMPLE: UNCERTAINTY ABOUT SALES DEMAND, COSTS AND PROFITS

Uncertainty about future sales demand, costs and profits can be brought into consideration. A company is trying to make a strategic decision about whether to introduce a new production process. The process would reduce unit variable costs of production significantly but would increase fixed costs of production substantially. Forecast sales demand is uncertain, for a range of different selling prices. Non-production costs were also uncertain. The key information in the question could be reduced to the following.

(a) **Option 1.** Keeping existing system

- Sales price could be anywhere in the range £9 - £10.5 per unit
- Sales quantity could be anywhere in the range 8.5 million to 11 million units
- Profits in £ would be $(PQ)^{0.8} - 0.2Q - 100,000$ where

P = price

Q = quantity sold.

(b) **Option 2.** Introduce new production system

- Sales price had to be £9 per unit or less

- Sales quantity could be anywhere above 11 million units at the chosen price
- Profit would be $(PQ)^{0.8} - 0.15Q - 400,000$.

2.17 A suitable approach to tackling this problem would be to consider the profits that would be earned at a number of different price/quantity combinations, for both Options 1 and 2. A 'worst possible' and 'best possible' estimate could have been made, and the various possible outcomes analysed and discussed. Some figures are shown below, for illustration purposes.

(a) **Option 1**

(i)	Worse possible price		£9
	Quantity		8.5 million
	Profit	$=$	$(9 \times 8.5 \text{ million})^{0.8} - 0.2 (8.5 \text{ million}) - 100,000$
		$=$	£227,351

(ii)	Best possible price		£10.5
	Quantity		11 million
	Profit	$=$	$(10.5 \times 11 \text{ million})^{0.8} - 0.2 (11 \text{ million}) - 100,000$
		$=$	£518,808

(b) **Option 2**

Best possible price		£9
Worst possible volume		11 million units
Profit	$=$	$(9 \times 11 \text{ million})^{0.8} - 0.15 (11 \text{ million}) - £400,000$
	$=$	£441,771

2.18 These could be used in a number of ways.

(a) If the probabilities of different outcomes were known they could be plotted on a **decision tree**.

(b) The outcomes might be used in a **decision matrix**, if they could be related to different sets of circumstances.

(c) An **assessment** of risk might be carried out.

3 DECISION TECHNIQUES

3.1 This section describes a number of techniques to enable a systematic approach to be taken to certain strategic decisions.

Decision trees

> **KEY TERM**
>
> **Decision tree.** 'A pictorial method of showing a sequence of interrelated decisions and their expected outcomes. Decision trees can incorporate both the probabilities of, and values of, expected outcomes, and are used in decision making.'
>
> (CIMA *Official Terminology*)

3.2 **The two stages in preparing a decision tree**

(a) **Drawing the tree itself**, to show all the choices and outcomes

(b) **Putting in the numbers:** the probabilities, outcome values and expected values (EVs). (Expected value is calculated as **probability × outcome**.) For example, if you have a 1% chance of winning £100, the expected value of the winning is £1.

3.3 EXAMPLE: A DECISION TREE

Beethoven Ltd has a new wonder product, the vylin, of which it expects great things. At the moment the company has two courses of action open to it, to test market the product or abandon it. If the company test markets it, the cost will be £100,000 and the market response could be positive or negative with probabilities of 0.60 and 0.40.

(a) If the response is positive the company could either abandon the product or market it full scale. If it markets the vylin full scale, the outcome might be low, medium or high demand, and the respective net payoffs would be (200), 200 or 1,000 in units of £1,000 (the result could range from a net loss of £200,000 to a gain of £1,000,000). These outcomes have probabilities of 0.20, 0.50 and 0.30 respectively.

(b) If the result of the test marketing is negative and the company goes ahead and markets the product, estimated losses would be £600,000. If, at any point, the company abandons the product, there would be a net gain of £50,000 from the sale of scrap. All the financial values have been discounted to the present.

3.4 SOLUTION

The starting point for the tree is to establish what decision has to be made now. What are the options? In this case, they are:

- To test market
- To abandon

The outcome of the 'abandon' option is known with certainty. There are two possible outcomes of the option to test market, positive response and negative response. Depending on the outcome of the test marketing, another decision will then be made, to abandon the product or to go ahead.

3.5   This is the decision tree.

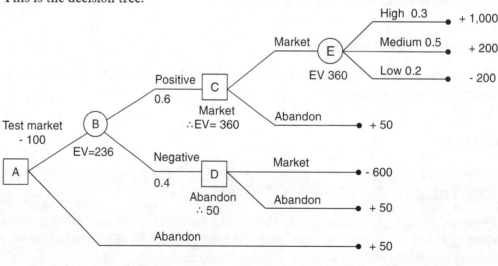

All values in £'000

☐ Decision point

◯ Outcome point

• Termination point

Evaluating the decision with a decision tree

3.6 The **expected value** (EV) of each decision option can be evaluated, using the decision tree to help with keeping the logic properly sorted out.

(a) Working from right to left, we calculate the EV of revenue, cost, contribution or profit at each outcome point on the tree. For example, at point E, £360,000 is the EV of the decision to market the product if the test shows positive response. It may help you to write the EV on the decision tree itself, at the appropriate outcome point (point E).

(b) We now make the second stage decisions. For example, at decision point C, the choice is:

- Market, EV + 360 (the EV at point E) or
- Abandon, value + 50

The choice would be to market the product, and so the EV at decision point C is +360.

(c) The evaluation of the decision tree is completed as follows.

   (i) Calculate the EV at outcome point B.
   (ii) Compare the options at point A, which are:
     (1) Test: EV = EV at B minus test marketing cost = 236 – 100 = 136;
     (2) Abandon: Value 50.

The choice would be to test market the product, because it has a higher EV of profit.

3.7 The role of decision trees then in strategic planning is to assess which choices are mutually exclusive, and to try and give them some quantitative value. As such, they are useful in:

- **Clarifying strategic decisions** when they are complex
- Using risk (in probability terms) as an **input** to quantifying the decision options
- Ranking the relative costs and benefits of the options

Cost/benefit analysis

3.8 **Cost/benefit analysis** is a strategy evaluation technique often used in the public sector, where many of the costs and benefits of a project are intangible.

> **KEY TERM**
>
> **Cost/benefit analysis** involves a comparison between the cost of the resources used, plus any other costs imposed by an activity (eg pollution, environmental damage) and the value of the financial and non-financial benefits derived.

3.9 In many public sector decisions, a cost/benefit analysis is conducted on the following basis.

(a) The project and its overall objectives are defined.

(b) The benefits, including social benefits, are analysed in detail. It is not always easy to put a value on social costs.

(c) The net benefits for the project are estimated, if possible. A road might reduce journey times, and so save money.

3.10 It can help businesses negotiate with public sector officials. For example, most large building projects have to get planning permission from the local authority. Local government officials will sometimes insist on certain social benefits to be included in a project.

Ranking and scoring

3.11 **Ranking and scoring methods** are less precise than decision trees. Some goals may be hard to quantify, and strategic decisions generally take more matters into account than can be dealt with by uncertain estimates of probability.

3.12 This is best illustrated by means of a simple example. The objectives are weighted in relative importance (so that minimising competitive threats is the most important).

Objectives Strategic option	Growth in profit by over 10%	Reduce dependence on suppliers	Minimise competitive threats	Score	Rank
Do nothing	X	X	X	-	
Cut costs by subcontracting	✓	X	X	4	3rd
Expand product range	✓	X	✓	9	1st
Offer discounts to customers for fixed term contract	X	X	✓	5	2nd
Objective weighting	4	3	5		

3.13 In the example, expanding the product range would be chosen as the firm believes this will enhance profits and minimise competitive threats. Note that this is a deliberately simple example. In many cases, the strategies may not be mutually exclusive.

Scenarios

3.14 **Scenario building** is the process of identifying alternative futures. A strategy can be evaluated in terms of the various models of the future a company has. For example, Shell in the 1980s (quoted by Johnson and Scholes) developed three scenarios of UK economic activity and government policy to try and estimate the likely demand for oil.

Decision matrices

3.15 A **decision matrix** is a way of comparing outcomes with a variety of circumstances. Outcomes can be selected on a number of bases, and the decision matrix clarifies the choice.

3.16 When a decision has to be made, there will be a range of possible actions. Each action will have certain consequences, or **payoffs**. The payoff from any given action will depend on the circumstances (for example, high demand or low demand).

3.17 For a decision with these elements, a **payoff table** can be prepared. This is simply a table with rows for circumstances and columns for actions (or vice versa) and the payoffs in the cells of the table. Here is an example.

Payoff table for decision on level of advertising expenditure: payoffs in £'000 of profit after advertising expenditure

		Actions: expenditure		
		High	Medium	Low
Circumstances	I	+50	+30	+15
of the economy	II	+20	+25	+5
	III	0	-10	-35

3.18 Having worked out the consequences of different actions under different circumstances, we need to select a criterion for making our decision. There are four criteria which each look at just one possible payoff for each circumstance, either the best or the worst: maximax, minimin, maximin and minimax.

(a) **Hope for the best**. The maximax and minimin criteria both look at the best possible payoffs.

- Maximax: maximise the maximum profit
- Minimin: minimise the minimum costs or losses

(b) **Expect the worst**. The maximin and minimax criteria both look at the worst possible payoffs.

- Maximin: maximise the minimum profit
- Minimax: minimise the maximum costs or losses

3.19 To consider only one payoff of each action may be thought unrealistic. The Hurwicz criterion seeks to remedy this by taking a **weighted average** of the best and worst payoffs of each action:

$$\text{Weighted payoff} = \alpha \times \text{worst payoff} \times (1 - \alpha) \times \text{best payoff}$$

α is a number between 0 and 1, sometimes called the **pessimism-optimism index**. The value chosen reflects one's attitude to the risk of poor payoffs and the chance of good payoffs. The action with the highest weighted payoff is selected.

3.20 Another possible approach is to consider the extent to which we might come to regret an action we had chosen.

Regret for any combination of action and circumstances	=	Payoff for best action in those circumstances	−	Payoff of the action actually taken in those circumstances

Sensitivity analysis

> ### KEY TERM
>
> **Sensitivity analysis** 'A modelling and risk assessment procedure in which changes are made to significant variables in order to determine the effect of these changes on the planned outcome. Particular attention is thereafter paid to variables identified as being of special significance.'
> (CIMA *Official Terminology*)

3.21 **Sensitivity analysis** involves asking 'what if?' questions, and so it can be used for strategic planning. By changing the value of different variables in a decision model, a number of **different outcomes** will be produced. For example, wage increases can be altered to 10% from 5%; demand for a product can be reduced from 100,000 to 80,000, the introduction of new processing equipment can be deferred by six months, on the revised assumption that there will be delays, and so on.

Unity Bicycles plc

(1) What sort of risks are associated with the acquisition of, and further investment in, the plant in Romania?

Chapter roundup

- Strategic decisions are fraught with **risk** and **uncertainty**.

- A number of **techniques** can be used to model the risk systematically and help with decision making.

- This chapter looked at the following:

  ° **relevant costs** and **DCF** techniques

  ° **strategic investment appraisal** (including expenditure on marketing)

  ° **risk and cost behaviour**

  ° **decision techniques:** decision trees, cost/benefit analysis, ranking and scoring, scenarios and decision matrices

Quick quiz

1 What is strategic value analysis?

2 List the steps for analysing strategic investment projects

3 Identify some types of risk.

4 Explain the relationship between risk and operational gearing.

5 Define cost/benefit analysis.

6 The marginal cost of capital is the cost of the extra capital required to finance a specific project.

☐ True
☐ False

7 CVP analysis is also known as .... analysis.

8 **Fill in the blanks** in the statements below

- The cost (1) .... of the business is a risk

- A high level of (2) .... costs means that large (3) .... are made if sales are less than breakeven.

- A high proportion of (4) .... product costs means that total costs are always sensitive to production (5) ....

9 How is 'expected value' calculated when preparing a decision tree?

10 To protect .... , it might be made a condition of all new investments that they should .... within a certain period of time.

Answers to quick quiz

1 Strategic value analysis is an approach which measures the potential financial benefit or loss to shareholders from pursuing strategic options.

2
- Determine the investment project to be analysed.
- Determine the strategic objectives for the project.
- Determine alternative ways of achieving the same strategic objectives.
- Analyse a small number of alternatives.
- Try and determine what will happen if nothing is done (but this does not mean that you assume that competitors will do nothing).
- Determine key internal and external assumptions.
- Collect data on areas of greatest uncertainty.
- Carry out sensitivity analysis tests.
- Redefine the project on the basis of 8.
- Expose key assumptions and debate them.

3 - Physical
  - Economic
  - Financial
  - Business
  - Stakeholder response risk

4 The business's operational gearing (the ratio of fixed to variable costs) is an important indicator of risk. Where there is a high proportion of fixed costs, a strategy might be more risky, although it promises a higher return. A high proportion of genuinely variable costs can mean more flexibility.

5 Cost/benefit analysis involves a comparison between the cost of the resources used, plus any other costs imposed by an activity (eg pollution, environmental damage) and the value of the financial and non-financial benefits derived

6 True

7 Breakeven

8 (1) structure (2) fixed (3) losses (4) variable (5) volumes

9 Probability × outcome

10 Cash flows, pay back

Unity Bicycles plc review

Question 1. The *business risk* is that the plant will fail, and that it will not provide an adequate return on the investment made in it. Quality concerns, or problems with local management, may lead UB to close the plant.

The *financial risk* is that if it fails the bank may call in its loan of £3m (assuming this is the source of the invested funds) and may have recourse to other secured assets, depending on the terms of the loan agreement. Using equity finance, as suggested by the finance director, would transfer some of the risk. Share capital gives UB more flexibility than if it borrows heavily.

There could be an element of *political risk,* for example in the target market of Russia.

Now try the question below from the Exam Question Bank

Question to try	Level	Marks	Time
10	Intermediate	n/a	30 mins

BPP
PUBLISHING

Chapter 12

ORGANISATION STRUCTURE AND STRATEGY

Topic list	Syllabus reference	Ability required
1 The design of organisations	(iv)	Evaluation
2 Divisionalisation and decentralisation	(iv)	Evaluation
3 Organisational growth and development	(iv)	Evaluation
4 Alternative forms of organisation	(iv)	Evaluation
5 Business process re-engineering	(iv)	Evaluation
6 Transaction cost analysis	(iv)	Evaluation
7 Networks	(iv)	Evaluation
8 Outsourcing	(iv)	Evaluation
9 Management by objectives	(iv)	Evaluation

Introduction

The general concept of **organisation structure** is reflected in a significant amount of the content for part (iv) of the *Business Strategy* syllabus, as detailed below, and all relate to the learning outcome of being able to 'evaluate and recommend appropriate changes in organisational structure'.

Section 1 describes how **organisational design** provides a framework for the co-ordination and achievement of **objectives**. The trend towards decentralisation is described in section 2. Greiner's organisational life cycle, which features on the pilot paper, is a model of organisational growth and development which is described in section 3.

In recent years **alternative forms** of organisation have evolved to meet changing business needs. In section 4 we look at issues of **workforce flexibility** as well as 'the virtual firm', and in section 5 business process re-engineering (BPR) is described.

Organisational structure, it is argued, is determined by the **relative cost of the alternatives**. This is the basis for **transaction cost analysis** (section 6) and **networks** (section 7). Companies are now tending to concentrate on their core competences and sub-contract peripheral, support functions to independent firms via **outsourcing** (section 8).

The behaviour of **individual managers** must be made **congruent** to organisational objectives. There is thus an organisation structure to allocate responsibilities and a hierarchy of objectives (section 9).

Learning outcomes covered in this chapter

- **Evaluate** and **recommend** appropriate changes in organisational structure

---

Syllabus content covered in this chapter

- The implications for the internal organisation of the entity of the environment and corporate objectives

- Alternative forms of organisation (core and non-core activities) and the effects of changes in technology (eg home working) and the labour market (flexible employment relationships)

- The application of business process re-engineering and the need for customer responsiveness

- The role of the management accounting and information systems in supporting management and the appropriateness of management accounting techniques for alternative organisational structures and philosophies

- The basics of transaction cost analysis and the implications for the location of assets, knowledge, people and activities inside or outside the organisation

- Contracting and outsourcing decisions and their financial effects

- The potential problems and advantages in contracting out the finance function as a whole or of some elements of the function

- The implications of the above for the Chartered Management Accountant and the management accounting information system

---

1 THE DESIGN OF ORGANISATIONS

1.1 Organisational design or structure implies a framework or mechanism intended to do the following.

(a) To **link individuals** in an established network of relationships so that authority, responsibility and communications can be controlled

(b) To **group together** (in any appropriate way) the **tasks** required to fulfil the objectives of the organisation, and allocate them to suitable individuals or groups

(c) To give each individual or group the **authority** required to perform the allocated functions, while **controlling behaviour and resources** in the interests of the organisation as a whole

(d) To **co-ordinate** the objectives and activities of separate units, so that overall aims are achieved without gaps or overlaps in the flow of work required

(e) To **facilitate the flow** of work, information and other resources required, through planning, control and other systems

1.2 **Basic approaches to departmentation and divisionalisation**

(a) **Function.** This is departmentation by type of work done (eg finance department, marketing department, production function).

(b) **Geographic area.** Reporting relationships are organised by geography. In each area functional specialists report to an area boss, who ensures co-ordination.

(c) **Product/brand.** A divisional manager for each product is responsible for marketing and production. Some divisions are effectively run as independent businesses, in which case the division's finance specialists will report to the division's head.

(d) **Customer/market segment.** Reporting relationships are structured by type of customer.

(e) **Hybrid designs.** In practice, organisations may draw on a number of these approaches. Product/brand departmentation for marketing and production, say, might be combined with a centralised R&D function. This is because some activities are better organised on a functional basis (for reasons of economies of scale) whereas others are more suited, say, to product/brand departmentation (eg marketing).

Influences on organisation design

1.3 Many factors influence the structural design of the organisation.

Factor	Detail
Size	As an organisation gets larger, its structure gets more complex: specialisation and subdivision are required. The more members there are, the more potential there is for interpersonal relationships and the development of the informal organisation.
Task (the nature of its work)	Structure is shaped by the division of work into functions and individual tasks, and how these tasks relate to each other.
Staff	The skills and abilities of staff will determine how the work is structured and the degree of autonomy or supervision required.
Legal, commercial, technical and social environment	Examples include: economic recession necessitating staff streamlining especially at middle management level, market pressures in the financial services sector encouraging a greater concentration of staff in specialised areas and at the bank/customer interface, technology reducing staff requirements but increasing specialisation.
Age	The time it has had to develop and grow, or decline, whether it is very set in its ways and traditional, or experimenting with new ways of doing things and making decisions.
Culture and management style	How willing management is to delegate authority at all levels, how skilled they are in organisation and communication (for example in handling a wider span of control), whether teamwork is favoured, or large, impersonal structures are accepted by the staff.

Question 1

Consider how each of the factors listed in Paragraph 1.3 might affect the structural design of a service organisation (for example, a bank) and a manufacturing organisation (for example, a cement manufacturer).

Answer

Just taking elements of the first two factors as an example, a small bank may have just one office located in the area where it does its business - probably the City of London - and employ fairly specialised autonomous staff. A large bank would need a network of branches and regional offices as well as a central HQ and would employ a larger proportion of relatively unskilled workers, with greater supervision.

A cement manufacturer would need to have its production facilities located on top of the natural resources used. Larger organisations might have administrative offices and distribution depots elsewhere. The distinction between 'productive' workers and administrative workers would be much more marked than in a bank, and these differences would be accentuated the larger the organisation was.

Delayering and empowerment

1.4 Many large organisations in the late 1980s and early 1990s recognised that their tall structure was leading to communication problems, overlapping responsibilities and problems with planning and control. The **economic recession** in this period led many companies to seek ways of **cutting costs**, and **developments in technology meant** that the **information processing traditionally done by middle managers could be done by computer** just as effectively.

> **KEY TERMS**
>
> **Delayering** is removing whole layers of middle management.
>
> **Downsizing** is 'organisational restructuring involving outsourcing activities, replacing permanent staff with contract employees and reducing the number of levels within the organisational hierarchy, with the intention of making the organisation more flexible, efficient and responsive to its environment.' *(CIMA Official Terminology)*
>
> **Empowerment** is allowing workers to have the freedom to decide how to do their own work and making those workers personally responsible for achieving production targets and for quality control.

Matrix organisation

1.5 In recent years there has been a new emphasis on **flexibility** and **adaptability** in organisational design, particularly since the **pace of the change in the technological and competitive environment** has put pressure on businesses to **innovate**, to adopt a **market orientation**.

1.6 Part of this shift in emphasis has been a trend towards **task-centred structures**, such as **multi-disciplinary project teams**, which draw experience, knowledge and expertise together from different functions to facilitate flexibility and innovation. In particular, the concept of **'matrix' organisation** emerged, **dividing authority** between functional managers and product or project managers or co-ordinators - thus challenging classical assumptions about 'one man one boss'.

1.7 The **advantages** of a matrix structure are said to be as follows.

- **Greater flexibility of people**
- **Greater flexibility of tasks and structure**
- **Re-orientation**
- A structure for **allocating responsibility** to managers for end-results
- **Inter-disciplinary co-operation** and a **mixing of skills and expertise**
- **Motivation of employees**

1.8 The **disadvantages** of matrix organisation are said to be as follows.

- **Dual authority** threatens a conflict between functional managers and product/project managers.

- One individual with two or more bosses is more likely to suffer **stress** at work

- Matrix management can be more **costly**

- It may be **difficult** for the management of an organisation **to accept a matrix structure and the culture** of participation

2 DIVISIONALISATION AND DECENTRALISATION

2.1 As Ezzamel (*Business Unit & Divisional Performance Measurement*, 1992) notes, divisionalisation and decentralisation are sometimes treated as if they are synonymous, but this is not strictly correct. Ezzamel makes a number of distinctions.

> ### KEY TERMS
>
> **Functional decentralisation** involves delegating decision-making power to lower levels on the basis of function specialisation.
>
> **Federal decentralisation** 'involves the partitioning of the firm into two or more quasi-autonomous sub-units ... for example divisions dealing with different product lines, different customers, or different geographical areas'.
>
> Divisions in some organisations are highly centralised, with decision-making authority delegated only as far as the divisional manager. Depending on one's perspective, the divisional managers could be seen as part of the centre of the organisation.

Traditional ideas

2.2 Arguments in **favour of centralisation** include the following.

- Decisions are made at one point and so control and co-ordination are easier
- Senior managers in an organisation can take a wider view of problems and consequences
- Senior management can keep a proper balance between different departments
- The quality of decisions is higher due to skills and experience
- It is possibly cheaper, by reducing the number of managers needed
- Crisis decisions are taken more quickly at the centre
- Policies, procedures and documentation can be standardised organisation-wide

2.3 Arguments in **favour of decentralisation** include the following.

- It avoids overburdening top managers, in terms of workload and stress
- It improves motivation of more junior managers who are given responsibility
- Decision makers have a greater awareness of local problems
- It allows greater speed of decision making, and response to changing events
- It helps junior managers to develop
- Separate spheres of responsibility can be identified
- Communication technology allows decisions to be made locally

Mintzberg

2.4 Mintzberg argues that the **divisional form emerges when the 'middle line' exerts a pull to 'balkanise'** - in other words to split into small self-managed units.

2.5 Mintzberg believes that any organisation is based on the following principles.

- Job specialisation (the number of tasks in a given job, the division of labour)
- Behaviour formalisation (in other words, the standardisation of work processes)
- Training (to enforce work standardisation)
- Indoctrination of employees (in the organisation's culture)
- Unit grouping (eg organisation by function, geographical area, or product)
- Unit size (eg span of control)
- Planning and control systems
- Liaison and communication devices (eg networks, committees, matrix structures)

2.6 These principles can be embodied in an organisation in a number of ways. In any organisation, Mintzberg identifies five possible component parts which are outlined in the diagram below (called an **organigram**).

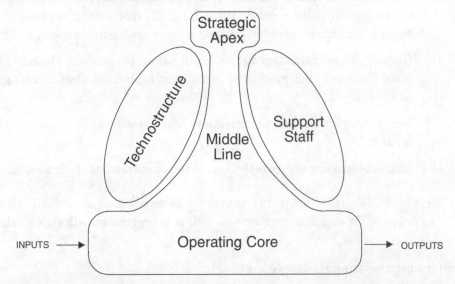

KEY TERMS

The **operating core** contains those people directly involved in production (ie in securing inputs and processing them into outputs and distributing those outputs).

The **strategic apex** emerges with the need for supervision and control. It ensures that the organisation follows its mission and serves the needs of its owners.

The **middle line** is the hierarchy of authority between the operating core and the strategic apex. People in this area administer the work done.

The **technostructure** standardises the work. Work-study analysts standardise work processes by analysing and determining the most efficient method of doing a job. Planners (eg quality staff, accountants) standardise outputs.

Support staff provide ancillary services such as public relations, legal counsel, the cafeteria.

3 ORGANISATIONAL GROWTH AND DEVELOPMENT

Growth

3.1 **Organisations grow in a number of ways.**

- Sales revenue (a growth in the number of markets served)
- Profitability (in absolute terms, and as a return on capital)
- Number of goods/services sold
- Number of outlets/sites
- Number of employees
- Number of countries

3.2 **Reasons for growth**

(a) **A genuine increasing demand for the products/services.** For example, there is likely to be a growth in the number of UK hospitals specialising in geriatric illnesses, simply because the number of elderly people in the population is expected to rise.

(b) **Growth can be necessary for an organisation to compete effectively. Economies of scale** can arise from producing in bulk, as high fixed costs can be spread over more units of output.

(c) **The managers of the organisation like growth,** as it increases their power and rewards.

(d) **Shareholders can see growth as a means of increasing their wealth,** in many cases.

3.3 Organisational growth in size can occur by **acquisition** or **organically** (ie generated by an expansion of the organisation's activities). It is to **organic growth** that we shall now turn.

Greiner's organisational life cycle model   Pilot paper

3.4 An **organisation life cycle model** was suggested by Greiner. It assumes that, as an organisation **ages**, it grows in **size**, measured, perhaps by the **number of employees** and **diversity** of activities. This growth takes place in discrete phases. Each phase is characterised by two things.

- **Evolution**: a distinctive factor that **directs** the organisation's **growth**

- **Revolution**: a **crisis**, through which the organisation must pass before starting the next phase

3.5 Greiner identified five phases.

(a) **Phase 1**

   (i) **Growth through creativity.** The organisation is small, and is managed in a personal and informal way. The founders of the business are actively involved in the operations, personnel issues and innovation. Apple Computers, for example, started up in a garage. The product range is probably limited. A key goal is survival.

   (ii) **Crisis of leadership.** Sooner or later there comes a need for **distinct** management skills, relating less to products and marketing issues and more to the co-ordination of the organisation's activities.

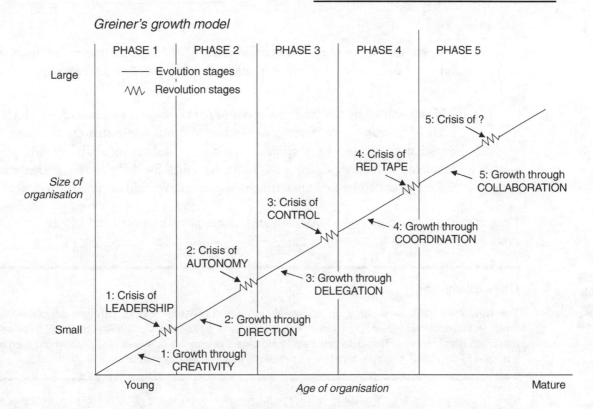

Greiner's growth model

(b) **Phase 2**

(i) **Growth through direction**. Clear direction is provided in response to the crisis of leadership by professionalising the management. At the same time, there are more employees. Their initial enthusiasm might be tempered by loss of autonomy and the growth of hierarchy.

(ii) **Crisis of autonomy**. Delegation becomes a problem. The top finds it harder and harder to keep in detailed control as there are too many activities, and it is easy to lose a sense of the wider picture. **Employees resent the lack of initiative and their performance falters**.

(c) **Phase 3**

(i) **Growth through delegation**. The response to the crisis of autonomy in Phase 2 is delegation. This has the advantage of decentralising decision-making and giving confidence to junior managers.

(ii) **Crisis of control**. Delegation leads to additional problems of co-ordination and control. **Over-delegation can result in different departments acting sub-optimally**, in other words pursuing their own departmental goals to the detriment of the organisation as a whole.

(d) **Phase 4**

(i) **Growth through co-ordination**. The addition of internal systems, procedures and so forth aims to ensure co-ordination of activities and optimal use of resources, without reverting to the detailed hands-on methods in Phase 1. You might expect to see more complex management accounting systems, transfer pricing procedures, and some central management functions.

(ii) **Crisis of red tape**. The new procedures *inhibit useful action*.

(e) **Phase 5**

  (i) **Growth through collaboration**. The crisis of red tape is resolved by increased informal collaboration. Control is cultural rather than formal. People participate in teams.

  (ii) This growth stage may lead to a '**crisis of psychological saturation**', in which all become exhausted by teamwork. (Greiner did not name this crisis, hence the question mark in the diagram.) Greiner postulates a sixth growth phase involving a dual organisation: a 'habit' structure for daily work routines and a 'reflective structure' for stimulating new perspectives and personal enrichment.

3.6 Greiner's model refers to evolutionary organisational growth punctuated by revolutionary crisis.

Case study link

The November 2001 case study on Intelligent Refrigeration Systems (IRS Ltd) was concerned with how an individual with specific market knowledge and a forceful personality built up a sizeable manufacturing business. The skills required to manage the growing business, the funding required and the need to develop a management team as markets matured also featured.

Exam focus point

The pilot paper ties the stages of Greiner's model to the differences in organisational objectives at different phases of company development.

3.7 A different approach, adopted by Quinn, was **logical incrementalism**. This means that businesses make small adjustments, building consistently on what they have, and adapting to the environment. Change is continuous and gradual. This alternative model was based, like Greiner's, on a study of real organisations.

Criticisms of organisation life cycle models

Formation

3.8 **Early stages**. Not all organisations are founded by a visionary controlling entrepreneur, selling a product or service.

(a) A new organisation can be formed from the **merger of two existing ones**.

(b) Two or more companies might **collaborate on a joint venture**. The Airbus project, for example, did not start as a small business, but as a result of co-operation between governments and existing companies.

(c) New organisations are created by existing ones and have a substantial complement of staff.

Too many issues

3.9 **The models combine too many issues**: organisation structure, organisation culture, product/market scope, leadership, management style and reward systems. A business can grow quickly in some aspects but not in others.

Growth is not the same as effectiveness

3.10 Many organisations can be effective without growth. In fact growth is not the normal state of affairs for many organisations.

No timescale

3.11 **It gives no idea of the timescale involved.**

(a) For example, the early stages (Phase 1) may be very rapid, or may take several years. The longer it takes, the easier it might be for the organisation to adjust, and no crises may punctuate the process.

(b) Growth models imply a **linear development** over time, whereas the organisation might enjoy different rates of growth at different times of the life cycle, and even decline.

Ignores environment and competition

3.12 The models do not clearly indicate the relationship with the environment. Organisational growth depends on environmental factors.

3.13 The growth of the business can be curtailed by the **growth of competition**. In other words, a business can be hemmed in, but still survive and even prosper.

Question 2

Heifetz and Kyung are partners in a business that makes violins and other stringed musical instruments. They are based in a small workshop in Stoke Newington, north London. They are both experts at their craft. They believe that their future is rosy: Kyung, in particular, realises that as western classical music becomes popular in China, Japan and other Asian countries, demand for instruments will pick up.

Although there is enough demand in the UK to keep them going, both want to expand the business. Kyung asks her brother, who lives in Hong Kong, to help them market their products to Asian orchestras and violinists. Kyung's brother has sent them a number of official forms relating to customs, import and export, and some ideas as to agents. With the global trade liberalisation, they assume that exporting will be easy. Heifetz and Kyung hire and train three more skilled instrument-makers.

Required

What issues relating to Greiner's life cycle model are raised by this scenario?

Answer

(a) Although the firm is small, it will very soon need specialist assistance. Despite trade liberalisation, exporting *inevitably* involves red tape: time must be spent dealing with bureaucracies, filling in VAT forms, and managing relationships with distributors. In addition, somebody has to look after the firm's accounts.

(b) The business shows characteristics of a pre-bureaucratic stage, but it needs detailed technical expertise as mentioned in (a) above. Operations will become *bureaucratic*, simply to deal with the export side of things.

Greiner's model cannot predict how *every* organisation will grow as each faces its own unique problems. But it does indicate some of the issues that can arise. You should treat it as a broad generalisation that admits of many exceptions, or as a tool to help you think about organisations, rather than a scientific law.

---

4   ALTERNATIVE FORMS OF ORGANISATION   Pilot paper

Workforce flexibility

4.1   Flexibility is an area of current interest in human resource management, as economic pressures require more **efficient** use of the workforce. It involves the development of **versatility** in the workforce.

4.2   For the organisation, it offers a cost effective, efficient way of utilising the workforce. With competitive pressure, technological innovation, and a variety of other changes, organisations need a flexible, 'lean' workforce for efficiency, control and predictability: the stability of the organisation in a volatile environment depends on its ability to adapt swiftly to meet changes, without incurring cost penalties or suffering waste.

4.3   Mechanisms for developing flexibility include the following.

    (a)   **The erosion of demarcations between job areas**. With the need for adaptability, rigid job descriptions and specialisation have gone out of fashion and versatility is much prized on the labour market.

    (b)   **Flexibility in the deployment of the workforce in terms of man hours**. With the shrinking demand for some categories of work, ideas about full employment, full-time employment and 'one man, one job' have had to be revised. There are various ways in which individuals can be given a flexible job - in terms of working hours - and organisations can avoid overstaffing and idle time. **Flexitime** is an area in which conventional rules and boundaries are increasingly bent or broken: the '9 to 5' is no longer the most effective scheme of working in large city areas where commuting is a problem, and in a workforce where parents and home makers are having to reconcile the requirements of family, household and work.

Flexible working methods

4.4   G A Cole (*Personnel Management: Theory and Practice*) sums up the pressures on managerial decisions about the size and nature of the workforce as follows.

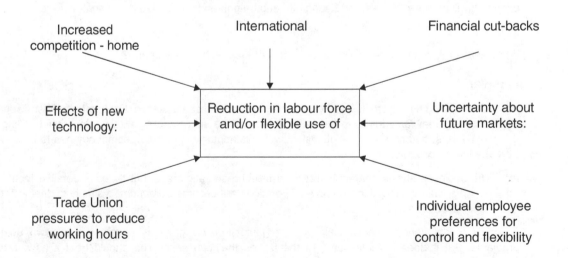

Teleworking and homeworking

4.5   The nature of work in many organisations has now changed so much that there is less dependence on a **particular location** where the work should be done. Many people can carry out their work independently, as long as they are connected to resources, colleagues, suppliers and customers through the telecommunications network. The exploitation of the **Internet** is central to this development.

4.6 **Teleworking** describes the process of working from home, or from a satellite office close to home, with the aid of computers, facsimile machines, modems or other forms of telecommunication equipment'. It offers benefits to the organisation.

- **Savings** on overheads, particularly premises costs
- Employing **skilled people** for whom traditional working practices are impracticable
- Elimination of the need to **commute**
- Potential **reduction in stress,** since there is less conflict with non-work goals

4.7 In addition to 'telecommuters', home workers can be of various types.

(a) Traditional **outworkers,** such as home typists or wordprocessors and envelope-fillers (for mailshots), writers and editors, tele-canvassers and market-researchers.

(b) **Itinerants** such as salesmen, who do not have a permanent presence in the office, and use their home (and even car) for working on the move.

(c) Those in **personal services,** like ironing and mending of clothes, out-of-salon hairdressing and music teaching.

4.8 There are certain problems associated with homeworking for both management and individuals.

- **Control**
- **Communication**
- **Co-ordination**
- **Employee appraisal and development**
- **Risks associated with 'networking'** eg computer viruses
- **Health and safety**

Case example

Rank Xerox launched a successful networking scheme as long ago as 1981. They closed down a central London office costing them £300,000 a year, 'fired' the staff and then re-engaged them on networking contracts: each became a separate company working from home, linked direct to HQ, and guaranteed income if they supplied work on time.

The advantages seemed to be that:

(a) As 'self-employed' workers, the networkers developed the discipline and motivation to work conscientiously

(b) The more they did, the more they earned, and the firm encouraged them to use their spare time to take on contracts outside Rank Xerox itself

(c) Networkers travelled in to Head Office only one day per week

(d) Some banded together to form multiple units, or shared office premises near their homes, thus overcoming any sense of isolation.

The virtual firm

4.9 An extreme example of an alternative form of organisation is the so-called **virtual company.** A virtual firm is at the opposite extreme from the sort of business most of us work for. The virtual firm does not really exist. It is created out of a network of alliances and subcontracting arrangements: it is as if most of the activities in a particular **value chain** are conducted by different firms, even though the process is loosely co-ordinated. We examine networks in more detail in Section 7.

Case study link

Molecular Allies, one of the divisions of Proton Quest in the May 2001 Final Level Case Study operated very much as a virtual company, managing large scale drug discovery projects.

4.10 As another example, assume you manufacture small toys. You could in theory outsource:

- The design to a consultancy
- Manufacturing to a subcontractor
- Delivery arrangements to a specialist logistics firm
- Debt collection to a bank (factoring)
- Filing, tax returns, bookkeeping to an accountancy firm

Case example

First Virtual Corporation, one of the few truly virtual organisations in existence, was set up in 1993 by Ralph Ungermann. With only 50 direct employees, it generates sales of its multimedia networking equipment of about $50m. Everything except the crucial design and development work is outsourced.

The company has two 'core competences' according to Ungermann: technical development and forging alliances with large companies.

The question is whether First Virtual will need to take tighter control of some functions as it grows.

4.11 Virtual corporations effectively put market forces in all linkages of the value chain - this has the advantage of creating incentives for suppliers, perhaps to take risks to produce a better product, but can lead to a loss of control.

4.12 A **core competence** should always be retained in-house, or else the firm is effectively surrendering its source of competitive advantage. It is part of the short versus long term debate: if all the knowledge needed to run a business is held 'outside' it, are short term improvements being made at the (long term) expense of the ability to innovate?

Outsourcing

4.13 This has been a significant trend, and involves companies and government bodies turning over **non-core functions** to specialist contractors. A company that earns its profits from , say, manufacturing bicycles, does not also need to have expertise in mass catering or office cleaning. Outsourcing is discussed in more detail in section 7 below.

5 BUSINESS PROCESS RE-ENGINEERING (BPR)

> **KEY TERM**
>
> **Business process re-engineering (BPR)** is 'the selection of areas of business activity in which repeatable and repeated sets of activity are undertaken, and the development of improved understanding of how they operate and the scope for radical redesign with a view to creating and delivering better customer value.' (CIMA *Official Terminology*)

5.1 According to Rupert Booth (*Management Accounting*, September 1994), there are **three common themes.**

(a) The **need to make radical changes to the entire organisation.** Changing conditions 'impact all functions of the company and lead to a radically different way of doing business, sweeping away the previous methods.' The chief BPR tool is a clean sheet of paper. In effect the question becomes 'If we were a new company, how would we run the place?' Other critical questions are:

- What is done?
- How is it done?
- Where is it done?
- When is it done?
- Who does it?

- Why do it?
- Why do it that way?
- Why do it there?
- Why do it then?
- Why that person?

(b) The **need to change functional hierarchies:** 'existing hierarchies have evolved into functional departments that encourage functional excellence but which do not work well together in meeting customers' requirements.

(c) The **need to address the problem of fragmented staff roles:** 'roles have become specialised with the result that staff are only responsible for a small part of an overall task.

5.2 Properly implemented BPR may help an organisation to reduce costs, improve customer services, cut down on the complexity of the business and improve internal communication. At best it may bring about new insights into the objectives of the organisation and how best to achieve them.

Contribution of the management accountant to the planning of a BPR programme

5.3 Having overall responsibility for the organisation's information systems, the **management accountant** will be the **main provider of the information required by the BPR programme.** Because BPR involves the introduction of significant changes to business processes, the organisation's information requirements are likely to change. Users will require alternative types of information in alternative formats.

(a) At the outset there will be no way of knowing for sure the precise information requirements of the organisation. It is only once the programme commences that precise information requirements will become clear.

(b) At the planning stage of a BPR programme the management accountant will therefore need to **liaise with all others on the team** and consider the changes that will be necessary to the organisation's information systems as a result of different ways of organising work.

(c) **Benchmarking** exercises may need to be set up, and the management accountant is likely to be heavily involved in devising ways of collecting and analysing data from such exercises.

(d) A **modelling approach** will help to assess the validity and consequences of alternative ways of re-engineering processes.

(e) **Costing systems** may need to be reappraised: for example it might be useful to set up activity based costing systems, but the consequent changes to information collection and analysis and to accounting software need to be thought through fully.

(f) For reporting purposes, **alternative performance measures** will need to be devised, since information will no longer be required on a departmental/functional basis but on a process basis.

Contribution of the management accountant to the implementation of a BPR programme

5.4 When the BPR programme is being implemented, the management accountant will need to ensure that **managers** within the organisation are **provided with the information they require**. It is likely that the management accounting function will need to provide a **broader range of information** than previously, but the emphasis must be on **user friendliness and sharing**. This is likely to mean the introduction of new software and telecommunications links, capable of handling different flows of information.

5.5 An important aspect of implementation will be **monitoring of progress**: are the expected benefits of BPR being realised, and if not what action is required? Indicators of success might include reduced costs, faster delivery, more satisfied customers and so on, but systems need to be in operation to measure such things.

Question 3

One way of grouping organisational activities is by product. Suggest six other ways and think of examples of organisations that might be organised in these ways.

Answer

Six ways of grouping activities are by numbers, by shifts, by function, by territory, by customer or market segment, and by equipment specialisation. Think of examples for yourself.

6 TRANSACTION COST ANALYSIS   5/02

6.1 What do people actually do in organisations? One point of view argues that **work is a series of transactions**. For example, A asks B to type up a letter. B provides this service (and others) for A in exchange for a monthly salary. In terms of what is achieved this is exactly the same as if A worked for one organisation and B worked for an independent typing bureau: A could engage in a transaction with the typing bureau to get the letter typed.

6.2 Organisation structure, it is argued, is determined by the **relative cost of the alternatives**: whether it is cheaper to complete the transaction through a **market** or to arrange it so that it takes place within an **hierarchical organisation**.

> **KEY TERMS**
>
> **Transaction costs** are the costs of using arm's length market exchange to carry out exchange of goods and services. The existence of significant transaction costs can explain why organisations sometimes carry out transactions internally rather than relying on market specialists.' (*Besanko et al*)
>
> **Transaction cost economics** is the theory that argues that organisation structure is determined by the relative costs of conducting activities through the market or through a hierarchy.

6.3 The main proponent of transaction cost economics was O E Williamson (*Markets and Hierarchies*, 1975). Williamson says that **transaction costs are influenced by three main factors.**

(a) **Bounded rationality.** Searching only until one finds an option which is satisfactory, though it may not be perfect.

(b) **Opportunism**. Often one person has better access to information than another, allowing them to act in their own interest. If B were the only person in the world who knew how to type this would significantly affect the cost of B's services.

(c) **Atmosphere**. Different people like different types of organisation and prefer to work with different types of people.

The M-form

6.4 Williamson then goes on to consider the impact of transaction cost economics at different levels of complexity. Williamson distinguishes between **U-form** and **M-form**.

> **KEY TERMS**
>
> **M-form** is a multidivisional organisational structure.
> **U-form** is a unitary or centralised organisational structure.

PEER GROUPS
Share expertise, information and physical assets

Chief Executive

Production   Marketing

U-FORM
At least two management layers. Increasing amounts of information. Loss of information due to
(a) communication up and down hierarchy
(b) bounded rationality

Board

Division A   Division B   Division C

M-FORM
Day-to-day operations are carried out at divisional level. The organisation as a whole is controlled from the centre. Information loss is reduced.

6.5 As the **level of complexity increases, transaction costs can be reduced by adopting some kind of hierarchy**. For example, this will reduce the costs of collecting sufficient information to know the best places to go in the market to conduct transactions. It will also cut the costs of entering into contracts with individuals to supply their labour: if individuals are employed on a continuing basis they can be required to perform a variety of tasks as the need arises.

6.6 As the level of complexity increases still further, however, these **savings are counterbalanced by the increasing costs of keeping control** because information tends to be lost or distorted as it passes through the hierarchy. This leads to the development of the M-form.

6.7 Williamson identifies the **attributes of the M-form organisation** as follows.

(a) Each division has quasi-autonomous status.

(b)   Strategic decisions are taken by senior managers (the hierarchy), while operational decisions are made by divisional managers (the market).

(c)   An incentive mechanism exists and is used to encourage divisional managers to share the interests of senior managers.

(d)   An internal audit system is in place, with performance measures to evaluate the success or otherwise, both of managers and of divisions.

(e)   There is a system of allocating resources whereby senior managers distinguish the most profitable alternatives from amongst **all** divisions.

6.8   As Berry, Broadbent and Otley say (with BPP's emphasis), 'The **M-form** of organisation can be seen to provide a **mixture of markets and hierarchical organisation**. The M-form organisation allows the mixing of the **hierarchy**, which **controls the strategic issues**, and the market, in which the **day-to-day activities** are placed. Thus at divisional level some **competition** takes place, not just between the divisions and their **external competitors**, but also between the divisions for **internal allocations of resources**.'

6.9   Besanko et al (*The Economics of Strategy, 2000*) identify three important concepts from transaction cost economics.

- **Relationship-specific assets**
- **Rents** and **quasi rents**
- The **holdup** problem

Relationship-specific assets

6.10   These are investments **made to support a particular transaction,** and are often essential for its efficiency, but have the effect of locking parties into a relationship to some degree. Besanko et al quote the example of a metal refining company making a relationship specific investment when it builds a refinery that can only accommodate a particular grade of ore. It cannot now easily replace its ore supplier, because it would need to reconfigure its plant to accept other grades. Asset specificity can take four forms.

(a)   **Site specificity.** Assets are located side by side to economise on transport or processing efficiencies.

(b)   **Physical assets specificity.** Asset properties are tailored to a specific transaction.

(c)   **Dedicated assets.** Investment is made in plant and equipment in order to serve a particular customer and complete a particular contract.

(d)   **Human assets specificity.** Workers acquire skills, know-how and information that is valuable to the organisation. This will cover such aspects as organisational routine and operating procedures, which will be vital for a particular organisation but less useful for any other. Besanko quotes the example of a defence contractor that is attempting to enter commercial markets. Successful management in defence contracting requires knowledge and expertise in lobbying government departments and understanding their processes (skills which are less valuable in the commercial environment).

(e)   **Brand name capital specificity.** Brands become associated with specific products or services, such as Rank Xerox photocopiers or Western Union money transfers.

(f)   **Temporal specificity.** This refers to the provision of services at a specific time. In an article in the March 2002 edition of *CIMA Insider*, the examiner notes the example of airlines needing to book landing slots at an airport to be able to provide their service to passengers. These slots are an asset for a short time only, until the landing has been made and the slot needs to be booked again for future flights.

Exam focus point

These 'specificities' were examined in May 2002: a straightforward question for those who had read and noted the examiner's article referred to in point (f) above.

Rents and quasi rents

6.11 To explain rent and quasi rent, we will use a numerical example.

6.12 EXAMPLE

A is thinking about building a factory to produce widgets specifically for B. One million of these widgets will be made, at a variable cost of £2.50 per unit.

The factory will be financed by a mortgage, the payment of which will be £3,000,000 annually.

The total cost of making one million widgets per year is therefore £5.5 million. ((£2.50 × 1 million units) + £3,000,000).

B is expected to buy the widgets at a profitable price, but if B plc does not buy A's widgets, A can sell them all to C, another company that will modify them for resale. The price A can get from another company is £4.00 per widget.

By selling the widgets for £4.00, A would not be covering its mortgage costs. The shortfall of £1,500,000 ((1,000,000 units × (£4.00 – £2.50)) – £3,000,000) represents a **relationship specific investment** with B, the amount of A's investment that it cannot recover if it does not do business with B. In these circumstances, it would not make sense for A to build the factory unless it fully expected to sell the widgets to B.

Rent

Suppose B plc agreed to buy one million widgets at £6 per widget, generating revenues of £6,000,000. A's **rent** is defined as the profit it expects to get when the factory is built, which is ((1,000,000 × (£6 – £2.50)) – £3,000,000) = £500,000.

Quasi rent

If the deal with B falls apart after the factory is built, should A still sell widgets to C? The answer is yes (assuming it is the next best deal available), because the factory investment is now a **sunk cost**. The sales to C will cover variable costs.

Quasi rent is the difference between the profit from selling to B and from selling to C. In this example it is: 1,000,000 units × (£6.00 – £4.00) = £2,000,000. It is the extra profit from the deal going ahead as planned when compared to the next best alternative.

The 'holdup' problem

6.13 A company may face what is termed a **holdup problem** when its trading partner attempts to renegotiate a deal and take advantage of the fact that the company has already invested in the specific asset.

6.14 If an asset is not relationship specific, its associated quasi rent is zero, but when quasi-rent is large, a company has a lot to lose by pursuing its second best alternative (in A's case above, £2,000,000).

6.15 From the example above, B may offer to pay £4.50 per widget rather than £6, as it knows that A will now accept anything above £4. B will be able to increase its profits at A's expense, and A will end up losing £1,000,000 ((1,000,000 units x (£4.50-£2.50)) - £3,000,000). Companies that are afraid of being 'held up' in this way may become reluctant to invest in specific assets in the first place.

POINT TO NOTE

The relevance of all of this for the study of organisational structure is that by placing the trading parties in the same organisation through **vertical integration**, opportunistic behaviour such as this may become less likely. Vertical integration would occur, for example, if A became the selling division of a vertically integrated firm that also included B. *Two divisions within the same organisation may be more likely to co-operate.* This will be influenced by various factors.

- Formal governance mechanisms such as the employer/employee relationship
- Social values
- Individual commitment to the organisation
- A corporate culture stressing teamwork and co-operation

Ouchi

6.16 Ouchi developed the ideas of transaction cost economics and identified three types of control.

(a) **Market control** is appropriate when it is **possible to measure outputs easily**. It is the use of the **price mechanism**, internally and externally, to control organisational behaviour. At the level of the entire organisation, 'market control' is always used: sales and profit information are published, and so the organisation's performance can be judged in comparison with other organisations, or with previous years. Internally, the price mechanism can be used as a means to control activities for example by using transfer prices or in compulsory competitive tendering exercises.

(b) **Bureaucratic control** is the use of '**rules, policies, hierarchies of authority, documentation**, and so forth' to standardise behaviour and assess performance.

(c) **Clan control** is control based on **corporate culture**.

6.17 Ouchi explains which form of control is appropriate in different circumstances in terms of the way in which organisations transform inputs into outputs. The **style of control** is **dependent upon** how easy it is to **understand the transformation process** and how easy it is to **measure outputs**.

		UNDERSTANDABILITY OF TRANSFORMATION PROCESS	
		Easy	*Not easy*
MEASURABILITY OF OUTPUTS	*Easy*	Market control OR Bureaucratic control	Market control
	Not easy	Bureaucratic control	Clan control

7 NETWORKS

> **KEY TERM**
>
> **Networks** are **groups** of firms making relational contracts with each other, who need to do business together in the long term, and who arguably depend on a common skills base.

7.1 You should now be familiar with the idea of interrelationships between different units of a business. We shall now explore the nature of some of these relationships. It is possible to contrast two types of **contract**.

(a) A **spot contract** is a one-off transaction. (When you buy a house, you do not expect to see the current owners again.)

(b) A **relational contract** contains parties doing business with each other in a long term relationship. Its provisions are only partly specified but it is enforced not by legal process but by the needs the parties have to go on doing business with each other .

7.2 These **relational contracts** may have a **legal basis**, but also include a **pattern of expectations** that the parties have of each other. For example, the **employment contract** is an important **relational contract**; it is impossible in a **legal** document to specify rigidly what an employee will do.

7.3 Firms may establish these relationships in two ways.

Internal networks ...with and among their employees (internal architecture)	Organisation structure and culture; job descriptions and work patterns to encourage development; employment contracts (eg employer commitment vs 'short term hire'); remuneration structure to encourage 'loyalty' 'creativity' and a willingness to satisfy individual preferences for the collective's benefit.
External networks ...with their suppliers or customers (external architecture) among firms engaged in related activities	Relationships with suppliers - eg long-term supply contracts, detailed design specifications - firms share knowledge and establish fast response times on the basis of relational contracts. A good example of this is Porter's clustering model discussed in Chapter 5.

7.4 It is clear that the idea of **networks of relational contracts** is very wide in scope. They are activities embedded in **business relationships** built up over time.

> **Exam focus point**
>
> The development of the network organisation was directly linked with transaction cost analysis in the May 2002 exam (see Section 8).

Networks and co-ordination

7.5 Trends in organisational structure include the following. All of them remove the activities of the organisation from hierarchical control.

Outsourcing	Third party firms take over some functions they can perform more effectively.
Growth of knowledge work	The environment of competition has been changed by the importance of knowledge a resource.
Delayering	A reduction in the number of levels in the management hierarchy.
Communications technology	Organisational life has been revolutionised by email and network technology.
Core/periphery	Some firms have been changing the structure of their workforces for the sake of greater flexibility, eg a core of full-time permanent staff and periphery part-timers and temporary or contract workers.

7.6   In terms of the management process it is arguable that, within the organisation, networking and networks can be of significant importance. Networks of contacts are often vital for the effective conduct of organisational decision making and activity. People and skills, from within and external to the organisation, are important and need to be contacted and brought into project teams.

7.7   Such networks of contacts and skills might **span the boundaries of the organisation**. Networking is necessary to draw people into temporary or semi-permanent work arrangements for planning, decision making and the production process. Where expertise or information is an important commodity, then networking is a means of obtaining such information.

7.8   Even in **large, more formal, organisations** there are still informal communication patterns and networks. They **ensure co-ordination of middle managers**, whose day-to-day jobs are important in the implementation of corporate plans and strategies. These middle managers are key tactical and operational decision-makers. They will not be functional heads, as such people are too far removed from the decisions under review.

7.9   Information and communications technology has also encouraged the use of networking. As the costs of communications have fallen, such networking arrangements are easier to set up and facilitate.

External networks

7.10   In an external network, relationships are conducted on a **relationship basis** rather than on a 'spot' or 'one-off' basis. The word relationships implies **continuing** involvement. Using relationships as an asset or a resource does require careful management. In many industries, **collaborative ventures** and **strategic alliances** are becoming increasingly common. Whilst some strategic alliances are relatively clear cut, other forms of networking activity and organisational relationships require new forms of dealing with the end-customer. Here is an example of the relative complexities of networks.

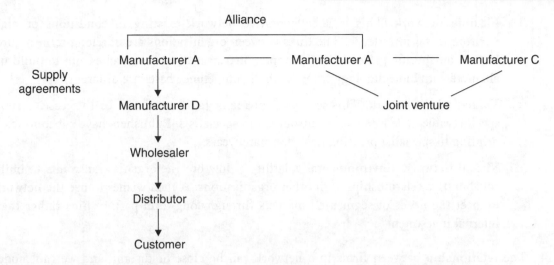

7.11 As we can see, there are many types of organisational forms that can be developed. Networks display, **horizontal** (eg joint ventures) and **vertical** (supply chain) linkages.

What is driving the development of networks?

7.12 Drivers of collaboration strategies that result in network arrangements can be characterised as follows.

(a) **Blurring of market boundaries** (eg convergence of telecommunications and computing). This increases the complexity of technologies.

(b) **Escalating customer diversity**: customers are becoming more demanding. In global markets, customers are more diverse almost by definition.

(c) **Skills and resource gaps**: firms need to collaborate in technologically demanding markets.

Types of external network

7.13 It is possible to model types of network on the axes of environmental volatility or turbulence and the type of network **relationship**, as in the diagram below. The type of network relationship can range from the **collaborative** to mainly **transactional** (just a buy-sell relationship). A **collaborative** network involves a great deal of co-operation, which may be enshrined in joint venture agreements. In a **transactional relationship**, there is no commitment to the long term.

	Environmental turbulence	
	Low	High
Collaborative	Virtual network	Flexible
Transactional	Value-added	Hollow

(a) A **hollow network** combines high environmental volatility with a transactional-based approach. The organisation draws heavily on other organisations to satisfy customer needs. Such organisations can be quite small, but have a large number of contacts. For example, in the publishing industry, there are print brokers who will deal with a variety of printing needs by accessing a network of subcontractors.

(b) **Flexible network.** This is a collaborative network existing in conditions of high environmental turbulence. The links between organisations are of a long-term nature, but are on specific projects. For example, pharmaceuticals companies aim to build up alliances with biotechnology firms (as their competence bases are different)

(c) **Value-added network.** This is typical of many Japanese firms. In this case, certain specific value added items are outsourced to specialists. Publishers have subcontracted printing to specialist printing firms for many years.

(d) **Virtual network.** Environmental volatility is low but the organisation wants to build collaborative relationships with other organisations. A firm wishes to use the network to meet the needs of segmented markets through long-term partnerships rather than internal investment.

7.14 The **relationship** between firms in a network can be close or distant, and we can model them as follows.

Distant   Outsourcing – Purchase of goods/services

                 Partnership – co-ordinated/integrated activities

                 Alliance – Joint ventures: shared ownership

Close   Ownership – for example, vertical integration

8 OUTSOURCING

8.1 A significant recent trend has been for companies and government bodies to **concentrate on their core competences** – what they are really good at (or set up to achieve) – and turn **other functions over to specialist contractors.**

8.2 Every activity of quoted companies is questioned by shareholders, in particular those activities which take up a lot of money. Research by PricewaterhouseCoopers (a major provider of outsourced services) has found that when most business processes are stripped down to their basics, about 70% of them can be found in every company. With the help of technology and telecommunications it is now possible for **one service provider** to devise a common process to deal with **many different local processes in a single location.**

Case example

The idea that companies should concentrate on a few core processes and buy in the rest has survived, despite the bursting of the dotcom bubble and the collapse of Enron. The dotcom era saw many businesses build rapidly with little capital investment, relying instead on the Internet to manage a network of relationships. Enron outsourced wherever possible: how far did such outsourcing undermine management control?

The breadth of services now being outsourced is much greater than in the past. The pressure to cut costs and maintain efficiency and competitiveness is intense, and Procter and Gamble is investigating outsourcing a range of processes across HR, supply chain and finance.

Most companies are trying to do three things well.

(i)   Manage customer relationships
(ii) Routine processing of information
(iii) Development of new products

It is likely that companies in the future will concentrate on just one, while buying in the others: 'it has become possible to design an organisation from scratch, just as you would a product.'

According to the FT, the notion that a company should concentrate on core activities is rooted in modern management theory:

(i)   *Capital efficiency*. The popularity of EVA (see Chapter 15) means that businesses are trying to get things off the balance sheet

(ii)   *Core competency*

(iii) *Process design*. Fads such as TQM (Chapter 13) and BPR (Business Processing Re-engineering, Chapter 12) encourage companies to make improvements to their processes to make them ever more efficient.

Information technology is crucial to the outsourcing market. The Internet has enabled suppliers to handle the work of several clients at big administrative centres.

Adapted from the FT, April 18 2002

KEY TERM

Outsourcing is 'The use of external suppliers as a source of finished products, components or services. This is also known as **contract manufacturing** or **sub-contracting.**'   (CIMA *Official Terminology*)

Exam focus point

Outsourcing is relevant to performance measurement and control issues.

- When the decision whether to contract out an activity is being considered, the organisation will want to know how well its in-house provider is performing in relation to potential external providers.

- Even if an activity has been contracted out the organisation will want to monitor the quality and value that it gets from the external provider.

Advantages and disadvantages

8.3   The **advantages** of outsourcing are as follows.

(a) It **frees up time** taken by existing staff on the contracted-out activities.

(b) It allows the company to **take advantage of specialist expertise and equipment** rather than investing in these facilities itself and underutilising them. If the contractor is judiciously chosen it is likely that the service will be performed more **quickly** and to a **higher standard** than is currently the case.

(c) It **frees up time spent supporting the contracted-out services** by staff not directly involved, for example supervisory staff, personnel staff. There may also be no need to provide facilities for the service to be performed (though not in all cases: a contracted-out canteen would still usually be located on the business premises of the workers it serves).

(d) It may be **cheaper,** once time savings and opportunity costs are taken into account

(e) It is particularly **appropriate** when an organisation is **attempting to expand in a time of uncertainty**

8.4   However there are also a number of **disadvantages**.

(a) Without monitoring there is **no guarantee** that the service will be **performed to the organisation's satisfaction**. There may be **penalty clauses** built into the contract for poor performance, but financial compensation will not necessarily undo the damage caused. However, if a contract has to be too closely monitored this weakens the argument for contracting out in the first place.

(b) There is a good chance that contracting out will be **more expensive** than providing the service in-house.

(c) By performing services itself the organisation retains or develops **skills** that may be needed in the future and will otherwise be **lost**.

(d) Contracting out any aspect of information-handling carries with it the possibility that **commercially sensitive data will get into the wrong hands.** The contractor will not be able to guarantee absolute security.

(e) There may be some **ethical reservations**. For example, contract cleaning companies are notorious for exploiting staff, offering inadequate pay and poor conditions.

(f) There will almost certainly be **opposition from employees** and their representatives if contracting out involves redundancies. Great care is needed in this area as the contracting-out organisation and the new supplier have statutory responsibilities under 'transfer of undertakings' legislation.

Criteria for selection

8.5 There are three main criteria for selection of a function or service to be contracted out.

(a) **Whether the organisation sees the activity in question as one that is part of its 'core business'.** Most organisations do not see the ability to clean offices as one of their main objectives and this is why this service is so commonly contracted out.

(b) The **relative costs** (staff, equipment and premises compared with the cost of the service), and **relative benefits** (in-house capabilities compared with external specialisms).

(c) The **consequences of mistakes**.

Exercising control over the cost of outsourced services

8.6 The most **significant controls** will need to be **implemented at the planning stage** of the process of outsourcing a service.

(a) The organisation should **document details** of the level and quality of the service it requires from the external organisation.

(b) External organisations should then be **invited to tender** for providing the service. A documented policy as to the tendering process is required and should cover factors such as the number of bids required, whether the bids should be sealed and so on.

(c) The organisation must **confirm a price** for the service with the successful bidder.

(d) **On-going control** involves ensuring that the service delivered is actually of the contracted level and quality.

(e) The organisation must also give consideration to drawing up **policies** to deal with problems which could arise in the following areas.

- Judging the quality of service provided
- Approving any costs in excess of those agreed
- Including a get-out clause in the contract
- Including a price increase clause in the contract
- Reducing prices if the level of service is lower than anticipated

Budgetary control within organisations using outsourcing

8.7 The basic budgetary control procedure will involve comparing actual costs with the budgeted cost based on the contracted price.

(a) If the actual level of service provided differs from the budgeted level and if the contracted price varies according to the level of service provided rather than being fixed, the budgeted cost will need to be flexed to the actual level of service.

(b) The comparison of actual and budgeted costs provides **no information as to the quality of the service provided,** however.

(c) There is therefore some value in operating a system of budgetary control over outsourced services but the **main thrust of any control procedures** should be at the stage of actually **planning** to outsource services.

Outsourcing the finance function

Exam focus point

The specific issue of outsourcing the finance function is addressed by the syllabus. A process for outsourcing the finance function is outlined below, which indicates some of the associated problems and advantages. The use of **benchmarking** (Chapter 7) is now tending to isolate the core activities of finance and suggest those support activities which should be outsourced.

8.8 As part of its **sourcing strategy,** a company may decide that its finance function or elements of it (such as financial accounting, payroll, creditor payments, debtors control) are non-core activities for the resources of the company, the outsourcing of which could generate savings and improve service levels.

8.9 **Sourcing preparation** establishes the levels of service needed in the outsourced function. This will involve collecting detailed information on how the function currently operates, including the costs associated with it.

(a) **Cost accounting principles,** such as consideration of the allocation of **fixed overheads,** need to be applied to be sure that any savings that are expected do indeed materialise. For example, certain fixed costs associated with the financial accounting function may not necessarily disappear when that function is outsourced.

(b) Some companies may use the outsourcing of the finance function as a solution to **administrative issues** where they lack expertise. An example is provided by the outsourcing of sales ledger administration in the UK, which could become increasingly appealing to companies worried about their ability to cope with invoicing in euros.

Case example

Start-up companies in high technology sectors are making extensive use of outsourcing, by keeping their core innovation and research activities in-house while they outsource accounting and other functions (such as human resources, internal audit, stationery buying) which they do not need to set up for themselves.

To quote from PricewaterhouseCoopers research: 'Existing companies have accumulated these [functions] as baggage over the years , from a time when they had no alternatives, and it is baggage which they now need to offload.'

8.10 **Supply selection** involves identifying the appropriate supplier for each service. Several finance-related functions can often be provided by one organisation. Some of the large accountancy practices and management consultancies provide comprehensive outsourcing services. Using a large and reputable organisation will help to ensure a quality service.

8.11 A **transition period** will be needed for the handover of the functions to the supplier(s). This may include a period of parallel running, for example of some period end reporting procedures.

8.12 The outsourcing contract will need to be **managed** and **monitored** to ensure satisfactory performance by the outsourcing organisation and compliance with the **supply contract**. This is probably one of the most complex areas as it will depend upon the negotiated terms and also upon accurate presentation of the **expected benefits** from the outsourcing programme.

   (a) Investment should be made in a staff team set up to manage the contract, which will cover roles such as managing the **financial control** of the contract, its **legal** aspects and the **technical** strategy.

   (b) For example, a company may want to see an improvement in **debtors collection** periods, and the outsourcing company will be expected to provide regular details such as aged debt reports. **Deadlines** for production of reports from the financial accounting function may be tighter than were imposed on the in-house service.

8.13 If the supplier performs well then the **reselection process** at the end of the contract will be smooth. A company may eventually decide to bring some of the functions back **in-house** if new resources (more space in a new building or the recruitment of a tax expert) become available.

8.14 A major concern when outsourcing elements of the finance function is the effect on the **annual audit**. Auditors may find it more difficult to obtain sufficient and appropriate audit evidence.

   (a) Companies have a responsibility to maintain control over their assets and maintain proper internal controls. This translates directly into the **legal responsibility** which directors have for maintaining **books and records**. When they outsource the accounting function or investment management activities, that has a direct impact on the evidence that the auditor needs, and may necessitate the auditor visiting the outsourcer.

   (b) There may also be loss of **internal skills** that may be needed in the future if employees are made redundant as a result of the outsourcing programme.

The management accountant's role

8.15 The role of the accountant in the outsourcing process takes several forms.

   • Provide relevant analysis
   • Provide decision-making support
   • Pricing mechanisms
   • Devise and monitor control strategies
   • Management of the relationship with the outsourcing supplier and its staff

9 MANAGEMENT BY OBJECTIVES

9.1 An approach to operations planning and control, which can be integrated with a system of budgeting, is **Management by Objectives** (MBO).

KEY TERM

Management by objectives (MBO) is a technique to tie individual managerial performance with overall corporate objectives by identifying key results for each manager, derived ultimately from strategic plans.

9.2 The hierarchy of objectives which emerges is as follows.

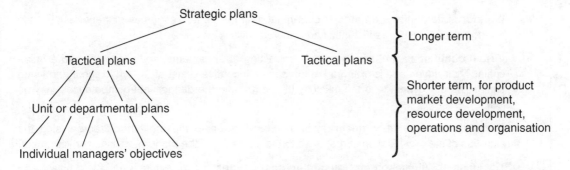

9.3 MBO provides a **link between corporate planning and the individual manager** in terms of the objectives that managers pursue and how managers relate to other managers.

9.4 Once the unit objectives have been identified, it is necessary to identify which individual managers within the unit are in a position to influence the achievement of each of them. Humble recommends the following.

(a) Clarify and agree with each manager the **key results and performance standards** he/she should achieve.

(b) Agree a **job improvement plan**.

(c) Provide **conditions and motivation** which will help managers to achieve their key results and job improvement plans.

(d) Have a systematic **performance review** of results.

Unity Bicycles plc

(1) Comment on Walter Drake's observations that the current divisional structure is not in line with how the business actually works.

BPP
PUBLISHING

Chapter roundup

- **Organisation structure** links individuals, groups tasks, assigns authority, co-ordinates activities, and facilitates flows of work and information.

- Modern trends favour **delayering** and **empowerment**, **matrix organisation** and re-organisation of **functions into 'processes'** designed to satisfy customers.

- **Decentralisation** (functional or federal) has pragmatic advantages and disadvantages.

- **Divisionalisation** occurs as organisations grow, because of the pull of the middle line in Mintzberg's terms, or because of the relative costs of controlling transactions in different ways. Information costs are highly significant.

- Organisations grow in a number of ways. Growth occurs by acquisition or organically. Greiner's **organisational life cycle model** says that an organisation grows in discrete phases.

- **Workforce flexibility** is an area of current interest for human resources management, as the workforce must be used efficiently and with versatility.

- **Virtual companies** are effectively subcontracting arrangements, spun together into a value chain. Their advantage is that market forces and incentives exist at every linkage in the value chain. The disadvantage is the difficulty of control, and the danger that competences may be lost.

- **Business process re-engineering** is the name given to the process of reorganising the activities of the organisation in response to the demands of the modern business environment.

- The ideas of **Williamson** on **transaction cost economics** (or markets and hierarchies) and of **Ouchi** on **transformation processes, outputs and types of control** are important to many of the more recent writings on management control.

- **Network** organisations are a recent development. Activities are being increasingly removed from traditional hierarchical control.

- This chapter also examined the issues behind the **outsourcing** of the finance function. As more and more companies undertake benchmarking exercises, they are identifying **non-core** activities which can be turned over to specialist contractors.

- **Management by objectives** is a technique which tries to link the overall strategic behaviour of the firm with the performance of departments and units, and ultimately with the performance of individual managers, by setting out a hierarchy of objectives.

Quick quiz

1   Departmentation by type of work done is known as .... departmentation

2   What are the five component parts of Mintzberg's 'organigram'?

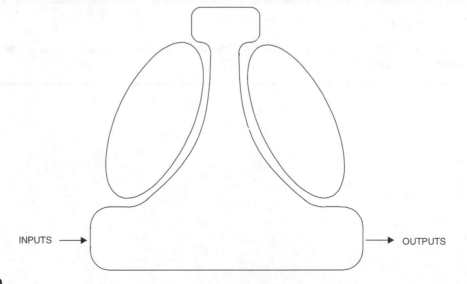

INPUTS ➞   ➞ OUTPUTS

3 Give three ways in which organisations grow.

4 What follows 'growth through delegation' in Greiner's model?

5 What is the key goal of workforce flexibility?

    A   Full employment

    B   Lower labour costs

    C   Efficient use of the workforce

    D   Reduction in trade union disputes

6 **Fill in the blanks**

The (1) .... does not really exist. It is really created out of a (2) .... of alliances and (3) .... arrangements. It is as if most of the activities in a (4) .... are conducted by different firms.

7 What is said to be the chief tool of BPR?

8 What are 'relationship specific assets'?

9 What is the driving force behind the growth of outsourcing?

    A   Aggressive marketing by outsourcing providers

    B   A trend towards delayering and downsizing

    C   It is always cheaper than in-house provision

    D   Increased concentration on core competences

10 MBO provides a link between (1) .... and the (2) .... in terms of the (3) .... that managers pursue.

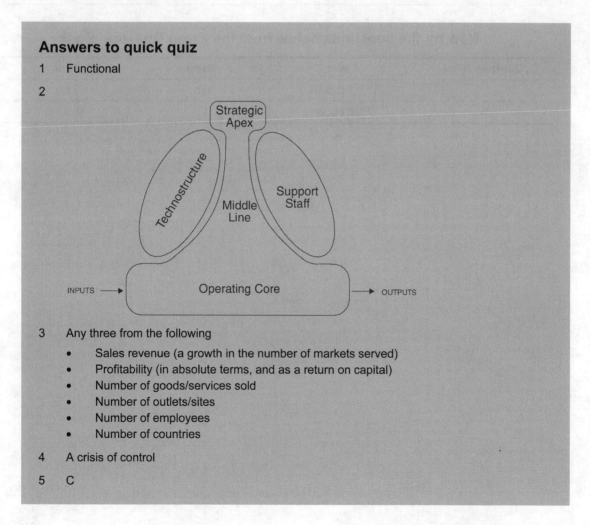

Answers to quick quiz

1 Functional

2

3 Any three from the following

    • Sales revenue (a growth in the number of markets served)
    • Profitability (in absolute terms, and as a return on capital)
    • Number of goods/services sold
    • Number of outlets/sites
    • Number of employees
    • Number of countries

4 A crisis of control

5 C

BPP PUBLISHING

6   (1) virtual firm (2) network (3) subcontracting (4) value chain

7   A clean sheet of paper.

8   Investments made to support a particular transaction.

9   D

10   (1)   corporate planning
     (2)   individual manager
     (3)   objectives

Unity Bicycles plc review

Question 1. Currently, UB is organised by divisions represented by the factories which, together with the purchasing office in Hong Kong, are the main profit/investment centres.

(a)   In practice, with the firm's global expansion, it might need a more sophisticated system, perhaps with marketing divisions set up by country. SBU organisation may not be appropriate: managers have little control over component costs - these are set centrally.

(b)   A US division could 'import' bikes from the UK and from Mexico: at the moment the marketing efforts of each factory are different. There could be a China division to monitor relationships with the subcontractors. On the other hand, the R&D department could become a profit or investment centre, as it might be selling ideas to the Chinese firms. It could charge internally for its 'services'.

Now try the questions below from the Exam Question Bank

Question to try	Level	Marks	Time
11	Pilot paper	25	45 mins
12	Pilot paper	25	45 mins

Factors influencing the design of a management accounting system

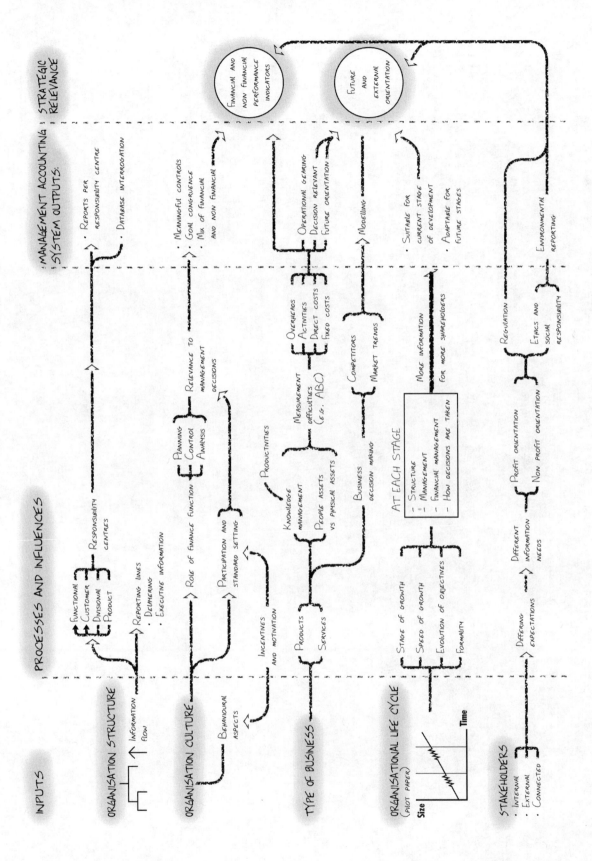

Part E
Implementing and controlling plans

Chapter 13

APPROACHES TO MEASURING PERFORMANCE I

Topic list		Syllabus reference	Ability required
1	Performance measurement	(v)	Evaluation
2	Strategic control and critical success factors	(v)	Evaluation
3	Budgetary control systems	(v)	Evaluation
4	Performance measures: financial and non-financial	(v)	Evaluation
5	The balanced scorecard	(v)	Analysis/evaluation
6	Other multidimensional measures of performance	(v)	Analysis/evaluation
7	Performance: service departments and firms	(v)	Evaluation
8	Performance: manufacturing	(v)	Evaluation
9	Activity based costing	(v)	Evaluation
10	Regulation and performance	(v)	Analysis

Introduction

Strategies can fail when they are **implemented. Feedback information** is needed. In the past, firms relied purely on financial measures, but this created some problems, particularly in relating the short term to the long term.

Performance measurement is all about **communicating the objectives** of the company and concentrating efforts towards them. **Strategic control** (section 2) indicates the need for a review of strategic performance over a whole host of measures, as opposed to just the numbers, although many companies still use the traditional **budgetary control process** as the main basis for measuring performance (section 3).

The aim of strategic control is to review **long term** indicators of the business. The **balanced scorecard** (section 5) is one way by which **financial and non-financial** (strategic) performance can be measured. Other multidimensional models of performance, chiefly the **performance pyramid,** are described in section 6.

At **operational level,** some useful indicators of performance are given for both service and manufacturing businesses (sections 7 and 8). ABC analysis is examined in section 9.

Finally, this chapter considers the impact of both legal and voluntary **regulation** on corporate performance. Corporate codes, for example on ethical issues, are becoming a feature of business strategy.

Learning outcomes covered in this chapter

- **Evaluate** and **recommend** appropriate control measures

- **Evaluate** and **produce** multidimensional models of performance measurement

- **Discuss** the effect of regulation on performance

> # Syllabus content covered in this chapter
>
> - The problem of assessing strategic performance; the use of profit and cash measures and the concept of appropriate measures for an industry and contingent on environmental factors
>
> - Non-financial measures and their interaction with financial measures. Consider the need for ethical and environmental measures
>
> - Multidimensional models of performance: including the balanced scorecard, the results and determinants framework (six dimensional performance matrix) and the performance pyramid
>
> - The effect of regulation, both voluntary and legal, on corporate performance

1 PERFORMANCE MEASUREMENT   Pilot paper, 5/01

1.1 **Performance measurement aims to establish how well something or somebody is doing in relation to previous or expected activity or in comparison with another thing or body.**

> ### KEY TERM
>
> **Performance measurement.** 'The process of assessing the proficiency with which a reporting entity succeeds, by the economic acquisition of resources and their efficient and effective development, in achieving its objectives. Performance measures may be based on non-financial as well as on financial information.'   (CIMA *Official Terminology*)

The aims of performance measurement

1.2 Performance measurement has become such an accepted part of business life that sometimes we lose sight of its aims.

- **Communicating the objectives** of the company
- **Concentrating efforts toward those objectives**
- It is **part of the control process where feedback is compared with the plan**

Approaches to performance measurement

1.3 There are a number of key areas to consider when determining the approach to adopt towards performance evaluation in a given set of circumstances.

Area to consider	Comments
What is evaluated?	Some approaches concentrate on the performance of the organisation as a whole, while others look at strategic business units, divisions, functions or the individual.
Who wants the evaluation?	Some approaches are based on the viewpoint of a single interest group such as investors. Others take in the views of various interest groups (for example employees).
What are the objectives of the organisation?	Is there a single goal or many goals? Are the goals short or long term?

Area to consider	Comments
Are quantitative measures or qualitative measures appropriate?	Quantitative measures (eg ROI or number of rejects) may not seem relevant but qualitative measures (eg customer satisfaction) are sometimes perceived to be too subjective.
What targets are used to assess performance?	Measures are meaningless unless they are compared against something. Common sources of comparison are historic figures, standards/budgets, similar external activities, similar internal activities, indices and trends over time.

Critical success factors

1.4 Critical success factors can be set and used by **identifying objectives and goals, determining which factors are critical for accomplishing each objective** and then determining a small number of performance measures for each factor.

Question 1

How could product leadership be measured, besides considering market share?

Answer

Qualitative measures ought to be available in the form of reviews by consumer magazines, newspapers, and trade press, awards, endorsement by public figures, and direct comment from customers.

2 STRATEGIC CONTROL AND CRITICAL SUCCESS FACTORS

2.1 Michael Goold and John J Quinn write: 'Most companies take pride in fostering a performance-driven culture that emphasises profitability as the key goal for business management ... [but] ... too much emphasis on budgetary control and short-term profit can disguise strategic problems.'

Gaps and false alarms

2.2 Many firms have spent time measuring the wrong things - the trick is to remove 'false alarms' from performance measures and replace them with measures that fill gaps in coverage. **Gaps** (important areas which are neglected) include:

- New product introduction
- Customer satisfaction
- Employee involvement

2.3 In *Management Accounting* (May 1995), Robert Booth identified the following problems.

- Short-term measures predominate over long-term measures
- Financial proxies (eg EPS) predominate over reality
- Efficiency takes precedence over effectiveness
- Economy takes precedence over efficiency
- Individual department performance measures take precedence over how departments are linked together to satisfy the customers

Strategic control systems

2.4 **Formal systems of strategic control are rare,** although more companies are adopting them.

(a) The formal process begins with a **strategy review**, perhaps each year. The key assumptions on which the strategy is based must be monitored.

(b) **Milestones of performance** both of a quantitative and qualitative nature are developed.

(c) **Strategic budgets** indicate the resources to be spent on strategic targets

2.5 **Informal systems of strategic control**. Many companies do not 'define explicit strategic objectives or milestones that are regularly and formally monitored as part of the ongoing management control process.'

- Informality promotes flexibility
- Formal systems can become over-bureaucratic
- Openness of communication is necessary
- A narrow focus on individual strategic objectives can blind managers to wider issues

2.6 The characteristics of strategic control systems can be measured on two axes: how formal is the process and how many milestones are identified for performance? Goold and Quinn recommend the following guidelines.

(a) **Linkages**. If there are important linkages among business units, the formality of the process should be low, to avoid undermining co-operation.

(b) **Diversity**. If there is a great deal of diversity, it is doubtful whether any overall strategic control system is appropriate.

(c) **Risk**. Firms whose strategic stance depends on high risk decisions which could destroy the company as a whole need strategic control systems which have a large number of performance criteria so that problems will be easily detected.

(d) **Change**. Fashion-goods manufacturers must respond to relatively high levels of environmental turbulence, and have to react quickly.

(e) **Competitive advantage**. For control purposes, it is useful to distinguish between two types of business.

    (i) Businesses with few sources of competitive advantage. In this case, perhaps market share or quality is the source of success.

    (ii) Businesses with many sources of advantage. In this case, success over a wider number of areas is necessary. The greatest dangers in this sort of business are misdirected effort and high cost.

2.7 The introduction of a formal or semi-formal strategic control system to monitor a firm's strategic position has certain advantages.

- Realism in planning
- The encouragement of higher performance standards
- More motivation for business units
- More timely intervention by senior management

2.8 Some CSFs which cover both **financial and non-financial criteria** are outlined below.

Sphere of activity	Critical factors
Marketing	Sales volume Market share Gross margins
Production	Capacity utilisation Quality standards
Logistics	Capacity utilisation Level of service

Some criteria which are regularly used in choosing between alternative plans for specific elements of the marketing mix are outlined below.

Activity	CSF
New product development	Trial rate Repurchase rate
Sales programmes	Contribution by region, salesperson Controllable margin as percentage of sales Number of new accounts Travel costs
Advertising programmes	Awareness levels Attribute ratings Cost levels
Pricing programmes	Price relative to industry average Price elasticity of demand
Distribution programmes	Number of distributors carrying the product

3 BUDGETARY CONTROL SYSTEMS

KEY TERM

Budgetary control. The establishment of budgets relating the responsibilities of executives to the requirements of a policy, and the continuous comparison of actual with budgeted results, either to secure by individual action the objectives of that policy or to provide a basis for its revision.' (CIMA *Official Terminology*)

3.1 A budget is a **plan expressed in monetary terms.** It is prepared and approved prior to the budget period and may show income, expenditure and capital to be employed.

3.2 Purpose of budgets

- To compel planning
- To co-ordinate activities
- To communicate ideas
- To provide a framework for responsibility accounting
- To motivate employees and management
- To evaluate performance

3.3 **Negative effects of budgets include**

- No incentive as the budget is unrealistic

- A manager may add 10% to his expenditure budget to ensure that he can meet the figure

- Manager achieves target but does no more

- A manager may go on a 'spending spree'

- Draws attention away from the longer term consequences

3.4 Problems with budgetary control

- The managers who set the budgets are often not responsible for attaining them.

- The goals of the organisation as a whole, expressed in the budget, may not coincide with the personal aspirations of the individual managers.

- Control is applied at different stages by different people.

3.5 How to improve behavioural aspects of budgetary control

- Develop a working relationship with operational managers
- Keeping accounting jargon to a minimum
- Making reports clear and to the point
- Providing control and information with a minimum of delay
- Ensuring actual costs are recorded accurately
- Allow for participation in the budgetary process

3.6 Limitations to the effectiveness of participation

- Some people prefer tough management
- A manager may build slack into his won budget
- Management feels that they have little scope to influence the final outcome

Activity based budgeting (ABB)

> **KEY TERM**
>
> **Activity-based budgeting.** 'A method of budgeting based on an activity framework and utilising cost driver data in the budget-setting and variance feedback processes.'
>
> (CIMA *Official Terminology*)

3.7 **Activity based budgeting** focuses on what the organisation actually does (its objectives) rather than on the resources it buys to do it.

3.8 If the objective of a production department is produce quality output, the techniques of ABB will focus on the activities rather than inputs.

Features of ABB

3.9   • It links strategic planning with operational decisions/control
     • It embodies the total quality management (TQM) philosophy
     • It seeks to detect and eliminate non value adding activities

Continuous rolling budget

KEY TERM

Rolling/continuous budget. 'A budget continuously updated by adding a further accounting period (month or quarter) when the earliest accounting period has expired. Its use is particularly beneficial where future costs and/or activities cannot be forecast accurately.' (CIMA *Official Terminology*)

Operating a rolling budget

3.10
- 12 month budget prepared – first quarter meticulously
- At the end of the first quarter the actuals are compared to budget
- Update the budgets for the next quarter with more detail

Advantages

3.11
- The company has a budget 12 months into the future
- Management are more accountable due to continuous review
- Budgets are more realistic and up to date
- New goals are communicated quicker

Disadvantages

3.12
- There is a lot of time and resource involved in the continuous updating of budgets
- Motivation to achieve the original budget is reduced

Zero based budgeting (ZBB)

KEY TERM

Zero based budgeting (ZBB). 'A method of budgeting which requires each cost element to be specifically justified, as though the activities to which the budget relates were being undertaken for the first time. Without approval, the budget allowance is zero.'
(CIMA *Official Terminology*)

Operating a zero based budget

3.13
- The budget for the next period is initially set at zero
- The choices are listed in accordance with cost benefit analysis
- The available resources are allocated based on ranking

Advantages of ZBB

3.14
- It can identify and remove inefficient or obsolete operations
- It can result in a more efficient allocation of resources
- It involves widespread participation
- It responds to changes in the environment

Disadvantages

3.15 • There is a large volume of paperwork
• There may be a lack of necessary skills in the management team
• It may emphasise short term benefits and ignore long term goals

Criticisms of traditional budgeting

3.16 According to an article in *CIMA Insider* in February 2001, 'traditional budgets hold companies back, restrict staff creativity and prevent them from responding to customers'. Jeremy Hope and Robin Fraser quote a 1998 survey which found that 88% of respondents were dissatisfied with the budgeting model. They also quote research which came up with some surprising statistics.

(a) 78% of companies do not change their budget during the annual cycle. Managers tend to 'manage around' their budgets.

(b) 60% do not link strategy and budgeting.

(c) 85% of management teams spend less than one hour a month discussing strategy.

3.17 Budgets tend to focus upon financial outputs rather than quantitative performance measures, and are not linked to employee performance. Hope and Fraser believe that organisational and behavioural changes are required, and they link these with the new business environment to suggest 'a management model that really supports strategy'. We summarise this in the table below.

Change in environment	How to succeed?	Key success factors	'Budget barriers'
• Rising uncertainty	• Cope with uncertainty by adapting quickly	• Devolve authority • Fast information • Strategy an adaptive process	• Too many rules • Restricted information flows • Fixed cycles are difficult to change
• Importance of intellectual capital	• Find (and retain) good people	• Recruit and develop good staff and set up a fair reward system	• Budgets tend to ignore people and lead to 'management by fear' and a cost-cutting mentality
• Increasing pace of innovation	• Create an innovative climate	• Share knowledge • See the business as a series of investments, not just components of a budget	• Central planning and bureaucracy encourage short-termism, and stifle creativity
• Falling prices and costs	• Operate with low costs	• Adopt a low cost network structure • Challenge costs • Align resources and costs with strategy	• Budgets prevent costs being challenged, they simply become 'entitlements'

Change in environment	How to succeed?	Key success factors	'Budget barriers'
• Declining customer loyalty	• Attract and keep the right customers	• Set up strong customer relationships • Establish a customer-facing strategy	• Budgeted sales targets and product focus tends to ignore customer needs
• More demanding shareholders	• Create consistent shareholder value	• Take a long term view of value creation • Base controls on performance	• Budgets tend to focus on the short term, with no future view

Case example

According to Hope and Fraser, 'giving managers control of their actions and using a few simple measures, based on key value drivers and geared to beating the competition, is all that most cases require'.

Challenging costs is inevitably part of such a process. Swedish bank Handelsbanken is a key exponent. Its low costs are the product of several factors, according to EVP finance Sven Grevelius.

(i) Small head office staff

(ii) People in regions and branches are self sufficient and are measured by competitive results, which has produced an attitude keen to weed out unwarranted expenses

(iii) Lower credit losses because front line staff feel more concerned to make sure that the information on which they base lending decisions is correct

(iv) Central services and costs are negotiated rather than allocated

(v) Internet technology is used to reduce costs, with the benefit accruing to the customer's own branch

'Devolving responsibility for results, turning cost centres into profit centres; squeezing central costs, using technology and … eradicating the budgeting "cost entitlement" mentality are just some of the actions we have taken to place costs under constant pressure,' says Grevelius.

4 PERFORMANCE MEASURES: FINANCIAL AND NON-FINANCIAL
Pilot paper

Deciding what measures to use

4.1 Clearly different measures are appropriate for different businesses. Determining which measures are used in a particular case will require **preliminary investigations** along the following lines.

(a) The **objectives/mission** of the organisation must be **clearly formulated** so that when the factors critical to the success of the mission have been identified they can be translated into performance indicators.

(b) **Measures** must be **relevant** to the way the organisation operates. Managers themselves must believe the indicators are useful.

(c) **The costs and benefits of providing resources** (people, equipment and time to collect and analyse information) to produce a performance indicator must be carefully **weighed up**.

BPP PUBLISHING

(d) **Performance must be measured in relation to something,** otherwise measurement is meaningless.

Financial modelling and performance measurement

4.2 **Financial modelling might assist in performance evaluation** in the following ways.

(a) **Identifying the variables** involved in performing tasks and the relationships between them. This is necessary so that the model can be built in the first place. Model building therefore shows what should be measured, helps to explain how a particular level of performance can be achieved, and identifies factors in performance that the organisation cannot expect to control.

(b) **Setting targets for future performance**. The most obvious example of this is the budgetary control system described above.

(c) **Monitoring actual performance**. A flexible budget is a good example of a financial model that is used in this way.

(d) **Co-ordinating long-term strategic plans with short term operational actions.** Modelling can reflect the dynamic nature of the real world and evaluate how likely it is that short-term actions will achieve the longer-term plan, given new conditions.

Profitability, activity and productivity

4.3 In general, there are three possible **points of reference for measurement**.

(a) **Profitability**

Profit has two components: **cost and income**. All parts of an organisation and all activities within it incur costs, and so their success needs to be judged in relation to cost. Only some parts of an organisation receive income, and their success should be judged in terms of both cost and income.

(b) **Activity**

All parts of an organisation are also engaged in activities (activities cause costs). Activity measures could include the following.

- Number of orders received from customers, a measure of the effectiveness of marketing

- Number of machine breakdowns attended to by the repairs and maintenance department

Each of these items could be measured in terms of **physical numbers, monetary value,** or **time spent**.

(c) **Productivity**

This is the **quantity of the product or service produced in relation to the resources put in,** for example so many units produced per hour or per employee. It defines **how efficiently resources are being used.**

The **dividing line between productivity and activity is thin,** because every activity could be said to have some 'product', or if not can be measured in terms of lost units of product or service.

Question 2

An invoicing assistant works in a department with three colleagues. She is paid £8,000 per annum. The department typically handles 10,000 invoices per week.

One morning she spends half an hour on the phone to her grandfather, who lives in Australia, at the company's expense. The cost of the call proves to be £32.

Required

From this scenario identify as many different performance measures as possible, explaining what each is intended to measure. Make any further assumptions you wish.

Answer

Invoices per employee per week: 2,500 (activity)
Staff cost per invoice: £0.06 (cost/profitability)
Invoices per hour: 2,500/(7 × 5) = 71.4 (productivity)
Cost of idle time: £32 + £2.14 = £34.14 (cost/profitability)

You may have thought of other measures and probably have slight rounding differences.

Financial performance measures

4.4 Financial measures (or **monetary measures**) are very familiar to you. Here are some examples, accompanied by comments from a single page of the *Financial Times*.

Measure	Comment
Profit	The commonest measure of all. Profit maximisation is usually cited as the main objective of most business organisations: 'ICI increased pre-tax profits to £233m'; 'General Motors... yesterday reported better-than-expected first-quarter net income of $513 (£333m) ...
Revenue	'the US businesses contributed £113.9m of total group turnover of £409m'
Costs	'Sterling's fall benefited pre-tax profits by about £50m while savings from the cost-cutting programme were running at around £100m a quarter'; 'The group interest charge rose from £48m to £61m'.
Share price	'The group's shares rose 31p to 1278p despite the market's fall'.
Cash flow	'Cash flow was also continuing to improve, with cash and marketable securities totalling $8.4bn on March 31, up from $8bn at December 31'.

4.5 The important point to note here is that the monetary amounts stated **are only given meaning in relation to something else**. Profits are higher than last year's; cashflow has improved compared with last quarter's.

4.6 We can generalise the above and give a list of **yard-sticks against which financial results are usually placed so as to become measures.**

- **Budgeted** sales, costs and profits
- **Standards** in a standard costing system
- The **trend** over time (last year/this year, say)
- The **results of other parts** of the business
- The **results of other businesses**
- The **economy** in general
- **Future potential** (eg a new business in terms of nearness to breaking even)

Question 3

Choose the appropriate word(s) in the following statements and decide whether each correct statement is an advantage or a disadvantage of the use of the profit measure.

(a) There is an advantage/there is no advantage in management science to specify a single objective.

(b) Encourages/does not encourage short-termism.

(c) Profit is always/not always a simple concept.

(d) It makes quantitative analysis possible/impossible.

(e) Non-financial factors are not important/are important in long-term performance measurement.

(f) It is a broad/narrow performance measure.

(g) It fails to allow for/enables decentralisation.

(h) It is/is not the sole short-term objective of a firm.

(i) Motivates/does not motivate cost centre managers.

(j) It enable/does not enable unlike units to be compared.

(k) It motivates and educates managers/does not motivate and educate managers.

(l) It is always/not always an effective measure for controlling managerial performance.

(m) Profit should be/should not be related to risk, as well as to capital employed.

Answer

Advantages

(a) There is an advantage in management science to specify a single objective.
(d) It makes quantitative analysis possible.
(f) It is a broad performance measure.
(g) It enables decentralisation.
(j) It enables unlike units to be compared.
(k) It motivates and educates managers.

Disadvantages

(b) It encourages short-termism.
(c) Profit is not always a simple concept.
(e) Non-financial factors are important in long-term performance measurement.
(h) It is not the sole short-term objective of a firm.
(i) It does not motivate cost centre managers.
(l) It is not always an effective measure for controlling managerial performance.
(n) Profit should be related to risk, as well as to capital employed.

The profit measure

4.7 This has advantages and disadvantages, as outlined in an article in the August 1998 *CIMA Student*.

Advantages	Comment
• Single criterion	Easier to manage, as the sole concern is the effect on the bottom line
• Analysis has a clear objective, ie the effect on future profits	Easier than cost/benefit analysis, for example
• A broad performance measure which incorporates all other measures	'If it does not affect profit it can be ignored.'

Advantages	Comment
• Enables decentralisation	Managers have the delegated powers to achieve divisional (and therefore group) profit
• Profitability measures (eg ROI) can compare all profit-making operations even if they are not alike	This ignores the balance between risk and return
• Management motivation and education	Bonuses based on simple profit targets are easy to understand

Disadvantages	Comment
• Encourages **short-termism** and focus on the annual cycle, at the expense of long term performance	Examples: cutting discretionary revenue investments, manipulating of accounting rules, building up stocks
• Profit differs from **economic income**	
• A firm has to satisfy **stakeholders** other than shareholders, such as the government and the local community	This may include environmental/ethical performance measures
• **Liquidity** is at least as important as profit	Most business failures derive from liquidity crises
• Profit should be related to **risk**, not just capital employed	Rarely done
• Profits can **fluctuate** in times of rapid change eg exchange rates	
• Profit measures cannot easily be used to motivate **cost centre** managers	

Ratios

4.8 Ratios are a **useful** way of measuring performance for a number of reasons.

(a) It is easier to look at **changes over time** by comparing ratios in one time period with the corresponding ratios for periods in the past.

(b) Ratios are often **easier to understand** than absolute measures of physical quantities or money values. For example, it is easier to understand that 'productivity in March was 94%' than 'there was an adverse labour efficiency variance in March of £3,600'.

(c) Ratios relate one item to another, and so help to **put performance into context**. For example the profit/sales ratio sets profit in the context of how much has been earned per £1 of sales, and so shows how wide or narrow profit margins are.

(d) Ratios can be **used as targets**. In particular, targets can be set for ROI, profit/sales, asset turnover, capacity fill and productivity. Managers will then take decisions which will enable them to achieve their targets.

(e) Ratios provide a way of **summarising an organisation's results**, and **comparing them with similar organisations**.

Percentages

4.9 A percentage expresses one number as a proportion of another and gives meaning to absolute numbers.

Example	Comment
Market share	A company may aim to achieve a 25% share of the total market for its product, and measure both its marketing department and the quality of the product against this.
Capacity levels	These are usually measured in percentages. 'Factory A is working at 20% below full capacity' is an example which indicates relative inefficiency.
Wastage	This is sometimes expressed in percentage terms. 'Normal loss' may be 10%, a measure of **in**efficiency.
Staff turnover	This is often measured in this way. In the catering industry for example, staff turnover is typically greater than 100%, and so a hotel with a lower percentage could take this as an indicator both of the experience of its staff and of how well it is treating them.

Quantitative and qualitative performance measures

4.10 It is possible to distinguish between **quantitative information**, which is **capable of being expressed in numbers**, and **qualitative information**, which **can only be expressed in numerical terms with difficulty.**

4.11 An example of a **quantitative performance measure** is '**You have been late for work twice this week and it's only Tuesday!**'. An example of a **qualitative performance measure** is '**My bed is very comfortable**'.

4.12 The first measure is likely to find its way into a staff appraisal report. The second would feature in a bed manufacturer's customer satisfaction survey. Both are indicators of whether their subjects are doing as good a job as they are required to do.

4.13 **Qualitative measures** are by nature **subjective and judgmental** but this does not mean that they are not valuable. They are especially valuable when they are derived from several different sources because then they can be expressed in a mixture of quantitative and qualitative terms which is more meaningful overall: 'seven out of ten customers think our beds are very comfortable' is a quantitative measure of customer satisfaction as well as a **qualitative** measure of the perceived performance of the beds.

Measuring performance in the new business environment

4.14 In the June 1998 edition of *Management Accounting*, Jeremy Hope and Robin Fraser argued that if organisations are serious about gaining real benefits from decentralisation and empowerment, they need to **change the way in which they set targets, measure performance and design reward systems.** (The emphasis is BPP's.)

> 'The SBU [strategic business unit] manager is once again asked for a '**stretch target**'. However, under this management model [suggested by Hope and Fraser] she knows that 'stretch' really means her best shot with **full support** from the centre (including investment funds and improvement programmes) and a sympathetic hearing should she fail to get all of the way. Moreover, she alone carries the **responsibility** for achieving these targets. There is neither any micro-management from above, nor any monthly 'actual versus budget' reports. **Targets are both**

strategic and financial, and they are underpinned by clear action plans that cascade down the organisation, building **ownership and commitment at every level**. Monthly reports comprise a **balanced scorecard set** of graphs, charts and trends that track progress (eg financial, customer satisfaction, speed, quality, service, and employee satisfaction) **compared with** last year and with other **SBUs within the group** and, where possible, with **competitors**. Quarterly **rolling forecasts** (broad-brush numbers only) are also prepared to help manage production scheduling and cash requirements but they are not part of the measurement and reward process.

Of course, if there is a significant blip in performance (and the fast/open information system would flag this immediately), then a performance review would be signalled. Such reviews focus on the effectiveness of action plans and what further improvements need to be made and maybe even whether the targets (and measures) themselves are still appropriate.'

4.15 There are a number of reasons why this approach is **successful**.

(a) Managers are **not punished for failing to reach the full target.**

(b) The use of the **balanced scorecard** ensures that all key perspectives are considered.

(c) Because managers set their own targets and plan the changes needed to achieve them, real **ownership and commitment** are built. Feedback and learning takes place as a result of the tracking of action plans. (Contrast this with numerical variances that tell managers nothing about what to do differently in the future).

(d) **Beating internal and external competitors is a constant spur to better performance.**

(e) Managers share in an bonus pool that is based on share price or **long-term performance** against a basket of competitors. **Resource and knowledge sharing** is therefore encouraged.

Non-financial performance measures   11/01

4.16 It is worth remembering that performance measures can be both financial and non financial.

> **KEY TERM**
>
> **Non-financial performance measures** are 'measures of performance based on non-financial information which may originate in and be used by operating departments to monitor and control their activities without any accounting input. Non-financial performance measures may give a more timely indication of the levels of performance achieved than do financial ratios, and may be less susceptible to distortion by factors such as uncontrollable variations in the effect of market forces on operations.'
>
> (CIMA *Official Terminology*)

Here are some examples of non-financial performance measures.

Areas assessed	Performance measure
Service quality	Number of complaints
	Proportion of repeat bookings
	Customer waiting time
	On-time deliveries
Production performance	Set-up times
	Number of suppliers
	Days' inventory in hand
	Output per employee
	Material yield percentage
	Schedule adherence
	Proportion of output requiring rework
	Manufacturing lead times
Marketing effectiveness	Trend in market share
	Sales volume growth
	Customer visits per salesperson
	Client contact hours per salesperson
	Sales volume forecast v actual
	Number of customers
	Customer survey response information
Personnel	Number of complaints received
	Staff turnover
	Days lost through absenteeism
	Days lost through accidents/sickness
	Training time per employee

Question 4

Draw up a list of performance criteria for a hotel.

Answer

Financial performance: profit and loss per department, variance analysis (eg expenditure on wages, power etc).

Competitive performance: market share (room occupied on a total percentage of rooms available locally); competitor occupancy; competitor prices; bookings; vacant rooms as a proportion of the total attitudes of particular market segments.

Resource utilisation: rooms occupied/rooms available service quality measure: complaints, room checks.

Quality of service: Complaints, results of questionnaires

4.17 The beauty of non-financial performance measures is that **anything can be compared if it is meaningful to do so**. The measures should be tailored to the circumstances so that, for example, number of coffee breaks per 20 pages of Study Text might indicate to you how hard you are studying!

The advantages and disadvantages of non-financial measures

4.18 Unlike traditional variance reports, they can be provided **quickly** for managers, per shift or on a daily or hourly basis as required. They are likely to be **easy to calculate**, and **easier for non-financial managers to understand** and therefore to use effectively.

4.19 There are problems associated with choosing the measures and there is a danger that **too many such measures could be reported**, overloading managers with information that is not truly useful, or that sends conflicting signals. There is clearly a need for the information provider to work more closely with the managers who will be using the information to make sure that their needs are properly understood.

4.20 Research on more than 3,000 companies in Europe and North America has shown that the strongest drivers of competitive achievement are the intangible factors, especially **intellectual property, innovation** and **quality.** Non-financial measures have been at the forefront of an increasing trend towards **customer focus** (such as TQM), **process re-engineering** programmes and the creation of **internal markets** within organisations.

4.21 Arguably, non-financial measures are **less likely to be manipulated** than traditional profit-related measures and they should, therefore, **offer a means of counteracting short-termism**, since short-term profit at any expense is rarely an advisable goal.

> **REMEMBER**
>
> The ultimate goal of commercial organisations in the long run is likely to remain the maximisation of profit, and so the **financial aspect cannot be ignored**.

4.22 A further danger is that they might lead managers to **pursue detailed operational goals and become blind to the overall strategy in which those goals are set. A combination of financial and non- financial measures is likely to be most successful.**

Value for money (VFM) audits

4.23 Value for money audits can be seen as being of particular relevance in not-for-profit organisations. Such an audit focuses on **economy, efficiency** and **effectiveness.** These measures may be in conflict with each other. To take the example of higher education, larger class sizes may be **economical** in their use of teaching resources, but are not necessarily **effective** in creating the best learning environment.

Case example

A recent study by the Public Management Foundation has found that public sector managers are concerned largely with 'making a difference' in the community. Improving services and increasing the satisfaction of those using them were the two most important goals.

While the introduction of private sector management techniques in the 1980s has served to sharpen the attention given to financial performance, public sector managers rated the value of financial management lower than service improvement.

---

5 THE BALANCED SCORECARD 11/01

5.1 A theme so far has been that financial measurements do not capture all the strategic realities of the business, but it is possible to go too far in this direction. A failure to attend to the 'numbers' can rapidly lead to a failure of the business.

Case example

The fall from grace of Digital Equipment, in the past second only to IBM in the world computer rankings, was examined in a *Financial Times* article. The downfall is blamed on Digital's failure to keep up with the development of the PC, but also on the company's culture.

The company was founded on brilliant creativity, but was insufficiently focused on the bottom line. Outside the finance department, monetary issues were considered vulgar and organisational structure was chaotic. Costs were not a core part of important decisions - 'if expenditure was higher than budget, the problem was simply a bad budget'. Ultimately the low-price world of lean competitors took its toll, leading to huge losses.

The balanced scorecard

5.2 Financial measurements do not capture all the strategic realities of a business. A technique which has been developed to integrate the various features (financial and non-financial) of corporate success is the **balanced scorecard**, developed by Robert Kaplan and publicised in the *Harvard Business Review* in 1992.

KEY TERM

The **balanced scorecard** approach is 'An approach to the provision of information to management to assist strategic policy formulation and achievement. It emphasises the need to provide the user with a set of information which addresses all relevant areas of performance in an objective and unbiased fashion. The information provided may include both financial and non-financial elements, and cover areas such as profitability, customer satisfaction, internal efficiency and innovation.' (CIMA *Official Terminology*)

5.3 The balanced scorecard focuses on **four different perspectives**, as follows.

Perspective	Question	Explanation
Customer	What do existing and new customers value from us?	Gives rise to targets that matter to customers: cost, quality, delivery, inspection, handling and so on.
Internal	What processes must we excel at to achieve our financial and customer objectives?	Aims to improve internal processes and decision making.
Innovation and learning	Can we continue to improve and create future value?	Considers the business's capacity to maintain its competitive position through the acquisition of new skills and the development of new products.
Financial	How do we create value for our shareholders?	Covers traditional measures such as growth, profitability and shareholder value but set through talking to the shareholder or shareholders direct.

Performance targets are set once the key areas for improvement have been identified, and the balanced scorecard is the **main monthly report**.

5.4 The scorecard is 'balanced' in the sense that managers are required to think in terms of all four perspectives, to **prevent improvements being made in one area at the expense of another.**

5.5 Broadbent and Cullen (in Berry, Broadbent and Otley, ed, *Management Control*, 1995) identify the following **important features** of this approach.

- It looks at both **internal and external matters** concerning the organisation
- It is **related to the key elements of a company's strategy**
- **Financial and non-financial measures** are linked together

Problems

5.6 As with all techniques, problems can arise when it is applied.

Problem	Explanation
Conflicting measures	Some measures in the scorecard such as research funding and cost reduction may naturally conflict. It is often difficult to determine the balance which will achieve the best results.
Selecting measures	Not only do appropriate measures have to be devised but the number of measures used must be agreed. Care must be taken that the impact of the results is not lost in a sea of information.
Expertise	Measurement is only useful if it initiates appropriate action. Non-financial managers may have difficulty with the usual profit measures. With more measures to consider this problem will be compounded.
Interpretation	Even a financially-trained manager may have difficulty in putting the figures into an overall perspective.

5.7 The scorecard should be used **flexibly.** The process of deciding **what to measure** forces a business to clarify its strategy. For example, a manufacturing company may find that 50% - 60% of costs are represented by bought-in components, so measurements relating to suppliers could usefully be added to the scorecard. These could include payment terms, lead times, or quality considerations.

5.8 An example of how a balanced scorecard might appear is offered below.

Balanced Scorecard

Financial Perspective	
GOALS	**MEASURES**
Survive	Cash flow
Succeed	Monthly sales growth and operating income by division
Prosper	Increase market share and ROI

Customer Perspective	
GOALS	**MEASURES**
New products	Percentage of sales from new products
Responsive supply	On-time delivery (defined by customer)
Preferred supplier	Share of key accounts' purchases
	Ranking by key accounts
Customer partnership	Number of cooperative engineering efforts

Internal Business Perspective	
GOALS	**MEASURES**
Technology capability	Manufacturing configuration vs competition
Manufacturing excellence	Cycle time
	Unit cost
	Yield
Design productivity	Silicon efficiency
	Engineering efficiency
New product introduction	Actual introduction schedule vs plan

Innovation and Learning Perspective	
GOALS	**MEASURES**
Technology leadership	Time to develop next generation of products
Manufacturing learning	Process time to maturity
Product focus	Percentage of products that equal 80% sales
Time to market	New product introduction vs competition

Case example

An oil company (quoted by Kaplan and Norton, Harvard Business Review) ties:

- 60% of its executives' bonuses to their achievement of ambitious financial targets on ROI, profitability, cash flow and operating cost

- 40% on indicators of customer satisfaction, retailer satisfaction, employee satisfaction and environmental responsibility

Exam focus point

The scorecard can be used both by profit and not-for-profit organisations because it acknowledges the fact that both financial and non-financial performance indicators are important in achieving strategic objectives. This point was examined in November 2001, but the examiner noted that many candidates concentrated too much upon profit-orientated organisations in their answers.

6 OTHER MULTIDIMENSIONAL MEASURES OF PERFORMANCE

6.1 There have been a number of ideas concerning the measurement of performance across a range of dimensions. For example, as long ago as 1952 General Electric undertook a measurements project which concluded that there were eight key results areas (or critical success factors).

- Profitability
- Market position

- Productivity
- Product leadership
- Personnel development
- Employee attitudes
- Public responsibility
- Short v long term balance

The performance pyramid

6.2 The **performance pyramid** derives from the idea that an organisation operates at different levels, each of which has different concerns which should nevertheless support each other in achieving business objectives.

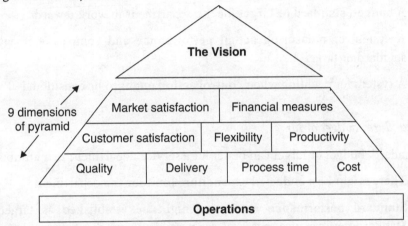

6.3 (a) At **corporate level**, financial and market objectives are set.

(b) At **strategic business unit** level, strategies are developed to achieve these financial and market objectives.

- **Customer satisfaction** is defined as meeting customer expectations
- **Flexibility** indicates responsiveness of the business operating system as a whole
- **Productivity** refers to the management of resources such as labour and time

(c) These in turn are supported by more specific **operational** criteria.

- **Quality** of the product or service, consistency of product and fit for the purpose
- **Delivery** of the product or service, ie the method of distribution, its speed and ease of management
- **Cycle time** of all processes from cash collection to order processing to recruitment
- **Cost** meaning the elimination of all non value added activities

6.4 The pyramid highlights the links running between the **vision for the company** and **functional objectives**. It hopes to ensure a consistency of performance across all business areas.

The results and determinants matrix

6.5 This is described in the following section where we look at measuring performance in the service sector.

7   PERFORMANCE: SERVICE DEPARTMENTS AND FIRMS

Service departments

7.1   Measuring performance in a service department will focus management attention on matters such as the following.

- How the service department is using up resources of the organisation
- What its resources are costing
- Whether the department should be capable of improved efficiency and lower costs

7.2   The principles of control theory still apply, so that a system of performance evaluation for service departments or selling activities needs:

(a)   A **budget, standard or target** for the department to work towards

(b)   A system of **measuring actual performance** and comparing it against the budget, standard or target

(c)   A system for deciding when **control action** ought to be considered

Setting a standard, budget or target

7.3   A standard, budget or target can be set for a service department in a number of ways.

(a)   There might be a budgeted expenditure limit for the department.

(b)   **Standard performance measures** might be established as targets for efficiency. Standard performance measures are possible where the department carries out routine activities for much of its work.

(c)   Targets or standards might be set for the **quality of the service**.

- To provide training to employees up to a quantifiable standard

- To respond to requests for help within a specified number of minutes, hours or days

- To respond to materials requisitions within a specified period of time

(d)   To perform a **targeted quantity of work** with a budgeted number of staff.

(e)   **To meet schedules for completing certain work**.

- Scheduled dates for completion of each stage in a product development project in the R & D department

- Scheduled dates for the DP department to complete each stage of a new computer project

(f)   **To make a profit**. A service department might be designated as a profit centre. It would charge other departments for the services it provides at a 'commercial' transfer price rate, and it would be expected to earn a 'profit' on the work it does.

Standards for cost or efficiency

7.4   Two methods of setting a standard measure of performance in a service department are:

- Standard cost per unit of activity
- Standard quantity of 'output' per unit of resource used up

With both methods, there has to be a measurable quantity or volume of activity in the department. Both types of standard can be employed within a control system, and they are not mutually exclusive.

7.5 Examples of standard **measures of performance in service departments** might be as follows.

(a) In the accounts receivable section of an accounts department, for example, the volume of activity could be measured by:

- Number or value of invoices issued
- Number or value of payments received
- The number or value of bad debts

A budget for the section could then establish a standard cost per invoice issued, or a standard cost per £1 received or receivable, or a standard % of bad debts. In addition, there could be standards for the number or value of invoices issued per man/day.

(b) In a sales department, activity could be measured by the number and value of orders taken, the number of customer visits, or the number of miles travelled by sales representatives. There could be a standard cost per customer visit, a standard cost per £1 of sales, and so on. Alternatively, standards could be set for the amount of work done per unit of resource consumed, and in a sales department, such standards include:

- Standard number of customer visits per salesperson per day
- Standard number and value of sales per customer visit
- Standard number of miles travelled per £1 of sales

(c) In a transport department, activity could be measured in tonne/miles (tonnes of goods delivered and miles travelled) and standards could be established for:

- Cost per tonne/mile
- Drivers' hours per tonne/mile
- Miles per gallon consumed

Measuring and evaluating performance

7.6 Once a target, budget or standard has been set, we have a basis for evaluating performance, by comparing actual results against the target.

Indices of 'output' in a service department

7.7 Standards for work done in a service department could be expressed as an index. For example, suppose that in a sales department, there is a standard target for sales representatives to make 25 customer visits per month each. The budget for May 19X5 might be for ten sales representatives to make 250 customer visits in total. Actual results in May might be that nine sales representatives made 234 visits in total. Performance could then be measured as:

Budget   100   (Standard = index 100)

Actual   104 $\left(\dfrac{234}{9 \times 25} \times 100 \right)$

This shows that 'productivity' per sales representative was actually 4% over budget.

7.8 **Advantages of indices are as follows.**

(a) They are easily understood.

(b) Once established, they can be used to evaluate:

- Actual results in a period against the standard
- Trends in productivity over time

(c) They can incorporate a 'basket' of different types of job. In the example of customer visits by sales representatives, not all customer visits are the same. Travelling time to some customers will be longer than to others, and some customers will take longer to deal with than others. With indexing, weightings can be given to different types of visit.

Exam focus point

Service departments vary between organisations, and in your examination you might be required to suggest standards of performance and methods of measuring and evaluating actual performance for a particular department in a particular type of organisation.

Selecting measures of performance

7.9 Key item(s) of performance to be measured should be identified. Examples include return, growth, productivity, market share, and cost control.

(a) Return can be measured as ROI, RI, profit and so on.

(b) Growth can be measured by sales growth, profit growth, investment spending, capacity fill and so on.

(c) Productivity measures can be applied to machinery as well as labour.

(d) Market position and status, or quality of product/service, could be measured by market research, or through customer responses and complaints.

(e) Cost control involves identifying the nature of the costs that ought to be controlled and comparing actual spending with budget.

7.10 A more elaborate approach was described in an article by Ken Slater on performance measurement of the finance function (*Management Accounting*, May 1991).

(a) **Define the boundaries** of the finance function. Does it include data processing, for example, or stock control or treasury management?

(b) **Define formal objectives** for the function as a whole, and then for each main section, for supervisory and managerial staff and for the operation of systems (for example payroll).

(c) Ascertain what **activities** each section does (or should do) to achieve its objectives.

(d) **Identify appropriate measures,** on the basis of the objectives and activities identified. The 'pyramid' approach should be used, with successively more detailed information for successively junior levels of staff.

(e) Select suitable **bases of comparison**. Possibilities are time, budgets, standards or targets, intra-group comparison, or intra-organisational comparison, if verifiably comparable data is available.

Performance measurement in service businesses

7.11 Lin Fitzgerald et al, (*Performance measurement in service businesses*, (CIMA, 1991)) identify three different types of service organisation, as follows.

(a) **Professional services**, for example a management consultancy. Such services are characterised as being highly adaptable to individual customer needs, dependent upon staff/customer contact, people-based and relying on short chains of command and highly autonomous employees.

(b) **Mass services**, for example rail travel. These involve little customisation and limited customer contact, they are predominantly equipment-based and require defined tasks and set procedures to be performed with little exercise of judgement.

(c) **Service shops**, for example, a bank. These fall between the above extremes in terms of customisation, customer contact, people/equipment and levels of staff discretion.

Dimensions of performance measurement

7.12 Fitzgerald et al advocate the use of a range of performance measures covering six 'dimensions' in what is known as the **results and determinants framework**.

(a) **Results**

(i) **Competitive performance**, focusing on factors such as sales growth and market share.

(ii) **Financial performance**, concentrating on profitability, liquidity, capital structure and market ratios.

(b) **Determinants** (of those results)

(i) **Quality of service** looks at matters like reliability, courtesy, competence and availability. These can be measured by customer satisfaction surveys.

(ii) **Flexibility** is an apt heading for assessing the organisation's ability to deliver at the right speed, to respond to precise customer specifications, and to cope with fluctuations in demand.

(iii) **Resource utilisation** considers how efficiently resources are being utilised. This can be problematic because of the complexity of the inputs to a service and the outputs from it and because some of the inputs are supplied by the customer.

(iv) **Innovation** is assessed in terms of both the innovation process and the success of individual innovations. Individual innovations can be measured in terms of whether they have improved the organisation's ability to meet the other five performance criteria.

8 PERFORMANCE: MANUFACTURING

8.1 A number of performance indicators can be used to assess operations. They are particularly relevant to the internal business and customer perspectives of the balanced scorecard.

- Quality
- Number of customer complaints and warranty claims
- Lead times
- Rework
- Delivery to time
- Non-productive hours
- System (machine) down time

BPP PUBLISHING

8.2 These indicators can also be expressed in the form of ratios or percentages for comparative purposes. Like physical measures, they can be produced quickly and trends can be identified and acted upon rapidly. Examples of useful ratios might be as follows.

(a) **Machine down time: total machine hours**. This ratio could be used to monitor machine availability and can provide a measure of machine usage and efficiency.

(b) **Component rejects: component purchases**. This ratio could be used to control the quality of components purchased from an external supplier. This measure can be used to monitor the performance of new suppliers.

(c) **Deliveries late: deliveries on schedule**. This ratio could be applied to sales made to customers as well as to receipts from suppliers.

(d) **Customer rejects/returns: total sales**. This ratio helps to monitor customer satisfaction, providing a check on the efficiency of quality control procedures.

(e) **Value added time: production cycle time**. Value added time is the direct production time during which the product is being made and value is therefore being added.

Advanced manufacturing technology

8.3 The advent of **advanced manufacturing technology (AMT)** has meant that many organisations will need to modify their performance measures so that the information they provide will be useful in controlling operations in the new manufacturing environment.

Performance measurement for manufacturing

8.4 Performance measurement in manufacturing is increasingly using non-financial measures. Malcolm Smith (*Management Accounting*, March 1997) identifies four over-arching measures for manufacturing environments.

- **Cost**: cost behaviour
- **Quality**: factors inhibiting performance
- **Time**: bottlenecks, inertia
- **Innovation**: new product flexibility

Cost

8.5 Possible non-financial or part-financial indicators are as follows.

Area	*Measure*
• Quantity of raw material inputs	Actual v target number
• Equipment productivity	Actual v standard units
• Maintenance efforts	No. of production units lost through maintenance
	No. of production units lost through failure
	No. of failures prior to schedule
• Overtime costs	Overtime hours/total hours
• Product complexity	No. of component parts
• Quantity of output	Actual v target completion
• Product obsolescence	% shrinkage
• Employees	% staff turnover
• Employee productivity	direct labour hours per unit
• Customer focus	% service calls; % claims

Quality

8.6 Integrating quality into a performance measurement system suggests attention to the following items.

Area	Measure
• Quality of purchased components	Zero defects
• Equipment failure	Downtime/total time
• Maintenance effort	Breakdown maintenance/total maintenance
• Waste	% defects; % scrap; % rework
• Quality of output	% yield
• Safety	Serious industrial injury rate
• Reliability	% warranty claims
• Quality commitment	% dependence on post-inspection
	% conformance to quality standards
• Employee morale	% absenteeism
• Leadership impact	% cancelled meetings
• Customer awareness	% repeat orders; number of complaints

> ## KEY TERMS
>
> **Total quality management (TQM).** 'An integrated and comprehensive system of planning and controlling all business functions so that products or services are produced which meet or exceed customer expectations. TQM is a philosophy of business behaviour, embracing principles such as employee involvement, continuous improvement at all levels and customer focus, as well as being a collection of related techniques aimed at improving quality such as full documentation of activities, clear goal setting and performance measurement from the customer perspective.'
>
> **World class manufacturing.** 'A position of international manufacturing excellence, achieved by developing a culture based on factors such as continuous improvement, problem prevention, zero defect tolerance, customer-driven JIT-based production and total quality management.' *(CIMA Official Terminology)*

Time

8.7 A truly just-in-time system is an ideal to which many manufacturing firms are striving. Time-based competition is also important for new product development, deliveries etc. The management accounting focus might be on throughput, bottlenecks, customer feedback and distribution.

Area	Measure
• Equipment failure	Time between failures
• Maintenance effort	Time spent on repeat work
• Throughput	Processing time/total time per unit
• Production flexibility	Set-up time
• Availability	% stockouts
• Labour effectiveness	Standard hours achieved/total hours worked
• Customer impact	No. of overdue deliveries
	Mean delivery delay

Innovation

8.8 Performance indicators for innovation can support the 'innovation and learning' perspective on the balanced scorecard. Some possible suggestions are outlined below.

Area	Measure
• The ability to introduce new products	% product obsolescence
	Number of new products launched
	Number of patents secured
	Time to launch new products

Area	Measure
• Flexibility to accommodate change	Number of new processes implemented
	Number of new process modifications
• Reputation for innovation	Media recognition for leadership
	Expert assessment of competence
	Demonstrable competitive advantage

Activity based measures of performance

8.9 Many writers have seen the potential of the activity-based approach to management accounting to provide new performance indicators. For example, if the number of purchase requisitions is a cost driver for a number of purchasing, receiving and accounting activities then it would be possible to compare the resources which ought to be employed to process a given number of requisitions with the resources actually employed. We look at ABC in more detail in the following section

KEY TERM

Activity based management (ABM). 'System of management which uses activity-based cost information for a variety of purposes including cost reduction, cost modelling and customer profitability analysis.' (CIMA *Official Terminology*)

Use of experience curves

8.10 As we have seen in Chapter 9, the **experience curve** can be used in strategic control of costs. It suggests that as output increases, the cost per unit of output falls. To recap, this results from:

(a) **Economies of scale** - in other words an increased volume of production leads to lower unit costs, as the firm approaches full capacity.

(b) A genuine '**learning effect**' as the workforce becomes familiar with the job and learns to carry out the task more efficiently. As a process is repeated, it is likely that costs will reduce due to **efficiency, discounts** and **reduced waste**.

(c) **Technological improvements**.

8.11 The **strategic importance** of experience curves are listed in Chapter 9, paragraph 1.10.

Target costing

8.12 This brings us on to **target costing**, an approach used in Japan. This is based on the principle that a product must have a target price that will succeed in winning a target share of the market.

8.13 When a product is first manufactured, the **target cost** will usually be well below the current cost, which is determined by current technology and processes, and experience effects. Management then sets benchmarks for improvement towards the target costs, by improving technologies and processes.

8.14 Target costing is thus in effect a process of establishing what the cost of the product should be over the entire **product life cycle**.

(a) In the short run, because of development costs and the learning time needed, costs are likely to exceed price.

(b) In the longer term, costs should come down (eg because of the experience curve) to their target level.

9 ACTIVITY BASED COSTING

> **KEY TERM**
>
> **Activity based costing (ABC).** An approach to the costing and monitoring of activities which involves tracing resource consumption and costing final outputs. Resources are assigned to activities and activities to cost objects based on consumption estimates. The latter utilise cost drivers to attach activity costs to outputs. *(CIMA Official Terminology)*

The reasons for the development of ABC

9.1 Traditional cost accumulation systems were developed when most organisations produced only a narrow range of products and overhead costs were only a **very small fraction** of total costs. Errors made in attributing overheads to projects were therefore not too significant.

9.2 Nowadays, however, overheads are likely to be far more important and in fact direct labour may account for as little as 5% of a product's cost. Material handling, setting up machines, scheduling production and inspection take up significant amounts of time. Moreover, **information technology** now allows more sophisticated overhead allocation methods.

9.3 It is difficult in such circumstances to justify the use of direct labour or direct material as the basis for allocating overheads or to believe that errors made in attributing overheads will not be significant. The demand for more accurate product costs has therefore increased. It was against this background that **activity based costing (ABC)** emerged a decade ago.

9.4 Earlier in the text we looked at the **value chain** for a typical modern firm. **Porter** identified nine **value-adding activities**. Four of these value-adding activities are labelled **support activities**, and are typically areas where major overhead costs are incurred: procurement, technology development, human resource management and infrastructure.

9.5 These support activities assist the efficient manufacture of a wide range of products and are not, in general, affected by changes in production volume. In traditional terms such costs would have been identified as fixed or semi-variable costs. The wider the range and the more complex the products, the more support services will be required.

9.6 The ideas behind **activity based costing** are as follows.

(a) **Activities drive costs**. Activities include ordering, materials handling, machining, assembly, production scheduling and despatching.

(b) **Producing products** creates demand for the activities.

(c) **Costs are assigned to a product** on the basis of the product's consumption of the activities.

It is therefore based upon identifying the drivers of cost and calculating the cost associated with them.

Outline of an ABC system

9.7 An ABC costing system operates as follows.

(a) *Step 1*

Identify an organisation's major activities.

(b) *Step 2*

Identify the factors which determine the size of the costs of an activity or drive the costs of an activity. These are known as **cost drivers**. Look at the following example of a company manufacturing kites.

Activity	Cost driver
Ordering of nylon and plastic	Number of orders
Materials handling	Number of production runs
Production scheduling	Number of production runs
Despatching of kites to retail outlets	Number of despatches

For those costs that vary with production levels in the short term, ABC uses volume-related cost drivers such as labour or machine hours. The cost of oil used as a lubricant on sewing machines would be added to kite costs on the basis of the number of machine hours, since oil would have to be used for each hour the machine ran.

(c) *Step 3*

Collect the costs of each activity into what are known as **cost pools**.

(d) *Step 4*

Charge support overheads to products on the basis of their usage of the activity. A product's usage of an activity is measured by the number of the activity's cost drivers it generates.

Suppose, for example, that the cost pool for the ordering of nylon and plastic activity totalled £10,000 and that there were 1,000 orders (the cost driver). Each product would therefore be charged with £10 for each order it required. A batch of kites requiring five orders would therefore be charged with £50.

9.8 ABC uses many cost drivers as absorption bases (number of orders, number of dispatches and so on). Absorption rates under ABC should therefore be more closely linked to the causes of overhead costs and hence produce more realistic product costs, especially where support overheads are high.

9.9 The diagram below shows how cost drivers may be applied to achieve a **product cost, product and customer profitability analysis** and **market segment profitability analysis**.

Cost Driver

1	Set-up time in minutes
2	Time in minutes for total operations
3	Number of batches
4	Material value as a percentage of product cost
5	Quality control testing time
6	Number of sales orders
7	Number of sales quotes
8	Number of sales visits
9	Number of customers served
10	Marketing support time

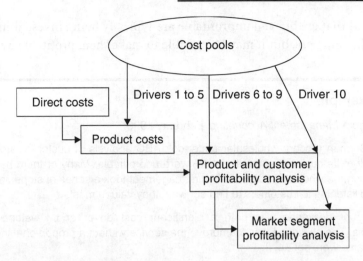

9.10 Activity based costing often confirms that some products and customers are profitable, but are **subsidising** those which make a loss. Not understanding customer and product profitability lays companies open to attack from competitors.

Case example

Siemens had a product range varying from simple toasters to complex tailor made machines. Overhead costs were allocated with little regard for these varying degrees of complexity, making some products overpriced. New entrants (especially from the Far East) were able to spot these niches and undercut Siemens. With ABC, Siemens could eventually see that some products were overpriced (thereby subsiding other products) and uncompetitive.

9.11 ABC gives strategists a clear picture of where to compete and encourages them to look at customers as a portfolio. Consider the diagram below.

The appropriate action is not merely to remove non-profitable customers or products

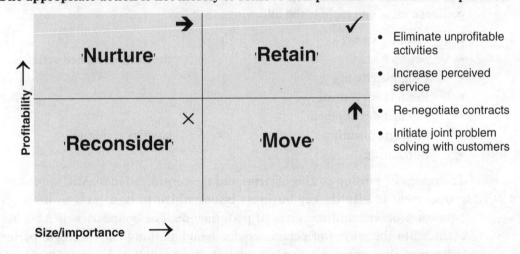

Adapted from 'Activity Based Costing: focusing on what counts' by Michael Gering (Management Accounting, February 1999).

9.12 To focus on the diagram, it shows:

(a) Customers and products that are both important and profitable must be retained.

(b) Those that are neither must be reconsidered, and possibly axed.

(c) Those that are small in size or importance, but very profitable, should be investigated and nurtured, possibly with cross-selling or other enhanced promotional techniques.

(d) Those that are big and unprofitable are typically being invested in for very little return to the company, but it may be possible to make them profitable by moving them.

Case example

Adapted from *Management Accounting*, February 1999:

A large German grocery wholesaler undertook ABC analysis of customer profitability and found that nearly half of its customers (retail outlets) were unprofitable. Many of them had negotiated deals that were costing the wholesaler dear. Senior management took a series of steps, including renegotiation of terms and listening to customers to find out what they valued most.

Frequency of deliveries was both a significant cost driver and keystone of customers service perceptions. The challenge was to improve the service without a proportional increase in cost. Problem solving teams were set up.

The merits of activity based costing

9.13 There is nothing difficult about ABC, once the necessary information has been obtained. This simplicity is part of its appeal. Further merits of ABC are as follows.

(a) ABC **focuses attention** on the nature of cost behaviour and attempts to provide meaningful product costs.

(b) In a more **competitive environment**, companies must be able to assess product and customer profitability realistically. To do this, they must have a good understanding of what drives overhead costs.

(c) ABC can give **valuable insights** into product design, product mix, processing methods, administration and pricing.

(d) ABC might be useful in contributing towards the control of **non-value-added** activities. These are activities that do not augment the customer's perception of a product's value and include the following.

- Holding stocks
- Set-up costs   } production-related activities
- Progress chasing
- Production control
- Product development
- Strategic planning   } support activities
- Purchasing

(e) The review of existing costing systems and the consideration of ABC approaches helps management to identify **key business issues** which in turn leads to investigation of business processes and measures of performance. The boundaries of ABC have been extended to the setting of parameters for **benchmarking** and **strategic performance indicators**, thus working towards a concept of **activity based management**. Managers are able to focus upon, and measure, those factors critical to the success of the firm.

9.14 We will now consider a full example comparing ABC and traditional overhead allocation methods. Our kite company manufactures two products: basic toy kites and competition kites. The toy kites are a standard high-volume product, but the competition kites are a low-volume product. For the purposes of our example, activity levels in 2001 are well in excess of those experienced in 2000, and basic data is as follows:

	Machine hours per product	Output units	Total machine hours	Purchase orders	Materials handling
Toy kite	4	10,000	40,000	20	10
Competition kite	20	1,000	20,000	20	20
			60,000	40	30

The overheads of the business are analysed as:

	£
Related to volume	120,000
Related to purchasing	60,000
Related to materials handling	120,000
	300,000

Overhead allocation under ABC would be:

	Volume	Purchasing	Materials handling	Total
Overheads	£120,000	£60,000	£120,000	
Cost drivers for the activity	60,000 machine hours	40 orders	30 requisitions	
Cost per unit	£2	£1,500	£4,000	
Costs charged to:				
Toy kites	40,000 x £2 = £80,000	20 x £1,500 = £30,000	10 x £4,000 = £40,000	£150,000
Competition kites	20,000 x £2 = £40,000	20 x £1,500 = £30,000	20 x £4,000 = £80,000	£150,000
				£300,000

Overhead allocated to:

Toy kites	£150,000 ÷ 10,000 units = £15 each
Competition kites	£150,000 ÷ 1,000 units = £150 each

This allocation reflects the use made of overhead activities by the two products. By contrast, traditional overhead absorption using a single **machine hour** rate on these figures would give:

Absorption rate per machine hour: £300,000 ÷ 60,000 hours = £5.00 per hour

Overhead absorbed per unit:

Toy kites	4 hrs x £5.00 = £20
Competition kites	20 hrs x £5.00 = £100

The traditional method charges more than ABC to the high-volume product (toy kites) because it is based only on machine hours. ABC uses cost drivers to relate the overheads to the use made by the product of those overhead-creating activities. The traditional method of cost allocation will lead to toy kites subsidising the competition kites and may make them uncompetitive if they are priced to reflect the extra £5 (£20 – £15) of overheads per unit.

Criticisms of ABC

9.15 It has been suggested by critics that activity based costing is flawed.

(a) It should not be introduced unless it can provide **additional information** for management to use in planning or control decisions.

(b) It is claimed by proponents of ABC that it provides more **accurate product costs**. This assumes that relevant cost drivers have been correctly identified.

(c) Any firm contemplating the introduction of ABC needs to consider the associated **systems** and **implementation cost**.

(d)   The benefits of ABC may be more meaningful to the **larger enterprise** than the small firm since overhead costs will probably constitute a higher proportion of total product cost in the larger firm.

Case example

Transco continues to refine its objectives in the light of the increasingly competitive market place for gas transportation services. To quote its management accounting manager: 'The need to create shareholder value is important to Transco. The use of emerging business appraisal and investment techniques such as shareholder or economic value added are widespread'.

These measures supplement the existing approaches such as ABC, used extensively at operational and strategic levels. ABC contributes to performance management by identifying cost drivers and relationships between inputs and outputs, and Transco uses it to ensure that prices reflect costs, to manage operations, for reporting purposes and to help develop and implement strategy.

9.16   Writing in the May 2000 edition of *Management Accounting*, Tom Kennedy says that ABC 'is not as popular in practice as its supporters would suggest.' He highlights **two conflicting views** in contemporary management accounting practice.

(a)   A number of US academics believe that traditional management accounting systems should be swept aside and replaced by ABC.

(b)   Academics from the London School of Economics in the UK suggest, on the other hand, a more careful and flexible approach to management accounting system design. ABC does not fit all organisations.

9.17   To quote Kennedy: 'Worldwide adoption rates for ABC have **peaked at 20%** and a declining number of firms are giving it further consideration.' Changes are indeed taking place in management accounting , but 'primarily in the way management accounting is used and not necessarily in the introduction of new systems or techniques.'

10   REGULATION AND PERFORMANCE

10.1   Modern society is very concerned to define for itself what is and what is not 'acceptable'. Businesses are taking this concern on board, and both **legal** and **voluntary** regulations will affect company performance.

Fiduciary obligations

10.2   **Directors, employees, agents, professional advisers** and others owe **fiduciary duties to those for whom they act**. It follows, for example, that **directors must act in good faith** in the best interests of their company. This obligation manifests itself in various way, for example **not to disclose confidential information, not to make secret profits** and **not to take bribes**. If a director places himself in a situation where there is a **conflict of interest and duty**, he must be sure to **disclose all relevant details** to the company in order to seek the company's approval and thereby avoid possible liability for breach of fiduciary duty.

Insider dealing

10.3   An individual who has information as an 'insider' is **guilty of insider dealing if he deals on a regulated market in securities that are price-affected securities in relation to the information**. An 'insider' is an individual who is, or has been within the previous six months, connected with a company and who knows that that is so. It follows that this includes directors, officers, employees and professional advisers. The relevant law is contained in the Criminal Justice Act 1993.

Fraudulent trading

10.4   The **Insolvency Act 1986** contains a range of provisions designed to impose personal liability on directors of insolvent companies who have engaged in some form of wrongdoing. The most important of these provisions are sections 213 and 214. **Section 213** imposes **personal liability on directors and others who have carried on business with intent to defraud the creditors**. Such 'fraudulent trading' also carries criminal sanctions in the form of fines and/or imprisonment. **Section 214** provides for the **imposition of personal liability on directors who engage in 'wrongful trading'**, ie continuing to trade after a time when the director(s) knew or ought to have known that there was no reasonable prospect of the company's avoiding insolvent liquidation. This provision carries civil liability only.

Directors who are caught by these provisions may also be disqualified from acting as directors under the Company Directors Disqualification Act 1986.

Organisational guidelines and corporate codes

10.5   Organisations are coming under increasing pressure from a number of **sources** to behave more ethically.

- **Government**
- UK and European **legislation**
- **Treaty obligations** (such as the Rio Summit)
- **Consumers**
- **Employers**
- **Pressure groups**

10.6   These sources of pressure expect an ethical attitude towards the following.

- **Stakeholders** (employees, customers, competitors, suppliers and society at large)
- **Animals**
- **Green issues** (such as pollution and the need for recycling)
- **The disadvantaged**
- Dealings with **unethical companies or countries**

10.7   Reidenbach and Robin usefully distinguish between **five different attitudes to corporate ethics**. The following is an adapted version of a report in the *Financial Times*.

(a)   **Amoral organisations**

Such organisations are prepared to **condone any actions that contribute to the corporate aims** (generally the owner's short-term greed).

(b)   **Legalistic organisations**

Such organisations **obey the letter of the law but not necessarily the spirit of it**, if that conflicts with economic performance. Ethical matters will be ignored until they become a problem.

(c)   **Responsive companies**

These organisations take the view - perhaps cynically, perhaps not - that there is **something to be gained from ethical behaviour**. It might be recognised, for example, that an enlightened attitude towards staff welfare enabled the company to attract and retain higher calibre staff.

(d) **Emerging ethical (or 'ethically engaged') organisations**

They take an **active** (rather than a reactive) **interest in ethical issues**.

(e) **Ethical organisations**

These organisations have a **'total ethical profile'**: a philosophy that informs everything that the company does and a commitment on the part of everyone to carefully selected core values.

Corporate codes and corporate culture

Case example

British Airways got caught in 1993 waging a 'dirty tricks' campaign against its competitor Virgin Atlantic. British Airways maintained that the offending actions (essentially, the poaching of Virgin's customers) were those of a small group of employees who overstepped the bounds of 'proper' behaviour in their eagerness to foster the interests of their employer.

An alternative view digs a little deeper. Some observers believed that the real villain of the piece was British Airways' abrasive corporate culture, inspired by the then chairman of BA, Lord King.

One of BA's responses to its defeat in the courts against Virgin and the bad publicity arising from the case was to introduce a code of ethics.

10.8 Many commentators would argue that the introduction of a code of ethics is **inadequate** on its own. To be effective a code needs to be accompanied by **positive attempts to foster guiding values, aspirations and patterns of thinking that support ethically sound behaviour** - in short a **change of culture**.

Company code of conduct

10.9 A **corporate code** typically contains a **series of statements setting out the company's values and explaining how it sees its responsibilities towards stakeholders**.

Question 5

How can an organisation influence employee behaviour towards ethical issues?

Answer

Here are some suggestions.

- Recruitment and selection policies and procedures
- Induction and training
- Objectives and reward schemes
- Ethical codes
- Threat of ethical audit

The impact of a corporate code

10.10 A code of conduct can set out the company's expectations, and in principle a code such as that outlined above addresses many of the problems that the organisations may experience. However, **merely issuing a code is not enough**.

(a) The **commitment of senior management** to the code needs to be real, and it needs to be very clearly communicated to all staff. Staff need to be persuaded that expectations really have changed.

(b) Measures need to be taken to **discourage previous behaviours** that conflict with the code.

(c) **Staff need to understand** that it is in the **organisation's best interests** to change behaviour, and become committed to the same ideals.

(d) Some employees – including very able ones - may find it very difficult to buy into a code that they **perceive may limit their own earnings** and/or restrict their freedom to do their job.

(e) In addition to a general statement of ethical conduct, **more detailed statements** (codes of practice) will be needed to set out formal procedures that must be followed.

Green and social issues and the management accountant

10.11 Recent issues of *Management Accounting* have seen a number of articles on green and social issues and their impact on management accountants.

10.12 Martin Bennett and Peter James ('The green bottom line: management accounting for environmental improvement and business benefit', November 1998) looked at the **ways in which a company's concern for the environment can impact on its performance.**

(a) **Short-term savings** through waste minimisation and energy efficiency schemes can be substantial.

(b) **Pressures on businesses** for environmental action are increasing.

(c) Companies with poor environmental performance may face **increased cost of capital** because investors and lenders demand a higher risk premium.

(d) There are a growing number of **energy and environmental taxes**, such as the UK's landfill tax.

(e) Accidents and long-term environmental effects can result in **large financial liabilities**.

(f) **Pressure group campaigns** can cause damage to reputation and/or additional costs.

(g) Environmental legislation may cause the '**sunsetting**' of products and opportunities for '**sunrise' replacements**.

(h) The cost of processing input which becomes **waste** is equivalent to 5-10% of some organisation's turnover.

(i) The phasing out of CFCs has led to markets for alternative products.

10.13 They go on to suggest six main ways in which business and environmental benefits can be achieved.

(a) **Integrating the environment into capital expenditure decisions** (by considering environmental opposition to projects which could affect cash flows, for example)

(b) **Understanding and managing environmental costs**. Environmental costs are often 'hidden' in overheads and environmental and energy costs are often not allocated to the relevant budgets.

(c) **Introducing waste minimisation schemes**

(d) **Understanding and managing life cycle costs.** For many products, the greatest environmental impact occurs upstream (such as mining raw materials) or downstream from production (such as energy to operate equipment). This has led to producers being made responsible for dealing with the disposal of products such as cars, and government and third party measures to influence raw material choices. Organisations therefore need to identify, control and make provision for environmental life cycle costs and work with suppliers and customers to identify environmental cost reduction opportunities.

(e) **Measuring environmental performance.** Business is under increasing pressure to measure all aspects of environmental performance, both for statutory disclosure reasons and due to demands for more environmental data from customers.

(f) **Involving management accountants in a strategic approach to environment-related management accounting and performance evaluation.** A 'green accounting team' incorporating the key functions should analyse the strategic picture and identify opportunities for practical initiatives. It should analyse the short-, medium- and long-term impact of possible changes in the following.

- **Government policies**, such as on transport
- **Legislation and regulation**
- **Supply conditions**, such as fewer landfill sites
- **Market conditions**, such as changing customer views
- **Social attitudes**, such as to factory farming
- **Competitor strategies**

Possible action includes the following.

(i) Designating an '**environmental champion**' within the strategic planning or accounting function to ensure that environmental considerations are fully considered.

(ii) Assessing whether **new data sources** are needed to collect more and better data

(iii) Making **comparisons** between sites/offices to highlight poor performance and generate peer pressure for action

(iv) Developing **checklists** for internal auditors

Such analysis and action should help organisations to better understand present and future environmental costs and benefits.

KEY TERM

Corporate social accounting. 'The reporting of the social and environmental impact of an entity's activities upon those who are directly associated with the entity (employees, customers, suppliers etc) or those who are in any way affected by the activities of the entity, as well as an assessment of the cost of compliance with relevant regulations in this area.'
(CIMA *Official Terminology*)

10.14 Lynne Paine (*Harvard Business Review*, March-April 1994) suggests that ethical decisions are becoming more important, as penalties, in the US at least, for companies which break the law are become tougher. Paine suggests that there are two approaches to the management of ethics in organisations:

(a) A **compliance-based** approach is primarily designed to ensure that the company and its personnel act within the letter of the law. Mere compliance is not an adequate means for addressing the full range of ethical issues that arise every day. This is especially the case in the UK, where **voluntary codes** of conduct and self-regulating institutes are perhaps more prevalent than the US.

(b) An **integrity-based approach** combines a concern for the law with an emphasis on managerial responsibility for ethical behaviour ... . When integrated into the day-to-day operations of an organisation, such strategies can help prevent damaging ethical lapses.

Codes of practice

10.15 It would seem to follow that the imposition of social and ethical responsibilities on its management should come from within the organisation itself, and the organisation should issue its own code of conduct for its employees.

10.16 One such set of guidelines was issued by United Biscuits plc as follows.

'These "guiding principles", taken in conjunction with our budget and strategic objectives, are important as a description of the way in which we operate.

United Biscuits' business ethics are not negotiable - a well-founded reputation for scrupulous dealing is itself a priceless company asset and the most important single factor in our success is faithful adherence to our beliefs. While our tactical plans and many other elements constantly change, our basic philosophy does not. To meet the challenges of a changing world, we are prepared to change everything about ourselves except our values.

Some employees might have the mistaken idea that we do not care how results are obtained, as long as we get results. This would be wrong: we do care how we get results. We expect compliance with our standard of integrity throughout the company, and we will support an employee who passes up an opportunity or advantage that can only be secured at the sacrifice of a principle.

While it is the responsibility of top management to keep a company honest and honourable, perpetuating ethical values is not a function only of the chief executive or a handful of senior managers. Every employee is expected to take on the responsibility of always behaving ethically whatever the circumstances. Beliefs and values must always come before policies, practices and goals; the latter must be altered if they violate fundamental beliefs.'

Professional directors

10.17 A director's role is distinct from the manager's role: the director is accountable to shareholders. Perhaps the best way to ensure that long-term owner value is maximised is for directors to have substantial shareholdings of their own. Owners, too, need to make more effort in ensuring businesses behave ethically.

Environmental reporting

10.18 The move to encourage **reporting** of the **environmental** or **ethical effects** of business activity is fairly new when compared to the long history of **financial** reporting.

10.19 The main problems in devising an appropriate **reporting system** seem to hinge on the following.

- Should reports stand alone, or form part of the year end accounts?

- Should the work be done by accountants, or environmental experts?

- What standard measures can be universally agreed? For example, could the Post Office be measured on pollutant emissions per delivery?

- What should be the framework of a report?

- How can environmental strategy be clearly linked to business drivers?

- Which stakeholders are being served?

- For what reasons are these reports to be produced?

10.20 Another major barrier is that environmental reporting necessitates a shift to **long-term** thinking. Businesses have many and diverse ways of looking at the future and their investments, and not all of them will have a corporate culture prepared to take a long term view.

10.21 The chief environmental reporters in the UK have been the big utilities, oil and chemical companies, who have a **direct concern** with the environment and are in the **political spotlight**.

10.22 In the UK, a regulation took force on 2 July 2000 which requires pension funds to describe the ethical parameters in their investment strategy. It could be that the pension funds will exert pressure, through analysts, to produce environmental assessments, but this is not guaranteed. In the long run, **statutory instruments** may be the only method by which all companies will get involved in environmental reporting.

Unity Bicycles plc

(1)   What sort of strategic control system is employed by UB? Could you improve it?

(2)   What do you think is meant by the 'fitness for use' of UB's products?

(3)   What do you think would be the most significant measures on a balanced scorecard for UB?

(4)   Indicate ways in which UB's management accounting procedures might have to change.

(5)   What problems can you envisage in the improvement of quality at the Mexican and Romanian plants?

Chapter roundup

- **Performance measurement** aims to establish how well something or somebody is doing in relation to previous or expected activity or in comparison with another thing or body.

- Performance measurement **aims** to

  ° **Communicate** the objectives of the company
  ° **Concentrate efforts** towards those objectives
  ° **Produce feedback** for comparison with the plan

- **Critical success factors** are the few key areas where things must go right for the organisation to flourish.

- **Strategic control** is bound up with measurement of performance, which often tends to be based on financial criteria. Techniques for strategic control suggest that companies develop strategic milestones (eg for market share) to monitor the achievement of strategic objectives, as a counterweight to purely financial issues.

- Some strategic control measures can be suggested by **benchmarking** competitors and similar firms.

- **Budgetary control systems** are subject to some criticism, but are still used by many companies to compel planning, co-ordinate activities and motivate employees, as well as to evaluate performance. Deviations from the plan are corrected via **control action.**

- Types of budgeting include ABB, continuous rolling budgets and ZBB

- Measures must be **relevant** to the way the organisation operates

- Growing dissatisfaction with financial performance measures has led to other measures being developed, based on **operational performance.**

- An approach which tries to integrate the different measures of performance is the **balanced scorecard**, where key linkages between operating and financial performance are brought to light. This offers four perspectives

  ° Financial
  ° Customer
  ° Innovation and learning
  ° Internal business

- Perhaps a good way to enforce the balanced scorecard is to relate it to **executive remuneration** and **performance appraisal**, or else decisions will be taken on purely financial criteria.

- The **performance pyramid** derives from the idea that an organisation operates at different levels, each of which has different (but supporting) concerns.

- The management accountant can still contribute to strategic control, as a financial perspective still has to be brought to bear.

- **Operational performance measures** for manufacturing include quality and production efficiency.

- **Activity based costing** (ABC) is an alternative to the more traditional absorption costing. ABC involves the identification of the factors **(cost drivers)** which cause the costs of an organisation's major activities. Support overheads are charged to products on the basis of their usage of an activity.

- When using ABC for costs that vary with production levels in the short term, the cost driver will be **volume related** (labour or machine hours). Overheads that vary with some other activity should be traced to products using **transaction-based** cost drivers such as production runs or number of orders received.

- For service departments, Fitzgerald et al advocate the use of the **results and determinants framework.**

- As well as legal **regulation** covering company activities, many companies have their own corporate **codes of conduct** and may also follow industry self regulating **codes of practice.**

BPP PUBLISHING

Quick quiz

1   **Fill in the blanks** in the statements below, using the words in the box.

The aims of performance measurement are as follows

- (1) .... the (2) .... of the company
- Concentrating (3) .... towards objectives
- Part of the (4) .... process where (5) .... is compared with the (6) ....

⊙ plan	⊙ objectives	⊙ control
○ feedback	⊙ efforts	⊙ communicating

2   What is an example of a critical success factor for the production function?

3   Which of the following is a perceived disadvantage of zero based budgeting (ZBB)?

A   There are no incentives as the budget is often unrealistic
B   The managers who set the budgets are not responsible for attaining them
C   Too many people are involved
D   It may emphasise short term benefits rather than long term goals

4   'In general, there are three possible points of reference for measurement'. What are they?

....

....

....

5   Give some examples of non-financial performance measures that can be applied to an assessment of marketing effectiveness.

6   What are the four perspectives on the balanced scorecard?

....

....

....

....

7   What are the specific operational criteria contained in the performance pyramid?

8   What have been seen as the four 'over-arching' measures for manufacturing environments?

9   **Fill in the blanks** in the statements below, using the words in the box.

A corporate (1) .... typically contains a series of (2) .... setting out the company's (3) .... and explaining how it sees its (4) .... towards (5) ....

⊙ stakeholders	⊙ code	○ statements
⊙ responsibilities	⊙ values	

10   What are some of the disadvantages of using profit as a performance measure?

Answers to quick quiz

1　(1) Communicating　(2) objectives　(3) efforts　(4) control　(5) feedback　(6) plan

2　Quality standards / capacity utilisation

3　D

4　Profitability
　Activity
　Productivity

5　Trend in market share
　Customer visits per salesperson
　Sales volume forecast v actual
　Customer survey response information

　Sales volume growth
　Client contact hours per salesperson
　Number of customers

6　Customer
　Internal
　Innovation/learning
　Financial

7　Quality
　Process time

　Delivery
　Cost

8　Cost
　Time

　Quality
　Innovation

9　(1) code　(2) statements　(3) values　(4) responsibilities　(5) stakeholders

10　Encourages short-termism and focus on the annual cycle, at the expense of long term performance

　Profit differs from economic income

　A firm has to satisfy stakeholders other than shareholders, such as the government and the local community

　Liquidity is at least as important as profit

　Profit should be related to risk, not just capital employed

　Profits can fluctuate in times of rapid change, eg exchange rates

　Profits measures cannot easily be used to motivate cost centre managers

BPP PUBLISHING

Unity Bicycles plc review

Question 1. At best UB has an informal system of strategic control, but there is no evidence to suggest that the issue has even been addressed. This is likely to be down to the dominance of Walter Drake, and a more formal system may be required as the company seeks expansion.

Question 2. Fitness for use is what is meant by quality – but ultimately this is determined by the customer. The 'quality' of a sports bike might be very different from the quality of a commuting bike, to be ridden in rural areas with poor roads. The design of the bikes must take the conditions in which they will be used into consideration.

Question 3. Balanced scorecard.

(a) Cash flow is important from the financial perspective.

(b) The customer perspective will vary from market to market.

(c) Internal perspective measures include efficiency in the use of scarce resources, and low-cost component supplies, providing quality does not suffer. Some cost/quality objectives are needed. Particular attention should be paid to the Romanian plant.

(d) *Innovation and learning:* the firm has only just started to address the issue. UB must bring the Romanian factory up to scratch. A measure might include the number of training schemes etc.

Question 4. UB is introducing advanced manufacturing technology which will change its cost structure. Perhaps it needs to introduce ABC or other approaches.

Question 5. Arguably the worst problem is in Romania, where local managers have to be taught the basic principles of profit and customer satisfaction. The Mexican plant is probably more attuned to these issues.

Now try the question below from the Exam Question Bank

Question to try	Level	Marks	Time
13	Pilot paper	25	45 mins

Chapter 14

APPROACHES TO MEASURING PERFORMANCE II

Topic list	Syllabus reference	Ability required
1 Using NPVs to control strategic investments	(v)	Analysis/evaluation
2 Using contribution margin as a measure of performance	(v)	Analysis/evaluation
3 Variance analysis	(v)	Analysis/evaluation
4 Divisional performance: Return on investment (ROI)	(v)	Analysis/evaluation
5 Divisional performance: Residual income (RI)	(v)	Analysis/evaluation
6 Comparing profit centre performance	(v)	Analysis/evaluation
7 Interfirm comparisons and performance ratios	(v)	Analysis/evaluation
8 Inflation	(v)	Analysis/evaluation

Introduction

In this chapter we concentrate on the **financial perspective** area of the balanced scorecard. Financial measures of performance are those you will be most likely to have a hand in.

The material in this chapter should present you with no problems. There are no techniques or concepts that you have not encountered earlier in your studies. The point is that management accounting and financial measures can be flexibly applied.

This chapter looks at three main areas. We start in Section 1 by reviewing the performance of **investment** decisions first. We also look at **contribution analysis** and **variance analysis** (sections 2 and 3). This should be mostly revision for you. Then we discuss appraisal of particular **business units and divisions** (Sections 4-6), and the **relationships** between them (Sections 7).

Although this chapter is in many respects concerned with **control**, we examine in detail why some 'control' measures can have a dysfunctional impact on strategic decision-making.

A general theme of this chapter is that accounting measures such as ROI (Section 4) must be used with some care, because:

- They reflect **organisation structure**, rather than business processes
- They are easily **manipulated** by accountants and managers
- They are rendered uncertain by **inflation** (Section 8)

This is an argument that they should be supplemented by other measures, as suggested in the previous chapter.

Learning outcomes covered in this chapter

- **Evaluate** and **recommend** appropriate control measures

- **Evaluate** and **produce** multidimensional models of performance measurement

---

Syllabus content covered in this chapter

- The problem of assessing strategic performance, the use of profit and cash measures and the concept of appropriate measures for an industry and contingent on environmental factors.

---

1   USING NPVs TO CONTROL STRATEGIC INVESTMENTS

Pilot paper, 11/01

1.1   The easiest form of strategic decision to control relates to **capital expenditure**, such as investment in machinery.

The control of capital expenditure

> **KEY TERM**
>
> **Capital projects** involve 'any long term commitments of funds undertaken now in anticipation of a potential inflow of funds at some time in the future.' (Hartley).

1.2   Once a project is given the go-ahead, with a spending ceiling of £x, the progress of the project should be monitored. Although **direct expenditure** can be monitored, it is not always easy to identify **additional indirect expenditures** and extra **working capital investment** as a direct cause of the project.

1.3   Assume a firm has a level of sales of £1,000,000 pa. It has a choice of two investments. Both involve saving costs, but neither will have an effect on sales revenue. Project A involves developing an exclusive distribution system, and has a positive NPV of £50,000. Project B involves investing in new production equipment and has an NPV of £100,000. Normally project B would be chosen, as it has the higher NPV, but if you were told that:

(a)   A new competitor had entered the market, threatening sales revenue by an undefined amount

(b)   Project A would raise barriers to entry

you might prefer Project A, as it has additional benefits in **protecting revenue**.

1.4   With long-term planning, capital expenditure decisions should be based on an evaluation of future cash flows, discounted at an appropriate cost of capital to an NPV.

Cash flows and NPVs for strategic control: shareholder wealth

1.5   Control at a strategic level should be based on measurements of **cash flows,** ie actual cash flows for the period just ended and revised forecasts of future cash flows. Since the objective of a company might be to maximise the wealth of its shareholders, a control technique based on the measurement of cash flows and their NPV could be a very useful technique to apply.

1.6   A numerical example might help to illustrate this point.

Suppose that ABC Ltd agrees to a strategic plan from 1 January 20X1 as follows.

Year	20X1	20X2	20X3	20X4	20X5	Total
Planned net cash inflow (£'000)	200	300	300	400	500	1,700
NPV at cost of capital 15%	174	227	197	229	249	1,076

1.7 Now suppose that ABC Ltd reviews its position one year later.

(a) It can measure its actual total cash flow in 20X1 - roughly speaking, this will be the funds generated from operations minus tax paid and minus expenditure on fixed assets and plus/minus changes in working capital.

(b) It can revise its forecast for the next few years.

We will assume that there has been no change in the cost of capital. Control information at the end of 20X1 might be as follows.

Year	20X1 (actual)	20X2 (forecast)	20X3	20X4	20X5	Total
Net cash inflow (£'000)	180	260	280	400	540	1,660
NPV at cost of capital 15%	180	226	212	263	309	1,190

1.8 A control summary comparing the situation at the start of 20X1 and the situation one year later would now be as follows.

	£'000
Expected NPV as at 1.1.20X1	1,076
Uplift by cost of capital 15%	161
	1,237
Expected NPV as at 1.1.20X2	1,190
Variance	47 (A)

The control information shows that by the end of 20X1, ABC Ltd shows signs of not achieving the strategic targets it set itself at the start of 20X1. This is partly because actual cash flows in 20X1 fell short of target by (200-180) £20,000, but also because the revised forecast for the future is not as good now either. In total, the company has a lower NPV by £47,000.

1.9 The reasons for the failure to achieve target should be investigated. Possible reasons include the following.

• A higher-than-expected pay award to employees, which will have repercussions for the future as well as in 20X1

• An increase in the rate of tax on profits

• A serious delay in the implementation of some major new projects

• The slower-than-expected growth of an important new market

Exam focus point

Do not be surprised if calculations are required in the exam: this is a management accounting subject. If calculations are required you will probably have to use or comment on them in support of an argument. This was the case in November 2001.

Reconciling successive NPVs: summary of the technique

1.10 Strategic progress can be measured by reconciling successive net present values and the intervening cash flows.

The arithmetic is straightforward and can be summed up as follows.

(a) The previous NPV is uplifted by the cost of capital applicable to the current period.

(b) From this uplifted figure is deducted the actual cash flow in the period.

(c) The result is the 'benchmark NPV' indicating what the new NPV needs to be if long-term health has been maintained.

(d) Comparison of the new NPV with the benchmark produces a variance which can be analysed by cause and by time frame.

1.11 Attempt your own solution to the following question.

Question 1

XYZ Ltd prepared the following strategic budget for a five-year period 20X3 - 20X7.

Year	Forecast cash flow £'000	Discount factor 18%	NPV £'000
20X3	360	0.847	305
20X4	400	0.718	287
20X5	440	0.609	268
20X6	500	0.516	258
20X7	600	0.437	262
			1,380

Actual cash flows in 20X3 were £400,000 and revised forecasts for the next five years are, in £'000: 20X4 - 420; 20X5 - 450; 20X6 - 480; 20X7 - 540; 20X8 - 560. As from 20X4, the cost of capital has been increased to 20%.

Required. Assess the strategic progress of XYZ Ltd.

Answer

We must compare the *same* period of time and so the new forecast for 20X8 should be ignored. Since 20X3 cash flows are 'actual' a discount factor of 1 is applied.

Year	Forecast cash flow £'000	Discount factor 20%	NPV £'000
20X3	400 *(actual)*	1.0	400
20X4	420	0.833	350
20X5	450	0.694	312
20X6	480	0.579	278
20X7	540	0.482	260
			1,600

Summary	£'000
Expected NPV as at beginning of 20X3	1,380
Uplift by cost of capital for 20X3 (18%)	248
'Benchmark' NPV	1,628
Expected NPV as per revised forecast, end of 20X3	1,600
Variance	28 (A)

The NPV has fallen by £28,000, in spite of the better-than-expected cash flow in 20X3, and the improved cash flow forecasts for 20X4 and 20X5. The increase in the cost of capital is clearly a major cause of the fall in NPV. (*Note.* The variance caused by the increase from 18% to 20% could be quantified, by re-evaluating the future cash flows in the revised forecast at 18%, but this calculation is not shown here.)

1.12 With the technique just described, it is necessary to obtain information about actual cash flows and forecast cash flows for the business as a whole. In theory, the same principles should apply to performance measurement for individual parts of a business. In practice, it is not often easy to identify the attributable cash flows for individual capital projects or individual profit centres, and so other financial measures of performance have to be applied. These are now described.

2 USING CONTRIBUTION MARGIN AS A MEASURE OF PERFORMANCE

> ## KEY TERM
>
> **Contribution margin** can be defined as 'the difference between sales volume and the variable cost of those sales, expressed either in absolute terms or as a contribution per unit.' (CIMA).

2.1 The contribution per unit is 'often related to a key or limiting factor to give a sum required to cover fixed overhead and profit, such as contribution per machine hour, per direct labour hour or per kilo of scarce raw material.'

    (a) A **contribution centre** is a profit centre where expenditure is calculated on a marginal cost basis.

    (b) **Contribution per unit of limiting factor** is a measurement for optimising the use of scarce resources.

2.2 Contribution margins are also used for measuring performance in terms of **breakeven analysis**.

Contribution and strategic decisions

Product market issues

2.3 Consider, for example, a situation where an automobile manufacturer wishes to launch a new model, the success of which is crucial to corporate survival. Fixed costs are the capital required to develop the vehicle and tool up, which will appear in the breakeven equation as depreciation, development costs and operational fixed costs. Variable costs will have been identified and reliable sales forecasts will have been obtained. From this data, two figures can be computed.

    (a) The number of vehicles required to **break even**.

    (b) The number of vehicles required to generate **adequate returns** over the life of the model or the investment, and, significantly, what this represents in terms of market penetration and market share.

2.4 Johnson and Scholes argue that breakeven analysis has a useful role to play in appraising and controlling strategy. Questions can be asked based on the breakeven model.

    • What is the **probability** of achieving the desired levels of market penetration?

    • Do the **conditions in the market** lend themselves to achieving that desired penetration?

    • Will the **competitors** allow a profitable entry?

- Are the **cost and quality** assumptions feasible?

- Are the **funds available,** not just to complete the development but to establish the production capacity and skilled manpower to achieve the desired penetration?

Exit

2.5 Firms with high exit barriers may use contribution as the main tool for decision making. Ward cites the example of a coal mine, as to the type of decisions taken. High exit barriers result from:

- The actual costs of closure, redundancy etc
- The cost of re-opening the mine, if demand for coal and prices picks up
- Costs which will not be avoided by the closure

Applying contribution margin accounting to divisional performance measurement

2.6 A danger with contribution margin analysis is that firms in a competitive industry might be tempted to sell at prices which cover marginal costs, but fail to earn an adequate return on **sunk fixed costs**.

2.7 Applying the principle that managers should only be made accountable for costs and revenues which they are in a position to control directly, it follows that short-term controls for profit centres should focus largely on contribution margins, because in the short run, only revenues and variable costs tend to be **controllable**.

2.8 However, some directly attributable fixed costs might also be controllable in the short term, or at least might be avoidable if the scale of business operations were to be reduced significantly. Fixed costs can therefore be classified as follows.

(a) Costs which are **directly attributable** to a particular activity, and which tend to rise or fall in steps as the scale of activities is increased or lowered.

(b) **Unavoidable costs**. Many fixed costs are committed, or not directly attributable to any particular activity.

2.9 One way of measuring profit for an investment centre or a profit centre is as follows.

	£
Sales revenue	X
less Variable cost of sales	(X)
equals Contribution	X
less Directly attributable fixed costs (avoidable/controllable)	(X)
equals Gross profit	X
less Share of unavoidable (committed*/uncontrollable*) fixed costs	(X)
equals Net profit	X

(* in the short term. In the long term, all fixed cost items should be controllable and 'variable').

3   VARIANCE ANALYSIS 5/01

> **KEY TERMS**
>
> **Variance** 'The difference between a planned, budgeted or standard cost and the actual cost incurred. The same comparisons may be made for revenues.'
>
> **Variance analysis.** 'The evaluation of performance by means of variances, whose timely reporting should maximise the opportunity for managerial action.'
>
> (CIMA *Official Terminology*)

3.1   **Variance analysis** is a method of identifying areas of possible weakness, where control action might be necessary. It does not provide a ready-made diagnosis of faults, nor does it provide management with a ready-made indication of what corrective action needs to be taken. It merely **highlights items for possible investigation**.

3.2   Variances might **occur for several reasons**.

(a)   A variance may be due to **normal fluctuations** around the standard cost, with variations above and below the average (adverse and favourable variances) cancelling each other out in the course of time. The trend should be observed, however. Where small variances are always slightly adverse in every control period they may indicate that the area is moving into an out of control situation.

(b)   A variance may indicate excessive (or favourable) **expenditure which is controllable.**

(c)   A variance may indicate excessive (or favourable) **expenditure which is uncontrollable**.

(i)   The variance may be uncontrollable **by the manager to whom it is reported**, although **controllable by a different manager**. In a well designed costing system, this should not happen.

(ii)   The variance **may not be controllable by anyone** within the company because it has been caused by factors beyond the company's control.

(d)   If the **standard cost is inaccurate**, variances which are reported will be unreliable. A standard may be inaccurate because of poor planning, or because a deliberately unrealistic ideal has been set in order to measure performance.

(e)   Quite possibly, individual variances should not be looked at in isolation. One variance might be **inter-related** with another, and much of it might have occurred only because the other, inter-related, variance occurred too.

> **POINT TO NOTE**
>
> The basic problem is **how to decide whether or not a reported variance is worthy of investigation.**

3.3   The problem varies according to who is using the variance information. Arguably, if a variance is reported to the local manager of a smallish unit it should not be news: the manager should already know that something is going wrong and be taking corrective action. If, however, variances are reported to senior managers who are not closely in touch with the operations of the business some kind of **decision rule is needed to trigger the variance investigation/explanation process.** Four types of model have been proposed.

Model 1: materiality significance model

3.4   If the **size of a variance is within a certain limit, it should be considered immaterial.** Only if it exceeds the limit should it be considered materially significant, and worthy of investigation. The limit can be set either as an **absolute size or as a percentage from standard** (say, 10%).

Model 2: the statistical significance model

3.5   If a standard is an expected average performance, variances over time will average out at zero, and there is an equal probability of variances being adverse or unfavourable. Historical data can be used to decide what size of variations around the average could be expected without control action being required. Statistically, the **historical data** would be used to **calculate the standard deviation of 'acceptable' or 'uncontrollable' variations,** which are **assumed to be distributed normally around the average cost.**

3.6   Applying this historical data as a predictor of future variances, the **theory of normal distribution** can be used to decide if a variance should be investigated (given a significance limit of say 1% or 5%, set by the organisation).

3.7   **Advantages** of the statistical significance rule over the fixed limit rule

(a)   Important costs that normally vary by only a small amount from standard will be signalled for investigation if variances increase significantly

(b)   Costs that usually fluctuate by large amounts will not be signalled for investigation unless variances are extremely large.

3.8   The main **disadvantage** of the statistical significance rule is the problem of assessing standard deviations in expenditure. Historical variations in actual costs might not provide a statistically reliable measurement of the standard deviation of future costs.

Model 3: control charts

3.9   The $\bar{x}$ **control chart** is based on the principle of the statistical significance model. For each cost item, a chart is kept of monthly, weekly or daily variances and tolerance limits are set at 1, 2 or 3 standard deviations.

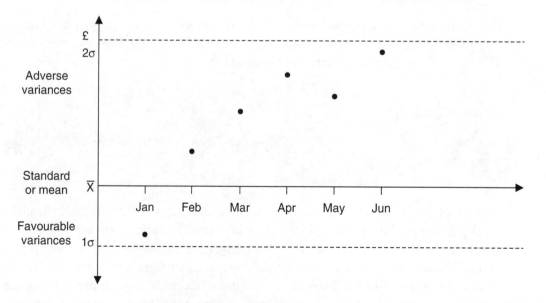

In this example, variances do not exceed the tolerance limits in any month, but the chart shows a worsening of variances over time, and so management might decide that an investigation is warranted, perhaps when it exceeds an inner warning limit.

3.10 With a **cusum chart** the variance in each period is taken as a 'partial sum' of the total variances over a longer period of time. If the variances are not significant, these 'partial sums' will simply fluctuate in a random walk above and below the average to give a total or cumulative sum of zero. But if **significant variances** occur, the **cumulative sum will start to develop a positive or negative drift**, and when it exceeds a set tolerance limit, the situation must be investigated, because control action is probably required.

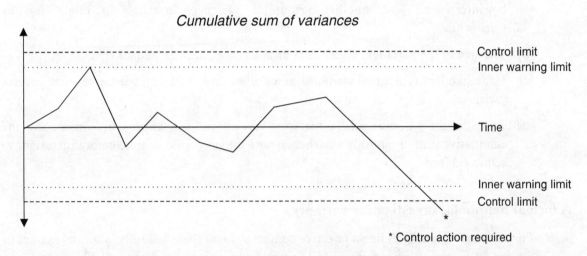

Cumulative sum of variances

3.11 The **advantage of the multiple period approach** over the single period approach is that **trends are detectable earlier,** and control action would be introduced sooner than might have been the case if only current-period variances were investigated.

Model 4: statistical decision theory

3.12 A further aspect of the problem of deciding whether a variance is worth investigating is the **expected costs of investigation and control, and the expected benefits from control action.**

3.13 Using the statistical decision theory approach, a **variance should be investigated if the expected value of the benefits exceeds the expected value of the costs,** that is, if:

$$pB \geq I + pC$$

where   p   is the probability that the process is out of control
              B   is the benefits from control action when the process is out of control
              I   is the cost of investigating the cause of a variance
              C   is the cost of control action when the process is out of control

Alternatively, the formula could be stated thus: a variance should be investigated if:

$$p(B-C) \geq I.$$

3.14 The costs and benefits approach has the **appeal** of being the **most financially aware** model, but it does have some severe **disadvantages**.

(a) It assumes that the probability that the process is out of control can be assessed.

(b) It assumes that the benefits of control action - even though these are ongoing from month to month - can be properly evaluated. Costs of investigation and control must also be assessed.

(c) It assumes that the costs of investigation and correction are constant.

- This might presuppose that the cause of a variance is the same every time.
- It does not allow for the process of learning from mistakes.

Other factors to consider

3.15 Mathematical decision rules should not obscure all the other factors which might be relevant to the decision.

(a) **Interdependence** between variances. If an adverse variance seems almost certainly to be interrelated with another favourable variance, investigation might not be worthwhile.

(b) The **size of the variance**, either in £s or as a percentage of standard cost.

(c) If the standard is an **ideal standard**, some allowance must be made for 'normal' adverse variances.

(d) There might be some advantage from a **wait-and-see approach**, considering the cumulative sum of monthly variances over a longer period of time before investigative action is taken.

A formal routine for investigating variances

3.16 For variance reporting to be an effective control system, there has to be a formal system or routine for investigating variances. The following procedures might be suitable.

(a) Managers should be **allowed to participate** in the budgeting and standard-setting process, and should then **accept their responsibility** for certain costs and revenues, and the variances associated with them.

(b) Standards and budgets should be **reviewed regularly** to keep them 'sensible'. Managers will not want to be made responsible for variances caused by inaccurate and unreliable standards.

(c) The doctrine of control, and the value of variances as control information, has to be properly understood. This might mean that managers should receive some **formal training** in the organisation's budgetary control systems.

(d) There should be an established and agreed **system for deciding which variances should be investigated.**

(e) **Actual costs** should be **accurately cost-coded**, so that they are charged to the correct cost centre, and so to the manager actually responsible for them.

(f) Periodic **variance reports** should be produced and **distributed promptly**. There should be variance reports at a **suitable level of detail** for all managers in the management hierarchy, for example for a divisional manager, for each of his or her departmental heads, and for each of their section heads.

(g) The reports should be clearly set out. The principle of **reporting by exception** should be applied, and variances that ought **to be investigated should be highlighted**.

(h) Variance reports should ideally include an **analysis of cumulative variances** or trends over time, not just single-period variances.

(i) When a variance is reported to the manager responsible for investigation, the **manager's superior should be notified too**, within the superior's variance report. The subordinate should then be required to report the results of his or her investigative action to the superior, who ought to be satisfied that suitable control action has been taken in appropriate cases

Planning and operational variances

3.17 The **cause of a total variance** might be one or both of the following.

- Adverse or favourable **operational performance**
- **Inaccurate planning**, or **faulty standards**

> ### KEY TERMS
>
> A **planning variance** compares an original standard cost with a revised standard cost that should and would have been used if planners had known what was going to happen in advance.
>
> Planning variances are sometimes called **revision variances**.
>
> An **operational variance** (or **operating variance**) compares actual cost with the revised standard cost.
>
> **Ex ante** means original budget/standard.
>
> **Ex post** means revised budget/standard.

3.18 **Traditional variance** reports imply that **'actual' performance is always at fault**. The **analysis of variances between operational and planning** factors means that **any failure to achieve budgeted profit because of faulty standards can be identified separately**.

Question 2

Jitt Ltd budgeted to make and sell 700 units of its product, in a four week period.

	£
Budgeted sales	70,000
Variable costs (700 units × £50)	35,000
Contribution	35,000
Fixed costs	15,000
Profit	20,000

At the beginning of the second week, production came to a halt because stocks of raw materials ran out, and a new supply was not received until the beginning of week 3. As a consequence, the company lost one week's production and sales. Actual results in the period were as follows.

	£
Sales (620 units)	62,000
Variable costs (620 units × £50)	31,000
Contribution	31,000
Fixed costs	15,000
Actual profit	16,000

In retrospect, it is decided that the optimum budget, given the loss of production facilities in the third week, would have been to sell only 600 units in the period.

Calculate variances in as meaningful a way as possible.

Answer

The **planning variance compares the revised budget with the original budget.**

	Units
Revised sales volume, given materials shortage	600
Original budgeted sales volume	700
Planning variance in units of sales	100 (A)
× standard contribution per unit	× £50
Planning variance in £	£5,000 (A)

Running out of raw materials is an operational error: the loss of sales volume and contribution from the materials shortage is an opportunity cost that could have been avoided with better purchasing arrangements. The **operational variances** are variances calculated in the usual way, except that **actual results are compared with the revised standard or budget.** There is a **sales volume variance** which is an **operational variance**, as follows.

	Units
Actual sales volume	620
Revised sales volume	600
Operational sales volume variance	20 (F)
(possibly due to production efficiency or marketing efficiency)	
× standard contribution per unit	× £50
	£1,000 (F)

These variances can be used as control information to **reconcile** budgeted and actual profit.

Operating statement	£		£	
Budgeted profit			20,000	
Planning variance	5,000	(A)		
Operational variance - sales volume	1,000	(F)		
			4,000	(A)
Actual profit in period			16,000	

Disadvantages

3.19 The limitations of planning and operational variances, which must be overcome if they are to be applied in practice, are as follows.

(a) The difficulties in **deciding in hindsight what the realistic standard should have been.** Some independent yardstick must be available, such as official commodity prices for certain raw materials.

(b) Establishing realistic revised standards and analysing the total variance into planning and operational variances can be a **time consuming** task, even if a spreadsheet package is devised.

(c) Even though the intention is to provide more meaningful information, **managers** may be **resistant to the very idea of variances** and refuse to see the virtues of the approach. Careful presentation and explanation will be required until managers are used to the concepts.

4 DIVISIONAL PERFORMANCE: RETURN ON INVESTMENT (ROI)

Pilot paper, 11/01

4.1 We have covered DCF and contribution margin accounting first of all for these reasons.

(a) Both techniques are in theory applicable to controlling and assessing strategies and can be applied to **divisional performance measurement**

(b) DCF addresses the issue in terms of **cash flows**

4.2 In practice, many firms use more 'traditional' accounting based measures, such as return on investment (ROI). First some definitions.

> ## KEY TERM
>
> **Return on investment (ROI)**
>
> $$\frac{\text{Profit before interest and tax} \times 100}{\text{Operations management capital employed}}$$
>
> A form of return on capital employed, which compares income with the operational assets used to generate that income. Profit is taken before tax and interest because tax is an appropriation of profit made from the use of the investment, and the introduction of interest charges introduces the effect of financing decisions into an appraisal of operating performance. (CIMA *Official Terminology*)

> ## KEY TERM
>
> **Return on capital employed (ROCE)**
>
> $$\frac{\text{Profit before interest and tax} \times 100}{\text{Average capital employed}}$$
>
> Indicates the productivity of capital employed. The denominator is normally calculated as the average of the capital employed at the beginning and end of the year. Problems of seasonality, new capital introduced or other factors may necessitate taking the average of a number of periods within the year. (CIMA *Official Terminology*)

4.3 ROI is normally used to apply to investment centres or profit centres. These normally reflect the existing organisation structure of the business.

4.4 ROI shows how much profit in accounting terms has been made in relation to the amount of capital invested. For example, suppose that a company has two investment centres A and B, which show results for the year as follows:

	A	B
	£	£
Profit after depreciation, before tax and interest	60,000	30,000
Assets generating income	400,000	120,000
ROI	15%	25%

Investment centre A has made double the profits of investment centre B, and in terms of profits alone has therefore been more 'successful'. However, B has earned a much higher ROI. This suggests that B has been a more successful investment than A.

4.5 The main reasons for the widespread use as a measure of ROI as a performance indicator are these.

(a) **Financial reporting**. It ties in directly with the accounting process, and is identifiable from the profit and loss account and balance sheet, the firm's most important communications media with investors.

(b) **Aggregation.** ROI is a very convenient method of measuring the performance for a division or company as an entire unit.

Measurement problems: fixed assets

4.6 The problems with ROI relate to accurate measurement.

Net assets

4.7 It is probably most common to use **return on net assets**. There are two main problems.

(a) If an investment centre maintains the same annual profit, and keeps the same assets without a policy of regular fixed asset replacement, its ROI will increase year by year as the assets get older. This can give a false impression of improving 'real' performance over time.

(b) It is not easy to **compare fairly** the performance of one investment centre with another. Fixed assets may be of different ages or may be depreciated in different ways.

Return on gross assets

4.8 (a) **Advantage.** Ignoring depreciation removes the problem of ROI increasing over time as fixed assets get older and get depreciated.

(b) **Disadvantages.**

(i) Measuring ROI as return on gross assets ignores the **age factor**. Older fixed assets usually cost more to repair and maintain. An investment centre with old assets may therefore have its profitability reduced by repair costs.

(ii) **Inflation and technological change** alter the cost of fixed assets. If one investment centre has fixed assets bought ten years ago with a gross cost of £1 million, and another investment centre, in the same area of business operations, has fixed assets bought very recently for £1 million, the quantity and technological character of the fixed assets of the two investment centres are likely to be very different.

ROI: replacement cost

4.9 The view that ROI should be measured in terms of **replacement cost** (either net or gross) is connected to the arguments in favour of **current cost accounting**. In a period of price inflation, ROI based on historical costs is difficult to interpret because it will become higher as assets get older, by virtue of the fact that profits will be measured in current-year money.

Measurement problems: what are 'assets' anyway?

4.10 Prudence and other accounting principles require that items such as research and development should only be carried forward as an investment in special circumstances.

4.11 Many 'costs' do have the effect of enhancing the long-term revenue-earning capacity of the business. A good example is **brands**: many firms have capitalised brands for this reason. For decision-making and control purposes, the expenditure on brands might be better treated as an investment.

The target return for a group of companies

4.12 If a group of companies sets a target return for the group as a whole, or if a company sets a target return for each SBU, it might be company policy that no investment project should go ahead in any subsidiary or investment centre unless the project promises to earn at least the target return. For example, it might be group policy that:

(a) There should be no new investment by any subsidiary in the group unless it is expected to earn at least a 15% return;

(b) Similarly, no fixed asset should be disposed of if the asset is currently earning a return in excess of 15% of its disposal value;

(c) Investments which promise a return of 15% or more ought to be undertaken.

4.13 Problems with such a policy are these.

(a) Investments are appraised by DCF whereas actual performance will probably be measured on the basis of ROI.

(b) The target return makes no allowance for the different risk of each investment centre.

(c) In a conglomerate an identical target return may be unsuitable to many businesses in a group.

Example: the problem with setting a target ROI

4.14 Suppose that an investment in a fixed asset would cost £100,000 and make a profit of £11,000 pa after depreciation. The asset would be depreciated by £25,000 pa for four years. It is group policy that investments must show a minimum return of 15%.

4.15 The DCF net present value of this investment would just about be positive, and so the investment ought to be approved if group policy is adhered to.

Year	Cash flow (profit before dep'n)	Discount factor at 15%		Present value
	£			£
0	(100,000)	1.000		(100,000)
1	36,000	0.870		31,320
2	36,000	0.756		27,216
3	36,000	0.658		23,688
4	36,000	0.572		20,592
			NPV	2,816

4.16 However, if the investment is measured year by year according to the accounting ROI it has earned, we find that its return is less than 15% in year 1, but more than 15% in years 2, 3 and 4.

Year	Profit	Net book value of equipment (mid-year value)	ROCE
	£	£	
1	11,000	87,500	12.6%
2	11,000	62,500	17.6%
3	11,000	37,500	29.3%
4	11,000	12,500	88.0%

4.17 In view of the low accounting ROI in year 1, should the investment be undertaken or not?

(a) Strictly speaking, investment decisions should be based on IRR, and should not be guided by short term accounting ROI.

(b) Even if accounting ROI is used as a guideline for investment decisions, ROI should be looked at over the full life of the investment, not just in the short term. In the short term (in the first year or so of a project's life) the accounting ROI is likely to be low because the net book value of the asset will still be high.

4.18 In our example, it is conceivable that the group's management might disapprove of the project because of its low accounting ROI in year 1. This approach is short-termist, but it nevertheless can make some sense to a company or group of companies which has to show a satisfactory profit and ROI in its published accounts each year, to keep its shareholders satisfied with performance.

Possible behavioural implications of ROI: short-termism and lack of goal congruence

4.19 Since managers will be judged on the basis of the ROI that their centre earns each year, they are likely to be motivated into taking those decisions which increase their centre's short-term ROI. An investment might be desirable from the group's point of view, but would not be in the individual investment centre's 'best interest' to undertake. Thus there is a lack of **goal congruence**.

4.20 In the short term, a desire to increase ROI might lead to projects being taken on without due regard to their risk.

4.21 Any decisions which benefit the company in the long term but which reduce the ROI in the immediate short term would reflect badly on the manager's reported performance.

Question 3

Describe any methods you can think of (and their implications) which managers would use to 'fiddle' the return on investment figures, if ROI was calculated as:

$$\text{Return on total assets} = \frac{\text{Profit before interest, tax, depreciation}}{\text{Gross fixed assets + total current assets}}$$

Answer

(a) Keep gross assets to a minimum

    (i) Avoid capital expenditure

    (ii) Acquire all assets on operating leases

(b) Manipulate current assets

    (i) Factor debtors (ie sell the debts)

    (ii) Introduce over-generous settlement discounts, set not by the prevailing interest rate (the true cost) but by divisional ROI targets to encourage early payment.

    (iii) Sell all stocks before the balance sheet date and repurchase them immediately after.

    (iv) Refuse credit.

(c) Manipulate the return by investing in projects with higher long-term risk even if they offered better short-term profits.

Compare these measures to the balanced scorecard: clearly they cause dysfunctional behaviour in customer relations and in internal processes (stock management). Too much effort is devoted to fiddling the books, not improving the business.

(Note. This exercise is based on an example cited by Ward in Strategic Management Accounting.)

ROI, strategy and product-market issues

ROI reflects organisation structure, not business processes

4.22 ROI is based on the existing organisation structure of a business.

(a) Business process re-engineering suggests that many organisation structures are badly designed in themselves.

(b) The use of ROI in a responsibility accounting framework perpetuates the bad effects of the existing organisation structure.

(c) All investment projects may involve the co-operation of many departments in a business, along the whole extent of the value chain.

Product life cycle: ROI is not suitable to all phases

4.23 Product-market issues are also relevant. ROI is suited to the **mature phase**, when the market is established. ROI is also best suited to cash cows on the BCG matrix.

ROI aggregates all products in a portfolio

4.24 We have seen that many firms have a **portfolio of products** in different stages of the life cycle - in fact this is necessary for the firm's long term survival. ROI does not suggest the right strategic action to be taken with regard to new products or declining products, rising stars, question marks or dogs.

5 DIVISIONAL PERFORMANCE: RESIDUAL INCOME (RI)   Pilot Paper

5.1 An alternative way of measuring the performance of an investment centre, instead of using ROI, is residual income (RI).

> **KEY TERM**
>
> **Residual income** is a measure of the centre's profits after deducting a notional or imputed interest cost.

5.2 The imputed cost of capital might be the organisation's cost of borrowing or its weighted average cost of capital. Alternatively, the cost of capital can be adjusted to allow for the risk characteristics of each investment centre, with a higher imputed interest rate being applied to higher risk centres.

The advantages and weaknesses of RI compared with ROI

5.3 The **advantages of using RI** are as follows.

(a) Residual income will increase when:

- Investments earning above the cost of capital are undertaken
- Investments earning below the cost of capital are eliminated

(b) Residual income is more flexible since a different cost of capital can be applied to investments with different risk characteristics.

5.4 The weakness of RI is that it does not facilitate comparisons between investment centres nor does it relate the size of a centre's income to the size of the investment, other than indirectly through the interest charge.

RI versus ROI: marginally profitable investments

5.5 Residual income will increase if a new investment is undertaken which earns a profit in excess of the imputed interest charge on the value of the asset acquired. When a manager is judged by ROI, a marginally profitable investment would be less likely to be undertaken because it would reduce the average ROI earned by the centre as a whole.

5.6 Residual income does not always point to the right decision, because notional interest on accounting capital employed is not the same as IRR on cash investment. However, residual income is more likely than ROI to improve when managers make correct investment/divestment decisions, and so is probably a 'safer' basis than ROI on which to measure performance.

Example: ROI versus residual income

5.7 Suppose that Department H has the following profit, assets employed and an imputed interest charge of 12% on operating assets.

	Department H	
	£	£
Operating profit	30,000	
Operating assets		100,000
Imputed interest (12%)	12,000	
Return on investment		30%
Residual income	18,000	

5.8 Suppose now that an additional investment of £10,000 is proposed, which will increase operating income in Department H by £1,400. The effect of the investment would be:

	£	£
Total operating income	31,400	
Total operating assets		110,000
Imputed interest (12%)	13,200	
Return on investment		28.5%
Residual income	18,200	

5.9 If the Department H manager is made responsible for the department's performance, he would resist the new investment if he were to be judged on ROI, but would welcome the investment if he were judged according to RI, since there would be a marginal increase of £200 in residual income from the investment, but a fall of 1.5% in ROI.

5.10 The marginal investment offers a return of 14% (£1,400 on an investment of £10,000) which is above the 'cut-off rate' of 12%. Since the original return on investment was 30%, the marginal investment will reduce the overall divisional performance. Indeed, any marginal investment offering an accounting rate of return of less than 30% in the year would reduce the overall performance.

5.11 Residual income should not be used as a means of making asset purchasing decisions; nevertheless, it may be a useful alternative to ROI where there is a conflict between purchase decisions indicated by a positive NPV in discounted cash flow, and the resulting reduction in divisional ROI which 'reflects badly' on management performance.

NPV, residual income, and annuity depreciation

5.12 Another approach to measuring divisional performance, which attempts to achieve consistency with the NPV rule, is to treat divisions as lessees of assets owned by head office. For each asset that it uses, the division will receive an annual **finance lease charge** for the life of the asset, which is calculated from:

- The cost/estimated residual value of the asset
- The asset's expected life
- A target cost of capital for the division

6   COMPARING PROFIT CENTRE PERFORMANCE

6.1 When departments within an organisation are set up as profit centres, their performance will be judged on the profit they earn. The performance of profit centres might be compared on the basis of profit/sales ratios, contribution earned per unit of scarce resource, or profit growth rates.

Dysfunctional decisions and goal congruence

6.2 A profit centre manager might take decisions that will improve his own centre's performance at the expense of other parts of the business.

- Profit centre managers tend to put their own profit performance above everything else.

- Profit centres are not isolated entities, but related divisions within a single organisation.

Question 4

What are the likely behavioural consequences of a head office continually imposing its own decisions on divisions?

Answer

Decentralisation recognises that those closest to a job are the best equipped to say how it should be done and that people tend to perform to a higher standard if they are given responsibility. Centrally imposed decisions are likely to make managers feel that they do not really have any authority and therefore that they cannot be held responsible for performance. They will therefore make less effort to perform well.

Comparing profit centre performance

6.3 Shillinglaw (1957) suggested that four profit concepts could be used to measure and report divisional profit internally within a company. Each has its own purpose.

(a) **Contribution**

(b) '**Controllable profit**' - contribution minus all the division's fixed costs controllable by the manager.

(c) **Controllable margin** - controllable profit minus all other costs directly traceable to the division.

(d) **Net profit or net contribution**, less a share of service centre costs and general management overhead. However, 'net profit' is the least useful of the four, because the allocation of general overhead costs must inevitably be largely arbitrary.

Contribution

6.4   A principle of responsibility accounting is that profit centre managers should only be held accountable for those revenues and costs that they are in a position to control. Increases in production volume, within the relevant range of output, will raise profit by the amount of increase in contribution.

6.5   A divisional performance statement based on contribution might appear as follows.

	Division A £'000	Division B £'000	Total £'000
Sales	80	100	180
Less variable costs	60	50	110
Contribution	20	50	70
Less fixed costs			50
Profit			20

(a)   Divisional performance can be improved by increasing the sales price, or volume of sales, or reducing the unit variable cost.

(b)   The relative profitability of divisions A and B could be compared by means of their C/S ratios (in this example, 25% and 50% respectively).

(c)   If there is a production limiting factor, performance could also be measured in terms of contribution per unit of limiting factor. In our example, if there is a shortage of cash for working capital acting as a restriction on output, and if divisions A and B use £2,500 and £8,000 in working capital respectively, the contribution per £1 of working capital employed would be £8 for division A and £6.25 for division B (so that a transfer of some production resources from B to A might be profitable under these circumstances).

Controllable profit

6.6   One drawback to using contribution alone as a measure of divisional performance is that although it indicates the short-term controllable results of the division, it gives no indication as **to longer-term underlying profitability**.

6.7   In the following example, closure of division X might be justified, since there would be a net saving in annual running costs of £5,000.

	Division X £'000	Division Y £'000	Total £'000
Sales	70	120	190
Less variable costs	50	80	130
Contribution	20	40	60
Less directly attributable fixed costs	25	25	50
Profit of the division	(5)	15	10
Less fixed costs (general)			8
Company profit			2

Controllable margin

6.8   A further refinement of this approach to profit centre accounting is to make a distinction between fixed costs over which the centre manager has short-run discretionary control, for example advertising costs and sales promotion expenditures, and fixed costs over which the manager has no personal control, such as his own salary, or depreciation of assets.

		Division X	Division Y	Total
		£'000	£'000	£'000
	Sales	70	120	190
	Less variable costs	50	80	130
(1)	Contribution	20	40	60
	Less fixed costs directly attributable to the manager's discretionary control	8	20	28
(2)	Profit attributable to the manager	12	20	32
	Less fixed costs directly attributable to the profit centre, outside the manager's control	17	5	22
(3)	Profit attributable to the profit centre	(5)	15	10
	Shared fixed costs			8
	Company profit			2

Net profit: after charging a proportion of shared fixed costs

6.9 An argument against measuring profit on the basis of contribution less directly attributable fixed costs is that no one is made responsible for earning a sufficiently large profit to ensure that shared fixed costs are covered, and that the organisation as a whole is profitable.

The problems of absorption costing

6.10 Absorption costing systems are perhaps the 'traditional' method of accounting for divisional performance, but they have some serious drawbacks.

(a) **They are not a method of responsibility accounting**, in that managers cannot control the general fixed costs charged to their division, and are not properly responsible for them.

(b) **The method of apportioning fixed costs can vary**, according to the basis chosen.

Residual income and interdepartmental comparisons

6.11 With a residual income method of reporting divisional profits, four different 'profit' figures can be identified, as follows. It is quite possible that divisions will do better or worse, in comparative terms, according to which measure is used.

			Division A
		£'000	£'000
	Sales: external		310
	internal transfers		210
			520
	Variable costs of goods sold internally and externally	220	
	Variable divisional expenses	20	
			240
(1)	**Controllable contribution**		280
	Controllable divisional overhead		90
(2)	**Controllable profit**		190
	Depreciation and other expenses on controllable fixed assets (eg lease costs)	50	
	Interest on controllable fixed assets	15	
			65
(3)	**Controllable residual income**		125
	Depreciation and other expenses on non-controllable fixed assets	20	
	Allocated central expenses	40	
	Interest on non-controllable fixed assets	10	
			70
(4)	**Net residual income**		55

Head office as a profit centre or investment centre: charging for services

6.12 One way of improving the responsibility accounting system might be to establish head office as a profit centre or investment centre in its own right.

Service departments

6.13 Just as it is important in measuring production performance to distinguish between fixed and variable costs, between directly attributable costs and shared general overheads and between controllable and uncontrollable costs, so too should these distinctions be made for service department costs.

(a) The department might incur costs that are variable with the volume of activity in the department. Variable costs should be identified, and control reporting should compare actual costs with a flexed budget.

(b) The department's directly attributable fixed costs should be identified, because these are the running costs that would be saved if the department were to be closed down.

Making fixed assets controllable

6.14 Fixed assets are 'controllable' by a divisional manager if he or she has the authority to purchase or dispose of assets. But suppose that a division has fixed assets that are temporarily surplus to requirements. Unless the divisional manager disposes of the asset, which might be inappropriate because the asset might be needed at some time in the future, the division's short term ROI or residual income will be reduced because of the surplus 'controllable' fixed assets. One method, used by some firms, of overcoming this problem of 'controllability' of fixed assets is to establish a head office 'pool' of fixed assets. Divisional managers can obtain fixed assets from this pool when they are needed, and return them when they become surplus to requirements.

Added value

> **KEY TERM**
>
> Although added value can be measured in different ways, the broad concept is that **added value** equals sales minus the costs of materials and bought-in services.

6.15 Managers are then made responsible for the following.

(a) Total value added earned.

(b) The way in which value added is divided between labour costs, fixed asset depreciation, profit.

(c) Value added earned per unit of key resource (per machine hour, say, or direct labour hour).

Division B

	£'000	£'000
Sales		400
Materials	160	
Bought-in services	80	
		240
Value added		160
Direct labour	70	
Indirect labour	50	
Depreciation	30	
		150
Profit		10

7 INTERFIRM COMPARISONS AND PERFORMANCE RATIOS

7.1 Interfirm comparisons are comparisons of the performance of different companies, subsidiaries or investment centres.

The purpose of interfirm comparisons

7.2 (a) One company can compare its performance against another, as part of **competitive analysis or benchmarking**.

   (b) **Senior management** can compare the performance of different subsidiary companies within their group.

   (c) **Investors** can compare different firms in an industry.

   (d) A company's **status** as a potential takeover target, or as a potential takeover threat, can be evaluated.

7.3 A financial comparison between rival public limited companies might cover:

   • The best profits record (ROI, growth in profits and EPS)
   • The best financial structure (financial gearing, debt ratio, interest cover)
   • The 'best quality' profits or best growth prospects (P/E ratio comparison)
   • The best cash flow position

Which firms should be compared with each other?

7.4 It is unrealistic to assume that all firms ought to be able to earn comparable ROI.

   • Some industries are more profitable than others
   • Some companies need a big investment in fixed assets

Schemes of interfirm comparison

7.5 There are occasional exercises to operate a scheme of interfirm comparisons (IFC). These schemes are operated by an independent body or a trade association.

7.6 There are a number of basic requirements before an IFC scheme will be successful.

   (a) Reports might be given in the form of lists of **ratios**. If ratios are to be helpful for control purposes, comparisons should be limited to companies of roughly the same size.

   (b) The companies compared must all belong to a **similar industry** to enable comparison.

(c) The results of each of the participants must be adjusted so that, as far as possible, the same **accounting policies** are used for each.

Uniform costing

7.7 **Uniform costing** takes a scheme of interfirm comparison even further. It is the use by several undertakings of the same costing systems, ie the same basic costing methods, principles and techniques.

7.8 An accurate comparison is only possible where companies in the scheme use the same accounting bases and conventions, and establish broadly similar cost systems. All of the companies must do the following.

- Value materials by the same method (eg LIFO/FIFO; absorption marginal costing)

- Classify fixed and variable costs in the same way (eg direct labour)

- Classify direct and indirect costs in the same way (eg treatment of overtime)

- Value assets in the same way; and use exactly the same depreciation method and estimated life of fixed assets

- Establish similar cost centres for allocating cost

- Apportion overheads on a similar basis

- Use the same absorption bases

Performance ratios

7.9 Ratios are useful in that they provide a means of comparison of actual results:

- With a budget, or desired target
- With ratios of previous years' results, in order to detect trends
- With ratios of other companies or divisions
- With industry or governmental indices.

Ratios from financial statements

7.10 You should be familiar with the principal balance sheet and P & L account ratios.

(a) **Profit and loss account ratios** include profit margin (profit/sales) which can be analysed as follows, in a hierarchy of subsidiary ratios.

(i) $\dfrac{\text{Production cost of sales}}{\text{Sales}}$ which can be broken down into:

(1) $\dfrac{\text{Material costs}}{\text{sales value of production}}$ or $\dfrac{\text{Material costs}}{\text{total costs of production}}$

(2) $\dfrac{\text{Works labour cost}}{\text{sales value of production}}$ or $\dfrac{\text{Labour costs}}{\text{total cost of production}}$

(3) $\dfrac{\text{Production overheads}}{\text{sales value of production}}$ or $\dfrac{\text{Production overheads}}{\text{total costs of production}}$

(ii) $\dfrac{\text{Distribution and marketing costs}}{\text{Sales}}$

(iii) $\dfrac{\text{Administrative costs}}{\text{Sales}}$

(b) **Balance sheet ratios** include the following, broken down further.

    (i)   **Asset turnover** (sales/capital employed), which can be analysed by class of asset (eg sales/fixed assets).

    (ii)   **Working capital ratios** covering liquidity (eg current ratio, current assets/current liabilities) and turnover periods for debtors, creditors and stock (eg credit period taken by debtors).

    (iii) Gearing ratios covering borrowings.

Question 6

What might be the strategic significance of the following, when compared to the industry average?

(a) A high fixed asset turnover.
(b) High gearing
(c) Far higher fixed assets but lower labour costs.

Answer

(a) The firm is using capital efficiently - or is operating at high capacity.

(b) The firm has to reach a high profit level to pay its lenders - it might have less flexibility in pricing than competitors.

(c) This might imply that the firm is more capital-intensive, in other words that perhaps it has invested in technology rather than labour. Given the high level of fixed costs which can be deduced from this, the firm might have to price aggressively to maintain market share.

Question 7

Calculate and compare the ROI, asset utilisation and profitability of the two subsidiaries whose results are shown below.

	A Ltd £	B Ltd £
Capital employed	300,000	800,000
Net profit	60,000	120,000
Sales	1,250,000	2,400,000

Answer

	A Ltd		B Ltd	
ROI	$\dfrac{\pounds 60,000}{\pounds 300,000}$	$\times 100\%$	$\dfrac{\pounds 120,000}{\pounds 800,000}$	$\times 100\%$
	$= 20\%$		$= 15\%$	
Asset turnover	$\dfrac{\pounds 1,250,000}{\pounds 300,000}$		$\dfrac{\pounds 2,400,000}{\pounds 800,000}$	
	$= 4.17$ times		$= 3$ times	
Profit/sales ratio	$\dfrac{\pounds 60,000}{\pounds 1,250,000}$	$\times 100\%$	$\dfrac{\pounds 120,000}{\pounds 2,400,000}$	$\times 100\%$
	$= 4.8\%$		$= 5\%$	

A Ltd has a higher ROI than B Ltd. This is because, although it earned a lower net profit per £1 of sales (4.8p compared with 5p) its capital employed generated more sales turnover, and its asset turnover was nearly 40% higher, at 4.17 times compared with 3 times for B Ltd.

The calculation of return on investment in interfirm comparisons

7.11 There are several issues to consider when deciding how to measure both the return and the capital employed.

Return

7.12 **Definition of return**. Return might be taken as profit after tax. However, when interfirm comparisons are being made, this would be unsuitable, for two reasons.

(a) The **tax rate** applicable to one company's profits may be different from the tax rate applicable to another's.

(b) One company might be financed largely by borrowing, receiving tax relief on interest payments. Another company might be entirely equity financed.

7.13 **Measuring return (profit)**. When there is a comparison between the results of subsidiaries within the same group or the results of investment centres within a single company, there may be a problem with **transfer prices**.

Capital employed/investment

7.14 Should assets be valued on the basis of historical cost, replacement cost, disposal value, current value or some other similar inflation-adjusted basis?

(a) Historical cost has the severe drawback that in a period of inflation, the balance sheet value of older fixed assets can fall below their 'realistic' current value, and so the measurement of ROI will give a misleading (excessively high) percentage return.

(b) Depreciation charges against fixed assets might also fail to reflect the loss of value from using the assets during the period, when historical cost accounting is used.

(c) Replacement cost or current cost might be difficult to estimate whereas historical cost is a readily-known value.

(d) Disposal value is only useful when the fixed assets are readily marketable (eg property) but in such cases a target return on disposal value represents an opportunity cost of the investment.

The accounting policies of different companies

7.15 Typical differences in accounting policies and asset acquisition methods between one firm and another are these.

- The assumed life of fixed assets
- The method of depreciation used
- Accounting for intangible fixed assets, such as development costs and goodwill
- Stock valuation methods
- Renting accommodation instead of buying the freehold or leasehold
- Purchasing operating fixed assets or leasing/renting them

8   INFLATION

8.1 When an organisation prepares its strategic plans, it will probably build some assumptions about the rate of inflation into the plan itself.

The consequences of inflation

8.2 The problem for performance measurement is to decide what the actual effect of inflation has been, how this compares with the plan, and what significance this might have for performance measures and control action.

(a) If a company operates in a competitive market, where customers resist price increases, it may be unable to pass on all its cost increases to the customer, and so the effect of inflation would be to reduce its profitability.

(b) If a company exports goods overseas, domestic price inflation will push up the cost of its goods to foreign buyers unless the exchange rate were to fall to compensate for the rate of inflation.

Controlling inflation

8.3 Inflationary pressures on costs ought to be kept as much under control as possible.

• Given anticipated material cost increases is there scope through exercising 'buyer power' over suppliers to keep them below the rate of inflation?

• Is the material being effectively used?

• Labour pay agreements should be competitive but kept as low as possible.

• Labour efficiency must match the competition.

• Expenses should be rigorously controlled.

• The timing of price increases should be monitored carefully.

Performance measurement and inflation

8.4 You should already know the argument that a major problem with the historical cost convention is that it can report that an organisation is making a profit, when it has in fact suffered a fall in its operating capacity. In other words, inflation can conceal poor performance.

8.5 There are five consequences of historical cost accounting which, because of price inflation, reduce the reliability of the information given in company accounts.

• Fixed asset values and depreciation.

• Cost of sales.

• Increase in working capital needed to support normal trading operations.

• Borrowing benefits.

• Comparability of figures from year to year (and also between one company and another).

Fixed asset values and depreciation

8.6 Using the historical cost accounting convention, a company might have assets in its balance sheet valued on the basis of costs dating back 5, 10, 20, 30, or even 40 years or more. The costs of these assets would not be comparable with each other, partly because of technological developments over time, but largely because of inflation.

BPP PUBLISHING

8.7 A numerical example might help to reinforce this point.

Suppose that Costin Moore Ltd has three identical items of machinery in operation, bought on 30 June 20X0, 20X4, and 20X8 respectively. 'Now' is 30 June 20X9. Because of inflation, the cost of each item was different, as follows.

Year of purchase	Purchase cost £
20X0	20,000
20X4	28,000
20X8	33,000

The equipment is depreciated to a nil residual value over 10 years at 10% (straight line) each year.

8.8 At 30 June 20X9, the balance sheet values of the equipment would be as follows.

	Bought in 20X0 (9 years old) £	Bought in 20X4 (5 years old) £	Bought in 20X8 (1 year old) £	Total £
At cost	20,000	28,000	33,000	81,000
Accumulated depreciation	18,000	14,000	3,300	35,300
Net book value	2,000	14,000	29,700	45,700

8.9 This example should suggest the following.

(a) The balance sheet net book value of a fixed asset is dependent on two factors

- Its economic life already used up
- The purchase cost, which in turn is dependent on price inflation over time

(b) The depreciation charge in the profit and loss account, because it is a function of the historical purchase price, is also dependent on price inflation over time. In our example, the depreciation charge per identical asset ranges from £2,000 to £3,300.

8.10 It is also worth asking yourself whether you think that the net book value of the three assets together, £45,700, has any real meaning to a reader of the company's accounts. In other words, does a statement of assets at cost less accumulated depreciation have any significance when cost is variable according to when the individual assets were acquired?

8.11 Most companies now recognise the need to state some fixed assets at a 'realistic' current value in their balance sheet, land and buildings in particular. It is therefore quite common for land and buildings to be revalued every one, two or three years or so, and stated in the balance sheet at the revalued amount.

The cost of sales and inflation

8.12 When the rate of inflation is low and stock turnover is quite fast, the historical cost of sale and the replacement cost of sale will be much the same, and so there is unlikely to be a serious problem. However, in the past, when the rate of inflation has been much higher, companies with a slow-ish stock turnover would have recorded a quite significantly higher profit using historical costs to value their cost of sales than if they had, more prudently, used the replacement cost of sales.

The need for working capital

8.13   In a period of inflation, companies need more working capital to finance their stocks and debtors. For example, suppose that a company has a stock turnover period of three months, a debt collection period of three months, and takes two months credit from suppliers. In 20X7 goods cost £12 per unit and were resold for £15 per unit: 10,000 units were sold in the year.

In 20X8, 10,000 units were sold again, but the cost of goods had risen to £14 and selling prices to £18 per unit. The working capital needed to support annual sales of 10,000 units would therefore rise between 20X7 and 20X8, as follows.

		20X7		*20X8*
		£		£
Stocks	(2,500 units × £12)	30,000	(2,500 units × £14)	35,000
Debtors	(2,500 units × £15)	37,500	(2,500 units × £18)	45,000
		67,500		80,000
Creditors	(10,000 ×2/12 × £12)	20,000	(10,000 × 2/12 × £14)	23,333
		47,500		56,667

8.14   This increase in working capital of £9,167 has to be financed somehow, and an obvious source of funds is profits. If we take profits in 20X8 to be £4 per unit or £40,000 in total, we could see that the increase in working capital the company needs would tie up funds that could have been used for other purposes.

	£
Cash profit in 20X8	40,000
Applied to finance working capital	9,167
Balance: increase in cash, perhaps used to pay a dividend	30,833

8.15   Inflation inevitably means that more working capital will be needed, and this will more often than not be funded out of profits. However, the historical cost accounting convention fails to draw any attention to this point; indeed, it ignores it completely.

Borrowing benefits in a period of inflation

8.16   Just as the historical cost accounting convention tends to overstate operating profit in a period of inflation, so too does it ignore the benefits of borrowing. In a period of inflation, the real value of loans decreases over time, and so a company that borrows will find that time erodes the real value of its balance sheet liabilities.

8.17   For example, if a company were to issue £500,000 of loan stock, repayable after ten years, the real cost of the loan would decline over the ten year period. When the loan stock is eventually redeemed after ten years, £500,000 will have much less purchasing power than when the loan was first raised. So the company would be benefiting at the expense of the loan stock investors.

8.18   Of course, the interest rate charged on loans should be high enough to compensate the investors for the loss in value of their capital - for example, with inflation at 3% pa, interest rates might be at, say, 7%, giving the investors a 'real' return of 4% on their investment. However, the benefit to the company of a decline in the real value of its liabilities is ignored.

Trends: comparability of figures over time

8.19   One method of measuring performance is to look at trends over a period of time; for example, the trend over a number of years in dividend per share, EPS, and sales volume (in

£s). An estimate of whether there has been 'real' growth in dividends, earnings or sales can be made simply by 'taking away' an estimate of the inflationary element in the growth. For example, given the following figures:

	Year		
	1	2	3
Earnings per share	40p	45p	55p
Retail price index	100	105	112

the rate of 'real' growth in EPS could be estimated approximately as follows.

(a) Year 2 compared with Year 1

    (i)   Total increase $\dfrac{45p}{40p} = 1.125$

    (ii)   Increase in RPI $\dfrac{105}{100} = 1.05$

    (iii)   'Real' increase $\dfrac{1.125}{1.05} = 1.071$ - ie 7.1%

(b) Year 3 compared with Year 2

    (i)   Total increase $\dfrac{55p}{45p} = 1.222$

    (ii)   Increase in RPI $\dfrac{112}{105} = 1.067$

    (iii)   'Real' increase $\dfrac{1.222}{1.067} = 1.145$ - ie 14.5%

Ratios for control

8.20 When ratio measurements are used as targets for control, they may be unaffected by inflation, because both sides of the ratio might be equally inflated.

(a) Accounting return on capital employed, ie:

$$\frac{\text{Profit}}{\text{Capital employed}}$$

If both profit and capital employed are equally affected by inflationary increases, the ROI ratio would be unaffected. However, if capital employed is not subject to the same inflationary increases as profit, trends in ROI would be misleading.

(b) Similarly, the profit/sales ratio would be unaffected as a control measure by inflation, provided that profits and sales were equally boosted by inflationary increases.

(c) The same argument would apply to a number of other ratios, such as asset turnover, average debtors' payment period, stock turnover, gearing ratio, and the current ratio etc.

Unity Bicycles plc

(1) What might be the drawbacks of using an ROI-based bonus scheme for Romania and Mexico?

(2) Why do you think the firm should be particularly concerned with cash flows?

(3) How would you go about comparing the performance of the various factories?

Chapter roundup

- There are many ways of measuring the **'financial perspective'** and financial measures are also brought into measuring **operational** performance.

- **Discounted cash flows** can be used to assess the performance of capital investment projects, by comparing anticipated and actual cash flows, discounted in an appropriate way. It is probably a lot harder, although not impossible, to apply these to profit centres.

- **Immaterial variances** are to be expected: **uncontrollable variances** are to be accounted for in the plan.

- Variances may have a variety of **sources**. The process of standard setting is as much a victim of uncertainty as the process of implementing standards by carrying out operations.

- There are several different **models** that may be used for variance investigation, employing a variety of management accounting techniques. In practise, however, managerial judgement is the most important factor.

- An **operational variance** compares actual results with a plan revised in hindsight. A **planning variance** compares the original plan with the revised plan. This may remind you of rolling budgets, but unlike these planning and operational variances keep an eye on the original plan which was, after all, set within the framework of a longer term strategic plan.

- **Profit centre organisation** reflects the structure of authority in the organisation, and managers are made accountable and rewarded on the basis of profit centre results.

- **Return on investment (ROI)** is a convenient measure, which ties in easily with the firm's accounts. However, there are measurement and valuation problems, especially in relation to fixed assets. These can encourage managers to take decisions which are not in the firm's best long-term interest. ROI does not easily account for risk.

- ROI is based on **organisation structure**, not business processes, and is only suitable to products at the mature phase of the life cycle.

- **Residual income** (RI) gets round some of the problems of ROI, by deducting from profit an imputed interest charge for the use of assets.

- **Profit centres** are often compared. Problems arise when managers are judged on matters they cannot control. A variety of measures involving **contribution** are used to isolate controllable costs.

- Problems in measuring **divisional performance** include allocation of head office costs, and different asset valuations.

- As well as comparing profit centres within a group, comparisons are also made between **companies in an industry**. Problems include a lack of information and different accounting polices. As well as monitoring performance from the investor's point of view, such schemes can be used in **competitive analysis. Ratio analysis** might be useful in this context.

- **Inflation** makes it harder to compare performance over time, as it affects accounting values, and hence measures of performance. It affects base line and comparative figures

BPP PUBLISHING

Quick quiz

1 Control of a strategic level should be based on measurements of ....

2 Define 'contribution margin'.

3 What is the main problem associated with ROI as a performance measure?

4 ROI is a form of ROCE

☐ True

☐ False

5 Residual income (RI) is a measure of the centre's profits after deducting a notional or imputed .... cost.

6 What do you understand by the term 'divisional autonomy'?

7 What are 'controllable profit' and 'controllable margin'?

8 Give a broad definition of 'added value'.

9 In what way can inflation conceal poor performance?

10 A division with capital employed of £400,000 currently earns a ROI of 22%. It can make an additional investment of £50,000 for a 5 year life with nil residual value. The average net profit from this investment would be £12,000 after depreciation. The division's cost of capital is 14%. Calculate the residual income before and after the investment.

Answers to quick quiz

1 Cash flows.

2 Contribution margin can be defined as 'the difference between sales volume and the variable cost of those sales, expressed either in absolute terms or as a contribution per unit.'

3 It is mainly to do with the problem of accurate measurement of the value of the assets used to produce the return. For example, it is probably most common to use return on net assets. Inflation and technological change alter the cost of fixed assets, so that it becomes difficult to compare the performance of different divisions.

4 True

5 Interest

6 The term refers to the right of a division to govern itself, that is, the freedom to make decisions without consulting a higher authority first and without interference from a higher body.

7 Controllable profit – contribution minus all the division's fixed costs controllable by the manager.

Controllable margin – controllable profit minus all other costs directly traceable to the division.

8 Added value equals sales minus the costs of materials and bought-in-services

9 An organisation may be making a profit, but have suffered a fall in its operating capacity. Using the historical cost accounting convention, a company might have assets in its balance sheet valued on the basis of costs dating back 5, 10, 20, 30, or even 40 years or more. The costs of these assets would not be comparable with each other, partly because of technological developments over time, but largely because of inflation.

10	Before investment £	After investment £
Divisional profit	88,000	100,000
Imputed interest		
(400,000 × 0.14)	56,000	
(450,000 × 0.14)		63,000
Residual income	32,000	37,000

Unity Bicycles plc review

Question 1. Appraising managers in Romania and Mexico on an ROI basis is not appropriate for the time being.

(a)   The managers had no control over the initial size of the investment. All these decisions are taken by head office.

(b)   They are not genuine divisions or SBUs, in that purchasing is a 'central' function for the group.

(c)   They are still climbing a learning curve, especially in Romania.

Question 2. The firm has to pay loan interest and repay capital for its investment projects.

Question 3. The factories are entirely different, serving different markets, with different levels of fixed assets and different 'cultural' inheritances. Providing they are all contributing to the group as a whole, there would be little point in comparing them at all, other than for operational measures such as quality, for the time being.

Now try the question below from the Exam Question Bank

Question to try	Level	Marks	Time
14	Exam	25	45 mins

Chapter 15

CONTROLLING PERFORMANCE

Topic list	Syllabus reference	Ability required
1 Strategic business units	(v)	Evaluation
2 International subsidiaries	(v)	Evaluation
3 Transfer pricing	(v)	Evaluation
4 Managerial performance: agency theory	(v)	Evaluation
and reward systems	(v)	Evaluation
5 Short versus long term achievement	(v)	Evaluation
6 Achieving success for the shareholder	(v)	Evaluation

Introduction

This final chapter of the Study Text describes some more themes in **controlling performance** with the ultimate aim of increasing **shareholder value**. Many large firms are organised into strategic business units, and multinational firms in particular have specific management problems in relation to setting **objectives** and **performance assessment** (section 2).

Transfer prices (section 3) are a way of promoting divisional autonomy, but the transfer price needs to be fair, neutral and administratively simple. Otherwise, prices may be set in such a way as to improve the results of one subsidiary at the expense of another.

Turning away from the performance of the **managed unit**, in section 4 we look at rewarding **managerial performance** itself. In this section we describe 'agency theory'. A typical plc has a large number of **owners** (or principals) who have no real idea what their **agents** (the directors/managers) are doing.

Rewarding managers for their performance is a method of **control** in the sense that managers will have some **incentive** to achieve the organisation's objectives if they can see a reward (large bonus, share options) at the end of it.

We conclude the chapter with a look at the considerations of **short versus long term** achievement (section 5) and its effect on decisions relating to capital investment, technology and outsourcing.

Section 6 describes some ways of measuring **shareholder value.**

Learning outcomes covered in this chapter

- **Identify** problems in performance measurement and **recommend** solutions
- **Evaluate** performance from different time and stakeholder perspectives
- **Evaluate** the use of shareholder value analysis

Syllabus content covered in this chapter

- Strategic business unit performance: transfer pricing, reward systems and agency theory
- The appraisal and comparison of international subsidiaries
- Short versus long term achievement: research and development, changing technology, outsourcing and capital investment
- The achieving of success for the shareholder: shareholder value analysis and value drivers. The strategic use of shareholder value analysis in resource allocation and rebalancing the portfolio

1 STRATEGIC BUSINESS UNITS

1.1 Many large firms are organised into **strategic business units** (SBUs).

> ## KEY TERM
>
> A **strategic business unit (SBU)** is a 'section, within a larger organisation, which is responsible for planning, developing, producing and marketing its own products or services'. *(CIMA Official Terminology)*
>
> A typical SBU is a division of the organisation 'where the managers have control over their own resources, and discretion over the deployment of resources within specified boundaries' (Ward).

2 INTERNATIONAL SUBSIDIARIES

2.1 The task of setting objectives within a multinational is complex, and several problems must be resolved.

> ## Exam focus point
>
> A question may require consideration of particular difficulties with performance measurement when plant and marketing operations are in various parts of the world.

(a) **Capital structure.** Where foreign subsidiaries are financed partly by loans, the differing rates of interest in each country might affect the relative profitability of subsidiaries.

(b) **Cost structure.** Overseas subsidiaries may have a different operational gearing.

(c) **Accounting policies.** In each country, the subsidiary may adopt a different rate of depreciation so that profits and asset values are not comparable. Profits can be transformed into losses by accounting policies.

(d) **Government policy.** There will be differences in the levels of grants or concessions from the national government and in the rate of taxation and interest.

(e) **Transfer prices** for goods and services between the subsidiaries may be set in such a way as to improve the results of one subsidiary (or head office) at the expense of another (eg if goods are transferred from a subsidiary to head office at cost, the subsidiary will get no profit and the head office will obtain the goods at a low price).

(f) **Workforce.** A justification for expanding into developing countries is to take advantage of lower wages.

(g) **Exchange rate fluctuations** may turn profits into losses and vice versa.

(h) **Risk.** Some overseas operations may be a greater risk than others so that higher returns may be required from them.

(i) **Life cycle.** The same product may be at different stages in its product life cycle in each country, as we have seen.

(j) **Transport.** If a subsidiary in, say, the United Kingdom is performing much worse, and incurring higher unit costs of production than a comparable subsidiary in, say, Germany, it may still be uneconomic to switch production from the United Kingdom to Germany because the extra costs of transport to the UK may exceed the savings in the costs of production.

(k) **Domestic competition.** The market of the overseas subsidiary may face a unique configuration of Porter's five forces.

(l) **Different economic conditions.**

International comparisons

2.2 If the firms or subsidiaries being compared operate in different countries there will be certain problems for performance measurement.

(a) **Realistic standards.** It may be difficult to establish realistic standards for each different country. Performance standards should take account of local conditions, considering local opportunities as well as any restrictions on the activities of an operating unit in a particular country.

(b) **Controllable cash flows.** Care must be taken to determine which cash flows are controllable and to separate these from the cash flows which are outside the control of local management. In particular the distortions caused by local taxation laws should be eliminated.

(c) **Currency conversion.** Considerable friction and difficulty in measuring performance can be caused by the use of inappropriate currency conversion rates.

(d) **Basis for comparison.** Following on from the problem of setting realistic standards of performance, central management must exercise care when attempting to compare performance between the different countries.

Exchange rates and transfer pricing

2.3 The most obvious problem is the exchange rate, but Ward argues that this may not be serious.

(a) A firm which makes an investment in a factory intends to use the factory, not sell it. So whilst changes in exchange rates alter the value of the original investment this does not matter so much in the long term, providing that the subsidiary is making a profit at the same rate, in local terms.

(b) This might seem a rather dangerous assertion; however, it is sometimes asserted that long-term differences in rates of exchange result from inflation.

2.4 In practice many companies have to budget for exchange rate changes which affect their plans. A firm can lock itself into particular exchange rate by hedging or other financing. Jaguar used this when, as an independent British company, most of its sales were in the US. Hedging instruments were used to protect its profits from any fall.

2.5 As well as operational issues, such as the acquisition of funds, hedging contracts etc, there is the obviously vexed problem of performance assessment.

2.6 It might be helpful to illustrate this with a question.

Question 1

Enharmonic Changes Ltd is a company with two European factories: at Sharp in the UK and at Pflatte in Austria. The company is facing overcapacity at Sharp even though it is the most productive plant. The company makes *Andantes*. The relative performance of each factory at rates of £1= 200 Yen and 14 Yen = 1 Austrian Schilling (ASch) is as follows.

		Sharp		*Pflatte*
	£	Yen equiv (200Y: £1)	Austrian Schillings	Yen equiv (14Y: 1 ASch)
Selling price	100	20,000	2,000	28,000
Cost of production	75	15,000	1,600	22,400
Gross profit	25	5,000	400	5,600
Margin		25%		20%

In Japanese Yen terms, the UK factory has a higher margin, but the actual profits from making and selling andantes in Austria are higher than in the UK.

(a) However, given the overcapacity in the UK, and given transportation cost at £10 per andante from the UK to Austria, should the UK factory be used as a sole source for the Austrian plant? Assume that the Pflatte pays Sharp in sterling for the andantes. Assume that profits are remitted to Japan to Austrian Shillings. Assume the £: Yen and ASch: Yen relationships are as above, but that £: ASch rates are as follows

(i) £1 = 20 ASch.
(ii) £1 = 15 ASch.

(b) What would be the position if Andantes were shipped over directly, and Pflatte did *not* pay Sharp any money for the components?

Answer

(a) (i) Pflatte sources from the UK (£1 = 20 ASch)

	£	*Pflatte* ASch	Yen equivalent
Selling price	-	2,000	28,000
Sourcing cost from UK	75 × 20	(1,500)	(21,000)
Transport from UK	10 × 20	(200)	(2,800)
Gross profit margin		300	4,200
Margin			15%

(ii) Pflatte sourcing from the UK (£1 =15 ASch)

	£	ASch	Yen
Selling price (ASch)		2,000	28,000
Sourcing cost from UK	75 × 15	(1,125)	(15,750)
Transport from UK	10 × 15	(150)	(2,100)
Gross profit margin		725	10,150
Margin			36.2%

(b)

	£	ASch	Yen
Revenue	-	2,000	28,000
Cost (UK)	(75)	-	15,000
Transport	(10)	-	2,000
Profit/(loss)	(85)	2,000	11,000

Tutorial note

Further permutations can be tried. For example the relative exchange rates between £ and Yen, and Sch and Yen would also affect the decision. So, even though greater Yen profit is made by Pflatte, the differences in production costs can, at *some* rates of exchange, make it easier for Pflatte merely to sell andantes imported from Sharp. In option (b), no currency changes hands between Pflatte and Sharp, but at prevailing rates of exchange, it is still better for Pflatte to sell andantes made at Sharp than to make them itself.

2.7 There are particular problems in the management of overseas subsidiaries.

(a) How much **control**? There is always a tension between autonomy and centralisation.

(b) **Staffing.** Expatriate managers are often expensive. Housing costs, school fees etc often have to be paid. In addition there are cultural problems in adjusting to the country and the way of doing business.

3 **TRANSFER PRICING** **Pilot paper**

> **KEY TERM**
>
> **Transfer price.** The price at which goods or services are transferred between different units of the same company. If those units are located within different countries, the term *international transfer pricing* is used.
>
> The extent to which the transfer price covers costs and contributes to (internal) profit is a matter of policy. A transfer price may, for example, be based upon marginal cost, full cost, market price or negotiation. Where the transferred products cross national boundaries, the transfer prices used may have to be agreed with the governments of the countries concerned.'
> (CIMA *Official Terminology*)

3.1 Where there are **transfers of goods or services between divisions**, the transfers could be made 'free' to the division receiving the benefit. For example, if a garage and car showroom has two divisions, one for car repairs and servicing and the other for sales, the servicing division will be required to service cars before they are sold. The servicing division could do its work for the car sales division without making any record of the work done. However, unless the cost or value of such work is recorded, management cannot keep a check on the amount of resources (such as labour time) being used up on new car servicing. It is necessary for control purposes that some record of the inter-divisional services should be kept. Inter-divisional work can be given a cost or charge: a **transfer price**.

3.2 Transfer prices are a way of promoting **divisional autonomy**, ideally without prejudicing the measurement of **divisional performance** or discouraging overall **corporate profit maximisation**. The management accountant therefore has to devise a method of transfer pricing which meets three criteria.

- Equity (provides a fair measure of divisional performance)
- Neutrality (avoids the distortion of business decision making)
- Administrative simplicity

3.3 The transfer price should provide an **'artificial' selling price** that enables the transferring division to earn a return for its efforts, and the receiving division to incur a cost for benefits received, and should be set at a level that enables profit centre performance to be measured 'commercially'. This means that the transfer price should be a **fair commercial price**.

Transfer pricing with constant unit variable costs and sales prices

3.4 An ideal transfer price should reflect **opportunity cost**.

3.5 Where a **perfect external market price exists** and unit variable costs and sales prices are constant, the opportunity cost of transfer will be one or other of the following

- External market price
- External market price less savings in selling costs

3.6 *Example: transferring goods at market price*

A company has two profit centres, A and B. Centre A sells half of its output on the open market and transfers the other half to B. Costs and external revenues in a period are as follows.

	A £	B £	Total £
External sales	8,000	24,000	32,000
Costs of production	12,000	10,000	22,000
Company profit			10,000

Required

What are the consequences of setting a transfer price at market price?

3.7 If the transfer price is at market price, A would be happy to sell the output to B for £8,000, which is what A would get by selling it externally.

	A £	A £	B £	B £	Total £
Market sales		8,000		24,000	32,000
Transfer sales		8,000		-	
		16,000		24,000	
Transfer costs	-		8,000		
Own costs	12,000		10,000		22,000
		12,000		18,000	
Profit		4,000		6,000	10,000

3.8 The consequences, therefore, are as follows.

(a) **A earns the same profit** on transfers as on external sales. B must pay a commercial price for transferred goods.

(b) A will be indifferent about selling externally or transferring goods to B because the profit is the same on both types of transaction. B can therefore ask for and obtain as many units as it wants from A.

Adjusted market price

3.9 Internal transfers in practice are often cheaper than external sales, with savings in selling and administration costs, bad debt risks and possibly transport/delivery costs. It would seem reasonable for the buying division to expect a **discount** on the external market price.

3.10 If profit centres are established, however, and unit variable costs and sales prices are constant, there are two possibilities.

(a) Where the supplying division has spare capacity the ideal transfer price will simply be the **standard variable cost of production.**

(b) When there is a scarce production resource, the ideal transfer price will be the variable cost of production plus the contribution forgone by using the scarce resource instead of putting it to its most profitable alternative use.

Cost-based approaches to transfer pricing

3.11 **Cost-based approaches to transfer pricing** are often used in practice, because there is often no external market for the product that is being transferred or because, although there is an external market, it is an imperfect one because there is only limited external demand.

Transfer prices based on full cost

3.12 Under this approach the full standard cost (including fixed overheads absorbed) that is incurred by the supplying division in making the product is charged to the receiving division. If a **full cost plus** approach is used, a profit margin is also included in this transfer price.

3.13 A company has 2 profit centres, A and B. Centre A can only sell half of its maximum output externally because of limited demand. It transfers the other half of its output to B which also faces limited demand. Costs and revenues in a period are as follows.

	A £	B £	Total £
External sales	8,000	24,000	32,000
Costs of production in the division	12,000	10,000	22,000
(Loss)/Profit	(4,000)	14,000	10,000

3.14 If the transfer price is at full cost, A in our example would have 'sales' to B of £6,000 (ie half of its total costs of production). This would be a cost to B, as follows.

	A £	A £	B £	B £	Company as a whole £
Open market sales		8,000		24,000	32,000
Transfer sales		6,000		-	
Total sales, inc transfers		14,000		24,000	
Transfer costs			6,000		
Own costs	12,000		10,000		22,000
Total costs, inc transfers		12,000		16,000	
Profit		2,000		8,000	10,000

The transfer sales of A are self-cancelling with the transfer costs of B so that total profits are unaffected. The transfer price simply spreads the total profit of £10,000 between A and B. Division A makes no profit on its work and using this method, would prefer to sell its output on the open market if it could.

Transfer prices based on full cost plus

3.15 If the transfers are at cost plus a margin of, say, 25%, A's sales to B would be £7,500.

	A £	A £	B £	B £	Total £
Open market sales		8,000		24,000	32,000
Transfer sales		7,500		-	
		15,500		24,000	
Transfer costs			7,500		
Own costs	12,000		10,000		22,000
		12,000		17,500	
Profit		3,500		6,500	10,000

3.16 Compared to a transfer price at cost, A gains some profit at the expense of B. However, A makes a bigger profit on external sales in this case because the profit mark-up of 25% is less than the profit mark-up on open market sales, which is (£8,000 – 6,000)/£6,000 = 33%. The transfer price does not give A fair revenue or charge B a reasonable cost, and so their profit performance is distorted. It would seem to give A an incentive to sell more goods externally and transfer less to B. This may or may not be in the best interests of the company as a whole.

3.17 Division A's total costs of £12,000 will include an element of fixed costs. Half of division A's total costs are transferred to division B. However from the point of view of division B the cost is entirely variable.

3.18 Suppose that the cost per unit to A is £15 and that this includes a fixed element of £6, while division B's own costs are £25 per unit, including a fixed element of £10. The total variable cost is really £9 + £15 = £24, but from division B's point of view the variable cost is £15 + £15 = £30. This means that division B will be unwilling to sell the final product for less than £30, whereas any price above £24 would make a contribution.

Transfer prices based on variable cost

3.19 A variable cost approach entails charging the variable cost that has been incurred by the supplying division to the receiving division. As above, we shall suppose that A's cost per unit is £15, of which £6 is fixed and £9 variable.

	A		B		Company as a whole	
	£	£	£	£	£	£
Market sales		8,000		24,000		32,000
Transfer sales at variable cost		3,600		-		
$\left(\frac{£9}{£15}\times 6,000\right)$						
		11,600		24,000		
Transfer costs		-	3,600			
Own variable costs	7,200		6,000		13,200	
Own fixed costs	4,800		4,000		8,800	
Total costs and transfers		12,000		13,600		22,000
(Loss)/Profit		(400)		10,400		10,000

3.20 The problem is that with a transfer price at variable cost the supplying division does not cover its fixed costs.

Transfer prices based on opportunity costs

3.21 It has been suggested that transfer prices can be set using the following rule.

Transfer price per unit = **standard variable cost** in the producing division plus the opportunity cost to the organisation of supplying the unit internally.

3.22 The opportunity cost will be one of the following.

(a) The maximum **contribution foregone** by the supplying division in transferring internally rather than selling externally

(b) The **contribution foregone** by not using the same facilities in the producing division for their next best alternative use

3.23 (a) If there is no external market for the item being transferred, and no alternative uses for the division's facilities, the transfer price = standard variable cost of production.

(b) If there is an external market for the item being transferred and no alternative use for the facilities, the transfer price = the market price.

Transfer pricing when unit variable costs and sales prices are not constant

3.24 When unit variable costs and/or unit selling prices are not constant there will be a profit-maximising level of output and the ideal transfer price will only be found by careful analysis and sensible negotiation.

(a) The starting point should be to establish the output and sales quantities that will optimise the profits of the company or group as a whole.

(b) The next step is to establish the transfer price at which both profit centres, the supply division and the buying division, would maximise their profits at this company-optimising output level.

(c) There may be a range of prices within which both profit centres can agree on the output level that would maximise their individual profits and the profits of the company as a whole. Any price within the range would then be 'ideal'.

3.25 **Problems in transfer pricing**

(a) If transfer prices are set at **full cost** the transferring division makes no profit.

(b) If **full cost plus** is used the problem is how to set the margin at a level that all parties perceive as being fair.

(c) If **variable cost** is used the transferring division does not cover its fixed costs but two-part prices (the variable cost transfer price plus a fixed annual fee) might be used to overcome this.

(d) Transfer prices based on **standard cost** are fairer than transfer prices based on actual costs because if actual costs are used the transferring division has no incentive to control its costs: it can pass on its inefficiencies to the receiving division.

(e) On the other hand, standards may become out of date so it is advisable to have an agreement to revise them periodically.

Negotiated transfer prices

3.26 When authority is decentralised to the extent that divisional managers negotiate transfer prices with each other, the agreed price may be finalised from a mixture of accounting arithmetic, politics and compromise.

3.27 Inter-departmental disputes about transfer prices are likely to arise and these may need the intervention of head office to settle the problem.

(a) **Head office imposition.** Head office management may impose a price which maximises the profit of the company as a whole.

(b) On the other hand, head office management might restrict its intervention to the task of **keeping negotiations in progress** until a transfer price is eventually settled.

3.28 Where **negotiation** is necessary there should be an understanding of the 'risk/return' profile. Tomkins suggests the following methodology, which head office can apply when mediating in disputes.

(a) **Identify the outer bounds of the transfer price**. In other words, at what transfer price does the buying division end up earning the entire group profit, and at what transfer price does the selling division earn the entire group profit?

(b) **Variability**. At each transfer price, compare each division's expected profits and the variability of the profits.

(c) Incorporate **risk attitudes** in a fair transfer price, so that the profit-share between divisions takes the riskiness of the project into consideration.

4 MANAGERIAL PERFORMANCE: AGENCY THEORY AND REWARD SYSTEMS

4.1 Special attention is required to the problems of segregating managerial performance from the economic performance of the managed unit. The distinction is very important. Horngren provides a good illustration.

> 'The most **skilful divisional manager is often put in charge of the sickest division in an attempt to change its fortunes**. Such an attempt may take years, not months. Furthermore the manager's efforts may merely result in bringing the division up to a minimum acceptable ROI. The division may continue to be a poor profit performer in comparison with other divisions. If top management relied solely on the absolute ROI to judge management, the skilful manager would be foolish to accept such a trouble-shooting assignment.'

4.2 It is difficult to devise performance measures that relate specifically to a manager to judge his or her performance as a manager. As soon as the issue of **ability as a manager** arises it is necessary to **consider him in relation to his area of responsibility**. If we want to know how good a manager is at marketing the only information there is to go on is the marketing performance of his division (which may or may not be traceable to his own efforts).

Uncontrollable factors

4.3 It is generally considered to be unreasonable to assess managers' performance in relation to matters that are beyond their control. Therefore **management performance measures** should **only include those items that are directly controllable by the manager** in question.

4.4 There are different degrees of controllability.

(a) A divisional manager may have no control over the level of head office costs. It may seem unfair that X division, say, is allocated 10% of £1m = £100,000, when it is actually demands made by division Y that caused costs to be that high rather than £500,000 (10% × £500,000 = £50,000).

However, X division does have control over the relative demands it places on head office. If it placed fewer demands perhaps its percentage contribution could fall, say, to 5%.

(b) Likewise a division may not have control over the overall level of a group's interest charge, which will depend on the source of funds and on other division's activities. However, it may have control over its working capital requirements and perhaps over capital expenditure.

Agency theory

4.5 Some accounting researchers have recently borrowed from economic theory the idea that the relationship between 'owners' and 'managers' is an example of an agency relationship. This is really little more than a different way of expressing ideas that will be very familiar to you already.

413

> **KEY TERM**
>
> **Agency theory** 'Hypothesis that attempts to explain elements of organisational behaviour through an understanding of the relationships between principals (such as shareholders) and agents (such as company managers and accountants). A conflict may exist between the actions undertaken by agents in furtherance of their own self-interest, and those required to promote the interests of the principals. Within the hierarchy of firms, the same goal incongruence may arise when divisional managers promote their own self-interest over those of other divisions and of the company generally.'
>
> (CIMA *Official Terminology*)

4.6 It is assumed that the principal forgoes certain benefits that should arise from the relationship (and hence incurs a **residual loss**) because the agent tries to maximise his own 'utility' rather than the principal's. Mathematical models have been developed to determine the magnitude of this 'residual loss'.

4.7 The theory makes certain **assumptions about individuals as agents,** listed in Wilson and Chua, *Managerial Accounting: Method and Meaning* (1993) as follows.

- They behave rationally in seeking to maximise their own utility

- They seek financial and non-financial rewards

- They tend to be risk-averse and, hence, reluctant to innovate

- Their individual interests will not always coincide with those of their principals

- They prefer leisure to hard work

- They have greater knowledge about their operating performance and actions than is available to their principals

4.8 Key issues in agency theory are **attitudes to risk** and the **observability of effort**.

(a) Conventional management accounting assumes that principals protect agents from risk - it only makes managers responsible for things they can control. Agency theory suggests that if principals are risk averse then they should share the risk with agents and this can increase the utility of both parties. Making a large part of an executive's potential reward subject to some profit target is a simple example of such a contract.

(b) The principal may find it difficult to observe the agent's efforts. Alternatively the principal may not be able to evaluate the effort because he does not possess the information on which the decision to expend that much effort was based.

4.9 The **relevance of agency theory to control** issues is made clear in an article in *CIMA Student*, by J G Williams: 'Corporate governance: aims and developments' (February 1996). The point is that a **typical plc has a large number of owners (shareholders) who have no real idea what their agents (the directors) are doing.**

> 'Agency theory gives a clear structure to the problems of a relationship between shareholders (principals) and directors (their agents) where the principals have the problem of motivating and controlling their agents to act in their interest.
>
> - Supervision is impracticable. It is impossible to see what the agents are doing, and what effort they are making.
>
> - The agents have superior knowledge of the situation and potential profits, and the agents may be motivated to act in their own interests rather than those of the shareholders.'

4.10 Many of the assumptions of agency theory are open to question, however. Wilson and Chua describe the **limitations** of agency theory as follows.

> 'Firstly, it is essentially a two-person analysis and, although it may be possible to extend it to a whole hierarchical organization, this has yet to be done. Secondly, it is a single period model which neglects the potential impact of a continuing employment relationship. Finally, the descriptive validity of the utility maximizing assumptions is open to question.'

4.11 In the context of agency theory some writers (including Emmanuel *et al*) refer to the contract between the organisation and the manager, meaning not only the legal employment contract, but the understanding between the two parties that is enforced by the organisation's administrative processes and by the forces of the labour market (how easy it is for managers to move elsewhere and for organisations to find replacements). There are strong **links with transaction cost economics**, described in Chapter 12.

4.12 The relevance of this to the role of the management accountant is that the needs of outsiders to the management team (the shareholders) must be taken into account, especially with regards to any risky decisions which may not yield a satisfactory return.

Possible management performance measures

4.13 In the light of the above the following can be suggested.

(a) **Subjective measures may** be used, for example ranking performance on a scale of 1 to 5. This approach is used in the civil service. It is obviously highly imprecise but if properly done it should avoid the problems that arise when a good manager is hampered by a poor division.

(b) **The judgement of outsiders can** be regarded as a measure of managerial performance. This may be difficult to implement for many companies but the method is used. A company might, for example, design a share option scheme so that directors could only exercise their options if the share price outperformed the FT-SE 100 index over, say, five years.

(c) **Upward appraisal** is used by some businesses. This involves staff giving their opinions on the performance of their managers.

(d) **Accounting measures** can be used, but must be tailored according to what or whom is being judged.

(e) **Non-financial measures** may include market share measurements or a variety of other qualitative criteria.

Reward systems

4.14 **Rewarding managers for their performance is a method of control** in the sense that it is **assumed that attempts will be made to achieve the organisation's objectives in return for rewards.** This, in turn, **derives from motivation theory,** which suggests that people have wants or desired outcomes and modify their behaviour accordingly.

What type of reward?

4.15 Money is not the only type of reward that managers might seek. Emmanuel *et al* cite Vancil's **categorisation of rewards** into three types.

- The **pleasure** that is derived from **managing one's own entity**
- The **power and status** that accompanies the position of being manager
- Rewards in the form of **money** or with **a monetary value**

How to link performance and rewards

4.16   A good reward system should have the following characteristics.

   (a)   It should **offer real incentives**, sufficiently high after tax to make extraordinary effort worthwhile.

   (b)   It should **relate payments to criteria over which the individual has control** (otherwise he will feel helpless to ensure his reward, and the expectancy element in motivation will be lacking).

   (c)   It should **make clear the basis on which payments are calculated**, and all the conditions that apply, so that individuals can make the calculation of whether the reward is worth the extra level of effort;

   (d)   It should be **flexible** enough to reward different levels of achievement in proportion, and with provision for regular review and adaptation to the changing needs of the organisation.

   (e)   It should be **cost effective** for the organisation.

Lower cut-off point

4.17   Emmanuel *et al* suggest that a **linear link** is the most common method of linking performance and reward, but with a lower cut-off point because organisations **do not want mediocre performance to be rewarded.**

Upper cut-off point

4.18   Most schemes also have upper cut-off points, for a variety of reasons.

   (a)   A fear that the **high bonuses that would be paid might not be deserved** because of:

   •   A windfall gain
   •   Increased current period reported profit at the expense of the long term
   •   A faulty plan design (the fear is greatest when the plan is new)

   (b)   A desire **not to encourage unsustainably high growth and profitability.**

   (c)   A desire not to pay lower-level managers more than upper-level managers earn **(vertical compensation equity).**

   (d)   A desire to **keep total compensation consistent over time,** so that managers are able to sustain their lifestyle.

   (e)   A desire to **adhere to standard corporate and industry practices.**

                                                                                                        (Emmanuel et al)

Common types of scheme

4.19   There are three common types of scheme.

   (a)   Under a **profit-related pay scheme**, pay (or part of it) is related to results achieved (performance to defined standards in key tasks, according to plan). A form of **management by objectives** will probably be applied (see Chapter 12).

   (b)   **Profit-sharing schemes** offer managers bonuses, perhaps in the form of shares in the company, related directly to profits.

   (c)   **Group incentive schemes** typically offer a bonus for a group (equally, or proportionately to the earnings or status of individuals) which achieves or exceeds specified targets.

4.20 Incentive and recognition schemes are **increasingly focused not on cash,** but on non-cash awards, such as gifts and travel vouchers. These are cheaper for the organisation, especially as they are regarded as 'won' rather than deserved by right.

4.21 Schemes should of course be **tailored to suit the circumstances.** A bonus scheme for part-time non-executive directors remunerated by fees under contract for a fixed term of years should ensure that they take a longer-term view of the organisation in the interests of shareholders.

Problems with incentive schemes

Short-termism

> ### Exam focus point
>
> There is an implicit assumption in the paragraphs above that short-termism should be avoided if possible. There may be occasions when short termism is to be encouraged, and this could be the topic of an exam question.

4.22 There are a number of problems associated with measures specifically designed to avoid short-termism.

  (a) The link between current expenditure or savings and long-term effect may not be clear.

  (b) There is a danger that over-investment for the future may have such an adverse impact on present performance that the future envisaged is impossible to achieve.

  (c) Incentive schemes for long-term achievements may not motivate since effort and reward are too distant in time from each other (or managers may not think that they will be around that long!).

Problems of measurement

4.23 Clearly the way in which measurements are taken could seriously affect the reward a manager receives. There are three main issues.

  (a) It is **questionable** whether any performance measures or set of measures can provide a **comprehensive assessment** of what a single person achieves for the organisation. There will always be the old chestnut of **lack of goal congruence,** employees being committed to what is measured, rather than the objectives of the organisation.

  (b) Particularly where performance has to be measured by **non financial performance measures** (such as in the public sector), the results are formed from **subjective judgement.**

  (c) It is difficult to **segregate the controllable component** of performance from the uncontrollable component.

Problems of motivation

4.24 Schemes will only work if **rewards** seem both **desirable and achievable.**

  (a) **Money is not the only motivator** - different individuals value different types of reward. Some people may be in a job because it offers 'job for life' security and a pension; although current working practices have made this less common it is still true in areas of the public sector and large 'institutionalised' companies. **Personal objectives** may also be important; public sector nurses or teachers may feel they are following a vocation regardless of the rewards offered.

(b) When an individual's work performance is dependent on work done by other people (and much work involves co-operation and interdependence with others), an **individual bonus scheme is not always effective**, since **individual performance can be impaired by what other people have done.**

(c) There is evidence that the **effectiveness** of incentive schemes **wears off over time**, as acceptable 'norms' of working are re-established.

(d) The **value of a reward may be affected by factors beyond the organisation's control.** For example a reward such as a company car (associated with achieving a certain status) may be so highly taxed that managers do not consider the effort of achieving the reward to be worthwhile.

Particular problems in the public sector

4.25 In addition to the general problems outlined above, performance-related reward schemes in the public sector have particular problems.

(a) **Timescale.** Many projects (for example, environmental programmes) can only be assessed for effectiveness in the longer term.

(b) **The political dimension.** A senior manager in the public sector may be set a goal which is highly undesirable from the point of view of opposition parties: if a change of power is imminent, might the manager later be rewarded for **not** achieving it!

5 SHORT VERSUS LONG TERM ACHIEVEMENT

Is short-termism a problem?

5.1 **Short-termism in current parlance** is used by industrialists who complain about difficulties in raising capital for investment, and by commentators who complain about the UK's record in R&D on the grounds that businesses do not invest for the long term.

5.2 Although short-termism is supposed to have impaired the performance of the UK and the US in relation to Japan and Germany since 1945, there are many factors which are conducive to a nation's competitive success. The UK was in relative decline since 1945 for many reasons. (We discuss the so-called 'competitive advantage of nations in Chapter 6.) There are a whole host of reasons relating to education, demography, marketing, social structure, government policy and industry structure which may cause a relative decline.

5.3 A proper accounting system should encourage **long-term performance assessment**. Companies which are well managed should withstand 'short-termist' views to cut back on such things as marketing and training, although arguably pressure to improve short-term results can lead to an increase in the number of investment projects and innovations undertaken.

Short-termism and capital investment

5.4 In the US and the UK, companies raise money from the stock market, where investors apply for new shares, and buy and sell existing ones. A high share price implies that a firm can raise capital cheaply. Does this encourage short-termism?

5.5 **Investors' needs.** Pension funds acquire stock market investments on behalf of individuals. To do this properly, they cannot risk the pension of their clients. You would expect a fairly cautious attitude to risk, as well as a desire to maximise the return on the investment. Fund managers are judged on overall performance of the shares.

5.6 **Financial reporting.** In the US, firms report on their performance every quarter whereas in the UK firms report only once or twice a year. The financial reporting cycle bears little relation to the underlying business cycle. An investment in advanced manufacturing technology may take a couple of years to put into effect, and there might be a **learning curve** of one or more accounting periods before its benefits are realised.

5.7 **Inflation.** Another reason is that if a return is volatile, the cost of capital will increase, so the **hurdle rates** for assessing investments will rise. The simple reason for this is **inflation**. Inflation creates uncertainties in future returns. Shareholders require a higher real return.

5.8 The experience of the US and the UK, which have capital markets which finance companies in a similar way, have been different. Arguably, the US system of quarterly reporting would encourage an even more short-termist attitude than in the UK. Yet the USA is still the world's most productive economy per capita, and its firms are some of the most innovative in the world (eg in biotechnology, computing and services).

Technology

5.9 Investment in technology often takes a long time to produce a return to the company (and its shareholders). New technology, especially production technology and information technology is changing the way that people do their work.

- Design work (computer-aided design)
- Planning and budgeting (using financial models or spreadsheet models)
- Creating and using a central 'database' of information
- Carrying out calculations
- Communicating via electronic mail
- Showing the progress of a production system
- Controlling production

5.10 The **purpose** of new technology might be the following.

- To reduce operating costs

- To increase flexibility. For example, computer-aided design helps a firm to experiment with more product designs before finally selecting an optimal design

- To improve the quality of a product or service

- To provide better control and integration

- To provide a better means of adding value to the production process

- To provide a new product which meets customer needs better than existing technology

5.11 These purposes are mostly long term in their nature and effects, but will require significant investment in the short term if the organisation is to maintain its innovative capacity.

BPP PUBLISHING

Outsourcing

5.12 This was examined in Chapter 12. It is relevant to the short versus long term debate because it allows the use of facilities on a short term (readily cancelled) basis which could only otherwise be available via the relatively long term investments of permanent employees and the training required. It is a way of **gaining all the benefits of extra capacity without having to find the full cost.**

5.13 A company considering outsourcing must however be careful that it is not overemphasising **short term shareholder concerns** at the expense of the overall **quality** of the company and the **sustainability** of its success in the long term. The correct balance of in house and outsourced service provision must be achieved.

5.14 Elmuti, Kathawala et al identify long term and short term reasons for outsourcing.

(a) **Long term**

- Freeing up resources for other purposes and core competences

- Sharing risks and enabling the organisation to keep up to date and remain adaptable

- Benefits from re-engineering when in-house services are not of a high enough standard

(b) **Short term**

- Increased efficiency

- Reducing the operating costs of supervision and management

- Generating cash by selling assets to an outsourcer

- Can have access to capital funds without supplying capital resources (such as buildings)

5.15 The non availability of resources may lead to outsourcing a service in the short term, but it may be more beneficial in the long term to bring that service back in-house, especially if **fixed costs are imposed** that cannot be avoided by outsourcing.

Performance measurement

5.16 As we have seen in this chapter, there is some evidence to suggest that a bias towards the short term is incorporated in some incentive systems for managers, linking results to performance.

5.17 The incentive systems of 30 UK, US and German companies were examined (in a study by J Cotes et al, Management Accounting Research) to see if there existed any bias towards the short or long term.

(a) In all companies, some measure of **profitability** was a primary corporate objective, measured as return on investment, earnings per share or some equivalent measure.

(b) **Marketing objectives** (eg sales growth, market share) came next, although German and US companies placed greater emphasis on these than UK firms.

5.18 **Short-termist incentive schemes** might include the following.

- **Share options**
- **Bottom line profits** in absolute terms

- **Returns on assets** - easily manipulated
- **Residual income**

5.19 **Long-termist schemes** are based perhaps on marketing/sales objectives, profit margin, and other measures related to **management by objectives**.

5.20 When should short-termism be **encouraged**? One way of answering this question is to be bloody-minded and make a case for **never** encouraging short-termism. A short-term approach may be appropriate in certain circumstances however.

- In **highly uncertain and changeable situations**, for example in the fashion industry

- When a short-term approach is **consistent with long-term goals** (for instance a business may make do with old, inefficient plant, awaiting the availability of a new technology)

- When **stakeholders also take a short-term view**

- When **competitors** do likewise

- Under **financial constraints** or difficulties such as workflow problems or insolvency

- Some organisations have **duties to maintain a certain financial position**

6 ACHIEVING SUCCESS FOR THE SHAREHOLDER   Pilot paper, 5/01, 11/01

Shareholder value

6.1 A management team is required by an **organisation's shareholders** to **maximise the value of their investment** in the organisation and a plethora of performance indicators is used to assess whether or not the management team is fulfilling this duty.

6.2 The majority of these **performance measures** are based on the information contained in the organisation's published accounts. Not only do these indicators often give **conflicting messages**, they can be easily **manipulated** and often provide **misleading** information. Earnings per share, for example, is reduced by capital-building investments in research and development and in marketing.

6.3 What is more, the **financial statements** themselves **do not provide a clear picture of whether or not shareholder value is being created or destroyed**. The **profit and loss account**, for example, indicates the quantity but not the quality of earnings and it does not distinguish between earnings derived from operating assets as opposed to non-operating assets. Moreover, **it ignores the cost of equity financing** and only takes into account the costs of debt financing, thereby penalising organisations which choose a mix of debt and equity finance. Neither does the cashflow statement provide particularly appropriate information. Cashflows can be large and positive if an organisation underspends on maintenance and undertakes little capital investment in an attempt to increase short-term profits at the expense of long-term success. On the other hand, an organisation can have large negative cashflows for several years and still be profitable.

6.4 The use of a **shareholder value approach** to performance measurement involves moving the focus of attention away from simply looking at short-term profits to a **longer-term view of value creation**, the motivation being that it will help the business stay ahead in an increasingly competitive world.

6.5 But what is meant by shareholder value? Quite simply, **shareholder value is in the eye of the shareholder:** different shareholders will value different aspects of performance.

- Financial returns in the short-term
- Short-term capital gains
- Long-term returns or capital gains
- Stability and security
- Achievements in products produced or services provided
- Ethical standards

(It is unlikely that the last two alone make a company valuable to an investor.)

6.6 These factors and others will all be reflected in a company's share price, but stock markets are notoriously fickle and tend to have a short-term outlook.

Shareholder value analysis

6.7 Wider share ownership and more knowledgeable investors are forcing companies to understand the techniques by which their companies are being judged. The terminology **shareholder value** is used widely to describe a range of shareholder focussed performance indicators developed by various consultancies.

6.8 One approach is **shareholder value analysis (SVA)**, devised by Alfred Rappaport (*Creating Shareholder Value*, 1986) and the subject of articles in *Management Accounting*.

KEY TERM

Shareholder value is 'the total return to the shareholders in terms of both dividends and share price growth, calculated as the present value of future free cash flows of the business discounted at the weighted average cost of the capital of the business less the market value of its debt.'   (CIMA *Official Terminology*)

6.9 The value of a corporation can be established by developing a future **cash flow forecast** and converting it into a present value. The total value of the business is then found by taking away the value of any debt and adding any value from external investments. Dividing the result by the number of shares gives the **shareholder value per share**. This technique has been used extensively in acquisition situations and is often known as **cash flow return on investment (CFROI)**.

6.10 Rappaport proposes that this **single figure value** for a business be calculated by **reference to seven 'value drivers'**, which drive the generation of **cash.**

- Sales growth
- Operating margin
- Fixed capital investment
- Working capital investment
- Cash taxes
- The planning period
- The cost of capital

6.11 According to Johnson and Scholes, applying SVA requires a whole new mindset, termed **value management**. Central to this way of thinking is the identification of the cash generators of the business, or **value drivers**, examples of which are listed above. These will be both external and internal. For example, **competitive rivalry** is a major external value driver because of its direct impact on margins.

6.12 All the consultants who have followed Rappaport's ideas work from the same principles.

(a) **Profit** has become discredited as a performance measure.

(b) The traditional cost of capital used in the P & L, interest, is inadequate. A composite measure taking into account the complex **capital structure** of a business is needed.

(c) What really needs to be measured is **how well the business is performing for the shareholders.**

Exam focus point

The November 2001 exam contained a question on using SVA to determine product and service development. The examiner commented on the 'abject lack of understanding of the concept of SVA'.

How does business strategy promote increased shareholder value?

6.13 A diagram helps to show how strategy drives the business towards what is a key objective.

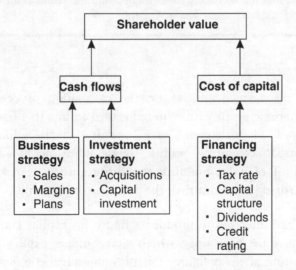

(Adapted from CIMA Insider, March 2001)

Case study link

Managing shareholder value and balancing the short and long term features in the May 2002 case study. The CEO realises that the stores in his charge need to modernise and invest to keep pace with industry developments, but he is also reluctant to cut the dividend. (Maintaining the dividend could mean restrained investment.)

BPP PUBLISHING

Case example

The Kingfisher group has announced that it is demerging its electrical division, in a bid to boost shareholder value by transforming it into a specialist DIY group. Sir Geoff Mulcahy, who is standing down as chief executive, said that the benefits of having a clear and focused DIY management outweighed the benefits of keeping the divisions together. He hopes that a standalone electricals business will be given a better rating by investors.

Case example

'For the last 15 years or so [shareholder value] ... has been the mantra for those who believe that companies should be run for the exclusive benefit of shareholders, with the interest of management aligned to shareholders through the use of stock options and similar equity-linked incentive schemes' (Edward Chancellor, *'Perverse Incentives'*, June 2002).

Chancellor believes that this idea should now come under closer scrutiny in the wake of the Enron collapse and other accounting scandals. Managers have often been guilty of earnings manipulation, inflating the share price and enriching themselves through the exercise of share options at the expense of shareholders. At Global Crossing, the telecoms firm, managers received billions of dollars in stock option profits while investors were left with worthless shares.

The shareholder value doctrine depends upon the efficient market hypothesis, which claims that a company's share price and market value is the same as its intrinsic value. The boom and bust in the 'dotcom' sector shows that shares may sometimes be over or under-valued, at least in the short run. Markets are constantly testing and discarding new ideas, so what may seem like a good idea one day is terrible the next. To quote again from Chancellor, 'Notable examples include the tens of billions of euros spent by European telecoms companies on licences to operate third generation mobile phone systems. Never mind that the technology was untried and the demand for the services unproven, the market was indicating that the money was well spent.'

Economic value management

6.14 Economic value management hinges on the calculation of **economic profit (EP)**. A comparison of economic profit with required return results in a figure for **economic value added or destroyed**. The calculation of EP requires several **adjustments** to be made to traditionally-reported accounting profits. These adjustments are made to **avoid the immediate write-off of value-building expenditure** such as research and development expenditure, advertising expenditure or the purchase of goodwill.

6.15 The adjustments are intended to produce a figure for capital employed which is a more accurate reflection of the **base upon which shareholders expect their returns to accrue** and to provide a profit after tax figure which is a more realistic measure of the **actual cash yield generated** for shareholders from recurring business activities.

6.16 EVA says that in order to add economic value, a project or business unit must deliver more net operating profit, after all taxes and costs, than it costs to have access to the total capital used to generate that profit.

6.17 The principles of EVA, devised by the US consultants Stern Stewart, are:
- Investment leads to assets regardless of accounting treatments
- Assets once created cannot be diminished by accounting action

KEY TERM

Economic value added (EVA) 'A measure which approximates a company's profit. Traditional financial statements are translated into EVA statements by reversing distortions in operating performance created by accounting rules and by charging operating profit for all of the capital employed. For example, written-off goodwill is capitalised, as are extraordinary losses and the present value of operating leases. Extraordinary gains reduce capital.' (CIMA *Official Terminology*)

6.18 Such an approach contrasts favourably with information based on traditional accounting concepts and conventions. The prudence concept, for example, requires revenue expenditure (such as maintenance expenditure on plant and machinery) to be written off to the profit and loss account in the accounting period in which it is incurred. This is to reflect the fact that such expenditure may have no long-term benefits. It is therefore not very surprising that if management are assessed using performance measures calculated using traditional accounting policies, they are unwilling to invest in or spend money on activities which immediately reduce current year's profit.

6.19 It is claimed that EP provides the basis for a useful management performance appraisal measure because **while EP increases, so does the market value added (MVA) for a company and shareholder value.**

6.20 EXAMPLE ON EVA

Recommend which plc, X or Y, to invest funds in. Justify your decision.

Profit and loss account for the previous year (£m's)

	X	Y
Sales	26.0	62.0
Cost of sales	18.0	47.0
Gross profit	8.0	15.0
Production overheads	1.2	2.4
Advertising	0.6	2.0
Depreciation	1.1	1.6
Training	0.1	1.8
R & D	0.6	2.0
Bad debt expense	0.2	0.3
PBIT	4.2	4.9
Investment base	26.5	40.6

6.21 SOLUTION

Traditional ROI techniques would give X plc 15.8% and Y plc 12.1%, and therefore choose X plc for investment. However this ignores the fact that Y is more heavily involved in developing the long term future of its company by spending on training, advertising and R & D. These items, under EVA, would be added back to obtain a comparison using operational expenses.

Adjusted ROI	X	Y
Original profit	4.2	4.9
Training	0.1	1.8
Advertising	0.6	2.0

R & D	0.6	2.0
New profit	5.5	10.7
New ROI	20.8%	26.4%

6.22 There is still a lack of information here to make a final decision, although the original analysis and decision to invest in X plc has been considerably refined. Business risk, market dynamics, previous year's results, competitor comparisons, and investment portfolio issues will all affect the analysis.

6.23 '**Economic value added** is the best indicator of business performance. When it is projected for future years and discounted to the present value, it represents the net present value of all past and future investments and cash flows. Therefore, by making increases in EP a priority, the economic value added of a company will increase, which will, in turn, lead to increases in a company's market value (and therefore its share price).'

(John Mayfield, 'Economic value management: the route to shareholder value',
Management Accounting, September 1997)

Market value added (MVA)

6.24 This is related to EVA, being the net present value created for shareholders over the life of the company.

> **KEY TERMS**
>
> **Market value added** is 'the difference between a company's fair market value, as reflected primarily in its stock price, and the economic book value of capital employed' (Stern Stewart). It is an external measure of how much better off shareholders now are.

6.25 Put another way, it is 'the difference between what investors put into the company as capital and what they could get out by selling at today's market price' (Al Ehrbar). If you look again at the statement on EVA contained in paragraph 6.23, its link with MVA is apparent. **MVA is the present value of all future EVAs**. However, market sentiment will always affect the share price too.

6.26 The difficulty with this measure is that while capital employed (monies invested by shareholders in the company) represents investments made in the **past**, market value is the present value of **future** cash flows. So what does MVA (ie, the difference between these two) really represent? In addition, shareholders are buying and selling shares all the time – there must be as many measures of MVA for a company as there are individual shareholders.

Total shareholder return (TSR)

6.27 Total shareholder return is defined as the **total percentage return to shareholders over a period** using the formula

$$\frac{\text{Dividend per share} + \text{Movement in share price}}{\text{Share price at the start of the period}}$$

6.28 This measure is very simple to calculate, and can be used to compare performance of similar companies. As with MVA, however, it is not immune to market sentiment.

Case example

Nokia, the Finnish mobile phone company, produced a total shareholder return (TSR) of 1,660 per cent over the years 1996-2001, putting it top of a recent FT European performance league table. In late 2000 it commanded 35 per cent of global mobile unit sales.

Characteristics of companies in the league table with high TSRs include:

- Strong management and clear strategy
- Strong communication with investors, customers and staff
- Ability to innovate (in technology, product design, customer service)
- Successful international expansion

Unity Bicycles plc

(1) Comment on the Hong Kong purchasing department's system of charging 10% on supplies transferred to the factories. Is this a suitable method of transfer pricing?

Chapter roundup

- The task of setting objectives within a **multinational** is complex, and several problems must be resolved. For example, setting up systems of **performance measurement** will need to consider:

  ° realistic **standards** country to country
  ° **controllability** of cash flows
  ° **currency conversion**

- **Transfer pricing** is used to encourage optimal performance by keeping track of costs incurred throughout a business. Ideally, prices should be set by reference to the **external market**, but where this is not possible transfer prices will have to be **negotiated**, or head office might **impose** a transfer price.

- **Managerial performance** should be assessed on those items that are directly **controllable** by the manager in question.

- **Agency theory** states that the agents (ie directors and managers) need to be motivated to act in the principals' interest. Making a large part of an executive's potential reward subject to some profit target is a simple example.

- **Rewarding managers** for their performance is a method of **control**, although money is not the only type of reward they may seek. Managers may also look for power, status and responsibility.

- This chapter also looked at the issue of **short termism** as applied to capital investment, technology, outsourcing and performance measurement.

- A management team is required by an **organisation's shareholders** to **maximise the value of their investment** in the organisation and a plethora of performance indicators is used to assess whether or not the management team is fulfilling this duty. This chapter looked at shareholder value analysis (SVA) and economic value added (EVA).

- **Economic value** management hinges in the idea of an **economic profit,** which is derived after adjusting traditional accounting profits for the write offs that are made for **value building expenditures** such as training and advertising. By adding such expenditures back to accounting profit, better comparison can be made between companies.

- **Market value added** (MVA) is the difference between the market value of a company and the economic book value of capital employed.

- **Total shareholder return** (TSR) is the total percentage return to shareholders over a given period.

Quick quiz

1   Profits can be transformed into losses by accounting policies

    ☐   True

    ☐   False

2   How might controllable cash flows vary between international subsidiaries?

3   When setting transfer prices, the management accountant has to devise a method which meets these three criteria:

    ....

    ....

    ....

4   A transfer price should be

(i)   An 'artificial' selling price

(ii) A fair commercial price

A   (i) only

B   (ii) only

C   both (i) and (ii)

D   neither (i) nor (ii)

5   How can the important distinction between managerial performance, and the economic performance of the managed unit, be illustrated?

6   Who is the principal and who is the agent in a company?

7   How can management by objectives be regarded as a system of control?

8   **Fill in the blanks**

A company considering outsourcing must be careful that it is not overemphasising .... shareholder concerns at the expense of the .... of its success in the long term.

9   What are some short term benefits of outsourcing?

10 Define 'shareholder value analysis'.

Answers to quick quiz

1   True

2   Local tax rates may differ

3   Equity or fairness
    Neutrality
    Administrative simplicity

4   C

5   The most skilful divisional manager is often put in charge of the sickest division in an attempt to change its fortunes. Such an attempt may take years, not months.

6   Principal = shareholder
    Agent = manager/director

7   Managers are required to specifically state the objectives that they expect to attain. Actual results can then be measured against these objectives.

8   Short term, sustainability

9   Increased efficiency
    Reducing the operating costs of supervision and management
    Generating cash by selling assets to an outsourcer
    Can have access to capital funds without supplying capital resources (such as buildings)

10 Shareholder value analysis is an approach to financial management which focuses on the creation of economic value for shareholders, as measured by share price performance and flow of dividends.

Unity Bicycles plc review

Question 1. The 10% mark up bears no relation to the total cost of the purchasing function, or the cost of servicing each order. Arguably, its costs should be treated as a corporate overhead.

Now try the questions below from the Exam Question Bank

Question to try	Level	Marks	Time
15	Exam	25	45 mins
17	Pilot paper	50	90 mins

We have analysed the requirements of question 17 in some detail, as it is a detailed case-study scenario which requires careful reading.

Exam question bank

1 STRATEGY AND INFORMATION

30 mins

(a) Distinguish between a strategic planning style, a financial control style and a strategic control style.

(b) What did Anthony mean by strategic planning information, management control information and operational control information?

(c) Describe a strategy to introduce strategic management accountancy into an organisation of your choice.

2 DEVELOPING A STRATEGY

30 mins

Discuss the main issues which need to be addressed in developing a corporate strategy for two of the following.

(a) A bank
(b) A building society
(c) A college
(d) A national charity
(e) A retail store
(f) A local authority

3 DEVELOPMENT AGENCIES

45 mins

A leading manufacturer of personal computers has set up its manufacturing operation in a region of the country which has seen a decline of its traditional industries, lower prosperity and higher unemployment than the rest of the country. Its decision was seen as a success for the Regional Development Agency, which had been hoping to attract such companies to the region.

Requirements

(a) What do you think would be the objectives of a Regional Development Agency (RDA), and how might its objectives and those of a manufacturer of high technology items be expected to coincide in the matter of choosing a location for the European manufacturing base? **10 Marks**

(b) Describe the environmental factors which you think might be influential in encouraging a high-tech manufacturer to locate its operations in an under-developed or declining region, and how the RDA might have tried to exploit these influences. **15 Marks**

Total marks = 25

4 U PLC

45 mins

The management accountant of U plc has evaluated the activities of two of its important competitors. Within their industry the three firms together share some 60% of the market supplying public authorities. It is suggested that the three firms' financial results can be represented as follows.

	Variable costs/ turnover	Operating profit/ turnover	Operating profit/ capital employed
A Limited	40%	10%	22½%
U plc	30%	7½%	15%
Z plc	25%	15%	20%

A Limited is thought to enjoy a 25% share of the market, Z plc some 20% and U plc 15%. It is also significant that U plc's price/earnings ratio is reported as 10.4 whereas shares in Z plc are fetching 17.3 times current earnings. This confirms the directors' belief that U plc's attempts to improve market share by promotional advertising and exhibition activity have been less effective than had been hoped for.

Senior sales personnel have argued that buyers' search costs are such that once a satisfactory vendor rating has been arrived at, it is difficult to persuade authorities to change their suppliers. It has also become apparent that several customers are merely using U plc's fine pricing to prise additional discounts from their regular supplier. This has had the effect of reducing competitors' return on capital employed below what would otherwise be regarded as reasonable.

Alternative marketing strategies have been proposed - one is that U plc should increase its prices in line with competition so that at least 12½% is earned on turnover. If, as is believed, customers will not readily change their suppliers, it is assumed that improved returns will become available to U plc. This would also bring U plc's variable costs' ratio more into line with those of Z plc.

An alternative argument is that U plc is out-of-date in its production procedures and that the difficulties arise mainly because its capital equipment cannot be adapted to product development sufficiently quickly. A Limited may use less capital-intensive production methods but it compensates for this by being able to adapt more readily to changes required by its customers.

Required

(a) Evaluate U plc's existing and the two proposed marketing strategies in terms of the likely effects on the company's financial results. **9 Marks**

(b) Recommend whether an offer by U plc of three of its shares for every two held in Z plc would be in the interest of the present shareholders of U plc. **8 Marks**

(c) Explain what further growth could be reasonably expected by U plc's shareholders were the merger to come about. **8 Marks**

Total marks = 25

5 **MARKETING ORIENTATION** *45 mins*

(a) Organisations which claim to be 'market orientated' attempt to define the nature of the business in which they are operating. Discuss the relevance of such a definition to an organisation which has its objective stated other than in profit terms. **13 Marks**

(b) In what ways does organisational buyer behaviour differ from consumer buyer behaviour?
12 Marks

Total marks = 25

6 **CORPORATE STRATEGY DEVELOPMENT** *30 mins*

In the context of the development of a company's corporate strategy, you are required to explain the composition and function of:

(a) A position audit

(b) A corporate appraisal

7 **CONTRACT CATERING** *45 mins*

Contract caterers are firms which supply food and drink to the employees of 'client firms'. Client firms might prefer to hire contract caterers instead of employing their own in-house catering staff.

The following data describes past trends and current developments in the contract catering industry.

(i) The early growth in contract catering was largely concentrated among companies employing between 100 and 1,500 people, of which there are about 22,000 in the UK. The 'average' current value of a catering contract is about £10,000 pa, which represents the provision of roughly 200 meals a day. About one-third of UK companies employing between 100 and 1,500 people use contract caterers. The rest prefer to provide their own in-house catering.

Organisations employing more than 1,500 people will normally be able to provide in-house catering more cheaply than the cost of contract catering.

(ii) Cook-chill catering has been developing in recent years. This is a process whereby contract caterers cook food in a central production unit and then blast-chill the food. The food is then distributed to the locations where it will be eaten and is regenerated in special ovens which heat the food quickly and without drying. In January 1987, a report by the London Food Commission made some warnings about the safety and quality of blast-chilled food.

(iii) There has been a significant shift over recent years towards consumer preference for vegetarian or other health foods. For example, a survey of students' eating habits found that 18% were either vegetarian or sought to avoid eating meat.

(iv) Crown immunity has been removed from hospitals, so that hospitals may now be liable for prosecution over inadequate hygiene standards in catering, in just the same way as cafes and restaurants in the private sector.

(v) Technological developments in automatic vending machines include vending machines allied to a microwave oven, controlled by a microprocessor, and able to accept plastic cards as payment instead of cash.

(vi) In the City of London, lunch time used to be regarded as the end of the effective working day, and many City managers had long and expensive lunches in City restaurants. Lunchtime has now changed its character, and has become a short break before the opening of the US financial markets.

Required

(a) Using the data given, analyse the threats and opportunities facing the various segments of the contract catering industry, and suggest how contract catering firms may choose to develop their products or markets in response to these opportunities or threats.

20 Marks

(b) Suppose that a client firm of a contract caterer is dissatisfied with the increasing costs of contract catering, and wishes to monitor the costs of the service. Recommend two performance measurements, any one of which might provide a suitable basis for setting a target and monitoring the actual costs of the service.

5 Marks

Total marks = 25

8 **LIFE CYCLES AND PRODUCT MARKET STRATEGY (Pilot Paper)**   *45 mins*

It has been stated that an industry or a market segment within an industry goes through four basic phases of development. These four phases – introduction, growth, maturity and decline – each has an implication for an organisation's development of growth and divestment strategies.

The following brief profiles relate to four commercial organisations, each of which operate in different industries.

- **Company A.** Established in the last year and manufactures state of the art door locks which replace the need for a key with computer image recognition of fingerprint patterns.

- **Company B.** A biotechnological product manufacturer established for three years and engaged in the rapidly expanding animal feedstuffs market.

- **Company C.** A confectionery manufacturer which has been established for many years and is now experiencing low sales growth but high market share in a long established industry.

- **Company D.** A retailing organisation which has been very profitable but is now experiencing a loss of market share with a consequent overall reduction in turnover.

Required

(a) Explain

(i) The concept of the industry life cycle, and

(ii) The phase of development in which each of the industries served by the four companies is positioned.   **7 Marks**

(b) Discuss how Ansoff's product market growth vector matrix may be applied by the firms in developing their growth and divestment strategies.   **18 Marks**

Total marks = 25

9 **GRIER AND BOX PLC**   *45 mins*

Grier and Box plc is a manufacturing company that has emerged from economic recession to earn a profit before interest and tax of £14.8 million last year. The company has six operating divisions, and the results for last year were as follows.

	Electrical equipment £m	Fluid controls £m	Metals £m	Division Industrial services £m	Bathroom accessories £m	Tubes £m	Total £m
Sales	40.0	25.2	17.1	33.7	7.0	6.0	129.0
Cost of sales							
Materials	34.7	20.3	8.0	14.7	4.5	1.5	83.7
Salaries and wages	1.2	1.8	2.1	3.0	1.0	2.4	11.5
Other costs	2.1	1.9	4.0	8.0	1.0	2.0	19.0
	38.0	24.0	14.1	25.7	6.5	5.9	114.2
Profit before interest and tax	2.0	1.2	3.0	8.0	0.5	0.1	14.8
Market share	40%	27%	30%	25%	8%	3%	

The company's summarised balance sheet as at the end of last year was:

	£m	£m
Net fixed assets		65.0
Current assets	35.0	
Current liabilities	20.0	
Net current assets		15.0
		80.0
Loan capital		48.0
		32.0
Share capital		10.0
Reserves		22.0
		32.0

You are asked to comment on each of the following matters that have been raised by the company's managing director.

(a)   He believes that some of the product divisions manufacture too many low value-added items which require huge working capital investments.

From the data given, which product divisions are these, and what are the implications of low value-added items for financial returns and profitability?

8 Marks

(b)   He wishes to make a strategic decision about the long-term viability of both the bathroom accessories division and the tubes division.

(i)   The bathroom accessories division produces bathroom fittings, which are sold to a manufacturer of bathroom ceramics (baths and washbasins etc). The division is still profitable, but there are indications that the manufacturers of bathroom ceramics are beginning to produce their own bathroom accessories, and market a total 'package' to their own customers.

(ii)   The tubes division is barely profitable and would need considerable capital expenditure to improve efficiency and make it more competitive.

What are the arguments for selling off these divisions now, even though both are profitable?
6 Marks

(c)   The company needs to reduce its financial gearing, which is too high. However, the company also needs to spend large sums of capital for equipment replacement and modernisation programmes, investments in new projects and new product developments. All capital investment projects should have a target payback period.

(i)   Discuss the factors which should influence how long the payback period should be for:

(1)   equipment replacement programmes
(2)   new development projects

(ii)   Discuss the relative importance of the strategic aim of reducing gearing and the aim to continue to invest in modernisation programmes. **5 Marks**

(d)   The company is about to introduce a decentralisation programme, in which decision making is pushed as far down the line as possible and head office staff is cut from 56 in number to just 20. The managing director believes that control can be exercised from head office by having a regular reporting system. 'There is much more attention in my mind to looking at ratios and questioning deviations from budget.'

What are the main dangers of relying on ratio analysis and budgetary control for co-ordination and control of the group? **6 Marks**

Total marks = 25

10   FG PLC *30 mins*

Following a review of its plans for expansion, FG plc carried out an assessment of its plant utilisation. The company is considering sub-contracting the work of those departments where plant utilisation is poor. The resources thus released could then be used to increase production capacity in those departments where shortages currently occur.

The following information is available.

(a)   Disposal of under-utilised plant is estimated to provide £100,000 net of demolition costs. This work is expected to take six months from the date of the decision.

(b)   Installation of the additional production equipment to overcome the current shortages will take two years. Stage payments will need to be made to specialist plant suppliers as follows.

	£
From the date of decision	
6 months	50,000
12 months	75,000
18 months	157,000
2 years	370,500
30 months	472,500

(c)   The net cash inflow from the additional production would amount to:

in year 3 from the date of the decision, to £450,000
in year 4 from the date of the decision, to £650,000
in year 5 from the date of the decision, to £700,000
After year 5 some undefined benefits may accrue.

(d)   The company's marginal cost of capital after allowing for taxation is at present 16% per annum. Were the project to be financed from borrowed funds it is thought that future borrowings would cost the company an additional 2% per annum.

Required

(a)   Provide a financial analysis of the proposal in order to determine whether the company should be advised to proceed with its implementation. **5 Marks**

(b)   Comment on factors significant for this decision which have not been provided in the information given. **7 Marks**

(c)   Comment on the helpfulness of an internal rate of return calculation to evaluate this proposal. **3 Marks**

Total marks = 15

11   OB (Pilot Paper) *45 mins*

Ob. is a trading company which has been in existence for five years. It achieved such high market growth and profitability that the founder (F) was able to quickly repay the bank loan which was taken out to start the business. The growth was achieved through F's creative and imaginative style of undertaking business. However two years ago the company encountered a crisis of leadership. This resulted in F recruiting managers to co-ordinate the activities of the business.

F still had the final word in strategic decisions affecting the business. More operational employees were recruited and the buildings extended to satisfy the increasing market demand.

F found that the initial enthusiasm displayed by the managers began to reduce. As they became more confident in their roles, the managers became frustrated and sought more autonomy in decision-making. F also found it more difficult to maintain full control and, as a consequence, delegated more responsibility for decision making to the managers. Ob. is now in phase 3 of Greiner's organisational life cycle model and the company is achieving growth through delegation.

It is clear to F that more capital needs to be injected in order to sustain the current level of growth. This will have to be obtained from an outside source as retained earnings are insufficient to finance this development. F has now appointed two of the managers to the respective positions of finance director and operations director to assist him with the strategic management of the company.

Required

Compare and contrast the likely approaches to establishing organisational objectives for Ob. At the beginning of its life, with its position now as an expanding business entity. Discuss briefly how Ob. can monitor and control progress towards the achievement of its objectives. **25 Marks**

12   MANAGEMENT ACCOUNTING INFORMATION (Pilot Paper)   *45 mins*

It has been said that management accounting has traditionally been concerned with providing information for decision making and controlling costs. It has often been criticised for not providing sufficient relevant information to management because it tends to impose general techniques as a solutions in situations which demand custom-designed (directly applicable) methods and specific information.

Required

(a) Discuss the validity of this criticism of management accounting.   **13 Marks**

To be relevant to the needs of the organisation, management accounting systems need to be designed to accommodate its specific requirements taking account of the circumstances of its particular business environment. One such circumstance may be the change in traditional working patterns. For example, it can no longer be assumed that all employees will be located on the organisation's premises in carrying out their duties. Some are likely to provide their services from remote locations.

Required

(b) Compare the approach to providing relevant management accounting information for strategic decision making purposes in

   (i) a manufacturing organisation which employs staff on site, with

   (ii) a service organisation which employs contractors. The contractors mainly work from home to provide technical solutions for customers engaged in large scale building projects.

12 Marks

Total marks = 25

13   FINANCIAL AND NON-FINANCIAL APPRAISAL (Pilot Paper)   *45 mins*

Capital investment appraisal is defined by CIMA as 'an evaluation of the costs and benefits of a proposed investment in operating assets'. Techniques of capital investment appraisal usually involve comparisons between the projected cash outflows and inflows from projects, and normally involve discounting those cash flows. Investment appraisal for strategic planning purposes involves other factors as well as consideration of cash flows.

The information below relates to proposed strategic investments in two different organisations:

(i) A private sector company which is proposing to increase its production capacity by enlarging its factory

(ii) A government funded school which intends to increase the range of its services by adding a new building to its present site.

The private sector organisation will obtain its funds for expansion from the capital market, while the school building project will be entirely funded by the government. You may assume that the school has no power to make any charge for the services it provides.

Required

Discuss the financial and non-financial factors that should be taken into account in appraising the proposed developments for each of the organisations. **25 Marks**

14   **NOMINEE HOLDINGS** *45 mins*

Nominee Holdings plc, an investment conglomerate, co-ordinates the capital expenditure proposals of its subsidiaries by:

(a)   Allowing each company to pledge its asset base as loan security where value is likely to be added to the equity provided the parent's resources are in no way jeopardised (eg by having to give any form of guarantee)

(b)   Ranking applications from subsidiaries for reinvestment of operating profits according to the premium available over the group's average cost of capital and their accord with its medium-term strategy.

Outline investment plans have been submitted for approval as follows.

	Dairy-P Ltd	Keen Casements	Flexi-Carbon Ltd
Project cost *	£150,000	£65,000	£125,000
(standard deviation)	£41,000	0 (ie firm)	£15,000
Profitability ratio			
(using DCF 19.5%)	1.41	1.28	1.35
Current Asset ratio			
(of project proposal)	1.70	0.65	1.21
Mortgage debentures outstanding	£200,000	nil	£150,000
Rate of interest	10%	-	15%
Second mortgage			
debentures outstanding	£50,000	nil	nil
Rate of interest	17%	-	-
Fixed assets at current valuation	£400,000	£15,000	£250,000

* mean of pessimistic, most likely and optimistic

The subsidiary companies are not aware of the parent company's directors' unhappiness about the future of Dairy-P Ltd. The parent board expects the European Union to continue inflating the cost of that company's inputs and is investigating the feasibility of moving the processing facilities to Greece as that country integrates its economy into the European Union. Nominee Holdings plc's cash and short-term deposits earn on average only 5% pa and amount to some 20% of the company's net worth according to its management accounts, which price non-monetary assets at replacement cost.

Required

(a)   Put forward appropriate recommendations for Nominee Holdings plc's directors to consider.

15 Marks

(b)   Explain how divisional performance should be measured in the interest of the group's shareholders. **5 Marks**

(c)   Propose the means of charge-out that would be appropriate for the parent company to debit subsidiaries for their capital employed. **5 Marks**

Total marks = 25

15   **RAPPAPORT LTD AND NFIs** *45 mins*

(a)   The management accountant of Rappaport Ltd started to calculate the value of the business last Friday afternoon. At the weekend he won the National Lottery and, although he has not returned to work, he has put in a bid for the company of £250,000.

You have his unfinished working papers which are shown below.

Required

Advise the shareholders of Rappaport Ltd whether to accept the former management accountant's offer. **15 Marks**

439

Value drivers

Sales growth rate	5%
Operating profit margin	10%
Cash tax rate	25%
Incremental fixed capital investment	10%
Incremental working capital investment	8%
Cost of capital	7%
Planning period (years)	5

Financial position at end of most recent year

	£	£
Fixed assets		80,000
Current assets	40,000	-
Current liabilities	20,000	-
Net current assets		20,000
		100,000
Long-term loan		16,000
		84,000
Share capital		72,000
Reserves		12,000
		84,000

	£
Sales value for most recent year	240,000
Depreciation for most recent year	8,000

(assumed to increase by £800 each year for the foreseeable future)

Cash flow projection

	Year 0 £	Year 1 £	Year 2 £	Year 3 £	Year 4 £	Year 5 £	Beyond* £
Sales	240,000	252,000					
Operating profit		25,200					
Tax		(6,300)					
Depreciation		8,000					
Operating cashflow		26,900					
Replacement capital expenditure (Note 1)		(8,000)	(8,800)				
Incremental fixed capital investment (Note 2)		(3,600)	(3,960)				0
Incremental working capital investment (Note 2)		(2,880)	(3,168)				0
Free cashflow		12,420					

* Assumed to be the same as Year 5 figures.

SVA Calculation

Year	Free cash flow £	Discount factor 7%	PV £
1	12,420	0.935	
2		0.873	
3		0.816	
4		0.763	
5		0.713	
Beyond (Note 3)		0.713	
Long-term debt			(16,000)
Shareholder value			

Notes

1 Replacement capital expenditure is assumed to equal depreciation

2 Additional Fixed capital needs are calculated as follows

Year 1 = 10% × (Net current assets + loan) = £3,600.

Year 2 = 10% × (Net current assets + loan + Year 1 needs)

= 10% × (20,000 + 16,000 + 3,600) = £3,960

and so on.

Additional working capital needs are calculated in a similar fashion

3 This is the value beyond year 5 expressed in PV terms: calculate the value of beyond year 5 free cash flow as a perpetuity at 7% and discount using the year 5 factor.

(b) One of Kaplan's proposals to improve management accounting was the greater use of non-financial indicators to control organisations.

You are required to explain and discuss the advantages and disadvantages of using non-financial indicators in control. **10 Marks**
Total Marks = 25

16   **MANAGEMENT AND SOCIAL RESPONSIBILITY**   *45 mins*

In what respects may the need to exercise social responsibility shape the relationship of management to stakeholders?   **25 Marks**

Approaching the answer

This is a difficult question, mainly because it seems very short, and possibly even a bit vague, and you may wonder how you can plan and write for 45 minutes on this topic. Thinking about the requirement should throw up several issues for you to consider. Let's look at it again.

In what respects may the need to exercise social responsibility shape the relationship of management to stakeholders?

> Who are the stakeholders likely to be affected? Not just talking about shareholders!

> Why is there ever a need to exercise social responsibility?

> What is social responsibility? A minefield! Different stakeholders define it in different terms. (But have a definition in your mind)

> What is the usual relationship between managers and stakeholders? Why are such relationships important?

Answer plan

Organise the things that you have noticed and your points arising into a coherent answer plan. Not all of the points may need to go into your answer, so spend some time thinking them through and prioritising them.

Definition of social responsibility – not just environmentalism, but also social issues. Organisation must be aware of wider society. This will sometimes have to override commercial pressures. There are costs and benefits.

Where are the limits? The world as a whole? Argument that businesses discharge some responsibility simply by creating wealth and paying taxes.

Pressures come from stakeholders – managers don't do it under their own steam.

Stakeholder analysis (for each one, describe the relationship, and their particular interest in social responsibility)

(a)   **Employees** – paid workers, but also members of society. Legal regulations such as health and safety

(b)   **Customers** – paying for goods and services. Can put pressure on products to set new standards eg 'dolphin friendly' tuna fishing

(c)   **Suppliers** – may impose restrictions

(d)   **Professional bodies** – ethical standards for management to follow

(e)   **Elected authorities** – can affect management in a number of ways (legislation, public opinion, influence over commercial organisations)

(f)   **Shareholders** – profit! Might not appreciate resources being used on worthy projects that earn no money.

Management issues – they need to weigh up the conflicting demands

(a)   Monitoring the expectations people have of the organisation

(b)   Achieving good publicity

(c)   Selecting socially responsible activities.

(i)   Ensuring core activities are conducted in a socially responsible way

(ii)   Supporting activities which are for public welfare (eg charitable donations)

(d)   Clearly knowing the minimum acceptable standards. Is it worth going further?

17   **THE S GROUP** (Pilot Paper)   *90 mins*

Company development

The headquarters of the S Group is located in K, a country which has experienced rapid economic growth in recent years.

S itself has been established for over 100 years. Two brothers first started trading in K and developed the group, which is now a highly profitable international conglomerate company. Its diverse business activities range from capital goods manufacture, through materials handling to operation of airlines and banking. Some of its activities involve the transfer of partly completed goods between manufacturing and assembly plants located in different countries. The group operates a divisional structure.

Economic circumstances

Over the last three years the region of the world in which K is located has been subject to serious economic difficulties. K itself has not been affected as much as some of its neighbours, owing to the fact that its independent currency is pegged to the US dollar.

There has been much activity and intervention by the monetary authorities in K to protect the value of the currency, and this has proved to be largely successful, despite the intense pressure exerted by foreign speculators. Nevertheless, the effects of the regional economic difficulties are being felt. This is exemplified by the recent emergence of unemployment after a period of 30 years of full employment and a dramatic fall in property prices.

Organisational economic objectives

Fifty five per cent of S's holding company shares are held within the families of the original founders. The remaining forty five per cent of the shares are mainly held by international banks and other financial institutions located all over the world. These institutional shareholders maintain constant pressure on the directors to improve earnings per share and increase dividend payments. The directors have stated that their main objective is to increase shareholder value. In satisfying the requirements of the shareholders the directors are conscious of the need for improved efficiency in the group's operations. Consequently, the holding company's board of directors carefully scrutinises the activities of the constituent subsidiary companies within the group.

Divisional performance measurement

S has always applied a traditional form of measurement to assess the performance of the group's subsidiaries. It uses return on capital employed (ROCE) and defines this as:

$$\frac{\text{Profit before interest and tax}}{\text{Average capital employed}} \times 100$$

(The capital employed value is the average of that shown at the beginning and end of the year.)

The performance of the divisional managers is strictly monitored on this basis and their remuneration increases if they achieve growth in their ROCE, which is measured annually. Inevitably, the divisional managers strive to improve their performance as measured by this method.

The Agricultural Equipment (AE) Division

The AE division, which is not located in K, assembles components into a single product. It receives the components from other subsidiaries in the group which are situated in other countries. The group as a whole has been able to benefit from economies of scale, as a result of other subsidiary divisions, which have long experience in manufacturing, supplying AE. Following assembly, AE ships the product to various customers throughout the world. The geographical location of the country in which AE is situated enables the product to be easily exported, but the division is subject to high levels of corporation tax.

The transfer prices of the components transferred to AE are set centrally by group head office located in K. The divisional manager of AE has no influence over them at all. The group head office may vary the transfer prices during the financial year.

Comparative results for the AE division over the last two years (translated into K's currency) are as follows:

443

	Last year		Previous year	
	K$m	K$m	K$m	K$m
Sales		800		750
Components	600		400	
Assembly costs	100		75	
		700		475
Gross profit		100		275
AE Division Head Office (all fixed)		75		75
Net profit before interest and tax		25		200
Average capital employed		2,020		2,000

Selling prices over the two years remained stable.

It may be assumed that the variable costs of the supplying division, relating to the transferred components, were neutral in respect of AE division's profitability over the two years.

The budgeted and actual selling price per unit was K$50,000 in each of the two years. The budgeted production and sales level for each year was 18,000 units. it can be assumed that there were no opening and closing stocks for finished goods or work in progress in either of the years.

The budgeted cost per unit for each of the last two years was as follows:

	Last year	Previous year
	K$	K$
Assembly	6,000	5,000
Components transferred	35,000	25,000
	41,000	30,000

It can be assumed that there was no change in the currency exchange rate between the AE division's host country and K$ in the last two years. There have been discussions at S Group headquarters regarding the deteriorating performance of AE and there is growing pressure to close it down. The AE divisional manager believes there is little he can do in the circumstances, where he only controls a small proportion of the total costs of the division.

Potential for growth in AE division

Despite the reduced profitability in the last financial year, the divisional manager of AE believes there is potential for growth. He has put forward plans to group headquarters to take over a competitor company in the country in which the division is situated. This would result in an increase for the division in world wide market share and provide the capacity to increase the range of agricultural equipment supplied in accordance with the divisional manager's perception of demand. To do this AE will need to obtain funds which will be secured against group assets.

Required

(a) State the sources from which the board of directors of S may obtain information relating to the group's business environment and how it might use that information for strategic management purposes. Explain how the board of directors might assure itself of the quality of that information for strategic management purposes. (You are not required to consider the ecological environment in answering this question.) **12 Marks**

(b) Making use of the information contained in the case, produce a critical appraisal of the method applied by S Group's directors to assess the performance of the AE division.

16 Marks

(c) Discuss the factors which should be taken into consideration by the directors of S in deciding whether the strategic development proposals put forward by AE's divisional manager should be pursued. **10 Marks**

(d) Assume that the AE division makes the acquisition as proposed by its divisional manager. Recommend how S Group's directors should improve the methods of measuring the performance of the AE division in order to assess its contribution to the group's strategic requirement to increase shareholder value. **12 Marks**

Total marks = 50

Approaching the answer

You should read through the requirement before working through and annotating the question as we have, so that you are aware of what things you are looking for. We have also prepared a precis of the case, which follows this annotated version, summarising the key issues.

Company development

The headquarters of the S Group is located in K, a country which has experienced rapid economic growth in recent years.

> Turbulent environment? Unstable? Good infrastructure? Or boom then bust?

> Long established indicates a certain stability

S itself has been established for over 100 years. Two brothers first started trading in K and developed the group, which is now a highly profitable international conglomerate company.

> Big numbers, although an unfashionable business model now

Its diverse business activities range from capital goods manufacture, through materials handling to operation of airlines and banking. Some of its activities involve the transfer of partly completed goods between manufacturing and assembly plants located in different countries. The group operates a divisional structure.

> Products and services – marketing/ branding issues?

> Transfer pricing issues

> Performance assessment

Economic circumstances

Over the last three years the region of the world in which K is located has been subject to serious economic difficulties. K itself has not been affected as much as some of its neighbours, owing to the fact that its independent currency is pegged to the US dollar.

> Will foreign exchange policy become an issue?

There has been much activity and intervention by the monetary authorities in K to protect the value of the currency, and this has proved to be largely successful, despite the intense pressure exerted by foreign speculators. Nevertheless, the effects of the regional economic difficulties are being felt. This is exemplified by the recent emergence of unemployment after a period of 30 years of full employment and a dramatic fall in property prices.

> Economic environment could become unfavourable

> Global profile

Organisational economic objectives

Fifty five per cent of S's holding company shares are held within the families of the original founders. The remaining forty five per cent of the shares are mainly held by international banks and other financial institutions located all over the world. These institutional shareholders maintain constant pressure on the directors to improve earnings per share and increase dividend payments. The directors have stated that their main objective is to increase shareholder value. In satisfying the requirements of the shareholders the directors are conscious of the need for improved efficiency in the group's operations. Consequently,

> Could this imply conservative management and resistance to change?

> Stakeholder analysis – short term interests?

> As would generally be expected).

> What does 'efficiency' mean? Cost control?

> **Tight central control?**

the holding company's board of directors carefully scrutinises the activities of the constituent subsidiary companies within the group.

Divisional performance measurement

S has always applied a traditional form of measurement to assess the performance of the group's subsidiaries. It uses return on capital employed (ROCE) a...

> **Advantages and disadvantages of this as a measure**

> **Note this for your calculations!**

$$\frac{\text{Profit before interest and tax}}{\text{Average capital employed}} \times 100$$

(The capital employed value is the average of that shown at the beginning and end of the year.)

> **Possible disadvantages here – disincentive to invest and thereby increase capital employed, for example**

The performance of the divisional managers is strictly monitored on this basis and their remuneration increases if they achieve growth in their ROCE, which is measured annually. Inevitably, the divisional managers strive to improve their performance as measured by this method.

The Agricultural Equipment (AE) Division

The AE division, which is not located in K, assembles components into a single product. It receives the components from other subsidiaries in the group which are situated in other countries. The group as a whole has been able to benefit from economies of scale, as a result of other subsidiary divisions, which have long experience in manufacturing, supplying

> **Interest from the tax authorities in the . transfer pricing, as a method of reducing profits?**

AE. Following assembly, AE ships the product to various customers throughout the world. The geographical location of the country in which AE is situated enables the product to be easily exported, but the division is subject to high levels of corporation tax.

> **No incentive to manage his costs as he does not control them, yet he is judged on them via ROCE!**

The transfer prices of the components transferred to AE are set centrally by group head office located in K. The divisional manager of AE has no influence over them at all. The group head office may vary the transfer prices during the financial year.

Comparative results for the AE division over the last two years (translated into K's currency) are as follows:

> **These numbers are vital for answering part (b)**

	Last year K$m	K$m	Previous year K$m	K$m
Sales		800		750
Components	600		400	
Assembly costs	100		75	
		700		475
Gross profit		100		275
AE Division Head Office (all fixed)		75		75
Net profit before interest and tax		25		200
Average capital employed		2,020		2,000

Selling prices over the two years remained stable.

It may be assumed that the variable costs of the supplying division, relating to the transferred components, were neutral in respect of AE division's profitability over the two years.

> What does this mean? Basically that the big increase in costs is not due to higher costs of the supplying division being passed on, but rather due to higher transfer prices. Is using ROCE in such circumstances a fair performance measure? There must be a better one!

The budgeted and actual selling price per unit was K$50,000 in each of the two years. The budgeted production and sales level for each year was 18,000 units. It can be assumed that there were no opening and closing stocks for finished goods or work in progress in either of the years.

The budgeted cost per unit for each of the last two years was as follows:

	Last year K$	Previous year K$
Assembly	6,000	5,000
Components transferred	35,000	25,000
	41,000	30,000

It can be assumed that there was no change in the currency exchange rate between the AE division's host country and K$ in the last two years. There have been discussions at S Group headquarters regarding the deteriorating performance of AE and there is growing pressure to close it down. The AE divisional manager believes there is little he can do in the circumstances, where he only controls a small proportion of the total costs of the division.

> Is it really deteriorating?

Potential for growth in AE division

Despite the reduced profitability in the last financial year, the divisional manager of AE believes there is potential for growth. He has put forward plans to group headquarters to take over a competitor company in the country in which the division is situated. This would result in an increase for the division in world wide market share and provide the capacity to increase the range of agricultural equipment supplied, in accordance with the divisional manager's perception of demand. To do this, AE will need to obtain funds which will be secured against group assets.

> Increased sales, profits, contribution to shareholder value

> But is this perception realistic?

> Cost of those funds?

Overall precis of the case

S Group, **highly profitable international conglomerate**, established for over 100 years. Located in K, a country which has experienced rapid economic growth (currency pegged to the US$), although the region it is in has been subject to difficulties recently: unemployment and falling property prices.

Business activities: capital goods manufacture, materials handling, operation of airlines, banking. Some **transfer of goods** between plants in different countries. The group operates a **divisional structure**.

Shareholders: 55% families of the original founders, 45% held by worldwide financial institutions who press for improved **eps** and increased **dividends**. Main **objective** of group is to **increase shareholder value**. Subsidiaries' activities closely scrutinised by centre.

Uses **ROCE** for performance measurement and for influencing manager remuneration, defined as:

$$\frac{\text{Profit before interest and tax}}{\text{Average capital employed}} \times 100$$

The **AE division** (not located in K) assembles components which it receives from other subsidiaries in other countries, and then ships the completed capital goods to customers. Group benefits from economies of scale. AE is subject to high levels of corporation tax.

Transfer prices of the components are set **centrally**. Divisional manager of AE has no influence.

(**Results** for the AE division are as in the tables above).

There have been discussions at head office regarding the **deteriorating performance** of AE, with pressure to close it down. AE divisional manager only controls a small proportion of his total costs, but remains committed - has put forward plans for **acquisition** of a domestic competitor to increase both AE's **global market share** and its **product range**, to be **financed** by funds secured against group assets.

What are the likely sources?

What information do they really need about the business environment?

Required

(a) State the sources from which the board of directors of S may obtain information relating to the group's business environment and how it might use that information for strategic management purposes. Explain how the board of directors might assure itself of the quality of that information for strategic management purposes. (You are not required to consider the ecological environment in answering this question.)

Why does strategic management need information?

Quality issues an unusual angle – internal checking, external verification?

Is ROCE a good method to apply, in the specific circumstances of the question?

Critical appraisal means 'analyse its good and bad points'.

Don't make things up! Use the information that you are given - the numbers are vital.

(b) Making use of the information contained in the case, produce a critical appraisal of the method applied by S Group's directors to assess the performance of the AE division.

No need to make any recommendations yourself!

Discuss – this is easiest if you categorise the factors. Which ones are more important?

(c) Discuss the factors which should be taken into consideration by the directors of S in deciding whether the strategic development proposals put forward by AE's divisional manager should be pursued.

Financial and non-financial is a useful basis upon which to structure your discussion.

> Recommend new divisional performance assessment methods – and give reasons.

> Indicate how appropriate your recommendation is to the need to monitor contributions towards shareholder value: ease of measurement, validity of calculations, fairness to the division...

(d)   Assume that the AE division makes the acquisition as proposed by its divisional manager. Recommend how S Group's directors should improve the methods of measuring the performance of the AE division in order to assess its contribution to the group's strategic requirement to increase shareholder value.

> It is irrelevant if you think it is a bad idea!

> Define shareholder value.

Answer plan

Think about the points you want to make, and prioritise them.

(a)   Importance of understanding the environment/trends – define **strategic intelligence** (**Maintain a database** – financial/non-financial indicators).

Sources of environmental information

(i)   **Internal sources** – staff, stakeholders

       Importance of management information system – info on sales, costs, market share

(ii)   **External sources** – media, consultants, academic/trade journals, trade bodies, Internet, government, public databases, stockbrokers

Using the information

Needs to be coherently organised and presented, as there will be a lot of it.

Strategy planning proces - involve divisional managers, who will have their own awareness of the environment

Quality of the information

Information must be accurate/reliable: **why** is it being collected, and **what** will it be used for?

Comparing information from various sources: more sources, and more checks, as time goes on.

(b)   ROCE an **historical measure** - no guide to future performance. Manager could consider only those decisions which increase AE's short term ROCE (at expense of group): lack of **goal congruence.**

ROCE calculations and analysis.

Fair comparison between divisions based on ROCE is difficult.

Analysis of **sales and profitability**, concentrating on **transfer pricing policy** (75% of sales value last year/53% in previous year).

Conclusion that the performance of AE is being assessed on factors beyond its control, using an unsatisfactory measure.

(c)   Key objective: **increase shareholder value.** Does acquisition fit in with the overall **strategic direction** of the group? Must understand reasons for it – do they balance the level of **risk**?

Possible problems/issues to consider:

(i) **Costs**
(ii) **Customers reaction/ market research**
(iii) **Incompatibilities**
(iv) **Lack of information**

Refer to the analysis in part (b) – AE is actually profitable, so should it risk that with this venture?

Non financial factors too – such as problems of **implementation** /human resources issues.

(d) **Performance measurement** should become more **forward looking.** Balance long v. short term.

Shareholder value analysis - definition

Factors to focus on re the AE division (Rappaport's value drivers):

(i) **Market share** forecasts and trends

(ii) Investment in **working capital**

(iii) **Cash flows**

(iv) **Corporation tax planning**

(v) **Cost of funding** (incremental value of the acquisition must exceed the cost of capital)

Economic value management - definition

Applied to the AE division – adjust for the transfer price.

Exam answer bank

1   STRATEGY AND INFORMATION

> **Tutorial note.** This is an introductory question covering some of the basics of management control and information, and particularly the ideas of Anthony and Goold and Campbell which are described in Chapter 1.
>
> Anthony's ideas about levels of decision making are best understood as a hierarchy.
>
>
>
> Information needs at these three levels will obviously differ, both in the type of information required and its ultimate purpose.
>
> The third part of the question is more difficult. Use Ward's critical success factors in your answer. The key to designing and implementing any new management accounting system is to be clear what the information requirements are. A specifically *strategic* management accounting information system must aid strategic decisions by drawing information from many sources.

(a) (i) **Strategic planning** entails the centre participating in and influencing the strategies of the core businesses. The centre establishes a planning process and contributes to strategic thinking. Rather less emphasis is placed on financial controls and performance targets are set flexibly and reviewed within the context of long-term progress.

(ii) **Financial control,** as the name suggests, focuses on annual profit targets. There are no long-term planning documents and no strategy documents. The role of the centre is limited to appraising budgets and monitoring performance.

(iii) **Strategic control** is concerned with the plans of its business units but believes in autonomy for business unit managers. Plans are therefore made locally but reviewed in a formal planning process to upgrade the quality of the thinking. The centre does not advocate strategies or interfere with major decisions but maintains control through financial targets and strategic objectives.

(b) (i) **Strategic planning information**

Strategic plans are those which set or change the objectives, or strategic targets of an organisation. They would include such matters as the selection of products and markets, the required levels of company profitability, the purchase and disposal of subsidiary companies or major fixed assets, whether there should be an employee share of company profits and so on.

Strategic planning information is obtained to some extent from internally-measured data, but to a far greater extent from outside - that is, external data about competitors, customers, suppliers, new technology, the state of markets and the economy, government legislation, political unrest and so on.

Such information includes overall profitability, the profitability of different segments of the business, future market prospects, the availability and cost of raising new funds, total cash needs, total manning levels and capital equipment needs. Much of this information must come from environmental sources, although internally generated information will always be used. Strategic information is prepared on an ad hoc basis. It also tends to be more approximate and imprecise than management control information.

(ii) **Management control information**

Management control is at the level below strategic planning in Anthony's decision-making hierarchy. Whilst strategic planning is concerned with setting objectives and strategic targets, management control is concerned with decisions about the efficient and effective use of an organisation's resources to achieve these objectives or targets.

(a) **Resources**, sometimes referred to as the '4 Ms', are men, materials, machines and money.

(b) **Efficiency** in the use of resources means that optimum **output** is achieved from the **input** resources used. It relates to the combinations of people, land and capital (for example how much production work should be automated) and to the productivity of labour, or material usage.

(c) **Effectiveness** in the use of resources means that the **outputs** obtained are in line with the intended **objectives** or targets.

The information required for management control embraces the entire organisation, just as the master budget includes all aspects of the organisation's activities. Control information provides a comparison between actual results and the plan. A system must exist for planning, measuring, comparing and controlling the efforts of every department or profit centre. The information is often quantitative (labour hours, quantities of materials consumed, volumes of sales and production) and is commonly expressed in money terms.

Such information includes productivity measurements, budgetary control or variance analysis reports, cash flow forecasts, manning levels, profit results within a particular department of the organisation, labour turnover statistics within a department, short-term purchasing requirements and so on. A large proportion of this information will be generated from within the organisation and it will often have an accounting emphasis. Tactical information is usually prepared regularly, perhaps weekly, or monthly.

Management control information may be analysed in several different ways, for example an analysis may be made of product costs or departmental costs, but the total costs will be the same, whatever analysis is used.

(iii) **Operational control information**

Operational information is information which is needed for the conduct of day-to-day implementation of plans. It will include much 'transaction data' such as data about customer orders, purchase orders, cash receipts and payments. Operating information must usually be consolidated into totals in management reports before it can be used to prepare management control information.

In the payroll office, for example, operational information relating to day-rate labour will include the hours worked each week by each employee, his or her rate of pay per hour, details of deductions, and for the purpose of wages analysis, details of the time each person spent on individual jobs during the week. In this example, the information is required weekly, but more urgent operational information, such as the amount of raw materials being input to a production process, may be required daily, hourly, or in the case of automated production, second by second.

The amount of *detail* provided in information is likely to vary with the purpose for which it is needed, and operational information is likely to go into much more detail than management control information, which in turn will be more detailed than strategic information.

Whereas tactical information for management control is often expressed in money terms, operational information, although quantitative, is more often expressed in terms of units, hours, quantities of material and so on.

(c) **Introducing a system of strategic management accounting**

The following factors should be considered when designing a management accounting system.

(i) **Output required**

The management accountant must identify the information needs of managers. If a particular manager finds pie-charts most useful, the system should be able to produce them.

(ii) **Response required**

A further, vitally important issue is how managers are likely to behave, depending on what factors or figures are stressed in the information they are given.

(iii)   **When the output is required**

If information is needed within the hour the system should be capable of producing it at this speed.

(iv)   **Sources of input information**

The production manager may require a report detailing the precise operations of his machines. The management accounting system could only acquire this information if suitable production technology had been installed.

(v)   **Processing involved**

This is generally a cost/benefit calculation: some of the information that could be provided would cost more to produce than the benefit obtained from having it.

A **strategic management accounting system** will have an **external and future focus**, but will be able to shed necessary light on internal processes to provide managers with strategic information. Whether the strategic management accounting system is tagged on to the existing one or whether the existing one would be modified to allow for greater flexibility is a question for implementation.

Most strategic decisions are unique: and hence is the information needed to support them. The accounting system should identify the type of information needed.

(i)   Decisions to enter or leave a business area, or to expand operations, should take account of avoidable and opportunity costs.

(ii)   The system should identify suitable performance measures.

(iii)   The system should be designed from the perspective of strategic decision-makers.

Designing a management accounting system effectively means devising ways to provide accounting information for managers to use. Remember however that managers need information that financial accounting systems and cost accounting systems on their own do not provide.

Ward (*Strategic Management Accounting*) argues that a successful strategic management accounting system will be judged on ten critical success factors.

- Aid to strategic decisions
- Close the communication gap
- Identify decision type
- Suitable financial performance indicators
- Economic vs managerial performance
- Only provide relevant information
- Separate committed from discretionary costs
- Distinguish discretionary from engineered costs
- Use standard costs strategically
- Allow for changes over time

2   DEVELOPING A CORPORATE STRATEGY

> **Tutorial note.** Another introductory question which nevertheless tests your ability to apply your knowledge of strategy development to particular scenarios.
>
> When you see the list of organisations, your mind should be automatically throwing out points that will influence strategy development in each case. For example:
>
> (a)   Bank – profit orientated. Bad press for overcharging small businesses: ethical considerations?
>
> (b)   Building Society – mutual, or demutualised?
>
> (c)   A college – objectives based upon efficient and effective use of teaching resources. Alternative revenue streams? Private or public sector?
>
> (d)   A national charity – needs to appeal to the donating public. How much to be spent on administration?
>
> (e)   A retail store – subject to consumer feelings about disposable income. Might be fashion-driven eg clothes. Highly market driven

Tutorial note continued

(f)   A local authority – provision of services using government funds. Transport, education, health

All of these types of organisation will ask themselves similar questions (as we have set out early in the suggested solutions) but the answers will be different. This answer sets out issues to be considered by each type of organisation. You needed to choose only two.

Introduction

All organisations need to **plan**. Strategic planning is the process they use to select goals and determine how to achieve them. A **corporate strategy** is a plan for the future of the organisation.

Developing a corporate strategy involves top management taking a view of the organisation, and the future that it is likely to encounter, and then attempting to organise the **structure and resources** of the organisation accordingly. Policies must be formulated and a set of medium/long term plans (probably 2-5 years ahead) developed.

The **issues** that need to be addressed and questions to be asked, are as follows.

- What is our business and what should it be?
- Who are our customers and who should they be?
- Where are we heading?
- What major competitive advantages do we enjoy?
- In what areas of competence do we excel?

Developing the strategy involves a process of **strategic planning.** The plan must embrace strategies covering funding, markets, products, technology and resources.

Developing a corporate strategy embraces the following.

(a)   Setting the corporate/strategic objectives which need to be expressed in quantitative terms with any constraints identified

(b)   From (a), establishing the corporate performance required

(c)   Internal appraisal, by means of assessing the organisation's current state in terms of resources and performance (SWOT analysis)

(d)   External appraisal, by means of a survey and analysis of the organisation's environment, including the competition

(e)   Forecasting future performance based on the information obtained from (c) and (d), initially as purely passive extrapolations into the future of past and current achievements

(f)   Analysing the gap between the results of (b) and (e)

(g)   Identifying and evaluating various strategies to reduce this 'performance gap' in order to meet strategic objectives

(h)   Choosing between alternative strategies

(i)   Preparing the final corporate plan, with divisions between short term and long term as appropriate

(j)   Evaluating actual performance against the corporate plan

Senior managers must be actively involved in developing the corporate strategy. This should create a unified direction and guide the deployment of resources.

(a)   **A bank**

The prime corporate objective of a bank will be financial (growth in profits). Banks are expected to uphold a high standard of ethical behaviour towards customers.

Clearing banks are very large, and so the problems of creating an effective, co-ordinated planning process are large. It is difficult to involve all the local branch managers in the corporate planning process, and so getting the commitment of branch managers to the bank's objectives might also be difficult.

Clearing banks are traditionally fairly staid and bureaucratic, but they have been faced with rapid changes in recent years, and this is likely to continue in the future. Examples of change include the following.

(i)   New technology - home banking and Internet services

(ii)   Changes in the law - banks can provide more financial services, but so too can building societies. Opportunities must be actively sought. A defensive corporate strategy of reacting to competition would prove ineffective

(iii)   Changes in the economy - for example, future bank lending will be dependent to some extent on future interest rates. Environmental analysis is required

Innovative thinking is essential for banks to maintain their status in financial markets.

(b) **A building society**

The principal purposes of building societies are raising, primarily from their members, funds for making advances to members secured upon land and buildings for their residential use.

Objectives to be met

(i)   Protection of the investments of its shareholders and depositors

(ii)   Promoting and securing financial stability

(iii)   Competing successfully with banks, insurance companies, estate agents and other building societies

Under the 1986 Building Societies Act there are provisions for a building society to become a public limited company and be therefore regulated by the Companies Act 1985. The Act also confers wide new powers on building societies to offer banking, insurance and estate agency services.

A corporate strategy must cover the change in the law and the widening of both the range of services to be offered and the activities of competitors.

(c) **A college**

The prime objective of a college should be to provide education, but in the corporate planning process, the college should give thought to the following issues.

- How much and what sort of education should it provide?
- To whom should it offer education?
- What standard of education should it provide?
- Who is the customer? Student, employer, government?

A local college of education, for example, could offer a wide range of courses. It will need funding.

- How much finance will it need - say for new buildings and equipment etc?

- How much funding will it expect to receive? What constraints will be attached?

- Can it supplement funding from the government with donations and grants from private companies?

The information needed by a college

- What will be the likely size and pattern of demand for education by students?

- What will be the demand for qualified students by employers?

- How will students want to study - part time, full time, by distance learning?

- Will rival colleges or universities offer similar courses of a better standard?

- How fast is the rate of change in demand for education, and how is this demand changing?

A private college will supply educational services and fix fees to meet market demand. Its strategy may be to earn an acceptable return on capital.

(d) **A national charity**

The purpose and values of a national charity will largely be social and ethical. Emphasis will be placed on developing a strategy covering the following.

- The type and quality of service provision

- Identifying worthwhile outlets for funds

- Identifying potential sources of funds and developing fund raising activities

- Arguing the case for political and social change to achieve the objectives of the charity

- Attracting managers, employees and unpaid helpers who hold the same values as the charity's patrons, sponsors and staff
- Generating good morale amongst the workforce

(e) **A retail store**

The strategic aim is to sell a wide range of merchandise to individuals.

- Increase turnover and volume of sales, in total and per area of selling space
- Control costs and stocks
- Earn a return on capital
- Predict what is going on in the market place - identify changes, growth in mail order business, falling market share
- Develop a profile of what competitors are doing and selling. Undertake market research and collect sales intelligence
- Decide on price, products and sales promotions

(f) **A local authority**

The prime objective should be to provide services to meet needs. The authority must consider the following.

- The range and quality of services to be provided (some will be mandatory and others discretionary).
- How much finance will be needed to meet expenditure?
- How much funding will it receive, or should it raise, from government grants, community charge and direct charges to service users?

The authority must develop a corporate strategy within a framework of political, legal, social and financial constraints. It must plan to provide cost-effective services whilst taking account of conflicting objectives.

Environmental appraisal is a crucial element in developing a strategy. Key factors include the following.

- Government policies, inflation and interest rates
- Media and public opinion
- Size/composition of the labour market
- Likely demand for services of different types
- Potential sources of finance

3 DEVELOPMENT AGENCIES

Tutorial note. This is a tricky question on the environment, which concentrates on the "P" of the PEST framework (the political/legal environment). A variety of incentives, funded by national governments, exist for locating capacity in a particular area. Think of the reasons why this might be, and do not let the specific language of the question (the Acronym 'RDA', for example) put you off providing a sensible answer. There are clues in the question scenario as to the issues involved.

In part (a) set out the objectives of the RDA, then those of the computer manufacturer, followed by your analysis of how they may be expected to coincide.

For part (b) we have offered six influential environmental factors, which would be enough to earn the 15 marks on offer, provided there is adequate explanation of the points given and they are not merely listed. Think of the important supporting factors for a business when setting up anywhere. They can be grouped into the following broad areas:

- Customers and markets
- Suppliers
- Competitors
- Labour and physical resources
- Finance

(a) The objective of a Regional Development Agency is to promote industrial and commercial growth and development in an underdeveloped or declining region, with a view to bringing more employment and economic wealth to relatively underdeveloped areas of the country.

The objective of the computer manufacturer would be primarily a financial one, to seek certain financial returns for its shareholders. The strategic decision to set up a computer manufacturing operation in Europe would seem to indicate the following about the manufacturer.

- Expects increasing sales in Europe
- Wishes to locate a manufacturing plant close to its European markets

The objective of the RDA and the objective of the computer manufacturer would coincide if a location in the region is the best location commercially for the manufacturer. The RDA should therefore have done its best to achieve the following.

- Bring the commercial advantages of the region to the manufacturer's attention
- Offer some commercial incentive itself, if possible
- Offer assistance to the manufacturer in identifying suitable sites

(b) The environmental factors might have been as follows.

(i) **The availability of components supplies**

A computer manufacturer will want supplies of components from external suppliers, and is likely to want the bulk of its supplies to be provided from local sources. Many components will be custom made for the specific manufacturer.

The RDA should have been able to:

(1) Obtain a list of the components that the manufacturer would want to buy locally

(2) race local suppliers able to supply the components and who would provide price quotations for them

(3) Provide this supplier and price information to the manufacturer.

(ii) **Other high-tech manufacturers in the area**

The existence of other high-tech manufacturers in the region would be an indication that there are good component suppliers in the region and that other environmental factors might be conducive to small computer manufacture in the area.

(iii) **Proximity to markets**

A manufacturing base should be fairly close to its major markets, so as to minimise distribution costs (provided, of course, that manufacturing costs are not so high in the area as to outweigh the advantages of proximity to markets). Geographical distance need not be a problem if there are efficient transport links.

(iv) **Productivity**

An important factor in keeping down manufacturing costs is productivity, especially amongst skilled workers. A reputation in high-tech industries for highly productive staff and good labour relations would be an advantage for the region.

(v) **The availability of a good site**

The site wanted by the computer manufacturer would presumably be close to a good transport system and a prestige location, to suit the corporate image of a major computer manufacturer. One of the key tasks of the RDA would be to help the manufacturer to locate such a site.

(vi) **Financial incentives**

The government (through the RDA) could offer certain financial incentives to encourage a manufacturer to set up operations in the region. The most obvious of these would be a cash grant, in the form perhaps of a regional development grant and selective regional assistance.

Financial incentives will therefore be a 'sweetener' for the computer manufacturer.

4   U PLC

> **Tutorial note.** The answer to part (a) examines the three strategies in turn.
>
> (i)   Existing promotional advertising and exhibitions
> (ii)   Raise prices
> (iii)   Adapting production procedures
>
> It looks at the potential risks and benefits of each, keeping in mind the objective of increasing market share, turnover and margins, and comes up with a conclusion.
>
> Other points to note are
>
> - The reaction of A Ltd and Z plc to any strategy change of U plc
> - The cost of the different options for U plc
> - The timescale needed to introduce major changes
> - The high investment risk in a major spending programme
> - Balancing long-term and short-term benefits for U plc
>
> It is not clear from the question whether the 'alternative' marketing strategies are mutually exclusive, or whether they should be considered in combination. This solution tries to adopt the view that the strategies could be considered either in isolation or in combination.
>
> Part (b) concludes that the offer described would not be good enough for acceptance by Z. Simple manipulation of the figures given in the question, with a basic assumption about turnover levels, shows that Z is a far stronger company. The question does ask whether it would be in the interest of U plc shareholders, so make sure that your answer includes reference to this (even though such a deal would be highly unlikely to take place!)
>
> In part (c) do not forget to mention the benefits of operating synergy (in addition to increased turnover, profit and ROCE). Marketing and production operations, for example, could be combined.

(a)   The existing strategy of attempting to **boost market share** by **promotional** advertising and exhibitions has not shown any success to date. It is difficult to relate advertising expenditure directly to higher sales, and it is possible that U plc's market share will improve in the course of time if advertising and exhibition displays are continued.

On the other hand, there may be a weakness in the nature of the advertising campaign - ie what is the objective of the campaign? - and the product might not be one which can be exhibited with any great success. The **reluctance of customers to switch** to a new supplier indicates that advertising might not be an effective marketing strategy at all.

Unless the promotional advertising and exhibitions can be expected to increase sales, or prevent a fall in sales, the expenditure involved in the current strategy will result in a lower **profit/turnover ratio** and lower **profit/capital employed ratio** than would otherwise be achievable.

The strategy to raise prices so as to achieve a minimum profit/sales ratio of 12½%, compared with the current 7½%, implies **price rises** of at least 5%. If the strategy were successful, profits would be about two-thirds higher, and so the profit/capital employed figure would also rise by about two-thirds to 25%. With an unchanged P/E ratio the **share price** of U plc shares would also rise by two-thirds.

Another advantage of this strategy, compared with the current one, is that the company would make savings in advertising and promotion costs.

The major drawback to this strategy is that U plc's current **low price strategy**, whilst not winning any new customers because of the reluctance of customers to change supplier, could mean that higher prices will result in some loss of business. If the demand for U plc's product is **inelastic**, the financial benefits of a price rise would exceed the drawback of some loss of market share. However, if demand at higher prices shows a **high elasticity**, (which is sometimes the case in oligopoly markets) the loss of sales and market share could be considerable, in which case the higher-price strategy would **fail to achieve the objective** of a 12½% profit/sales ratio.

The third marketing strategy of adapting **production procedures** so as to become more flexible, **responsive to customer demands** and capable of faster **product development**, would presumably have the objective of increasing market share. A Ltd, which has the greatest flexibility of the three companies, has the biggest market share but also the highest variable costs. This strategy, were it successful, might eventually succeed in improving U plc's results so as to become comparable to A Ltd's. However, it is not clear how easily U plc could switch to a strategy of greater flexibility, and what this might involve in terms of scrapping existing capital equipment and converting to a less capital-intensive system of operating.

The third strategy would take longer to implement than the other two, and so its benefits would be longer in coming. It would also be the highest-risk strategy of the three, if a large amount of **capital expenditure** were involved.

The choice of strategy must also take account of **competitors'** reactions. Presumably they have already reacted to the current strategy. A price increase by U plc should not be a direct threat to the others. A change in production methods, though, would be more threatening, and Z plc and A Ltd might take counter-measures of some kind.

Of the three strategies, a strategy of increasing prices might seem to offer the best immediate prospects of improved financial results, but the consequences of higher prices on sales volume ought to be investigated closely before such a strategy is adopted. The strategy of adapting production procedures might offer the best long-term prospects, but it is a high-risk strategy, especially if competitors take successful counter-measures.

(b) It is assumed that the three companies specialise in the single market and that their financial results do not include results from any other trading activities.

A 'takeover' of Z plc by U plc would then appear to be an unusual suggestion, and one that would be most unlikely to succeed.

Suppose, for the purpose of illustration, that the total market were worth £10 million in sales turnover. The results of U plc and Z plc could then be compared as follows:

	Turnover £m		Profit £		Capital employed £	P/E ratio	Market capitalisation £m
U plc	1.5	(7.5%)	112,500	(÷ 15%)	750,000	10.4	1.17
Z plc	2.0	(15%)	300,000	(÷ 20%)	1,500,000	17.3	5.19
			412,500		2,250,000		

On the basis of the figures, it would seem that Z plc has twice the **capital employed** of U plc and over four times the current **market capitalisation**. An offer of only three shares in U plc for two shares in Z plc would be impossibly low.

The offer would be in the interests of U plc shareholders, were it to succeed, because the **ROCE** of the new company would be higher (about 18.3% on the basis of the figures above). Since U plc would be offering three of its shares (currently priced on a P/E of 10.4) for two shares in Z plc (currently on a P/E of 17.3) there would also be a small improvement in the **EPS** for U plc shareholders. This in turn would result in a higher share price, even if the P/E ratio of the new company remained at 10.4.

In order to afford the takeover, U plc would almost certainly have to **issue new shares**, and **control** of the company would be affected. This might not be in the interest of existing shareholders, especially any major shareholder in the company.

As indicated earlier, however, this is not an offer that Z's board of directors or shareholders should wish to accept.

(c) The growth that might be expected would be as follows:

(i)   Without synergy and without growth, the combined company's **profits and ROCE** would be higher than for U plc on its own.

(ii)   The combined **market share** of the merged company would start at 35%. If the sales turnover of the total market is rising annually, the company's **turnover** would also increase. This should result in a higher total **contribution** and **operating profit**, a higher **profit/sales ratio** and a higher **ROCE**.

(iii) The combined company might hope to succeed in improving its results through **synergy**.

(1)   **Marketing operations** could be combined, with some savings in costs. There would also be the possibility of more effective sales and promotional activities, resulting in new clients and a bigger market share.

(2)   **Production operations** might be rationalised with some savings in **capital equipment**. This would improve the profit/capital employed ratio and the ROCE.

(3) There might be some synergy with **R & D activities**, enabling the combined company to develop **new products** more successfully, thus rivalling A Ltd in this respect and so perhaps winning some customers from A Ltd.

5   MARKETING ORIENTATION

> **Tutorial note.** The essence of a market orientation is to find out what the customer needs and attempt to satisfy those needs, rather than to devise a product or service and then offer it for use.
>
> A non-profit organisation will have 'customers' too. Our answer to part (a) indicates that a bit of re-thinking can help any organisation to focus its effort on its customers. We include three examples. You may have thought of others.
>
> Part (b) is a straightforward examination of the differences between consumer and industrial marketing. It is worth learning these differences, but the concept of the DMU is the most important element to mention.

(a) **Marketing orientation**' is a management philosophy which holds that the key task of an organisation is to identify the needs and wants of **customers** in a **target market**, and to adapt the organisation to satisfying them **effectively and efficiently**. An organisation whose objective is to make profits would be market-oriented in order to satisfy customers and thereby be more profitable than it could by means of any other policy.

An organisation which does not have a profit objective may be a charity, an organisation formed to promote a cause (for example a political party) or an organisation which is established to provide a certain non-commercial service (for example a club or a government department). These organisations still have 'target markets' and 'customers' with needs to satisfy, and therefore a market-oriented approach by the management of the organisation is a feasible proposition.

An initial **definition of the nature of the business** in which an organisation operates is useful because it helps the business to focus on the interests of the consumer. For example, as profit-making organisations, Hollywood film companies eventually realised that they were not film-makers but firms in the entertainment market. As a result, instead of competing unsuccessfully with television, they switched profitably into the production of television programmes.

A similar exercise might help **non-profit-motivated organisations** to re-assess their future. For example, the fire department of a local authority might redefine its purpose from fighting fires to 'being in the business of minimising injury and damage through fire or other accidents'. This redefinition, if it is in keeping with the needs of customers, would extend the activities of the department to fire prevention, rescuing victims from accidents etc.

Another example might be a public swimming pool, which defines its business, not as providing a facility for swimming but as swimming for general recreation and life protection. In this way, the pool's management might extend its activities into swimming classes, life-saving classes, opening a swimming club for sports competition etc.

As a final example, a charitable organisation might define itself, not in terms of raising funds and providing food to help a starving population in an overseas country, (product or service orientation) but in terms of the business of providing for the health and security of the population in the short term and for the improvement of the population's well-being in the longer term (ie market orientation). In this way the charity's management might actively seek ways, not only of providing food and medical supplies, but also of providing funds for education and investment in agricultural machinery, or even an infrastructure of roads and communications for the country concerned.

(b) An understanding of who buys your product, how they buy it and what influences the buying process is fundamental to establishing marketing strategy for both **consumer** and **industrial** marketing managers. There is, however, general agreement that there are certain features in **organisational buying** that are not found in consumer markets and that these features have implications for sales strategy. These are as follows.

(i) **Fewer potential organisational buyers**. Often 80% of output is sold to relatively few organisations. In consumer selling, the presence of intermediaries (ie wholesalers/retailers) can mean there are relatively few direct buyers, although the ultimate number of end consumers can amount to millions.

(ii) **Organisational buyers are more rational.** Although people buying for organisations are only human and may, as individuals, prefer the colour of a particular product, on the whole the buying behaviour is more rational. Economic criteria tend to be used. Also, the buying decision has to be justified to other parts of the organisation.

(iii) **Organisational buying may be to satisfy specific requirements.** Often buyers determine product specifications and so the seller must tailor the product to meet them. In consumer marketing, products are rarely geared to individual customers.

(iv) **Reciprocal buying may be important.** For example, a company supplying business documentation (eg invoices) to a chain of garages may only get the business if they have all their company cars serviced there.

(v) **Organisational buying can be more risky.** Often the contract is agreed before the product is made. Technical problems could arise later which could make the product uneconomic to produce. In addition, very large sums of money are often involved, such as with the purchase of a new computer system.

(vi) **Organisational buying is usually more complex than consumer buying.** Many people could potentially get involved - engineers, directors, marketing people. It may therefore be necessary to sell as a team. The main way in which the decision making process varies is that a **group** of people, rather than an individual consumer, will normally be involved. This is known as the Decision Making Unit (DMU). The DMU is usually made up of:

- Users (often initiators, for example production)
- Deciders (those with authority, for example directors)
- Influencers (marketing, research and development, other managers)
- Buyers (who execute the purchase)
- Gatekeepers (for example, secretaries, receptionists)

(vii) **Organisational buying has a different buying motive** or need. Consumer buying is usually for personal consumption whereas industrial buying is not. The development of formal specifications and the review of potential supplier proposals, together with the development of an order routine, make the process more formal and tangible.

6 CORPORATE STRATEGY DEVELOPMENT

> **Tutorial note.** A very straightforward question on the position audit and SWOT that should require no additional explanation. The models described are important tools when assessing a business and its position and are often used in examination questions to apply to particular scenarios. The Ms model featured in the May 2002 exam, although the CIMA definition is the more important list to learn. It is also more concise.

(a) A **position audit** is a detailed review of an organisation's current position, and is a useful starting point for developing strategies for the future. Position audit is defined in the CIMA's **Official Terminology** as:

'Part of the planning process which examines the current state of the entity in respect of:

- Resources of tangible and intangible assets and finance
- Products, brands and markets
- Operating systems such as production and distribution
- Internal organisation
- Current results
- Returns to stockholders'

It can also be described using the M's model:

- Men
- Money
- Management
- Make-up
- Machinery
- Methods
- Markets
- Materials
- Management Information

The position audit can be split into a marketing audit and a resources audit.

(i) The **marketing audit** will establish information about **market share** for the company's products, the size of its **customer base**, the size and frequency of **orders**, the split of sales between **exports and domestic** markets, sales and contribution **growth** over the past few years, current sales **revenue** and **profitability** for each product, product group and in total etc.

(ii) A **resource audit** will provide information about the resources that the organisation uses, such as the number of **materials** suppliers, prices for materials, **supplier** reliability and quality, the size and skills of the labour force, **wages** costs, labour efficiency, labour **turnover**, industrial relations, the cost, age and efficiency of **machines** and other fixed assets, fixed asset utilisation, management experience and skills, **working capital** requirements, periods of credit given and taken, **stock levels** and turnover, **financial resources**, and intangible items such as **brands**, patents and goodwill.'

(b) A **corporate appraisal** (**SWOT analysis**) follows on from a position audit and environmental analysis. Corporate appraisal is defined in the CIMA's **Official Terminology** as:

'A critical assessment of the strengths and weaknesses, opportunities and threats (SWOT analysis) in relation to the internal and environmental factors affecting an entity in order to establish its condition prior to the preparation of the long term plan.'

Strengths and weaknesses analysis involves looking at the (internal) particular strengths and weaknesses of the organisation and its product/service range.

(i) The strengths and weaknesses analysis is **internal** to the company but is intended to shape its approach to the **external** world. For instance, the identification of shortcomings in skills or resources could lead to a planned acquisition programme or to more staff recruitment and training.

(ii) In essence, an internal appraisal seeks to identify:

(1) Shortcomings in the company's present skills and resources
(2) Strengths which the company should seek to exploit

The **external appraisal** of **opportunities** and **threats** follows on from the environmental analysis and position audit.

(i) The analysis of opportunities would involve:

(1) Identifying business opportunities and their inherent potential (eg for making profits)

(2) Assessing whether the organisation has sufficient strengths to exploit these opportunities, and whether competitors are better placed to exploit them.

(ii) The analysis of threats involves identifying potential threats to the organisation, from economic change, government regulations, competitors, technological change, social/demographic changes and so on.

SWOT analysis should help the planners to develop strategies that will **exploit** attractive opportunities, **take defensive measures** against threats, **exploit** strengths and **reduce** weaknesses.

7   CONTRACT CATERING

Tutorial note. Part (a) of this question is all about converting threats into opportunities. The answer has been structured around the points (i) to (vi) outlined in the question data. The threats (and the opportunities they could create) are then set out. For example, the 'threat' of increasing vegetarianism and health consciousness can be converted into an opportunity to expand the product ranges offered.

Increasing food regulation could also bring opportunities to service markets now wary of being caught in violation of the rules.

In part (b) we have come up with two simple cost measures as required by the question. You may have thought of others. The important thing is to have come up with examples that can represent a *target* to work towards. They should not be over-complicated.

(a) **Threats and opportunities** (numbers refer to factors identified in question)

(i) It would seem that most large organisations should be able to provide their own in-house catering more cheaply. Even so, there might be possible clients amongst larger firms, and a contract caterer with sufficient resources to service a large client might see an opportunity in a direct marketing approach to these firms.

The sales and profit potential for contract catering to smaller firms is not clear from the data given in the question. This potential market segment might be profitable as developments in cook-chill catering and automatic vending machines continue.

(ii) Cook-chill catering appears to bring both opportunities and threats to the market. The **cost advantages** of producing food in a central production unit will include:

- Saving in kitchen space at distribution points
- Less capital expenditure on catering equipment
- Lower maintenance costs
- Fewer catering staff

Cook-chill food can be prepared during normal working hours and, on re-heating, served up at any time of the day. This should reduce labour costs of overtime working in cases where food has to be provided to shift workers or at odd times of the day.

However, the **safety aspect** of cook-chill foods should be considered, and any firm which invests in cook-chill production methods will find itself liable to its customers and their employees, especially in cases where there is inadequate management and operational controls over the chilling, re-heating or shelf life of the food. There is an opportunity here to improve customer service and client satisfaction (and hence return business) by strict adherence to safety standards that go beyond the minimum required by law.

(iii) The growing preference for health foods suggests that there will be continuing opportunities to develop new or more **varied ranges** of foods in a catering service. The corresponding threat of this development is that any contract catering firm which does not offer vegetarian meals or other health food might eventually find that it loses some customers.

(iv) The removal of Crown immunity from hospitals is likely to make hospitals much more wary about preparing food for patients, or washing up crockery and cutlery by 'traditional' domestic methods. In many hospitals there could be a switch to using 'disposable' food products and disposable plates and cups etc - for example, cook-chill foods, supplied perhaps by contract caterers.

The drawback for firms in this sector will be the need for hospitals to keep their costs under control, so that they are unlikely to buy disposable food products from caterers unless at a low price.

(v) Vending machines linked to a microwave oven can provide a round-the-clock food and drinks service offering a wide range of products. Plastic cards used as 'payment' have the advantage that machines do not have to be continually emptied of money.

Provided that vending machines are clean, efficient and provide a varied product range, there is likely to be a growth market in the vending machine market sector. Many people are fairly casual about eating, and might prefer a vending machine service to a sit-down three course meal in the works canteen or office cafeteria.

(vi) Changing work habits in the City of London creates threats for city restaurateurs who might lose lunchtime business. Restaurants might however be able to attract more evening business, as City workers finally end their day in the early to late evening.

The changing habits might also create opportunities for contract caterers to provide palatable food which can be served quickly to City workers in their work premises during a short lunch break.

Many City firms might increasingly award contracts to such caterers and so this market segment should provide opportunities for rapid growth.

(b) It is assumed that the contract caterer's customers will subsidise the cost of the meals to their employees, so that the meals are sold below cost. Two possible measures of performance.

(i) The **food cost recovery rate** as a percentage of contractor's charges. For example, if meals cost the employer £10,000 and employees pay £3,000 in meal prices, the food cost recovery rate would be 30%. Actual results would be compared against a target food cost recovery rate.

(ii) The **cost per employee** of the catering service. Actual cost would be compared against a target.

8 LIFE CYCLES AND PRODUCT MARKET STRATEGY

> **Tutorial note.** This question requires practical application of two syllabus models to various companies in different industries, and as such it is typical of questions at this level. You must be able to analyse the information presented, in this case identifying the phase of development reached by each industry, then applying Ansoff's matrix. You may have been distracted by the phrase 'industry' life cycle, but this is no different in principle to the product life cycle with which you should be familiar. Being able to tie the industries in question to the respective life cycle phases in part (a) should cause few problems, and indeed is not worth too many marks.
>
> Part (b) is more challenging. We have opened our answer with a diagram to link the narrative to, as it makes the answer easier to follow. You may have done the same, as it helps to focus the mind!
>
> In summary, our conclusions for part (b) were broadly as follows
>
> | | Key feature | Option |
> |---|---|---|
> | • Company A | Innovation | Product development |
> | • Company B | Growing market | Product development and/or market penetration |
> | • Company C | Mature market | Market development |
> | • Company D | Weak position, with sales down | Divestment to free resources before fighting on where possible |

(a) (i) The **industry life cycle** reflects the fact that the profitability and sales of an industry can be expected to change over time. It is an attempt to recognise distinct stages in an industry's sales history. The classic **life cycle pattern** is commonly described by a curve as follows.

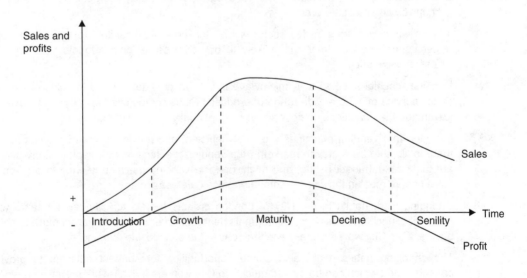

Introduction

(1) A new industry product takes time to find acceptance by would-be purchasers and there is a slow growth in sales. Unit costs are high because of low output and expensive sales promotion.

(2) There may be early teething troubles with technology.

(3) The industry for the time being is a loss-maker.

Growth

(1) With market acceptance, sales will eventually rise more sharply, and profits will rise.
(2) Competitors are attracted. As sales and production rise, unit costs fall.

Maturity

(1) The rate of sales growth slows down and the industry reaches a period of maturity which is probably the longest period of a successful industry's life. Innovation may have slowed down by this stage.

(2) Most products on the market will be at the mature stage of their life. Profits are good.

Decline

(1) Sales will begin to decline so that there is over-capacity of production in the industry. Severe competition occurs, profits fall and some producers leave the market.

(2) The remaining producers seek means of prolonging product life by modification and searching for new market segments. Many producers are reluctant to leave the market, although some inevitably do because of market fragmentation and falling profits.

(ii) The industries in which each of the companies appear to be operating are as follows.

(1) **Company A**. This is operating in the introductory phase of what is a very new innovation, but this innovation is located within a very old industry.

(2) **Company B**. This is positioned in a rapidly expanding and relatively young industry, experiencing a growth phase.

(3) **Company C**. This company is in a mature industry, as witnessed by the low growth but high market share. Profits are likely to be good.

(4) **Company D**. While the retailing industry itself is not in decline, this company appears to be, as it is losing ground to competitors in what is a highly competitive industry. The competitors may be larger companies able to compete more effectively on marketing mix issues such as price.

(b) **Ansoff** drew up a **growth vector matrix**, describing a combination of a firm's activities in current and new markets, with existing and new products. The matrix can be represented diagrammatically as follows.

		Product	
		Present	*New*
Market	*Present*	Market penetration; (for growth) or consolidation (to maintain position) or withdrawal	Product development
	New	Market development	Diversification

Company A is involved with launching a very **innovative** product to revolutionise an existing market (home security). Such product development forces competitors to innovate and may provide initial barriers to entry, with newcomers to the industry being discouraged. This will give Company A the chance to build up rapid **market penetration**, but as competitors enter the market, it must make sure that it keeps household and commercial customers interested via constant innovation. The drawback to this is the related **expense and risk**. Company A must also make sure that it has enough resources to satisfy demand so that competitors cannot poach market share.

Product improvements will be necessary to sustain the market, so Company A must make sure that enough resources are given to **research and development** of new technologies (and hence new products) in its field, as well as to maintaining sufficient production capacity to satisfy current demand.

Company B is engaged in a rapidly expanding market that is likely to attract many **competitors** keen for their own share of the market and profits. The growth strategy is limited to the current agricultural market, so referring to the Ansoff matrix above, the company is going to be mainly concerned with

market penetration and **product development**, with an emphasis on the latter to make life more difficult for new competitors. By investing in product development, the company will see a necessary expansion in its R&D facility. To keep the new products and the company itself in the public eye, it may need to invest more in **marketing** and **promotion.**

With **market penetration**, the company will aim to achieve the following.

- Maintain or increase its **share** of the current market with its current products, for example through competitive pricing, advertising, sales promotion and quality control

- Secure **dominance** of the market and drive out competitors

- Increase **usage by existing and new customers**. The customer base is likely to be expanding

Company C is in the **mature phase** of its life cycle. As the current market is mature, the company can achieve growth via the investigation of **new markets**. Referring to the Ansoff matrix, this means pursuing a strategy of **market development.** Seeing as the current market is mature, with satisfied customers and little innovation, there is small scope for market development, unless it is via short term aggressive tactics such as cuts in prices.

Selling current products to new markets is likely to be more successful, and may include one or more of the following strategies.

- New **geographical areas** and export markets
- **Different package sizes** for food and other domestic items
- **New distribution channels** to attract new customers
- **Differential pricing policies** to attract different types of customer and create new market segments
- **Mass marketing techniques** that encourage customers to switch brands

The company may also investigate the possibility of developing **new products** to make up for those that are in the **decline phase** of the life cycle. This may lead to the creation of more **cash cows**.

Company D is in a difficult position, with a weak position in a well established market. It needs to undertake some rigorous **analysis of costs**. A strategy of **divestment** may be advised to enable it to reduce costs and concentrate on more profitable areas of activity. **Resource limitations** mean that less profitable outlets or products may have to be abandoned. This could involve analysis of individual contributions, perhaps using **direct product profitability** techniques.

The market has become less attractive and Company D needs to assess its image and profitability. It is likely that customers have become more discerning on price, as has happened in the UK retailing sector in the past few years. When some product areas have been divested, the company may find that it has the **resources** to pursue strategies of **market penetration** for some products and **new product development** to improve its image with customers.

A strategy of **total withdrawal**, and **diversification** into wholly new industries is not seen as appropriate for any of the companies described in the question. It could not be recommended because of the attendant **risks**.

Company D does need to be careful, and it is facing the most difficult situation of all the companies that have been described. As **Johnson and Scholes** point out, it is one thing to eliminate unprofitable products but will there be sufficient growth potential among the products that remain in the product range?

In addition, new products require some initial **capital expenditure**. Retained profits are by far the most significant source of new funds for companies. A company investing in the medium to long term which does not have enough **current income from existing products** will go into liquidation, in spite of its future prospects.

9   GRIER AND BOX PLC

> **Tutorial note.** This is a 'bitty' question that needs to be approached stage by stage.
>
> In part (a), given that 'value added' is a simple measure of the value earned by a company from selling a product, over and above the direct material costs of production, some simple analysis will show us the worst performing divisions. Low value added items drag down profitability, and it is often difficult to turn their performance around because if materials costs are high (no matter how efficient you are), then the only way to achieve better profitability is to obtain cheaper supplies if you can.
>
> Part (b) is concerned with the rationale for a divestment. We have referred to the threat from competitors and small market shares to conclude that a significant investment would be needed to establish these divisions more firmly in their markets. Note here that you are not asked to recommend whether or not to sell the divisions. The question almost assumes that such a decision has already been made, by asking you **why** they *should* be sold off.
>
> When answering part (c) (i) the key factor to consider is the relative risk of the two types of investment. For part (ii) make use of the numbers given and take note of the need to balance the aims of reducing gearing and continuing to modernise. Which option represents the better use of cash resources? We show in our answer that both options are valid, but Grier and Box should certainly reduce their gearing to improve their interest cover.
>
> Part (d) is a more general question on performance control using traditional methods of ratio analysis and budgetary control. Such systems must provide regular and up-to-date information if they are to be effective. Annual budgets are becoming notorious for their inflexibility and many companies now prepare revised forecasts every quarter.

(a) **Value added** is 'the increase in realisable value resulting from an alteration in form, location or availability of a product or service, excluding the cost of purchased materials or services' (CIMA). In a simplified definition, value added is measured as **sales minus materials costs.**

Division	Value added £m	Value added/sales ratio
Electrical equipment	5.3	13.25%
Fluid controls	4.9	19.44%
Metals	9.1	53.22%
Industrial services	19.0	56.38%
Bathroom accessories	2.5	35.71%
Tubes	4.5	75.00%

The MD would appear to be referring to the electrical equipment and fluid controls divisions, whose value added is only about 13% and 19% of sales value respectively. The implications of making and selling low value added items are the following.

(i)   **Profit/sales ratios** will be small because materials costs are a large proportion of total sales value. For electrical equipment, this was 5% last year, ignoring interest on capital, and for fluid controls, it was 4.8%.

(ii)   Attempts to **improve efficiency and reduce labour costs** will therefore have only a small effect on profit/sales ratios.

(iii)   Improving **profitability** will rely largely on reducing materials costs or increasing sales.

(iv)   A very **large increase in sales** would be needed to earn a sizeable increase in profits.

(v)   The **working capital investment** in the products will be high, because of the high materials cost of production.

(vi)   For reasons (i) and (v), **ROCE** will be low.

(b) The fundamental question in both cases is whether each business can make an effective **contribution** to the company in the future. Both divisions are currently earning profits, but if they are unlikely to contribute significantly to the group in future the following will occur.

(i)   Any capital invested in the division will be tied up, earning relatively low returns.

(ii)   It is therefore be more appropriate to sell the businesses now, to obtain a reasonable price whilst they are profitable, and to use the revenue earned from the sales to invest in projects that would earn a better return.

The bathroom accessories division faces the prospect of having to compete in its market with companies which are currently its customers. The threat of backward vertical integration by manufacturers of bathroom ceramics suggests that the division:

- Might struggle to retain its market share
- Might even lose market share

The long-term prospects for profit and sales growth are therefore poor.

The tubes division has a very small share of its market. It is doubtful whether the capital investment needed to improve efficiency would be justified (although a DCF evaluation should be made) and in view of the very small market share, the long term prospects for the product are probably poor.

In terms of **BCG classification**, tubes and bathroom accessories are probably '**dog**' products for the company and should be sold off.

(c) (i) **Capital expenditure on replacement equipment** to manufacture well-established products should have a **short payback period**, because the products ought to be earning good profits and cash inflows. A payback period of about 2 - 3 years might be suitable.

Capital expenditure on new development projects will be **high risk spending** and so should perhaps be evaluated at a higher DCF cost of capital. However, new projects take time to become established, and so their payback period will be longer than for equipment replacement projects.

A suitable payback period would depend on the nature of the business and the 'normal' time for new projects to become established in the marketplace.

(ii) If the company wishes to **reduce its gearing**, which is currently high at 60%, a suitable balance should be made in the company's strategic plans between using cash inflows to **reduce borrowing** and using cash inflows to **invest** in modernisation programmes.

Manufacturing companies must remain efficient to be competitive and profitable, and effective modernisation programmes should be an essential feature of their strategic plans. There is no reason why Grier and Box plc cannot use its earnings partly to repay debt and partly for new investments.

The need to reduce gearing from 60% is a valid **strategic aim**. Taking the company's average interest cost of debt is 10%, then the current level of debt would be £4.8m per annum which gives the company an interest cover of only (14.8 ÷ 4.8) 3.1 times.

(d) There are several main **dangers**.

(i) The **reporting system**, using performance ratios and budget variances, might be inadequate. It must be capable of providing regular and up-to-date reports which:

(1) Report **key performance measures**
(2) Draw management attention to **significant divergences** between actual and plan.

(ii) The **budget** itself might be built on incorrect assumptions and so budget **variances** might be misleading and incorrect.

(iii) Budgets get **out of date**. There would probably need to be an additional system whereby revised forecasts are prepared, perhaps every three months, and actual results compared against the revised forecast in reports to head office.

(iv) There has to be a **retained authority** for head office staff to insist on control measures being taken by line managers, when they consider that actual performance indicates a need for **control action**.

10   FG PLC

> **Tutorial note**. The complication with this example is that some of the cash flows are given at half yearly intervals, whereas the tables of discount factors assume that cash flows occur at the year end. A reasonable approximation could be obtained by halving the interest rate and taking each six month period as a year.
>
> Alternatively, the conservative viewpoint could be taken by assuming that cash flows occur at the end of the year. If the project is still viable with this assumption then it may be worthwhile.
>
> This probably seems rather unscientific, but the question in part (a) does ask us to analyse the proposal and not to calculate the exact NPV of the project.

> **Tutorial note continued**
>
> Other factors to consider are based on the uncertainties about the project. It is risky, and we do not know if the cash inflows are accurate forecasts. Moreover, it is not known how the project is to be financed.
>
> Non-financial factors also need to be considered. The physical inconvenience of the proposed building work should also be noted. This may go on for a long time as there is no guarantee that suppliers will be reliable. In addition, the outsourcing of some production will mean that FG loses some control over its customer relationships in the areas affected.

(a) A discount rate of 18% will be used since this gives the worst possible outcome. It is assumed that the cash flows are given net of taxation.

Year	Cash inflow £'000	Cash outflow £'000	Net cash flow £'000	18% discount factor	Present value £
1	100	(125.0)	(25.0)	0.847	(21,175)
2	-	(527.5)	(527.5)	0.718	(378,745)
3	450	(472.5)	(22.5)	0.609	(13,702)
4	650	-	650.0	0.516	335,400
5	700	-	700.0	0.437	305,900
				Net present value	227,678

The project produces a net present value of almost £230,000. It pays back during the fourth year, probably towards the end of the year if the cash inflow occurs evenly.

The project therefore seems viable despite the conservative views taken on cash flows and should proceed. However management should be aware of the following points arising from the information supplied.

(i) The **payback period** is very long and this increases the risk associated with the project.

(ii) There is no information as to how the **net cash inflow** from the additional production has been derived. If it has been assumed that all output can be sold at current prices then this may be over-optimistic.

(iii) If the project were to be financed from borrowed funds this may cause an unacceptable increase in the company's **gearing**.

(iv) The project may produce a higher NPV than shown because of the undefined benefits which may accrue after year 5.

(b) Other factors to be considered include the following.

(i) **Reliability of the plant suppliers**. The project has a long payback period therefore any delay could be critical and would increase the risk substantially. The contract should include penalty clauses to protect FG from the cost of delays, or more than one supplier could be used.

(ii) **Disruption caused by building work**. This may cause lost production in other departments if their activities are disturbed.

(iii) **Staff redeployment**. It may be necessary to make staff redundant or to retrain them, both of which have inherent cost implications.

(iv) **Use of sub-contractors**. FG's customers may not be happy to hear that a third party is now manufacturing the product. It will probably depend on the importance of the product to the customer. FG must have adequate control over the quality and reliability of supply and must instigate appropriate quality control procedures. Clarification is also needed on stock policy - would finished stocks be held by the sub-contractor, and if so, what are the cash flow implications for FG?

(c) The **internal rate of return** (IRR) suffers from a number of **interpretation problems**, particularly with this project. The forecast cash flows are non-conventional in that they do not become positive until year 4. These non-conventional cash flows will result in more than one IRR for the project, which would be difficult for management to interpret.

Another problem with both the IRR and the NPV is that they do not take account of **risk**.

For this simple accept/reject decision, the **large NPV** combined with a consideration of the **qualitative factors** should provide enough information for managers to make their decision.

11   OB

> **Tutorial note.** This question relates to a very specific syllabus topic within the Setting Objectives section. Greiner's organisational life cycle model demonstrates the phases that a company goes through as it grows. The focus of this question is the effect that such growth has upon the approach to setting corporate objectives at the various growth stages.
>
> Our suggested solution does not include a diagram of the model, as this is rather involved and would take up too much time. Rather, we have concentrated on a clear explanation of the model's phases, as they apply to the scenario. This gives a structure to the answer.
>
> The broad distinction to be made is that between an ad-hoc approach to objective setting when the company is young, and a more formal approach, involving more layers of management as the company grows and objectives become more 'advanced' (eg finance for a capital injection).
>
> Note that our answer also includes examples of objectives at each stage, how such objectives are set and how they could be measured. For example:
>
> | Model | Objective | Set by | Measurement |
> |---|---|---|---|
> | • Phase 1 | • Basic survival | • Incrementalism or freewheeling | • Profitability/Liquidity |
> | ↓ | | | |
> | • Phase 3 | • More investment in plant and equipment | • Co-ordinated at board level | • Investment appraisal analysis |

An organisation **grows** in a number of ways, and one of the main reasons for growth is an increasing **demand** for its products and services. This **market growth** will stimulate sales revenue, profitability, product range, number of outlets and the number of employees. Attendant on this growth will be a periodic revision in the **focus of organisational objectives** at each stage, from the beginning of a company's life to its position as a successful and expanding business entity.

An **organisational life cycle model** was suggested by **Greiner** (as referred to in the question scenario). It assumes that, as an organisation ages, it grows in size, perhaps by the **number of employees** (in the example, more managers and operational employees have been recruited by F) and by **diversity or scope of activity**. Ob's market demand is increasing such that it needs more capital if growth is to be sustained.

Establishing objectives in the early stages

Phase 3 of Greiner's model has seen Ob arrive at the stage where it is achieving **growth through delegation**. Phase 1, **growth through creativity**, saw Ob as a small company, managed in a personal and informal way and influenced strongly by the creativity of its founder, F. The founder will have been actively involved in all aspects of the operations, personnel issues and innovation.

A key goal at this stage is **basic company survival**. The establishment of objectives will have been largely in the domain of F, although he will have had to take account of the need to satisfy **connected stakeholders** such as customers, suppliers and investors (chiefly the providers of the loan finance, who needed reassurance about the security for their loan). These stakeholders are likely to have been small in number in the early stages of the company's life, and F may have felt that he had almost an entirely free hand in the running of the company so long as he was able in the longer term to pay off the bank loan.

Objective setting in such an organisation is unlikely to have followed a logical or predictable pattern, driven as it was mainly by the personal ambition of the sole founder. Although it is not clear from the scenario which industry Ob operates in, objectives were probably set out in broad terms that were necessary for the business plan that F would have put together when looking for his bank loan, such as **profitability and liquidity forecasts**, maybe over the following five to ten years.

Any development of objectives beyond these broad measures is likely to have been via a process of **incrementalism** or **freewheeling opportunism**, with F taking advantage of good opportunities as they presented themselves to him. Adoption of strategies will have mainly depended on whether or not F thought them to be a good idea at the time. They are likely to have related mainly to **product** and **marketing** issues.

With the growth of the business, new managers and employees were recruited and the number of **internal stakeholders** grew. There will have emerged a need for distinct **management skills**, relating less to product and marketing issues and more to the **co-ordination** of the expanding company activity. Greiner calls this a 'crisis of leadership'.

By professionalising the management, better direction is given. This is **Phase 2** of Greiner's model. However, the initial enthusiasm of Ob's new managers has been tempered by a loss of autonomy. Their ability to contribute to the overall decision making has declined, relative to their growing confidence in handling the business. At the same time, F has found it harder and harder to keep in detailed control.

More **delegation** has now taken place **(Phase 3)** and there are two new board members to assist F in strategic planning. Objectives are likely to now be **formally set** at **board** rather than **operational** level, and there is going to be more discussion of **strategic direction** as there is now more than one viewpoint to be taken into consideration.

Approaches to setting objectives in the later stages

Objectives are likely to now be **co-ordinated** more strongly from board level, although overall objectives in terms of **profitability** and **returns to shareholders** are likely to be unchanged. Survival is still a key objective for what is still a young company.

Board policy will be to further these objectives, and a wider group of stakeholders now needs to be taken into consideration, as the company has grown and no doubt attracted **new customers** and forged relationships with **new suppliers**. As more finance is being sought to fund future expansion, future **growth in earnings** must be emphasised, to ensure the ability to pay interest in the short term and eventually repay the loan when required. This will involve **increased revenues** and **strict cost control.**

It is also likely that long term objectives will gain more prominence to focus on company survival. **More investment** may be required in plant and equipment, and maybe a long term **research and development** programme or marketing campaign. Such investments would need to be subjected to **investment appraisal analysis** which Ob may not have had to undertake in its early days.

The organisational structure is likely to become more **hierarchical** as a result of greater **delegation** and a more obvious division between strategy setting at board level (F and his two fellow directors) and the operational managers. This will mean that objectives need to be **clearly communicated**, and a **reporting system** set up which monitors progress towards their achievement.

If we look to the next phase of Greiner's model, we can anticipate that the company may next face a **crisis of control**, where delegation leads to different departments acting sub-optimally, pursuing their own goals to the detriment of Ob as a whole. Greater effort at co-ordination will therefore be needed, but the company will need to be careful that there is not too much centralisation as this may hinder growth.

Departments are less likely to operate sub-optimally if the objectives of the organisation are clearly established, and uncontrolled, emergent strategies are increasingly seen as inappropriate to the future planned development and growth of the organisation.

12   MANAGEMENT ACCOUNTING INFORMATION

> **Tutorial note.** This is a familiar topic for examination questions at this level. The relevance of management accounting information has troubled academics and practitioners alike, and has been influential in the development of new techniques (such as ABC or the balanced scorecard) over the past decade or so, in an effort to make management accounting seem more relevant to modern business.
>
> The question is broken down into two parts. The first requires an analysis of the validity of the criticism that management accounting information is irrelevant for decision making. The second part asks you to think about the provision of management accounting information in two different types of organisation.
>
> Our answer to the first part takes the stance that while new techniques are available, many firms do not sufficiently tailor their information collection to specific decisions, and need to develop systems to make sure that they are able to undertake financial analysis, planning and control. No one solution will suit all businesses.
>
> Our answer to the second part considers issues of financial v non-financial information, organisational structure and performance measurement. These will vary between the two organisations concerned.

(a)   In 1987 **Kaplan and Johnson** wrote a stinging critique of the management accounting profession in *Relevance Lost*. Seeing the challenge facing management accountants as being one of providing more **relevant** information for decision making, they argued that traditional management accounting systems may not always provide this. Management accounting information is often biased towards the **past** rather than the future, and management accounting systems do not always detect **strategic issues**.

Decision making is a **forward** and **outward** looking process, and management accounting information has been too inward looking and directed largely towards **financial reporting**. Historical costs are necessary to report to shareholders, but the classifications of transactions for reporting purposes are not necessarily relevant to decision making.

Much management accounting information is devised for **internal consumption**. However, strategic management involves looking at the **external environment**, and strategy is pursued in relation to **competitors**. Their actions need to be understood and quantified to be able to devise appropriate response activity.

Some management accounting techniques such as **variance analysis** are seen as too simplistic and largely irrelevant for decision making in a 21st century business. Modern business is embracing new ways of working, including **outsourcing** and **homeworking**, and there is constant pressure to improve quality and service and reduce costs. Some techniques such as **activity based costing** have been developed which are designed to take specific business processes and cost drivers into account when measuring profitability and performance. Techniques such as **customer account profitability and direct product profitability** attempt to replace general analysis with specifics, but in general many firms continue to use old costing systems which are too general in their application to be able to support specific strategic decisions.

It could be argued, that the production of more relevant costs does not necessarily make the management accountant a strategic partner for the chief executive overnight. Management accountants do however need to tackle this issue of the relevance of the information they provide for **strategy formulation** and **control decisions** at higher levels in the organisation. Strategic plans may cover a long period into the future, and often involve big changes and new ventures. How can the management accountant support such developments?

CIMA has defined '**strategic management accounting**' as 'a form of management accounting in which emphasis is placed on information which relates to factors external to the firm, as well as to non-financial information and internally generated information.' Ward suggests that the role of the strategic management accountant can be analysed as being split between **financial analysis, financial planning** and **financial control**. These roles encompass the current **position** of the business, its **goals** and **objectives** and its **feedback** mechanisms, which compare planned with actual performance. They may involve obtaining information from other **functions** in the organisation, such as production, distribution or marketing.

Contingency theory is a theory that has been developed which states that there is no universally applicable best practice in the design of control systems such as management accounting systems. Specific **business** and **environmental** factors will influence the operation of the system, such as organisational structure, technology and the market. The management accountant needs to analyse and present information which takes these specifics into account.

(b) Both types of organisation are going to be interested in the provision of a range of both **financial** and **non-financial information.** On the financial side, both organisations will be interested in measures such as cost control, contribution, profits, return on investment, cash flow measures, liquidity, competitiveness and market share. Non-financial measures will include issues such as product or service quality, levels of innovation, customer satisfaction and flexibility in meeting customer needs quickly.

The main distinction between the two companies is in **organisational structure**. One of the companies operates from one site. Usual methods of cost collection, reporting and profitability analysis will be able to be employed. The other is highly fragmented and so information collection may require more detailed systems and closer monitoring of the operatives working from home.

Performance appraisal of staff will be easier for the manufacturing company, and it may be that the staff identify with the company more strongly and are more motivated to achieve **company objectives**, both because they are contracted employees in the traditional sense and because they work together at one site each day. The homeworking contractors may have less sense of such loyalty and could be motivated mainly by considerations such as adding to their own stock of experience and their hourly rate.

The homeworkers are also likely to be working on their own individual projects or tasks, and could all be facing different problems and issues in the effective performance of their work. The standard management accounting system will not necessarily recognise this. It is also possible that they are being paid at different rates according to their experience (this is less likely to be sustainable in a one-site company), making comparisons of individual profitability more complex.

Many organisations operate with off-site employees, and it is becoming increasingly common to employ **outworkers** as traditional working methods are replaced. Standard reports on activities and profitability, both historical and future, are still capable of being produced despite the fact that off-site employees are now more common. The **collection** of such information may be more complicated, but advances in **technology** and computer links should enable information to be logged from remote sites all over the world if necessary.

This scenario provides an example of how management accounting systems need to be **adapted** to organisational realities. Some techniques may be consistently applied in all organisations (measuring employee productivity, for example) while others will be adapted. The one-site company may find it easier than the fragmented one to establish, define (and therefore control) meaningful **cost centres**. Individual **contract profitability** should be easily measurable by both companies, regardless of staff location, although comparing the costs of off-site employees may need to take pay rate differentials into account, as mentioned above.

Measures such as **return on investment** will be more easily defined in the manufacturing company because it is likely to have significant investment in plant and equipment. For the service company on the other hand, the chief asset is its body of professional staff, which may have a high turnover and which is less capable of being assessed in this way. As ROI is normally used to apply to investment centres or profit centres it generally reflects the **organisation structure** of the business. As mentioned previously, such centres are more likely to be a feature of the site-based company.

13 FINANCIAL AND NON-FINANCIAL APPRAISAL

> **Tutorial note**. This question brings in both investment appraisal and the distinction between public and private sector organisations in such circumstances. You are not required to critically evaluate capital investment appraisal methods, but rather to apply your knowledge to varying business environments.
>
> Cashflows are important to both public and private sector organisations, but do not forget to state in your answer that some public sector services will be required regardless of financial viability. However, some kind of statement of costs, against which to measure the likely benefits of service provision, will be needed. With resources in short supply, the public funds must be seen to be applied in the best way (by looking at the three Es, for example). For the private company, non-financial indicators such as quality will be important.

The easiest form of strategic decision to control relates to **capital expenditure**, such as investment in new factory premises or buildings. Capital projects of this nature involve long term **commitment of funds**, in anticipation of a potential **future inflow of cash**. Capital expenditure decisions should be based on an evaluation of future cash flows, **discounted** at an appropriate cost of capital, to arrive at a net present value of the investment. A positive **net present value** indicates a financially viable project.

When looking at the differing objectives of private and public sector organisations, the financial viability (or otherwise) of a project will be more readily associated with private sector preoccupations with **profitability** and **return to shareholders**. A public sector organisation such as a school does however need to ensure that it makes proper use of the **resources** made available to it, so an assessment of the cost of an investment project is going to be important if it is going to be able to measure whether or not it is making the best use of these resources within its necessarily **limited budget**.

That said, **social provision** of school services will be required **regardless of financial viability**, for example in deprived areas, or areas of the community which need special facilities. The return made by the school in such circumstances is more difficult to quantify and therefore measure.

Private sector company

The private sector company is seeking to increase its production capacity with an enlarged factory. This is likely to have been stimulated by **increased demand**, or at least an expectation of **increased future sales** and **market share**. The company may even be finding that it is having to turn customers away because of a lack of capacity. It is driven by clearly **commercial considerations**.

The **incremental** discounted cash flows (both in and out) associated with the factory extension need to be positive if the project is going to add to **shareholder value** and be viable in the financial sense. If the cost of building the extension exceeds the possible future cash flows (taking all expected revenues and tax breaks into account) then the project is simply not worth doing.

The company may expect **economies of scale** to result from the new premises, which will improve profitability via **lower unit costs**. If the industry has high **fixed costs**, significant reductions in unit costs can be achieved by producing on a larger scale.

Non financial considerations for the private sector company may include **quality concerns**. Quality is a key performance measure for manufacturing companies. Without the new premises, future improvements in quality may be compromised. The ability to stay ahead of the competition via **innovation** and **new product development** may also be seen as an important role for the planned new capacity. These factors will not be easily assessed by standard capital appraisal methods, although the company is likely to have some idea of what will be happening to the market in the future, and the likely impact on market share if the company does not keep up on quality, innovation and satisfying customer demand.

In other words, the longer term implications of the project need to be considered.

Publicly funded school

The school will not be charging for its services, so there is no revenue stream by which profitability or financial viability of the project can be measured. However, some kind of **return to the stakeholders** in the school (the local community, the government, the taxpayers) needs to be assessed. A starting point will be an assessment of the costs of the project in **net present value** terms, using an appropriate cost of capital. This can then be assessed against the perceived **benefit** of the school service, or maybe even the cost of putting the services out to **tender** to a private organisation.

Because public sector funds are limited, the expenditure on school buildings is likely to be diverting funds away from other local projects. The providers of the funds must decide whether the school services are an **appropriate use of money**. Could it be better spent elsewhere, such as on a new wing for the local library? How would the community benefit from the new services (or suffer if they are not provided)? As can be seen, non-financial criteria are very much to the fore.

The new school building may be assessed using a **value for money** audit. Such an audit focuses on **economy, efficiency** and **effectiveness**. Economy and efficiency refer to the way in which the school services will be provided, and effectiveness measures the school's performance in achieving its objectives of bringing educational services to the community. This latter measure is likely to be the most visible and important one in the public sector, where the effectiveness of service provision of all kinds is always under public scrutiny and expectations get higher and higher with each new service provided.

14   NOMINEE HOLDINGS

Tutorial note. This is a question which includes elements of financial management and management accounting (DCF, performance measurement). Indeed, the DCF rate of return or 'charge out' rate for capital is relevant to quantifying a company's long-term objectives.

The need to balance risk and return is an idea strongly suggested by the data in the question, and this touches on the overall objectives of the group. Sources of finance and gearing have to be considered, and these are problems of financial strategy as well as financial management.

The possible closure of a subsidiary is also a feature of the question, with emphasis on the strategic planning considerations.

It is necessary for some assumptions to be made.

It is not clear whether the project cost is the cost of the initial fixed asset expenditure, or whether it also includes the required investment in working capital.

It is also not clear what is meant by a 'current asset ratio'. If the question intended this to be the current ratio - ie the ratio of current assets to current liabilities, a current ratio of over 1 would indicate that some investment in working capital would be needed in addition to the fixed asset expenditure. A current ratio of less than 1 would indicate that current liabilities would help to finance the fixed assets.

(a)   To: directors of Nominee Holdings

Recommendations to consider

(i)   Three subsidiaries have submitted capital expenditure proposals, all of which would probably add value to the holding company's equity. The nature of the projects should be studied, to ensure that each project is in accord with the group's medium-term strategy. In the case of the Dairy-P project, this might not be so, since the group's strategy might favour a move of processing facilities to Greece. Clearly, if it is the group's intention to close down Dairy-P, the Dairy-P project should not be approved.

(ii)   The holding company's cash and short-term deposits amount to some 20% of its net worth, which is a very high proportion. The company is cash rich. However, its return on its cash and short-term deposits is exceedingly low, at 5%. This poor return compares most unfavourably with the company's average cost of capital (19.5%) and mortgage debenture nominal rates of interest (10% - 17%).

The holding company ought to investigate its cash management, with a view to:

(1)   Improving the return to much more than 5%.

(2)   Using some cash to finance investments by subsidiaries. It is an unsatisfactory situation when the holding company employs its assets to earn 5% whilst subsidiaries are having to borrow at 10% - 17% gross (6.5% - 11% net of tax relief, taking the rate of corporation tax to be 35%) to finance new projects.

(3)   Using some surplus cash to buy back and cancel some ordinary shares in the company. Authority for the company to purchase its own shares would have to be obtained from the shareholders in general meeting.

(iii)   Subsidiaries are required to justify projects financially, using DCF and the group's weighted average cost of capital, on the grounds that each project holds prospects of a positive NPV. The group should re-assess whether the weighted average cost of capital ought to be used. (Further recommendations about this are given in part (c)).

(iv)   **Dairy-P Ltd project**

This is a risky project. The estimated PV of benefits is (£150,000 × 1.41) = £211,500 and the NPV is £61,500. However, the project cost of £150,000 has a standard deviation of £41,000 and so if the actual project cost turns out to be 1.5 standard deviations above the mean, the project's NPV would be negative.

Assuming a normal distribution for project costs, the probability of a negative NPV would be (0.5 - 0.4332) = 0.0668, or 6.68%.

Dairy-P's fixed assets are currently valued at £400,000, and it is not stated how many of these assets provide the security for the first and second mortgage debentures, totalling £250,000. If the project were to go ahead, costing £150,000 in fixed assets plus the need for some working capital investment, Dairy-P might not be able to raise the finance by borrowing without a guarantee being given to the lender from Nominee Holdings. This appears to be unacceptable to the group. Dairy-P would therefore need finance from the cash resources of the holding company.

In view of the uncertain future of Dairy-P anyway, this project appears to be too risky, and incapable of attracting suitable finance at an acceptable rate of interest. Unless the group decides not to switch operations to Greece, and to risk some of its own cash in the project, the Dairy-P Ltd proposal should be turned down.

(v)   **Keen Casements project**

This is a fairly small project, which promises to earn an NPV of (0.28 × £65,000) £18,200 on an investment of £65,000.

There is a problem, however, with financing the project. The subsidiary has no loan capital outstanding, but if it had to finance the project by borrowing, it is unlikely that fixed assets worth £15,000 plus the fixed assets bought for the project (up to £65,000) would provide adequate security. Indeed, if the subsidiary has a bank overdraft as part of its negative net current assets (current ratio = 0.65) the bank might already have a fixed and floating charge over the existing assets.

It is assumed that the management of Keen Casements has the ability to invest successfully in a project costing over 400% more than the value of its entire fixed assets at current valuation.

(vi) **Flexi-Carbon project**

This project involves some risk. The estimated NPV is $(0.35 \times £125,000)$ £43,750. The standard deviation of the project cost is £15,000, and so the actual cost would have to be 2.92 standard deviations above the mean before the NPV became negative. The probability that this would occur is negligible - $(0.5 - 0.4983) = 0.0017$ or 0.17%, assuming that the potential project cost is normally distributed.

Flexi-Carbon's gearing level is already quite high. It has fixed assets currently valued at £250,000, a fairly low current ratio (1.21 for the proposed project) and yet mortgage debenture borrowings of £150,000. Further borrowing from external lenders would be difficult, and as with the Keen Casements project, it is doubtful whether the subsidiary could raise the finance unless the holding company itself provided the funds, or at least a guarantee for further borrowing.

(vii) In conclusion, it is recommended that the holding company should finance all (or most) of the Keen Casements and Flexi-Carbon projects, provided that they are in accord with the group's medium-term strategy.

In contrast, the Dairy-P project is more risky, and Dairy-P's future is uncertain. The expectation of higher input costs and the possibility of moving operations to Greece are two aspects of the same problem. If the Dairy-P project is rejected, the group's directors should perhaps initiate discussions with the subsidiary's board about Dairy-P's problems and future.

(b) **Divisional performance** should be measured in such a way as to indicate what sort of return each subsidiary is making on the **shareholders**' investment. Shareholders themselves are likely to be interested in the performance of the group as a whole, measured in terms of return on shareholders' capital, earnings per share, dividend yield, and growth in earnings and dividends.

These performance ratios cannot be used for subsidiaries in the group, and so an alternative measure has to be selected, which compares the return from the subsidiary with the value of the investment in the subsidiary.

Two performance measures could be used which provide a suitable indication of performance from the point of view of the group's shareholders.

(i) **Return on capital employed**, which from the shareholders' point of view would be:

$$\frac{\text{profit after interest}}{\text{net assets at current valuation minus long-term liabilities}}$$
(eg long-term borrowings)

(ii) Alternatively, **residual income** could be used. This can be measured as:

| profit before interest (controllable by the subsidiary's management) |

minus | a notional interest charge on the controllable investments of the subsidiary |

equals | residual income. |

Each subsidiary would be able to increase its residual income if it earned an **incremental profit in excess of the notional interest charge on its incremental investments** - ie in effect, if it added to the value of the group's equity.

(c) It is assumed that the rate of charge-out should apply to the reinvestment of operating profits of the group.

It seems that at the moment the subsidiaries are expected to earn a return on their investments in excess of the group's weighted average cost of capital (WACC), in other words the return that the market expects (currently 19.5%). This is not satisfactory, for two separate reasons.

(i) The WACC is not the group's marginal cost of extra capital. Decisions ought to be made on an **incremental** principle, so that if the incremental return from a project exceeds its incremental costs, allowing for the incremental cost of the capital needed to finance it, the project should go ahead. In the case of Nominee Holdings, a cash rich company, the marginal cost of capital at the moment would appear to be the opportunity cost of the cash and short-term investments, which is only 5%.

(ii) Each subsidiary is likely to have different **risk characteristics**. Investments in some subsidiaries will be more risky than investments in others. Investments that are more risky should be expected to promise a higher return, if the principle of the Capital Asset Pricing Model is applied, and arguably, each subsidiary ought to be set its own **target rate** of **return** to allow for its particular risk characteristics.

If the 'risk free' rate of return is taken as 5% - ie the return earned by the group's cash resources, a suitable premium over this rate might be worked out for each subsidiary.

15 RAPPAPORT LTD AND NFI's

Tutorial note. Part (a) is based closely on an article by Mills and Print, 'Strategic Value analysis', *Management Accounting*, February 1995. However, it is not unlike some questions that have been set in the past in which students are given some 'unusual ' calculations to do but also given strong hints on how to do them. In an exam you would probably be expected to provide some commentary too.

You may be interested in MIlls and Print's brief commentary on their example.

'SVA is reliant on determining a free cashflow profile into the future which is discounted to a present value. Overall it is analogous with the net present value (NPV) approach well known within the context of project appraisal. The NPV approach will typically be applied to a project over a planning period related to its expected useful economic life. Any value of the project remaining will normally be included in the cashflows for the last year of the projection, typically in the form of the realisable value of fixed assets and working capital released. In SVA the base case assumption for deriving value at the end of the period covered by the forecast is the perpetuity, although for some businesses the realisable value of assets or some other method may be more appropriate.'

When the SV is divided by the number of ordinary shares (if a limited-liability company) it gives a value per share. For a quoted company this can then be compared with the quoted share price to see if there is any evidence of a 'value gap'.

(a) The bid should not be accepted. You should have the following figures.

	Year 0	Year 1	Year 2	Year 3	Year 4	Year 5	Beyond*
	£	£	£	£	£	£	£
Sales (W1)	240,000	252,000	264,600	277,830	291,722	306,308	306,308
Operating profit (W2)		25,200	26,460	27,783	29,172	30,631	30,631
Tax (W3)		(6,300)	(6,615)	(6,946)	(7,293)	(7,658)	(7,658)
Depreciation (W4)		8,000	8,800	9,600	10,400	11,200	11,200
Operating cashflow		26,900	28,645	30,437	32,279	34,173	34,173
Replacement capital expenditure (Note 1)		(8,000)	(8,800)	(9,600)	(10,400)	(11,200)	(11,200)
Incremental fixed capital investment (Note 2)		(3,600)	(3,960)	(4,356)	(4,792)	(5,271)	0
Incremental working capital investment (Note 2)		(2,880))	(3,168)	(3,485)	(3,833)	(4,217)	0
Free cashflow		12,420	12,717	12,996	13,254	13,486	22,973

Year	Free cash flow	Discount factor	PV
	£	7%	£
1	12,420	0.935	11,613
2	12,717	0.873	11,102
3	12,996	0.816	10,605
4	13,254	0.763	10,113
5	13,486	0.713	9,615
Beyond (W5)	22,973	0.713	233,997
			287,045
Long-term debt			(16,000)
Shareholder value	(greater than the offer)		271,045

Workings

1 Sales increase each year by 5%
2 10% of sales each year
3 25% of operating profit
4 Depreciation is assumed to increase by £800 per annum, as explained in the question.
5 £22,973 ÷ 0.07 = £328,186 and £328,186 × 0.713 = £233,997.

(b) Management information can usefully be provided in **non-monetary terms**. Instead of valuing items such as output and stocks in financial terms, managers can be provided with information in the form of physical measures such as kilograms, tonnes or litres, or in terms of time or units of output.

Advantages of non-financial indicators.

(i) They can be provided **quickly**, per shift, or on a daily or even an hourly basis as required.

(ii) They are likely to be **easy to work out,** or at least easier than traditional financial measures.

(iii) They are expressed in terms that non-financial managers understand and they are therefore **easier to use effectively**. They will prompt the appropriate corrective action.

(iv) They can be expressed in the form of ratios or percentages for **comparative purposes** (with other divisions or periods or with competitors).

(v) Arguably, NFIs are **less likely to be manipulated** than traditional profit-related measures and they should, therefore, offer a means of counteracting short-termism, since short-term profit is not the goal.

Disadvantages of NFIs

(i) There is a danger that too many such measures could be reported, **overloading** managers with information that is not truly useful, or that sends conflicting signals.

(ii) NFIs may lead managers to pursue detailed operational goals and become blind to the overall strategy in which those goals are set.

A combination of financial and non-financial indicators is thus likely to be most successful.

6 MANAGEMENT AND SOCIAL RESPONSIBILITY

Social responsibility is a hard term to define, but many would say it means acting with regard to social welfare. No organisation would ever admit to be socially irresponsible. Organisations claim to act responsibly on social issues, whether this means using social issues in a marketing campaign (such as 'Computers for Schools' vouchers handed out by supermarkets), or the widespread claims of **environmentalism** (claimed by many organisations, from petrol companies to 'dolphin-friendly' tuna fleets) .

> Start off with a definition, and try to come up with an example

In brief, for an organisation to act with social responsibility, it should align its goals with those of the wider society in which it is a part. However, the **purpose and direction of society**, not to mention its goals, are generally political decisions, rather than obviously commercial ones. Any company these days has to overcome an almost inbuilt public distrust and cynicism about corporate objectives. Many simply will not believe that a company is operating other than purely for the benefit of its shareholders and senior managers. Recent scandals such as Enron have not helped.

Moreover, is the wider society limited to the national economy or the world as a whole? The consequences of a **global corporation** acting with 'social responsibility' in one society may cause it to act without social responsibility in another (eg shipping hazardous waste from a country with tough environmental legislation, to one with few controls).

> As we said, this area is a minefield! Try not to be too controversial with opinions or political allegiances. Refer instead to the obvious difficulties faced by an organisation charged with corporate social responsibility

So we can see that in multinational corporations, the exercise of social responsibility is distributed over several countries, but again, management will only let it override commercial objectives if it either is part of the inbuilt culture of the firm, or if the voice of public opinion in the market is strong. An example is the use of rainforest hardwoods: some consumer organisations are suggesting boycotting these products.

A business almost certainly has objectives, which, in the long term, it can claim will enhance social welfare - the creation of wealth as a result of business activities is felt to be of benefit to society as a whole.

The managers of organisations which seek to be socially responsible rarely start off with a theoretical notion of social responsibility which they then seek to implement. Rather, organisations which act responsibly do so in response to **pressures from their various stakeholders**. Some of these pressures are outlined below.

> Refer to the specifics of the manager's role, as this is what the question is asking. It is pressure from stakeholders that we are really concerned with.

> Make sure that you know who the relevant stakeholders are!

Employees

Employees are stakeholders. Their relationship is twofold. Firstly, it is their labour which keeps the organisation in operational existence, despite the impact of technology. Secondly, as citizens they are members of the wider society in which the organisation operates.

Employees value certainty and regularity of wages, in other words that the employing organisation will honour the contract of employment. Secondly, to act with social responsibility implies a concern and respect for safety in the workplace, whether this be equipment, buildings, or hours worked. (It is believed that repetitive strain injury arises from too much uninterrupted time at the word processor.)

> What are their concerns?

Social responsibility towards workers can also include a coherent career and training structure so that people can better themselves. It is believed that an economy's productivity is affected by the level of workforce skill, and so training is both beneficial for the trainee and for the company as a whole.

Other aspects include adapting to other pressures on employee's lifestyles. Workplace crèches, for example, are of great assistance to great numbers of working women, but employers are unlikely to introduce them if there is no commercial benefit.

> Show some awareness of current workplace issues – social changes and the law are fruitful areas for discussion. (You do <u>not</u> need detailed knowledge of employment legislation)

Management has a certain amount of discretion, but this is circumscribed by law. Health and safety for example is subject of regulation, as it was felt that commercial imperatives would not justify the expense, and that employers are not necessarily altruistic. Other benefits are won as the result of the relationship between management and organised labour.

So, the exercise of social responsibility towards the workforce is constrained by the law, by organised labour, and in some instances by the recognition that social responsibility can be of benefit in encouraging employee loyalty and skill.

Customers

> For each stakeholder that you note in your answer, explain the relevance of social responsibility for them. Give examples where you can

Customers are stakeholders in that they pay for the organisation's output of goods and services. They generally want quality products for as low a price as possible, but it can get more complex than that. In some consumer goods sectors, public attitudes - with some direction from government and lobby groups - have made the environmental impact of an organisation's activities open to public comment. This has led suppliers to reduce CFCs in aerosol cans, and to introduce ranges of goods which are supposed to be friendly to the environment.

Suppliers

Social responsibility towards suppliers may include the simple procedure of paying them on time. Many small businesses fail, and people lose their jobs, because of liquidity issues connected with late payment by business customers.

A supplier may also make restrictions on the end-use of products a condition of sale. For example, a supplier of high-technology items may require that these are not re-exported to the enemies of the nation where the supplier is based.

Professional bodies

Control is exercised over certain members of management by their membership of professional bodies, which have standards of ethics and conduct

Elected authorities

Society's elected political representatives can affect management in a number of ways, by legislation as has already been mentioned, by influencing the climate of public opinion, or by trying to persuade commercial organisations to follow a particular line or policy. An example is business sponsorship of the arts in the UK. The tenor of government policy was to reduce government funding and to encourage commercial organisations to avail themselves of the marketing opportunities thereby provided.

For example, if a firm bids for a contract from a local authority, contract compliance (by which the contract is only awarded to a firm which operates an equal opportunities policy) could affect the actions of management.

Elected authorities can also compel social authority by legislation (eg anti-pollution legislation), 'contract compliance' rules, or even taxation. Company reporting requirements might include a 'social audit'.

Shareholders

The main interest of shareholders is profit, and they might have objections to money being spent on projects which are socially responsible, as such profits reduce the return on the investment. As many shareholders are large institutions like pension funds, their duties can be adversely affected by the use of organisational resources on activities which do not make a profit.

It is possible that some shareholders, and other commentators, would assert that the creation of wealth is the only desirable social objective, and anything which intervenes in this objective is damaging in the long run.

Management options

Social responsibility has costs and benefits for an organisation, and management have to weigh up the **conflicting demands** of different stakeholders. With this must be balanced the duty of managing the business so that the most **effective use is made of the resources** allocated for the purpose. In the context of social responsibility, this can involve the following initiatives.

> Now go back to considerations of management – there are costs and benefits to be weighed up

> What can managers do to take note of social responsibility issues, while continuing in their general duty of managing the resources available to them?

(a)   Monitoring the **expectations** people have of the organisation, as an enterprise which trumpets its environmental friendliness will be expected to live up to its claims in all areas.

(b)   Achieving maximum **good publicity** for any project.

(c)   Selecting **appropriate socially responsible activities**.

    (i)   Ensuring that the firm's **core activities** are conducted in a socially responsible way

    (ii)   **Subsidising, supporting or sponsoring** those activities which are for public welfare (eg charitable donations, Prince's Trust)

> There is a fine line to tread – it's possible to do too much!

(d)   Clearly distinguishing between what are the **minimum acceptable standards** in a particular situation, and what are **additional** to them.

(e)   Reporting the **social audit** has been suggested as a means to monitor the wider record of companies and their responsibilities (eg number of industrial accidents).

> Why is it important to have good information, and where will it be needed?

17   THE S GROUP

A key task in the strategic management of any company is a willingness and an ability to understand the environment and anticipate future trends. Information will be required at both strategic and operational level. This is known as **strategic intelligence**, which can be defined as what a company needs to know about its business environment in order to be able to anticipate change and come up with appropriate strategies for the future.

> Define strategic intelligence

> Use the question wording to break your answer in this part down to:
> • Sources of information
> • Using the information
> • Quality of the information

There are many sources of environmental information..

Internal sources, or sources relatively close to the company, may include the sales force. It deals with the customers and so is in a position to obtain customer and competitor information. Stakeholders in the business such as employees, management and shareholders will influence the business and so are also a good source of internal information. It will be appropriate to set up a **database** for this information, containing both financial and non-financial indicators.

> Broadly, there are internal and external sources for a company to choose from

The **management information system** may generate information about the environment as well as information on sales, costs, market share and profitability.

> Think of plenty of examples to use in your answer, guided of course by the number of marks that are available

External sources of information are various. The media (newspapers, periodicals and television) offer many types of environmental information covering all kinds of environmental issues: social, political, economic and technological. Export consultants might specialise in dealing with particular countries (possibly relevant to a multinational like the S Group thinking about new markets), and academic or trade journals will give information about a wide variety of relevant issues to a particular industry. The S Group is likely to subscribe to some of these. As a large multinational, it may be represented on a trade body (an example is the British Retail Consortium in the UK) where it can meet competitors and discuss issues of interest. The **Internet** is also a fruitful source of information.

The **government** and public **databases** can be a source of statistical data, maybe relating to the money supply, the trade balance and so forth. Stockbrokers provide investment reports which often contain detailed analysis of industries and countries, and specialist consultancy firms can provide information. Universities and academic journals publish research results, with projects often being sponsored by large companies like the S Group.

Using the information

> The key to using information and being confident about its quality is being absolutely sure what the information is to be used for. This will influence its presentation

The information can be used in **devising appropriate strategies** for the future direction of the business environment. It is easy to be overwhelmed by the volume of relevant environmental information on offer and the variety of data that could be used, so S must make sure that the information it collects is collated and presented in a **coherent** fashion. This will enable the directors of S to assess the current position of the company and decide upon future strategies appropriate to the business environment.

Assuming that a company the size of S has some kind of **strategic planning function**, then it must make sure that the strategy planning process involves the divisional managers, who will be able to see that the business environment (of which they will be keenly aware) is being taken account of in strategy formulation.

Quality of the information

To be relevant and useful for decision making, the information gathered by S, both internal and external, must be **accurate** and **reliable**. A key priority is an understanding of **why** the information is being collected, and **what** it will be used for. This will indicate the level of detail required.

> Departmental specialists will be very important in ensuring accuracy

To be sure of the reliability and accuracy of internal information, **specialists** from the relevant company departments may be required to give assurances on the accuracy of information provided by their systems. Staff 'on the ground', such as the sales staff mentioned earlier, will have a far better knowledge of individual markets and competition activity than strategy setters higher up in the organisation.

Databases must be used with care as they can rapidly go out of date and must be regularly maintained. S should assure itself of the quality of data from both its internal and external databases. Comparing information from various sources can provide checks as to accuracy. As time goes on and S develops more and more **information sources**, it is likely that these sources will fluctuate in number as the less reliable sources are replaced with more accurate ones, and new methods of collecting information are devised.

> Important to note that information sources are not static, they will change and evolve with time

(a) **ROCE**

This part brings in performance appraisal, and you are required to assess the method by which one of the company divisions is measured. Our answer considers ROCE and its limitations, and includes some basic numerical analysis

By using return on capital employed (ROCE) as a performance measure, S is using an **historical measure** which is no guide to future performance and shows a lack of a forward looking perspective. **Past results** are not necessarily an indication of **future profitability**. Since the manager of AE is judged on this basis, he may be tempted into decisions which increase AE's short term ROCE. An investment might be desirable from the group's point of view, but would not be in the individual manager's interest to undertake. Thus there is a lack of **goal congruence**. A desire to increase ROCE might lead to projects being taken on without due regard to their **risk.**

If we look at ROCE for the AE division for last year and the previous year, we can see that it has decreased from 10% to 1.24%. This has very little to do with an increase in average capital employed (which has only increased by 1.1% over the year) and everything to do with an erosion in gross profit from 36.7% to 12.5% (see below).

Numerical analysis

The tiny increase in capital employed probably reflects the fact that there is little incentive for the manager to invest (assuming the investment decision is his to take) because any decisions which reduce ROCE in the short term will reflect badly on his reported performance. It is difficult to comment further on this small increase in capital employed, as no information is given in the scenario.

Further limitations of ROCE

A **fair comparison** between different divisions using ROCE is not easily achieved. Fixed assets may be of different ages or may be depreciated in different ways. If a division maintains the same annual profit, and keeps the same assets without a policy of replacement, its ROCE will increase year by year as the assets get older. This can give a false impression of improving 'real' performance over time.

Sales and profitability

AE has suffered a reduction in gross profit from $275m to $100m, a decrease of 64%. Head office fixed costs remained constant, but budgeted costs per unit increased from 63% of sales value to 87.5%. This can be attributed to **transfer pricing policy** (see below).

Despite this, it can be demonstrated that the performance of the division last year was an improvement on the previous year in terms of **sales.**

You will need to consider the sales and profitability of the division, and the importance of transfer pricing issues. Some basic number work should be included to support your analysis

	Last year	*Previous year*
Budgeted sales	K$900m	K$900m
Actual sales	K$800m	K$750m
Increase on previous year	6.67%	-
Actual volumes	16,000 units	15,000 units
% short of revenue target	11.1%	16.7%
Contribution volume variance	K$18m (A)	K$60m (A)

Assembly costs increased by 33.3% across the year, which is surprising given the much smaller increase in sales revenue, and the fact that the budgeted increase was 20%. No more information is given on assembly costs to enable further comment, although the divisional manager should certainly examine these costs as they fall under his control.

485

The **contribution volume variance** is calculated by multiplying the shortfall in unit sales volume from budget by the budgeted contribution per unit. Performance by this measure appears to be much better than the previous year, but it is probably unwise to read too much into this figure as the unit cost structures in both years are so different, with the budgeted contribution being dramatically reduced last year (from $20,000 to $9,000) after the rise in components transfer costs (which are in any case beyond the control of the divisional manager).

Transfer pricing policy

This is the area of prime concern as regards impact on AE division profitability. Transfer costs have risen to 75% of sales value last year, which compares with 53% in the previous year. They were budgeted at 70% of selling price (50% in the previous year). Total components costs have increased by 50% over the year, with sales up only around 7%.

> It should not be difficult to agree with our conclusion that the transfer pricing policy is punitive. Why do you think such a policy has been imposed upon AE?

Questions need to be asked about how the transfer price is being set. If the transferring division is inefficient, it is transferring those inefficiencies to AE, and AE's profitability is being severely affected. Alternatively the head office of S, under pressure to increase returns to its shareholders, may be deliberately imposing a large transfer price in order to cut AE division profits and **minimise its tax** bill in what is a high rate regime. This is likely to be investigated by tax authorities, especially since there has been a big year-on-year increase.

Either way, the performance of AE is being assessed on factors beyond its control. From the figures given in the question, the transfer pricing policy has contributed to 86% of the division's unit costs and is therefore a highly significant factor in assessing its performance. The board must consider AE's longer term potential for adding to shareholder value. Assessing its performance using ROCE alone, especially when that return is rendered artificially low by high transfer prices, will be to ignore its future profit potential.

> This part of the question requires consideration of a strategic development proposal. Key issues to consider are goal congruence, strategic 'fit' and the level of risk involved

The key objective of the board of S is to **increase shareholder value** and it must ensure that the AE divisional manager's plans fit in with the overall **strategic direction** of the group. Some acquisitions are driven by the personal goals of the acquiring company's managers. Again, the issue of **goal congruence** needs to be addressed. If it is true that the acquisition will enable AE division to increase market share then the board should give the proposal serious consideration.

It is important for the company to understand its reasons for acquisition, and that these reasons should be valid in terms of its strategic plan. The acquisition may give the AE division a new product range, heightened market presence and enable it to consolidate its distribution process, for example. However, the board of S must consider the level of **risk** involved. Acquiring companies in overseas markets is risky.

The divisional manager of AE is likely to believe, seeing as his division is under threat of closure, that the **opportunities** offered by the acquisition cannot be found within AE itself. However, acquisitions do have associated problems and the board of S may have to consider the following issues.

> Acquisitions do have their problems and our answer includes a consideration of some of these

(i)   **Cost.** The deal may be too expensive, or resisted by the target company. The necessary funds may have to be diverted from other group operations. Advice fees (bankers, corporate financiers) may be high.

(ii)   The **customers** of the target company may go elsewhere and the promised market share fail to materialise. Has enough **market research** been carried out?

(iii)   **Incompatibility**. In general, the problems of assimilating new products, customers, suppliers, markets, employees and different management systems might create problems of 'overload' for AE.

(iv)   **Lack of information**. Will the improvements in market share really be achieved? How strong is the competition? Does the AE division have the skills and experience to see the plan through? It has failed to achieve its own turnover targets, so can it manage those of an entirely new company?

> You might want to refer back to part (b) and reinforce the point that AE is not doing as badly as the initial analysis suggested

Following the analysis presented in part (b), it should be clear to the directors of S that the AE division is improving its performance, despite the transfer pricing policy. This profitability may be jeopardised by the acquisition.

Aside from financial factors such as **expected costs and revenues** (which S must be fully satisfied on if it is to commit funds which could, after all, be deployed elsewhere in the group), the group should bear in mind **non-financial factors** regarding the takeover.

Some major problems of **implementation** may arise relating to human resources and personnel issues, such as morale, performance assessment and culture. If key managers or personnel leave, the business will suffer and future development of the new entity (maybe into more new markets) may be compromised.

> Remember that the issues to consider are not always financial ones!

This acquisition may well be an opportunity not to be missed, but S must make sure that this is indeed the case and that **market development** is likely to flow from it.

> This is a basic necessity

(d) **Performance measurement** should become more **forward looking** than merely placing a reliance on historical measures such as ROCE. In this way the future of the AE division can be planned with more clarity, and its contribution to increasing shareholder value will be considered over the longer term, although this may clash with some investors who are looking for a **short term return.**

> This revisits the ground covered in part (b) and asks for better ways of measuring the contribution of the AE division.

As an increase in shareholder value is a key objective of the business, performance indicators will be required to assess whether or not the management team is fulfilling this duty. The use of what is known as a **shareholder value approach** to performance measurement involves moving the focus of attention away from simply looking at short term profits to a longer term view of **value creation**, the motivation being that it will help the business stay ahead in an increasingly competitive market. The success (or otherwise) of the new AE division will contribute to the determination of shareholder value.

Shareholder value analysis

This is defined as 'an approach to financial management which focuses on the creation of economic value for shareholders, as measured by share price performance and flow of dividends'. The main premise is that a business is worth the net present value of its **future cash flows**, and these are driven by the following factors: sales growth, operating margin, fixed capital investment, working capital investment, cash taxes, the planning period and the cost of capital.

> Our answer examines SVA and EVA approaches

It follows that these are therefore the factors that the directors of S need to focus on when measuring the performance of the AE division.

When looking at future sales growth and margin, the directors will want to see whether the divisional manager's forecasts of increased **market share** have been realised, but will also need to extrapolate **forecast trends** in the market. This may include a consideration of new products.

Investment in both fixed and working capital will be required if growth is to be **sustained**. Forecast cash flows may need to be revised if growth and return to shareholders is to be achieved. Additional funding may be required.

The level of **corporation tax** borne by the AE division has been high in the past. S has sought to mitigate its effects via its transfer pricing policy, but this may not be viable in the longer term (the policy is onerous, as we saw in part (b)) and S may need to look again at **tax planning** for the division.

> Evidence of wider commercial thinking

The cost of funding the project is fundamental to its success in increasing shareholder value. If the **incremental value** of the acquisition is in excess of the **cost of capital**, then **shareholder value** will be added. The cost of capital should be minimised, and any changes to it reflected in revised NPV calculations.

> Show that you understand how SVA is applied

Economic value management

This is another form of strategic value analysis and hinges on the calculation of **economic profit (EP).** The calculation of EP requires several **adjustments** to be made to **traditionally reported accounting profits**. These are intended to produce a figure for capital employed which is a more accurate reflection of the base upon which shareholders except their returns to accrue, and to provide a figure which is a more realistic measure of the **actual cash generated** for shareholders from recurring business activities.

In the case of the AE division, adjustments could be made to take the transfer price items out of the calculation and apply a **notional cost of capital** to the adjusted profit This would eliminate the somewhat artificial (and high) transfer price from the consideration of the **economic value added** by the division. The figures would read as follows.

		Last year	Previous year
		K$m	K$m
Sales		800	750
Division costs	-assembly	(100)	(75)
	-head office	(75)	(75)
Cost of capital (say 12%)		(242)	(240)
EVA		383	360

This analysis can be carried further and presented in terms of future expectations for the new division. This will enable future performance to be planned and any action taken that may be necessary to ensure that the acquisition continues to deliver acceptable results.

> With more forward looking information, it will be easier for the S group to plan future divisional performance

Appendix: Mathematical tables

FINANCIAL MATHEMATICS

Annuity

Present value of an annuity of £1 per annum, receivable or payable for n years, commencing in one year, discounted at r% per annum:

$$PV = \frac{1}{r}\left[1 - \frac{1}{[1+r]^n}\right]$$

Perpetuity

Present value of £1 per annum, payable or receivable in perpetuity, commencing in one year, discounted at r% per annum:

$$PV = \frac{1}{r}$$

Growing Perpetuity

Present value of £1 per annum, receivable or payable, commencing in one year, growing in perpetuity at a constant rate of g% per annum, discounted at r% per annum:

$$PV = \frac{1}{r - g}$$

Equivalent Annual Cost

An asset with a life of n years has an equivalent annual cost of:

$$\frac{PV \text{ of costs over n years}}{n \text{ year annuity factor}}$$

Mathematical tables

PRESENT VALUE TABLE

Present value of £1 ie $(1+r)^{-n}$ where r = interest rate, n = number of periods until payment or receipt

Periods					Interest rates (r)					
(n)	1%	2%	3%	4%	5%	6%	7%	8%	9%	10%
1	0.990	0.980	0.971	0.962	0.952	0.943	0.935	0.926	0.917	0.909
2	0.980	0.961	0.943	0.925	0.907	0.890	0.873	0.857	0.842	0.826
3	0.971	0.942	0.915	0.889	0.864	0.840	0.816	0.794	0.772	0.751
4	0.961	0.924	0.888	0.855	0.823	0.792	0.763	0.735	0.708	0.683
5	0.951	0.906	0.863	0.822	0.784	0.747	0.713	0.681	0.650	0.621
6	0.942	0.888	0.837	0.790	0.746	0.705	0.666	0.630	0.596	0.564
7	0.933	0.871	0.813	0.760	0.711	0.665	0.623	0.583	0.547	0.513
8	0.923	0.853	0.789	0.731	0.677	0.627	0.582	0.540	0.502	0.467
9	0.914	0.837	0.766	0.703	0.645	0.592	0.544	0.500	0.460	0.424
10	0.905	0.820	0.744	0.676	0.614	0.558	0.508	0.463	0.422	0.386
11	0.896	0.804	0.722	0.650	0.585	0.527	0.475	0.429	0.388	0.350
12	0.887	0.788	0.701	0.625	0.557	0.497	0.444	0.397	0.356	0.319
13	0.879	0.773	0.681	0.601	0.530	0.469	0.415	0.368	0.326	0.290
14	0.870	0.758	0.661	0.577	0.505	0.442	0.388	0.340	0.299	0.263
15	0.861	0.743	0.642	0.555	0.481	0.417	0.362	0.315	0.275	0.239
16	0.853	0.728	0.623	0.534	0.458	0.394	0.339	0.292	0.252	0.218
17	0.844	0.714	0.605	0.513	0.436	0.371	0.317	0.270	0.231	0.198
18	0.836	0.700	0.587	0.494	0.416	0.350	0.296	0.250	0.212	0.180
19	0.828	0.686	0.570	0.475	0.396	0.331	0.277	0.232	0.194	0.164
20	0.820	0.673	0.554	0.456	0.377	0.312	0.258	0.215	0.178	0.149

Periods					Interest rates (r)					
(n)	11%	12%	13%	14%	15%	16%	17%	18%	19%	20%
1	0.901	0.893	0.885	0.877	0.870	0.862	0.855	0.847	0.840	0.833
2	0.812	0.797	0.783	0.769	0.756	0.743	0.731	0.718	0.706	0.694
3	0.731	0.712	0.693	0.675	0.658	0.641	0.624	0.609	0.593	0.579
4	0.659	0.636	0.613	0.592	0.572	0.552	0.534	0.516	0.499	0.482
5	0.593	0.567	0.543	0.519	0.497	0.476	0.456	0.437	0.419	0.402
6	0.535	0.507	0.480	0.456	0.432	0.410	0.390	0.370	0.352	0.335
7	0.482	0.452	0.425	0.400	0.376	0.354	0.333	0.314	0.296	0.279
8	0.434	0.404	0.376	0.351	0.327	0.305	0.285	0.266	0.249	0.233
9	0.391	0.361	0.333	0.308	0.284	0.263	0.243	0.225	0.209	0.194
10	0.352	0.322	0.295	0.270	0.247	0.227	0.208	0.191	0.176	0.162
11	0.317	0.287	0.261	0.237	0.215	0.195	0.178	0.162	0.148	0.135
12	0.286	0.257	0.231	0.208	0.187	0.168	0.152	0.137	0.124	0.112
13	0.258	0.229	0.204	0.182	0.163	0.145	0.130	0.116	0.104	0.093
14	0.232	0.205	0.181	0.160	0.141	0.125	0.111	0.099	0.088	0.078
15	0.209	0.183	0.160	0.140	0.123	0.108	0.095	0.084	0.074	0.065
16	0.188	0.163	0.141	0.123	0.107	0.093	0.081	0.071	0.062	0.054
17	0.170	0.146	0.125	0.108	0.093	0.080	0.069	0.060	0.052	0.045
18	0.153	0.130	0.111	0.095	0.081	0.069	0.059	0.051	0.044	0.038
19	0.138	0.116	0.098	0.083	0.070	0.060	0.051	0.043	0.037	0.031
20	0.124	0.104	0.087	0.073	0.061	0.051	0.043	0.037	0.031	0.026

CUMULATIVE PRESENT VALUE TABLE

This table shows the present value of £1 per annum, receivable or payable at the end of each year for *n* years.

$$\frac{1-(1+r)^{-n}}{r}$$

Periods					Interest rates (r)					
(n)	1%	2%	3%	4%	5%	6%	7%	8%	9%	10%
1	0.990	0.980	0.971	0.962	0.952	0.943	0.935	0.926	0.917	0.909
2	1.970	1.942	1.913	1.886	1.859	1.833	1.808	1.783	1.759	1.736
3	2.941	2.884	2.829	2.775	2.723	2.673	2.624	2.577	2.531	2.487
4	3.902	3.808	3.717	3.630	3.546	3.465	3.387	3.312	3.240	3.170
5	4.853	4.713	4.580	4.452	4.329	4.212	4.100	3.993	3.890	3.791
6	5.795	5.601	5.417	5.242	5.076	4.917	4.767	4.623	4.486	4.355
7	6.728	6.472	6.230	6.002	5.786	5.582	5.389	5.206	5.033	4.868
8	7.652	7.325	7.020	6.733	6.463	6.210	5.971	5.747	5.535	5.335
9	8.566	8.162	7.786	7.435	7.108	6.802	6.515	6.247	5.995	5.759
10	9.471	8.983	8.530	8.111	7.722	7.360	7.024	6.710	6.418	6.145
11	10.368	9.787	9.253	8.760	8.306	7.887	7.499	7.139	6.805	6.495
12	11.255	10.575	9.954	9.385	8.863	8.384	7.943	7.536	7.161	6.814
13	12.134	11.348	10.635	9.986	9.394	8.853	8.358	7.904	7.487	7.103
14	13.004	12.106	11.296	10.563	9.899	9.295	8.745	8.244	7.786	7.367
15	13.865	12.849	11.938	11.118	10.380	9.712	9.108	8.559	8.061	7.606
16	14.718	13.578	12.561	11.652	10.838	10.106	9.447	8.851	8.313	7.824
17	15.562	14.292	13.166	12.166	11.274	10.477	9.763	9.122	8.544	8.022
18	16.398	14.992	13.754	12.659	11.690	10.828	10.059	9.372	8.756	8.201
19	17.226	15.679	14.324	13.134	12.085	11.158	10.336	9.604	8.950	8.365
20	18.046	16.351	14.878	13.590	12.462	11.470	10.594	9.818	9.129	8.514

Periods					Interest rates (r)					
(n)	11%	12%	13%	14%	15%	16%	17%	18%	19%	20%
1	0.901	0.893	0.885	0.877	0.870	0.862	0.855	0.847	0.840	0.833
2	1.713	1.690	1.668	1.647	1.626	1.605	1.585	1.566	1.547	1.528
3	2.444	2.402	2.361	2.322	2.283	2.246	2.210	2.174	2.140	2.106
4	3.102	3.037	2.974	2.914	2.855	2.798	2.743	2.690	2.639	2.589
5	3.696	3.605	3.517	3.433	3.352	3.274	3.199	3.127	3.058	2.991
6	4.231	4.111	3.998	3.889	3.784	3.685	3.589	3.498	3.410	3.326
7	4.712	4.564	4.423	4.288	4.160	4.039	3.922	3.812	3.706	3.605
8	5.146	4.968	4.799	4.639	4.487	4.344	4.207	4.078	3.954	3.837
9	5.537	5.328	5.132	4.946	4.772	4.607	4.451	4.303	4.163	4.031
10	5.889	5.650	5.426	5.216	5.019	4.833	4.659	4.494	4.339	4.192
11	6.207	5.938	5.687	5.453	5.234	5.029	4.836	4.656	4.486	4.327
12	6.492	6.194	5.918	5.660	5.421	5.197	4.988	4.793	4.611	4.439
13	6.750	6.424	6.122	5.842	5.583	5.342	5.118	4.910	4.715	4.533
14	6.982	6.628	6.302	6.002	5.724	5.468	5.229	5.008	4.802	4.611
15	7.191	6.811	6.462	6.142	5.847	5.575	5.324	5.092	4.876	4.675
16	7.379	6.974	6.604	6.265	5.954	5.668	5.405	5.162	4.938	4.730
17	7.549	7.120	6.729	6.373	6.047	5.749	5.475	5.222	4.990	4.775
18	7.702	7.250	6.840	6.467	6.128	5.818	5.534	5.273	5.033	4.812
19	7.839	7.366	6.938	6.550	6.198	5.877	5.584	5.316	5.070	4.843
20	7.963	7.469	7.025	6.623	6.259	5.929	5.628	5.353	5.101	4.870

List of key terms
and index

> Note: **Key Terms** and their page references are given in **bold**.

BPP PUBLISHING

See overleaf for information on other
BPP products and how to order

CIMA Order

To BPP Publishing Ltd, Aldine Place, London W12 8AW
Tel: 020 8740 2211. Fax: 020 8740 1184
www.bpp.com   Email publishing@bpp.com
Order online www.bpp.com

Mr/Mrs/Ms (Full name)

Daytime delivery address

Postcode

Daytime Tel

Email

Date of exam (month/year)

POSTAGE & PACKING

Study Texts

	First	Each extra
UK	£3.00	£2.00 £
Europe***	£5.00	£4.00 £
Rest of world	£20.00	£10.00 £

Kits/Passcards/Success Tapes

	First	Each extra
UK	£2.00	£1.00 £
Europe*	£2.50	£1.00 £
Rest of world	£15.00	£8.00 £

MCQ cards

	First	Each extra
	£1.00	£1.00 £

CDs each

	First	
UK		£2.00
Europe*		£2.00
Rest of world		£10.00

Breakthrough Videos

	First	Each extra
UK	£2.00	£2.00 £
Europe*	£2.00	£2.00 £
Rest of world	£20.00	£10.00 £

Grand Total (Cheques to *BPP Publishing*) I enclose a

cheque for (incl. Postage)   £

Or charge to Access/Visa/Switch

Card Number

Expiry date   Start Date

Issue Number (Switch Only)

Signature

	7/02 Texts	1/02 Kits	1/02 Passcards	9/00 Tapes	7/00 Videos	Virtual Campus	7/02 i-Pass	7/02 i-Learn	7/02 MCQ cards
FOUNDATION									
1 Financial Accounting Fundamentals	£20.95	£10.95	£6.95	£12.95	£25.95	£50	£24.95	£34.95	£5.95
2 Management Accounting Fundamentals	£20.95	£10.95	£6.95	£12.95	£25.95	£50	£24.95		£5.95
3A Economics for Business	£20.95	£10.95	£6.95	£12.95	£25.95	£50	£24.95	£34.95	£5.95
3B Business Law	£20.95	£10.95	£6.95	£12.95	£25.95	£50	£24.95	£34.95	£5.95
3C Business Mathematics	£20.95	£10.95	£6.95	£12.95	£25.95	£50	£24.95	£34.95	£5.95
INTERMEDIATE									
4 Finance	£20.95	£10.95	£6.95	£12.95	£25.95	£80	£24.95	£34.95	£5.95
5 Business Tax (FA 2002)	£20.95 (10/02)	£10.95	£6.95	£12.95	£25.95	£80	£24.95	£34.95	£5.95
6 Financial Accounting	£20.95	£10.95	£6.95	£12.95	£25.95	£80	£24.95	£34.95	£5.95
6i Financial Accounting International	£20.95	£10.95	£6.95	£12.95	£25.95	£80	£24.95		£5.95
7 Financial Reporting	£20.95	£10.95	£6.95	£12.95	£25.95	£80	£24.95	£34.95	£5.95
7i Financial Reporting International	£20.95	£10.95	£6.95	£12.95	£25.95	£80	£24.95		£5.95
8 Management Accounting – Performance Management	£20.95 *	£10.95	£6.95	£12.95	£25.95	£80	£24.95	£34.95 *	£5.95
9 Management Accounting – Decision Making	£20.95 *	£10.95	£6.95	£12.95	£25.95	£80	£24.95	£34.95 *	£5.95
10 Systems and Project Management	£20.95	£10.95	£6.95	£12.95	£25.95	£80	£24.95	£34.95	£5.95
11 Organisational Management	£20.95	£10.95	£6.95	£12.95	£25.95	£80	£24.95	£34.95	£5.95
FINAL									
12 Management Accounting – Business Strategy	£20.95	£10.95	£6.95	£12.95	£25.95		£24.95	£34.95	£5.95
13 Management Accounting – Financial Strategy	£20.95	£10.95	£6.95	£12.95	£25.95		£24.95	£34.95	£5.95
14 Management Accounting – Information Strategy	£20.95	£10.95	£6.95	£12.95	£25.95		£24.95	£34.95	£5.95
15 Case Study	£20.95			£12.95	£25.95				
(1) Workbook		£19.95							
(2) Toolkit									
Learning to Learn (7/02)	£9.95								

(For 11/02: available 9/02. For 5/03: available 3/03)

	11/02	5/03

* For paper 8 and 9, separate editions are available for the November 2002 and May 2003 exams. Please tick the exam you will be sitting.

Total

REVIEW FORM & FREE PRIZE DRAW

All original review forms from the entire BPP range, completed with genuine comments, will be entered into one of two draws on 31 January 2003 and 31 July 2003. The names on the first four forms picked out on each occasion will be sent a cheque for £50.

Name: _____   Address: _____

_____

How have you used this Text?
(Tick one box only)

☐ Self study (book only)

☐ On a course: college (please state)_____

_____

☐ With 'correspondence' package

☐ Other _____

Why did you decide to purchase this Text?
(Tick one box only)

☐ Have used BPP Texts in the past

☐ Recommendation by friend/colleague

☐ Recommendation by a lecturer at college

☐ Saw advertising

☐ Other _____

During the past six months do you recall seeing/receiving any of the following?
(Tick as many boxes as are relevant)

☐ Our advertisement in CIMA *Insider*

☐ Our advertisement in *Financial Management*

☐ Our advertisement in *Pass*

☐ Our brochure with a letter through the post

☐ Our website www.bpp.com

Which (if any) aspects of our advertising do you find useful?
(Tick as many boxes as are relevant)

☐ Prices and publication dates of new editions

☐ Information on product content

☐ Facility to order books off-the-page

☐ None of the above

Which BPP products have you used?

Text	☐	**MCQ cards**	☐	**i-Learn**	☐
Kit	☐	**Tape**	☐	**i-Pass**	☐
Passcard	☐	**Video**	☐	**Virtual Campus**	☐

Your ratings, comments and suggestions would be appreciated on the following areas.

	Very useful	Useful	Not useful
Introductory section (Key study steps, personal study)	☐	☐	☐
Chapter introductions	☐	☐	☐
Key terms	☐	☐	☐
Quality of explanations	☐	☐	☐
Case examples and other examples	☐	☐	☐
Questions and answers in each chapter	☐	☐	☐
Chapter roundups	☐	☐	☐
Quick quizzes	☐	☐	☐
Exam focus points	☐	☐	☐
Question bank	☐	☐	☐
Answer bank	☐	☐	☐
Index	☐	☐	☐
Icons	☐	☐	☐
Mind maps	☐	☐	☐

Overall opinion of this Study Text   Excellent ☐   Good ☐   Adequate ☐   Poor ☐

Do you intend to continue using BPP products?   Yes ☐   No ☐

On the reverse of this page are noted particular areas of the text about which we would welcome your feedback.

Please note any further comments and suggestions/errors on the reverse of this page. The BPP author of this edition can be e-mailed at: katemachattie@bpp.com

Please return this form to: Nick Weller, CIMA Range Manager, BPP Publishing Ltd, FREEPOST, London, W12 8BR

TELL US WHAT YOU THINK

Because the following specific areas of the text contain both tricky and highly examinable topics, your comments on their usefulness are particularly welcome.

- Design of information systems (Chapter 1)

- Transaction cost analysis (Chapter 12)

- Approaches to measuring and controlling performance (Chapters 13-15)

Please note any further comments and suggestions/errors below.

FREE PRIZE DRAW RULES

1 Closing date for 31 January 2003 draw is 31 December 2002. Closing date for 31 July 2003 draw is 30 June 2003.

2 Restricted to entries with UK and Eire addresses only. BPP employees, their families and business associates are excluded.

3 No purchase necessary. Entry forms are available upon request from BPP Publishing. No more than one entry per title, per person. Draw restricted to persons aged 16 and over.

4 Winners will be notified by post and receive their cheques not later than 6 weeks after the relevant draw date.

5 The decision of the promoter in all matters is final and binding. No correspondence will be entered into.